The Editor

MATTHEW WILSON SMITH is Associate Professor of Comparative Literature at Cornell University. He is the author of *The Total Work of Art: From Bayreuth to Cyberspace.*

A NORTON CRITICAL EDITION

Georg Büchner:
THE MAJOR WORKS

CONTEXTS

CRITICISM

Edited by

MATTHEW WILSON SMITH
CORNELL UNIVERSITY

Texts of the major works translated by

HENRY J. SCHMIDT

W · W · NORTON & COMPANY · *New York* · *London*

The text of this book is composed in Fairfield Medium with the display set in Bernhard Modern.
Composition by Westchester
Manufacturing by Maple-Vail
Production manager: Sean Mintus.
Book design by Antonina Krass

Library of Congress Cataloging-in-Publication Data

Büchner, Georg, 1813–1837.
    [Works. Selections. English. 2012]
    Georg Büchner : the major works, contexts, criticism / edited by Matthew
Wilson Smith ; texts of the major works translated by Henry J. Schmidt. —
First edition.
        pages cm. — (A Norton critical edition)
    Includes bibliographical references.
    ISBN 978-0-393-93351-2 (pbk.)
    1. Büchner, Georg, 1813–1837—Translations into English.
2. Büchner, Georg, 1813–1837—Criticism and interpretation.
I. Smith, Matthew Wilson. II. Schmidt, Henry J. III. Title.
    PT1828.B6A28 2012
    832'.7—dc23

                                                                    2011048260

W. W. Norton & Company, Inc., 500 Fifth Avenue, New York,
NY 10110-0017

wwnorton.com

W. W. Norton & Company Ltd., Castle House, 75/76 Wells Street, London
W1T 3QT

1 2 3 4 5 6 7 8 9 0

Contents

Illustrations

Introduction

A coauthored pamphlet, a short story with a section missing, two plays, four fragmentary drafts toward another play: these are the principal works of Georg Büchner. Never has so much been made of so little. Despite the incomplete and mangled forms in which they reach us, these few works have transformed literature and theater ever since their rediscovery in the late nineteenth century, thanks largely to the editorial labors of Karl Emil Franzos, whose edition of the collected works appeared in 1879. The highest literary honor for German-language writers is now called the Georg Büchner Prize, and the full extent of his influence—from Gerhart Hauptmann to Christa Wolf, Max Reinhardt to Robert Wilson, Alban Berg to Tom Waits—defies catalog.

Karl Georg Büchner was born on October 17, 1813, in the town of Goddelau in the Grand Duchy of Hesse-Darmstadt. He was the first of six children, several of whom would also achieve fame. His father, Ernst Karl Büchner, was a prominent surgeon whose generally conservative views and admiration for Napoleon often conflicted with the politics of his son. His mother, Caroline (née Reuss), had a warmer temperament and more liberal leanings and sparked in him a love for the folk songs that weave through his works. The memory of these songs never left him; in one of his last letters, Büchner asked his fiancée to "learn to sing the *folk songs* by Easter, if it doesn't fatigue you" and lamented that "One doesn't hear any voices here; the *folk* don't sing."

A sense of belatedness haunted many in Büchner's generation. In the previous quarter century, Germany had witnessed Beethoven and Schubert, Goethe and Schiller, Kant and Hegel, while France saw Robespierre give way to Napoleon and an empire that recalled the Caesars. On the day of Büchner's birth, however, the Grand Army found itself mired in the Battle of Leipzig, a four-day slaughterhouse that would prove the bloodiest European battle until World War I. It was also a decisive defeat that would quickly lead to Napoleon's abdication and exile to Elba. The age of the Romantic titans was lurching to an end.

After graduating from high school (or *Gymnasium*) in Darmstadt, Büchner at first followed his father's path, enrolling as a medical student at the University of Strassburg in November of 1831. His two years in the French city marked the happiest period of his life, and it is there that he met Wilhelmine ("Minna") Jaeglé, the daughter of his landlord, to whom he became secretly engaged. With its cosmopolitan blend of French, German, and Alsatian cultures, Strassburg struck Büchner as everything Hesse was not. In opposition to the more or less conservative regimes governing from Paris, Strassburg had emerged as a hotbed of political radicalism, with mainstream republicanism striking up against the proto-communist theories of radicals such as Philippe Buonarroti and Auguste Blanqui.

It was here that Büchner first experienced the force of a potentially revolutionary mass. The occasion was a controversial visit to the city by the freedom fighter Girolamo Ramorino, a former Napoleonic officer who represented for many the promise of the pan-European uprisings of 1830. His arrival was greeted by a phalanx of students that included Büchner; despite government attempts to stop it, the march only gained strength as students were joined by soldiers of the National Guard. The united front then marched into Strassburg, beneath kerchiefs waving from city windows, amid rounds of "La Marseillaise" and cries of *"Vive la liberté! Vive Ramorino!"* Büchner describes the stirring scene in a letter home to his parents only to undercut it with a final gesture that foreshadows the ambivalence of *Danton's Death*: "Ramorino appears on the balcony, thanks the crowd, it cries 'Vivat!'—and the comedy is complete."

Regulations on students studying abroad forced Büchner to return to his homeland in October 1833, and with reluctance he consented to continue his studies at the more local University of Giessen. Compared to the University of Strassburg, Giessen was a provincial institution in a place Büchner regarded as oppressively backward. The distaste was mutual. "Frankly, we didn't like this Georg Büchner," recalled his fellow medical student Karl Vogt. "He wore a big top hat that always sat back on his neck, constantly made a face like a cat in a thunderstorm, kept completely to himself." A bout with meningitis confined Büchner to his bed for five weeks and only deepened his isolation, though it may also have sharpened his edge. In March 1834 he organized a revolutionary group in Giessen that he dubbed the "Society of Human Rights" (*Gesellschaft der Menschenrechte*) and two months later founded another branch in Darmstadt. During this time he also met and befriended a radical pastor and schoolteacher named Friedrich Ludwig Weidig, with whom he would compose a revolutionary pamphlet titled *The Hessian Messenger* (*Der Hessische Landbote*).

Darmstadt, ca. 1816.

The Hessian Messenger, which anticipates elements of Marx and Engels's *Communist Manifesto* of 1848, remains one of the most important works of German revolutionary propaganda. It is written at a pitch of fury, heaping insult on the ruling nobility and exhorting the downtrodden to rise up against their oppressors. Insisting that the state and its laws should benefit the people as a whole, the work systematically argues that the precise opposite is the case, that the state is in fact a hammer wielded by the ruling class to beat lower orders into submission. The pamphlet draws the sharpest of dichotomies, juxtaposing icons of brutalized peasants against grotesques of bloodsucking ministers and aristocrats greasing their faces with the tears of orphans. Büchner's contributions included the use of statistical evidence drawn from official ducal sources, while Weidig hurled firebrand rhetoric drawn from Old Testament prophets and the Book of Revelation. The intertwining of these two rhetorical styles in many ways reflects the complex and even contradictory intellectual environments of the pamphlet's intended audiences. Speaking by turns the languages of science and scripture, commerce and prophesy, *The Hessian Messenger* is a ferocious appeal to laborers and peasants to recognize their common cause and revolt.

Coming at a time when the German Confederation was in full-scale reaction against democratic forces, it was also too much too early, and the work's publication was a tragedy that very nearly brought down Büchner with it. The conspirators had been infiltrated by a police informer, and soon after the secret printing of the manuscript in Offenbach the Hessian police descended in force. Büchner's rooms were illegally searched, and several of his comrades were arrested, imprisoned, and in some cases submitted to long periods of torture. Weidig remained free just long enough to print off, with defiance, a second edition of the *Messenger*, but in April 1835 he too was rounded up. Two years later, he was found dead in his cell, his wrists slashed with a piece of glass, the words "As the enemy denies me any defense, I have freely chosen an ignominious death" scrawled in blood over his body. Officials quickly deemed it a suicide, though murder at the hands of the police cannot be ruled out.

Lying low in his parents' house in Darmstadt, Büchner had a rope ladder readied near the garden wall in case he had to flee at a moment's notice. At one point he was summoned to court, but sent his brother Wilhelm in his stead. The matter, this time, came to nothing, but Büchner rightly assumed that he could not simply bide his time until the storm passed. Hoping to raise enough money to support an escape, he turned to the unlikely source of writing a play about the French Revolution. Büchner composed the drama at terrific speed, completing it in about five weeks and then sending it off to Karl Gutzkow, a leader of the Young Germany group of writers and the publisher of a journal called *Phönix*. Gutzkow liked it and arranged for publication, even sending a little money as payment. But Büchner had already left for the French border: in early March he reentered the city of Strassburg, and three months later Hessen police issued a warrant for his arrest. He was now officially a fugitive.

Büchner titled his drama *Danton's Death* (*Dantons Tod*), and it is hardly conceivable that its author had never written—and for all we know may never have even seen—a play before. With his first dramatic work, Büchner produced one of the most troubling meditations on revolution ever composed. With its parallel plotting, its sudden shifts in genre and tone from high tragedy to documentary history to low comedy, and its panoply of characters from varied orders of society, the work owes much to Shakespeare, whom Büchner read in the standard German translation by A. W. Schlegel and Ludwig Tieck and admired above all other writers. The echoes can be heard as well in Lucile's Lear-like mourning for Camille, Danton's Macbeth-like meditations on nothingness, and the ennui and death-drive that bring Danton so close to Hamlet.

Death, in fact, hovers over the whole play, and not only in the obvious sense that it is set during the Reign of Terror. Lacroix jokes that Danton is "making a mosaic" from the body parts of the whores of Paris, but in fact the whole Revolution has become a matter of cobbling together shards of ancient memory. "The Revolution is like the daughters of Pelias: it cuts humanity in pieces to rejuvenate it," shouts St. Just to a crowd of applauding Deputies at the end of act 2. "Humanity will rise up with mighty limbs out of this cauldron of blood, like the earth out of the waters of the Flood, as if it has been newly created." St. Just's primary allusion is to the legendary King Pelias. Longing to regain his youth, Pelias turned to the witch Medea, who advised his daughters to chop up their father and boil the body parts in a cauldron; rather than restoring Pelias to life, the remedy had the more predictable effect of simply reducing the king to cooked meat and his daughters to patricides. The irony here is that the reference is more apt than St. Just realizes, and his coupling of it with the biblical story of the Flood may similarly suggest the ways in which apocalyptic narratives of total destruction and rebirth are invariably followed by something less than paradisiacal. Allusion is both the labyrinth and the trailing string, and Büchner's decision simply to cut and paste large swaths from his historical sources—especially for the speeches of Robespierre, whose rhetoric paradoxically becomes more citational as it becomes more radical—is less a mark of immaturity than a herald of *The Waste Land*. Most of those we see onstage will either be guillotined with Danton by the end of the play or guillotined with Robespierre a few weeks later, and all these specters of men and words remind us that *revolution* can mean either forcible overthrow or simple rotation. Those who forget the past are of course doomed to repeat it, but the same may also be said for those who remember too well.

Danton's Death makes a poor play for polemics, and critics who take sides in the debate over which viewpoint the play espouses, Robespierre's or Danton's, are likely arguing in vain. Others have read the play not as an endorsement of either antagonist but as a refusal of politics altogether. In this reading, the play marks Büchner's rejection of his revolutionary period and his embrace of nihilism, with Danton's cry of despair—"We are puppets, our strings are pulled by unknown forces, we ourselves are nothing, nothing!"—elevated to the status of authorial voice (indeed, the cry partly echoes a line from Büchner's own letter to Minna of March 10, 1834). But we search for a raisonneur in Büchner at our peril. In this case Büchner is careful to situate Danton's lament in context, placing it at the end of a scene in which the character is wrestling with the guilt of his participation in the prison massacres of September 1792. Danton's surrender of agency seems, at least in part, a self-serving gesture, a way of granting himself, and perhaps the Revolution as a whole, absolution. In this refusal to render any final verdict on the figures and forces of history, Büchner once again shows how much he has learned from Shakespeare.

After the debacle of *The Hessian Messenger*, Büchner better understood the lethal risks of revolution and was relieved to have escaped Danton's fate. "Since I crossed the border, I'm in high spirits," Büchner wrote to his parents from Strassburg in March 1835; "I'm now completely alone, but that increases my energy." At the same time, he continued to be deeply troubled by the fate of his comrades, especially his school friend Karl von Minnigerode, one of those arrested as a courier of *The Hessian Messenger*. Reports from fellow refugees brought disturbing news. "I know for certain that Minnigerode's hands were chained in Friedberg; I know it from someone who was imprisoned with him," reads a letter of Büchner's from early August 1835. "He's said to be mortally ill; would to heavens his sufferings would cease! It's established that the prisoners are given prison rations and have neither light nor books." (A year later Büchner would believe a false, though plausible, rumor that Minnigerode had been tortured to death.) Powerless to help his companions, he resumed his studies at the University, concentrating on anatomy and philosophy. Alongside his research he continued to write, composing the novella *Lenz* in the spring of 1835 and working on the plays *Leonce and Lena* and *Woyzeck* in the summer and fall of the following year. This last, Büchner's most famous work, he never completed; all that survived his death were four fragmentary manuscript drafts, composed in a semilegible scrawl and occasionally accompanied by doodles.

The thin line between sanity and madness is a leitmotif of all Büchner's work, and in *Lenz* and *Woyzeck* he draws on accounts of historical figures who have been retrospectively diagnosed as likely schizophrenics. Inspired by Johann Friedrich Oberlin's account of the Sturm-und-Drang writer J. M. R. Lenz, Büchner paints a portrait of a mind torn. Here Büchner adopts a narrative voice that shifts with dizzying suddenness from clinical dispassion to radical embodiment; we seem—alternately or at one and the same time—to be seeing the world from on high and feeling it through Lenz's skin. "On the 20th Lenz went through the mountains," is the story's matter-of-fact opening—but thereafter the words quickly reproduce until we are confronted by blooming sentences that sprout off clauses like fungal spores:

> He went upstairs, it was cold up there, a large room, empty, a high bed in the background, he placed the lamp on the table and walked up and down, he recalled the day just passed, how he had come here, where he was, the room in the parsonage with its lights and dear faces, on the mountain, but he could no longer fill the void with anything, the light was out, darkness swallowed everything; an unnamable fear seized him, he jumped up, . . .

And so on—until suddenly we are returned to: "The next day went well." The phrasing, billowing and stoic, free-associative and plain-spoken, frustrates our ability to draw clean lines of judgment in and about the text at the same time that it winds a path within and around the title character.

The work also assiduously avoids the typical, and by the 1830s already clichéd, association of the madman-artist with the satanic rebel. To some of the late-Romantic temperament, harmonies between the lunatic, the lover, and the poet were cause for midnight revels, while to the broader public, as well as to much of the medical community, insanity appeared as a sign of divine punishment or moral degeneracy. But Lenz's brilliant madness appears as neither gloriously nor damnably nefarious, and for all its vertigo and horror the story resists the Gothic. In the end, we discover that unlikeliest of things in a narrative of chronic estrangement: a kind of pitiless sympathy.

Pitiless sympathy, though critics are generally reluctant to discuss it, also slips through the mill wheel of *Woyzeck*. Again Büchner draws on contemporary accounts of a historical figure, and in this case his principal sources are a pair of official evaluations by Dr. Johann Christian August Clarus, a Leipzig professor who served as a medical examiner for the trial of Johann Christian Woyzeck. An unemployed mercenary, Woyzeck murdered his some-time lover in 1821; subsequent reports indicate that he had been experiencing hallucinations, including voices commanding him to stab the victim to death. The play—with its blowhard army captain, its strutting drum major, its piss-obsessed doctor, and the rest of its cast of meat puppets—certainly has a sharp bite, but in the end it is slipperier than simple satire. "People call me a *scoffer*," Büchner wrote to his parents in February 1834. "That's true, I often laugh; but I do not laugh *about* a human being but *because* he is a human being, which he cannot help, and I thereby laugh about myself, for I share his fate."

Woyzeck does not so much satirize society as stage its disappearance. As with *Lenz*, the play systematically disorders our very capacity to know. At times it seems to contain no real character at all, to be so driven by relentless compulsion that all are equally driving and equally driven and the true protagonist seems less a "he" or a "she" than an "it," an invisible force simultaneously elsewhere and everywhere. One is tempted to dub the play's protagonist not "Woyzeck" but "*immer zu,*" a virtually untranslatable phrase that may be rendered as "on and on" or "ever onwards" and that emerges as a pulsing rhythm beginning with Marie's dance with the Drum Major. Alternately, the play's protagonist might be described as simply the noises, lights, and motions that plague Woyzeck and construct the stage space: the bang of the army drum; the flash of Marie's mirror; the "weird" sound, "too clear, too loud," that follows Marie's murder; the whole vortex of artificial and natural, real and hallucinated sensations that directly play on the nerves of the audience as of the title character. Almost exactly a century after Büchner's death, Antonin Artaud would call for a "Theatre of Cruelty" to overwhelm the spectator's nervous system through a whirlwind of stimuli, and so force its purgation; *Woyzeck* was one of the few plays he held up as a model.

Woyzeck's madness is also inseparable from the greater madness of his playworld, and it is no accident that Büchner altered the historical record somewhat to put Woyzeck in an army uniform at the time of the murder. What we witness in this play is not only the systematic degradation of theatre's first proletarian protagonist but also the emergence of a range of disciplinary mechanisms aimed at transforming the human body into an object for use by political power. The subjugation and control of bodies in the play is made only more intolerable by the occasional signs of resistance we glimpse in Woyzeck and Marie. "The likes of us are wretched in this world and in the next; I guess if we ever got to Heaven, we'd have to help with the thunder," says Woyzeck to the Captain, to which the latter responds simply, "Woyzeck, you have no virtue, you're not a virtuous person." *"Bin ich ein Mensch?"* demands Marie of Woyzeck, using a word that means both "person" and (colloquially) "prostitute," in a question that simultaneously translates as "What am I—a human being?" and "What am I—a whore?" In such protests and double-meanings lie traces of character not yet fully erased.

But *Leonce and Lena* (*Leonce und Lena*) may complete the erasure. Written for a playwriting competition sponsored by the Cotta publishing house, the play arrived past the deadline and was returned to the author unread. If *Woyzeck's* incompletion oddly suits its subject matter, then the same is true of *Leonce and Lena's* belatedness. This is a comedy of inertia and irrelevance—which is not to condemn it but to say that it prefigures Oscar Wilde's *Importance of Being Earnest,* Alfred Jarry's *Ubu Roi*, and the anti-dramas of Eugène Ionesco. All of Büchner's works involve heavy borrowing, and *Leonce and Lena* is no exception: the play alludes to (among other sources) Shakespeare's *As You Like It*, Goethe's *The Sorrows of Young Werther*, various dramas of Alfred de Musset, and the conventions of *commedia dell'arte*. If the characters of *Woyzeck* are fragments, then the inhabitants of Popo and Peepee are mere figments, and the play's title page, with its fake quotations from the Italian dramatists Vittorio Alfieri and Carlo Gozzi, sets a tone of artifice that runs right through to Valerio's curtain-closing command to "lie in the shade and ask God for macaroni, melons, and figs." And yet even this fairy-tale world is not so weightless that we cannot recognize Büchner's bitter scorn for this blinkered little kingdom in which the monarch spouts pseudo-Kantian gobbledygook, officials perform fawning court rituals, starving peasants are mustered as scenic backdrops to royal functions, and pampered aesthetes tour Italy to forget the awful boredom of it all. *The Hessian Messenger* waits in the wings of even this most playful of plays.

Büchner's artistic accomplishments during this second Strassburg period are so remarkable that it is easy to forget that most of his time was actually spent on scientific research. The anatomy and morphology of the nervous system particularly fascinated him. He spent the winter of 1835–36 working on his *Dissertation on the Nervous System of the Barbel Fish* (*Mémoire sur le système nerveux du barbeau*), which, in spring of 1836, won him entry into the Natural History Society of Strassburg as a corresponding member. Soon thereafter he was awarded a doctorate by the University of Zurich, which allowed him to teach there, and he moved to Zurich in October 1836, hoping to secure a lectureship at the University. One last hurdle remained: Büchner had to present to the faculty a "trial lecture" based on his dissertation. The lecture, titled "On Cranial Nerves" ("*Über Schädelnerven*"), helped win him the position, and in November Büchner began teaching anatomy at the University, with the hope of eventually adding courses in philosophy as well.

Scholars have only recently begun taking seriously the significance of Büchner's scientific research for his broader oeuvre. As a scientist, Büchner was heavily indebted to an offshoot of German idealism called *Naturphilosophie*, which rejected dominant empirical methods as reductively "mechanical" and advocated instead a more holistic (and even mystical) vision of the cosmos as a harmoniously interconnected organism. The irony is that, for all of the avant-garde experimentation of his plays and fiction, Büchner's scientific method was actually somewhat rearguard in its attachment to a waning form of idealist science. This paradox has led the scholar John Reddick to argue convincingly that much of the force of Büchner's creative work stems from the painful shattering of this idealism. At the same time, it would be a mistake to dismiss Büchner's anatomical work as entirely behind the times, as his interest in the nature and function of the nervous system arose in concert with the emergence of empirical psychology in the early nineteenth century. Büchner's dissertation drew heavily on one of the founders of modern empirical psychology, Johannes Müller, and Müller (whose relations to *Naturphilosophie* were similarly complex) returned the favor by writing an admiring review of the dissertation. Even long after Freud, the sharply physiological conception of the psyche that runs through Büchner's work—from the mental effects of Woyzeck's diet and military regimen to Danton's comment that we must "pull each other's thoughts out of the brain fibers"—continues to pummel any sweetly spiritual sense of self.

Employed now as a lecturer at the University of Zurich, Büchner had attained a degree of security he had not enjoyed since his escape from Hesse two years earlier. But the respite would prove brief. On January 20, 1837, he wrote Minna to say that he had caught a cold. A week later he wrote her again to say, "*I have no desire to die and am as healthy as ever*," and to joke that he had been "cured by the fear of the medical care here." In fact the condition continued to worsen, and a diagnosis was soon given of typhus. Minna arrived at his bedside on February 17, but by that point he was fading rapidly. Two days later he was dead, at the age of twenty-three.

Acknowledgments

Special thanks to Laura Ginters, Martin Puchner, Christine Schott, Peter Schwartz, Laurence Senelick, and Tamra Wysocki-Niimi for their assistance in assembling and editing this edition. My thanks also to my excellent Norton editors, Carol Bemis and Rivka Genesen. I owe a further debt of gratitude for the research support provided by Boston University and Cornell University and for the encouragement of friends and colleagues in the U.S., Germany, and elsewhere. Above all, I am profoundly grateful for the help, encouragement, and enduring love of my wife Bernadette Meyler; thank you, Bernie.

This book is dedicated to Calliope, born into a world every bit as troubled as Büchner's own. May her beautiful voice carry.

Lithograph portrait of Büchner by A. Hoffmann.

The Texts of
BÜCHNER'S MAJOR WORKS

The Hessian Messenger

Historical Background

Germany in Büchner's time was a hodgepodge of kingdoms, duchies, grand duchies, and free cities, each with its own authorities, customs, and laws and with commerce between states choked by tariffs and red tape. Napoleon's military adventure and ultimate defeat only strengthened the power of local nobility, many of whom now viewed all calls for social reform as French imperialism by other means. Even by the standards of the time, Büchner's home of the Grand Duchy of Hesse-Darmstadt was provincial. Exceptionally small and almost entirely agrarian, with only two towns (Darmstadt and Mainz) of more than twenty thousand inhabitants, the state largely consisted of peasants lorded over by a particularly stiff-necked nobility. Widespread starvation aggravated by heavy taxation helped spark a peasant uprising, which authorities brutally crushed in September 1830.

In short, much of Hesse-Darmstadt would have been familiar to a time traveler from the Middle Ages. Cosmopolitan families such as the Büchners were thus oddly suspended, like so many German bourgeois, between medieval social structures and the revolutions of modernity. While the Hessian bourgeoisie was generally far more interested in forming what alliances it could with the ruling aristocracy rather than calling for broader political reforms—a conservatism that enraged Büchner—the class did have its share of dissidents. Büchner himself had been radicalized during his time at the University of Strassburg in 1831–33, and when he returned to the University of Giessen in 1833 he brought this radicalism with him. Borrowing from French revolutionary practice, he founded a secret insurrectionist group dubbed the Society of Human Rights, organizing one cell in Giessen in March 1834 and another in Darmstadt two months later. It was during this time that he met Ludwig Weidig, twenty-two years his senior, an evangelical pastor, schoolteacher, and active revolutionary.

Manuscript and Publication

The Hessian Messenger is a collaborative work authored by Büchner and Weidig. In May 1834, Büchner completed the original draft, which Weidig then heavily rewrote. Büchner was infuriated by the alterations, though not so disapproving that he withdrew from the project. As the original manuscripts are now lost, distinguishing between the Büchner and Weidig sections is largely a matter of educated guesswork. We do, however, know that Weidig changed Büchner's references to "the rich" to "the aristocrats," and it seems clear that the statistical and analytic sections owe more to Büchner and the biblical rhetoric to Weidig. The title and preface are also almost certainly Weidig's.

In July 1834 Büchner smuggled the manuscript to a basement printing press in the town of Offenbach (near Frankfurt). Three hundred copies were soon run off and collected by three conspirators, each of whom departed in a different direction. But the conspiracy was already doomed: a police informer had infiltrated their ranks and betrayed them to the authorities. Karl Minnigerode, one of the couriers, was quickly arrested, and Büchner went to Offenbach and Frankfurt to warn others. Authorities arrested many of the conspirators, and Büchner's rooms were illegally searched. Weidig managed to keep his freedom long enough to print a second edition of the *Messenger* in November 1834. Weidig's luck would run out the next April, however, when authorities would arrest and imprison him as well. Brutally interrogated and tortured, he died in his cell on February 23, 1837; the official ruling was suicide.

Büchner was more fortunate. Returning first to his parents' home in Darmstadt, he was called to appear in court and, with the last door to freedom about to close, slipped through it. Fleeing to France, he arrived in Strassburg in the beginning of March. A warrant for his arrest was issued on June 13, 1835. He would never return to Germany.

THE HESSIAN MESSENGER[†]

First Message

Darmstadt,[1] July 1834

Preface[2]

This paper intends to reveal the truth to the State of Hesse, but he who speaks the truth will be hanged; yes, even he who reads the truth might be punished by corrupt judges. Therefore anyone receiving this paper must take note of the following:

1) He must hide this paper carefully outside his house from the police;
2) he may only pass it on to trusted friends;
3) he may only pass it on anonymously to those who cannot be trusted as one trusts one's own self;
4) if this paper is found in the possession of anyone who has read it, he must confess he was just about to bring it to the District Council;
5) if this paper is found with anyone who has not read it, then he is of course innocent.

* * *

Peace to the huts! War on the palaces![3]

In the year 1834 it looks as if the Bible had been lying. It looks as if God had created peasants and laborers on the fifth day and princes and aristocrats on the sixth, saying to the latter: have dominion over every creeping thing that creepeth upon the earth—and had included peasants and the middle classes among the creeping things.[4] The life of aristocrats is a long Sunday; they live in beautiful houses, they wear elegant clothing, they have well-fed faces, and they speak their own language, while the people lie before them like manure on the field. The peasant walks behind his plow, but behind him walks the aristocrat, driving him on with the oxen, taking the grain and leaving the stubble to the peasant. The life of the peasant

---

[†] Translated by Henry J. Schmidt.

1. Actually printed in secret in Offenbach am Main, a Hessian town some twenty-five miles (forty kilometers) from Darmstadt. The error may be a deliberate attempt to confuse authorities.

2. The preface does not appear in the second edition of November 1834.

3. *Friede den Hütten! Krieg den Palästen!* in German; a translation of the French revolutionary slogan, "*Guerre aux châteaux! Paix aux chaumières!*"

4. In Genesis, God creates birds and sea creatures on the fifth day and land animals and humans on the sixth day. He gives man and woman "dominion" over all animals, including "every thing that creepeth upon the earth" (1:30).

is a long workday; strangers devour his land in his presence,[5] his body is a callus, his sweat is the salt on the aristocrat's table.

The Grand Duchy of Hesse has 718,373 inhabitants who pay the state 6,363,364 florins [sic] every year as follows:

1)	Direct taxes	2,128,131 fl.
2)	Indirect taxes	2,478,264 fl.
3)	Rent (for use of royal lands)	1,547,394 fl.
4)	Royal prerogatives[6]	46,938 fl.
5)	Fines	98,511 fl.
6)	Various sources	64,198 fl.
		6,363,363 fl. [sic]
		[6,363,436 fl.]

This money is the blood-tithe taken from the body of the people. Some seven hundred thousand human beings sweat, moan, and starve because of it. It is extorted in the name of the state, the extortionists claim to be authorized by the government, and the government says this is necessary to preserve order in the state. Now what kind of powerful thing is this: the state? If a number of people live in a country and regulations or laws exist to which everyone must conform, this is called a state. The state is therefore *everyone*; the regulators within the state are the laws which secure the well-being of *all*, and which should arise from the well-being of *all*.—Now see what has become of the state in the Grand Duchy; see what it means to preserve order in the state! Seven hundred thousand people pay six million for it, that means they are transformed into plowhorses and oxen so that they live in order. Living in order means starving and being oppressed.

Who are they who have created this order and who watch over its preservation? The Grand Ducal government. The government consists of the Grand Duke and his highest officials. The other officials are men appointed by the government to maintain order. Their number is legion:[7] state and government officials, county and district officials, church and school officials, treasury and forestry officials, etc., all with their armies of secretaries, etc. The people are their flock, they are its shepherds, milkers, and fleecers; they wear the peasants' skins, the spoil of the poor is in their houses;[8] the tears of widows and orphans are the grease on their faces; they rule freely

---

5. "Your country is desolate, your cities are burned with fire: your land, strangers devour it in your presence, and it is desolate, as overthrown by strangers" (Isaiah 1:7).
6. Fees collected by the sovereign from a range of industries.
7. When Jesus heals a man possessed by a devil, the devil tells Jesus, "My name is Legion: for we are many" (Mark 5:9).
8. "The Lord will enter into judgment with the ancients of his people, and the princes thereof: for ye have eaten up the vineyard; the spoil of the poor is in your houses" (Isaiah 3:14).

and exhort the people to servitude. To them you pay your 6,000,000 florins in fees; for that they have the task of governing you; that is, to be fed by you and to rob you of your human and civil rights. Now see the harvest of your sweat.

The Ministries of the Interior and Justice are paid 1,110,607 florins. For that you have a chaos of laws accumulated from arbitrary ordinances of all centuries, written mostly in a foreign language. You have thereby inherited the nonsense of all previous generations; the burden that crushed them is pressing upon you. The law is the property of an insignificant class of aristocrats and intellectuals who grant themselves authority through their own machinations. This justice is merely a means to keep you under control, so that you can be more easily oppressed; it acts according to laws that you do not understand, principles about which you know nothing, judgments that you cannot comprehend. It is incorruptible, for it lets itself be paid just dearly enough not to need any bribes. But most of its servants have sold body and soul to the government. Their armchairs stand on a pile of 461,373 florins (total expenses for the courts and penal institutions). The frock coats, canes, and sabers of their inviolable servants are lined with the silver of 197,502 florins (total cost of the police force, constabulary, etc.). In Germany justice has been for centuries the whore of the German princes. You must pave each step toward her with silver and pay for her verdict with poverty and humiliation. Think of the stamp taxes, think of cringing in offices and standing sentry duty before them. Think of the fees for scribes and bailiffs. You may sue your neighbor for stealing a potato, but just try to sue for the larceny committed on your property every day on behalf of the state in the form of fees and taxes, so that a legion of useless officials may fatten themselves on your sweat; try to sue because you are subject to the whims of a few potbellies and because these whims are called law; sue because you are the plowhorses of the state; sue for your lost human rights: where are the courts that will hear your suit, where are the judges who will administer justice?—The chains of your fellow citizens of Vogelsberg who were dragged off to Rokkenburg[9] will give you an answer.

And if at last one of those few judges or other officials who holds justice and the common good dearer than his belly and Mammon[1] wants to aid instead of persecute the people, then he himself will be persecuted by the prince's highest officials.

For the Finance Ministry 1,551,502 florins.

---

9. Parts of Vogelsberg engaged in a peasants' revolt that swept across upper Hesse in September 1830. Some insurrectionists were subsequently imprisoned near Rokkenburg.
1. Greed, often personified as the devil.

This pays the salaries of the treasury officials, chief revenue officials, tax collectors, and their subordinates. For this they calculate the yield of your fields and count your heads. The ground beneath your feet, the bite of food between your teeth is taxed. For this the lords sit together in frock coats and the people stand naked and cringing before them, the lords lay their hands on the people's thighs and shoulders and calculate how much they still can carry, and if the lords are merciful, it is like sparing an animal that should not be overly fatigued.

For the military 914,820 florins.

For that your sons get a colorful coat for their bodies, a gun or a drum on their shoulders, and every autumn they may shoot blanks, and they tell you how the lords of the royal court and the misbegotten sons of nobility take precedence over all children of honest people, and they march around with them on broad city streets with drums and trumpets. For those 900,000 florins your sons must swear allegiance to the tyrants and stand guard at their palaces. With their drums they drown out your groans, with their clubs they smash your skulls when you dare to think you are free men. They are legal murderers protecting legal thieves, think of Södel! There your brothers, your children were killers of brothers and fathers.

For pensions 480,000 florins.

For that the officials are put in easy-chairs after they have served the state loyally for a certain time, that means after they have been zealous hacks serving in that organized oppression called law and order.

For the Ministry of State and the State Council 174,600 florins.

Just about everywhere now in Germany the biggest rascals stand closest to the princes, at least in the Grand Duchy. If an honest man were to appear in a State Council, he would be thrown out. But if an honest man could indeed become and remain a minister, as matters now stand in Germany he would merely be a puppet on strings pulled by a princely puppet, and the princely dummy is being manipulated by a valet or a coachman or his wife and her favorite, or his half-brother—or all together. The situation in Germany is now as the Prophet Micah writes, Chapter 7, Verses 3 and 4: "The great man, he uttereth his mischievous desire: so they wrap it up. The best of them is as a brier: the most upright is sharper than a thorn hedge." You must pay dearly for the briers and thorn hedges, for in addition you must pay 827,772 florins for the Grand Ducal house and royal court.

The institutions, the people of which I have spoken up to now are merely tools, merely servants. They do nothing in their own name; under their appointment to office stands an "L.," that means *Ludwig*[2]

---

2. Ludwig II (1777–1848), Grand Duke of Hesse and by Rhine.

by the Grace of God, and they say with reverence: "in the name of the Grand Duke." This is their battle cry when they auction off your equipment, drive off your cattle, throw you in jail. In the name of the Grand Duke, they say, and this man is called: inviolable, holy, sovereign, Royal Highness. Yet approach this child of man and look through his princely cloak. He eats when he is hungry and sleeps when his eyes grow heavy. Behold, like you he crept naked and soft into the world and like you he will be carried from it hard and stiff, and yet his foot is on your neck, seven hundred thousand human beings are hitched to his plow, his ministers are responsible for his actions, he controls your property through the taxes he decrees, he controls your lives through the laws he makes, around him are noblemen and women known as the royal court, and his divine power is passed on to his children through women of equally superhuman stock.

Woe unto you idolaters!—You are like the heathens who pray to the crocodile that tears them apart. You place a crown on his head, but it is a crown of thorns that you are pressing onto your own heads; you place a scepter in his hand, but it is a rod that flogs you; you place him on your throne, but it is a rack of torture for you and your children. The prince is the head of the bloodsucker that crawls over you, the ministers are its teeth and the officials its tail. The hungry bellies of all highborn gentlemen to whom he gives high positions are the cupping glasses which he applies to the body of the land. That "L." on his decrees is the mark of the beast[3] worshiped by the idolaters of our time. The princely cloak is the carpet on which the lords and ladies of nobility and the court roll over each other in their lust—they cover their abscesses with medals and ribbons, and they cover their leprous bodies with costly garments. The daughters of the people are their maids and whores, the sons of the people their lackeys and soldiers. Go to Darmstadt once and see how the lords are amusing themselves there with your money, and then tell your starving wives and children that strangers' bellies are thriving marvelously on their bread, tell them about the beautiful clothes dyed in their sweat and the dainty ribbons cut from the calluses on their hands, tell about the stately houses built from the bones of the people; and then crawl into your smoky huts and bend over your stony fields, so that for once your children can go there too when a royal heir and a royal heiress want advice and counsel on the production of another royal heir, and your children can look through the open glass doors and see the tablecloth on which the lords dine and smell the lamps that burn from the fat of the peasants. You endure all that because rascals tell you: "This

3. A sign of apocalypse described in Revelation 13:17–18, 16:2, and 19:20.

government is ordained of God."[4] This government is ordained not of God but of the Father of Lies. These German princes have no legitimate power; to the contrary, for centuries they have scorned and finally betrayed legitimate power, namely the German Emperor, who was formerly freely chosen by the people. The power of the German princes is based on treason and perjury, not on the people's choice, and therefore their ways and doings are cursed by God; their wisdom is illusion, their justice is oppression. They beat down the land and grind the faces of the poor.[5] You blaspheme against God if you call one of these princes the Lord's anointed, this means God has anointed devils and made them rulers over German soil. These princes have torn apart Germany, our dear Fatherland, they have betrayed the Emperor elected by our free forefathers, and now these traitors and torturers demand your loyalty!—But the kingdom of darkness is coming to an end. Now oppressed by the princes, Germany will soon arise again as a free state with a government elected by the people. The Scriptures say: "Render unto Caesar the things which are Caesar's."[6] But what things belong to the princes, to the traitors?—*Judas's share!*[7]

For the legislatures 16,000 florins.

In 1789[8] the people of France were tired of being their king's whipping boy. They rose up and nominated trustworthy men who came together and said: a king is a man like any other, he is merely the first servant of the state, he must be accountable to the people, and if he does his job poorly, he should be punished. They then defined the rights of man: "No one shall inherit by birth any rights or titles over another, no one shall gain rights over another through property. Supreme power lies in the will of all or of the majority. This will is law, it manifests itself through legislatures or through the people's representatives, elected by all, and anyone may be elected; the elected express the will of their constituents, and the will of the elected majority thus corresponds to the will of the majority of the people; the king is merely responsible for the execution of the laws they enact."[9] The king swore to uphold this constitution, but he perjured himself before the people, and the people sentenced him to die as is proper for a traitor. The French then abolished hereditary monarchy and freely elected a new government, to

---

4. "The powers that be are ordained of God" (Romans 13:1).
5. " 'What mean ye that ye beat my people to pieces, and grind the faces of the poor?' saith the Lord God of hosts" (Isaiah 3:15).
6. Words of Jesus in Mark 12:17 and Matthew 22:21.
7. Matthew 26 describes Judas's betrayal of Jesus for thirty pieces of silver.
8. The beginning of the French Revolution.
9. Not an actual quotation but rather an invention of Büchner and/or Weidig.

which every nation is entitled according to reason and Holy Writ. The men who were to supervise the execution of the laws were elected by the assembly of people's representatives, they formed the new government. Executive and legislative government was thus elected by the people and France was a free state.

But the remaining monarchs were terrified of the power of the French people; they thought they might all break their necks on that first royal corpse, and their mistreated subjects might awaken at the French call to freedom. With giant war machines and cavalry they descended upon France from all sides, and a large number of nobles and aristocrats bestirred themselves and joined the enemy. Then the people grew angry and arose in their strength. They crushed the traitors and annihilated the monarchs' mercenaries. This newborn freedom thrived in the blood of tyrants, and thrones trembled and nations exulted in its voice. But the French sold even their newborn freedom for the glory offered them by Napoleon, and they crowned him Emperor.—Thereupon the Almighty allowed the Emperor's army to freeze to death in Russia and lashed France with cossacks' whips and gave the French potbellied Bourbon kings again, so that France would convert from idolizing hereditary monarchy to serving the god who had created men free and equal. But when France had paid its penalty and brave men chased the corrupt Charles the Tenth out of the country in July 1830, liberated France nevertheless turned once again to *semi-hereditary* monarchy and set a new scourge on its back in the person of the hypocrite Louis Philippe. There was great joy in Germany and all of Europe, however, when Charles the Tenth was deposed, and the suppressed German states prepared to fight for freedom. Then the princes deliberated how to avoid the wrath of the people, and the cunning ones among them said: let us give up part of our power to save the rest. And they appeared before the people and spoke: we shall grant you the freedom you mean to fight for.—And trembling with fear they threw down a few scraps and spoke of their charity. Unfortunately the people trusted them and were pacified.—And thus was Germany deceived like France.

What in fact are these constitutions in Germany? Nothing but empty straw from which the princes have threshed the grain for themselves. What are our legislatures? Nothing but slow-moving vehicles which can perhaps be used once or twice to block the rapacity of the princes and their ministers, but which can never be used to build a mighty fortress for German freedom. What are our election laws? Nothing but violations of most Germans' civil and human rights. Think of the election laws in the Grand Duchy, where no one may be elected who is not well-to-do, no matter how upright and well-intentioned he may be, yet Grolmann, who wanted to steal two million from you is elected.[1] Think of the constitution of the Grand Duchy.—According to its articles, the Grand Duke is inviolable, holy, and accountable to no one. His high position is hereditary, he has the right to wage war and has exclusive control over the military. He convenes, adjourns, or dissolves the legislatures. The legislatures may not originate laws but must request them, and it is left completely up to the prince's discretion to grant or deny them. He retains possession of nearly unlimited power, except that he may not enact new laws and impose new taxes without the approval of the legislatures. Yet often he does not adhere to this approval, often he is satisfied with the old laws deriving from princely power, and he therefore needs no new laws. Such a constitution is a miserable, deplorable thing. What can be expected from legislatures restricted by such a constitution? Even if there were no betrayers of the people nor craven cowards among the elected, even if they consisted only of determined friends of the people?! What can be expected from legislatures hardly able to defend the miserable tatters of a wretched constitution!—The only opposition they were able to muster was the denial of the two million florins the Grand Duke wanted as a gift from the heavily indebted nation for the payment of his debts. But even if the Grand Duchy's legislatures had sufficient rights, and the Grand Duchy—but the Grand Duchy alone—had a true constitution, this marvel would soon come to an end. The vultures in Vienna and Berlin would stretch their hangmen's claws and destroy this little freedom root and branch. The entire German nation must win this freedom. And this time, dear fellow citizens, is not far off.—The Lord has delivered the beautiful land of Germany—for many centuries the most glorious empire on earth—into the hands of foreign and native oppressors, because in their hearts the German people had forsaken the freedom and equality of their ancestors and forsaken the fear of the Lord, because you devoted yourselves to idolizing those many petty lords, dukes, and kinglets.

The Lord who smashed the rod of the foreign oppressor Napoleon[2] shall also destroy the images of our native tyrants through the hands of the people. These images may glitter with gold and jewels, medals and decorations, but inside them *the worm does not die, and their feet are of clay.*—God will give you strength to smite their feet

1. A proposal was made in 1830 to transfer two million gulden of the duke's personal debt to the state treasury. The reference is likely to Friedrich von Grolmann, a member of Parliament, though Karl von Grolmann, the chief minister of Hesse until 1829, is possibly intended, and the author(s) may be confusing the two.
2. "For thou hast broken the yoke of his burden, and the staff of his shoulder, the rod of his oppressor" (Isaiah 9:4).

as soon as you repent the error of your ways and know the truth: "that there is only one God and no other gods before him who let themselves be called Highness and Most High,[3] divine and accountable to no one; that God created all men free and equal in their rights; that no government has God's blessing unless it is based on the people's trust and is expressly or tacitly elected by them; but that a government with power but no rights over a nation is ordained of God only as the Devil is ordained of God; that obedience to such a devil's government is only valid until its devil's might can be broken; that God, who united a nation into one body through a common language, shall punish in this life and eternally hereafter as murderers of the people and tyrants those rulers who draw and quarter the nation or even tear it into thirty pieces, for the Scriptures say: what God hath joined together, let not man put asunder;[4] and that the Almighty, who can create a paradise from a desert, can also transform a land of distress and misery into a paradise, like our treasured Germany before its princes tore it apart and flayed it."

Since the German Empire was decayed and rotten, and the Germans had forsaken God and freedom, God let the Empire go to ruin in order to regenerate it as a free state. For a time He gave "Satan's angels" the power to beat Germany with their fists, He gave "principalities and powers, the rulers of the darkness of this world, spiritual wickedness in high places" (Ephesians 6:12), power to torment citizens and peasants and suck their blood and do mischief to all who love justice and freedom more than injustice and servitude.—But their cup is full!

Look at that monster branded by God, King Ludwig of Bavaria, the blasphemer who forces honest men to kneel before his image and allows corrupt judges to imprison those who speak the truth; the swine who rolled in every puddle of vice in Italy, the wolf who makes corrupt legislatures allot five million every year to his Baal-court,[5] and then ask: "Is this a government with God's blessing?"

---

3. The passage contains numerous biblical allusions, including the First Commandment: "Thou shalt have no other gods before me" (Exodus 20:30, Deuteronomy 5:7). In Isaiah 66:24, God says of transgressors that "their worm shall not die, neither shall their fire be quenched; and they shall be an abhorring unto all flesh" (cf. Mark 9). In Daniel 2, the Babylonian king Nebuchadnezzar dreams of a great idol composed of four metals and feet made of iron and clay; a stone smites the feet and destroys the idol. Daniel interprets the dream to represent successive kingdoms, each of which will be shattered until a kingdom comes that will last forever.

4. Jesus' prohibition of divorce in Matthew 19:6: "What therefore God hath joined together, let not man put asunder." "Thirty pieces": after the Congress of Vienna in 1815, Germany consisted of thirty-eight states.

5. In the Hebrew Bible, "Baal" designates a false god or idol. "That monster": after the July Revolution in France in 1830, the relatively liberal policies of Ludwig I (1786–1868) turned sharply repressive.

> Ha! you'd be a governor of God?
> God bestows on us his grace;
> You rob, oppress, imprison us,
> You're not of God, tyrant!

I say to you: the cup of the prince and his like is full. God, who has used these princes to punish Germany for its sins, shall heal it again. "He shall go through the briers and thorns and burn them together" (Isaiah 27:4).

Just as the hunchback with which God has branded this King Ludwig can grow no larger,[6] so can the atrocities of these princes no longer increase. Their cup is full. God will smash their fortresses, and life and strength, the blessing of freedom, shall then bloom again in Germany. The princes have transformed German soil into a great field of corpses, as Ezekiel writes in Chapter 37: "The Lord set me down in the midst of the valley which was full of bones, and lo, they were very dry." But what is God's Word about these dry bones: "Behold, I will lay sinews upon you, and will bring up flesh upon you, and cover you with skin, and put breath in you, and ye shall live; and ye shall know that I am the Lord." And God's Word shall truly come to pass in Germany as well, as the Prophet says: "There was a noise, and behold a shaking, and the bones came together, bone to his bone.—And the breath came into them, and they lived, and stood up upon their feet, an exceeding great army."

As the Prophet writes, so it was until now in Germany: your bones are dry, for the order in which you live is sheer oppression. In the Grand Duchy you pay six million to a handful of people whose whims govern your life and property, and it is the same for others in fragmented Germany. You are nothing, you have nothing! You are without rights. You must give whatever your insatiable oppressors demand and carry whatever they load upon you. As far as a tyrant can see— and Germany has about thirty of them—land and people wither. But as the Prophet writes, so shall it soon be in Germany: the Day of Resurrection[7] is at hand. On the field of corpses there shall be a noise and a shaking, and there will be a great army of the resurrected.

Lift up your eyes and count the little band of your oppressors, who are strong only through the blood they suck from you and through your arms which you lend them against your will. There are about ten thousand of them and seven hundred thousand of you in the Grand Duchy, and that is the ratio of people to their oppressors in the rest of Germany as well. They may threaten with royal

6. Ludwig's hunchback was a propagandistic invention.
7. The end of time when the dead will rise up to be judged by Christ.

armaments and cavalry, but I say to you: all they that take the sword against the people shall perish with the sword of the people.[8] Germany is now a field of corpses, soon it shall be a paradise. The German nation is one body, you are a limb of that body. It makes no difference where the apparently dead body begins to twitch. When the Lord gives you his signs through the men through whom he shall lead nations from bondage to freedom, then arise, and the whole body will rise up with you.

You cringed for long years in the thorny fields of servitude,[9] then you will sweat for one summer in the vineyard of freedom and shall be free unto the thousandth generation.

Throughout a long life you dug up the earth, then you shall dig your tyrants' grave. You built the fortresses, then you shall destroy them and build the house of freedom. Then you shall be able to baptize your children freely with the water of life. And until the Lord calls you through his messengers and signs, be watchful, prepare yourselves in spirit, pray, and teach your children to pray: "Lord, break the rod of our oppressors and let Thy kingdom come,[1] the kingdom of righteousness. Amen."

---

8. "All they that take the sword shall perish with the sword" (Matthew 26:52). "I say to you": *ich sage euch* in German; a phrase frequently used by Jesus in the Gospels.
9. After exiling Adam and Eve from Eden, God made them toil in thorny fields (Genesis 3).
1. An echo of the Lord's Prayer (Matthew 6:10).

Danton's Death

Historical Context

Danton's Death takes place at the climax of the Reign of Terror, an especially violent period of the French Revolution. Louis XVI had been guillotined more than a year earlier, and the government was now in the hands of the Jacobins, a faction of revolutionary radicals led by Maximilien de Robespierre. This faction led a campaign to fundamentally transform French society, a campaign that included the expropriation of property to the poor and the creation of a new calendar marking the beginning of the Revolution as Year I. The Jacobins carried out this wholesale transformation while at the same time defending the infant Republic against a host of internal and external enemies. To resist these enemies Robespierre transformed the Republic into a virtual dictatorship. The fountainhead of state power now lay with the Committee of Public Safety, a body largely controlled by Robespierre and his supporters.

The play occupies roughly two weeks, from late March to early April of 1794, a fortnight that comprehended two crucial phases in the Reign of Terror. The first phase involved the arrest and execution of members of the Hébertists, an ultra-radical faction regarded by Robespierre as a threat from the left. Though Büchner does not stage this event, we witness its effects on the characters and their world. The second event, staged by Büchner with help from his historical sources, is the imprisonment, trial, and execution of Danton and his allies. A Jacobin himself, Danton had nevertheless become increasingly critical of the dictatorial and terroristic direction of the Robespierre regime. His struggle with Robespierre forms the backbone of the drama.

For more details about the historical period, see the Character Descriptions on p. 18, particularly the entries for the play's central antagonists: Danton and Robespierre.

Sources

While Büchner took many liberties with the historical record, he also borrowed heavily from a variety of sources. The most prominent of these are Adolphe Thiers's *Histoire de la Révolution française* (*History of the French Revolution*, 1823–27) and *Die Geschichte unserer Zeit* (*The History of Our Age*, 1826–30, edited by Carl Strahlheim). Among other works he consulted was one written by a character who also appears in the play: Louis-Sébastien Mercier's *Le Nouveau Paris* (*New Paris*, 1799).

Manuscript, Publication, and Premiere

A complete manuscript of the play survives, though scholars debate whether this represents a final version. In addition, Büchner's supporter Karl Gutzkow published a censored version in the journal *Phönix* in 1835, and two extant copies of this version include Büchner's handwritten corrections. In assembling the play, editors must therefore pick and choose among the manuscript, the published version, and Büchner's various corrections.

The play was premiered by the Volksbühne at the Belle-Alliance Theater in Berlin on January 5, 1902. It was the enormous success of Max Reinhardt's 1916 production at the Deutsches Theater in Berlin, however, that gained it widespread attention and assured it a place in the European repertoire.

Character Descriptions

Almost all of the characters in Büchner's play are based on historical figures, many of whom have since fallen into obscurity. Below are descriptions of all the historical figures in the play. The overrepresentation of one particular profession in the group might lead one to think of the Revolution as an unyielding decision to take literally Dick's injunction from *Henry VI, Part 2*: "The first thing we do, let's kill all the lawyers." Above all, it reminds us that revolutionary leadership largely derived from the legal segment of the bourgeoisie.

Amar: Jean-Baptiste-André Amar (1755–1816), a lawyer, strong supporter of Robespierre, and President of the National Convention in April 1794.

Barère: Bertrand Barère de Vieuzac (1755–1841), a lawyer, radical propagandist, and member of the Committee of Public Safety.

Billaud-Varennes: Jacques-Nicolas Billaud-Varenne (1756–1819), a lawyer and member of the Committee of Public Safety. Influential in instigating the September massacres of 1792.

Chaumette: Pierre-Gaspard Chaumette (1763–1794), a radical revolutionary and leader in the Paris Commune. Participated in the September massacres and championed the Cult of Reason; guillotined in April 1794 for his connections to the ultra-radical Hébertists.

Collot d'Herbois: Jean-Marie Collot d'Herbois (1750–1796), an actor, writer, radical revolutionary, and member of the Committee of Public Safety; notoriously ordered summary mass executions of suspected counterrevolutionaries in Lyon.

Danton: Georges Jacques Danton (1759–1794), a lawyer, popular orator, and one of the central figures of the French Revolution. Danton claimed responsibility for the Storming of the Tuileries on August 10, 1792, an event that led to the overthrow of the monarchy. Whatever the truth of this claim, Danton was appointed Minister of Justice of the new Republic in 1792. The Republic was in a desperate position, threatened from within by enemies, spies, and a factional government and from without by the combined armies of Austria, Spain, and England, to name but three. Terrified of the enemy within, mobs broke into the prisons of Paris in early September 1792 and slaughtered roughly half the inmates, a population of perhaps fourteen hundred. Though Danton was likely responsible only for indulging the mobs rather than inciting them, some moderates accused him of orchestrating the September massacre. There is, however, no historical evidence that his acts during the massacre subsequently provoked in him a crisis of conscience of the sort depicted in the play. A year later, in April 1793, Danton joined the first Committee of Public Safety and soon emerged as its leader. From that position, he attempted to deal with the Revolution's foreign enemies through diplomacy and compromise, a stance regarded by radicals as overly conciliatory. When the National Convention elected a new Committee of Public Safety on July 10, 1793, Danton was not included. From an increasingly marginal position, Danton sought to temper the bloodthirstiness of the Reign of Terror, and eventually widened his object of criticism from the terror itself to the whole government of Robespierre. By the time of his arrest, on the night of March 29–30, 1794, he was widely regarded as the leader of the moderate opposition. Drawing on his famous oratorical skills, Danton defended himself before the Revolutionary Tribunal, but Robespierre already held him in checkmate. Danton was guillotined on April 5, 1794, saying to the executioner, "Show my head to the people; it is well worth seeing."

Danton, Julie: An invention of Büchner's. Danton's second wife was actually Sébastienne-Louise Danton (née Gély), who bears little resemblance to Büchner's character.

Desmoulins, Camille: A lawyer and revolutionary journalist (1760–1794). He was friends with Robespierre from their school days in the Collège Louis-le-Grand in Paris. He helped instigate the storming of the Bastille in July 1789 and became famous as a radical pamphleteer. He became Danton's Secretary-General at the Ministry of Justice, and became allied with him. By December 1793 Desmoulins and Danton were widely regarded as leaders of the moderate wing of the Jacobins. His journal *Le Vieux Cordelier* opposed actions of the Robespierre regime with increasing vehemence, and Robespierre had him guillotined with Danton on April 5, 1794.

Desmoulins, Lucile: Wife of Camille, whom she married in 1790 (1771–94). Her death in the play is an invention; in reality she was arrested eight days after her husband's death and guillotined.

Dillon: Arthur Dillon (1750–1794), an Irish-born aristocrat and general who served the ancien régime and later commanded an army of the Republic. He was arrested on charges of royalist sympathies and guillotined on April 13, 1794.

Dumas: René François Dumas (1758–1794), a priest-turned-lawyer and a hardline follower of Robespierre. Guillotined with Robespierre and his circle.

Fabre d'Églantine: Philippe Fabre d'Églantine (1750–1794), poet, playwright, and the author of the names of the months and days of the revolutionary calendar. A friend of Danton, he was accused for involvement in a forgery scandal (see p. 42, n. 4) and guillotined.

Fouquier-Tinville: Antoine Quentin Fouquier-Tinville (1746–1795), a lawyer and public prosecutor of the Revolutionary Tribunal from March 1793 to July 1794. A particularly merciless inquisitor, he was himself guillotined after Robespierre's fall.

Hérault-Séchelles: Marie-Jean Hérault de Séchelles (1759–1794), an aristocratic lawyer and member of the Committee of Public Safety. Accused of conspiring with the ultra-radical Hébertists and foreign agents against the government, he was guillotined with Danton.

Herman: Martial Joseph Armand Herman (1749–1795), a lawyer who served as President of the Revolutionary Tribunal until replaced by Dumas. Guillotined after the fall of Robespierre.

Lacroix: Jean-François Delacroix (1753–1794), a lawyer and member of the first Committee of Public Safety. An ally of Danton, he was guillotined with him.

Legendre: Louis Legendre (1752–1797), a butcher and prominent Jacobin who had taken part in the storming of the Tuileries in 1792. An ally of Danton, he initially defended him before the Revolutionary Tribunal, but retreated in the face of threats. After Robespierre's death he would become a reactionary and serve as president of the National Convention.

Mercier: Louis-Sébastien Mercier (1740–1814), a writer. Arrested in 1793 as a moderate, he was released from prison after Robespierre's fall. His account of the political events and the daily life of the revolution appeared in 1799 as *Le Nouveau Paris*, which Büchner used as a source for *Danton's Death*.

Paris: Félix Paris, a member of the Revolutionary Tribunal who adopted the name "Fabricius" in 1793. He warned Danton of his impending arrest, but was imprisoned in 1795 as a follower of Robespierre.

Paine: Thomas Paine (1737–1809), English writer and philosopher, and one of the most influential propagandists in history. His pamphlet *Common Sense* (1776) helped spark the American Revolution, in which he also fought. His *Rights of Man* (1791) defended the French Revolution and caused him to be indicted for treason in England. Resettling in France, he was elected to a seat in the National Convention. While he favored the abolition of the monarchy, he opposed the King's execution. He would suffer the consequence of such moderation when Robespierre came to power, languishing in prison for much of 1794. During the period of his imprisonment the first part of his book *The Age of Reason* appeared; though the book largely espoused deistic principles, it earned him a reputation as an atheist. He was released after Robespierre's fall from power and readmitted to the National Convention.

Philippeau: Pierre Philippeaux (1756–1794), a lawyer, journalist, and member of the National Convention. An ally of Danton, he was guillotined alongside him.

Robespierre: Maximilien de Robespierre (1758–1794), a lawyer, radical Jacobin leader, and one of the central figures of the French Revolution. Born in the French provincial city of Arras, he obtained a scholarship to study law at the elite Collège Louis-le-Grand in Paris, where he befriended Camille Desmoulins. He was involved in the Revolution from the beginning, as a representative to the Estates General and various other assemblies from 1789 onward. He became known for his democratic political principles (including universal suffrage, an end to slavery in the colonies, and the abolition of the monarchy) and his austere personal behavior, which earned him the nickname "The Incorruptible." Robespierre's base of power was the Jacobin Club, a radically egalitarian political organization in Paris. Elected to the National Convention in September 1792, he became a leader of the radical Jacobin faction (called "The Mountain") and demanded the execution of Louis XVI. After the King's execution, the Jacobins managed to defeat their antagonists, the moderate Girondists, many of whom were arrested and executed. In June 1793 the Jacobins came fully into power, but their republic was teetering on the verge of civil war and actively defending itself against foreign armies. Robespierre answered the threat by establishing a virtual dictatorship, at the heart of which was the Committee of Public Safety. Acting as a leader of this Committee from mid-1793 to mid-1794, Robespierre became the single most powerful person in France, and began a systematic campaign of summary trial and execution against perceived enemies from both the left and the right. The former included the ultra-radical Hébertist faction, which he crushed in March 1794, and the latter included a group of moderate Jacobins, the most famous of whom was Danton. The persecution of this group, which took place from late March to early April 1794, is the subject of Büchner's play. Robespierre would not outlive his enemies long; just a few weeks later, on July 27, he was arrested, and the next day guillotined.

St. Just: Louis de Saint-Just (1767–1794), a lawyer, Jacobin hardliner, and zealous devotee of Robespierre. One of the youngest of the revolutionary leaders, he was elected to the National Convention in 1792. He quickly distinguished himself as an orator and firebrand by eloquently calling for the execution without trial of Louis XVI. He was elected to the Committee of Public Safety in 1793 and subsequently to the position of President of the National Convention. His brief tenure in power was distinguished by some of the most radical legislative acts of the Revolution (e.g., the Ventôse Decrees, which expropriated land from "enemies of the Republic" to "patriots") as well as by merciless extermination of perceived enemies. He was arrested at the beginning of the Thermidorian Reaction, on July 27, 1794, and guillotined alongside Robespierre.

Vouland: Jean-Henri Voulland (1751–1801), a lawyer and member of the Committee of General Security. Though he helped prosecute the Reign of Terror, he was nevertheless an opponent of Robespierre and helped overthrow him.

DANTON'S DEATH[†]

Characters

GEORGE DANTON
LEGENDRE
CAMILLE DESMOULINS
HÉRAULT-SÉCHELLES
LACROIX　　　　　　　　　} *deputies of the National Convention*[1]
PHILIPPEAU
FABRE D'ÉGLANTINE
MERCIER
THOMAS PAINE

ROBESPIERRE
ST. JUST
BARÈRE　　　　　　　} *members of the Committee*
COLLOT D'HERBOIS　　　*of Public Safety*[2]
BILLAUD-VARENNES

CHAUMETTE, *procurator of the Commune*[3]
DILLON, *a general*
FOUQUIER-TINVILLE, *public prosecutor*
AMAR
VOULAND　　} *members of the Committee of General Security*[4]
HERMAN
DUMAS　　} *presidents of the Revolutionary Tribunal*[5]
PARIS, *a friend of Danton*
SIMON, *a prompter*
SIMON'S WIFE
LAFLOTTE
JULIE, *Danton's wife*
LUCILE, *wife of Camille Desmoulins*
ROSALIE
ADELAIDE　} *grisettes*
MARION
LADIES *at card tables,* GENTLEMEN *and* LADIES *as well as a* YOUNG
GENTLEMAN *and* EUGÉNIE *on a promenade,* CITIZENS, CITIZEN-

---

† Translated by Henry J. Schmidt.
1. Elected assembly that governed France from September 1792 to October 1795.
2. The most powerful political body in France during the Reign of Terror (September
   1793 to July 1794); charged with national defense against foreign and domestic enemies and ultimately granted dictatorial powers.
3. The revolutionary government of Paris.
4. Organ of the revolutionary government especially charged with police functions;
   alongside the Committee of Public Safety, directed much of the Reign of Terror.
5. Revolutionary court for political crimes.

SOLDIERS, DEPUTIES FROM LYONS *and other* DEPUTIES, JACOBINS, PRESIDENTS OF THE JACOBIN CLUB *and the* NATIONAL CONVENTION, JAILERS, EXECUTIONERS, *and* DRIVERS, MEN *and* WOMEN *of the people*, GRISETTES, BALLADEER, BEGGAR, *etc.*

Act One

I

HÉRAULT-SÉCHELLES, *a few women at a card table.* DANTON, JULIE *somewhat farther off,* DANTON *on a footstool at* JULIE'S *feet.*

DANTON Look at the pretty lady—how neatly she plays her cards. She knows how, all right—they say she always gives her husband a heart and others a diamond. You women could even make us fall in love with a lie.

JULIE Do you believe in me?

DANTON How do I know? We know little about each other. We're all thick-skinned, we reach for each other, but it's all in vain, we just rub the rough leather off . . . we are very lonely.

JULIE You know me, Danton.

DANTON Yes, whatever "knowing" means. You have dark eyes and curly hair and a nice complexion and you always say to me: dear George. But (*He points to her forehead and eyes.*) there—there: what's behind that? No, our senses are coarse. Know each other? We'd have to break open our skulls and pull each other's thoughts out of the brain fibers.

A WOMAN (*To* HÉRAULT.) What are you doing with your fingers?

HÉRAULT Nothing!

WOMAN Don't twist your thumb under like that! I can't stand it.

HÉRAULT Just look, it has a very peculiar physiognomy.

DANTON No, Julie, I love you like the grave.

JULIE (*Turning away.*) Oh!

DANTON No, listen! They say in the grave there is peace, and grave and peace are one. If that's so, then in your lap I'm already lying under the earth. You sweet grave—your lips are funeral bells, your voice my death knell, your breasts my burial mound, and your heart my coffin.

WOMAN You lose!

HÉRAULT That was an adventure of love. It costs money as they all do.

WOMAN Then you made your declarations of love with your fingers, like a deaf-mute.

HÉRAULT And why not? Some say that fingers are the easiest to understand. I plotted an affair with a queen, my fingers were princes changed into spiders, you, Madame, were the good fairy, but it didn't work: the queen was always with child, bearing jacks by the minute. I wouldn't let my daughter play games like that. The kings and queens fall on top of each other so indecently and the jacks pop up right after.

(CAMILLE DESMOULINS *and* PHILIPPEAU *enter.*)

HÉRAULT   Philippeau, what sad eyes! Did you rip a hole in your red cap, did Saint Jacob[6] look angry, did it rain during the guillotining or did you get a bad seat and not see anything?

CAMILLE   You're parodying Socrates. Do you know what the divine man asked Alcibiades[7] when he found him gloomy and depressed one day? "Did you lose your shield in battle, did you lose a race or a sword fight? Did someone else sing better or play the zither better than you?" What classic republicans![8] Just compare that to our guillotine-romanticism!

PHILIPPEAU   Another twenty victims today. We were wrong: the Hébertists[9] were sent to the scaffold because they weren't systematic enough. Maybe also because the decemvirs[1] thought they'd be lost if just for a week there were men who were more feared than they.

HÉRAULT   They want to change us into cavemen. St. Just would be happy to see us crawling around on all fours so that the lawyer from Arras could invent beanies, school benches, and a God according to the formulas of the watchmaker from Geneva.[2]

PHILIPPEAU   They wouldn't be afraid to add a few more zeros to Marat's calculations.[3] How much longer should we be dirty and bloody like newborn children, having coffins as cradles and playing with human heads? We must act. The Committee of Clemency must be established and the expelled deputies reinstated.

HÉRAULT   The Revolution has reached the stage of reorganization. The Revolution must stop and the Republic must begin. In our constitution, right must prevail over duty, well-being over virtue, and self-defense over punishment. Everyone must be able to assert

---

6. Reference to the Jacobins, a violently egalitarian political club that was instrumental to the Reign of Terror. They acquired their name from their meeting place, a former monastery on the rue Saint-Jacques in Paris. "Red cap": an emblem of the Revolution.
7. The reference is to the *Second Alcibiades*, a Platonic dialogue. "Divine man": Socrates.
8. Büchner derived Camille's opening lines from Adolphe Thiers's *Histoire de la révolution française* (1823–27).
9. Extremist revolutionaries, led by Jacques-René Hébert, who demanded forcible de-Christianization and the extermination of moderates. Robespierre and the Committee of Public Safety perceived them as too radical and guillotined eighteen Hébertists, including Hébert himself, on March 24, 1794.
1. Name for the Committee of Public Safety. The name was inspired by the *decemviri legibus scribundis*, a group of ten men formed in 451 B.C.E. to construct a new code of laws for Rome.
2. Jean-Jacques Rousseau. "Lawyer from Arras": Robespierre.
3. Jean-Paul Marat (1743–1793), a radical revolutionary, had claimed that the security of the republic could be won at the cost of "five or six hundred heads."

himself and live according to his nature. Be he reasonable or unreasonable, educated or uneducated, good or evil—that's not the state's business. We are all fools: no one has the right to impose his own folly on anyone else. Everyone must be allowed to enjoy himself as he likes, but not at the expense of others nor by disturbing their personal enjoyment.

CAMILLE   The government must be a transparent gown that clings closely to the body of the people. Every pulsing vein, flexing muscle, twitching sinew must leave its imprint. Its appearance may be beautiful or ugly—it has the right to be as it is. We don't have the right to cut a dress for it as we see fit. We will rap the knuckles of those who wish to throw a nun's veil over the naked shoulders of that dearest sinner, France. We want naked gods and bacchantes, Olympic games, and from melodic lips the words: "Ah, uninhibiting wicked love!"[4] We won't prevent the Romans[5] from sitting in a corner and cooking their turnips, but they are not to give us any more gladiatorial games. The divine Epicurus and Venus with the beautiful ass must replace Saints Marat and Chalier[6] as doorkeepers of the Republic.

Danton, you will lead the attack in the Convention.

DANTON   I will, you will, he will. If you live that long, as the old women say. In an hour sixty minutes will have gone by. Right, my boy?

CAMILLE   What's all that for? That's obvious.

DANTON   Oh, everything is obvious. Who's going to accomplish all these beautiful things?

PHILIPPEAU   We and the respectable people.

DANTON   That "and" there is a long word, it holds us pretty far apart. The road is long and respectability runs out of breath before we come together. And what if we do!—to those respectable people you can lend money, be their godfather, give them your daughters in marriage, but that's all!

CAMILLE   If you know all that, why did you begin the fight?

DANTON   Because I loathed those people. I could never look at such pompous Catonians[7] without giving them a kick. That's the way I am. (*He rises.*)

4. A quotation from the Greek poet Sappho.
5. I.e., Robespierre and his circle, who, like ancient Roman Stoics, cultivated moral austerity.
6. Joseph Chalier (1747–1794), a radical revolutionary whose execution by conservative forces made him a martyr in the eyes of the Jacobins. Epicurus was a Greek philosopher, often portrayed as teaching the importance of sensual pleasures. "Venus": The *Venus Kallipygos,* or "Venus of the Beautiful Buttocks," was one of the most famous sculptural depictions of the Greek goddess of love.
7. Reference to Cato the Younger, the stoic Republican of ancient Rome, known, like Robespierre, for his incorruptibility.

JULIE   You're going?

DANTON (*To* JULIE.)   I have to, their politics are getting on my nerves. (*While leaving.*) A final prophecy: the statue of freedom is not yet cast, the furnace is glowing, we can all still burn our fingers. (*Exits.*)

CAMILLE   Let him go, do you really think he could stay away once the action starts?

HÉRAULT   Yes, but just to pass the time, like playing chess.

2

A *street.*

SIMON. *His* WIFE.

SIMON (*Beats his* WIFE.)   Thou panderer, thou wrinkled contraceptive, thou worm-eaten apple of sin!

WIFE   Hey, help! Help!

PEOPLE (*Running in.*)   Get them apart! Get them apart!

SIMON   No—let me be, Romans! I will smite this skeleton to the earth! Thou vestal virgin![8]

WIFE   Me a vestal virgin? We'll see about that!

SIMON   Thus I tear thy raiment from thy shoulders,
            Thy naked carcass I cast into the sun.
Thou bed of prostitution, in every wrinkle of thy body lurketh lechery.

      (*They are separated.*)

FIRST CITIZEN   What's going on?

SIMON   Where is the virgin? Speak! No, I cannot call her that. The maid! No, not that either. The woman, the wife! Not that, not that either. Only one name is left. Oh, it chokes me! I have no breath for it.

SECOND CITIZEN   That's good, otherwise the name would stink from brandy.

SIMON   Old Virginius,[9] cover thy bare pate. The raven of shame perches upon it and stabs at thine eyes. Give me a knife, Romans! (*He collapses.*)

WIFE   Oh, usually he's a good man, but when he drinks too much, brandy sticks out a leg and trips him up.

SECOND CITIZEN   Then he walks on three legs.

WIFE   No, he falls.

SECOND CITIZEN   Right. First he walks on three and then he falls on the third until the third falls too.

SIMON   Thou art the vampire's tongue that drinketh the warmest blood of my heart.

---

8. A virginal Roman priestess.
9. Roman officer who stabbed his daughter Virginia to death to prevent her from being enslaved to the lecherous decemvir Appius Claudius Crassus.

WIFE   Leave him be—about this time he always gets sentimental. He'll get over it.

FIRST CITIZEN   What happened?

WIFE   You see, I was sitting in the sun on a rock, keeping warm, you see, 'cause we don't have any wood, you see . . .

SECOND CITIZEN   So use your husband's nose.

WIFE   . . . and my daughter had gone around the corner—she's a good girl and supports her parents.

SIMON   Ha, she confesses!

WIFE   You Judas, would you have a pair of pants to pull *up* if the young gentlemen didn't pull theirs *down* with her? You barrel of brandy, do you want to die of thirst when the little spring stops running, hey? We have to work with all our limbs—why not with *that* too? Her mother worked with it when she was born, and it hurt. Can't she work for her mother with it, too, hey? And does it hurt her, hey? You idiot!

SIMON   Ha, Lucretia![1] A knife, give me a knife, Romans! Ha, Appius Claudius![2]

FIRST CITIZEN   Yes, a knife, but not for the poor whore. What did she do wrong? Nothing! It's her hunger that goes whoring and begging. A knife for those who buy the flesh of our wives and daughters! Down with those who prostitute the daughters of the people! You have hunger pains and they have gas pains, you have holes in your jackets and they have warm coats, you have calluses and they have velvet hands. Ergo: you work and they do nothing; ergo: you earn it and they steal it; ergo: if you want to get a few cents back from your stolen property, you have to go whoring and begging; ergo: they are thieves and must be killed.

THIRD CITIZEN   All the blood they have in their veins they sucked out of ours. They told us: kill the aristocrats, they are wolves! We strung up the aristocrats on the lampposts. They said the Veto eats up your bread; we killed the Veto.[3] They said the Girondists[4] are starving you out; we guillotined the Girondists. But they took the clothes off the dead and we go barefoot and freeze, the same as before. We want to pull the skin off their thighs and make pants out of it, we want to melt off their fat and blend it into our soups. Let's go! Kill anyone without a hole in his coat!

FIRST CITIZEN   Kill anyone who can read and write!

---

1. Roman matron raped by Sextus Tarquinius, son of the Etruscan king. According to legend, the rape and subsequent suicide sparked the revolt that toppled the monarchy and established the Roman Republic.
2. See p. 27, n. 9.
3. The 1791 constitution granted the King the right to veto legislation, but that right was stripped in 1792.
4. Moderate revolutionary faction chiefly allied with the middle classes.

SECOND CITIZEN   Kill anyone who turns up his toes when he walks!
ALL (*Screaming.*)   Kill them, kill them!
     (*A* YOUNG MAN *is dragged in.*)
A FEW VOICES   He's got a handkerchief! An aristocrat! String him
   up! String him up!
SECOND CITIZEN   What? He doesn't blow his nose with his fingers?
   String him up on the lamppost!
YOUNG MAN   Oh, gentlemen!
SECOND CITIZEN   There aren't any gentlemen here. String him up!
A FEW (*Sing.*)

> If you lie within the earth,
> The worms will soon invade your berth.
> Hanging is a better lot,
> Than lying in a grave to rot.

YOUNG MAN   Mercy!
THIRD CITIZEN   It's only a little game with a bit of hemp around
   your neck. It'll only take a second—we're more merciful than the
   likes of you. Our life is murder by work; we hang on the ropes for
   sixty years and twitch, but we'll cut ourselves loose. String him
   up on the lamppost!
YOUNG MAN   All right, but that won't make things any brighter.
THE OTHERS   Bravo, bravo!
A FEW VOICES   Let him go! (*He escapes.*)
   (ROBESPIERRE *enters, accompanied by women and sansculottes.*)
ROBESPIERRE   What's the matter, citizen?
THIRD CITIZEN   What's the next step? Those few drops of blood
   from August and September[5] haven't reddened the cheeks of the
   people. The guillotine is too slow. We need a downpour.
FIRST CITIZEN   Our wives and children cry out for bread, we want
   to feed them with the flesh of the aristocrats. Hey! Kill anyone
   without a hole in his coat!
ALL   Kill them! Kill them!
ROBESPIERRE   In the name of the law!
FIRST CITIZEN   What's the law?
ROBESPIERRE   The will of the people.
FIRST CITIZEN   We are the people, and we don't want any law, ergo:
   this will is law, ergo: in the name of the law there is no more law,
   ergo: kill them!
SEVERAL VOICES   Listen to Aristides![6] Listen to the Incorruptible!

---

5. On August 10, 1792, a revolutionary crowd besieged the Tuileries Palace and massacred the Swiss Guard. Over the course of about five days in early September, roughly half the prison population of Paris was butchered by mob violence.
6. Athenian statesman and general, dubbed "The Just."

A WOMAN   Listen to the Messiah, who has been sent to choose and to judge. He will destroy the wicked with his sharp sword. His eyes are the eyes of selection, his hands are the hands of judgment.

ROBESPIERRE   Poor, virtuous people! You do your duty, you sacrifice your enemies. People, you are mighty. You reveal yourselves in lightning and thunder. But you must not be wounded by your own blows; you kill yourselves in your own wrath. You can fall only through your own strength. Your enemies know that. Your lawmakers are watchful, they will guide your hands. Their eyes are infallible, your hands are inescapable. Come with me to the Jacobins. Your comrades will open their arms to you, we will hold a bloody judgment over our enemies.

MANY VOICES   To the Jacobins! Long live Robespierre! (*They all exit.*)

SIMON   Woe is me, abandoned! (*He tries to get up.*)

HIS WIFE   There! (*She helps him.*)

SIMON   Oh, my Baucis,[7] thou heapest coals of fire on my head.

WIFE   There—stand up.

SIMON   Thou turnest away? Ha, canst thou forgive me, Portia?[8] Did I smite thee? 'Twas not my hand, 'twas not my arm, 'twas my madness.

> His madness is poor Hamlet's enemy.
> Then Hamlet does it not, Hamlet denies it.[9]

Where is our daughter, where is my Susie?

WIFE   There—around the corner.

SIMON   Let's go to her. Come, my virtuous spouse. (*Both exit.*)

3

The Jacobin Club.

A MAN FROM LYONS   Our brothers in Lyons have sent us to pour their bitter indignation in your ears. We do not know whether or not the cart on which Ronsin[1] rode to the guillotine was the hearse of liberty, but we do know that since that day Chalier's murderers again walk the earth as if there were no grave for them. Have you forgotten that Lyons is a blot on French soil, which we must cover with the corpses of traitors? Have you forgotten that this whore of kings[2] can wash away her leprosy only

---

7. A poor but kindly old wife from Greco-Roman myth.
8. Daughter of Cato the Younger and wife of Marcus Brutus who killed herself upon the death of her husband.
9. From *Hamlet* 5.2.
1. Revolutionary commandant who won a major victory against counterrevolutionary forces in Lyon, but was executed in turn by the Jacobins as an Hébertist.
2. I.e., Lyon.

in the waters of the Rhone? Have you forgotten that this revolutionary torrent must make Pitt's Mediterranean fleets run aground upon the corpses of the aristocrats? Your clemency is murdering the Revolution. The breath of an aristocrat is the death rattle of liberty. Only a coward dies for the Republic; a Jacobin kills for it. We tell you this: if we no longer find in you the vigor of the men of the 10th of August, of September, and of the 31st of May, then, like the patriot Gaillard, we can turn only to Cato's dagger.[3] (*Applause and confused cries.*)

A JACOBIN   We will drink the cup of Socrates[4] with you!

LEGENDRE   (*Jumps onto the tribune.*)   We do not need to turn our eyes to Lyons. For several days now those who wear silk clothes, ride in carriages, sit in theater loges, and speak according to the Dictionary of the Academy have felt their heads to be secure on their shoulders. They make clever remarks, saying that Marat and Chalier should be helped to a double martyrdom by guillotining them in effigy. (*Violent commotion in the assembly.*)

SEVERAL VOICES   They are dead men. Their tongues guillotine them.

LEGENDRE   May the blood of these saints come over them! I ask you members of the Committee of Public Safety: since when have your ears become so deaf . . .

COLLOT D'HERBOIS   (*Interrupts him.*)   And I ask you, Legendre: whose voice has given breath to such thoughts so that they come to life and dare to speak? It is time to tear off masks. Listen! The cause accuses its effect, the shout its echo, and the premise its conclusion. The Committee of Public Safety is more logical than that, Legendre! Be quiet. The busts of the saints will remain untouched, like Medusa-heads they will turn the traitors into stone.[5]

ROBESPIERRE   I wish to speak.

THE JACOBINS   Listen! Listen to the Incorruptible!

ROBESPIERRE[6]   We were waiting only for the cry of discontent to ring out from all sides before we speak. Our eyes were open, we watched the enemy arming himself and rising up, but we did not sound the alarm. We let the people be their own guard; they have not slept, they have taken up arms. We let the enemy emerge from his cover, we let him advance; now he stands exposed in broad daylight, every blow will strike him, he is dead as soon as you have caught sight of him.

---

3. Cato the Younger committed suicide rather than submit to the dictatorship of Julius Caesar. On May 31, 1793, the Jacobins began their campaign against the Girondists. Gaillard was an Hébertist who committed suicide.
4. Socrates was sentenced to die by drinking a cup of hemlock.
5. Medusa was a mythical monster whose head turned onlookers to stone.
6. Büchner derives much of this speech from his historical sources, principally *Die Geschichte unserer Zeit* (1826–30), edited by Carl Strahlheim.

I have told you once before that the internal enemies of the Republic are split into two factions, like two armies. Under banners of various colors and on quite different paths they all rush toward the same goal. One of these factions[7] no longer exists. In its presumptuous madness it tried to cast aside the most proven patriots, branding them worn-out weaklings in order to rob the Republic of its strongest arms. It declared war on the Deity and on property in order to create a diversion on behalf of the kings. It parodied the exalted drama of the Revolution in order to compromise it through premeditated excesses. Hébert's triumph would have turned the Republic into chaos, and despotism would have been satisfied. The sword of judgment has struck the traitor down. But what does it matter to our foreign enemies when criminals of another sort remain to accomplish the same purpose? We have achieved nothing so long as another faction[8] remains to be destroyed. This one is the opposite of the first. It leads us to weakness; its battle cry is: mercy! It intends to rob the people of their weapons and of their strength to fight in order to deliver them up to the kings, naked and unnerved.

The weapon of the Republic is terror, the strength of the Republic is virtue. Virtue: for without it, terror is corruptible; terror: for without it, virtue is powerless. Terror is an outgrowth of virtue; it is nothing more than swift, rigorous, and inflexible justice. Some say terror is the weapon of a despotic government, therefore ours resembles despotism. True, but in the way a sword in the hand of a hero of liberty resembles a saber in the hand of a tyrant's minion. If a tyrant rules his brutish subjects through terror, that is his right as a despot; if you destroy through terror the enemies of liberty, you, the founders of the Republic, are no less right. The Revolutionary government is the despotism of liberty against tyranny.

Mercy to the royalists! certain people cry. Mercy to the wicked? No! Mercy to the innocent, mercy to the weak, mercy to the unfortunate, mercy to humanity! Only the peaceful citizen deserves the protection of society. In a republic only republicans are citizens, royalists and foreigners are enemies. To punish the oppressors of mankind is charity, to pardon them is barbarity. I regard all traces of false sentimentality as sighs that fly to England or Austria.

Yet not content to disarm the people, some try to poison the most sacred sources of its strength through vice. This is the most subtle, most dangerous, and most deplorable attack against lib-

---

7. I.e., the Hébertists.
8. I.e., the Dantonists.

erty. Vice is the mark of Cain on the aristocracy. Within a republic it is not only a moral but a political crime; the vice-ridden are the political enemies of liberty; the more they seem to accomplish in its service, the more dangerous they are. The most dangerous citizen is the one who wears out a dozen red caps more easily than doing one good deed.

You will understand me readily when you think about those who used to live in a garret and now ride in a carriage and fornicate with former marchionesses and baronesses. We may well ask: have the people been robbed or have we grasped the golden hands of the kings when we, the people's lawmakers, display all the vices and luxuries of former courtiers, when we see these marquises and barons of the Revolution marrying rich wives, giving sumptuous banquets, gambling, keeping servants and wearing expensive clothes? We may well be surprised when we hear them being witty, playing the snob, and adopting elegant manners. Lately someone shamelessly parodied Tacitus—I could answer like Sallust, and travesty Catiline;[9] but no more brushstrokes are necessary, the portraits are complete.

Let there be no compromise, no truce with those who were only set on robbing the people, who hoped to rob them unpunished, for whom the Republic was business speculation and the Revolution a trade. Frightened by the rushing torrent of the examples we have set, they now very quietly seek to cool down our justice. We are to believe that they say to themselves: "We are not virtuous enough to be so terrible. Philosophic lawmakers, have mercy on our weakness! I don't dare to tell you that I am so wicked, so I'd rather tell you, don't be inhuman!"

Calm yourselves, virtuous people, calm yourselves, patriots: tell your brothers in Lyons that the sword of justice will not rust in the hands of those to whom you have entrusted it.—We will set a great example for the Republic. (*General applause.*)

MANY VOICES   Long live the Republic, long live Robespierre!

PRESIDENT   The meeting is adjourned.

4

A street.

LACROIX. LEGENDRE.

LACROIX   What have you done, Legendre? Do you realize whose head you're knocking off with those busts of yours?

---

9. Sallust was a Roman historian who described a conspiracy by the corrupt politician Catiline to overthrow the state. Tacitus was a Roman historian who depicted the emperor Tiberius as a tyrant. Camille Desmoulins attacked Robespierre by citing Tacitus's portrait of Tiberius.

LEGENDRE   The heads of a few playboys and elegant women, that's all.

LACROIX   You're suicidal, a shadow that murders its origin and thereby itself.

LEGENDRE   I don't understand.

LACROIX   I thought Collot had made himself clear.

LEGENDRE   What difference does it make? He was drunk, as usual.

LACROIX   Fools, children, and—well?—drunks speak the truth. Who do you think Robespierre was talking about with his Catiline?

LEGENDRE   Well?

LACROIX   It's very simple: the atheists and the ultrarevolutionaries have been sent to the scaffold, but the people haven't been helped; they still go barefoot in the streets and want to make shoes out of aristocratic leather. The guillotine thermometer must not drop—a few degrees lower and the Committee of Public Safety can seek its bed on the Square of the Revolution.[1]

LEGENDRE   What do my busts have to do with that?

LACROIX   Don't you see it yet? You have officially announced the counterrevolution; you have forced the decemvirs to act; you have led their hand. The people are a Minotaur[2] that must have a weekly supply of corpses if it is not to devour its leaders.

LEGENDRE   Where is Danton?

LACROIX   How should I know? He's searching for the Venus de Medici piece by piece among all the grisettes of the Palais Royal.[3] He's making a mosaic, as he says; heaven knows what limb he's at right now. It's a shame that nature has cut up beauty into pieces, like Medea[4] her brother, and has put the fragments into our bodies.

   Let's go to the Palais Royal. (*Both exit.*)

5

   A room.

   DANTON, MARION.

MARION   No, let me be. Here at your feet. I want to tell you a story.

DANTON   You could use your lips in better ways.

MARION   No, let me stay like this. My mother was a smart woman, she always said chastity was a fine virtue—when people came to

---

1. The location of the guillotine.
2. Mythical monster that lived off the flesh of youths sacrificed to it.
3. Converted during the revolutionary period into a place of shops and casinos, often frequented by prostitutes. "Venus de Medici": famous statue of the Greek goddess of love.
4. A woman from Greek myth who fled her homeland with her lover, Jason. Pursued across the sea by her father, she killed her brother and then cast pieces of his corpse into the water. Her father was compelled to retrieve each of the dismembered pieces from the water, thus enabling the lovers' escape.

the house and started talking about certain things, she told me to
leave the room; when I asked what they wanted, she said I ought
to be ashamed of myself; when she gave me a book to read,
I almost always had to skip a few pages. But I read the Bible whenever I liked—there everything was holy; but there were things in
there that I didn't understand, and I didn't want to ask anyone;
I brooded about them by myself. Then spring came, and all around
me things were going on that I didn't take part in. I found myself
in a strange atmosphere, it almost choked me; I looked at my
body, sometimes I felt I was double and then melted again into
one. At that time a young man came to our house—he was good-
looking and often said crazy things; I wasn't sure what he wanted,
but I had to laugh. My mother invited him often—both he and
I liked that. Finally we couldn't see why we might not just as well
lie together between two sheets as sit next to each other in two
chairs. I enjoyed that more than our conversations, and I didn't
understand why one would allow the smaller pleasure and deny
the greater one. We did it secretly. It went on like that. But
I became like an ocean, consuming everything and swirling deeper
and deeper. For me there was only one opposite: all men melted
into one body. That was my nature—who can escape it? Finally
he realized it. He came one morning and kissed me as if he
wanted to choke me, his arms wrapped tight around my neck.
I was terribly afraid. Then he let me go and laughed and said he
had almost done a foolish thing, I ought to keep my dress and use
it, it would wear out by itself, he didn't want to spoil my fun just
yet, it was all I had. Then he left, and again I didn't know what he
wanted. That evening I was sitting at the window; I'm very sensitive, and I relate to everything around me only through feeling.
I became absorbed in the waves of the sunset. Then a group of
people came down the street, children in front, women looking
out of their windows. I looked down—they were carrying him by
in a basket, the moon shone on his pale forehead, his hair was
damp, he had drowned himself. I had to cry. That was the only
break in my being. Other people have Sundays and working days,
they work for six days and pray on the seventh; once a year, on
their birthdays, they get sentimental, and every year on New Year's
Day they reflect. I don't understand all that. For me there is no
stopping, no changing. I'm always the same, an endless longing
and grasping, a fire, a torrent. My mother died of grief, people
point at me. That's silly. It's all the same, whatever we enjoy: bodies, icons, flowers, or toys, it's all the same feeling; whoever enjoys
the most prays the most.

DANTON   Why can't I contain your beauty in me completely, surround it entirely?

MARION   Danton, your lips have eyes.

DANTON   I wish I were a part of the ether so that I could bathe you in my flood and break on every wave of your beautiful body.

(LACROIX, ADELAIDE, ROSALIE *enter.*)

LACROIX (*Remains at the door.*)   Oh, that was funny!

DANTON (*Indignantly.*)   Well?

LACROIX   The street!

DANTON   And?

LACROIX   There were dogs on the street, a Great Dane and an Italian lapdog—they were trying to have a go at it.

DANTON   So what?

LACROIX   I just thought of that and I had to laugh. That was edifying! Girls were looking out of the windows—one ought to be careful and not let them sit in the sun or the flies will do it on their hands[5]—that's food for thought.

Legendre and I went through almost every cell—the little Sisters of the Revelation Through the Flesh were hanging on our coattails and wanted a blessing. Legendre is making one do penance, but he'll have to abstain for a month for that. Here are two priestesses of the body.

MARION   Hello, Miss Adelaide, hello, Miss Rosalie.

ROSALIE   We haven't seen you for a long time.

MARION   Yes, I'm sorry.

ADELAIDE   Oh God, we're busy night and day.

DANTON (*To* ROSALIE.)   Say, little one, your hips are getting softer.

ROSALIE   Oh yes, every day we get more perfect.

LACROIX   What's the difference between an antique and a modern Adonis?[6]

DANTON   And Adelaide has gotten virtuous—how interesting! A fascinating change. Her face looks like a fig leaf which she holds in front of her whole body. A fig tree like that on such a frequented street throws a refreshing shadow.

ADELAIDE   I'd be a cowpath, if Monsieur . . .

DANTON   I understand, just don't get angry, my dear.

LACROIX   Listen! A modern Adonis isn't torn to pieces by a boar but by sows, he isn't wounded in the thigh but in the groin, and it's not roses that sprout from his blood but buds of mercury.[7]

DANTON   Miss Rosalie is a restored torso, only her hips and feet are antique. She's a magnetized needle: what the headpole repels, the footpole attracts; her middle is an equator where everyone who crosses the line gets a sublimate baptism.

---

5. Cf. *Woyzeck* 4,11: "Do it in broad daylight, do it on our hands, like flies."
6. In Greco-Roman myth, a beautiful young man who was killed by a wild boar. Flowers bloomed from the blood that flowed from his wounded thigh.
7. A common treatment for syphilis.

LACROIX   Two Sisters of Mercy—each serves in her own hospital, that is, in her own body.

ROSALIE   You ought to be ashamed! You're making our ears red.

ADELAIDE   You should have better manners.

(ADELAIDE *and* ROSALIE *exit.*)

DANTON   Good night, you beautiful children!

LACROIX   Good night, you pits of mercury!

DANTON   I'm sorry for them, they'll miss dinner.

LACROIX   Listen, Danton, I just came from the Jacobins.

DANTON   Is that all?

LACROIX   The Lyonists read a proclamation, saying that all they could do was to wrap themselves in a toga. Everybody made a face as if he wanted to say to his neighbor: Paetus, it doesn't hurt![8] Legendre cried that some want to shatter the busts of Chalier and Marat. I think he wants to redden his face again, he's completely turned away from the Terror—on the street children tug at his coat.

DANTON   And Robespierre?

LACROIX   Drummed on the tribune and said, "Virtue must rule through terror." That phrase made my neck hurt.

DANTON   It's planing boards for the guillotine.

LACROIX   And Collot yelled like a madman that it's time to tear off masks.

DANTON   The faces will come off with them.

(PARIS *enters.*)

LACROIX   What's new, Fabricius?[9]

PARIS   From the Jacobins I went to Robespierre. I demanded an explanation. He tried to make a face like Brutus sacrificing his sons.[1] He spoke in generalities about duty, said that concerning liberty he makes no compromises, he would sacrifice anyone— himself, his brother, his friends.

DANTON   That was clear. If you reverse the order, he'll stand below and hold the ladder[2] for his friends. We owe Legendre thanks, he made them talk.

LACROIX   The Hébertists aren't dead yet and the people are impoverished—that's a terrible lever. The scale of blood must not rise lest it become a lamppost for the Committee of Public Safety. It needs ballast, it needs a weighty head.

---

8. Condemned to death, Caecina Paetus attempted to commit suicide but his nerve failed him; his wife Arria then stabbed herself and handed him the dagger with these words.
9. Paris's adopted name, inspired by Gaius Fabricius Luscinus, a Roman statesman famous for honesty.
1. Lucius Junius Brutus is a legendary figure who overthrew the monarchy and established the Roman Republic. He had his own two sons executed for treason.
2. I.e., to the scaffold.

DANTON   I know that—the Revolution is like Saturn,[3] it devours its own children. (*After some thought.*) But they won't dare.

LACROIX   Danton, you are a dead saint, but the Revolution is not interested in relics; it has thrown the bones of kings out into the street and all the statues out of the churches. Do you think they'd let you stand as a monument?

DANTON   My name! The people!

LACROIX   Your name! You are a moderate, I am one. Camille, Philippeau, Hérault. For the masses weakness and moderation are the same. They kill the stragglers. The tailors of the red-cap faction will feel all of Roman history in their needles if the Man of September[4] appears as a moderate to them.

DANTON   Very true, and besides—the people are like children, they have to break everything open to see what's inside.

LACROIX   And besides, Danton, we are vice-ridden, as Robespierre says, that is, we enjoy ourselves; and the people are virtuous, that is, they don't enjoy themselves, because work deadens their organs of pleasure. They don't get drunk because they don't have any money, and they don't go to whorehouses because their breath stinks of cheese and herring and that disgusts the girls.

DANTON   They hate the pleasure seekers as a eunuch hates men.

LACROIX   They call us scoundrels, and (*Leaning toward* DANTON's *ear.*) between us, there's a grain of truth to that. Robespierre and the people will be virtuous, St. Just will write a novel, and Barère will tailor a carmagnole and hang a mantle of blood over the Convention and . . . I see it all.

DANTON   You're dreaming. They never had courage without me, they won't have any against me. The Revolution isn't over yet, they might still need me—they'll keep me in the arsenal.

LACROIX   We must act.

DANTON   We'll see.

LACROIX   You'll see when we're lost.

MARION (*To* DANTON.)   Your lips have grown cold, your words have stifled your kisses.

DANTON (*To* MARION.)   To have lost so much time! As if it were worth it! (*To* LACROIX.) Tomorrow I'll go to Robespierre—I'll provoke him, then he can't remain silent. Until tomorrow! Good night, my friends, good night, I thank you.

---

3. Roman name for the Greek god Cronus, the ruler of the universe who was prophesied to be overthrown by his own son. Attempting to avoid this fate, he ate each of his children at birth, until his son Jupiter escaped and realized the prophesy.
4. I.e., Danton.

LACROIX   Out, my good friends, out! Good night, Danton, the thighs of that woman will guillotine you, the mons veneris will be your Tarpeian Rock.[5] (*Exit.*)

6

A room.
ROBESPIERRE. DANTON. PARIS.

ROBESPIERRE   I tell you, whoever tries to stop me when I pull my sword is my enemy, his intention is of no concern. Whoever prevents me from defending myself kills me as surely as if he attacked me.

DANTON   Murder begins where self-defense stops; I see no reason to continue the executions.

ROBESPIERRE   The social revolution is not yet achieved; whoever carries out a revolution only halfway, digs his own grave. The privileged are not dead yet, the healthy strength of the people must replace this class, decadent in all respects. Vice must be punished, virtue must rule through terror.

DANTON   I don't understand the word "punishment."

You and your "virtue," Robespierre! You've never taken money, you've never been in debt, you've never slept with a woman, you've always worn a decent coat, and you've never gotten drunk. Robespierre, you are appallingly upright. I'd be ashamed to walk around between heaven and earth for thirty years with that righteous face just for the miserable pleasure of finding others worse than I.

Isn't there something in you that sometimes whispers secretly: you lie, you lie!

ROBESPIERRE   My conscience is clean.

DANTON   Conscience is a mirror before which an ape torments itself; we preen ourselves as best we can, and we go looking for pleasure each in our own way. As if it were worth the trouble to get in each other's hair. Everyone can defend himself when someone else spoils his fun. Do you have the right to make the guillotine a basket for other people's dirty laundry and to make their decapitated heads into scrubbing balls for their dirty clothes, just because you always wear a cleanly brushed coat? Yes, you can defend yourself when they spit on it or tear holes in it, but what difference does it make to you as long as they leave you alone? If they don't mind walking around as they do, do you have the right to lock them up in a grave? Are you the military policeman of heaven? And if you can't stand the sight of it, as God can, then put a handkerchief over your eyes.

---

5. The cliff in ancient Rome from which traitors were hurled.

ROBESPIERRE   You deny virtue?

DANTON   And vice. There are only epicureans, either crude or refined, Christ was the most refined of all; that's the only difference I can discern among human beings. Everyone acts according to his nature, that means he does what is good for him.

Isn't it cruel, Mr. Incorruptible, to pull the rug out from under you like this?

ROBESPIERRE   Danton, at certain times vice can be high treason.

DANTON   You can't outlaw it, for heaven's sake—that would be ungrateful; you owe vice too much for providing a contrast to you.

By the way, in keeping with your terminology, our blows must serve the Republic: the innocent must not be struck down with the guilty.

ROBESPIERRE   Whoever said that an innocent person was struck down?

DANTON   Do you hear that, Fabricius? No innocent person was killed! (*Leaving, to* PARIS.) We don't have a moment to lose, we must show ourselves! (DANTON *and* PARIS *exit.*)

ROBESPIERRE (*Alone.*)   Go ahead! He wants to stop the horses of the Revolution at the whorehouse, like a coachman his trained nags; they'll have enough strength to drag him to the Square of the Revolution.

"To pull the rug out from under me!" "In keeping with your terminology!" Wait! Wait! Is it really that? They will say his gigantic figure threw too much of a shadow on me, and for that I ordered him out of the sunlight.

And if they're right?

Is it really that necessary? Yes, yes! The Republic! He must go.

It's ridiculous how my thoughts watch over each other. He must go. Whoever stands still in a mass moving forward opposes it as much as if he were moving against it; he'll be trampled.

We will not let the ship of the Revolution be stranded on the shallow calculations and the mudbanks of these people; we must cut off the hand that tries to stop it, and even if he seized it with his teeth!

Down with a society that took the clothes away from the dead aristocracy and inherited its leprosy!

"No virtue!" "Virtue: a rug under me!" "In keeping with my terminology!"

How that keeps coming back.

Why can't I escape that thought? It's always pointing there, there! with a bloody finger. No matter how many rags I wrap around it, the blood keeps seeping through. (*After a pause.*) I can't tell what part of me is deceiving the other.

(*He steps to the window.*) Night snores over the earth and wallows in wild dreams. Thoughts, hardly perceived wishes, confused and formless, having crept shyly from daylight, now take shape and steal into the silent house of dreams. They open doors, they look out of windows, they become almost flesh, their limbs stretch out in sleep, their lips murmur.—And isn't our waking a more lucid dream, aren't we sleepwalkers, aren't our actions dreamlike, only clearer, more precise, more complete? Who can reproach us for that? The mind accomplishes in one hour more acts of thought than the sluggish organism of our body can carry out in years. The sin is in our thoughts. Whether thought becomes action, whether the body carries it out—that is pure chance.

(ST. JUST *enters.*)

ROBESPIERRE   Hey—who's there, in the dark? Hey—lights, lights!

ST. JUST   Do you know my voice?

ROBESPIERRE   Oh, it's you, St. Just! (*A maid brings a light.*)

ST. JUST   Were you alone?

ROBESPIERRE   Danton just left.

ST. JUST   I met him on the way in the Palais Royal. He made his revolutionary face and spoke in epigrams; he spoke familiarly with the sansculottes, the grisettes[6] were at his heels, and people were standing around whispering in each other's ears what he had said.

    We will lose the advantage of the attack. How much longer are you going to hesitate? We will act without you. We are resolved.

ROBESPIERRE   What do you want to do?

ST. JUST   We will call a formal session of the Committees of Legislation, General Security, and Public Safety.

ROBESPIERRE   Quite a bother.

ST. JUST   We must bury the great corpse with proper decorum, like priests, not murderers. We dare not chop it up; all its limbs must fall with it.

ROBESPIERRE   Speak more clearly.

ST. JUST   We must bury him in full armor and slaughter his horses and slaves on his burial mound: Lacroix . . .

ROBESPIERRE   A confirmed scoundrel, formerly a law clerk, presently Lieutenant General of France. Go on.

ST. JUST   Hérault-Séchelles.[7]

ROBESPIERRE   A handsome head.

---

6. Working-class women. "Sanscullottes": radical revolutionaries, often coming from the lower classes.
7. A member of the Committee of Public Safety and the principle drafter of the Jacobin constitution in 1793. He was suspected of treason that same year and subsequently guillotined.

ST. JUST   He was the beautifully painted first letter of the Constitution; we have no further need of such ornaments, he will be
erased. Philippeau, Camille . . .

ROBESPIERRE   He too?

ST. JUST (*Hands him a piece of paper.*)   I thought so. Read that!

ROBESPIERRE   Aha, *The Old Franciscan*,[8] is that all? He's a child,
he was laughing at you.

ST. JUST   Read it, here, here! (*He points to a passage.*)

ROBESPIERRE (*Reads.*)   "Robespierre, this Messiah of Blood on his
Calvary between the two thieves Couthon and Collot,[9] upon which
he sacrifices and is not sacrificed. The worshipful Sisters of the
Guillotine stand below like Mary and Magdalene. St. Just lies at his
heart like St. John and reveals to the Convention the apocalyptic
revelations of the Master. He carries his head like a monstrance."[1]

ST. JUST   I will make him carry his like St. Denis.[2]

ROBESPIERRE (*Reads on.*)   "Are we to believe that the clean shirt of
the Messiah is the shroud of France and that his thin fingers,
fidgeting on the tribune, are guillotine blades?

And you, Barère, who said our coinage is being minted on the
Square of the Revolution. Yet—I don't want to dig up that old sack
again.[3] He is a widow who had half a dozen husbands and helped
bury them all. Who can help that? That is his talent: he sees a
death's head on people half a year before they die. Who would
want to sit with corpses and smell the stench?"

You too, then, Camille?

Away with them! Quickly! Only the dead do not return. Have
you prepared the indictment?

ST. JUST   It will be easy. You made allusions to it at the Jacobins.

ROBESPIERRE   I wanted to scare them.

ST. JUST   I merely have to carry out your threats; the Forgers[4] are
the appetizer and the Foreigners the dessert. They will die from
the meal, I promise you.

---

8. Journal edited by Desmoulins and supported by Danton that opposed the Reign of
Terror.
9. Collot d'Herbois was a member of the Committee of Public Safety. Georges Couthon
was a close ally of Robespierre throughout the Reign of Terror and was guillotined
alongside him.
1. In the Roman Catholic Church, the container in which the consecrated host is exhibited.
2. First bishop of Paris and patron saint of France. Beheaded in 258, he supposedly carried his head under his arm.
3. A pun on Barère de Vieuzac, a member of the Committee of Public Safety occasionally
suspected of shifting loyalties with political winds.
4. A group of Jacobins who falsified documents related to the liquidation of the French
East India Company in 1793. Danton was accused, on scant evidence, of involvement in
the scandal, though he escaped prosecution. More damaging to Danton was the fact
that his friend and ally Fabre d'Églantine almost certainly was involved, for which crime
he was guillotined.

ROBESPIERRE   Then quickly, tomorrow. No long death agony! I've become sensitive lately. Quickly!

(ST. JUST *exits*.)

ROBESPIERRE (*Alone*.)   That's true, Messiah of Blood who sacrifices and is not sacrificed—He redeemed them with His blood and I redeem them with their own. He allowed them to sin and I take the sin upon myself. He had the ecstasy of pain, and I the agony of the executioner.

Who renounced more, I or He?

And yet there is something foolish in that thought.

Why do we always look only toward Him? Truly the Son of Man is crucified in each of us, we all struggle in bloody sweat in the Garden of Gethsemane,[5] but not one of us redeems the other with his wounds.—My Camille!—They're all leaving me—all is desolate and empty—I am alone.

Act Two

I

A room.

DANTON. LACROIX. PHILIPPEAU. PARIS. CAMILLE DESMOULINS.

CAMILLE   Hurry, Danton, we have no time to lose.

DANTON (*Getting dressed*.)   But time loses us.

It's very boring, always putting on the shirt first and the pants over it and going to bed at night and crawling out again in the morning and always putting one foot before the other—there's no hope that it will ever be any different. It's very sad; and that millions have done it this way and millions will keep on doing it—and, above all, that we're made up of two halves which do the same thing so that everything happens twice—that's very sad.

CAMILLE   You're talking like a child.

DANTON   The dying often become childish.

LACROIX   Your hesitation is dragging you down to destruction, you're taking all your friends with you. Let the cowards know that it's time to rally around you; summon them from the Plain and from the Mountain.[6] Cry out against the tyranny of the decemvirs, speak of daggers, call on Brutus[7]—then you will frighten the tribunes and even gather up those who are denounced as accomplices of Hébert. You must give way to your anger! At

---

5. Where Jesus prayed on the night before his arrest.
6. Moderate forces at the National Convention occupied seats along the floor of the hall, and so became known as "The Plain." Radical Jacobins occupied higher benches and so became "The Mountain."
7. Marcus Junius Brutus, Caesar's most famous assassin.

least don't let us die defenseless and humiliated like the disgraceful Hébert.

DANTON   You have a poor memory, you called me a dead saint. You
were right, even more than you realized. I was at the Section
meetings—they were respectful but like undertakers. I am a relic
and relics are thrown into the street, you were right.

LACROIX   Why did you let it come to that?

DANTON   To that? Yes, that's true, I was finally bored with it all.
Always walking around in the same coat and making the same
face! That's pitiful. To be such a wretched instrument, on which
one string always sounds just one note.

I can't bear it. I wanted to make it easy for myself. I was successful: the Revolution is letting me retire, but not in the way
I expected.

Besides, what can we rely on? Our whores could still compete
with the worshipful Sisters of the Guillotine; that's all I can
think of. I can count it all off on my fingers: the Jacobins have
announced that virtue is now the order of the day, the Cordeliers
call me Hébert's executioner, the Commune does penance,[8] the
Convention—that might still be a way! But there'd be a 31st of
May,[9] they wouldn't withdraw without a fight. Robespierre is the
dogma of the Revolution, it cannot be erased. That wouldn't work
either. We haven't made the Revolution; the Revolution has made
us.

And even if it worked—I would rather be guillotined than guillotine others. I'm sick of it—why should we human beings fight
each other? We should sit down with each other in peace. A mistake was made when we were created—something is missing.
I have no name for it. We won't rip it out of each other's intestines,
so why should we break open each other's bodies? Oh, we are miserable alchemists.

CAMILLE   To say it in a more sublime way: how long should humanity devour its own limbs in eternal hunger? Or: how long should
we, stranded on a wreck, suck blood out of each other's veins
with unquenchable thirst? Or: how long should we algebraists of
the flesh write our calculations with mangled limbs while searching for the unknown, eternally withheld X?

DANTON   You are a strong echo.

CAMILLE   Yes, a pistol shot resounds as loudly as a thunderclap,
doesn't it? So much the better for you, you should always have me
with you.

8. The Paris Commune had previously supported the Hébertists; "Cordeliers": followers
of Hébert.
9. See p. 31, n. 3.

PHILIPPEAU   And France is left with her executioners?

DANTON   What's the difference? The people are very comfortable with them. They aren't well off; can one ask for more in order to be moved, noble, virtuous, or witty, or never to be bored?

What's the difference if they die under the guillotine or from a fever or from old age? As long as they can walk offstage nimbly and can make nice gestures and hear the audience clap as they exit. That's very proper and suits us well—we're always on stage, even if we're finally stabbed to death in earnest.

It's a good thing that our life span is being shortened a little; the coat was too long, our bodies couldn't fill it out. Life becomes an epigram—that's not so bad; whoever has enough breath and spirit for an epic poem in fifty or sixty cantos? It's time that we drink that little bit of essence not out of tubs but out of liqueur glasses, that will still fill our mouths; before, we could hardly get a few drops to run together in that bulky container.

Finally—I ought to cry out, but that's too much trouble; life isn't worth the effort we make to maintain it.

PARIS   Then escape, Danton!

DANTON   Do we take our homeland along on the soles of our shoes? And finally—and that's the main point: they won't dare. (*To* CAMILLE.) Come, my boy, I tell you, they won't dare. Adieu. Adieu!

(DANTON *and* CAMILLE *exit.*)

PHILIPPEAU   There he goes.

LACROIX   And he doesn't believe a word he's said. Nothing but laziness! He would rather let himself be guillotined than make a speech.

PARIS   What do we do now?

LACROIX   We'll go home and think like Lucretia[1] about an honorable death.

2

A promenade.

PASSERSBY.

A CITIZEN   My good Jacqueline—I mean, Corn . . . uh, Cor . . .

SIMON   Cornelia, citizen, Cornelia.[2]

CITIZEN   My good Cornelia has blessed me with a little boy.

SIMON   Has borne a son for the Republic.

CITIZEN   . . . for the Republic—that's too general, one might say . . .

SIMON   That's just it, the part must succumb to the whole . . .

1. See p. 28, n. 1.
2. A virtuous wife and mother of the Roman Republic. It was a sign of revolutionary fervor to adopt names of great republicans from antiquity.

CITIZEN   Oh, yes, my wife says the same thing.

BALLADEER   Tell me, tell me everyone,
                        What's man's joy, what's his fun?[3]

CITIZEN   Oh, but his name, I just can't think of anything.

SIMON   Call him Pike, Marat.

BALLADEER
                        With sorrow and with care he's worn,
                        Working from the early morn,
                        Till the day is done.

CITIZEN   Three'd be better, there's something about the number three—and then something useful and something just. I've got it: Plow, Robespierre. And then the third?

SIMON   Pike.

CITIZEN   Thank you, neighbor. Pike, Plow, Robespierre, those are pretty names, that'll be nice.

SIMON   I tell you, the breast of your Cornelia will be like the udder of the Roman she-wolf—no, that won't do—Romulus was a tyrant, that won't do.[4] (*They pass on.*)

A BEGGAR   A handful of earth
                        And a little bit of moss . . .
        Dear sirs, kind ladies!

FIRST GENTLEMAN   Go and work, you dog, you look very well fed.

SECOND GENTLEMAN   There! (*He gives him money.*) His hand's like velvet. What impudence!

BEGGAR   Sir, how did you get that coat of yours?

SECOND GENTLEMAN   Work, work! You could have one just like it. I'll give you a job. Call on me—I live at . . .

BEGGAR   Sir, why did you work?

SECOND GENTLEMAN   So I could have the coat, idiot.

BEGGAR   You tortured yourself for a piece of pleasure. A coat like that's a pleasure, so's a rag.

SECOND GENTLEMAN   Certainly, there's no other way.

BEGGAR   If I were such a fool! It all balances out.
        The sun's shining warm on the corner and that's easy to enjoy.
    (*Sings.*)   A handful of earth
                        And a little bit of moss . . .

ROSALIE (*To* ADELAIDE.)   Hurry up, there come the soldiers, we haven't had anything warm in our bodies since yesterday.

BEGGAR   . . . Is all I'll have left
                        When I lie beneath the cross!
        Gentlemen, ladies!

---

3. From a Swabian folk song.
4. Romulus and his brother Remus, the legendary founders of Rome, were suckled by a she-wolf as babies. Romulus killed Remus and proclaimed himself king.

SOLDIER Wait! Where are you off to, my dears? (*To* ROSALIE.)
    How old are you?

ROSALIE As old as my pinkie.

SOLDIER You're very sharp.

ROSALIE You're very blunt.

SOLDIER So I'll have to whet myself on you. (*He sings.*)
    Christina, O Christina dear,
    Does the pain make you sore, make you sore,
    Make you sore, make you sore?

ROSALIE (*Sings.*)
    Oh no, dear soldiers,
    All I say is: give me more, give me more,
    Give me more, give me more!
    (DANTON *and* CAMILLE *enter.*)

DANTON Isn't that amusing!
    I sense something in the atmosphere—it's as if the sun were
    breeding lechery.
    Don't you feel like jumping into the middle of it, tearing off
    your pants and copulating from the rear like dogs in the street?
    (*They go past.*)

YOUNG GENTLEMAN Ah, Madame, the tolling of a bell, twilight on
    the treetops, a twinkling star . . .

MADAME A flower's scent! These natural pleasures, this pure
    enjoyment of nature! (*To her daughter.*) You see, Eugénie, only
    virtue has eyes for such things.

EUGÉNIE (*Kisses her mother's hand.*) Oh, Mama, I see only you!

MADAME Good girl!

YOUNG GENTLEMAN (*Whispers into* EUGÉNIE'*s ear.*) Do you see that
    pretty lady over there with the old gentleman?

EUGÉNIE I know her.

YOUNG GENTLEMAN They say her hairdresser did her hair "à l'enfant."

EUGÉNIE (*Laughs.*) Naughty tongues.

YOUNG GENTLEMAN The old gentleman walks with her, he sees the
    little bud swelling and takes it for a walk in the sun, thinking he
    was the thundershower that made it grow.

EUGÉNIE How shameful! I almost feel like blushing.

YOUNG GENTLEMAN That could make me turn pale.

DANTON (*To* CAMILLE.) Don't expect me to be serious. I can't
    understand why people don't stop on the street and laugh in each
    other's faces. I'd think they'd have to laugh out of the windows
    and out of the graves, and the heavens would burst and the earth
    would be convulsed with laughter.

FIRST GENTLEMAN An extraordinary discovery, I assure you. All
    the technical arts will acquire a new look. The human race is mak-
    ing giant strides toward its great destiny.

SECOND GENTLEMAN   Have you seen the new play? A Tower of Baby-
lon! A maze of arches, stairways, halls—and it's all blown up with
the greatest of ease. You get dizzy at every step.[5]
   A bizarre idea! (*He stops in embarrassment.*)
FIRST GENTLEMAN   What's the matter?
SECOND GENTLEMAN   Oh, nothing! Your arm, sir! The puddle—
there! Thank you. I barely managed it—that could have been
dangerous!
FIRST GENTLEMAN   You weren't afraid?
SECOND GENTLEMAN   Yes, the earth is a thin crust. I always think
I'll fall through a hole like that.
   You have to walk carefully—you might break through. But go
to the theater—take my advice.

3

   A room.
   DANTON. CAMILLE. LUCILE.

CAMILLE   I tell you, if they aren't given everything in wooden copies,
scattered about in theaters, concerts, and art exhibits, they'll have
neither eyes nor ears for it. Let someone whittle a marionette
where the strings pulling it are plainly visible and whose joints
crack at every step in iambic pentameter: what a character, what
consistency! Let someone take a little bit of feeling, an aphorism, a
concept, and clothe it in a coat and pants, give it hands and feet,
color its face and let the thing torment itself through three acts
until it finally marries or shoots itself: an ideal! Let someone fiddle
an opera which reflects the rising and sinking of the human spirit
the way a clay pipe with water imitates a nightingale: oh, art!

   Take people out of the theater and put them in the street: oh,
miserable reality! They forget their Creator because of His poor
imitators. They see and hear nothing of Creation, which renews
itself every moment in and around them, glowing, rushing, lumi-
nous. They go to the theater, read poetry and novels, make faces
like the masks they find there, and say to God's creatures: how
ordinary!

   The Greeks knew what they were saying when they declared
that Pygmalion's statue did indeed come to life but never had any
children.[6]

---

5. The target of Büchner's satire here is likely the popular theater of his own time rather
   than that of Danton's. By the 1830s, dramas featuring spectacular recreations of legendary and historical disasters were in vogue across Europe.
6. In Greco-Roman myth, Pygmalion was a man who fell in love with a statue of a woman;
   in answer to his prayer, the goddess Aphrodite endowed the statue with life. Cf. Lenz's
   reflections on art (p. 91) and Büchner's letter of July 28, 1835 (p. 188).

DANTON   And the artists treat nature like David, who cold-bloodedly sketched those murdered in September as they were being thrown out of the Force Prison onto the streets, and said: I am capturing the last spasms of life in these villains. (DANTON *is called out.*)

CAMILLE   What do you think, Lucile?

LUCILE   Nothing, I like to watch you talk.

CAMILLE   Do you listen to what I say, too?

LUCILE   Yes, of course.

CAMILLE   Was I right? Did you understand what I said?

LUCILE   No—not at all. (DANTON *returns.*)

CAMILLE   What's the matter?

DANTON   The Committee of Public Safety has decided to arrest me. I've been warned and offered a place of refuge.

They're after my head—so what? I'm sick of all the fuss. Let them have it. What will it matter? I'll know how to die bravely—that's easier than living.

CAMILLE   Danton, there's still time.

DANTON   Impossible—but I wouldn't have thought . . .

CAMILLE   Your laziness!

DANTON   I'm not lazy, just tired. The soles of my feet are on fire.

CAMILLE   Where will you go?

DANTON   Yes, if I only knew.

CAMILLE   Seriously, where?

DANTON   For a walk, my boy, for a walk. (*He goes.*)

LUCILE   Oh, Camille!

CAMILLE   Don't worry, my dear.

LUCILE   When I think that this head—Camille! That's nonsense, right? Am I crazy to think it?

CAMILLE   Don't worry. Danton and I are not the same person.

LUCILE   The world is large and there are many things on it—why just this one? Who would take this from me? That would be awful. What good would it do them?

CAMILLE   I'm telling you, it'll be all right. Yesterday I talked to Robespierre, he was friendly. Things are a little strained, that's true—differing opinions, that's all.

LUCILE   Go look for him.

CAMILLE   We sat next to each other in school. He was always gloomy and aloof. I was the only one who went to him and made him laugh sometimes. He's always showed me great affection. I'll go.

LUCILE   Off so fast, my friend? Go ahead! Come here! Just that (*She kisses him.*) and that! Go! Go! (CAMILLE *exits.*)

These are terrible times. But that's the way it is. Who can change it? You have to live with it. (*Sings.*)

> Oh, parting, oh parting, oh parting,
> Whoever invented parting?[7]

Why did I just think of that? That's not good, if it simply comes out by itself that way.

When he left it seemed as if he could never turn back and had to go farther and farther away from me, farther and farther away.

The room's so empty, the windows are open, as if a dead person had been lying here. I can't stand it up here. (*She leaves.*)

4

Open field.

DANTON   I don't want to go on. I don't want to break this silence with my clattering footsteps and my panting breath. (*He sits. After a pause.*)

I've heard of a sickness that makes one lose one's memory. Death, they say, is like that. Then I hope sometimes that death would be even stronger and make one lose *everything.* If only that were so!

Then I'd run like a Christian to save my enemy—that is, my memory.

That place is supposed to be safe; maybe for my memory, but not for me—the grave would be safer. At least it would make me *forget.* It would kill my memory. But there my memory will live on and kill me. I or it? The answer is easy. (*He rises and turns around.*)

I'm flirting with death; it's pleasant to ogle him like this through an eyeglass from a distance. Actually, the whole affair makes me laugh. There's a feeling of permanence in me which says that tomorrow will be the same as today, and the day after and all the days to come will be alike. It's all empty noise, they want to scare me, they won't dare. (*Exit.*)

5

A room. Night.

DANTON. JULIE.

DANTON (*At the window.*)   Won't it ever stop? Won't the light ever fade, the sound die away, won't it ever become quiet and dark so that we don't hear and see each other's ugly sins?—September![8]—

JULIE (*Calls from inside.*)   Danton! Danton!

DANTON   Yes?

JULIE (*Enters.*)   What did you shout?

---

7. From a Hessian folk song.
8. Danton is haunted by his involvement in the September prison massacres.

DANTON   Did I shout?

JULIE   You talked of ugly sins and then you moaned, "September!"

DANTON   Did I? No, I didn't say it. I hardly thought it; those were just very quiet, secret thoughts.

JULIE   You're trembling, Danton.

DANTON   And shouldn't I tremble when the walls begin to talk? When my body is so shattered that my uncertain, wavering thoughts speak with the lips of stones? That's strange.

JULIE   George, my George!

DANTON   Yes, Julie, that's very strange. I'd like to stop thinking when they speak like that. There are thoughts, Julie, for which there shouldn't be any ears. It's not good that they scream at birth like children. That's not good.

JULIE   May God keep you in your right mind, George. George, do you recognize me?

DANTON   Oh, why not? You are a human being, a woman, and finally my wife, and the earth has five continents, Europe, Asia, Africa, America, Australia; and two times two is four. I haven't lost my mind, you see. Didn't something scream "September"? Isn't that what you said?

JULIE   Yes, Danton, I heard it through all the rooms.

DANTON   As I came to the window—(*He looks out.*) the city is quiet, the lights are out . . .

JULIE   A child is crying nearby.

DANTON   As I came to the window—through all the streets it cried and shrieked—"September!"

JULIE   You were dreaming, Danton. Get hold of yourself.

DANTON   Dreaming? Yes, I was dreaming—but it was different— I'll tell you right away, my poor head is weak—right away! There— now I've got it! Beneath me the earth was panting in its flight, I had seized it like a wild horse, with immense limbs I rooted in its mane and pressed its ribs, with my head bent down, my hair streaming out over the abyss. I was being dragged along. Then I screamed in fear and awoke. I went to the window—and that's when I heard it, Julie.

What does that word want from me? Why just that, what do I have to do with that? Why does it stretch out its bloody hands toward me? I didn't strike it down.

Oh, help me, Julie, my senses are dull. Wasn't it in September, Julie?

JULIE   The kings were just forty hours from Paris . . .

DANTON   The defenses had fallen, the aristocrats were in the city . . .

JULIE   The Republic was lost.

DANTON   Yes, lost. We couldn't ignore the enemy at our backs, we
would have been fools—two enemies at once, we or they, the
stronger strikes down the weaker, isn't that reasonable?

JULIE   Yes, yes.

DANTON   We killed them. That was not murder, that was internal
warfare.

JULIE   You saved the country.

DANTON   Yes, I did. It was self-defense, we had to. The Man on the
Cross made it easy for Himself: "It must needs be that offenses
come, but woe to that man by whom the offense cometh."[9]

It must—it was this "must." Who would curse the hand on
which the curse of "must" has fallen? Who has spoken this "must,"
who? What is it in us that whores, lies, steals, and murders?[1]

We are puppets, our strings are pulled by unknown forces, we
ourselves are nothing, nothing! Swords that spirits fight with—
you just don't see any hands, as in a fairy tale.

Now I'm calm.

JULIE   Quite calm, dear?

DANTON   Yes, Julie, come to bed.

6

Street in front of DANTON'S *house.*
SIMON. CIVILIAN TROOPS.

SIMON   How far into the night?

FIRST CITIZEN   What into the night?

SIMON   How far are we into the night?

FIRST CITIZEN   As far as between sunset and sunrise.

SIMON   Idiot, what time is it?

FIRST CITIZEN   Look on your dial. It's the time when perpendicu-
lars rise up under the bed sheets.

SIMON   Let's go up! Onward, citizens! We'll stake our heads on it.
Dead or alive! He's very strong. I'll go first, citizens.

Make way for freedom.

Look to my wife! I'll bequeath her a wreath of oak leaves.

FIRST CITIZEN   With acorns on them? Enough acorns fall into her
lap every day.[2]

SIMON   Onward, citizens! The country will be grateful for your
service!

SECOND CITIZEN   I wish the country would serve *us*; with all those
holes we make in other people's bodies, not a single one in our
pants has been mended.

9. Cf. Matthew 18:7.
1. Cf. Büchner's letter to Minna Jaeglé written after March 10, 1834 (p. 185).
2. In German, "acorn" (*Eichel*) can also refer to the glans penis.

FIRST CITIZEN   Do you want your fly sewed up? Heh, heh, heh!

THE OTHERS   Heh, heh, heh!

SIMON   Let's go, let's go! (*They force their way into* DANTON's *house*.)

7

The National Convention.
A group of DEPUTIES.

LEGENDRE   When will this slaughtering of deputies stop? Who is safe if Danton falls?

A DEPUTY   What can we do?

ANOTHER DEPUTY   He must be heard before the Convention. It's bound to work; how can they compete against his voice?

ANOTHER DEPUTY   Impossible. A decree prohibits it.[3]

LEGENDRE   It must be repealed or an exception must be granted. I'll make the motion. I'm counting on your support.

PRESIDENT   The session is opened.

LEGENDRE[4] (*Ascends the tribune*.)   Four members of the National Convention were arrested last night. I know that Danton is one of them; I do not know the names of the others. Whoever they may be, I demand that they be heard here. Citizens, I declare Danton to be as innocent as myself, and I believe my record to be beyond reproach. I do not wish to accuse any member of the Committees of Public Safety or General Security, but for well-founded reasons I fear that personal enmity and emotion could deprive liberty of men who have served it well. The man whose energy saved France in 1792 deserves to be heard; he must be allowed to account for himself when he is accused of high treason. (*Great commotion*.)

SEVERAL VOICES   We support Legendre's motion.

A DEPUTY   We are here in the name of the people, we cannot be deprived of our seats without the consent of the electorate.

ANOTHER DEPUTY   Your words smell of corpses. You took them from the mouths of the Girondists. Are you asking for privileges? The ax of the law hangs over all heads.

ANOTHER DEPUTY   We cannot allow our committees to send our legislators from the immunity of the law to the guillotine.

ANOTHER DEPUTY   Crime knows no immunity, only royal crimes find it on the throne.

ANOTHER   Only scoundrels appeal to the right of immunity.

ANOTHER   Only murderers refuse to recognize it.

---

3. I.e., one stripping deputies of their constitutional immunity.
4. This speech is largely derived from Büchner's historical sources.

ROBESPIERRE[5]   Such disorder, unknown in this assembly for a long time, proves that weighty matters are at stake. It shall be decided today whether a few men will stand as victors over the fatherland. How can you compromise your principles to such an extent that you grant a few individuals today what you refused Chabot, Delaunai, and Fabre[6] yesterday? Why should these men be treated differently? What do I care about the eulogies one showers upon oneself and upon one's friends? Only too many experiences have shown us what to think of that. We do not ask whether a man has performed this or that patriotic act; we inquire about his entire political career.

Legendre does not appear to know the names of those who were arrested; the entire Convention knows them. His friend Lacroix is among them. Why does Legendre appear not to know that? Because he knows that only shamelessness can defend Lacroix. He named only Danton because he believes that this name demands special privileges. No, we want no privileges, we want no idols! (*Applause.*)

What distinguishes Danton from Lafayette, from Dumouriez, from Brissot,[7] Fabre, Chabot, Hébert? What was said about them that you could not also say about him? Did you spare them? Why should he be favored above his fellow citizens? Possibly because a few deceived individuals and others who did not let themselves be deceived gathered around him as his followers in order to rush into the arms of fortune and power? The more he has deceived patriots who trusted him, the more forcefully he must feel the severity of the friends of liberty.

They want to make you fear the misuse of power which you yourselves have wielded. They cry out against the despotism of the committees, as if the trust which the people have placed in you and which you have delegated to these committees were not a certain guarantee of patriotism. They pretend to tremble. But I say that whoever trembles at this moment is guilty, for innocence never trembles before the watchful eye of the public. (*General applause.*)

They tried to intimidate me: I was led to understand that the danger which threatens Danton might extend to me.

---

5. This speech is largely derived from Büchner's historical sources.
6. Three of the Forgers referred to earlier (see p. 42, n. 4).
7. Lafayette was a liberal aristocrat who supported the constitutional monarchy; after the execution of the King, he defected to the Austrians. Dumouriez was a general and leading Girondist (a moderate, bourgeois faction) who similarly defected to the Austrians. Brissot, the leader of the Girondists, was guillotined in 1793.

They wrote me that Danton's friends had besieged me in the belief that a memory of old ties, a blind faith in simulated virtues could induce me to moderate my zeal and passion for liberty.

Thus I declare that nothing shall stop me, even if Danton's danger should become my own. We all need some courage and magnanimity. Only criminals and base souls fear to see their allies fall at their side, for when they are no longer hidden by a crowd of accomplices, they are exposed to the light of truth. Yet if there are such souls in this assembly, there are also heroic ones here. The number of villains is not great. We need only strike down a few heads, and the fatherland is saved. (*Applause.*)

I demand that Legendre's motion be defeated. (*The* DEPUTIES *rise together as a sign of universal approval.*)

ST. JUST   There appear to be in this assembly a number of sensitive ears that cannot endure the word "blood." May a few general observations convince them that we are no crueler than nature and time. Nature follows its laws serenely and irresistibly; man is destroyed when he comes in conflict with them. A change in the elements of the atmosphere, an eruption of tellurian fires, a fluctuation in the balance of a body of water, a plague, a volcanic eruption, a flood bury thousands. What is the result? An insignificant, barely noticeable change of physical nature that would have passed almost without a trace, were not corpses lying in its path.

I ask you now: should moral nature in its revolutions be more considerate than physical nature? Should not an idea be permitted to destroy its opposition just as well as a law of physics? Should any event whatsoever that transforms the shape of moral nature—that is, humanity—not be permitted to shed blood? The world spirit[8] makes use of our arms in the sphere of the intellect just as in the physical sphere it generates volcanic eruptions or floods. What does it matter if men die from a plague or a revolution?

The strides of humanity are slow, they can only be counted in centuries; behind each rise the graves of generations. The achievement of the simplest inventions or principles has cost the lives of millions who died along the way. Is it then not obvious that at a time when the course of history accelerates, more people lose their breath?

---

8. *Weltgeist* in German; a central term in Hegelian philosophy that Büchner perhaps inserts as a sly anachronism.

We will conclude quickly and simply: since everyone was created under the same conditions, all are therefore equal, aside
from the differences caused by nature itself.

Therefore everyone may enjoy advantages, yet no one may
enjoy privileges, neither an individual nor a smaller nor a greater
class of individuals. Every portion of our proposition, applied in
reality, has killed its human beings. The 14th of July, the 10th of
August, the 31st of May are its punctuation marks.[9] It needed
four years to be realized in the physical world, and under normal
conditions it would have required a century and would have been
punctuated with generations. Is it therefore so surprising that the
flow of the revolution throws out its corpses at every dip, at every
new turn?

We have yet to add several conclusions to our proposition;
shall a few hundred corpses prevent us from doing so?

Moses led his people through the Red Sea and into the desert
until the old corrupt generation had destroyed itself, before he
founded the new state.[1] Legislators! We have neither a Red Sea
nor a desert, but we have the war and the guillotine.

The Revolution is like the daughters of Pelias:[2] it cuts humanity in pieces to rejuvenate it. Humanity will rise up with mighty
limbs out of this cauldron of blood, like the earth out of the waters
of the Flood, as if it had been newly created. (*Long, sustained
applause. Several* DEPUTIES *rise in enthusiasm.*)

We summon all secret enemies of tyranny, who in Europe and
in the entire world carry the dagger of Brutus beneath their
cloaks, to share with us this sublime hour! (*The spectators and
the* DEPUTIES *begin the Marseillaise.*)

Act Three

I

The Luxembourg prison. A room with prisoners.
CHAUMETTE. PAINE. MERCIER. HÉRAULT-SÉCHELLES. *Other
prisoners.*
CHAUMETTE (*Tugs at* PAINE's *sleeve.*) Listen, Paine, it could be
that way after all, something came over me a while ago. Today

---

9. References to the storming of the Bastille (1789), the storming of the Tuileries (1792),
  and the beginning of the anti-Girondist campaign (1793), respectively.
1. Events described in the Book of Exodus.
2. According to Greek myth, the sorceress Medea persuaded Pelias that he could magically regain his youth by being dismembered and boiled. His daughters carried out the
  grisly deed, to no avail.

I have a headache; help me a little with your syllogisms, I feel very peculiar.

PAINE   Come then, philosopher Anaxagoras,[3] I will catechize you. *There is no God*, because: either God created the world or He did not. If He did not, then the world has its cause within itself and there is no God, since God only becomes God in that He contains the cause of all existence. However, God cannot have created the world, for Creation is either eternal like God or it has a beginning. If the latter be true, then God must have created it at a specific moment. Thus, having been idle for an eternity, God must have become active at a certain point; He must therefore have experienced a change within Himself, which subjects Him to the concept of *time*. Both these points contradict the nature of God. God therefore cannot have created the world. Since we know very well, however, that the world or at least our own self exists, and, according to the above, must contain its cause within itself or within something that is not God, God therefore cannot exist. Quod erat demonstrandum.[4]

CHAUMETTE   Yes, indeed, that makes it all very clear again, thank you, thank you.

MERCIER   Just a moment, Paine. What if Creation is eternal?

PAINE   Then it is no longer Creation, then it is one with God or an attribute of God, as Spinoza[5] says; then God is in everything, in you, my dear friend, in the philosopher Anaxagoras here, and in me. That would not be so objectionable, but you must admit that the Heavenly Majesty wouldn't amount to much if our dear Lord could suffer a toothache, get the clap, or be buried alive along with each of us—or could at least have the very unpleasant conceptions of these miseries.

MERCIER   But a cause must exist.

PAINE   Who denies that? But who can claim that this cause is that which we imagine to be God—that is, perfection? Do you think the world is perfect?

MERCIER   No.

PAINE   Then how can you postulate a perfect cause from an imperfect effect?

---

3. Chaumette had changed his first name to Anaxagoras in honor of the Greek philosopher who was sentenced to exile for impiety.
4. That which was to be demonstrated (Latin, literal translation), usually abbreviated Q.E.D. and used at the conclusion of a mathematical or philosophical proof.
5. Seventeenth-century Jewish Dutch philosopher and seminal figure of the Enlightenment; the idea mentioned here is found in his *Ethics*, Part I.

Voltaire[6] dared to offend God as little as the kings, that's why *he* did it. One who has nothing but his reason and doesn't even know or dare to use it logically is a bungler.

MERCIER   To that I ask: can a perfect cause have a perfect effect— that is, can perfection create perfection? Isn't that impossible because the created object can never have its cause within itself, which, however, as you said, is a part of perfection?

CHAUMETTE   Be quiet! Be quiet!

PAINE   Calm yourself, philosopher. You are right; but if God were once to create and could only create imperfection, He had better forget about it entirely. Isn't it very human to be able to think of God only as a Creator? Just because we always have to stretch and shake ourselves only in order to say, "we exist," do we also have to attribute this miserable necessity to God? When our spirit becomes absorbed in the essence of an everlasting bliss, harmoniously at rest within itself, must we immediately assume that it has to stretch out its fingers and knead little men of dough on the table? It's because of a boundless need of love, as we secretly whisper into each other's ears. Must we do this just to make ourselves sons of God? I am satisfied with a lesser father; at least, I won't be able to blame him for raising me beneath his station in pigsties or in galleys.

Eliminate imperfection; only then can you demonstrate God, Spinoza tried it. One may deny evil but not pain; only reason can prove the existence of God, our feelings rebel against it. Note this, Anaxagoras: why do I suffer? That is the rock of atheism. The smallest twinge of pain—and may it stir only in a single atom— makes a rent in Creation from top to bottom.

MERCIER   And what of morality?

PAINE   First you prove God from morality and then morality from God. What do you want with your morality? I don't know if in fact good or evil exist, and therefore I certainly don't need to change my way of life. I act according to my nature; whatever suits it is good for me, and I do it, and whatever is contrary to it is bad for me, and I don't do it, and I defend myself against it when it gets in my way.[7] One can remain virtuous, as they say, and resist so-called vice without having to despise one's opponents—which is really a sad feeling.

CHAUMETTE   True, very true!

---

6. Eighteenth-century Deistic French poet, playwright, historian, and philosopher and a central figure of the Enlightenment.
7. A passage possibly inspired by the philosophy of Thomas Hobbes's *Leviathan*, first translated into German in 1793.

HÉRAULT   Oh, philosopher Anaxagoras, one could, however, also say that if God were to be all things, He would also have to be His own opposite—that is, perfect and imperfect, evil and good, blissful and suffering. The result would certainly equal zero, it would cancel itself out, we would come to nothing. Be happy, you'll survive; you can go on worshiping nature's masterpiece in Madame Momoro—at least she has left rosaries for it in your groin.[8]

CHAUMETTE   I'm much obliged to you, gentlemen. (*Exits.*)

PAINE   He still doesn't believe it—in the end he'll take extreme unction, turn his feet toward Mecca, and get circumcised so he doesn't miss a chance.

(DANTON, LACROIX, CAMILLE, PHILIPPEAU *are led in.*)

HÉRAULT (*Goes up to* DANTON *and embraces him.*)   Good morning—good night, I should say. I can't ask how you've slept. How will you sleep?

DANTON   Well—one has to go to bed laughing.

MERCIER (*To* PAINE.)   This bloodhound with dove's wings! He's the evil genius of the Revolution, he ventured against his mother, but she was stronger than he.

PAINE   His life and death are equally unfortunate.

LACROIX (*To* DANTON.)   I didn't think that they would come so quickly.

DANTON   I knew it, I had been warned.

LACROIX   And you said nothing?

DANTON   What for? A stroke is the best death; would you rather be sick before it? And—I didn't believe they would dare. (*To* HÉRAULT) It's better to lie down in the earth than to get corns walking on it; I'd rather have it as a pillow than a footstool.

HÉRAULT   At least we won't stroke the cheeks of the fair Lady Decay with callused fingers.

CAMILLE (*To* DANTON.)   Don't trouble yourself. You can hang your tongue out as far as you like and you still won't be able to lick the sweat of death from your brow. Oh, Lucile! It's a great pity.

(*The prisoners crowd around the new arrivals.*)

DANTON (*To* PAINE.)   What you have done for the good of your country, I have tried to do for mine. I wasn't as lucky; they're sending me to the scaffold—so what, I won't stumble.

MERCIER (*To* DANTON.)   The blood of the twenty-two is drowning you.[9]

---

8. I.e., the marks of syphilis. The actress Sophie Momoro played the Goddess of Reason in the Hébertists' Cult of Reason.
9. A reference to the execution of Girondins in October 1793.

A PRISONER (*To* HÉRAULT.)   "The power of the people and the power of reason are one."[1]

ANOTHER (*To* CAMILLE.)   Well, High Commissioner of the Lamppost, your improvement of street lighting hasn't made things any brighter in France.[2]

ANOTHER   Let him be! Those are the lips that spoke the word "mercy."[3] (*He embraces* CAMILLE, *several prisoners follow his example.*)

PHILIPPEAU   We are priests who have prayed with the dying; we have been infected and will die of the same plague.

SEVERAL VOICES   The blow that strikes you kills us all.

CAMILLE   Gentlemen, I regret that our efforts were so fruitless. I go to the scaffold because my eyes grew moist at the fate of some unfortunates.

2

A room.

FOUQUIER-TINVILLE. HERMAN.

FOUQUIER   Is everything ready?

HERMAN   It'll be hard to make it stick; if Danton weren't among them, it would be easy.

FOUQUIER   He'll have to lead the dance.

HERMAN   He'll frighten the jury; he's the scarecrow of the Revolution.

FOUQUIER   The jury must will it.

HERMAN   I know of a way, but it would violate legal formality.

FOUQUIER   Go ahead.

HERMAN   We won't draw lots, but we'll pick out the reliable ones.

FOUQUIER   That will have to work. We'll have a nice shooting gallery. There are nineteen of them, a cleverly mixed group. The four forgers,[4] then a few bankers and foreigners. It's a spicy meal—the people need things like that. Dependable people, then! Who, for instance?

HERMAN   Leroi—he's deaf and won't hear a word from the defendants. Danton can shout himself hoarse at him.

FOUQUIER   Very good. Go on.

---

1. These words were originally Hérault's; the Prisoner is throwing them back in his face.
2. Desmoulins was known for his 1789 revolutionary pamphlet "The Streetlamp's Address to the Parisians" ("*Discours de la lanterne aux Parisiens*").
3. Desmoulins supported Danton's idea of a Committee of Clemency that might moderate the Reign of Terror.
4. See p. 42, n. 4.

HERMAN Vilatte and Lumière. The one's always sitting in a tavern and the other's always asleep; they open their mouths only to say the word "guilty."

Girard maintains that no one who has been brought before the Tribunal may go free. Renaudin . . .

FOUQUIER He, too? He once spared a few priests.

HERMAN Don't worry, he came to me a few days ago demanding that all who are to be executed should be bled beforehand to weaken them, because their usually defiant attitude annoys him.

FOUQUIER Oh, very good. Then I'll count on you.

HERMAN Leave it up to me.

3

The Conciergerie.[5] A corridor.

LACROIX, DANTON, MERCIER, *and other prisoners are walking up and down.*

LACROIX (*To a prisoner.*) What, are there so many unfortunates, and in such miserable condition?

PRISONER Didn't the guillotine carts ever tell you that Paris is a slaughterhouse?

MERCIER That's true, Lacroix. Equality swings its sickle over all our heads, the lava of the Revolution flows, the guillotine republicanizes! The galleries clap and the Romans rub their hands, but they don't hear that each of these words is the death rattle of a victim. Try following your rhetoric to the point where it becomes flesh and blood.

Look around you: all this you have spoken; here is a visual translation of your words. These wretches, their hangmen, and the guillotine are your speeches come to life. You built your systems, like Bayezid[6] his pyramids, out of human heads.

DANTON You're right. These days everything is worked in human flesh. That's the curse of our times. Now my body will be used up, too.

One year ago I created the Revolutionary Tribunal. I ask God and mankind to forgive me for that; I wanted to prevent new September massacres, I hoped to save the innocent, but this gradual murder with its formalities is more horrible and just as inevitable. Gentlemen, I hoped to help you leave this place.

MERCIER Oh, we'll leave it all right.

DANTON Now I'm here with you. Heaven knows how this will end.

---

5. A Paris prison, formerly a royal palace; used as a holding pen for prisoners before transport to the guillotine.
6. Ottoman sultan (1360–1403).

4

The Revolutionary Tribunal.

HERMAN (*To* DANTON.)   Your name, citizen.

DANTON   The Revolution calls out my name. My residence will soon be in nothingness and my name in the Pantheon of history.

HERMAN   Danton, the Convention accuses you of having conspired with Mirabeau, with Dumouriez, with Orléans,[7] with the Girondists, with foreigners, and with the faction of Louis XVII.

DANTON   My voice, which has so often rung out on behalf of the people, will easily refute this slander. Let the wretches who accuse me appear here and I will cover them with disgrace. Let the committees appear; I will only answer before them. I need them as accusers and witnesses.

Let them show themselves.

Besides, why should I care about you or your judgment? I have already told you: nothingness will soon be my abode—life is a burden, let them tear it from me; I long to shake it off.

HERMAN   Danton, audacity suits a crime, calmness reflects innocence.

DANTON   Personal audacity certainly deserves reproach, but national audacity, which I have shown so often, with which I have so often fought for liberty, is the worthiest of all virtues. This is my audacity, I use it here for the sake of the Republic against my wretched accusers. Can I control myself when I see myself slandered so basely? One cannot expect a dispassionate defense from a revolutionary such as I. Men of my sort are invaluable in revolutions, on our brows hovers the spirit of liberty. (*Signs of applause among the spectators.*)

They accuse me of conspiring with Mirabeau, with Dumouriez, with Orléans; of crawling to the feet of wretched despots; they challenge me to answer before inescapable, unbending justice.

You, miserable St. Just, will answer to posterity for this slander!

HERMAN   I demand that you answer calmly. Remember Marat—he appeared before his judges with respect.

DANTON   They have laid hands on my whole life, so let it arise and confront them; I will bury them under the weight of my every deed.

I am not proud about this. Fate guides our arm, but only powerful natures are its instruments.

On the Field of Mars I declared war on the monarchy; I defeated it on the 10th of August, I killed it on the 21st of January

---

7. Revolutionary leaders considered traitors by the Jacobins.

and threw a king's head down as a gauntlet before all monarchs.[8] (*Repeated signs of applause. He takes the papers of indictment.*) When I glance at these slanderous words, I feel my whole being tremble. Who are they, who had to force Danton to appear on that memorable day, the 10th of August? Who are the privileged beings, from whom he borrowed his energy? Let my accusers come forth! This is a most reasonable demand. I will unmask these base scoundrels and hurl them back into the nothingness out of which they never should have crept.

HERMAN (*Rings a bell.*) Don't you hear the bell?

DANTON The voice of a man who defends his honor and his life will drown out your bell.

In September I gorged the young brood of the Revolution with the dismembered corpses of the aristocrats. My voice forged weapons for the people out of the gold of the aristocrats and the rich. My voice was the typhoon that buried the minions of despotism under waves of bayonets. (*Loud applause.*)

HERMAN Danton, your voice is worn out, you are far too emotional. At the next meeting you will conclude your defense. You are in need of rest.

The session is adjourned.

DANTON Now you know Danton; in a few hours he will fall asleep in the arms of glory.

5

The Luxembourg prison. A cell.
DILLON. LAFLOTTE. A JAILER.

DILLON Hey, stop shining your nose in my face. Heh, heh, heh!

LAFLOTTE Keep your mouth shut—your moon has a halo. Heh, heh, heh!

JAILER Heh, heh, heh! Sir, do you think you could read by its light? (*Points to a paper in his hand.*)

DILLON Give it here!

JAILER Sir, my moon's brought on a low tide.

LAFLOTTE From the looks of your pants I'd say a high tide.

JAILER No, my moon attracts water. (*To* DILLON.) It's hidden itself away from your sun, sir. You'll have to give me something to fire it up again if you want to read by its light.

DILLON Here, take this! Now get out. (*He gives him money. Exit* JAILER. DILLON *reads.*) Danton has frightened the Tribunal, the jury wavers, the spectators were grumbling. The crowds were

---

8. References to Danton's call for the abolition of the monarchy on July 17, 1791, to the storming of the Tuileries, and to the execution of the King, respectively.

enormous. The people massed around the Palace of Justice out to the bridges. A handful of money, a willing arm—hm, hm! (*He walks back and forth, drinking out of a bottle from time to time.*) If only I had one foot in the street. I won't let myself be slaughtered like this. Yes, just one foot in the street!

LAFLOTTE   And on the guillotine cart, it's all the same.

DILLON   You think so? There'd still be a few steps in between, long enough to measure with the corpses of the decemvirs.—It's high time that the honest people raise their heads.

LAFLOTTE (*To himself.*)   So much the better, that makes it easier to cut them off. Keep it up, old man, a few more glasses and my ship will be afloat.

DILLON   The rascals, the fools—they'll end up guillotining each other. (*He walks up and down.*)

LAFLOTTE (*Aside.*)   One could really love life again, like one's own child, if one presents it to oneself. It doesn't happen often that one can commit incest with chance and become one's own father. Father and child at the same time. A pleasant Oedipus![9]

DILLON   The people can't be fed with corpses; Danton's and Camille's wives ought to throw money to the people, that's better than heads.

LAFLOTTE   But I wouldn't tear out my eyes afterward. I might need them to mourn for the good general.

DILLON   Laying their hands on Danton! Who is still safe? Fear will unite them.

LAFLOTTE   He's lost anyway. What does it matter if I step on a corpse in order to climb out of the grave?

DILLON   Just one foot in the street! I'll find enough people, old soldiers, Girondists, former noblemen—we'll storm the prisons; we must unite with the prisoners.

LAFLOTTE   Well, yes, it smells a little like villainy. So what? I feel like trying that for once, up to now I was too one-sided. I'll have conscience pangs, but that's a change too; it's not so unpleasant to smell one's own stench.

   The prospect of the guillotine has gotten boring; to have to wait for it so long! I've experienced it in my mind twenty times already. It's not even enticing anymore; it's gotten quite ordinary.

DILLON   We must send a letter to Danton's wife.

LAFLOTTE   And then—I'm not afraid of death, but of pain. It could hurt—who is to answer for that? They say it's only for an instant, but pain measures time more finely, it splits a fraction of a second. No! Pain is the only sin and suffering the only vice; I'll remain virtuous.

---

9. Because Oedipus married his mother, he was, in a sense, his own father.

DILLON   Listen, Laflotte, where did that fellow go? I've got money, that'll have to work; we must strike while the iron is hot, my plan is complete.

LAFLOTTE   Right away, right away. I know the jailer, I'll speak to him. You can count on me, general. We'll get out of this hole (*To himself as he leaves.*) and enter into another, I into the largest, the world; he into the smallest, the grave.

6

The Committee of Public Safety.

ST. JUST. BARÈRE. COLLOT D'HERBOIS. BILLAUD-VARENNES.

BARÈRE   What does Fouquier write?

ST. JUST   The second hearing is over. The prisoners demand the appearance of several members of the Convention and of the Committee of Public Safety. They appeal to the people because they are being denied witnesses. The excitement among the people is said to be indescribable. Danton parodied Jupiter[1] and shook his locks.

COLLOT   All the more easily will Samson[2] grasp hold of them.

BARÈRE   We dare not show ourselves. The fishwives and the rag-pickers might find us less impressive.

BILLAUD   The people have an instinct for letting themselves be stepped upon, be it only with a glance; they love insolent faces such as his. Such brows are worse than a noble coat of arms. The refined aristocratic scorn of humanity sits upon them. Everyone who resents being looked down on should help smash them in.

BARÈRE   He's like the horn-skinned Siegfried[3]—the blood of the September massacres has made him invulnerable.

What does Robespierre say?

ST. JUST   He acts as if he had something to say.

The jury must declare itself to be sufficiently informed and close the debate.

BARÈRE   Impossible, that can't be done.

ST. JUST   They must be taken care of at all costs, even if we have to strangle them with our own hands. "Dare!" Let it not be said that Danton taught us this word in vain.[4] The Revolution will not stumble over their dead bodies, but if Danton remains alive, he

---

1. The king of the gods in Roman myth.
2. Reference to Charles Henri Sanson, the foremost executioner of the French Revolution. The name change was likely erroneous, or Büchner may have intended to reference the biblical hero Samson (see p. 77, n. 7).
3. Germanic hero who became nearly invulnerable after bathing in dragon's blood.
4. Danton famously said of the enemies of the Republic, "To conquer them we must dare, dare again, always dare, and France is saved!"

will catch it by the robe, and he has something about him that could ravish liberty itself. (ST. JUST *is called out.*)

    (*A* JAILER *enters.*)

JAILER   In St. Pelagie prisoners are dying, they are calling for a doctor.

BILLAUD   That's unnecessary; less work for the executioner.

JAILER   There are pregnant women among them.

BILLAUD   So much the better; their children won't need a coffin.

BARÈRE   A consumptive aristocrat saves the Revolutionary Tribunal a session. Any medical help would be counterrevolutionary.

COLLOT (*Takes a paper.*)   A petition, a woman's name!

BARÈRE   Probably one of those who would like to be forced to choose between the board of the guillotine and the bed of a Jacobin. They will die like Lucretia[5] after being dishonored, but a little later than the Roman—namely, in childbirth, or from cancer or old age. It might not be so unpleasant to drive a Tarquinius out of the virtuous republic of a virgin.

COLLOT   She is too old. Madame demands death, she knows how to express herself—the prison rests upon her like the lid of a coffin. She's been there only four weeks. The answer is easy. (*He writes and reads.*) "Citizen, you have not wished for death long enough."

BARÈRE   Well said. But Collot, it's not good if the guillotine begins to laugh; the people will no longer fear it. One shouldn't be so familiar.

    (ST. JUST *returns.*)

ST. JUST   I've just received a denunciation. There's a conspiracy in the prisons; a young man named Laflotte discovered it all. He sat in the same room with Dillon, Dillon was drinking and chattering.

BARÈRE   He cuts off his head with his bottle, that's happened before.

ST. JUST   The wives of Danton and Camille are to throw money among the people, Dillon is to escape, the prisoners will be set free, the Convention blown up.

BARÈRE   Those are fairy tales.

ST. JUST   We will put them to sleep with this fairy tale. The denunciation I have right here; then the impudence of the accused, the unrest among the people, the consternation of the jury—I'll make a report.

BARÈRE   Yes, go, St. Just, and spin your phrases, where each comma is a swordstroke and each period a decapitated head.

---

5. See p. 28, n. 1.

ST. JUST   The Convention must decree that the Tribunal should continue the trial without interruption and may exclude from debate any of the accused who infringes upon the respect due to the court or creates a disturbance.

BARÈRE   You have a revolutionary instinct; that sounds very moderate, but it will have its effect. They cannot remain silent; Danton will have to shout.

ST. JUST   I will count on your support. There are people in the Convention who are as sick as Danton and are afraid of getting a similar cure. They have taken courage again, they will scream about violation of rules . . .

BARÈRE   (*Interrupting him.*)   I will tell them: in Rome the consul who had discovered the Catiline conspiracy[6] and had executed the criminals on the spot was accused of violating rules. Who were his accusers?

COLLOT   (*With pathos.*)   Go, St. Just. The lava of the Revolution is flowing. Liberty will strangle in its embrace those weaklings who tried to fertilize its mighty womb; the majesty of the people will appear to them in thunder and lightning like Jupiter to Semele and reduce them to ashes.[7] Go, St. Just, we will help you hurl the thunderbolt upon the heads of the cowards. (ST. JUST *exits.*)

BARÈRE   Did you hear the word "cure"? They'll manage to turn the guillotine into medication against venereal disease. They're not fighting the moderates, they're fighting vice.

BILLAUD   Up to now the two have followed the same path.

BARÈRE   Robespierre wants to turn the Revolution into a lecture hall for morality and the guillotine into a pulpit.

BILLAUD   Or a church pew.

COLLOT   On which he'll eventually lie rather than kneel.

BARÈRE   That will be easy. The world would have to be upside down if the so-called scoundrels are to be hanged by the so-called righteous people.

COLLOT   (*To* BARÈRE.)   When will you come again to Clichy?[8]

BARÈRE   When the doctor stops coming to me.

COLLOT   Yes, indeed, there's a comet over that place whose scorching rays dry out your spinal fluid.[9]

---

6. See p. 33, n. 9.
7. When Jupiter appeared to his mortal lover Semele in all his glory, the sublime vision consumed the woman in flame.
8. A Paris suburb where some prominent revolutionaries acquired country houses, several of which were rumored sites of debauchery.
9. Two double-entendres. "Comet": *Haarstern* in German (literally, "hair star"), has the suggestion of pubic hair. "Spinal fluid": syphilis particularly attacks the spinal cord.

BILLAUD Soon the pretty fingers of the charming Demahy[1] will pull it out of its case and make it hang down over his back like a braid.

BARÈRE (*Shrugs his shoulders.*) Shh! The Incorruptible must not know about that.

BILLAUD He is an impotent Mohammed.[2] (BILLAUD *and* COLLOT *leave.*)

BARÈRE (*Alone.*) The monsters! "You have not wished for death long enough!" Those words should have withered the tongue that spoke them.

And what about me?

When the September murderers forced their way into the prisons, a prisoner grabs his knife, mingles with the killers, plunges it into the breast of a priest—he is saved! Who can object to that? Now what if I mingle with the killers or join the Committee of Public Safety? What if I use a guillotine blade or a pocketknife? The situation remains the same, only with somewhat more complicated circumstances; the basic principles are the same.

And if he could murder one—what about two, or three, or more? Where does it stop? Here come the barleycorns—are two a pile, three, four—how many then? Come, conscience, come, my little chicken, come, cluck, cluck, cluck—here's food for you.

And yet—was I ever a prisoner? I was suspect, that's the same thing, my death was certain. (*Exits.*)

7

The Conciergerie.

LACROIX. DANTON. PHILIPPEAU. CAMILLE.

LACROIX Well roared, Danton. If you had agonized about your life a little sooner, things would be different now. It's bad, isn't it, when death comes so shamefully close and its breath stinks and it becomes ever more insistent?

CAMILLE If only it would ravish us and tear its prey from our hot bodies in a fierce fight! But with all these formalities, it's like marrying an old woman, with the contracts drawn up, the witnesses called, amen said, and then the bed sheets are raised and she crawls in with her cold limbs!

DANTON If only it were a fight with hands and feet! But I feel as if I've fallen into a mill and my limbs were slowly, systemati-

---

1. Barère's mistress at his country house in Clichy.
2. Particularly after Voltaire's 1736 play *Fanaticism, or Mahomet the Prophet* (*Le fanatisme, ou Mahomet le Prophète*), the name of the founder of Islam became an epithet for a zealot.

cally being twisted off by cold physical force. To be killed so
mechanically!

CAMILLE   To lie there alone, cold, stiff, in the rotting dampness;
it's possible that death slowly tortures life out of our fibers, perhaps to rot away consciously.

PHILIPPEAU   Be calm, my friends. We are like the autumn crocus
which only goes to seed after winter is over. We differ from trans-
planted flowers only in that we stink a little from the experiment.
Is that so bad?

DANTON   An edifying prospect! From one dungheap to another!
The divine theory of classes, right? From first grade to second,
from second to third, and so on? I'm sick of school benches, I've
gotten calluses on my ass like a monkey from sitting on them.

PHILIPPEAU   Then what do you want?

DANTON   Peace.

PHILIPPEAU   Peace is in God.

DANTON   In nothingness. Try to immerse yourself in something
more peaceful than nothingness, and if God is the greatest
peace, isn't nothingness God? But I'm an atheist. Those cursed
words: something cannot become nothing! And I am something,
that's the pity of it!

Creation has spread itself out so far that nothing is empty, it's
all a swarm.

Nothingness has killed itself, Creation is its wound, we are its
drops of blood, the world is the grave in which it rots.

That sounds crazy, but there's some truth to it.

CAMILLE   The world is the Wandering Jew,[3] nothingness is death,
but death is impossible. Oh, that I cannot die, that I cannot die,
as the song says.[4]

DANTON   We are all buried alive and entombed like kings in triple
or quadruple coffins—under the sky, in our houses, in our coats
and shirts.

For fifty years we scratch on the lid of the coffin. Oh, to
believe in obliteration—that would help.

There's no hope in death; it's only a simpler—and life a
more complicated, organized—form of decay; that's the only
difference!

But I just happen to be used to this kind of decay; the devil
only knows how I could adjust to another.

Oh, Julie! If I had to go *alone*! If she were to abandon me!

3. A legendary figure cursed to wander the world until the end of time because he taunted
Jesus on the road to Calvary.
4. Two sources have been suggested for this line. Christian Friedrich Daniel Schubart's
"The Eternal Jew" (*Der ewige Jude*, 1783) and Adelbert von Chamisso's "The New
Ahasverus" (*Der neue Ahasverus*, 1836).

And if I decomposed entirely, dissolved completely—I'd be a handful of tormented dust; each of my atoms could find peace only with her.

I can't die, no, I cannot die. We must cry out; they will have to tear out every drop of life from my limbs.

8

A room.

FOUQUIER. AMAR. VOULAND.

FOUQUIER   I no longer know how to answer; they demand a commission.[5]

AMAR   We've got the scoundrels. Here's what you need. (*He gives* FOUQUIER *a paper.*)

VOULAND   This will satisfy you.

FOUQUIER   You're right, we needed that.

AMAR   Now go to work, so all of us can get this thing off our necks.

9

The Revolutionary Tribunal.[6]

DANTON   The Republic is in danger and he has no instructions! We appeal to the people—my voice is still strong enough to hold a funeral oration for the decemvirs. I repeat: we demand a commission; we have important revelations to make. I shall withdraw into the citadel of reason, I shall burst forth with the cannon of truth and crush my enemies. (*Signs of applause.*)

(FOUQUIER, AMAR, VOULAND *enter.*)

FOUQUIER   Silence in the name of the Republic, reverence before the law!

The Convention has resolved:

whereas signs of mutiny are evident in the prisons; whereas the wives of Danton and Camille are throwing money to the people and General Dillon is to escape and become the leader of the insurgents in order to free the accused; whereas the latter have acted in a disorderly fashion and have attempted to libel the Tribunal, the Tribunal is hereby authorized to continue the investigation without interruption and bar from debate any of the accused who neglects the respect due to the law.

DANTON   I ask those present if we have libeled the Tribunal, the people, or the National Convention?

MANY VOICES   No! No!

---

5. The accused men had demanded a commission to review their charge that the Committee was planning a dictatorship.
6. Until Danton's "I accuse Robespierre," this scene is largely derived from Büchner's historical sources.

CAMILLE   The wretches, they want to murder my Lucile!

DANTON   Someday the truth will come to light. I see great misfortune coming over France. This is dictatorship—it has torn off its veil, it carries its head high, it strides over our dead bodies. (*Pointing to* AMAR *and* VOULAND.) Look there at the cowardly murderers, look at the scavengers of the Committee of Public Safety!

I accuse Robespierre, St. Just, and their hangmen of high treason.

They want to choke the Republic in blood. The tracks of the guillotine carts are the highways upon which the foreign powers will penetrate into the heart of the fatherland.

How much longer should the footprints of liberty be graves?

You want bread and they throw you heads. You are thirsty and they make you lick the blood from the steps of the guillotine.

(*Great agitation among the spectators, shouts of approval.*)

MANY VOICES   Long live Danton, down with the decemvirs! (*The prisoners are forcibly led away.*)

10

Square before the Palace of Justice.
A crowd of people.

SEVERAL VOICES   Down with the decemvirs! Long live Danton!

FIRST CITIZEN   Yes, that's right, heads instead of bread, blood instead of wine.

SEVERAL WOMEN   The guillotine is a bad mill and Samson is a bad baker's helper—we want bread, bread!

SECOND CITIZEN   Danton gobbled up your bread; his head will give bread to all of you again, he was right.

FIRST CITIZEN   Danton was with us on the 10th of August, Danton was with us in September. Where were those who accused him?

SECOND CITIZEN   And Lafayette was with you at Versailles and was a traitor anyway.

FIRST CITIZEN   Who says Danton is a traitor?

SECOND CITIZEN   Robespierre.

FIRST CITIZEN   And Robespierre is a traitor.

SECOND CITIZEN   Who says that?

FIRST CITIZEN   Danton.

SECOND CITIZEN   Danton has fancy clothes, Danton has a nice house. Danton has a beautiful wife, he bathes in Burgundy wine, eats venison from silver plates, and sleeps with your wives and daughters when he's drunk.

Danton was poor like you. Where did he get all this?

The Veto bought it for him so he would save the crown.

The duke of Orléans gave it to him so Danton would steal the crown for him.

That foreigner[7] gave it to him so he would betray you all.

What does Robespierre have? The virtuous Robespierre. You all know him.

ALL   Long live Robespierre! Down with Danton! Down with the traitor!

Act Four

1

A room.

JULIE. A BOY.

JULIE   It's all over. They were trembling before him. They'll kill him out of fear. Go! I've seen him for the last time—tell him I couldn't see him this way. (*She gives the* BOY *a lock of her hair.*)

There, bring him that and tell him he won't go alone. He'll understand—and then come back quickly. I want to read his glances in your eyes.

2

A street.

DUMAS. A CITIZEN.

CITIZEN   How can they condemn so many unfortunate people to death after such a trial?

DUMAS   That is unusual, to be sure, but the men of the Revolution have an instinct which is lacking in other men, and this instinct never deceives them.

CITIZEN   That is the instinct of a tiger.—You have a wife.

DUMAS   I shall soon have had one.

CITIZEN   So it's true!

DUMAS   The Revolutionary Tribunal will announce our divorce, the guillotine will separate us from bed and board.

CITIZEN   You are a monster!

DUMAS   Idiot! You admire Brutus?

CITIZEN   With all my heart.

DUMAS   Must one be a Roman consul and cover his head with a toga[8] in order to sacrifice his beloved to the fatherland? I shall wipe my eyes with the sleeve of my red coat, that's the only difference.

CITIZEN   That's horrible.

DUMAS   Go on, you don't understand me. (*They exit.*)

---

7. Presumably William Pitt the Younger, British Prime Minister during the French Revolution and a frequent object of Jacobin fears; Danton was one of many accused of being his hireling.

8. When he realized that he was mortally wounded, Julius Caesar is said to have covered his head with his toga.

3

The Conciergerie.
LACROIX, HÉRAULT *on a bed.* DANTON, CAMILLE *on another.*

LACROIX   It's really shameful how one's hair and nails grow here.

HÉRAULT   Watch out—you're sneezing sand into my face.

LACROIX   And please don't step on my feet like that, friend, I've got corns.

HÉRAULT   You've got lice besides.

LACROIX   Oh, if I could only get rid of the worms.

HÉRAULT   Sleep well, now—we'll have to see how we can work this out, we've got little space.

Don't scratch me with your fingernails while you sleep. There! Don't tug at your shroud, it's cold down there.

DANTON   Yes, Camille, tomorrow we'll be worn-out shoes that are thrown into the lap of that beggar, earth.

CAMILLE   The cowhide from which, according to Plato, the angels cut out slippers to trot around on the earth.[9] No wonder things are so bad. My Lucile!

DANTON   Calm down, my boy.

CAMILLE   Can I? Do you really think so, Danton? Can I? They cannot lay hands on her. The light of beauty that radiates from her sweet body is inextinguishable. Impossible! Look, the earth wouldn't dare cover her, it would arch around her, the mist of the grave would sparkle on her eyelashes like dew, crystals would sprout around her limbs like flowers, and bright springs would lull her to sleep.

DANTON   Sleep, my boy, sleep.

CAMILLE   Listen, Danton, between you and me—it's so miserable to have to die. It's of no use either. I want to steal the last glances from life's beautiful eyes; I want to keep my eyes open.

DANTON   They'll stay open on their own. Samson won't close them for us. Sleep is kinder. Sleep, my boy, sleep.

CAMILLE   Lucile, your kisses are floating on my lips; every kiss becomes a dream, my eyes sink down and enclose it tightly.

DANTON   Why doesn't the clock stop? With every tick it moves the walls closer around me until they're as tight as a coffin.

I once read a story like that as a child; my hair stood on end.

Yes, as a child! Was it worth the trouble to let me grow up and keep me warm? Just more work for the gravedigger!

9. A reference to the Greek philosopher's idea that the immortal soul is temporarily housed in a mundane body.

It's as if I'm smelling already. My dear body, I'll hold my nose and imagine that you're a woman, sweating and stinking after the dance, and pay you compliments. We've often passed the time with each other already.

Tomorrow you'll be a shattered violin; the melody is played out. Tomorrow you'll be an empty bottle; the wine has been drunk, but it hasn't made me drunk and I'll go to bed sober. Happy are they who can still get drunk. Tomorrow you'll be a worn-out pair of pants; you'll be thrown into the closet and the moths will eat you, no matter how much you stink.

Oh, that doesn't help. Yes, it's so miserable to have to die. Death apes birth: dying we're just as helpless and naked as new-born children.

Indeed, our shroud is our diaper. What's the use? We can whimper in the grave as well as in the cradle.

Camille! He's asleep. (*Bending over him.*) A dream is dancing under his eyelashes. I won't brush the golden dew of sleep from his eyes.

(*He gets up and goes to the window.*) I won't go alone—thank you, Julie. And yet I'd have liked to die in another way, as effortlessly as a falling star, as an expiring tone kissing itself dead with its own lips, as a ray of light burying itself in clear waters.—

The stars are scattered over the sky like shimmering tears; there must be deep sorrow in the eye from which they trickled.

CAMILLE   Oh! (*He has gotten up and is reaching toward the ceiling.*)

DANTON   What's the matter, Camille?

CAMILLE   Oh, oh!

DANTON (*Shakes him.*)   Do you want to tear down the ceiling?

CAMILLE   Oh, you, you—oh, hold me—say something, Danton!

DANTON   You're trembling all over, there's sweat on your brow.

CAMILLE   That's you—this is me—there! This is my hand! Yes, now I remember. Oh, Danton, that was terrifying.

DANTON   What was?

CAMILLE   I was half dreaming, half awake. Then the ceiling disappeared and the moon sank down very near, very close, my hand seized it. The sky with its lights had come down, I beat against it, I touched the stars, I reeled like a man drowning under a layer of ice. That was terrifying, Danton.

DANTON   The lamp is throwing a round beam at the ceiling, that's what you saw.

CAMILLE   For all I care—you don't need much to lose the little bit of saneness you have. Insanity grabbed me by the hair. (*He gets up.*) I don't want to sleep anymore, I don't want to go mad. (*He reaches for a book.*)

DANTON   What are you reading?

CAMILLE   The *Night Thoughts*.[1]

DANTON   Do you want to die prematurely? I'll read *La Pucelle*.[2] I don't want to sneak out of life from a church pew but from the bed of a Sister of Mercy. Life's a whore, it fornicates with the whole world.

4

Square in front of the Conciergerie.
A JAILER. *Two* DRIVERS *with carts.* Women.

JAILER   Who called you here?

FIRST DRIVER   I'm not called Here, that's a funny name.

JAILER   Stupid, who gave you the order to come?

FIRST DRIVER   I don't get any ordure, just ten sous a head.

SECOND DRIVER   That dog wants to take the bread out of my mouth.

FIRST DRIVER   What do you mean, your bread? (*Pointing to the prison windows.*) There's food for worms.

SECOND DRIVER   My kids are worms too and they want their share. Oh, things are bad in our profession, and yet we're the best drivers.

FIRST DRIVER   How's that?

SECOND DRIVER   Who is the best driver?

FIRST DRIVER   Whoever drives farthest and fastest.

SECOND DRIVER   Now, you ass, who drives farther than a man who drives someone out of this world, and who's faster than the man who does it in fifteen minutes? It's exactly fifteen minutes from here to the Square of the Revolution.

JAILER   Hurry up, you bums! Closer to the gate! Make room, girls!

FIRST DRIVER   Stay where you are—you don't drive around a girl, but always right through the middle.

SECOND DRIVER   Yeah, I'll believe that, you can drive in with cart and horse, you'll find good tracks, but when you come out, you'll have to go into quarantine.
    (*They drive up.*)

SECOND DRIVER (*To the women.*)   What are you staring at?

A WOMAN   We're waiting for old customers.

SECOND DRIVER   You think my cart is a whorehouse? It's a respectable cart—it's carried the king and all the elegant men of Paris to the table.

LUCILE (*Enters. She sits on a rock under the prison windows.*)

---

1. Edward Young's *The Complaint, or Night Thoughts on Life, Death, and Immortality* (1742–45) was a long pedagogical poem popular throughout eighteenth-century Europe.
2. Voltaire's *La Pucelle d'Orléans* (1762) was a burlesque epic about Joan of Arc.

Camille, Camille! (CAMILLE *appears at a window.*)

Listen, Camille, you make me laugh with your long coat of stone and your iron mask over your face—can't you bend down? Where are your arms?

I want to lure you down, dear bird. (*Sings.*)

> Two little stars shine in the sky
> Shining brighter than the moon,
> One shines at my dear love's window,
> The other at her chamber door.[3]

Come, come, my friend! Up the steps, quietly—they're all asleep. The moon helps me in my long wait. But you can't get through the gate, that's an unbearable costume you have. It's too nasty for a joke, please stop it. But you aren't moving either—why don't you say anything? You're making me afraid. Listen! People say you must die, and they make such somber faces.

Die! The faces make me laugh. Die! What kind of a word is that? Tell me, Camille. Die. I'll think about it. There—there it is. I want to run after it, come, sweet friend, help me catch it, come, come! (*She runs off.*)

CAMILLE (*Calls out.*)   Lucile! Lucile!

5

The Conciergerie.

DANTON *at a window that opens into the next room.* CAMILLE. PHILIPPEAU. LACROIX. HÉRAULT.

DANTON   You're quiet now, Fabre.

A VOICE (*From inside.*)   Dying.

DANTON   Do you know what we'll do now?

THE VOICE   Well?

DANTON   What you did all your life—*des vers.*[4]

CAMILLE (*To himself.*)   Insanity lurked behind her eyes. She isn't the first to go insane, that's the way of the world. What can we do about it? We wash our hands of it. It's better that way.

DANTON   I'm leaving everything behind in terrible confusion. No one knows how to govern. Things might still work out if I left Robespierre my whores and Couthon my legs.[5]

LACROIX   We would have made a whore out of liberty.

DANTON   What's the difference? Whores and liberty are the most cosmopolitan things under the sun. Liberty will now respectably

---

3. Popular verses found in many German folk songs.
4. French for both "verses" and "worms."
5. Georges Couthon's legs were paralyzed.

prostitute herself in the marital bed of the lawyer of Arras. But I imagine she'll play Clytemnestra to him;[6] I don't give him six months, I'm dragging him down with me.

CAMILLE (*To himself.*) May heaven help her to a comfortable delusion. The usual delusions we call sound reason are unbearably dull. The happiest of all people was the one who could imagine he was God the Father, the Son, and the Holy Ghost.

LACROIX The asses will bray "Long live the Republic!" as we go by.

DANTON What does it matter? The flood of the Revolution can discharge our corpses wherever it wants; they'll still be able to smash the heads of all kings with our fossilized bones.

HÉRAULT Yes, if a Samson turns up for our jawbones.[7]

DANTON They are brothers of Cain.[8]

LACROIX There's no better proof that Robespierre is a Nero[9] than the fact that he was never friendlier to Camille than he was two days before Camille's arrest. Isn't that so, Camille?

CAMILLE If you like—what does it matter to me?

(*To himself.*) What a beautiful child she has borne of insanity. Why must I leave now? We would have laughed with it, cradled it, kissed it.

DANTON If history ever opens its graves, despotism can still suffocate from the stench of our dead bodies.

HÉRAULT We stank well enough while alive.

This is all rhetoric for posterity, isn't it, Danton? It means nothing to us.

CAMILLE He's making a face as if it should turn to stone to be dug up by posterity as an antique.

Is it worth the trouble to put on false smiles and rogue and speak with a good accent? We ought to take the masks off for once: as in a room with mirrors we would see everywhere only the same age-old, numberless, indestructible muttonhead, no more, no less. The differences aren't so great; we're all villains and angels, fools and geniuses—and all that in one. These four things find enough space in the same body, they aren't as large as one thinks.

Sleeping, digesting, making children—that's what we all do; all other things are merely variations in different keys on the

---

6. In Greek myth, Clytemnestra murdered her husband.
7. According to Judges 15:15, he (in Büchner's German: *Simson*) slaughtered a thousand Philistines with the jawbone of an ass. A reference to the Revolution's chief executioner, Sanson, is also intended.
8. Firstborn son of Adam and Eve, who slew his brother Abel.
9. Roman emperor notorious for debauchery and misrule.

same theme. Is that why we stand on tiptoe and make faces, is that why we're self-conscious in front of each other? We've all eaten ourselves sick at the same table and have a bellyache. Why are you holding your napkins in front of your faces? Just scream and whine as it suits you.

Just don't make such virtuous and witty and heroic and intelligent faces—we know each other, after all; save yourselves the trouble.

HÉRAULT   Yes, Camille, we'll sit down together and cry out; there's nothing more stupid than to press one's lips together when something hurts.

Greeks and gods cried out, Romans and Stoics put on a heroic front.

DANTON   The ones were just as good epicureans as the others. They worked out for themselves a very comfortable feeling of self-satisfaction. It's not such a bad idea to drape yourself in a toga and look around to see if you throw a long shadow. Why should we be at odds? Does it matter if we cover our shame with laurel leaves, rose wreaths, or vine leaves, or if we carry the ugly thing openly and let the dogs lick at it?

PHILIPPEAU   My friends, one needn't stand very far above the earth to blot out all this confused wavering and flickering and to have one's eyes filled with a few great, divine forms. There is an ear for which cacophony and deafening outcries are a stream of harmonies.

DANTON   But we are the poor musicians and our bodies the instruments. Are those horrible sounds they scratch out only meant to rise up higher and higher and finally die away as a sensual breath in heavenly ears?

HÉRAULT   Are we like suckling pigs that are beaten to death with rods for royal dinners so that their meat is tastier?

DANTON   Are we children who are roasted in the fiery Moloch[1] arms of this world and are tickled with light rays so that the gods can enjoy their laughter?

CAMILLE   Is the ether with its golden eyes a bowl of golden carp, which stands at the table of the blessed gods, and the blessed gods laugh eternally and the fish die eternally and the gods eternally enjoy the iridescence of the death battle?

DANTON   The world is chaos. Nothingness is the world-god yet to be born.

(The JAILER enters.)

JAILER   Gentlemen, you may depart. The carts are at the door.

---

1. Babylonian god to which children were sacrificed by fire.

PHILIPPEAU   Good night, my friends. Let us pull the great blanket over ourselves under which all hearts stop beating and all eyes fall shut. (*They embrace each other.*)

HÉRAULT (*Takes* CAMILLE's *arm.*)   Be happy, Camille, the night will be beautiful. The clouds hang in the quiet evening sky like a dying Olympus with fading, sinking, godlike forms. (*They exit.*)

6

A room.

JULIE   The people were running through the streets, now all is quiet.

I don't want to keep him waiting for a moment.

(*She takes out a vial.*) Come, dearest priest, your amen makes us go to sleep.

(*She goes to the window.*) Parting is so pleasant; I only have to close the door behind me. (*She drinks.*)

I'd like to stand here like this forever.

The sun has set. The earth's features were so sharp in its light, but now her face is as still and serious as that of a dying person. How beautifully the evening light plays on her forehead and cheeks.

She's becoming ever paler; she's sinking like a corpse into the flood of the ether. Will no arm catch her by her golden locks and pull her from the stream and bury her?

I'll leave quietly. I won't kiss her, so that no breath, no sigh will wake her from her slumber.

Sleep, sleep. (*She dies.*)

7

The Square of the Revolution.
   The carts drive up and stop before the guillotine. Men and women sing and dance the carmagnole.[2] The prisoners sing the Marseillaise.[3]

A WOMAN WITH CHILDREN   Make room! Make room! The children are crying, they're hungry. I have to let them look, so they'll be quiet. Make room!

A WOMAN   Hey, Danton, now you can fornicate with the worms.

ANOTHER WOMAN   Hérault, I'll have a wig made out of your pretty hair.

HÉRAULT   I don't have enough foliage for such a barren mound of Venus.

---

2. Revolutionary song and dance especially popular during the Reign of Terror.
3. The most famous anthem of the Revolution.

CAMILLE   Damned witches! You'll be screaming, "Fall on us, you mountains!"[4]

A WOMAN   The mountain's already on you, or rather you fell from it.[5]

DANTON (*To* CAMILLE.)   Easy, my boy, you've screamed yourself hoarse.

CAMILLE (*Gives the driver money.*)   There, old Charon,[6] your cart is a good serving platter.

   Gentlemen, I'll serve myself first. This is a classic meal: we'll lie in our places and shed a little blood as a libation. Adieu, Danton. (*He ascends the scaffold. The prisoners follow him one after the other.* DANTON *is the last to ascend.*)

LACROIX (*To the people.*)   You kill us on the day when you have lost your reason; you'll kill *them* on the day when you've regained it.

SEVERAL VOICES   We've heard that before! How dull!

LACROIX   The tyrants will break their necks on our graves.

HÉRAULT (*To* DANTON.)   He thinks his dead body will be a hotbed of liberty.

PHILIPPEAU (*On the scaffold.*)   I forgive you—I hope that your last hour be no more bitter than mine.

HÉRAULT   I thought so; once again he has to bare his chest to show the people down there that he has clean linen.

FABRE   Farewell, Danton. I'm dying twice.

DANTON   Adieu, my friend. The guillotine is the best doctor.

HÉRAULT (*Tries to embrace* DANTON.)   Oh, Danton, I can't even make a joke anymore. Then it's time. (*An* EXECUTIONER *pushes him back.*)

DANTON (*To the* EXECUTIONER.)   Do you want to be crueler than death?

   Can you prevent our heads from kissing at the bottom of the basket?

8

   A street.

LUCILE   There seems to be something serious about it. I'll have to think about that. I'm beginning to understand it. To die—to die . . .

   Everything may live, everything, the little fly there, the bird. Why not he? The stream of life ought to stop short if that one drop were spilled. The earth ought to be wounded from the blow.

---

4. The phrase appears in Hosea 10:8, Luke 23:30, and Revelation 6:16.
5. I.e., the radical Jacobins (see p. 43, n. 6).
6. In Greek myth, the ferryman who carried the dead over the river Styx to the underworld.

Everything moves, clocks tick, bells ring, people walk around, water runs—it all keeps going up to that point—no! It mustn't happen, no—I'll sit on the ground and scream so that everything will stop in fear—everything will stand still, nothing will move. (*She sits down, covers her eyes and screams. After a pause she arises.*)

It doesn't help—it's all still the same, the houses, the street, the wind blows, the clouds move.—I suppose we must bear it.

(*Several women come down the street.*)

FIRST WOMAN   A good-looking man, that Hérault.

SECOND WOMAN   When he stood at the Arch of Triumph during the Constitutional Celebration, I thought, "He'll look good next to the guillotine, he will." That was sort of a hunch.

THIRD WOMAN   Yes, you got to see people in all kinds of situations. It's good that dying has become so public now. (*They go past.*)

LUCILE   My Camille! Where should I look for you now?

9

The Square of the Revolution.
Two EXECUTIONERS *busy at the guillotine.*
FIRST EXECUTIONER (*Stands on the guillotine and sings.*)

> And when I'm off to bed,
> The moon shines on my head . . . [7]

SECOND EXECUTIONER   Hey! You! Finished soon?
FIRST EXECUTIONER   Right away, take it easy. (*Sings.*)

> My grandpa says when I come,
> "Been with the whores, ya bum?"

Come on! Gimme my jacket! (*They go off singing.*)

> And when I'm off to bed,
> The moon shines on my head.

LUCILE (*Enters and sits on the steps of the guillotine.*)   I'm sitting in your lap, you silent angel of death. (*She sings.*)

> There's a reaper, Death's his name,
> His might is from the Lord God's flame.

You dear cradle, who lulled my Camille to sleep, who smothered him under your roses.

You death knell, who sang him to the grave with your sweet tongue. (*She sings.*)

---

7. From a folk song from the Mosel-Saar region of Germany.

> A hundred thousand, big and small,
> His sickle always makes them fall.[8]

(*A patrol appears.*)

A CITIZEN   Hey—who's there?

LUCILE   Long live the king!

CITIZEN   In the name of the Republic! (*She is surrounded by the watch and is led off.*)

---

8. From a folk song and Catholic hymn from the early seventeenth century, included in the collection *Des Knaben Wunderhorn* (1805–08).

Lenz

Historical Background

Alongside Goethe and Schiller, Jacob Michael Lenz (1751–1792) was one of the greatest dramatists of the Sturm und Drang (Storm and Stress), a German literary movement of the late eighteenth century. Inspired by Shakespeare and Rousseau, Sturm und Drang writers rejected neoclassical unities in favor of fluid narrative structures driven by restless emotions. In many ways Lenz not only participated in but actually embodied the movement. Lenz studied theology at Königsberg University, briefly attending lectures by Immanuel Kant before dropping out to pursue a vocation as a writer. He joined the Strassburg literary circle of Friedrich Rudolf Salzmann in 1771, where he met the young Goethe, whom he at once idolized and attempted to rival. While in Strassburg he wrote his two most famous plays—*The Tutor, or The Advantages of Private Education* (*Der Hofmeister, oder Vorteile der Privaterziehung*, 1774) and *The Soldiers* (*Die Soldaten*, 1776)—as well as a work of dramatic theory, *Observations on the Theatre* (*Anmerkungen übers Theater*, 1774). Already showing signs of mental instability when he visited Goethe's circle in Weimar in 1776, he soon became notorious for outlandish behavior and was expelled from the city, possibly for insulting Goethe's ducal patron. For several months he wandered across southern Germany and Switzerland before suffering a major mental breakdown in 1777.

Büchner's story begins in January of the following year, and its basic elements are historically accurate. Lenz did indeed make his way alone through the Vosges Mountains in eastern France to find Johann Friedrich Oberlin in Walderbach in the Steinthal (an area about forty miles, or sixty kilometers, west of Strassburg). A Lutheran pastor who welcomed Calvinists and Roman Catholics and a mystic who pioneered educational and agricultural reform among the poor, Oberlin harmonized disparate intellectual currents. For many at the time, he was the paragon of the engaged Christian humanist, at once active and contemplative, ecumenical and pious, progressive and rooted in tradition. As Büchner's story relates, Oberlin attempted

in vain to cure Lenz through spiritual means before eventually taking him to Strassburg in February 1778.

Lenz's postscript is a grim one. From Strassburg he resumed his
travels again, this time moving east through his birthplace of Lat-
via to Russia. In 1792 his body, ravaged by poverty and madness,
was found dead in a Moscow street.

Sources

Büchner's story is most heavily indebted to Oberlin's diary account
of his experience with Lenz. Büchner read a manuscript copy, which
was later published in installments by Büchner's friend August
Stöber in the journal *Erwinia* from 1838 to 1839. The story roughly
follows the events of Oberlin's account. As there is a significant gap
in Büchner's text, the corresponding section of Oberlin's account is
of particular interest. A translation of this part of Oberlin's diary
appears in the "Context" section of this volume.

Manuscript and Publication

We have no manuscript of *Lenz*, and the story was not published
until 1839, two years after Büchner's death. The editor, Karl Gutzkow, based his edition on a copy made by Büchner's fiancée, Minna
Jaeglé.

LENZ[†]

On the 20th Lenz went through the mountains. The peaks and
high slopes in snow, gray rock down into the valleys, green fields,
boulders, and pine trees. It was cold and damp, water trickled down
the rocks and sprang over the path. Pine branches hung down heavily in the moist air. Gray clouds moved across the sky, but everything
so dense, and then the fog steamed up, and trailed, oppressive and
damp, through the bushes, so sluggish, so shapeless. He went on
indifferently, the path did not matter to him, sometimes up, sometimes down. He felt no fatigue, but at times he was irritated that he
could not walk on his head. At first he felt tension in his chest when
stones jumped away, when the gray forest shivered beneath him,
when at times the fog enveloped the shapes or partly revealed the
powerful branches; he felt an urge, he searched for something, as

[†]   Translated by Henry J. Schmidt.

though for lost dreams, but he found nothing. Everything seemed to him to be so small, so close, so wet, he would have liked to set the earth behind the stove, he could not understand why he needed so much time to climb down a steep slope, to reach a distant point; he felt he should be able to cover any distance in a few steps. Only at times when the storm hurled the clouds into the valley, and the forest steamed up, and voices awakened on the rocks, often like thunder echoing in the distance and then raging up violently, as if they wanted to celebrate the earth in their wild rejoicing, and the clouds galloped along like wild neighing horses, and sunshine pierced through them and emerged and drew its flashing sword along the snowy slopes, so that a bright, blinding light cut across the peaks down into the valleys; or when the storm forced the clouds downward and tore a light blue sea into them, and then the wind died down, humming up like a lullaby and chiming bells from deep within the ravines, from the tops of the pine trees, and when a soft red glow arose against the deep blue, and tiny clouds fled by on silver wings, and all the mountain peaks, sharp and firm, gleamed and flashed far across the countryside: then pain tore through his chest, he stood, panting, his body bent forward, eyes and mouth wide open, he thought he must draw the storm into himself, contain all within him, he stretched out and lay over the earth, he burrowed into the cosmos, it was a pleasure that hurt him; or he stood still and rested his head on the moss and half-closed his eyes, and then it all moved far away from him, the earth receded below him, it grew small like a wandering star and plunged into a rushing stream flowing limpidly beneath him. But these were only moments, and then he rose, calm, steady, quiet, as if phantoms had passed before him, he remembered nothing. Toward evening he came to the mountain ridge, to the snowfield from which one descended again to the plain in the west, he sat down at the top. It had become more peaceful toward evening: the clouds hung firm and motionless against the sky, as far as the eye could see, nothing but mountaintops, with broad slopes leading down, and all so quiet, gray, in twilight; he became terribly lonely, he was alone, all alone, he wanted to talk to himself, but he could not breathe, he hardly dared, the creak of his foot below him sounded like thunder, he had to sit down; a nameless fear seized him in this nothingness, he was in a void, he jumped up and raced down the slope. It had grown dark, heaven and earth melted together. It seemed as if something were following him, as if something horrible would overtake him, something that humans cannot endure, as if insanity were pursuing him on horseback. At last he heard voices, he saw lights, he was relieved, he was told it was another half hour to Waldbach. He went through the village, lights shone through the windows, he looked in as he passed by, children at the table, old women, girls, all calm, quiet faces, it seemed to him as if the light must be radiating from them, he felt at ease, he was soon in the parsonage at Waldbach. They were sitting at the table, he went in; his blond curls hung around his pale face, his eyes and mouth twitched, his clothes were torn. Oberlin welcomed him, he took him for a laborer "Welcome, although I don't know you." I am a friend of + + +[1] and bring you greetings from him. "Your name, if you please?" Lenz. "Ha, ha, ha, hasn't it appeared in print? Haven't I read several dramas ascribed to a man of that name?" Yes, but I beg you not to judge me by them. They continued talking, he searched for words and spoke rapidly but in torment; gradually he became calm, the cozy room and the quiet faces emerging from the shadows, the child's bright face, on which all light seemed to rest, looking up curiously, trustingly, finally the mother, sitting quietly back in the shadows like an angel. He began to tell of his homeland; he drew all sorts of costumes, they gathered around him with interest, he felt right at home, his pale child's face, smiling now, his lively narration; he grew calm, it seemed to him as if old shapes, forgotten faces were stepping out of the dark once again, old songs awoke, he was far, far, away. At last it was time to leave, he was led across the street, the parsonage was too small, he was given a room in the schoolhouse. He went upstairs, it was cold up there, a large room, empty, a high bed in the background, he placed the lamp on the table and walked up and down, he recalled the day just past, how he had come here, where he was, the room in the parsonage with its lights and dear faces, it was like a shadow to him, a dream, and he felt empty again like on the mountain, but he could no longer fill the void with anything, the light was out, darkness swallowed everything; an unnameable fear seized him, he jumped up, he ran through the room, down the stairs, in front of the house; but in vain, all was dark, nothing, he felt himself to be a dream, isolated thoughts flitted by, he held them fast, he felt he had to keep saying "Our Father"; he could no longer find himself, an obscure instinct urged him to save himself, he beat against the stones, he tore at himself with his fingernails, the pain began to restore him to consciousness, he threw himself into the basin of the fountain, but the water was not deep, he splashed around in it. Then people came, they had heard this, they called out to him. Oberlin came running; Lenz had come to his senses again, fully aware of his situation, he was at ease again, now he was ashamed and sorry to have frightened these good people, he told

1. Christoph Kaufmann (1753–1795), a friend of many of the major figures of the Sturm und Drang period.

them he was used to taking cold baths, and went back up; exhaustion finally allowed him to rest.

The next day went well. With Oberlin through the valley on horseback; broad mountain slopes contracting from a great height into a narrow, winding valley that led high up into the mountains in many directions, large masses of rock, spreading out toward the base, few woods, but all in a gray, somber hue, a view toward the west into the country and to the mountain range running straight from south to north, immense, grave or silent peaks standing like a dusky dream. Huge masses of light gushing at times from the valleys like a golden river, then clouds again, hanging on the highest peak, then climbing down the forest slowly into the valley or sinking and rising in the sunbeams like a flying silvery web; not a sound, no movement, no birds, nothing but the wailing of the wind, sometimes near, sometimes far. Dots also appeared, skeletons of huts, boards covered with straw, a somber black in color. People, silent and grave, as though not daring to disturb the peace of their valley, greeted them quietly as they rode past. The huts were full of life, people crowded around Oberlin, he instructed, gave advice, consoled; everywhere trusting glances, prayer. People told of dreams, premonitions. Then quickly to practical affairs, laying roads, digging canals, visiting the school. Oberlin was tireless. Lenz his constant companion, at times conversing, attending to business, absorbed in nature. It all had a beneficial and soothing effect on him, he often had to look into Oberlin's eyes, and the immense peace that comes upon us in nature at rest, in the deep forest, in moonlit, melting summer nights seemed even nearer to him in these calm eyes, this noble, serious face. He was shy, but he made remarks, he spoke, Oberlin enjoyed his conversation and Lenz's charming child's face delighted him. But he could bear it only as long as the light remained in the valley; toward evening a strange fear came over him, he felt like chasing after the sun; as objects gradually became more shadowy, everything seemed so dreamlike, so abhorrent, he felt the fear of a child sleeping in the dark; he seemed to be going blind; now it grew, the demon of insanity sat at his feet, the hopeless thought that all was but a dream gaped before him, he clung to all objects, shapes rushed past him, he pressed up against them, they were shadows, life drained from him, and his limbs were quite rigid. He spoke, he sang, he recited passages from Shakespeare, he clutched at everything that used to make his blood run faster, he tried everything, but cold, cold. Then he had to go out into the open, when his eyes had gotten used to the dark, the weak light diffused through the night restored him, he threw himself into the fountain, the harsh effect of the water restored him, he also secretly hoped to fall ill, he now bathed with less noise. Yet the more he accustomed himself to this way of life, the calmer he became, he assisted Oberlin, drew, read the Bible; old, long gone hopes reawakened in him; the New Testament was so near to him here, and one morning he went out. When Oberlin told him how an irresistible hand had stopped him on the bridge, how a dazzling light on the heights had blinded him, how he had heard a voice, how it had spoken to him at night, and how God had entered into him so completely that he took his Bible verse from his pocket like a child in order to know what to do, this faith, this eternal Heaven in life, this being in God; now for the first time he comprehended the Scriptures. How close nature came to these people, all in heavenly mystery; yet not overpoweringly majestic, but still familiar!—He went out in the morning, snow had fallen that night, bright sunshine lay in the valley, but farther off the landscape partly in fog. He soon left the path, up a gradual slope, no more sign of footprints, past a pine forest, the sun formed crystals, the snow was light and fluffy, here and there on the snow light traces of wild animals leading up into the mountains. No movement in the air except for a soft breeze, the rustle of a bird lightly dusting snowflakes from its tail. All so quiet, and into the distance, trees with swaying white feathers in the deep blue air. Gradually it all became comfortable to him, hidden were those massive, uniform planes and lines that at times seemed to be speaking to him in mighty sounds, a cozy Christmas spirit crept over him, sometimes he thought his mother would step out from behind a tree, tall, and tell him she had given all this to him as a gift; as he went down, he saw that a rainbow of rays surrounded his shadow, something seemed to have touched his forehead, the being spoke to him. He came back down. Oberlin was in the room, Lenz went up to him cheerfully, saying he would like to hold a sermon sometime. "Are you a theologian?" Yes!—"Good, then next Sunday." Lenz went happily to his room, he thought about a text for his sermon and grew pensive, and his nights became peaceful. Sunday morning came, a thaw had set in. Clouds streaming by, blue in between, the church stood on a rise on the mountainside, the churchyard around it. Lenz stood up above as the churchbell rang, and the congregation came from various directions on the narrow paths up and down among the rocks, women and girls in their somber black dresses, a folded white handkerchief on the hymnal and a sprig of rosemary. Patches of sunshine lay at times on the valley, the warm air moved slowly, the countryside swam in a haze, distant church bells, it seemed as if everything were dissolving into one harmonious wave.

The snow had disappeared from the little churchyard, dark moss under the black crosses, a late rosebush leaned against the church-

yard wall, late flowers coming up through the moss, sometimes sunshine, then darkness again. The service began, voices joined in clear,
bright sound; an effect like looking into a pure mountain spring. The
singing died away, Lenz spoke, he was shy, the music had calmed his
convulsions entirely, all his pain awakened now and settled in his
heart. A sweet feeling of endless well-being crept over him. He spoke
simply to the people, they all suffered with him, and it was a comfort
to him when he could bring sleep to several eyes tired from crying,
bring peace to tortured hearts, direct toward Heaven this existence
tormented by material needs, these weighty afflictions. He had
grown stronger toward the end, then the voices began again:

> Burst, o divine woe,
> The floodgates of my soul;
> May pain be my reward,
> Through pain I love my Lord.[2]

The urge in him, the music, the pain shattered him. For him
there were wounds in the universe; he felt deep, inexpressible grief
because of it. Now, another existence, divine, twitching lips bent
over him and sucked on his lips; he went up to his lonely room. He
was alone, alone! Then the spring rushed forth, torrents broke from
his eyes, his body convulsed, his limbs twitched, he felt as if he
must dissolve, he could find no end to this ecstasy; finally his mind
cleared, he felt a quiet, deep pity for himself, he cried over himself,
his head sank on his chest, he fell asleep, the full moon hung in the
sky, his curls fell over his temples and his face, tears hung on his
eyelashes and dried on his cheeks, so he lay there alone, and all was
calm and silent and cold, and the moon shone all night and hung
over the mountains.

Next morning he came down, he told Oberlin quite calmly how
during the night his mother had appeared to him; she had stepped
out from the dark churchyard wall in a white dress, and had a white
and a red rose on her breast; then she had sunk down in a corner,
and the roses had slowly grown over her, she was surely dead; he
was quite calm about it. Then Oberlin told him how he had been
alone on a field when his father died, and he had then heard a
voice, so that he knew his father was dead, and when he came
home it was so. That led them further, Oberlin also spoke about the
people in the mountains, about girls who sensed water and metals
under the earth, about men who had been seized on certain mountaintops and had wrestled with a spirit; he told him too how in the
mountains he had once fallen into a kind of somnambulism by
looking into a clear, deep mountain pool. Lenz said that the spirit

2. Cf. *Woyzeck* 4,17.

of the water had come over him, that he had at that moment sensed
something of his unique being. He continued: the simplest, purest
character was closest to elemental nature, the more sophisticated a
person's intellectual feelings and life, the duller is this elemental
sense; he did not consider it to be an elevated state of being, it was
not independent enough, but he believed it must be boundless
ecstasy to be touched in this way by the unique life of every form;
to commune with rocks, metals, water, and plants; to assimilate each
being in nature as in a dream, as flowers take in air with the waxing
and waning of the moon.

He continued to speak his mind, how in all things there was an
inexpressible harmony, a tone, a blissfulness that in higher forms of
life reaches out, resounds, comprehends with more organs but was
consequently far more sensitive, whereas in the lower forms everything was more repressed, limited but was therefore far more at
peace with itself. He continued this further. Oberlin broke it off, it
led too far from his simple ways. Another time Oberlin showed him
color charts, telling him the relationship of each color to human
beings, he brought out twelve Apostles, each represented by a color.
Lenz understood, he carried the idea further, came to have frightening dreams and began like Stilling to read the Apocalypse,[3] and
read much in the Bible.

Around this time Kaufmann came to the Steintal with his fiancée. At first Lenz was troubled by the encounter, he had created a
small place for himself, that little bit of peace was so valuable to
him, and now someone was coming who reminded him of so much,
with whom he had to speak, converse, who knew his situation. Oberlin knew nothing of all this; he had taken him in, cared for him; he
saw this as the will of God, who had sent him this unfortunate one,
he loved him dearly. Besides, it was necessary that he was there, he
belonged to them as though he had been there for a long time, and
no one asked where he came from and where he would go. At table
Lenz was in a good mood again, they talked about literature, he was
in his element; the idealistic period was beginning then, Kaufmann
was one of its supporters, Lenz disagreed vehemently. He said: the
poets who supposedly give us reality actually have no idea of it, yet
they are still more bearable than those who wish to transfigure it.
He said: the good Lord has certainly made the world as it should
be, and we surely cannot scrawl out anything better, our only goal
should be to imitate Him a little. In all, I demand—life, the possibility of existence, and then all is well; we must not ask whether it
is beautiful or ugly, the feeling that the work of art has life stands

3. I.e., the Book of Revelation. Heinrich Stilling (1740–1817), author and Christian
   apologist.

above these two qualities and is the sole criterion of art. Moreover, we encounter it rarely, we find it in Shakespeare, and it resounds fully in folk songs, sometimes in Goethe. All the rest can be thrown in the fire. Those people cannot even draw a doghouse. They wanted idealistic figures, but all I have seen of them are wooden puppets. This idealism is the most disgraceful mockery of human nature. They ought to try immersing themselves for once in the life of the most insignificant person and reproduce it, in the palpitations, the intimations, the most subtle, scarcely perceptible gestures; he had attempted this in *The Tutor* and *The Soldiers*.[4] These are the most prosaic people under the sun; but the vein of sensitivity is alike in nearly all human beings, all that varies is the thickness of the crust through which it must break. One need only have eyes and ears for it. As I went by the valley yesterday, I saw two girls sitting on a rock, one was putting up her hair, the other was helping her; and the golden hair hung down, and a serious, pale face, and yet so young, and the black dress, and the other one working with such care. The most beautiful, most intimate paintings of the Old German School[5] barely hint at it. At times one would like to be a Medusa's[6] head in order to transform such a group into stone and summon everyone to see it. They stood up, the beautiful group was destroyed; but as they climbed down among the rocks they formed another picture. The most beautiful pictures, the richest sounds group together and dissolve. Only one thing remains, an endless beauty moving from one form to another, eternally unfolding, changing, one surely cannot always hold it fast and put it into museums and write it out in notes and then summon young and old and let boys and old men chatter about it and go into raptures. One must love humanity in order to penetrate into the unique essence of each individual, no one can be too low or too ugly, only then can one understand them; the most insignificant face makes a deeper impression than the mere sensation of beauty, and one can let the figures emerge without copying anything into them from the outside, where no life, no muscles, no pulse swells and beats. Kaufmann objected that he would find no prototype in reality for an Apollo of Belvedere or a Raphael Madonna.[7] What does it matter, he answered, I must admit they make me feel quite lifeless, if I delve into myself, I may indeed feel something, but then I do most of the work. I most prefer the poet or painter who makes nature most real to me, so that I respond emotionally to his portrayal, everything else disturbs me. I prefer the

---

4. Plays by Lenz.
5. I.e., the German painting tradition of the fifteenth and sixteenth centuries.
6. Mythical monster whose head turned onlookers to stone.
7. The Roman statue Apollo Belvedere and Raphael's paintings of the Madonna were often viewed as epitomes of Classical and Renaissance art, respectively.

Dutch painters to the Italians,[8] they alone are accessible; I know of only two paintings, by Dutchmen, which gave me the same impression as the New Testament; one is, I don't know by whom, "Christ and the Disciples at Emmaus."[9] When you read how the disciples went forth, all nature is in those few words. It's a gloomy, dusky evening, a straight red streak on the horizon, the street half dark, a stranger comes to them, they talk, he breaks bread, then they recognize him in a simple, human way, and his divine, suffering features speak distinctly to them, and they are afraid because it has grown dark, and something incomprehensible has neared them, but it is no spectral terror; it is as though a beloved dead man had come to them in his accustomed way at twilight, that's what the painting is like, with its uniform, brown mood, the gloomy, quiet evening. Then another.[1] A woman sits in her room holding a prayer book. Everything is cleaned up for Sunday, the sand strewn on the floor, so comfortably clean and warm. The woman was unable to go to church, and she performs her devotions at home, the window is open, she sits turned toward it, and it seems as if the sound of the bells from the village were floating over the wide, flat landscape into the window, and from the church the singing of the nearby congregation were drifting over to her, and the woman is following the text.—He continued in this manner, the others listened attentively, much was to the point, his face had flushed from speaking, and often smiling, often serious, he shook his blond curls. He had totally forgotten himself. After the meal Kaufmann took him aside. He had received letters from Lenz's father, his son should return, should support him. Kaufmann told him how he was throwing away his life here, wasting it fruitlessly, he should set a goal for himself, and more of the same. Lenz snapped at him: away from here, away! Go home? Go mad there? You know I can't stand it anywhere but here, in this area; if I couldn't go up a mountain and see the countryside and then back into the house, walk through the garden and look in through the window. I'd go mad! Mad! Leave me in peace! Just a little peace, now that I'm beginning to feel a little better! Away from here? I don't understand that, those three words ruin the world. Everyone needs something; if he can rest, what more

8. I.e., the Dutch realist painters of the seventeenth century, such as Vermeer, rather than painters of the Italian Renaissance.
9. Luke 24:13–49 describes two disciples who encounter Jesus on their way to Emmaus. As Jesus had already been crucified, they do not initially recognize him, but later, over supper at Emmaus, their eyes are opened to the truth of the resurrected Christ. The supper was an especially popular artistic subject in the sixteenth and seventeenth centuries, and the painting referred to here is almost certainly one that Büchner had seen in the Hessisches Landesmuseum Darmstadt, painted by a pupil of Rembrandt named Carel van Savoy (1621–1665). The painting is reproduced in this volume, p. 103.
1. Possibly a painting in the Schlossmuseum in Gotha by Nicholas Maes (1634–1693), another pupil of Rembrandt.

could he have! Always climbing, struggling, and thereby eternally throwing away all that the moment can offer and always starving just to enjoy something for once; thirsting while bright springs leap across one's path. I can bear it now, and I want to stay here; why? Why? Because I feel comfortable here; what does my father want? What can he give me? Impossible! Leave me in peace. He became vehement, Kaufmann left, Lenz was upset.

On the following day Kaufmann wanted to leave, he convinced Oberlin to accompany him to Switzerland. He was persuaded by the desire to meet Lavater[2] in person, whom he had known for a long time through correspondence. He agreed to go. Preparations kept them waiting an extra day. Lenz was struck to the heart, he had anxiously clung to everything to be rid of his endless torment; at certain moments he felt deeply how he was merely deceiving himself; he treated himself like a sick child, he rid himself of certain thoughts, powerful feelings only with the greatest fear, then he was driven back to them again with boundless force, he trembled, his hair almost stood on end, until he conquered it with incredible exertion. He found refuge in an image that always floated before his eyes, and in Oberlin; his words, his face did him a world of good. So he was apprehensive about his departure. Lenz now found it intolerable to remain in the house alone. The weather had become mild, he decided to accompany Oberlin into the mountains. On the other side where the valleys opened into a plain, they parted. He went back alone. He wandered through the mountains in various directions, broad slopes led down into the valleys, few woods, nothing but mighty lines, and farther out the broad, smoking plain, a strong wind, not a trace of people except for an occasional deserted hut resting against the slopes where shepherds spent the summer. He grew still, perhaps almost dreaming, everything seemed to melt into a single line like a rising and falling wave between heaven and earth, it seemed as though he were lying at an endless sea that gently rose and fell. Sometimes he sat, then he went on again, but slowly, dreaming. He did not look for a path. It was dark when he came to an inhabited hut on a slope toward the Steintal. The door was locked, he went to the window, through which faint light came. A lamp illuminated little more than one spot, its light fell on the pale face of a girl resting behind it, eyes half open, softly moving her lips. Farther off an old woman sat in the dark, singing from a hymnal in a droning voice. After much knocking she opened; she was partly deaf, she served Lenz some food and showed him to a place to sleep, singing her song continuously. The girl had not moved. A little later a man entered, he was tall and thin, traces of

2. Johann Caspar Lavater (1741–1801), Swiss pastor and mystic.

gray hair, with a restless, perplexed face. He approached the girl, she gave a start and became restless. He took a dried herb from the wall and put the leaves on her hand to calm her, and she crooned intelligible words in sustained, piercing tones. He told of hearing a voice in the mountains and then seeing sheet lightning over the valleys, it had seized him too, and he had wrestled with it like Jacob.[3] He dropped to his knees and prayed softly with fervor while the sick girl sang in a sustained, softly lingering voice. Then he went to sleep.

Lenz fell asleep dreaming, and then he heard the clock ticking in his sleep. The rushing wind sounded sometimes near, sometimes far through the girl's soft singing and the old woman's voice, and the moon, now bright, now hidden, cast its changing light dreamlike into the room. At one point the sounds grew louder, the girl spoke intelligibly and decisively, she said that a church stood on the cliff opposite. Lenz looked up and she was sitting upright behind the table with her eyes wide open, and the moon cast its quiet light on her features, which seemed to radiate an uncanny glow, while the old woman droned on, and during this changing and sinking of light, tones, and voices, Lenz fell at last into a deep sleep.

He awoke early, everyone was asleep in the dim room, even the girl had become quiet, she was leaning back, hands folded under her left cheek; the ghostly look had vanished from her features, she now had an expression of indescribable suffering. He went to the window and opened it, the cold morning air struck him. The house lay at the end of a narrow, deep valley open toward the east, red rays shot through the gray morning sky into the half-lit valley lying in white mist, and they sparkled on gray rocks and shone through the windows of the huts. The man awoke, his eyes met an illuminated picture on the wall, he stared at it fixedly, then he began to move his lips and pray softly, then ever louder. Meanwhile people entered the hut, they sat down in silence. The girl was in convulsions, the old woman droned her song and chatted with the neighbors. The people told Lenz that the man had come into the region a long time ago, no one knew from where; he was said to be a saint, he could see water underground and conjure up spirits, and people made pilgrimages to him. At the same time Lenz discovered that he had strayed farther away from the Steintal, he left with several woodsmen going in that direction. It did him good to find company; he now felt ill at ease with that powerful man who seemed at times to be speaking in horrendous tones. Besides, he was afraid of himself when he was alone.

---

3. Genesis 32:24–29 describes Jacob wrestling with an angel until daybreak, releasing the angel only when the angel blesses him.

He came home. Yet the past night had left a powerful impression on him. The world had seemed bright to him, and within himself he felt a stirring and crawling toward an abyss to which an inexorable power was drawing him. Now he burrowed within himself. He ate little; half the night in prayer and feverish dreams. A powerful urge, then beaten back in exhaustion; he lay bathed in the hottest tears, and then suddenly strength returned, and he arose cold and indifferent, his tears were like ice then, he had to laugh. The higher he raised himself up, the deeper he fell. Everything streamed together again. Visions of his former state flashed through his mind and threw searchlights into the wild chaos of his spirit. During the day he usually sat in the room downstairs, Madame Oberlin went back and forth, he drew, painted, read, clutched at every diversion, always hastily from one thing to another. Now he attached himself to Madame Oberlin, especially when she sat there, her black hymnal before her, next to a plant grown in the room, her youngest child between her knees; he also spent much time with the child. Once when he was sitting there he grew anxious, jumped up, paced back and forth. The door ajar, he heard the maid singing, first unintelligibly, then the words came:

> In all this world no joy for me,
> I have a love, far off is he.

This crushed him, he almost dissolved from the sound. Madame Oberlin looked at him. He steeled himself, he could no longer remain silent, he had to talk about it. Dearest Madame Oberlin, can't you tell me how the lady[4] is, whose fate lies like a hundredweight on my heart? "But Mr. Lenz, I know nothing about it."

He fell silent again and paced hastily back and forth in the room; then he began again: you see, I want to leave; God, these are the only people whom I can bear, and yet—yet I must go, to *her*—but I can't, I mustn't.—He was highly agitated and went out. Toward evening Lenz returned, the room was in twilight; he sat down beside Madame Oberlin. You see, he began again, when she used to walk through the room like that, and singing half to herself, and each step was music, there was such happiness in her, and it overflowed into me. I was always at peace when I looked at her or when she leaned her head against me like this, and—God! God—I haven't been at peace for a long time [. . .][5] Completely like a child; it was as if the world were too vast for her, she withdrew into herself so,

4. I.e., Friederike Brion (1752–1813), who had been Goethe's lover in 1771 and was left by
   him that same year. Lenz fell in love with her, unrequitedly, in 1772.
5. Words missing in the text.

she looked for the smallest place in the whole house, and there she sat as if all her happiness were focused on one little spot, and then I felt the same; then I could have played like a child. Now I feel so confined, so confined, you see, sometimes it's as if my hands were hitting the sky; oh, I'm suffocating! Sometimes I feel as if I'm in physical pain, here on the left side, in the arm that used to embrace her. But I can't visualize her anymore, the image escapes me, and that torments me, only sometimes when my mind is completely clear do I feel much better. —He often spoke about this afterwards with Madame Oberlin, but mostly only in fragmented sentences; she could say only little in response, but it did him good.

Meanwhile his religious torments continued. The emptier, the colder, the deader he felt inwardly, the more he felt urged to ignite a blaze within himself, he remembered the times when everything seethed within him, when he panted under the weight of all his sensations; and now so dead. He despaired of himself, then he threw himself down, he wrung his hands, he stirred up everything inside him; but dead! Dead! Then he begged God for a sign, then he burrowed within himself, fasted, lay dreaming on the floor. On the third of February he heard that a child had died in Fouday, he took this up like an obsession. He retired to his room and fasted for a day. On the fourth he suddenly entered the room where Madame Oberlin was, he had smeared his face with ashes and demanded an old sack; she was alarmed, he was given what he wanted. He wrapped the sack around himself like a penitent and set out for Fouday. The people in the valley were already used to him; they told all sorts of strange stories about him. He came into the house where the child lay. The people went about their business indifferently; they showed him to a room, the child lay in a nightgown on straw, on a wooden table. Lenz shuddered as he touched the cold limbs and saw the half-opened, glassy eyes. The child seemed so abandoned, and he so alone and lonely; he threw himself over the corpse; death frightened him, violent pain seized him, these features, this quiet face must decay, he dropped to his knees, he prayed in all the misery of despair that God should grant him a sign and revive the child, how weak and unhappy he was; then he sank into himself completely and focussed all of his willpower on one point, he sat rigidly like this for a long time. Then he rose and grasped the child's hands and said loudly and firmly: arise and walk! But the echo from the sober walls seemed to mock him, and the corpse remained cold. He collapsed, half insane, then he was driven up, out into the mountains. Clouds moved swiftly across the moon; at times all was dark, at times in the moonlight the landscape was revealed, shrouded in fog. He ran up and down. Hell's song of triumph was in his breast. The wind sounded like a song of titans, he felt as if he could thrust a gigantic fist up into

Heaven and tear God down and drag Him through His clouds; as if he could grind up the world in his teeth and spit it into the Creator's face; he swore, he blasphemed. So he came to the crest of the mountain ridge, and the uncertain light spread down to the white masses of stone, and the sky was a stupid blue eye and the moon hung in it most ludicrously, foolishly. Lenz had to laugh out loud, and in that laughter atheism seized and held him quite securely and calmly and firmly. He no longer knew what had disturbed him so before, he was freezing, he thought he would go to bed now, and he went coldly and stolidly through the uncanny darkness—all seemed empty and hollow to him, he had to run and went to bed.

The following day great horror overcame him because of his state the day before, he was now standing at the abyss, where a mad desire urged him to look down into it again and again and to relive this torment. Then his fear increased, the sin against the Holy Ghost loomed before him.

A few days later Oberlin returned from Switzerland, much earlier than expected. This disturbed Lenz. But he cheered up when Oberlin told him about his friends in Alsace. Oberlin went back and forth in the room meanwhile, unpacked, put things away. He talked about Pfeffel[6] praising the happy life of a country pastor. He admonished him to comply with his father's wishes, to live in keeping with his profession, to return home. He told him: "Honor your father and mother" and more of the same. During the conversation Lenz grew highly agitated; he sighed deeply, tears welled from his eyes, he spoke disjointedly. Yes, but I won't be able to bear it; do you want to turn me out? In you alone is the way to God. But it's all over with me! I have sinned, I'm damned for eternity, I'm the Wandering Jew.[7] Oberlin told him Christ had died for that, he should turn to Him with all his heart and he would partake of His grace.

Lenz raised his head, wrung his hands and said: ah! Ah! Divine consolation. Then suddenly he asked affably how the lady was. Oberlin said he knew nothing about this, yet he would help and advise him in all things, but he must tell him the place, circumstances, and the name. He answered only in broken words: ah, she's dead! Is she still alive? You angel, she loved me—I loved her, she was worthy of it, oh, you angel. Damned jealousy, I sacrificed her—she still loved another[8]—I loved her, she was worthy of it—oh, good mother, she loved me too. I'm a murderer. Oberlin answered: perhaps all these people were still alive, perhaps content; be that as it may, if he would turn to God, then God could and would do them so much good that

6. Gottlieb Konrad Pfeffel (1736–1809), German writer, educator, and poet.
7. Legendary figure cursed to wander the world until the end of time because he taunted Jesus on the road to Calvary.
8. I.e., Goethe.

the benefit they would gain through Lenz's prayers and tears would perhaps far outweigh the injury he had inflicted upon them. He gradually grew quieter and went back to his painting.

He returned in the afternoon with a piece of fur on his left shoulder and a bundle of rods in his hand, which had been given to Oberlin along with a letter for Lenz. He handed Oberlin the rods with the request that he should beat him with them. Oberlin took the rods from his hand, pressed several kisses on his mouth and said: these are the blows he would give him, he should be calm, settle his affairs alone with God, no amount of blows would erase a single sin; Jesus had seen to that, to Him should he turn. He went away.

At supper he was somewhat pensive as usual. Yet he talked about all sorts of things, but in anxious haste. At midnight Oberlin was awakened by a noise. Lenz was running through the yard, calling out the name Friederike in a hollow, harsh voice with extreme rapidity, confusion, and despair, then he threw himself into the basin of the fountain, splashed around, out again and up to his room, down again into the basin, and so on several times, finally he grew quiet. The maids who slept in the nursery below him said they had often, but especially that night, heard a droning sound that they could compare only to the sound of a shepherd's pipe. Perhaps it was his whining in a hollow, ghastly, despairing voice.

Next morning Lenz did not appear for a long time. Finally Oberlin went up to his room, he was lying quietly and motionless in bed. Oberlin questioned him repeatedly before he received an answer; at last he said: yes, Pastor, you see, boredom! Boredom! Oh! So boring. I no longer know what to say, I've already drawn all sorts of figures on the wall. Oberlin told him to turn to God; he laughed at that and said: yes, if I were as happy as you to have found such a comforting pastime, yes, one could indeed spend one's time that way. Everything out of boredom. For most people pray out of boredom; others fall in love out of boredom, a third group is virtuous, a fourth corrupt, and I'm nothing, nothing at all. I don't even want to kill myself: it's too boring!

> O God, Thy waves of radiant light,
> Thy glowing midday shining bright,
> Have made my watchful eyes so sore,
> Will not the night come evermore?

Oberlin looked at him angrily and started to go. Lenz rushed after him and, looking at him with haunted eyes: you see, now I've finally thought of something, if I could only determine whether I'm dreaming or awake: you see, that's very true, we must look into it; then he rushed back to bed. That afternoon Oberlin wanted to pay a visit nearby; his wife had already left; he was just about to leave when there was a knock at his door and Lenz entered, his body bent forward, his head hanging down, ashes all over his face and here and there on his clothes, holding his left arm with his right hand. He asked Oberlin to pull on his arm, he had sprained it, he had thrown himself from the window, but since no one had seen it, he did not want to tell anyone. Oberlin was seriously alarmed, but he said nothing, he did what Lenz asked, at the same time he wrote to the schoolmaster at Bellefosse, asking him to come down and giving him instructions. Then he rode off. The man came. Lenz had already seen him often and had grown attached to him. He pretended he had wanted to discuss something with Oberlin, then started to leave again. Lenz asked him to stay, and so they remained together. Lenz suggested a walk to Fouday. He visited the grave of the child he had tried to resurrect, knelt down several times, kissed the earth on the grave, seemed to be praying, though in great confusion, tore off part of the bouquet of flowers on the grave as a souvenir, returned to Waldbach, turned back again and Sebastian[9] with him. At times he walked slowly and complained about great weakness in his limbs, then he walked in desperate haste, the landscape frightened him, it was so confining that he was afraid of bumping into everything. An indescribable feeling of discomfort came over him, his companion finally got on his nerves, he probably guessed his purpose and looked for a way to be rid of him. Sebastian appeared to give in to him but secretly found a way to inform his brothers of the danger, and now Lenz had two guardians instead of one. He continued to lead them around, finally he returned to Waldbach, and as they neared the village he turned like a flash and ran like a deer back toward Fouday. The men chased after him. While they were looking for him in Fouday, two shopkeepers came and told them that a stranger who called himself a murderer had been tied up in a house, but he could not possibly be a murderer. They ran into the house and found it was so. A young man had been frightened into tying him up at his vehement insistence. They untied him and brought him safely to Waldbach, where Oberlin had since returned with his wife. He looked confused, but when he noticed he was received with kindness and friendship, he took courage, his expression changed for the better, he thanked his two companions affably and tenderly and the evening passed quietly. Oberlin implored him not to take any more baths, to spend the night quietly in bed, and if he could not sleep, to converse with God. He promised and did so that night, the maids heard him praying almost all night long.—Next morning he came to Oberlin's room looking cheerful. After they had discussed various things, he said with exceptional friendliness: dear

9. Sebastian Scheidecker, a teacher in Steinthal.

Pastor, the lady I was telling you about has died, yes, died, the angel. "How do you know that?"—Hieroglyphics, hieroglyphics—and then looking up to heaven, and again: yes, died—hieroglyphics. Then nothing else could be gotten out of him. He sat down and wrote several letters and gave them to Oberlin, asking him to add a few lines.

Meanwhile his condition had become ever bleaker, all the peace he had derived from Oberlin's nearness and the valley's stillness was gone; the world he had wished to serve had a gigantic crack, he felt no hate, no love, no hope, a terrible void and yet a tormenting anxiety to fill it. He had *nothing*. Whatever he did, he did consciously and yet an inner instinct drove him on. Whenever he was alone, he was so horribly lonely that he constantly talked out loud to himself, called out, and then he was startled again, and it seemed as if a strange voice had been speaking with him. He often stammered in conversation, an indescribable fear came over him, he had lost the end of his sentence; then he thought he ought to hold on to the last word spoken and keep repeating it, only with great effort did he suppress these desires. The good people were deeply concerned when at times in quiet moments he was sitting with them and speaking freely, and then he stammered and an unspeakable fear came over his features, he convulsively seized the arms of those sitting closest to him and only gradually came to his senses. When he was alone, or reading, it was even worse, at times all his mental activity would hang on one thought; if he thought about or visualized another person vividly, it seemed as if he were becoming that person, he became utterly confused, and at the same time he had a boundless urge to internalize everything around him arbitrarily; nature, people, Oberlin alone excepted, everything dreamlike, cold; he amused himself by standing houses on their roofs, dressing and undressing people, concocting the maddest pranks imaginable. At times he felt an irresistible urge to do something, and then he made horrible faces. Once he was sitting next to Oberlin, the cat was lying on a chair opposite, suddenly his eyes became fixed, he held them riveted on the animal, then he slipped slowly off the chair, so did the cat, as if transfixed by his gaze, it grew terribly frightened, it bristled with fear, Lenz making the same sounds, with a horribly distorted face, they threw themselves at each other as though in desperation, then finally Madame Oberlin rose to separate them. Once again he was deeply ashamed. The attacks during the night increased dreadfully. He fell asleep only with the greatest effort after he had attempted to fill the dreadful void. Then, between sleep and waking, he entered into a horrifying state; he bumped against something hideous, horrible, insanity seized him, he started up with terrible screams, drenched in sweat, and only gradually he found himself again. He then had to begin with the simplest things in order to come to his senses again. It was actually not he who did this but a powerful instinct of self-preservation, it seemed as if he were double and one part were trying to save the other, and called out to itself; he told stories, he recited poems in the most acute fear until he came to his senses again. These attacks occurred also during the day, then they were even more appalling; previously daylight had protected him from them. Then he seemed to be existing alone, as if the world were merely in his imagination, as if there were nothing besides him, he was the eternally damned, he was Satan; alone with his tormenting fantasies. He rushed with blinding speed through his past life and then he said: consistent, consistent; when someone said something: inconsistent, inconsistent; it was the abyss of incurable insanity, an insanity throughout eternity. The instinct of preserving his mind aroused him; he flung himself into Oberlin's arms, he clung to him as if he wanted to force himself into him, he was the only being who was alive for him and through whom life was revealed to him. Gradually Oberlin's words brought him to his senses, he knelt before Oberlin, his hands in Oberlin's hands, his face drenched in cold sweat in his lap, his whole body trembling and shivering. Oberlin felt boundless compassion, the family knelt and prayed for the unfortunate one, the maids fled and thought he was possessed. And when he calmed down it was like a child's misery, he sobbed, he felt deep, deep pity for himself; these were also his happiest moments. Oberlin talked to him about God. Lenz quietly drew away and looked at him with an expression of endless suffering and finally said: but I, if I were almighty, you see, if I were, and I couldn't bear this suffering, I would save, save, I just want nothing but peace, peace, just a little peace and to be able to sleep. Oberlin said this was blasphemy. Lenz shook his head dejectedly. His half-hearted suicide attempts that he undertook regularly were not wholly serious, it was less a wish to die, for him there was after all no peace nor hope in death; it was more an attempt to bring himself to his senses through physical pain in moments of most terrifying fear or of apathetic inactivity bordering on nonexistence. Those moments when his mind seemed to be riding on some sort of insane idea were still the happiest ones. That provided at least some peace, and his wild look was not as terrible as that fear thirsting for salvation, the eternal torment of anxiety! He often beat his head against the wall or inflicted violent physical pain on himself in other ways.

On the morning of the 8th he remained in bed, Oberlin went up; he was lying in bed nearly naked and was violently agitated. Oberlin wanted to cover him, but he complained much about how heavy everything was, so heavy, he doubted greatly he could walk, now at last he felt the immense weight of the air. Oberlin urged him to take courage. But he remained in this condition for most of the day, and he ate nothing. Toward evening Oberlin was called to visit a sick person in Bellefosse. The weather was mild and there was moonlight. On the way back Lenz met him. He seemed quite rational and spoke calmly and affably with Oberlin. Oberlin begged him not to go too far, he promised; walking away, he suddenly turned and came up very close to Oberlin again and said quickly: you see, Pastor, if only I didn't have to hear that anymore, that would do me good. "Hear what, my dear friend?" Don't you hear anything, don't you hear the terrible voice, usually called silence, screaming around the entire horizon, ever since I've been in this silent valley I always hear it, it won't let me sleep, yes, Pastor, if only I could sleep once again. Then he went away shaking his head. Oberlin went back to Waldbach and was about to send someone after him when he heard him going upstairs to his room. A moment later something crashed in the yard with such a loud noise that Oberlin thought it could not possibly have been caused by a falling human body. The nursemaid came, deathly pale and trembling all over. [. . .][1]

In cold resignation he sat in the coach as they rode out of the valley toward the west. He did not care where they were taking him; several times when the coach was endangered by the bad road he remained sitting quite calmly; he was totally indifferent. In this state he traveled through the mountains. Toward evening they were in the Rhine valley. Gradually they left the mountains behind, which now rose up like a deep blue crystal wave into the sunset, and on its warm flood the red rays of evening played; above the plain at the foot of the mountains lay a shimmering, bluish web. It grew darker as they approached Strassburg; a high full moon, all distant objects in the dark, only the mountain nearby formed a sharp line, the earth was like a golden bowl from which the foaming golden waves of the moon overflowed. Lenz stared out quietly, no perception, no impulse; only a dull fear grew in him the more things became lost in darkness. They had to stop for the night; again he made several attempts on his life but he was too closely watched. Next morning he arrived in Strassburg in dreary, rainy weather. He seemed quite rational, spoke with people; he acted like everyone else, yet there was a terrible void within him, he no longer felt any fear, any desire; his existence was a necessary burden.—So he lived on.

---

1. A gap in the text owing to missing pages. It is impossible to know precisely how much of the work is missing, but the corresponding section in Oberlin's account is almost a third of his narrative, so the missing pages may have been a substantial portion of Büchner's story. For the passage in Oberlin's account that corresponds to the missing section, see p. 195.

Christ at Emmaus, by Carel van Savoy (1621–1665).

Pastor Oberlin's house in the Steinthal, ca. 1840.

Leonce and Lena

Manuscript, Publication, and Premiere

Büchner wrote *Leonce and Lena* in 1836 for a competition sponsored by the Cotta publishing house for "the best one or two act comedy in prose or verse." As no complete manuscript survives, editors are almost entirely reliant on two versions edited by men who saw some more or less complete manuscript: Karl Gutzkow's version in *Telegraph für Deutschland* in 1838, and Ludwig Büchner's version in his 1850 edition of his brother's works. Both versions have problems, however, as Gutzkow cut passages from the play and Ludwig bowdlerized it throughout. As usual with Büchner, reconstruction is a frustrating affair of probability, uncertainty, and loss.

The play was privately premiered on May 31, 1895, at the Intimes Theater in Munich, and received its first public performance at the Residenztheater in Vienna on December 31, 1911.

LEONCE AND LENA[†]

A Comedy

PROLOGUE

Alfieri: "E la fama?"
Gozzi: "E la fame?"[1]

Characters

KING PETER *of the Kingdom of Popo*[2]
PRINCE LEONCE, *his son, engaged to*
PRINCESS LENA *of the Kingdom of Peepee*
VALERIO

[†] Translated by Henry J. Schmidt.
1. "And fame?" / "And hunger?" These supposed quotations from the eighteenth-century Italian dramatists Vittorio Alfieri and Carlo Gozzi were in fact invented by Büchner.
2. In German, a children's word for buttocks.

THE GOVERNESS
THE TUTOR
THE MASTER OF CEREMONIES
THE PRESIDENT OF THE STATE COUNCIL
THE COURT CHAPLAIN
THE DISTRICT MAGISTRATE
THE SCHOOLMASTER
ROSETTA
SERVANTS, COUNCILLORS, PEASANTS, *etc.*

Act One

> O that I were a fool!
> I am ambitious for a motley coat.
> —*As You Like It*

I

A garden.
   LEONCE *reclining on a bench. The* TUTOR.

LEONCE   Sir, what do you want from me? To prepare me for my profession? I have my hands full, I'm so busy I don't know which way to turn. Look, first I have to spit on this stone here three hundred sixty-five times in a row. Haven't you tried it yet? Do it, it's uniquely entertaining. Then—you see this handful of sand?— (*He picks up some sand, throws it in the air and catches it on the back of his hand.*)—Now I'll throw it in the air. Shall we bet? How many grains do I now have on the back of my hand? Odd or even?—What? You don't want to bet? Are you a heathen? Do you believe in God? I usually bet with myself and can keep it up for days. If you could find me someone who would like to bet with me, I'd be much obliged. Then—I must figure out how I could manage to see the top of my head for once.—Oh, if only a person could see the top of his head for once! That's one of my ideals. That would do me good. And then—and then more of the same, endlessly.—Am I an idler? Don't I have anything to do?—Yes, it's sad . . .

TUTOR   Very sad, Your Highness.

LEONCE   That the clouds have been moving from west to east for three weeks now. It's making me quite melancholy.

TUTOR   A very well-founded melancholy.

LEONCE   Why don't you contradict me, man? You have urgent business, don't you? I'm sorry I've detained you so long. (*The* TUTOR *exits with a deep bow.*) Sir, I congratulate you on the beautiful parentheses your legs make when you bow. (*Alone,* LEONCE *stretches out on the bench.*) The bees sit so slothfully on the flowers, and the sunshine lies so lazily on the ground. A horrible idleness prevails.—Idleness is the root of all evil.—What people won't do out of boredom! They study out of boredom, they pray out of boredom, they fall in love, marry, and reproduce out of boredom and finally die out of boredom, and—and that's the humor of it—they do everything with the most serious faces, without realizing why and God knows what they mean by it. All these heroes, these geniuses, these idiots, these saints, these sinners, these fathers of families are basically nothing but refined idlers.—Why must *I* be the one to know this? Why can't I take myself seriously and dress this poor puppet in tails and put an umbrella in its hand so that it will become very proper and very useful and very moral?—That man who just left me—I envied him, I could have beaten him out of envy. Oh, to be someone else for once! Just for one minute.—(VALERIO, *half drunk, comes running in.*) How that man runs! If only I knew of one thing under the sun that could still make me run.

VALERIO (*Stands close to* LEONCE, *puts a finger next to his nose and stares at him.*)   Yes!

LEONCE (*Does the same.*)   Correct!

VALERIO   You understand?

LEONCE   Perfectly.

VALERIO   Well, then let's change the subject. (*He lies down in the grass.*) Meanwhile I'll lie in the grass and let my nose bloom through the blades and inhale romantic sensations when the bees and butterflies sway on it as on a rose.

LEONCE   But don't sniff so hard, my dear fellow, or the bees and butterflies will starve because you're inhaling immense pinches of pollen from the flowers.

VALERIO   Ah, my Lord, what a feeling I have for nature! The grass looks so beautiful that I wish I were an ox so I could eat it, and then a human being again to eat the ox that has eaten such grass.

LEONCE   Unhappy man, you too seem to be suffering from ideals.

VALERIO   What a pity. You can't jump off a church steeple without breaking your neck. You can't eat four pounds of cherries with the pits without getting a bellyache. Look, my Lord, I could sit in a corner and sing from morning to night: "Hey, there's a fly on the wall! Fly on the wall! Fly on the wall!" and so on for the rest of my life.

LEONCE   Shut up with your song, it could turn a man into a fool.

VALERIO   Then at least he'd be something. A fool! A fool! Who will trade his folly for my reason? Ha, I'm Alexander the Great! Look how the sun shines a golden crown in my hair, how my uniform glitters! Generalissimo Grasshopper, let the troops advance!

Finance Minister Spider, I need money! Dear Lady Dragonfly, how is my beloved wife, Beanstalk? Ah, dear Royal Physician Spanish Fly, I need an heir to the throne. And on top of these delicious fantasies you get a good soup, good meat, good bread, a good bed, and a free haircut—in the madhouse, that is—while I with my sound mind could at best hire myself out to a cherry tree as a promoter of ripening in order to—well?—in order to?

LEONCE   In order to make the cherries red with shame at the holes in your pants. But, noblest sir, your trade, your profession, your occupation, your rank, your art?

VALERIO (*With dignity.*)   My Lord, I have the great occupation of being idle, I am incredibly skilled in doing nothing, I have an enormous capacity for laziness. No callus desecrates my hands, the earth has not drunk a drop of sweat from my brow; as for work, I'm a virgin, and if it weren't too much trouble, I would take the trouble to expound on these merits in greater detail.

LEONCE (*With comic enthusiasm.*)   Come to my bosom! Are you one of those godlike beings who wander effortlessly with a clear brow through sweat and dust on the highway of life and who enter Olympus with gleaming feet and glowing bodies like the blessed gods? Come! Come!

VALERIO (*Sings as he leaves.*)   Hey! There's a fly on the wall! Fly on the wall! Fly on the wall! (*They go off arm in arm.*)

2

A room.

KING PETER *is being dressed by two valets.*

KING PETER (*While being dressed.*)   Man must think, and I must think for my subjects, for they do not think, they do not think.— The substance is the "thing-in-itself,"[3] that is I. (*He runs around the room almost naked.*) Understood? In-itself is in-itself, you understand? Now for my attributes, modifications, affections, and accessories: where is my shirt, my pants?—Stop! Ugh! Free will is wide open here in front. Where is morality, where are my cuffs? The categories are in the most scandalous disorder, two buttons too many are buttoned, the snuffbox is in the right-hand pocket. My whole system is ruined.—Ha, what is the meaning of this knot in my handkerchief? Varlet, what does the knot mean, what did I want to remind myself of?

FIRST VALET   When Your Majesty deigned to tie this knot in your handkerchief, you wished . . .

KING PETER   Well?

_____

3. *Ding an sich* in German; a key term in Kantian philosophy.

FIRST VALET   To remind yourself of something.

KING PETER   A complicated answer!—My! Well, what do *you* think?

SECOND VALET   Your Majesty wished to remind yourself of something when you deigned to tie this knot in your handkerchief.

KING PETER (*Runs up and down.*)   What? What? These people mix me up, I am utterly confused. I am at my wit's end. (*A servant enters.*)

SERVANT   Your Majesty, the State Council is assembled.

KING PETER (*Happily.*)   Yes, that's it, that's it—I wanted to remind myself of my people! Come, gentlemen! Walk symmetrically. Isn't it very hot? Take your handkerchiefs and wipe your faces. I am always so embarrassed when I have to speak in public. (*All go off.*)

KING PETER. *The State Council.*

KING PETER   My dear and faithful subjects, I wish you to know by these presents, to know by these presents—because either my son marries or not (*Puts a finger next to his nose.*)—either, or— you understand, of course? There is no third possibility. Man must think. (*Stands musing for a while.*) When I speak out loud like that, I don't know who it really is—I or someone else: that frightens me. (*After long reflection.*) I am I.—What do you think of that, President?

PRESIDENT (*Slowly, with gravity.*)   Your Majesty, perhaps it is so, but perhaps it is also not so.

THE STATE COUNCIL (*In chorus.*)   Yes, perhaps it is so, but perhaps it is also not so.

KING PETER (*Emotionally.*)   Oh, my wise men!—Now what were we talking about? What did I want to say? President, how can you have such a short memory on such a solemn occasion? The meeting is adjourned. (*He leaves solemnly, the State Council follows him.*)

3

A richly decorated hall with burning candles.

LEONCE *with several servants.*

LEONCE   Are all the shutters closed? Light the candles! Away with day! I want night, deep, ambrosial night. Put the lamps under crystal globes among the oleanders, so that they peer out dreamily like girls' eyes under leafy lashes. Bring the roses nearer, so that the wine may sparkle on their petals like dewdrops. Music! Where are the violins? Where is Rosetta? Away! Everybody out! (*The servants go off.* LEONCE *stretches out on a couch.* ROSETTA *enters, prettily dressed. Music in the distance.*)

ROSETTA (*Approaches coquettishly.*)   Leonce!

LEONCE   Rosetta!

ROSETTA   Leonce!

LEONCE   Rosetta!

ROSETTA   Your lips are lazy. From kissing?

LEONCE   From yawning!

ROSETTA   Oh!

LEONCE   Ah, Rosetta, I have the terrible chore . . .

ROSETTA   Well?

LEONCE   Of doing nothing . . .

ROSETTA   Besides loving?

LEONCE   That's certainly a chore!

ROSETTA (*Insulted.*)   Leonce!

LEONCE   Or an occupation.

ROSETTA   Or idleness.

LEONCE   You're right as usual. You're a clever girl, and I admire your keenness.

ROSETTA   So you love me out of boredom?

LEONCE   No, I'm bored because I love you. But I love my boredom as I love you. You are one and the same. *O dolce far niente,*[4] I dream about your eyes as magical springs, deep and hidden; your caressing lips lull me to sleep like murmuring waves. (*He embraces her.*) Come, dear boredom, your kisses are voluptuous yawns and your steps a delicate hiatus.

ROSETTA   You love me, Leonce?

LEONCE   Why not?

ROSETTA   And forever?

LEONCE   That's a long word: forever! Now if I love you for five thousand years and seven months, is that enough? It's far less than forever, of course, but it's still a considerable length of time, and we can take time to love each other.

ROSETTA   Or time can take love from us.

LEONCE   Or love can take time from us. Dance, Rosetta, dance, let time pass to the beat of your dainty feet!

ROSETTA   My feet would rather pass out of time. (*She dances and sings.*)

> O tired feet, why must you dance
> In shoes so bright?
> You'd rather lie, so deep, so deep
> In earth's dark night.
>
> O fiery cheeks, why must you burn
> In wild delight?
> You'd rather bloom, not roses red,
> But roses white.

4. Oh, sweet idleness (Italian).

> O poor dear eyes, why must you gleam
> In candle's glow?
> You'd rather sleep, until is gone
> All pain and woe.

LEONCE (*Dreamily to himself meanwhile.*) Oh, a dying love is more beautiful than a growing one. I'm a Roman; for dessert at our lavish banquet, golden fish play in their death's colors. How her red cheeks fade, how softly her eyes dim, how gently her swaying limbs rise and fall! *Addio, addio,*[5] my love, I shall love your dead body. (ROSETTA *approaches him again.*) Tears, Rosetta? A fine Epicureanism[6]—to be able to cry. Go stand in the sun and let the precious drops crystallize, they'll be magnificent diamonds. You can have a necklace made of them.

ROSETTA Yes, diamonds. They're cutting my eyes. Oh, Leonce! (*Tries to embrace him.*)

LEONCE Careful! My head! I've buried our love in it. Look into the windows of my eyes. Do you see how nice and dead the poor thing is? Do you see the two white roses on its cheeks and the two red roses on its breast? Don't nudge me, or a little arm might break off, that would be a pity. I must carry my head straight on my shoulders, like a mourning woman with a child's coffin.

ROSETTA (*Jokingly.*) Fool!

LEONCE Rosetta! (ROSETTA *makes a face.*) Thank God! (*Covers his eyes.*)

ROSETTA (*Frightened.*) Leonce, look at me.

LEONCE Not for the world.

ROSETTA Just one look!

LEONCE Not one! Are you crying? The slightest thing would bring my beloved love to life again. I'm happy to have buried it. I'll retain the impression.

ROSETTA (*Goes off sadly and slowly, singing.*)

> I'm a poor orphan girl,
> Afraid and all alone.
> Ah, sorrow, dear,
> Will you not see me home?

LEONCE (*Alone.*) Love is a peculiar thing. You lie half-asleep in bed for a year, then one fine morning you wake up, drink a glass of water, get dressed, and run your hand across your forehead and come to your senses—and come to your senses.—My God, how many women does one need to sing up and down the scale of

---

5. Farewell (Italian).
6. Greek philosophical school often portrayed as teaching the importance of sensual pleasures.

love? One woman is scarcely enough for a single note. Why is the mist above the earth a prism that breaks the white-hot ray of love into a rainbow?—(*He drinks.*) Which bottle contains the wine that will make me drunk today? Can't I even get that far anymore? It's as if I were sitting under a vacuum pump. The air so sharp and thin that I'm freezing, as if I were going ice skating in cotton pants.—Gentlemen, gentlemen, do you know what Caligula and Nero[7] were? I know.—Come, Leonce, let's have a soliloquy, I'll listen. My life yawns at me like a large white sheet of paper that I have to fill, but I can't write a single letter. My head is an empty dance hall, a few withered roses and crumpled ribbons on the floor, broken violins in the corner, the last dancers have taken off their masks and look at each other with dead-tired eyes. I turn myself inside out twenty-four times a day, like a glove. Oh, I know myself, I know what I'll be thinking and dreaming in a quarter of an hour, in a week, in a year. God, what have I done that you make me recite my lesson so often like a schoolboy?—

Bravo, Leonce! Bravo! (*He applauds.*) It does me good to cheer for myself like this. Hey! Leonce! Leonce!

VALERIO (*From under a table.*) Your Highness really seems to be well on the way to becoming a genuine fool.

LEONCE Yes, seen in that light it looks the same to me.

VALERIO Wait, we'll discuss this in detail in a minute. I just have to finish a piece of roast beef I stole from the kitchen, and some wine I stole from your table. I'm almost through.

LEONCE How he smacks his lips. That fellow brings on the most idyllic feelings; I could begin again with the simplest things, I could eat cheese, drink beer, smoke tobacco. Hurry up, don't grunt like that with your snout and don't rattle your tusks.

VALERIO Most worthy Adonis, do you fear for your thighs?[8] Don't worry. I'm neither a broommaker nor a schoolmaster. I need no twigs for my rods.

LEONCE You're never at a loss.

VALERIO I wish it were the same with you, my Lord.

LEONCE So that you'll get a thrashing, you mean? Are you so concerned about your education?

VALERIO Oh heavens, procreation is easier to come by than education. It's a pity that propagation can cause such a sorry situation! What labor have I known since my mother was in labor! What good have I received from being conceived?

---

7. Roman emperors notorious for debauchery and misrule.
8. In Greco-Roman myth, Adonis was a beautiful young man who was mortally wounded in the thigh by a boar.

LEONCE   Concerning your conception, its enunciation deserves repression. Improve your expression, or you'll experience a most unpleasant impression of my negative reception.

VALERIO   When my mother sailed around the Cape of Good Hope . . .

LEONCE   And your father was shipwrecked on Cape Horn . . .

VALERIO   Right, for he was a nightwatchman. But he didn't put the horn to his lips as often as to the foreheads of fathers of well-born sons.[9]

LEONCE   Man, your impertinence is sublime. I feel a certain desire to become more closely acquainted with it. I have a passion to thrash you.

VALERIO   That is a striking response and an impressive proof.

LEONCE (*Goes after him.*)   Or you are a stricken response. Because you'll be struck for your response.

VALERIO (*Runs away,* LEONCE *trips and falls.*)   And you are a proof that remains to be proven, because it trips over its own legs, which are fundamentally unproven as yet. These are highly improbable calves and very problematic thighs. (*The State Council enters.* LEONCE *remains seated on the floor.*)

PRESIDENT   Pardon me, Your Highness . . .

LEONCE   And myself! And myself! I pardon myself for being kind enough to listen to you. Won't you take a seat, gentlemen?— What faces people make when they hear the word "seat"! Just sit on the ground and make yourselves at home. After all, that's the last seat you'll ever have, but it's of no value to anyone besides the gravedigger.

PRESIDENT (*Snapping his fingers in embarrassment.*)   May it please Your Highness . . .

LEONCE   But don't snap your fingers like that, unless you want to make a murderer of me.

PRESIDENT (*Snapping ever more violently.*)   If Your Highness would most graciously consider . . .

LEONCE   My God, put your hands in your pockets or sit on them. He's ready to burst. Pull yourself together.

VALERIO   Children must not be interrupted while they are pissing, or they'll become repressed.

LEONCE   Control yourself, man. Think of your family and the state. You'll risk a stroke if you hold back your speech.

---

9. A series of double-entendres. The Cape of Good Hope is a point near the southern tip of Africa, but "to be of good hope" (*guter Hoffnung sein*) is also a German euphemism for pregnancy. Cape Horn is the southern tip of South America, but a cuckold is also said to have horns. The nightwatchman traditionally carried a horn.

PRESIDENT (*Pulls a piece of paper from his pocket.*)   May it please Your Highness . . .

LEONCE   What, you can read? Well now . . .

PRESIDENT   His Royal Majesty desires to inform Your Highness that the awaited arrival of Your Highness's betrothed, Her Most Serene Highness, Princess Lena of Peepee, is to take place tomorrow.

LEONCE   If my betrothed awaits me, then I'll do as she wishes and let her wait. I saw her last night in a dream, her eyes were so large that my Rosetta's dancing shoes could have fit as eyebrows, and instead of dimples her cheeks had drainage ditches for her laughter. I believe in dreams. Do you ever dream, President? Do you have premonitions?

VALERIO   Of course. Every night before a roast for His Majesty's table burns, a capon drops dead, or His Royal Majesty gets a bellyache.

LEONCE   Apropos, didn't you have something else on the tip of your tongue? Go ahead, relieve yourself of everything.

PRESIDENT   On the wedding day it is the intention of the Highest Will to transmit the exalted disposition of His Will to Your Highness's hands.

LEONCE   Tell the Highest Will that I shall do anything except that which I forbear to do, which, however, shall in any case not be as much as if it were twice as much.—Gentlemen, you will excuse me if I do not see you out, right now I have a passion for sitting, but my goodwill is so great that I can't possibly measure it with my legs. (*He spreads his legs.*) President, measure this so you can remind me of it later. Valerio, bring the gentlemen out.

VALERIO   Ring them out? Shall I hang a bell on the President? Shall I direct them as if they could not walk erect?

LEONCE   Man, you are nothing more than a bad pun. You have neither father nor mother—the five vowels gave birth to you.

VALERIO   And you, Prince, are a book without letters, with nothing but dashes.—Now come, gentlemen! It's a pity about the word "come": if you want an income, you must steal; you won't come up in the world except when you're hanged; your only accommodation is a comedown to the grave; and a shortcoming is the lack of an accomplished comeback, when one is completely at a loss for words, as I am now, and as you are *before* you commence to speak. Discomfited by such a comeuppance, you are commanded to come away. (*The State Council and* VALERIO *go off.*)

LEONCE (*Alone.*)   How vilely I played the cavalier to those poor devils! And yet there's a kind of pleasure in a certain kind of vileness.—Hm! To marry! In other words, to drink a well dry. Oh,

Shandy, old Shandy, if only I had your clock[1]—(VALERIO *returns.*)
Ah, Valerio, did you hear that?

VALERIO   Well, you're to be king—that's a lot of fun. You can ride
around all day and make people wear out their hats because they
have to take them off all the time; you can carve decent soldiers out
of decent people, so that will become the natural order of things;
you can turn black frock coats and white ties into state officials,
and when you die every shiny button will tarnish and the bell-ropes
will tear like threads from all that tolling. Isn't that entertaining?

LEONCE   Valerio! Valerio! We've got to find something else to do.
Think!

VALERIO   Ah, science, science! Let's be scholars! A *priori?* Or *a
posteriori?*[2]

LEONCE   A *priori* you can learn from my father, and *a posteriori*
always begins like an old fairy tale: once upon a time!

VALERIO   Then let's be heroes. (*He marches up and down trumpet-
ing and drumming.*) Trara-ta-ta!

LEONCE   But heroism stinks terribly of liquor and gets hospital
fever and can't exist without lieutenants and recruits. Get away
with your Alexander and Napoleon romanticism!

VALERIO   Then let's be geniuses.

LEONCE   The nightingale of poetry warbles over our heads all day
long, but the best of it goes to the devil until we tear out its feathers and dip them into ink or paint.

VALERIO   Then let's be useful members of human society.

LEONCE   I'd rather resign from the human race.

VALERIO   Then let's go to the devil.

LEONCE   Oh, the devil exists only for the sake of contrast, so that
we'll believe there's something to the idea of Heaven. (*Jumping
up.*) Ah, Valerio, now I've got it! Don't you feel the breeze from the
south? Don't you feel the surging, deep blue, glowing ether, the
light flashing from the golden, sunny earth, from the holy salt
sea and the marble columns and statues? Great Pan sleeps, and
in the shade above the deep, rushing waves, bronze figures dream
of the old magician Virgil,[3] of tarantellas and tambourines and
dark, wild nights, full of masks, torches, and guitars. A *lazzarone!*[4]
Valerio! A *lazzarone!* We're going to Italy.

---

1. In Laurence Sterne's *Tristram Shandy* (1759–67), Shandy's father, a man of extraordi-
   narily regular habits, systematically wound the family clock once a month and pro-
   ceeded to perform his sexual obligations to his wife.
2. Two forms of logical reasoning.
3. In his *Eclogues*, the Roman poet Virgil imagined Arcadia, an idealized harmony of
   humanity and nature. Pan was the fertility god of Greek myth.
4. One of the lower-class street people of Naples.

4

A garden.

PRINCESS LENA *in bridal clothes. The* GOVERNESS.

LENA   Yes, now! Here it is. Up to now I didn't think about anything. Time passed, and suddenly *that* day looms before me. The bridal wreath is in my hair—and the bells, the bells! (*She leans back and shuts her eyes.*) Look, I wish the grass would grow over me and the bees would hum above me. Look, now I'm all dressed and have rosemary in my hair. Isn't there an old song:

> In the earth I'd lay my head
> Like a child in its bed . . .

GOVERNESS   Poor child, how pale you are under your glittering jewels.

LENA   Oh God, I could love, why not? We walk all alone and reach out for a hand to hold until the undertaker separates the hands and folds them over our breasts. But why drive a nail through two hands that weren't searching for each other? What has my poor hand done? (*She draws a ring from her finger.*) This ring stings me like a viper.

GOVERNESS   And yet—they say he's a real Don Carlos.[5]

LENA   But—a man—

GOVERNESS   Well?

LENA   Whom I don't love. (*She rises.*) Bah! You see, I'm ashamed.—Tomorrow I'll be stripped of all fragrance and luster. Am I like a poor, helpless stream whose quiet depths must reflect every image that bends over it? Flowers open and shut to the morning sun and evening breeze as they please. Is a king's daughter less than a flower?

GOVERNESS (*Weeping.*)   Dear angel, you're really a sacrificial lamb.

LENA   Yes—and the priest is already raising his knife.—My God, my God, is it true that we must redeem ourselves through pain?[6] Is it true that the world is a crucified Savior, the sun its crown of thorns, and the stars the nails and spears in its feet and sides?

GOVERNESS   My child, my child! I can't bear to see you like this. This can't go on, it will kill you. Perhaps, who knows! I've got an idea. We'll see. Come! (*She leads the* PRINCESS *away.*)

---

5. Hero of Schiller's tragedy of the same name.
6. In Matthew 27:46 and Mark 15:34, Jesus' last words are "My God, my God, why hast thou forsaken me?"

Act Two

Did not once a voice resound
Deep within me,
And instantly within me drowned
All my memory.
—Adelbert von Chamisso[7]

I

Open field. An inn in the background.
Enter LEONCE *and* VALERIO, *carrying a pack.*

VALERIO (*Panting.*)   On my honor, Prince, the world is an incredibly spacious building.

LEONCE   Not at all! Not at all! I hardly dare stretch out my hands, as if I were in a narrow room of mirrors, afraid of bumping against everything—then the beautiful figures would lie in fragments on the floor and I'd be standing before the bare, naked wall.

VALERIO   I'm lost.

LEONCE   That's a loss only to whoever finds you.

VALERIO   Soon I'll go stand in the shadow of my shadow.

LEONCE   You're evaporating in the sun. Do you see that beautiful cloud up there? At least a quarter of it is from you. It's looking down quite contentedly at your grosser material substance.

VALERIO   That cloud would do your head no harm if your head were shaved and the cloud were to drip on it, drop by drop.—A delightful thought. We've walked through a dozen principalities, half a dozen duchies, and several kingdoms with the greatest haste in half a day, and why? Because you're to become king and marry a beautiful princess. And in such a situation you're still alive? I can't understand your resignation. I can't understand why you haven't taken arsenic, climbed on a parapet of a church steeple, and put a bullet through your head, just to be on the safe side.

LEONCE   But Valerio, my ideals! I have the ideal woman in my mind, and I must search for her. She's infinitely beautiful and infinitely stupid. Her beauty is so helpless, so touching, like a newborn child. The contrast is exquisite. Those gloriously stupid eyes, that divinely simple mouth, that mutton-headed Greek profile, that spiritual death in that spiritual body.

VALERIO   Damn! Here we're at a border again; this country is like an onion, nothing but skins—or like boxes, one inside another: in the largest there's nothing but boxes and in the smallest, nothing at all. (*He throws down his pack.*) Shall this pack be my tombstone? Look, Prince, I'm getting philosophical—an image of human

---

7. Altered lines from "The Blind Girl" (*Die Blinde,* 1834).

existence: I haul this pack with sore feet through frost and broiling sun because I want to put on a clean shirt in the evening, and when the evening finally comes, my brow is wrinkled, my cheeks are hollow, my eye is dim, and I just have enough time to put on my shirt as a shroud. Now wouldn't it have been smarter to take my bundle off its stick and sell it in the nearest bar, and get drunk and sleep in the shade till evening—without sweating and getting corns on my feet? And now, Prince, the practical application: out of sheer modesty we shall now clothe the inner man and put on a coat and pants internally. (*Both go toward the inn.*) Hey, you dear pack, what a delicious aroma, what scents of wine and roast beef! Hey, you dear pants, how you root in the earth and turn green and bloom, and the long, heavy grapes hang into my mouth, and the new wine ferments in the winepress. (*They go off.*)

(PRINCESS LENA *and the* GOVERNESS *enter.*)

GOVERNESS   The day must be bewitched; the sun won't set, and it's been an eternity since we ran off.

LENA   Not at all, my dear; the flowers I picked as we left the garden have hardly wilted.

GOVERNESS   And where will we rest? We haven't come across a thing. I see no convent, no hermit, no shepherd.

LENA   I guess we dreamed things differently behind our garden wall with our books, among the myrtles and oleanders.

GOVERNESS   Oh, the world is horrible! We can't begin to think about a stray prince.

LENA   Oh, the world is beautiful and so vast, so infinitely vast. I'd like to go on like this day and night.

Nothing is stirring. Look how the red glow from the orchids plays over the meadow and the distant mountains lie on the earth like resting clouds.

GOVERNESS   Jesus, what will people say? And yet, it's all so delicate and feminine! It's a renunciation. It's like the flight of Saint Odilia.[8] But we must look for shelter. Night is coming!

LENA   Yes, the plants are closing their leaves in sleep and the sunbeams are swaying on blades of grass like weary dragonflies.

2

The inn on a hill beside a river, wide view.
The garden in front of the inn.
VALERIO. LEONCE.

---

8. Alsatian saint who hid in a cave while fleeing her father.

VALERIO Well, Prince, don't your pants provide a delicious drink? Don't your boots slide down your throat with the greatest of ease?

LEONCE Look at those old trees, the hedges, the flowers. They all have their legends, their dear, secret legends. Look at the old, friendly faces under the vines at the front door. How they sit holding hands, afraid because they're so old and the world is still so young. Oh, Valerio, and I'm so young, and the world is so old. Sometimes I'm afraid for myself and could sit in a corner and weep hot tears in self-pity.

VALERIO (*Gives him a glass.*) Take this bell, this diving-bell, and immerse yourself in the sea of wine till bubbles foam over you. Look how the elves float over the flowers of the wine-bouquet, in golden shoes, clashing their cymbals.

LEONCE (*Jumping up.*) Come, Valerio, we've got to do something, do something. Let's busy ourselves with profound thoughts: let's investigate why a stool stands on three legs but not on two, why we blow our noses with our hands and not with our feet as flies do. Come, let's dissect ants, count flower filaments; I'll manage to find some kind of princely hobby yet. I'll find a child's rattle that will fall from my hand only when I'm woolgathering and plucking at the blanket on my deathbed. I still have a certain dose of enthusiasm to use up, but when I've warmed everything up, it takes me an eternity to find a spoon for the meal, and it goes stale.

VALERIO *Ergo bibamus.*[9] This bottle is not a mistress, not an idea, it causes no labor pains, it won't be boring nor unfaithful—it stays the same from the first to the last drop. You break the seal and all the dreams slumbering inside bubble out at you.

LEONCE Oh God! I'll spend half my life in prayer if I could only have a blade of straw on which to ride as on a splendid steed, until I lie on the straw myself.—What an uncanny evening! Down there everything is quiet, and up there the clouds change and drift and the sunshine comes and goes. Look what strange shapes chase each other up there, look at the long white shadows with horribly skinny legs and bats' wings—and all so swift, so chaotic, and down there not a leaf, not a blade of grass is stirring. The earth has curled up like a frightened child, and ghosts stalk over its cradle.

VALERIO I don't know what you're after—I feel quite comfortable. The sun looks like the sign of an inn and the fiery clouds over it like the inscription: "Inn of the Golden Sun." The earth and the water down there are like wine spilled on a table, and we lie on it

9. Therefore let's drink! (Latin), a famous student song by Goethe.

like playing cards, with which God and the Devil are playing a game out of boredom, and you're the king and I'm the jack, and all we need is a queen, a beautiful queen with a large gingerbread heart on her breast and with a giant tulip, into which her long nose sentimentally sinks. . . . (*The* GOVERNESS *and the* PRINCESS *enter.*) . . . and—by God, there she is! But it's not really a tulip but a pinch of snuff, and it's not really a nose but a trunk. (*To the* GOVERNESS.) Why do you walk so fast, gracious lady, that one can see your former calves up to your respectable garters?

GOVERNESS (*Very angry, stops.*)   Why do you, most honorable sir, open your mouth so wide that you tear a hole in the landscape?

VALERIO   So that you, honorable madam, won't bloody your nose on the horizon. Thy nose is as the tower of Lebanon which looketh toward Damascus.[1]

LENA (*To the* GOVERNESS.)   My dear, is the way so long?

LEONCE (*Musing to himself.*)   Oh, every way is long! The ticking of the death-watch beetle in our breast is slow, and each drop of blood measures its time, and our life is a lingering fever. For tired feet every way is too long . . .

LENA (*Listening to him anxiously, pensively.*)   And for tired eyes every light is too bright and for tired lips every breath too heavy, (*Smiling.*) and for tired ears every word too much. (*She enters the inn with the* GOVERNESS.)

LEONCE   Oh, dear Valerio! Couldn't I, too, say: "Would not this and a forest of feathers with two Provincial roses on my razed shoes—"?[2] I believe I said it quite melancholically. Thank God I'm beginning to come down with a case of melancholy. The air isn't so clear and cold anymore, the glowing sky is sinking down closely around me, and heavy drops are falling.—Oh, that voice: "Is the way so long?" Many voices talk about the world, and you'd think they're speaking of other things, but I understood it. It rests upon me like the Spirit moving upon the face of the waters before there was light.[3] What ferment in the depths, what growth in me, how the voice pours through space!—"Is the way so long?" (*Exit.*)

VALERIO   No. The way to the madhouse is not so long, it's easy to find; I know every footpath, every highway and byway leading to it. I can see him now: going there down a broad avenue on an icy winter day, his hat under his arm, standing in the long shadows under the bare trees, fanning himself with his handkerchief.— He's a fool! (*Follows him.*)

---

1. Song of Solomon 7:4.
2. Altered quotation from *Hamlet* 3.2.
3. "And the Spirit of God moved upon the face of the waters" (Genesis 1:2).

3

A room.
LENA. *The* GOVERNESS.

GOVERNESS   Don't think about him.

LENA   He was so old under his blond curls. Spring on his cheeks and winter in his heart. That's sad. A tired body finds a pillow everywhere, but when the spirit is tired, where shall it rest? I've just had a horrible thought: I think there are people who are unhappy, incurable, just because they *exist*. (*She rises.*)

GOVERNESS   Where are you off to, my child?

LENA   I want to go down to the garden.

GOVERNESS   But . . .

LENA   But, dear mother—I should have been placed in a flowerpot, you know. I need dew and night air, like flowers. Do you hear the evening harmonies? How the crickets sing the day to sleep and the violets lull it with their fragrance! I can't stay in this room. The walls are falling in on me.

4

The garden. Night and moonlight.
LENA *is sitting on the grass.*

VALERIO (*At a certain distance.*)   Nature is a pleasant thing, but it would be even more pleasant if there weren't any gnats, if the beds in the inn were a little cleaner, and the death-watch beetles wouldn't tick so in the walls. Inside, people are snoring and outside, frogs are croaking; inside, house crickets are chirping and outside, it's the field crickets. Dear ground, this is a well-grounded decision. (*He lies down on the grass.*)

LEONCE (*Enters.*)   O night, balmy as the first that descended on Paradise. (*He notices the* PRINCESS *and approaches her quietly.*)

LENA (*To herself.*)   The warbler chirped in its dreams, the night sleeps more deeply, its cheeks grow paler and its breath calmer. The moon is like a sleeping child, its golden curls have fallen over its dear face.—Oh, its sleep is death. Look how the dead angel rests on its dark pillow and the stars burn around it like candles. Poor child, will the bogeymen come to get you soon? Where is your mother? Doesn't she want to kiss you once more? Ah, it's sad, dead and so alone.

LEONCE   Arise in your white dress and follow the corpse through the night and sing its requiem.

LENA   Who said that?

LEONCE   A dream.

LENA   Dreams are blessed.

LEONCE   Then dream yourself blessed and let me be your blessed dream.

LENA   Death is the most blessed dream.

LEONCE   Then let me be your angel of death. Let my lips sink like its wings onto your eyes. (*He kisses her.*) Dear corpse, you rest so beautifully on the black pall of night that nature begins to hate life and falls in love with death.

LENA   No, let me be. (*She jumps up and rushes off.*)

LEONCE   Too much! Too much! My whole being is in this one moment. Now die. More is impossible. How Creation struggles out of Chaos toward me, breathing freshly, glowing beautifully! The earth is a bowl of dark gold—how the light foams in it and overflows and the stars bubble out brightly. My lips suck their fill; this one drop of bliss turns me into a priceless vessel. Down with you, holy chalice! (*He tries to throw himself into the river.*)

VALERIO   (*Jumps up and grabs him.*)   Stop, my Serene Highness!

LEONCE   Let me be!

VALERIO   I'll let you be as soon as you let yourself be calm and promise to let the water be.

LEONCE   Idiot!

VALERIO   Hasn't Your Highness outgrown that lieutenants' romanticism yet—throwing the glass out of the window after you've drunk to your sweetheart's health?

LEONCE   I almost think you're right.

VALERIO   Console yourself. Even if you won't sleep *under* the grass tonight, at least you'll sleep *on* it. It would be an equally suicidal venture to sleep on one of those beds. You lie on the straw like a dead man and the fleas bite you like a living one.

LEONCE   All right. (*He lies down in the grass.*) Man, you ruined a most beautiful suicide. I'll never find such a marvelous moment for it again in my whole life, and the weather is so perfect. Now I'm not in the mood anymore. That fellow with his yellow vest and his sky-blue pants[4] spoiled everything for me.—Heaven grant me a good and healthy, solid sleep.

VALERIO   Amen.—And I've saved a human life, and I'll keep myself warm tonight with my good conscience. To your health, Valerio!

---

4. The protagonist of Goethe's *The Sorrows of Young Werther* (1774) wears such an outfit. A sensitive, poetic youth, Werther kills himself for love.

Act Three

1

LEONCE. VALERIO.

VALERIO Marriage? Since when has Your Highness decided to be bound by a perpetual calendar?

LEONCE Do you know, Valerio, that even the most insignificant human being is so great that life is far too short to love him? And yet I can say to those people who imagine that nothing is so beautiful and holy that they can't make it even more beautiful and holier: go ahead and enjoy yourselves. There's a certain pleasure in this dear arrogance. Why shouldn't I indulge them?

VALERIO Very humane and philobestial.[5] But does she know who you are?

LEONCE She knows only that she loves me.

VALERIO And does Your Highness know who she is?

LEONCE Idiot! Try asking a carnation and a dewdrop what their names are.

VALERIO That is, assuming she's anything at all, if that isn't already too indelicate and smacks of personal description.—But what then? Hm!—Prince, will I be your Minister of State when you are joined today before your father in holy matrimony with the unspeakable, nameless one? Your word on that?

LEONCE I give you my word.

VALERIO The poor devil Valerio takes his leave of His Excellency the Minister of State, Valerio of Valerianshire.—"What does the fellow want? I do not know him. Off with you, rascal!" (*He runs off,* LEONCE *follows.*)

2

Open square before KING PETER'*s palace.*
The DISTRICT MAGISTRATE. *The* SCHOOLMASTER. *Peasants in Sunday clothes, holding pine branches.*

MAGISTRATE How are your people holding up, schoolmaster?

SCHOOLMASTER They're holding up so well in their suffering that for quite a while they've been holding on to each other. They're downing a lot of liquor, otherwise they couldn't possibly hold out in this heat. Courage, people! Hold your branches out straight, so they'll think you're a pine forest and your noses the strawberries and your three-cornered hats the antlers and your leather pants the moonlight in it, and remember: the last one always walks

---

5. *Philobestialisch* in German, a neologism meaning "beast loving."

ahead of the first, so that it looks as if your number had been squared.

MAGISTRATE   And, you, schoolmaster, stand for sobriety.

SCHOOLMASTER   That's understood, since I'm so sober I can hardly stand.

MAGISTRATE   Pay attention, people. The program states: "All subjects shall voluntarily assemble along the highway, neatly dressed, well fed, and with contented faces." Don't give us a bad name!

SCHOOLMASTER   Stand firm! Don't scratch behind your ears and don't blow your noses with your fingers while the royal couple rides past, and show proper emotion, or we'll use emotive means on you. Look what we're doing for you: we've placed you so the breeze from the kitchen passes over you, and for once in your life you'll smell a roast. Do you still know your lesson? Hey? Vi!

PEASANTS   Vi!

SCHOOLMASTER   Vat!

PEASANTS   Vat!

SCHOOLMASTER   Vivat![6]

PEASANTS   Vivat!

SCHOOLMASTER   There, Mr. Magistrate. You see how intelligence is on the upswing. Just think, it's *Latin*. Besides, tonight we'll hold a transparent ball thanks to the holes in our jackets and pants, and we'll beat rosettes onto our heads with our fists.

3

Large hall.
Well-dressed gentlemen and ladies, carefully arranged in groups. The MASTER OF CEREMONIES *with several servants in the foreground.*

MASTER OF CEREMONIES   What a shame! Everything's going to pot. The roasts are drying up. Congratulations are going stale. Stand-up collars are all bending over like melancholy pigs' ears. The peasants' nails and beards are growing again. The soldiers' curls are drooping. Among the twelve bridesmaids there is none who wouldn't prefer a horizontal position to a vertical one. In their white dresses they look like exhausted Angora rabbits, and the Court Poet grunts around them like a distressed guinea pig. The officers are going limp. (*To a servant.*) Go tell our curate to let his boys make water.—The poor Court Chaplain! His frock coat is hanging its tails most dejectedly. I think he has ideals and is changing all the chamberlains into chamber stools. He's tired of standing.

6. Long live! (Latin).

FIRST SERVANT   All meat spoils from standing. The Court Chaplain is at a stale standstill too, after standing up this morning.

MASTER OF CEREMONIES   The ladies-in-waiting stand there like saltworks, the salt is crystallizing on their necklaces.

SECOND SERVANT   At least they're making themselves comfortable. You can't accuse them of bearing a weight on their shoulders. If they aren't exactly openhearted, at least they're open down to the heart.

MASTER OF CEREMONIES   Yes, they're good maps of the Turkish Empire—you can see the Dardanelles and the Sea of Marmara. Out, you rascals! To the windows! Here comes His Majesty! (KING PETER *and the State Council enter.*)

KING PETER   So the Princess has disappeared as well? Has no trace been found of our beloved Crown Prince? Have my orders been carried out? Are the borders being watched?

MASTER OF CEREMONIES   Yes, Your Majesty. The view from this hall allows us the strictest surveillance. (*To the* FIRST SERVANT.) What have you seen?

FIRST SERVANT   A dog ran through the kingdom looking for its master.

MASTER OF CEREMONIES (*To another.*)   And you?

SECOND SERVANT   Someone is taking a walk on the northern border, but it's not the prince, I'd recognize him.

MASTER OF CEREMONIES   And you?

THIRD SERVANT   Begging your pardon, nothing.

MASTER OF CEREMONIES   That's very little. And you?

FOURTH SERVANT   Nothing either.

MASTER OF CEREMONIES   That's even less.

KING PETER   But Council, have I not resolved that My Royal Majesty shall rejoice today and that the wedding shall be celebrated? Was this not our most solemn resolution?

PRESIDENT   Yes, Your Majesty, it is so registered and recorded.

KING PETER   And would I not compromise myself, if I did not carry out my resolution?

PRESIDENT   If it were at all possible for Your Majesty to compromise yourself, this would be an instance in which Your Majesty could compromise yourself.

KING PETER   Have I not given my Royal Word? Yes, I shall carry out my resolution immediately: I shall rejoice. (*He rubs his hands.*) Oh, I am exceptionally happy!

PRESIDENT   We join in sharing Your Majesty's emotion, insofar as it is possible and proper for subjects to do so.

KING PETER   Oh, I am beside myself with joy. I shall have red coats made for my chamberlains, I shall promote some cadets to lieutenants, I shall permit my subjects to—but, but, the wedding?

Does not the other half of the resolution state that the wedding shall be celebrated?

PRESIDENT   Yes, Your Majesty.

KING PETER   Yes, but if the Prince does not come and neither does the Princess?

PRESIDENT   Yes, if the Prince does not come and neither does the Princess—then—then—

KING PETER   Then, then?

PRESIDENT   Then indeed they cannot get married.

KING PETER   Wait, is the conclusion logical? If—then.—Correct! But my Word, my Royal Word!

PRESIDENT   Take comfort, Your Majesty, with other majesties. A Royal Word is a thing—a thing—a thing—of nothing.[7]

KING PETER (*To the servants.*)   Do you see anything yet?

SERVANTS   Nothing, Your Majesty, nothing at all.

KING PETER   And I had resolved to be so happy. I wanted to begin at the stroke of twelve and wanted to rejoice a full twelve hours.—I am becoming quite melancholy.

PRESIDENT   All subjects are commanded to share the feelings of His Majesty.

MASTER OF CEREMONIES   For the sake of decorum, those who carry no handkerchiefs are nonetheless forbidden to cry.

FIRST SERVANT   Wait! I see something! It's something like a protuberance, like a nose—the rest isn't over the border yet—and now I see another man and two people of the opposite sex.

MASTER OF CEREMONIES   In which direction?

FIRST SERVANT   They're coming closer. They're approaching the palace. Here they are. (VALERIO, LEONCE, *the* GOVERNESS, *and the* PRINCESS *enter, masked.*)

KING PETER   Who are you?

VALERIO   Do I know? (*He slowly takes off several masks, one after another.*) Am I this? Or this? Or this? I'm truly afraid I could peel myself away completely like this.

KING PETER (*Confused.*)   But—but you must be something, after all?

VALERIO   If Your Majesty commands it. But gentlemen, then turn the mirrors around and hide your shiny buttons somewhat and don't look at me so that I'm mirrored in your eyes, or I'll really no longer know who I actually am.

KING PETER   This man makes me confused, desperate. I am thoroughly mixed up.

---

7. HAMLET (4.2): "The king is a thing—" / GUILDENSTERN: "A thing, my lord!" / HAMLET: "Of nothing."

VALERIO But actually I wanted to announce to this exalted and honored company that the two world-famous automatons have arrived, and that I'm perhaps the third and most peculiar of them all, if only I really knew who I am, which by the way shouldn't surprise you, since I myself don't know what I'm talking about—in fact, I don't even know that I don't know it, so that it's highly probable that I'm merely being *made* to speak, and it's actually nothing but cylinders and air hoses that are saying all this. (*In a strident voice.*) Ladies and gentlemen, here you see two persons of opposite sexes, a male and a female, a gentleman and a lady. Nothing but art and machinery, nothing but cardboard and watchsprings. Each one has a tiny, tiny ruby spring under the nail of the little toe of the right foot—press on it gently and the mechanism runs a full fifty years. These persons are so perfectly constructed that one couldn't distinguish them from other people if one didn't know that they're simply cardboard; you could actually make them members of human society.[8] They are very noble, for they speak the Queen's English. They are very moral, for they get up punctually, eat lunch punctually, and go to bed punctually; they also have a good digestion, which proves they have a good conscience. They have a fine sense of propriety, for the lady has no word for the concept "pants," and it is absolutely impossible for the gentleman to follow a lady going upstairs or to precede her downstairs. They are highly educated, for the lady sings all the new operas and the gentleman wears cuffs. Take note, ladies and gentlemen: they are now in an interesting state. The mechanism of love is beginning to function: the gentleman has already carried the lady's shawl several times, the lady has turned her eyes up to heaven. Both have whispered more than once: "Faith, hope, charity!" Both already appear to be completely in accord; all that is lacking is the tiny word "amen."

KING PETER (*Puts a finger next to his nose.*) In effigy? In effigy? President, if you hang a man in effigy, isn't that just as good as hanging him properly?

PRESIDENT Begging Your Majesty's pardon, it's very much better, because no harm comes to him, yet he is hanged nevertheless.

KING PETER Now I've got it. We shall celebrate the wedding in effigy. (*Pointing to* LEONCE *and* LENA.) This is the Prince, this is the Princess. I shall carry out my resolution—I shall rejoice. Let the bells ring, prepare your congratulations! Quickly, Court Chaplain! (*The* COURT CHAPLAIN *steps forward, clears his throat, looks toward heaven several times.*)

VALERIO Begin! Leave thy damnable faces, and begin![9] Come on!

---

8. Cf. Büchner's letter of around March 10, 1834, to Minna Jaeglé (p. 184).
9. *Hamlet* 3.2.

COURT CHAPLAIN (*In the greatest confusion.*)   When we—or—but—

VALERIO   Whereas and because—

COURT CHAPLAIN   For—

VALERIO   It was before the creation of the world—

COURT CHAPLAIN   That—

VALERIO   God was bored—

KING PETER   Just make it short, my good man.

COURT CHAPLAIN (*Composing himself.*)   May it please Your Highness Prince Leonce from the Kingdom of Popo and may it please Your Highness Princess Lena from the Kingdom of Peepee, and may it please Your Highnesses mutually to want each other respectively, then say a loud and audible "I do."

LENA AND LEONCE   I do.

COURT CHAPLAIN   Then I say amen.

VALERIO   Well done, short and sweet—thus man and woman are created and all the animals of paradise surround them. (LEONCE *takes off his mask.*)

ALL   The Prince!

KING PETER   The Prince! My son! I'm lost, I've been deceived! (*He rushes over to the* PRINCESS.) Who is this person? I shall declare everything invalid.

GOVERNESS (*Takes off the* PRINCESS's *mask, triumphantly.*)   The Princess!

LEONCE   Lena?

LENA   Leonce?

LEONCE   Why Lena, I think that was an escape into paradise. I've been deceived.

LENA   I've been deceived.

LEONCE   Oh, Fortune!

LENA   Oh, Providence!

VALERIO   I can't help laughing. I can't help laughing. Fate has certainly been fortuitous for the two of you. I hope Your Highnesses will be so fortunate as to find favor with each other forthwith.

GOVERNESS   That my old eyes could see this! A wandering prince! Now I can die in peace.

KING PETER   My children, I am deeply moved, I am almost beside myself with emotion. I am the happiest of all men! I shall now, however, most solemnly place the kingdom in your hands, my son, and shall immediately begin to do nothing but think without interruption. My son, you will leave me these wise men (*He points to the State Council.*), so they can support me in my efforts. Come, gentlemen, we must think, think without interruption. (*He leaves with the State Council.*) That person confused me before—I must find my way out again.

LEONCE (*To those present.*)   Gentlemen, my spouse and I are terribly sorry that you have had to attend us for so long today. Your
deportment is so tenuous that we do not intend to test your
tenacity any longer. Go home now, but don't forget your speeches,
sermons, and verses, because tomorrow, in peace and comfort,
we'll begin the game all over again. Good-bye! (*All leave except*
LEONCE, LENA, VALERIO, *and the* GOVERNESS.)

LEONCE   Well, Lena, now do you see how our pockets are full of
dolls and toys? What shall we do with them? Shall we give them
beards and hang swords on them? Or shall we dress them up in
tails and let them play at protozoan politics and diplomacy and
watch them through a microscope? Or would you prefer a barrel
organ on which milk-white aesthetic shrews are scurrying about?
Shall we build a theater? (LENA *leans against him and shakes her
head.*) But I know what you really want: we'll have all the clocks
smashed, all calendars prohibited, and we'll count hours and
months only by flower-clocks, only by blossoms and fruit. And then
we'll surround the little country with heat reflectors so there'll be
no more winter, and in the summer we'll make it as warm as
Ischia and Capri, and we'll spend the whole year among roses and
violets, among oranges and laurels.

VALERIO   And I'll be Minister of State, and it shall be decreed that
whoever gets calluses on his hands shall be placed in custody,
that whoever works himself sick shall be criminally prosecuted,
that anyone who boasts of eating his bread in the sweat of his
brow shall be declared insane and dangerous to human society,
and then we'll lie in the shade and ask God for macaroni, melons,
and figs, for musical voices, classical bodies, and a comfortable
religion!

Variant to Act One, Scene 1

I

. . . [*The beginning of the variant is almost identical to the
later version on page 107*].

VALERIO   Ah, my Lord, what a feeling I have for nature! The grass
looks so beautiful that I wish I were an ox so I could eat it, and
then a human being again to eat the ox that has eaten such grass.

LEONCE   Unhappy man, you too seem to be suffering from ideals.

VALERIO   Oh God! For a week I've been running after an ideal
roast beef without finding it anywhere in reality. (*He sings.*)

> Our hostess has a pretty maid,
> She's in her garden night and day,
> She sits inside her garden,

Until the bells have all struck twelve
And stares at all the soo-ooldiers.[1]

(*He sits on the ground.*) Look at these ants, dear children, it's amazing what instinct is in these little creatures—order, diligence—My Lord, there are only four ways a man can earn money: find it, win it in a lottery, inherit it, or steal it in God's name, if you're clever enough not to suffer any conscience pangs.

LEONCE   You've grown rather old on these principles without dying of hunger or on the gallows.

VALERIO (*Always staring at him.*)   Yes, my Lord, and I maintain that whoever earns money in any other way is a scoundrel.

LEONCE   Because one who works is subtly committing suicide, and a suicide is a criminal, and a criminal is a scoundrel: therefore whoever works is a scoundrel.

VALERIO   Yes.—All the same, ants are most useful pests, but they'd be even more useful if they didn't do any damage. Nevertheless, most honored vermin, I can't deny myself the pleasure of kicking a few of you in the ass with my heel, blowing your noses and cutting your nails. (*Two policemen enter.*)

FIRST POLICEMAN   Halt—where's the rascal?

SECOND POLICEMAN   There are two over there.

FIRST POLICEMAN   Check if either of them is running away.

SECOND POLICEMAN   I don't think anyone is running away.

FIRST POLICEMAN   Then we'll have to interrogate them both.— Gentlemen, we're looking for someone—a subject, an individual, a person, a delinquent, a suspect, a rascal. (*To the other policeman.*) Check if either of them is blushing.

SECOND POLICEMAN   Nobody blushed.

FIRST POLICEMAN   Then we'll have to try something else.—Where's the warrant, the description, the certificate? (*The* SECOND POLICEMAN *takes a paper out of his pocket and hands it over.*) Inspect the subjects as I read: a human being—

SECOND POLICEMAN   Doesn't match, there are two of them.

FIRST POLICEMAN   Idiot!—walks on two feet, has two arms; in addition, a mouth, a nose, two eyes, two ears. Distinguishing characteristics: is a highly dangerous individual.

SECOND POLICEMAN   That fits both. Shall I arrest them both?

FIRST POLICEMAN   Two—that's dangerous—there are only two of us. But I'll make a report. It's a case of highly criminal complexity or highly complex criminality. For if I get drunk and lie down in bed, that's my affair and doesn't concern anyone, but if I squander my bed on drink, whose affair is that, you rogue?

---

1. Cf. *Woyzeck* 4,10.

SECOND POLICEMAN   Well, I don't know.

FIRST POLICEMAN   Well, I don't know either, but that's the point. (*They go off.*)

VALERIO   Just try to deny destiny. Look what one can accomplish with a flea. If it hadn't crawled over me last night, I wouldn't have carried my bed into the sun this morning, and if I hadn't carried it into the sun, I wouldn't have ended up with it next to the Inn of the Moon, and if sun and moon hadn't shone on it, I couldn't have pressed any wine out of my straw mattress and gotten drunk from it—and if all that hadn't happened I wouldn't be in your company now, most honored ants, letting you strip me to a skeleton and being dried up by the sun, but I'd be carving up a piece of meat and drying up a bottle of wine—in the hospital, namely.

LEONCE   A pleasant way of life.

VALERIO   I have a racy way of life. Because only my racing in the course of the war saved me from receiving a round of rifle bullets in my ribs. As a result of this rescue, I got a rasping cough, and the doctor resolved that my racing had become a galloping and that I had galloping consumption. But since I realized I had nothing to consume, I fell into or rather upon a consuming fever, during which I was required to eat good soup, good beef, good bread and drink good wine every day in order to sustain myself as a defender of the Fatherland.

LEONCE   But, noblest sir, your trade, your métier, your profession, your occupation, your rank, your art?

VALERIO   My Lord, I have the great occupation of being idle, I am incredibly skilled in doing nothing, I have an enormous capacity for laziness.

Woyzeck

Historical Context

The protagonist of this play is based on the historical Johann Christian Woyzeck (1780–1824), who killed his lover by stabbing her seven times with a broken sword blade. Had it not been for this sensational murder, Woyzeck would have lived and died as one of the numberless forgotten pawns of the world. Orphaned at the age of thirteen, he largely made his living as a mercenary, serving in a variety of German and Swedish units across Europe. At one point he fathered a child by a woman named Wienberg, but faulty personal papers prevented a marriage, and he subsequently deserted lover and child. Remorse for this act seems to have haunted him ever afterward. Woyzeck eventually returned to his native city of Leipzig, where he found intermittent work as a barber, wigmaker, and odd-jobs man. Problems with his personal papers once again thwarted him; this time, improper documentation denied him entry into the Leipzig militia. Taking increasingly to drink, he became involved with one Frau Woost, who enjoyed the company of soldiers and refused to remain faithful to him. Mad with jealousy and maybe simply mad, Woyzeck murdered her on June 21, 1821.

While his guilt was never in question, his sanity was, and the Leipzig court consulted a respected Leipzig professor, Dr. Johann Christian August Clarus, to examine Woyzeck and assess his mental state. Clarus ultimately issued two reports, both of which conceded that Woyzeck suffered from hallucinations as well as other mental disturbances, but which also concluded that Woyzeck was essentially sane and therefore accountable for his actions. Sentence quickly followed, and Woyzeck was beheaded in Leipzig on August 27, 1824. It was the city's first execution in several decades, and it proved an enormously popular spectacle.

Sources

Though Woyzeck's murder of Frau Woost was the principal influence for the play, Büchner may have also drawn on two related incidents for inspiration. The first of these was Daniel Schmolling's murder of his mistress near Berlin in 1817 (documented in the *Archiv für medizinische Erfahrung* in 1820) and the second was Johann Diess's murder of his mistress near Darmstadt in 1830 (documented in the *Zeitschrift für Staatsarzneikunde* in 1830). Still, Büchner's main source for *Woyzeck* was clearly Dr. Clarus's medical examination of Woyzeck, excerpts of which appear in the "Contexts" section of this edition. Not only did Büchner borrow a number of details from Clarus's two reports, but he also appears inspired by Clarus's general interest in Woyzeck's autonomy. While Clarus argued that Woyzeck, despite his condition, was a free agent and therefore responsible for his actions, Büchner's play questions such tidy distinctions. Where in this play might one draw the line between madness and sanity, between compulsion and freedom?

Clarus's unwitting contribution to the play may go even further than supplying so much of its source material; he may also have provided a model for the character of the Doctor. If so, then he shares this dubious honor with Johann Bernhard Wilbrand, Büchner's anatomy professor at the University of Giessen and another possible inspiration for the role.

Manuscript, Publication, and Premiere

Woyzeck is not a finished play; it is a collection of fragments. More precisely, it is a set of four manuscript drafts (only one of which seems to have a beginning, a middle, and an end), which Büchner left behind him at his death in 1837. The drafts languished in oblivion for decades. When Georg Büchner's brother Ludwig published the first edition of works in 1850, *Woyzeck* went missing and unmentioned, an omission that reflected Ludwig's sense that the work was riddled with "cynicism" and "trivialities," as well as being virtually illegible. The work was not found again until the Austrian novelist Karl Emil Franzos discovered, deciphered, and ultimately published it in the Viennese newspaper *Neue Freie Presse* in 1875. Four years later, he would include it in his complete edition of Büchner's works. The title Franzos used, based on a misreading, was *"Wozzeck."* Franzos introduced other confusions as well, including a free rendering of the text and, more seriously, the use of a chemical on the manuscript that had the effect of making the ink easier to read in the short run but even more muddled and blobbed forever after.

The result is a tragic, though perhaps fitting, mess. Optimists like to point to a letter dated a few weeks before Büchner's death, in which he wrote that he would "release *Leonce and Lena* along with two other dramas for publication in a week at most." The other dramas are presumably *Woyzeck* and the missing *Pietro Aretino,* leading some to believe that the last (and most complete) draft of *Woyzeck* represents something close to a final version. And indeed most translators, including the present one, use that draft as a principal guide to a reconstruction of the play. But even if one privileges the fourth draft, large mysteries remain: scenes may be missing, scene order is by no means clear, and those maddening ink blotches persist.

There are as many *Woyzecks* as there are translators. Henry J. Schmidt's reconstruction (printed here) differs from some, however, in that he makes his choices clear to the reader and includes all omitted material in a supplemental section. Each scene opens with a heading that lists the draft number, followed by the scene number in that draft.

The play premiered at the Munich Kammerspiele on November 8, 1913, in a production directed by Eugen Kilian. As with *Danton's Death,* however, the play had to wait for a successful Max Reinhardt staging to achieve its place in the theatrical canon. Reinhardt's production opened at the Deutsches Theater in Berlin on April 5, 1921, to wide acclaim. Basing his libretto on the Franzos version, Alban Berg composed the opera *Wozzeck* between 1914 and 1922, and it received its premiere in Berlin on December 14, 1925.

WOYZECK[†]

A Reconstruction

*[consisting of Büchner's incomplete revision
(Fourth Draft), scenes from the First Draft,
and two optional scenes]*

CHARACTERS[1]

Franz Woyzeck	First Apprentice
Marie	Second Apprentice
Captain	Karl, *an idiot*
Doctor	Katey
Drum Major	Grandmother
Sergeant	First Child
Andres	Second Child
Margret	First Person
Barker	Second Person
Announcer	Court Clerk
Old Man	Judge
Child	Soldiers, Students, Young
Jew	Men, Girls, Children
Innkeeper	

4,1.[2]

Open field. The town in the distance.

WOYZECK *and* ANDRES *are cutting branches[3] in the bushes.*

WOYZECK   Yes, Andres—that stripe there across the grass, that's where heads roll at night; once somebody picked one up, he thought it was a hedgehog. Three days and three nights, and he was lying in a coffin. (*Softly.*) Andres, it was the Freemasons, that's it, the Freemasons—shh![4]

ANDRES (*Sings.*)

[†] Translated by Henry J. Schmidt.

1. Compiled by the translator; Büchner includes no character list.

2. The translator's notation, indicating the draft from which this scene is taken, followed by the scene of that draft. This scene is therefore the first scene of the fourth draft. Four fragmentary drafts, the third of which consists of only two short scenes (or sketches toward scenes), are all that remain of Büchner's plans for *Woyzeck*.

3. *Stöcke* in German; such branches were often used to flog soldiers.

4. Büchner derives details such as Woyzeck's noticing the stripe across the grass and his fear of the Freemasons (a secretive fraternal order and frequent object of suspicion at the time) from Dr. Clarus's medical evaluations of the historical Woyzeck. Woyzeck's visions toward the end of this scene are also indebted to Clarus (see the "Contexts" section of this volume).

> I saw two big rabbits
> Chewing up the green, green grass[5] . . .

WOYZECK   Shh! Something's moving!

ANDRES   Chewing up the green, green grass
        Till it was all gone.

WOYZECK   Something's moving behind me, under me. (*Stamps on the ground.*) Hollow—you hear that? It's all hollow down there. The Freemasons!

ANDRES   I'm scared.

WOYZECK   It's so strangely quiet. You feel like holding your breath. Andres!

ANDRES   What?

WOYZECK   Say something! (*Stares off into the distance.*) Andres! Look how bright it is! There's fire raging around the sky, and a noise is coming down like trumpets. It's coming closer! Let's go! Don't look back! (*Drags him into the bushes.*)

ANDRES   (*After a pause.*)   Woyzeck! Do you still hear it?

WOYZECK   Quiet, it's all quiet, like the world was dead.

ANDRES   Listen! They're drumming. We've got to get back.

4,2.

[*The town.*][6]

MARIE *with her* CHILD *at the window.* MARGRET. *A military patrol goes by, the* DRUM MAJOR *leading.*

MARIE   (*Rocking the* CHILD *in her arms.*)   Hey, boy! Ta-ra-ra-ra! You hear it? They're coming.

MARGRET   What a man, like a tree!

MARIE   He stands on his feet like a lion. (*The* DRUM MAJOR *greets them.*)

MARGRET   Say, what a friendly look you gave him, neighbor—we're not used to that from you.

MARIE   (*Sings.*)

> A soldier is a handsome fellow . . .

MARGRET   Your eyes are still shining.

MARIE   So what? Why don't you take *your* eyes to the Jew and have them polished—maybe they'll shine enough to sell as two buttons.

MARGRET   What? Why, Mrs. Virgin, I'm a decent woman, but you—you can stare through seven pairs of leather pants!

---

5. From the folk song "*Zwischen Berg und tiefem, tiefem Tal.*"
6. Brackets indicate textual additions by the translator (as here) or uncertain readings.

MARIE   Bitch! (*Slams the window shut.*) Come, my boy. What do they want from us, anyway? You're only the poor child of a whore, and you make your mother happy with your bastard face. Ta-ta! (*Sings.*)

> Maiden, now what's to be done?
> You've got no ring, you've a son.
> Oh, why worry my head,
> I'll sing here at your bed:
> Rockabye baby, my baby are you,
> Nobody cares what I do.
>
> Johnny, hitch up your six horses fleet,
> Go bring them something to eat.
> From oats they will turn,
> From water they'll turn,
> Only cool wine will be fine, hooray!
> Only cool wine will be fine.

(*A knock at the window.*)

MARIE   Who's that? Is that you, Franz? Come on in!

WOYZECK   I can't. Have to go to roll call.

MARIE   What's the matter with you, Franz?

WOYZECK   (*Mysteriously.*)   Marie, there was something out there again—a lot. Isn't it written: "And lo, the smoke of the country went up as the smoke of a furnace"?[7]

MARIE   Man alive!

WOYZECK   It followed me until I reached town. What's going to happen?

MARIE   Franz!

WOYZECK   I've got to go. (*He leaves.*)

MARIE   That man! He's so upset. He didn't look at his own child. He'll go crazy with those thoughts of his. Why are you so quiet, son? Are you scared? It's getting so dark, you'd think you were blind. Usually there's a light shining in. I can't stand it. I'm frightened. (*Goes off.*)

4,3.

Carnival booths. Lights. People.[8]

OLD MAN   DANCING CHILD

> How long we live, just time will tell,
> We all have got to die,
> We know that very well!

---

7. From Genesis 19:28, describing the destruction of Sodom and Gomorrah; the image returns in Revelation 9:2.
8. In the fourth draft, Büchner wrote only this title and left one and a half pages blank. This scene is a reconstruction by the translator based on earlier drafts.

[WOYZECK]   Hey! Whee! Poor man, old man! Poor child! Young
child! Hey, Marie, shall I carry you? . . . Beautiful world!
CARNIVAL BARKER *(In front of a booth.)*   Gentlemen! Gentlemen!
[*(Points to a monkey.)*] Look at this creature, as God made it:
he's nothing, nothing at all. Now see the effect of art: he walks
upright, wears coat and pants, carries a sword! Ho! Take a bow!
Good boy. Give me a kiss! (*[Monkey] trumpets.*) The little dummy
is musical!

Ladies and gentlemen, here is to be seen the astronomical
horse and the little cannery-birds[9]—they're favorites of all potentates of Europe and members of all learned societies. They'll tell
you everything: how old you are, how many children you have,
what kind of illnesses. [*(Points to the monkey.)*] He shoots a pistol, stands on one leg. It's all a matter of upbringing; he has
merely a beastly reason, or rather a very reasonable beastliness—
he's no brutish individual like a lot of people, present company
excepted. Enter! The presentation will begin. The commencement of the beginning will start immediately.

Observe the progress of civilization. Everything progresses—a
horse, a monkey, a cannery-bird. The monkey is already a
soldier—that's not much, it's the lowest level of the human race!
[WOYZECK] Want to?
MARIE   All right. It ought to be good. Look at his tassels, and the
woman's got pants on!
        (SERGEANT. DRUM MAJOR. [MARIE. WOYZECK.])
SERGEANT   Hold it! Over there. Look at her! What a piece!
DRUM MAJOR   Damn! Good enough for the propagation of cavalry
regiments and the breeding of drum majors.
SERGEANT   Look how she holds her head—you'd think that black
hair would pull her down like a weight. And those eyes, black . . .
DRUM MAJOR   It's like looking down a well or a chimney. Come on,
after her!
MARIE   Those lights!
WOYZECK   Yeah, like a big black cat with fiery eyes. Hey, what a
night!
        (Inside the booth.)
CARNIVAL ANNOUNCER   [*Presenting a horse.*] Show your talent!
Show your beastly wisdom! Put human society to shame! Gentlemen, this animal that you see here, with a tail on his body, with
his four hooves, is a member of all learned societies, is a professor
at our university, with whom the students learn to ride and fight
duels. That was simple comprehension! Now think with double

---

9. *Canaillevogel* in German; a neologism combining *Kanarienvogel* ("canary") and
Canaille ("rascal").

raison. What do you do when you think with double *raison?* Is
there in the learned *société* an ass? (*The horse shakes its head.*)
Now you understand double *raison!* That is beastiognomy.[1] Yes,
that's no brutish individual, that's a person! A human being, a
beastly human being, but still an animal, a *bête.*[2] (*The horse
behaves improperly.*) That's right, put *société* to shame! You see,
the beast is still nature, unspoiled nature! Take a lesson from
him. Go ask the doctor, it's very unhealthy! It is written: man, be
natural; you were created from dust, sand, dirt. Do you want to
be more than dust, sand, dirt? Observe his power of reason! He
can add, but he can't count on his fingers—why is that? He simply can't express himself, explain himself—he's a transformed
person! Tell the gentlemen what time it is. Who among the ladies
and gentlemen has a watch—a watch?

DRUM MAJOR   A watch! (*Slowly and grandly he pulls a watch out of
his pocket.*) There you are, sir.

MARIE   This I've got to see. (*She climbs into the first row. The* DRUM
MAJOR *helps her.*)

4,4.

[*Room.*]

MARIE *sits with her* CHILD *on her lap, a piece of mirror in her
hand.*

MARIE (*Looks at herself in the mirror.*)   These stones really sparkle!
What kind are they? What did he say?—Go to sleep, son! Shut
your eyes tight. (*The* CHILD *covers his eyes with his hands.*)
Tighter—stay quiet or he'll come get you. (*Sings.*)

> Close up your shop, fair maid,
> A gypsy boy's in the glade.
> He'll lead you by the hand
> Off into gypsyland.[3]

(*Looks in the mirror again.*) It must be gold. The likes of us only
have a little corner in the world and a little piece of mirror, but
I have just as red a mouth as the great ladies with their mirrors
from top to toe and their handsome lords who kiss their hands.
I'm just a poor woman. (*The* CHILD *sits up.*) Shh, son, eyes shut—
look, the sandman! He's running along the wall. (*She flashes
with the mirror.*) Eyes shut, or he'll look into them, and you'll go
blind.

---

1. *Viehsionomik* in German; a neologism combining *Vieh* ("beast") and *Physiognomie*
("physiognomy").
2. *Raison, société, bête:* reason, society, beast (French).
3. Folk song from Franz M. Böhme's *Deutsches Kinderlied und Kinderspiel* (1897).

(WOYZECK *enters behind her. She jumps up with her hands over her ears.*)

WOYZECK   What's that you got there?

MARIE   Nothing.

WOYZECK   Something's shining under your fingers.

MARIE   An earring—I found it.

WOYZECK   I've never found anything like that. Two at once.

MARIE   What am I—a whore?[4]

WOYZECK   It's all right, Marie.—Look, the boy's asleep. Lift him up under his arms, the chair's hurting him. There are shiny drops on his forehead; everything under the sun is work—sweat, even in our sleep. Us poor people! Here's some more money, Marie, my pay and some from my captain.

MARIE   Bless you, Franz.

WOYZECK   I have to go. See you tonight, Marie. Bye.

MARIE   (*Alone, after a pause.*)   What a bitch I am. I could stab myself.—Oh, what a world! Everything goes to hell anyhow, man and woman alike.

4,5.[5]

The CAPTAIN. WOYZECK.

The CAPTAIN *in a chair,* WOYZECK *shaves him.*

CAPTAIN   Take it easy, Woyzeck, take it easy. One thing at a time; you're making me quite dizzy.[6] You're going to finish early today— what am I supposed to do with the extra ten minutes? Woyzeck, just think, you've still got a good thirty years to live, thirty years! That's 360 months, and days, hours, minutes! What are you going to do with that ungodly amount of time? Get organized, Woyzeck.

WOYZECK   Yes, Cap'n.

CAPTAIN   I fear for the world when I think about eternity. Activity, Woyzeck, activity! Eternal, that's eternal, that's eternal—you realize that, of course. But then again it's not eternal, it's only a

---

4. *Bin ich ein Mensch?* "*Mensch*" literally means "person" but is translated here in its slang sense of "whore." The double meaning recurs a few lines later in "*Ich bin doch ein schlecht Mensch*," translated as "What a bitch I am."

5. Karl Emile Franzos' reconstruction of the play, which first appeared in 1875 under the title *Wozzeck*, placed this scene first, and Alban Berg's 1923 libretto, based on Franzos' reconstruction, also begins here. Most scholars now find 4,1 a more plausible opening for the play.

6. The play's hierarchical modes of address resist translation into English. The Captain addresses Woyzeck with the third person singular, using the pronoun *Er* ("he"). His line therefore literally reads, "He's making me quite dizzy." This was at the time a customary way for superiors to speak to subordinates, especially in the military. For his part, Woyzeck addresses members of his own class (such as Marie and Andres) with *du*, using the informal form of the second person. He addresses his superiors with *Sie*, using the formal form of the second person.

moment, yes, a moment.—Woyzeck, it frightens me to think that
the earth rotates in one day—what a waste of time, what will
come of that? Woyzeck, I can't look at a mill wheel anymore or
I get melancholy.

WOYZECK   Yes, Cap'n.

CAPTAIN   Woyzeck, you always look so upset. A good man doesn't
act like that, a good man with a good conscience. Say something,
Woyzeck. What's the weather like today?

WOYZECK   It's bad, Cap'n, bad—wind.

CAPTAIN   I can feel it, there's something rapid out there. A wind
like that reminds me of a mouse. (*Cunningly.*) I believe it's coming from the south-north.

WOYZECK   Yes, Cap'n.

CAPTAIN   Ha! Ha! Ha! South-north! Ha! Ha! Ha! Oh, are you stupid, terribly stupid. (*Sentimentally.*) Woyzeck, you're a good man,
a good man—(*With dignity.*) but Woyzeck, you've got no morality.
Morality—that's when you are moral, you understand. It's a good
word. You have a child without the blessing of the church, as our
Reverend Chaplain says, without the blessing of the church—
I didn't say it.

WOYZECK   Cap'n, the good Lord isn't going to look at a poor little
kid only because amen was said over it before it was created. The
Lord said: "Suffer little children to come unto me."[7]

CAPTAIN   What's that you're saying? What kind of a crazy answer is
that? You're getting me all confused with your answer. When I
say *you,* I mean you—you!

WOYZECK   Us poor people. You see, Cap'n—money, money. If you
don't have money. Just try to raise your own kind of morality in this
world. After all, we're flesh and blood. The likes of us are wretched
in this world and in the next; I guess if we ever got to Heaven,
we'd have to help with the thunder.

CAPTAIN   Woyzeck, you have no virtue, you're not a virtuous person. Flesh and blood? When I'm lying at the window after it has
rained, and I watch the white stockings as they go tripping down
the street—damn it, Woyzeck, then love comes all over me. I've got
flesh and blood, too. But Woyzeck, virtue, virtue! How else could
I make time go by? I always say to myself: you're a virtuous man,
(*Sentimentally.*) a good man, a good man.

WOYZECK   Yes, Cap'n, virtue! I haven't figured it out yet. You see,
us common people, we don't have virtue, we act like nature tells
us—but if I was a gentleman, and had a hat and a watch and an
overcoat and could talk refined, then I'd be virtuous, too. Virtue
must be nice, Cap'n. But I'm just a poor guy.

7. Words of Jesus found in the Gospels (Matthew 19:14, Mark 10:14, Luke 18:16).

CAPTAIN   That's fine, Woyzeck. You're a good man, a good man. But you think too much, that's unhealthy—you always look so upset. This discussion has really worn me out. You can go now— and don't run like that! Slow, nice and slow down the street.

4,6.

MARIE. DRUM MAJOR.

DRUM MAJOR   Marie!

MARIE (*Looking at him expressively.*)   Go march up and down for me.—A chest like a bull and a beard like a lion. Nobody else is like that.—No woman is prouder than me.

DRUM MAJOR   Sundays when I have my plumed helmet and my white gloves—goddamn, Marie! The prince always says: man, you're quite a guy!

MARIE (*Mockingly.*)   Aw, go on! (*Goes up to him.*) What a man!

DRUM MAJOR   What a woman! Hell, let's breed a race of drum majors, hey? (*He embraces her.*)

MARIE (*Moody.*)   Leave me alone!

DRUM MAJOR   You wildcat!

MARIE (*Violently.*)   Just try to touch me!

DRUM MAJOR   Is the devil in your eyes?

MARIE   For all I care. What does it matter?

4,7.

MARIE. WOYZECK.

WOYZECK (*Stares at her, shakes his head.*)   Hm! I don't see anything, I don't see anything. Oh, I should be able to see it; I should be able to grab it with my fists.

MARIE (*Intimidated.*)   What's the matter, Franz? You're out of your mind, Franz.

WOYZECK   A sin so fat and so wide—it stinks enough to smoke the angels out of Heaven. You've got a red mouth, Marie. No blister on it? Good-bye, Marie, you're as beautiful as sin.—Can mortal sin be so beautiful?

MARIE   Franz, you're delirious.

WOYZECK   Damn it!—Was he standing here like this, like this?

MARIE   As the day is long and the world is old, lots of people can stand on one spot, one after another.

WOYZECK   I saw him.

MARIE   You can see all sorts of things if you've got two eyes and aren't blind, and the sun is shining.

WOYZECK   [With my own eyes!]

MARIE (*Fresh.*)   So what!

4,8.

WOYZECK. *The* DOCTOR.

DOCTOR   What's this I saw, Woyzeck? A man of his word!

WOYZECK   What is it, Doctor?

DOCTOR   I saw it, Woyzeck—you pissed on the street, you pissed on the wall like a dog. And even though you get two cents a day. Woyzeck, that's bad. The world's getting bad, very bad.

WOYZECK   But Doctor, the call of nature . . .

DOCTOR   The call of nature, the call of nature! Nature! Haven't I proved that the *musculus constrictor vesicae*[8] is subject to the will? Nature! Woyzeck, man is free; in man alone is individuality exalted to freedom. Couldn't hold it in! (*Shakes his head, puts his hands behind his back, and paces back and forth.*) Did you eat your peas already, Woyzeck?—I'm revolutionizing science, I'll blow it sky-high. Urea ten per cent, ammonium chloride, hyperoxidic. Woyzeck, don't you have to piss again? Go in there and try.

WOYZECK   I can't, Doctor.

DOCTOR (*With emotion.*)   But pissing on the wall! I have it in writing, here's the contract. I saw it all, saw it with my own eyes— I was just holding my nose out the window, letting the sun's rays hit it, so as to examine the process of sneezing. (*Starts kicking him.*) No, Woyzeck, I'm not getting angry; anger is unhealthy, unscientific. I am calm, perfectly calm—my pulse is beating at its usual sixty, and I'm telling you this in all cold-bloodedness! Who on earth would get excited about a human being, a human being! Now if it were a Proteus lizard that were dying! But you shouldn't have pissed on the wall . . .

WOYZECK   You see, Doctor, sometimes you've got a certain character, a certain structure.—But with nature, that's something else, you see, with nature—(*He cracks his knuckles.*) that's like—how should I put it—for example . . .

DOCTOR   Woyzeck, you're philosophizing again.

WOYZECK (*Confidingly.*)   Doctor, have you ever seen anything of double nature? When the sun's standing high at noon and the world seems to be going up in flames, I've heard a terrible voice talking to me!

DOCTOR   Woyzeck, you've got an *aberratio!*

WOYZECK (*Puts his finger to his nose.*)   The toadstools, Doctor. There—that's where it is. Have you seen how they grow in patterns? If only someone could read that.

8. Urinary bladder muscle.

DOCTOR   Woyzeck, you've got a marvelous *aberratio mentalis partialis*,[9] second species, beautifully developed. Woyzeck, you're getting a raise. Second species: obsession with a generally rational condition. You're doing everything as usual—shaving your captain?

WOYZECK   Yes, sir.

DOCTOR   Eating your peas?

WOYZECK   Same as ever, Doctor. My wife gets the money for the household.

DOCTOR   Going on duty?

WOYZECK   Yes, sir.

DOCTOR   You're an interesting case. Subject Woyzeck, you're getting a raise. Now behave yourself. Show me your pulse! Yes.

4,9.

CAPTAIN. DOCTOR.

CAPTAIN   Doctor, I'm afraid for the horses when I think that the poor beasts have to go everywhere on foot. Don't run like that! Don't wave your cane around in the air like that! You'll run yourself to death that way. A good man with a good conscience doesn't go so fast. A good man. (*He catches the* DOCTOR *by the coat.*) Doctor, allow me to save a human life. You're racing . . .
Doctor, I'm so melancholy, I get so emotional, I always start crying when I see my coat hanging on the wall—there it is.

DOCTOR   Hm! Bloated, fat, thick neck, apoplectic constitution. Yes, Captain, you might be stricken by an *apoplexia cerebralis.* But you might get it just on one side and be half paralyzed, or—best of all—you might become mentally affected and just vegetate from then on: those are approximately your prospects for the next four weeks. Moreover, I can assure you that you will be a most interesting case, and if, God willing, your tongue is partially paralyzed, we'll make immortal experiments.

CAPTAIN   Doctor, don't frighten me! People have been known to die of fright, of pure, sheer fright.—I can see them now, with their hats in their hands[1]—but they'll say, he was a good man, a good man.—You damn coffin nail!

DOCTOR   [(*Holds out his hat.*)] What's this, Captain? That's brainless!

CAPTAIN (*Makes a crease.*)   What's this, Doctor? That's in-crease!

DOCTOR   I take my leave, most honorable Mr. Drillprick.

CAPTAIN   Likewise, dearest Mr. Coffin Nail.

---

9. Partial mental aberration.
1. Literally, "with lemons in their hands"; it was customary to hold a lemon at a funeral as a sign of mourning.

4,10.

The guardroom.
WOYZECK. ANDRES.
ANDRES (*Sings.*)

> Our hostess has a pretty maid,
> She's in her garden night and day,
> She sits inside her garden[2] . . .

WOYZECK   Andres!
ANDRES   Huh?
WOYZECK   Nice weather.
ANDRES   Sunday weather. There's music outside town. All the broads are out there already, everybody's sweating—it's really moving along.
WOYZECK   (*Restlessly.*)   A dance, Andres, they're dancing.
ANDRES   Yeah, at the Horse and at the Star.
WOYZECK   Dancing, dancing.
ANDRES   Big deal. (*Sings.*)

> She sits inside her garden,
> Until the bells have all struck twelve,
> And stares at all the soo-ooldiers.

WOYZECK   Andres, I can't keep still.
ANDRES   Fool!
WOYZECK   I've got to get out of here. Everything's spinning before my eyes. How hot their hands are. Damn it, Andres!
ANDRES   What do you want?
WOYZECK   I've got to go.
ANDRES   With that whore.
WOYZECK   I've got to get out. It's so hot in here.

4,11.

Inn.
The windows are open, a dance. Benches in front of the house.
APPRENTICES.
FIRST APPRENTICE

> This shirt I've got, I don't know whose,
> My soul it stinks like booze . . .

---

2. From the folk song *"Es steht ein Wirtshaus an der Lahn."* Cf. *Leonce and Lena* Variant to 1.1.

SECOND APPRENTICE   Brother, shall I in friendship bore a hole in
your nature? Dammit, I want to bore a hole in your nature. I'm
quite a guy, too, you know—I'm going to kill all the fleas on his
body.

FIRST APPRENTICE   My soul, my soul it stinks like booze.—Even
money eventually decays. Forget-me-not! Oh, how beautiful this
world is. Brother, I could cry a rain barrel full of tears. I wish our
noses were two bottles and we could pour them down each other's throats.

OTHERS (*In chorus.*)

> A hunter from the west
> Once went riding through the woods.
> Hip-hip, hooray! A hunter has a merry life,
> O'er meadow and o'er stream,
> Oh, hunting is my dream![3]

(WOYZECK *stands at the window.* MARIE *and the* DRUM MAJOR
dance past without seeing him.)

MARIE (*Dancing by.*)   On! and on, on and on![4]

WOYZECK (*Chokes.*)   On and on—on and on! (*Jumps up violently
and sinks back on the bench.*) On and on, on and on. (*Beats his
hands together.*) Spin around, roll around. Why doesn't God blow
out the sun so that everything can roll around in lust, man and
woman, man and beast. Do it in broad daylight, do it on our
hands, like flies.[5]—Woman!—That woman is hot, hot! On and
on, on and on. (*Jumps up.*) The bastard! Look how he's grabbing
her, grabbing her body! He—he's got her now, [like I used to have
her.][6]

FIRST APPRENTICE (*Preaches on the table.*)   Yet when a wanderer
stands leaning against the stream of time or gives answer for the
wisdom of God, asking himself: Why does man exist? Why does
man exist?—But verily I say unto you: how could the farmer, the
cooper, the shoemaker, the doctor exist if God hadn't created
man? How could the tailor exist if God hadn't given man a feeling
of shame? How could the soldier exist, if men didn't feel the necessity of killing one another? Therefore, do not ye despair, yes, yes,
it is good and pleasant, yet all that is earthly is passing, even
money eventually decays.—In conclusion, my dear friends, let us
piss crosswise so that a Jew will die.

---

3. From the folk song "*Ein Jäger aus Kurpfalz.*"
4. *Immer zu* in German; according to Clarus's account, Woyzeck heard these words in his
head.
5. Cf. Lacroix's words in *Danton's Death* 1.5: "the flies will do it on their hands."
6. Or: "like it always is in the beginning!" [translator's note].

4,12.

Open field.

WOYZECK   On and on! On and on! Shh—music. (*Stretches out on the ground.*) Ha—what, what are you saying? Louder, louder—stab, stab the bitch[7] to death? Stab, stab the bitch to death. Should I? Must I? Do I hear it over there too, is the wind saying it too? Do I hear it on and on—stab her to death, to death.

4,13.

Night.

ANDRES *and* WOYZECK *in a bed.*

WOYZECK   (*Shakes* ANDRES.)   Andres! Andres! I can't sleep—when I close my eyes, everything starts spinning, and I hear the fiddles, on and on, on and on. And then there's a voice from the wall—don't you hear anything?

ANDRES   Oh, yeah—let them dance! God bless us, amen. (*Falls asleep again.*)

WOYZECK   And it floats between my eyes like a knife.

ANDRES   Drink some brandy with a painkiller in it. That'll bring your fever down.

4,14.

Inn.

DRUM MAJOR. WOYZECK. PEOPLE.

DRUM MAJOR   I'm a man! (*Pounds his chest.*) A man, I say. Who wants to start something? If you're not drunk as a lord, stay away from me. I'll shove your nose up your ass. I'll . . . (*To* WOYZECK.) Man, have a drink. A man gotta drink. I wish the world was booze, booze.

WOYZECK   (*Whistles.*)

DRUM MAJOR   You bastard, you want me to pull your tongue out of your throat and wrap it around you? (*They wrestle,* WOYZECK *loses.*) Shall I leave you as much breath as an old woman's fart? Shall I?

(WOYZECK *sits on the bench, exhausted and trembling.*)

DRUM MAJOR   He can whistle till he's blue in the face.[8] Ha!

---

7. *Zickwolfin* in German, a neologism that literally means "she-goat-wolf." It is possible that the word simply denotes Marie's surname (the feminine ending "-in" was commonly added to women's surnames), but more likely it is a brutal epithet of Woyzeck's invention. Two elements of this monologue—Woyzeck hearing a voice ordering him to stab his mistress dead and Woyzeck interrogating this inner voice—correspond with Clarus's report of the historical Woyzeck.

8. Cf. Clarus's quotation from the historical Woyzeck in his medical reports (p. 203 in this volume).

> Oh, brandy, that's my life,
> Oh, brandy gives me courage!

A PERSON   He sure got what was coming to him.
ANOTHER   He's bleeding.
WOYZECK   One thing after another.

4,15.

WOYZECK. *The* JEW.

WOYZECK   The pistol costs too much.

JEW   Well, do you want it or don't you?

WOYZECK   How much is the knife?

JEW   It's good and straight. You want to cut your throat with it? Well, how about it? I'll give it to you as cheap as anybody else; your death'll be cheap, but not for nothing. How about it? You'll have an economical death.

WOYZECK   That can cut more than just bread.

JEW   Two cents.

WOYZECK   There! (*Goes off.*)

JEW   There! Like it was nothing. But it's money! The dog.

4,16.

[MARIE. KARL, *the idiot.* CHILD.]

MARIE (*Leafs through the Bible.*)   "And no guile is found in his mouth"[9] . . . My God, my God! Don't look at me. (*Pages further.*) "And the scribes and Pharisees brought unto him a woman taken in adultery, and set her in the midst . . . And Jesus said unto her, 'Neither do I condemn thee: go, and sin no more.'"[1] (*Clasps her hands together.*) My God! My God! I can't. God, just give me enough strength to pray. (*The* CHILD *snuggles up to her.*) The boy is like a knife in my heart. [Karl! He's sunning himself!]

KARL (*Lies on the ground and tells himself fairy tales on his fingers.*)   This one has a golden crown—he's a king. Tomorrow I'll go get the queen's child.[2] Blood sausage says, come, liver sausage! (*He takes the* CHILD *and is quiet.*)

[MARIE]   Franz hasn't come, not yesterday, not today. It's getting hot in here. (*She opens the window.*) "And stood at his feet weeping, and began to wash his feet with tears, and did wipe them with the hairs of her head, and kissed his feet, and anointed them

---

9. From Isaiah 53:9 and 1 Peter 2:22.
1. From John 8:3 and 8:11.
2. Rumpelstiltskin says this in the fairy tale.

with ointment."[3] (*Beats her breast.*) It's all dead! Savior, Savior, I wish I could anoint your feet.

4,17.

The barracks.

ANDRES. WOYZECK *rummages through his things.*

WOYZECK   This jacket isn't part of the uniform, Andres; you can use it, Andres. The crucifix is my sister's, and the little ring. I've got an icon, too—two hearts and nice gold. It was in my mother's Bible, and it says:

> May pain be my reward,
> Through pain I love my Lord.[4]
> Lord, like Thy body, red and sore,
> So be my heart forevermore.

My mother can only feel the sun shining on her hands now. That doesn't matter.

ANDRES (*Blankly, answers to everything.*)   Yeah.

WOYZECK (*Pulls out a piece of paper.*)   Friedrich Johann Franz Woyzeck, enlisted infantryman in the second regiment, second battalion, fourth company, born . . . Today[5] I'm thirty years, seven months, and twelve days old.

ANDRES   Franz, you better go to the infirmary. You poor guy— drink brandy with a painkiller in it. That'll kill the fever.

WOYZECK   You know, Andres, when the carpenter nails those boards together, nobody knows who'll be laying his head on them.

[End of Büchner's revision.]
[Scenes from the First Draft:]

1,14.

[Street.]

MARIE *with girls in front of the house door.* [GRANDMOTHER. *Then* WOYZECK.]

GIRLS   How bright the sun on Candlemas Day,
> On fields of golden grain.
> As two by two they marched along
> Down the country lane.
> The pipers up in front,

---

3. Luke 7:38.
4. These lines from a Pietistic hymn return in *Lenz* (see p. 89).
5. The original draft adds: "on the Feast of the Annunciation, the 20th of July"; actually held on March 25, the feast celebrates the announcement of the Incarnation to the Virgin Mary.

The fiddlers in a chain.
Their red socks . . .

FIRST CHILD   That's not nice.
SECOND CHILD   What do you want, anyway?
[OTHERS]   Why'd you start it?

Yeah, why?

I can't.

Because!

Who's going to sing?

Why because?

Marie, you sing to us.
MARIE   Come, you little shrimps.
   ([*Children's games:*] *"Ring-around-a-rosy"* and *"King Herod."*)
   Grandmother, tell a story.
GRANDMOTHER   Once upon a time there was a poor child with no
   father and no mother, everything was dead, and no one was left in
   the whole world. Everything was dead, and it went and searched
   day and night. And since nobody was left on the earth, it wanted
   to go up to the heavens, and the moon was looking at it so friendly,
   and when it finally got to the moon, the moon was a piece of rotten wood and then it went to the sun and when it got there, the sun
   was a wilted sunflower and when it got to the stars, they were little
   golden flies stuck up there like the shrike[6] sticks 'em on the black-
   thorn and when it wanted to go back down to the earth, the earth
   was an overturned pot and was all alone and it sat down and
   cried and there it sits to this day, all alone.
WOYZECK[7]   Marie!
MARIE (*Startled.*)   What is it?
WOYZECK   Marie, we have to go. It's time.
MARIE   Where to?
WOYZECK   How do I know?

I,15.

   MARIE *and* WOYZECK.
MARIE   So the town is over there—it's dark.
WOYZECK   Stay here. Come on, sit down.
MARIE   But I have to get back.
WOYZECK   You won't get sore feet.
MARIE   What's gotten into you!
WOYZECK   Do you know how long it's been, Marie?

6. A bird that uses thorns as meat hooks to impale its prey.
7. Translator's emendation; in this draft, Woyzeck is originally named "Louis" and Marie
   is named "Margret."

MARIE   Two years since Pentecost.

WOYZECK   And do you know how long it's going to be?

MARIE   I've got to go, the evening dew is falling.

WOYZECK   Are you freezing, Marie? But you're warm. How hot your lips are!—Hot, the hot breath of a whore—and yet I'd give heaven and earth to kiss them once more. And when you're cold, you don't freeze anymore. The morning dew won't make you freeze.

MARIE   What are you talking about?

WOYZECK   Nothing. (*Silence.*)

MARIE   Look how red the moon is.

WOYZECK   Like a bloody blade.

MARIE   What are you up to? Franz, you're so pale. (*He pulls out the knife.*) Franz—wait! For God's sake—help!

WOYZECK   Take that and that! Can't you die? There! There! Ah— she's still twitching—not yet? Not yet? Still alive? (*Stabs once again.*) Are you dead? Dead! Dead! (*People approach, he runs off.*)

1,16.

Two people.

FIRST PERSON   Wait!

SECOND PERSON   You hear it? Shh! Over there.

FIRST PERSON   Ooh! There! What a sound.

SECOND PERSON   That's the water, it's calling. Nobody has drowned for a long time. Let's go—it's bad to hear things like that.

FIRST PERSON   Ooh! There it is again. Like someone dying.

SECOND PERSON   It's weird. It's so fragrant—some gray fog, and the beetles humming like broken bells. Let's get out of here!

FIRST PERSON   No—it's too clear, too loud. Up this way. Come on.

1,17.

The inn.

[WOYZECK. KATEY. KARL. INNKEEPER. *People.*]

WOYZECK   Dance, all of you, on and on, sweat and stink—he'll get you all in the end. (*Sings.*)

> Our hostess has a pretty maid,
> She's in her garden night and day,
> She sits inside her garden,
> Until the bells have all struck twelve,
> And stares at all the soldiers.[8]

---

8. From the folk song "*Es steht ein Wirtshaus an der Lahn.*"

(*He dances.*) Come on, Katey! Sit down! I'm hot! Hot. (*He takes off his jacket.*) That's the way it is: the devil takes one and lets the other go. Katey, you're hot! Why? Katey, you'll be cold someday, too. Be reasonable. Can't you sing something?

[KATEY]   For Swabian hills I do not yearn,
               And flowing gowns I always spurn,
               For flowing gowns and pointed shoes
               A servant girl should never choose.[9]

[WOYZECK]   No, no shoes—you can go to hell without shoes, too.

[KATEY]   For shame, my love, I'm not your own,
               Just keep your money and sleep alone.

[WOYZECK]   Yes, that's right, I don't want to make myself bloody.

KATEY   But what's that on your hand?

WOYZECK   Who? Me?

KATEY   Red! Blood! (*People gather around.*)

WOYZECK   Blood? Blood?

INNKEEPER   Ooh, blood.

WOYZECK   I guess I must have cut myself, there on my right hand.

INNKEEPER   But how'd it get on your elbow?

WOYZECK   I wiped it off.

INNKEEPER   What, with your right hand on your right elbow? You're talented.

KARL   And then the giant said: I smell, I smell, I smell human flesh. Phew! That stinks already.

WOYZECK   Damn it, what do you want? What's it got to do with you? Get away, or the first one who—damn it! You think I killed someone? Am I a murderer? What are you staring at? Look at yourselves! Out of my way! (*He runs out.*)

1,18.

Children.

FIRST CHILD   Come on! Marie!

SECOND CHILD   What is it?

FIRST CHILD   Don't you know? Everybody's gone out there already. Someone's lying there!

SECOND CHILD   Where?

FIRST CHILD   To the left through the trench, near the red cross.

SECOND CHILD   Let's go, so we can still see something. Otherwise they'll carry her away.

---

9. From the folk song *"Auf dieser Welt hab ich kein Freud."*

1,19.

WOYZECK *alone.*

WOYZECK   The knife? Where's the knife? Here's where I left it. It'll
give me away! Closer, still closer! What kind of a place is this?
What's that I hear? Something's moving. Shh! Over there. Marie?
Ah—Marie! Quiet. Everything's quiet! Why are you so pale,
Marie? Why is that red thread around your neck? Who helped
you earn that necklace, with your sins? They made you black,
black! Now I've made you white. Why does your black hair hang
so wild? Didn't you do your braids today? Something's lying over
there! Cold, wet, still. Got to get away from here. The knife, the
knife—is that it? There! People—over there. (*He runs off.*)

1,20.

WOYZECK *at a pond.*

WOYZECK   Down it goes! (*He throws the knife in.*) It sinks into the
dark water like a stone! The moon is like a bloody blade! Is the
whole world going to give me away? No, it's too far in front—when
people go swimming—(*He goes into the pond and throws it far out.*)
All right, now—but in the summer, when they go diving for shells—
bah, it'll rust. Who'll recognize it? I wish I'd smashed it! Am I still
bloody? I've got to wash myself. There's a spot—and there's another.

1,21.

COURT CLERK. BARBER. DOCTOR. JUDGE.

[CLERK]   A good murder, a real murder, a beautiful murder—as
good a murder as you'd ever want to see. We haven't had one like
this for a long time.

[Optional Scenes]

3,1.

The PROFESSOR's[1] *courtyard.*

STUDENTS *below, the* PROFESSOR *at the attic window.*

[PROFESSOR]   Gentlemen, I am on the roof like David when he saw
Bathsheba,[2] but all I see is underwear on a clothesline in the
garden of the girls' boarding house. Gentlemen, we are dealing

---

1. The Professor and the Doctor are probably the same character in this scene, though it
is possible that Büchner intended them to be separate.
2. Samuel 11:2 describes how David, walking on the roof of the king's house, saw Bathsheba bathing and desired her.

with the important question of the relationship of subject to object. If we take only one of the things in which the organic self-affirmation of the Divine manifests itself to a high degree, and examine its relationship to space, to the earth, to the planetary system—gentlemen, if I throw this cat out of the window, how will this organism relate to the *centrum gravitationis* and to its own instinct? Hey, Woyzeck. (*Shouts.*) Woyzeck!

WOYZECK   Professor, it bites!

PROFESSOR   The fellow holds the beast so tenderly, like it was his grandmother!

WOYZECK   Doctor [*sic*], I've got the shivers.

DOCTOR (*Elated.*)   Say, that's wonderful, Woyzeck! (*Rubs his hands. He takes the cat.*) What's this I see, gentlemen—a new species of rabbit louse, a beautiful species, quite different, deep in the fur. (*He pulls out a magnifying glass.*) Ricinus,[3] gentlemen! (*The cat runs off.*) Gentlemen, that animal has no scientific instinct. Ricinus— the best examples—bring your fur collars. Gentlemen, instead of that you can see something else: take note of this man—for a quarter of a year he hasn't eaten anything but peas. Notice the result— feel how uneven his pulse is. There—and the eyes.

WOYZECK   Doctor, everything's getting black. (*He sits down.*)

DOCTOR   Courage, Woyzeck—just a few more days, and then it'll be all over. Feel him, gentlemen, feel him. (STUDENTS *feel his temples, pulse, and chest.*) Apropos, Woyzeck, wiggle your ears for the gentlemen; I meant to show it to you before. He uses two muscles. Come on, hop to it!

WOYZECK   Oh, Doctor!

DOCTOR   You dog, shall I wiggle them for you, are you going to act like the cat? So, gentlemen, this represents a transition to the donkey, frequently resulting from being brought up by women and from the use of the mother tongue.[4] How much hair has your mother pulled out for a tender memory? It's gotten very thin in the last few days. Yes, the peas, gentlemen.

3,2.

[KARL,] *the idiot. The* CHILD. WOYZECK.

KARL (*Holds the* CHILD *on his lap.*)   He fell in the water, he fell in the water, he fell in the water.[5]

WOYZECK   Son—Christian!

KARL (*Stares at him.*)   He fell in the water.

WOYZECK (*Wants to caress the* CHILD, *who turns away and screams.*)

---

3. Latin term for a parasite.
4. I.e., rather than Latin, the language of German universities at the time.
5. The first line of a children's *Fingerspiel*, or finger-counting game.

My God!

KARL He fell in the water.

WOYZECK Christian, you'll get a hobbyhorse. Da-da! (*The* CHILD *resists. To* KARL.) Here, go buy the boy a hobbyhorse.

KARL (*Stares at him.*)

WOYZECK Hop! Hop! Horsey!

KARL (*Cheers.*) Hop! Hop! Horsey! Horsey! (*Runs off with the* CHILD.)

Synopsis:

CORRESPONDENCES AMONG DRAFTS

PRELIMINARY DRAFTS	REVISION
Scene(s): 2,1.	Scene: 4,1. *Open field.*
2,2.	4,2. *The town.*
1,1; 1,2; 2,3; (2,5).	(4,3. *Carnival booths. Lights. People.*)
	4,4. *Room.*
	4,5. *The* CAPTAIN. WOYZECK.
	4,6. MARIE. DRUM MAJOR.
2,8.	4,7. MARIE. WOYZECK.
2,6.	4,8. WOYZECK. *The* DOCTOR.
2,7.	4,9. CAPTAIN. DOCTOR.
1,4.	4,10. *The guardroom.*
1,5; 2,4.	4,11. *Inn.*
1,6.	4,12. *Open field.*
1,7; 1,8; 1,13.	4,13. *Night.*
(1,10).	4,14. *Inn.*
	4,15. WOYZECK. *The* JEW.
(2,9).	4,16. MARIE. KARL, *the idiot.* CHILD.
	4,17. *The barracks.*
1,14. *Street.*	
1,15. MARIE *and* WOYZECK.	
1,16. *Two people.*	
1,17. *The inn.*	
1,18. *Children.*	
1,19. WOYZECK *alone.*	
1,20. WOYZECK *at a pond.*	
1,21. COURT CLERK. BARBER. DOCTOR. JUDGE.	
3,1. *The* PROFESSOR'*s courtyard.*	
3,2. KARL, *the idiot. The* CHILD. WOYZECK.	

The Drafts

First Draft

1,1. *Booths. People.*

CARNIVAL BARKER (*In front of a booth.*)   Gentlemen! Gentlemen! Look at this creature as God made it: he's nothing, nothing at all. Now see the effect of art: he walks upright, wears coat and pants, carries a sword! Ho! Take a bow! Good boy. Give me a kiss! (*He trumpets.*) The little dummy is musical! Ladies and gentlemen, here is to be seen the astronomical horse and the little cannery-birds—they're favorites of all crowned heads. The presentation will begin! The beginning of the beginning! The commencement of the commencement will start immediately!

SOLDIER   Want to?

MARGRET[6]   All right. It ought to be good. Look at his tassels, and the woman's got pants on!

1,2. *Inside the booth.*

CARNIVAL ANNOUNCER   Show your talent! Show your beastly wisdom! Put human society to shame! Gentlemen, this animal that you see here, with a tail on his body, with his four hooves, is a member of all learned societies, is a professor at our university, with whom the students learn to ride and fight duels. That was simple comprehension! Now think with double *raison*. What do you do when you think with double *raison?* Is there in the learned *société* an ass? (*The horse shakes its head.*) Now you understand double *raison!* That is beastiognomy. Yes, that's no brutish individual, that's a person! A human being, a beastly human being, but still an animal, a *bête*. (*The horse behaves improperly.*) That's right, put *société* to shame. You see, the beast is still nature, unspoiled nature! Take a lesson from him. Go ask the doctor, it's very unhealthy! It is written: man, be natural; you were created from dust, sand, dirt. Do you want to be more than dust, sand, dirt? Observe his power of reason! He can add, but he can't count on his fingers—why is that? He simply can't express himself, explain himself—he's a transformed person! Tell the gentlemen what time it is. Who among the ladies and gentlemen has a watch—a watch?

SERGEANT   A watch! (*Slowly and grandly he pulls a watch out of his pocket.*) There you are, sir. (What a piece! She can stare through seven layers of leather pants!)

---

6. I.e., Marie.

MARGRET   This I've got to see. (*She climbs into the first row. The* SERGEANT *helps her.*)
SERGEANT   —

1,3. MARGRET *alone.*[7]

MARGRET   The other one gave him an order and he had to go. Ha! What a man!

1,4. *Barracks courtyard.*[*]

ANDRES. LOUIS.[8]
ANDRES (*Sings.*)

> Our hostess has a pretty maid,
> She's in her garden night and day,
> She sits inside her garden,
> Until the bells have all struck twelve,
> And stares at all the soldiers.

LOUIS   Hey, Andres, I can't keep still.
ANDRES   Fool!
LOUIS   What do you know about it? So tell me!
ANDRES   Well?
LOUIS   Why do you think I'm here?
ANDRES   'Cause it's nice weather and they're dancing today.
LOUIS   I've got to get out there, got to see it!
ANDRES   What do you want?
LOUIS   To get out there!
ANDRES   You spoilsport, because of that whore?
LOUIS   I've got to get out.

1,5. *Inn.*[*]

The windows are open. People are dancing. On the bench in front of the house LOUIS *looks through the window.*
LOUIS   It's him—with her! Hell! (*He sits down, shivering. He goes to the window again.*) They're really moving! Yeah, roll around on each other! Look at her—on! and on, on and on.
IDIOT   Phew! That stinks!
LOUIS   Yeah, that stinks! She's got red, red cheeks, but why does she stink already? Karl, what's on your mind?
IDIOT   I smell, I smell blood.

7. An asterisk indicates that Büchner crossed out the scene while he was revising the play [translator's note].
8. I.e., Woyzeck.

LOUIS   Blood? Why is everything turning red in front of my eyes?
It's like they were rolling around in a sea of blood, all of them
together! Ha! a red sea!

1,6. *Open field.**

LOUIS   On! and on!—On and on! Shssh, shssh, that's how the fiddles and flutes go. On and on! On and on! What's that talking
down there? There—out of the earth, very softly, something.
What? (*He stoops down.*) Stab! Stab! Stab the Woyzeck woman to
death. Stab, stab the Woyzeck woman to death. It's hissing and
moaning and thundering.

1,7. *A room.**

LOUIS *and* ANDRES.

ANDRES   Hey!
LOUIS   Andres!
ANDRES   (*Mumbles in his sleep.*)
LOUIS   Hey, Andres!
ANDRES   Well, what is it?
LOUIS   I can't keep still, I keep hearing it, the fiddling and the
jumping, on and on! On and on! And then when I shut my eyes,
I see flashes, and there's a big broad knife lying on a table by the
window—it's in a dark alley and an old man is sitting behind the
table. And the knife's always between my eyes.
ANDRES   Go to sleep, fool!

1,8. *Barracks courtyard.*

LOUIS   Didn't you hear anything?
ANDRES   He went past with a friend.
LOUIS   He said something.
ANDRES   How do you know? How shall I say it? Well, he laughed, and
then he said: "What a piece! She's got thighs, and it's all so firm!"
LOUIS (*Very coldly.*)   So that's what he said? What was I dreaming
about last night? Wasn't it about a knife? What foolish dreams we
get.
ANDRES   Where're you going, friend?
LOUIS   To get wine for my officer.—But Andres, she was one in
a million.
ANDRES   Who was?
LOUIS   Never mind. Bye.

1,9. *The* OFFICER. LOUIS.*

LOUIS (*Alone.*)   What did he say? Well, don't count your chickens.

1,10. *An inn.**

BARBER. SERGEANT.

BARBER   Oh daughter, dear daughter,
                    What's got into you?
                    You took up with coachmen
                    And stablemen too!

What is it that God can't do, huh? Undo what's been done, that's
what. Heh heh heh!—But that's the way it is, and that's good. But
just to be on the safe side. (*Sings.*)

                    Booze, that's my life,
                    Booze gives me courage.

And a decent person loves life, and a person who loves life has no
courage, a virtuous person has no courage. Whoever's got courage is a dog.

SERGEANT (*With dignity.*) You're forgetting yourself in the presence of a brave man.

BARBER   I'm not speaking politely, like the French do, and it was
nice of you.—But whoever's got courage is a dog!

SERGEANT   Damn you! You broken shaving basin, you stale soap-
suds! I'll make you drink your piss and swallow your razor!

BARBER   Sir, you're wronging yourself! Was I talking about you, did I
say that you had courage? Sir, leave me alone! I am science. Every
week I get half a florin for my scientific self—don't break me apart
or I'll go hungry. I am a *spinosa pericyclyda*; I have a Latin backbone. I'm a living skeleton, all mankind studies me.—What is man?
Bones! Dust, sand, dirt. What is nature? Dust, sand, dirt. But those
stupid people, those stupid people. Let's be friends. If I had no
courage, there wouldn't be any science. Only nature, no amputa-
tion. What is an arm, flesh, bones, veins? What is dirt? Where will
it be sticking in the dirt? So should I cut my arm off? No, man is
egoistic, but he hits, shoots, stabs. There, now. We must. Friends,
I'm touched. Look, I wish our noses were two bottles and we could
pour them down each other's throats. Oh, how beautiful the world
is! Friend! My friend! The world! (*Moved.*) Look how the sun's coming out of the clouds, like a bedpan being emptied out. (*He cries.*)

1,11. *The inn.*

LOUIS *sits in front of the inn. People go out.* ANDRES.

ANDRES   What are you doing there?

LOUIS   What time is it?

ANDRES   —

LOUIS Isn't it later than that? I thought it would go faster, and I wish it was the day after tomorrow.

ANDRES Why?

LOUIS Then it'd be over.

ANDRES What?

LOUIS Scram.

[ANDRES] Why're you sitting there in front of the door?

LOUIS I'm all right sitting here, and I know it, but lots of people sit in front of a door and they *don't* know it; a lot get carried out the door feet first.

[ANDRES] Come on, let's go!

[LOUIS] I'm all right sitting here, and I'd be even better lying here. If everybody knew what time it is, they'd get undressed and put on a clean shirt and have their coffin measured.

[ANDRES] He's drunk.

LOUIS What's that lying over there? It's flashing. It's always floating between my eyes. Look how it's shining. I got to have it.

1,12. *Open field.*

LOUIS (*Lays the knife in a hole.*) Thou shalt not kill. Stay there! Got to get out of here! (*He runs off quickly.*)

1,13. *Night. Moonlight.*

ANDRES *and* LOUIS *in a bed.*

LOUIS (*Softly.*) Andres!

ANDRES (*Dreams.*) There! Wait!—Yes.

LOUIS Hey, Andres!

ANDRES Well?

LOUIS I can't keep still! Andres.

ANDRES You had a nightmare?

LOUIS Something's lying out there. In the earth. They're always pointing to it. You hear that—and that? How they're knocking inside the walls? One of them just looked in at the window. Don't you hear it? I hear it all day long. On and on. Stab, stab the Woyzeck woman.

ANDRES Lie down, Louis. You better go to the infirmary. Drink some brandy with a painkiller in it; that'll bring the fever down.

[For 1,14 to 1,21: see Reconstruction, pp. 150–54.][9]

---

9. Note to Scene 1,21: after the Clerk's words, this fragment contains the following: "Barber. Tall, haggard, cowardly" [translator's note].

Second Draft

2,1. *Open field. The town in the distance.**

WOYZECK. ANDRES. *They are cutting branches in the bushes.*
ANDRES (*Whistles and sings.*)

> A hunter's life for me,
> A hunter's always free;
> Where I can hunt
> That's where I'll go.
>
> One day a rabbit I did see,
> "Are you a hunter?" he asked me.
> A hunter I used to be,
> But shooting I can't do.

WOYZECK   Yeah, Andres, it really is—this place is haunted. Do you see that shining stripe there across the grass, where the toadstools are growing? That's where heads roll at night; once somebody picked one up, thought it was a hedgehog. Three days and two nights, and he was dead. (*Softly.*) It was the Freemasons, I figured it out.

ANDRES   It's getting dark. You're almost making me scared. (*He sings.*)

WOYZECK (*Grabs him.*)   You hear it, Andres? Do you hear it, it's moving! Next to us, under us. Let's go—the ground's swaying under our feet. The Freemasons! How they're burrowing underground! (*He drags him away.*)

ANDRES   Leave me alone! Are you crazy? Damn it!

WOYZECK   Are you a mole, are your ears full of sand? Don't you hear that terrible noise in the sky? Over the town it's all in flames! Don't look back. Look how it's shooting up, and everything's thundering.

ANDRES   You're scaring me.

WOYZECK   Don't look back. (*They hide in the bushes.*)

ANDRES   Woyzeck, I can't hear anything anymore.

WOYZECK   Quiet, all quiet, like death.

ANDRES   They're drumming. We've got to get back.

2,2. *The town.**

LOUISE.[1] MARGRET *at the window. A military patrol goes by, the* DRUM MAJOR *leading.*

LOUISE   Hey, boy! Tra-ra-ra-ra!

MARGRET   A handsome man!

---

1. I.e., Marie.

LOUISE   Like a tree. (*The* DRUM MAJOR *greets them.*)

MARGRET   Say, what a friendly look you gave him, neighbor—we're not used to that from you.

LOUISE   A soldier is a handsome fellow . . .

MARGRET   Your eyes are still shining!

LOUISE   What's it to you? Why don't you take your eyes to the Jew and have them polished—maybe they'll shine enough to sell as two buttons.

MARGRET   Why, Mrs. Virgin! I'm a decent woman, but you—everybody knows you can stare through seven pairs of leather pants!

LOUISE   Bitch! (*Slams the window shut.*) Come, my boy, shall I sing you something? What do they want from us, anyway? You're only the child of a whore, and you make your mother happy with your bastard face.

> Johnny, hitch up your six horses fleet,
> Go bring them something to eat.
> From oats they will turn,
> From water they'll turn,
> Only cool wine will be fine, hooray!
> Only cool wine will be fine.

> Maiden, now what's to be done?
> You've got no ring, you've a son.
> Oh, why worry my head,
> I'll sing here at your bed:
> Rockabye baby, my baby are you,
> Nobody cares what I do.

(*A knock at the window.*)
Is that you, Franz? Come on in.

WOYZECK   I can't. Have to go to roll call.

LOUISE   Did you cut wood for the major?

WOYZECK   Yes, Louise.

LOUISE   What's the matter with you, Franz? You look so upset.

WOYZECK   Shh! Quiet! I figured it out. The Freemasons! There was a terrible noise in the sky and everything was in flames! I'm on the track of something! Something big!

LOUISE   Fool!

WOYZECK   Don't you think so? Look around! Everything's rigid, hard, dark—something's moving behind it all. Something that we don't understand, that drives us insane, but I figured it out. I've got to go!

LOUISE   And your child?

WOYZECK   Oh, the boy! Tonight—at the carnival. I saved something up again. (*Goes off.*)

LOUISE   That man'll go crazy. He frightened me. It's eerie—I don't
like to stay around when it gets dark, I think I'm going blind, I
catch it from him. Usually there's a light shining in. Oh, us poor
people. (*She sings.*)

> Rockabye baby, on the treetop,
> When the wind blows, your cradle will rock.

(*She goes off.*)

2,3. *Open square. Booths. Lights.*

OLD MAN   DANCING CHILD

> How long we live, just time will tell,
> We all have got to die,
> We know that very well!

———— Hey! Whee! Poor man, old man! Poor child! Young child!
Cares and fairs! Hey, Louise, shall I carry you? . . . Beautiful
world!

CARNIVAL BARKER (*In front of a booth.*)   Ladies and gentlemen,
here is to be seen the astronomical horse and the little cannery-
birds—they're favorites of all potentates of Europe and members
of all learned societies. They'll tell you everything: how old you
are, how many children you have, what kind of illnesses. He
shoots a pistol, stands on one leg. It's all a matter of upbringing;
he has merely a beastly reason, or rather a very reasonable
beastliness—he's no brutish individual like a lot of people, present company excepted. Enter! The presentation will begin. The
commencement of the beginning will start immediately.
   Observe the progress of civilization. Everything progresses—a
horse, a monkey, a cannery-bird! The monkey is already a
soldier—that's not much, it's the lowest level of the human race!
———— Are you an atheist, too? I'm a dogmatic atheist.
———— Is it grotesque? I'm a friend of the grotesque. You see that?
What a grotesque effect.
———— I'm a dogmatic atheist. Grotesque!

2,4. APPRENTICES.*

[AN APPRENTICE]   Brother! Forget-me-not! Friendship! I could cry a
rain barrel full. Sadness! If I only had another one! I think it
stinks, it smells. Why is this world so beautiful? If I close one eye
and look out over my nose, then everything's red as a rose. Brandy,
that's my life.

ANOTHER   He'll see everything red as a rose when a cross is looking over his nose.

[AN APPRENTICE]   It's all out of order! Why did the street-lamp
cleaner forget to sweep out my eyes—it's all dark. May God go to
the devil! I'm lying in my own way and have to jump over myself.
What happened to my shadow? There's no safety in this stable
anymore. Somebody shine the moon between my legs to see if
I've still got my shadow.

> Chewing up the green, green grass,
> Chewing up the green, green grass
> Till all the grass was go-o-ne.

Shooting star, I have to blow the noses of all the stars.

[ANOTHER]   Don't make a hole in nature.

[AN APPRENTICE]   Why did God create man? That has its reasons:
what would the farmer, the shoemaker, the tailor do, if he couldn't
make shoes or pants for people? Why did God give man a feeling
of shame? So that the tailor can exist. Yes! Yes! So there! That's
why! For that reason! Therefore! Or, on the other hand, if He
hadn't done it—but in that we see His wisdom, that the animals
He created would be respected by man, because mankind would
otherwise have eaten up the animals. This infant, this weak,
helpless creature, this infant.—Now let's piss crosswise so that a
Jew will die.

> Brandy, that's my life,
> Brandy gives me courage.

2,5. SERGEANT. DRUM MAJOR.

SERGEANT   Hold it! Over there. Look at her! What a piece!

DRUM MAJOR   Damn! Good enough for the propagation of cavalry
regiments and the breeding of drum majors!

SERGEANT   Look how she holds her head—you'd think that black
hair would pull her down like a weight. And those eyes, black . . .

DRUM MAJOR   It's like looking down a well or a chimney. Come on,
after her!

LOUISE   Those lights!

FRANZ   Yeah, like a big black cat with fiery eyes. Hey, what a
night!

2,6. WOYZECK. DOCTOR.*

DOCTOR   What's this I saw, Woyzeck? A man of his word? You! You!
You?

WOYZECK   What is it, Doctor?

DOCTOR   I saw it, Woyzeck! You pissed on the street like a dog. For that I give you three cents and board every day? The world's getting bad, very bad, bad, I say. Oh! Woyzeck, that's bad.

WOYZECK   But Doctor, if you can't help it?

DOCTOR   Can't help it, can't help it. Superstition, horrible superstition! Haven't I proved that the *musculus constrictor vesicae* is subject to the will? Woyzeck, man is free, in man individuality is exalted to freedom.—Couldn't hold it in! That's cheating, Woyzeck. Did you eat your peas already? Nothing but peas, nothing but legumes, *cruciferae*—remember that. Then next week we'll start on mutton. Don't you have to go to the toilet? Go ahead. I'm telling you to. I'm revolutionizing science. A revolution! According to yesterday's report: ten per cent urea, and ammonium chloride . . . But I saw how you pissed on the wall! I was just holding my head outside . . . Did you catch some frogs for me? Got any fish eggs? No fresh-water polyps? No hydra, *vestillae, cristatellae*? Don't bump into my microscope. I've just got the left molar of a protozoon under it. I'll blow them sky-high, all of them together. Woyzeck, no spiders' eggs, no toads? But pissing on the wall! I saw it. (*Starts kicking him.*) No, Woyzeck, I'm not getting angry; anger is unhealthy, unscientific. I am calm, perfectly calm, and I'm telling you this in all cold-bloodedness. Who on earth would get excited about a human being! A human being! Now if it were a Proteus lizard that were dying! But you shouldn't have pissed on the wall.

WOYZECK   Yes, nature, Doctor, when nature has run out.

DOCTOR   What's that when nature has run out?

WOYZECK   When nature has run out, that's when nature has run out! When the world gets so dark that you have to feel your way around it with your hands, and you think it'll dissolve like spiderwebs! That's when something is and yet isn't. When everything is dark and there's only a red glow in the west, like from a furnace. When . . . (*Paces up and down in the room.*)

DOCTOR   Man, you're tapping around with your feet like a spider.

WOYZECK (*Stands rigidly.*)   Have you seen the rings of toadstools on the ground yet? Long lines, crooked circles, figures—that's where it is! There! If only someone could read that. When the sun's standing high and bright at noon and the world seems to be going up in flames. Don't you hear anything? When the world speaks, you see, the long lines, it's like someone's talking with a terrible voice.

DOCTOR   Woyzeck! You're going to the insane asylum. You've got a beautiful obsession, a marvelous *alienatio mentis*. Look at me—now what are you supposed to do? Eat your peas, then eat your mutton, polish your rifle; you know all that. And then the obsessions. That's good, Woyzeck! You'll get a raise of one cent a week. My theory, my new theory—brave, eternally youthful. Woyzeck, I'll be immortal. Show me your pulse! I have to feel your pulse mornings and evenings.

2,7. *Street.*

CAPTAIN. DOCTOR. *The* CAPTAIN *comes panting down the street, stops, pants, looks around.*

CAPTAIN   Where to so fast, most honorable Mr. Coffin Nail?

DOCTOR   Where to so slowly, most honorable Mr. Drillprick?

CAPTAIN   Take your time, honorable tombstone.

DOCTOR   I don't waste my time like you, honorable . . .

CAPTAIN   Don't run like that, Doctor—a good man doesn't go so fast, sir, a good man. (*Pants.*) A good man. You'll run yourself to death that way. You're really frightening me.

DOCTOR   I'm in a hurry, Captain, I'm in a hurry.

CAPTAIN   Mr. Coffin Nail, you're wearing out your little legs on the pavement. Don't ride off in the air on your cane.

DOCTOR   She'll be dead in four weeks. She's in her seventh month— I've had twenty patients like that already. In four weeks—you can count on that.

CAPTAIN   Doctor, don't frighten me—people have been known to die of fright, of pure, sheer fright!

DOCTOR   In four weeks, the stupid beast. She'll be an interesting specimen. I'm telling you . . .

CAPTAIN   May you get struck by lightning! I'll hold you by the wing, I won't let you go. Dammit, four weeks? Doctor, coffin nail, shroud, I'll [live] as long as I exist—four weeks—and the people with their hats in their hands, but they'll say, he was a good man, a good man.

DOCTOR   Say, good morning, Captain. (*Swinging his hat and cane.*) Cock-a-doodle-doo! My pleasure! My pleasure! (*Holds out his hat.*) What's this, Captain? That's brain-less. Ha?

CAPTAIN   (*Makes a crease.*)   What's this, Doctor? That's an increase! Ha-ha-ha! No harm meant. I'm a good man—but I can when I want to, Doctor, ha-ha-ha, when I want to. [WOYZECK *comes running down the street.*] Hey, Woyzeck, why are you running past me like that? Stay here, Woyzeck. You're running around like an open razor blade—you might cut someone! You're running like you had to shave a regiment of Cossacks[2] and would be hanged by the last hair. But about those long beards—what was I going to say? Woyzeck—those long beards . . .

---

2. *Kosack* in German; an almost illegible smudge that has also been deciphered as *Kastrirte* (eunuchs).

DOCTOR   A long beard on the chin—Pliny already speaks of it. Soldiers should be made to give them up.[3]

CAPTAIN (*Continues.*)   Hey? What about those long beards? Say, Woyzeck, haven't you found a hair from a beard in your soup bowl yet? Hey? You understand of course, a human hair, from the beard of an engineer, a sergeant, a—a drum major? Hey, Woyzeck? But you've got a decent wife. Not like others.

WOYZECK   Yes, sir! What are you trying to say, Cap'n?

CAPTAIN   Look at the face he's making! Now, it doesn't necessarily have to be in the soup, but if you hurry around the corner, you might find one on a pair of lips—a pair of lips, Woyzeck. I know what love is, too, Woyzeck. Say! You're as white as chalk!

WOYZECK   Cap'n, I'm just a poor devil—and that's all I have in the world. Cap'n, if you're joking . . .

CAPTAIN   Joking? Me? Who do you think you are?

DOCTOR   Your pulse, Woyzeck, your pulse—short, hard, skipping, irregular.

WOYZECK   Cap'n, the earth is hot as hell—for me it's ice cold, ice cold—hell is cold, I'll bet. It can't be! God! God! It can't be!

CAPTAIN   Listen, fellow, how'd you like to be shot, how'd you like to have a couple of bullets in your head? You're looking daggers at me, but I only mean well, because you're a good man, Woyzeck, a good man.

DOCTOR   Facial muscles rigid, tense, occasionally twitching. Posture tense.

WOYZECK   I'm going. A lot is possible. A human being! A lot is possible. The weather's nice, Cap'n. Look: such a beautiful, hard, gray sky—you'd almost feel like pounding a block of wood into it and hanging yourself on it, only because of the hyphen between yes and no—yes and no. Cap'n, yes and no? Is no to blame for yes, or yes for no? I'll have to think about that. (*Goes off with long strides, first slowly, then ever faster.*)

DOCTOR (*Races after him.*)   A phenomenon, Woyzeck! A raise!

CAPTAIN   These people make me dizzy. Look at them go—that tall rascal takes off like the shadow before a spider, and the short one—he's trotting along. The tall one is lightning and the short one is thunder. Ha-ha! After them. I don't like that! A good man loves life, a good man has no courage! A scoundrel has courage! I just went to war to strengthen my love for life . . . Grotesque! Grotesque!

---

3. A confusion between the Roman writer Pliny and the Greek historian Plutarch, the latter of whom describes how Alexander the Great compelled his soldiers to shave.

2,8. WOYZECK. LOUISE.*

LOUISE Hello, Franz.

FRANZ (*Looking at her.*) Oh, it's you! Well, well! No, I don't see anything, I should be able to see it! Louise, you're beautiful!

LOUISE Why are you looking so strange, Franz? I'm scared.

FRANZ What a nice street—you can get corns walking on it. But it's good to stand on the street, and good to be in society.

LOUISE Society?

FRANZ Lots of people go through the streets, don't they? And you can talk to anyone you want; that's none of my business! Was he standing here like this? Like this? Close to you like this? I wish I'd been him.

LOUISE What "he"? I can't tell anybody to stay off the streets or leave their mouths at home when they go past.

FRANZ Or their lips at home. That'd be a shame—they're so beautiful. But wasps like to sit on them.

LOUISE And what kind of wasp stung you? You look as crazy as a cow chased by hornets.

FRANZ Whore! (*Goes after her.*)

LOUISE Don't you touch me, Franz! I'd rather have a knife in my body than your hand on mine. When I was ten years old, my father didn't dare touch me when I looked at him.

FRANZ Woman!—No, it should show on you! Everyone's an abyss—you get dizzy when you look down into it. It could be! She looks like Innocence herself. Now, Innocence, you have a mark on you. Do I know it? Do I know it? Who can tell?

2,9. LOUISE *alone. Prayer.*

LOUISE And no guile is found in his mouth. My God!

Third Draft

[See "Optional Scenes" 3,1 and 3,2 on pp. 154–56.]

Fourth Draft

[See Scenes 4,1–17 of the Reconstruction.]

I. C. WOYCECK.

geboren in Leipzig Aⁿᵒ 1780.

Portrait of Johann Christian Woyzeck, 1824.

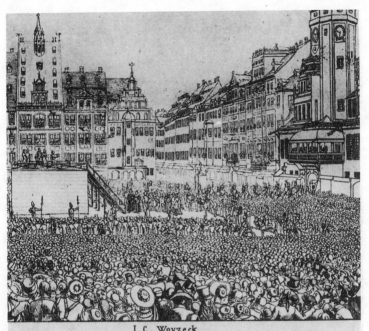

I. C. Woyzeck.
Geht seinem Tode als reuevoller Christ entgegen, auf dem Marktplatze zu Leipzig, den 27 August 1824.

The execution of Woyzeck in Leipzig on August 27, 1824. Lithograph by C. G. H. Geissler.

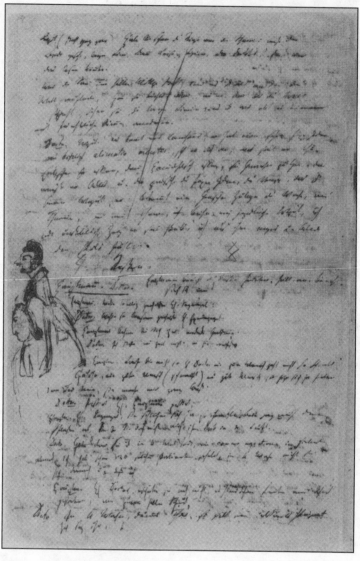

Manuscript page from *Woyzeck*.

Introduction to *On Cranial Nerves*

Historical Background

In 1836 Büchner completed his dissertation, a study of the nervous system of the barbel fish. He hoped to obtain a teaching position at the University of Zurich, but before he could be awarded the job, he had to deliver a "trial lecture" (*Probevorlesung*) before assembled faculty. Largely a technical discussion of the findings of his dissertation, the trial lecture, titled *On Cranial Nerves* (*Über Schädelnerven*), nevertheless opens with a provocative philosophical introduction. This overture, which develops motifs found throughout Büchner's artistic work, has an importance that goes beyond nineteenth-century neurology.

At its heart is a struggle between two conflicting notions of science—and indeed of the universe. The first, which Büchner dubs the "teleological" view, regarded the parts of the natural world as entities directed toward particular ends. This view tended to separate nature into discrete elements, which were then understood in terms of the separate functions they perform. Commonly associated with British and French empiricism, the method was challenged in the early nineteenth century by a number of German thinkers who stressed the organic wholeness of nature. This opposing conception, variously held by Goethe, Schelling, and Hegel, among others, held that teleological science mangled and misunderstood the universe by atomizing it and forcing it to conform to its mechanistic explanations. Often dubbed *Naturphilosophie*, the German approach argued that empirical scientific study ought to be integrated into a broader vision of nature as a seamless web of connections and an end in itself. This holistic and even mystical conception of nature Büchner dubs the "philosophical," and it is clearly the one he favors in the lecture. It was also the one favored at the University of Zurich, where one of the most prominent philosophical scientists of the age, Lorenz Oken, attended Büchner's trial lecture. Oken was sufficiently impressed that, after Büchner's appointment, he recommended that his own son take a course with the young academic.

Manuscript and Publication

Part of this text appeared in the 1850 edition of Büchner's work edited by Georg's brother Ludwig, and the rest exists in manuscript form.

INTRODUCTION TO *ON CRANIAL NERVES*[†]

Gentlemen!

In the field of the physiological and anatomical sciences we encounter two contradictory fundamental assumptions, which even have a national character in that one predominates in England and France, the other in Germany. The first looks at all phenomena of organic life from a *teleological* standpoint; it finds the solution to the riddle in the purpose of the effect, in the functional usefulness of an organ. It understands the individual only as something that achieves a purpose beyond itself, and only in its attempt to assert itself—partly as an individual, partly as a species—in the outside world. For those who hold this view, every organism is a complex machine provided with the artificial means to preserve itself, up to a point. The unveiling of the most beautiful and pure forms in man, the perfection of the noblest organs, in which the spirit seems almost to break through matter and to move behind the thinnest veil: all of this is for them merely the maximization of a machine. They make the skull an artificial vault with buttresses to protect its occupant, the brain,—cheeks and lips a chewing- and respiration-apparatus,—the eyes a complex lens,—the eyelids and eyelashes its curtains;—and tears are only water-drops that keep it moist. It is an enormous leap from this to the enthusiasm with which Lavater[1] counts himself lucky that he may speak of something so godly as lips.

The teleological method moves in an eternal circle in which it takes the effects of organs to be their purposes. It says, for example: if the eye is to perform its function, then the cornea must be kept moist, and to that end a tear gland is necessary. The tear gland therefore exists to keep the eye moist, and in this way the manner of this organ is explained; there is nothing more to ask.[2] The opposing view argues against this: the tear-gland is not there to moisten the eye, but rather the eye becomes moist because a tear gland is there, or, to give another example, we do not have hands so that we

---

[†] Translated by Matthew Wilson Smith.
1. Johann Caspar Lavater (1741–1801), Swiss pastor, poet, mystic, and physiognomist; author of *Physiognomische Fragmente* (*Physiognomical Fragments*, 1775–78), an influential attempt to understand psychological character through facial features.
2. Cf. the First Apprentice's speech at the end of *Woyzeck* 4,11 (p. 147).

can grip things, but rather we grip things because we have hands. The *greatest possible purposiveness* is the single law of the teleological method; but then one naturally asks about the purpose of this purpose and so this method, too, moves with every question into a *progressus ad infinitum*.[3]

Nature does not act according to purposes, it does not exhaust itself in an unending chain of purposes, each determined by another; rather it is immediately *self-sufficient* in all its manifestations. All that is, is for its own sake. To seek the law of this Being is the aim of the anti-teleological view, a view I will call the *philosophical*. Everything that is for *the former* a purpose, is for *the latter* an effect. At the point where the teleological school contents itself with its answer, the question begins for the philosophical. This question, which speaks to us at every point, can find its solution only in a fundamental law that applies to the entire organization, and so for the philosophical method the complete bodily existence of the individual is not devoted to its own preservation, but rather becomes the manifestation of a primordial law, a law of beauty, which produces the highest and purest forms from the simplest plans and outlines. According to this view, everything, form and matter, is bound by this law. All functions are its effects; they are not determined by purposes beyond themselves, and their so-called purposive interaction and cooperation is nothing more than a necessary harmony in the expressions of that same law, the effects of which of course do not negate one another.

The search for such a law has naturally led to two wellsprings by which the enthusiasm for absolute knowledge has forever intoxicated itself: the vision of the mystic and the dogmatism of the rational philosopher. Until now it has proven impossible to build a bridge between the latter and natural life, as we perceive it through immediate experience. *A priori* philosophy[4] still sits in a desolate desert; there is a great distance between it and fresh green life, and it is a real question whether it can traverse this distance. For all its ingenious attempts to advance, it has had to resign itself to the fact that the point of all its striving has not been the attainment of its goal but simply striving itself.

While they achieved absolutely nothing satisfactory, the thrust of these efforts was nevertheless enough to transform the study of nature. Even if no one had found the wellspring, still in many places

3. Progression without end (Latin). "Purposiveness": *Zweckmäßigkeit* in German, a key term in Kant's *Critique of Judgment* (*Kritik der Urteilskraft*, 1790).
4. The philosophical practice of reasoning from principles independent of experience. Büchner is primarily thinking here of Descartes and his heirs. Büchner's scorn for the aridity of this method is also evident in *Leonce and Lena* 1.2 and the letter to Wilhelm Büchner of September 2, 1836.

one heard the stream roaring deep below, and at some points the water burst forth, fresh and clear. In particular, botany and zoology, physiology and comparative anatomy enjoyed significant progress. From an immense mass of material, accumulated through the hard labor of centuries and scarcely even ordered into a catalogue, simple, natural groups formed; a tangle of strange forms with the most exotic names resolved themselves into beautiful symmetry; a mass of things that previously weighed down the memory as discrete, widely separated facts, came together, developed divergently, or placed themselves in antithetical relations. Even if no one has grasped the whole, coherent pieces have still come to light and the eye that tires in the face of innumerable facts rests with pleasure on such beautiful points as the metamorphosis of the plant out of the leaf, the derivation of the skeleton from the vertebra; the metamorphosis, indeed the metempsychosis of the foetus during gestation; Oken's idea of representation in the classification of the animal kingdom,[5] etc. In comparative anatomy everything was striving toward a certain unity, toward the derivation of all forms from the simplest primitive type. Thus the meaning of the structure of the vegetative nervous system for the development of the skeleton was soon discovered; only with regard to the brain has no such happy outcome emerged until now. Once Oken stated that the skull is a spinal column,[6] it necessarily followed that the brain is a metamorphosed spinal cord, and that the nerves of the brain are spinal nerves. But how this might actually be proven has remained until now a difficult riddle. How can brain mass be traced back to the simple form of the spinal cord? How can one compare the nerves of the brain, so tangled in their origin and course, with the spinal nerves, which arise so uniformly from their double row of roots along the spinal cord and which altogether run such a simple and regular course? And how, finally, to demonstrate the relationship of the cranial nerves to the cranial vertebrae? Several answers have been ventured to this question. Carus[7] devoted particular pains to it.

---

5. Lorenz Oken (1779–1851), prominent anatomist and proponent of *Naturphilosophie*, argued that all zoology, culminating in humanity, is a manifestation of God and that each of the levels of the animal kingdom mirrors the senses and attributes of the human being. "Metempsychosis": the transmigration of the soul after death from one body to another.
6. The theory that the skull was an extension of the spinal column was advanced by both Oken and Goethe.
7. Carl Gustav Carus (1789–1869), a prominent physiologist, pioneering psychologist, and proponent of *Naturphilosophie*.

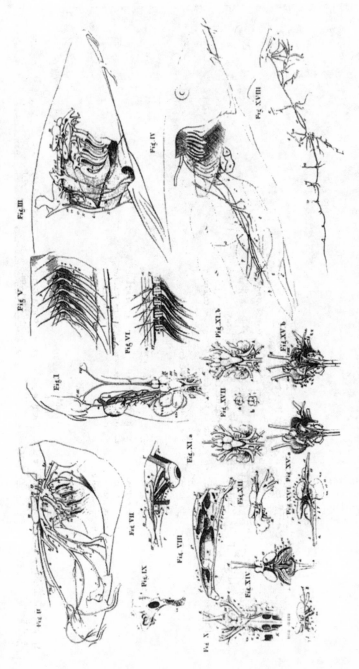

Büchner's illustration of the nervous system of the barbel fish, from his dissertation.

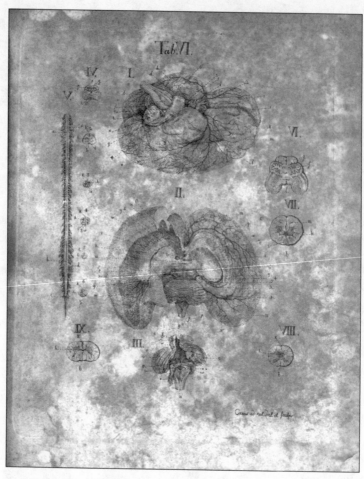

Illustration of the brain and spinal cord, from the appendix of Carl Gustav Carus, *Versuch einer Darstellung des Nervensystems* (Leipzig: Breitkopf und Härtel, 1814). Büchner consulted this text for his own research into the nervous system.

CONTEXTS

Selected Letters[†]

To His Parents

Strassburg, [after December 4] 1831

[. . .][1] When the rumor spread that Ramorino would pass through Strassburg, the students immediately organized a march in his direction with a black flag. Finally we heard the news that Ramorino[2] would arrive during the afternoon with Generals Schneider and Langermann. We immediately gathered in the academy, but as we attempted to march through the gate, the officer whom the government had ordered not to let us pass with our flag stationed the armed watch across our path. But we forced our way through, and three to four hundred of us assembled at the great bridge over the Rhine. The National Guard joined us. Finally Ramorino appeared, accompanied by a number of cavalry; a student makes a speech, which he answers, so does a soldier of the National Guard. The Guard surrounds his coach and pulls it, we join the head of the parade with our flag, a large musical choir precedes us. We march into town like this, accompanied by a huge crowd singing the Marseillaise and the Carmagnole;[3] everywhere the cry resounds: "Vive la liberté! Vive Ramorino! A bas les ministres! A bas le juste milieu!"[4] The city is illuminated, women wave their kerchiefs at their windows, and Ramorino is borne in triumph to the inn, where our flagbearer presents him the flag with the wish that this flag of mourning would soon be transformed into Poland's flag of freedom. Then Ramorino appears on the balcony, thanks the crowd, it cries "Vivat!"—and the comedy is complete. [. . .]

To His Parents

Strassburg, April 5, 1833

Today I received your letter with the news from Frankfurt.[5] My opinion is this: if anything can help in these times, it is *violence.*

[†] Translated by Henry J. Schmidt.

1. Deletions date from Ludwig Büchner's original edition of his brother's letters.

2. Girolamo Ramorino (1792–1849), a former Napoleonic officer and military adventurer who aided Polish freedom fighters in their failed 1830 uprising against Russian occupation [*Editor*].

3. French revolutionary songs [*Editor*].

4. "Long live liberty! Long live Ramorino! Down with the ministers! Down with *le juste milieu!*" "*Le juste milieu,*" or "middle way," was a moderate political philosophy advocated by King Louis Philippe, who ruled France from 1830 to 1848 [*Editor*].

5. On April 3, 1833, armed students stormed the main guardhouse in Frankfurt in an action known as the "*Frankfurter Wachensturm,*" "Storming of the Frankfurt Guardhouse." Their immediate intent was to free political prisoners and their broader intent was to spark a pan-German revolution. The uprising was quickly quelled by soldiers [*Editor*].

We know what to expect from our princes. All they have granted us has been forced from them by necessity. And even their concessions were thrown at our feet like a favor we had begged for, like a wretched child's toy, to make that eternal monkey, the German folk, forget its too tightly wrapped swaddling clothes. Only a German could indulge in the absurdity of playing soldier with a tin rifle and a wooden sword. Our legislatures are a satire against good sense; we could continue like this for another century, and the people would still end up paying more for their representatives' beautiful speeches than did the Roman emperor who gave his court poet twenty thousand florins for two broken verses. Young people are accused of using violence. But aren't we in an eternal state of violence? Because we were born and raised in a prison, we no longer realize that we're trapped in a hole with fettered hands and feet and with gags in our mouths. What do you call a *lawful state*? A law that transforms the great masses of citizens into toiling cattle in order to satisfy the unnatural needs of an unimportant and decadent minority? Supported by raw military might and by the stupid conniving of its agents, this law is *eternal, brute force*, insulting justice and good sense, and I will fight *tooth and nail* against it wherever I can. If I do not take part in whatever has happened or might happen, I do so neither out of disapproval nor out of fear, but only because at the present time I regard any revolutionary movement as a futile undertaking, and I do not share the delusion of those who see in the Germans a people ready to fight for its rights. This foolish idea led to the events in Frankfurt, and the error was dearly paid for. Error is no sin, incidentally, and the indifference of the Germans really thwarts every plan. I deeply pity the unfortunate ones. Might any of my friends have been involved in the incident? [. . .]

To His Parents

Strassburg, June 1833

[. . .] I shall always act according to my principles, but I have recently learned that only the essential needs of the masses can bring about change, that all activity and shouting by *individuals* is vain folly. They write but are not read; they cry out but are not heard; they act but are not helped.—You can imagine that I won't become involved in clandestine politics and revolutionary children's pranks in Giessen.

To August Stöber[6]

Darmstadt, December 9, 1833

*   *   *

I'm throwing myself with all my might into philosophy, the technical language is atrocious, for human affairs I think one should find human expressions; but that doesn't bother me, I laugh about my folly and tell myself that basically I'm doing nothing but cracking hollow nuts. But one has to choose an ass to ride under the sun, and so in God's name I'm saddling mine up; I'm not worried about fodder, there won't be a shortage of thistleheads, as long as the book printing business thrives. Farewell, good fellow. Greet our friends from me, then it will happen twice, for I've also asked Boeckel[7] to do it.

The political situation could drive me insane. The poor people patiently draw the cart upon which the princes and the liberals play their comedy of apes. Every night I pray to the hangman's rope and to the lampposts.

*   *   *

To His Parents

Giessen, February 1834

[. . .] *I scorn no one*, least of all for his intellect or his education, for it lies in no one's power not to become an idiot or a criminal, because in similar circumstances we would all be equal and because the circumstances lie outside ourselves. *Intellect* is in fact only a very small part of our mental self, and education is only an incidental form of it. Whoever accuses me of such scorn maintains that I would kick a man because he wears a shabby coat. This kind of brutality, which one would never be considered capable of in the physical sense, is here transposed into the sphere of the mind, where it is all the more base. I can call someone an idiot without *scorning* him for that; idiocy belongs to the general characteristics of human nature. I can't change their character, but no one can keep me from calling everything that exists by its rightful name or from avoiding whatever I don't like. To offend someone is cruel, but to seek him out or avoid him is up to me. *That* explains my behavior toward old friends; I offended no one and spared myself much boredom. If they call me arrogant when I show a dislike for their entertainments or occupations, that's unjust; I would never think of reproaching anyone else for this reason. People call me a *scoffer*. That's true, I often laugh; but I do not laugh *about* a human being

6. A close friend of Büchner's in Strassburg [*Editor*].
7. Eugen Boeckel, a close friend of Büchner's [*Editor*].

but *because* he is a human being, which he cannot help, and I thereby laugh about myself, for I share his fate. People call that ridicule; they do not tolerate it if one acts like a fool and talks to them familiarly. They are arrogant scorners and scoffers because they search for folly only *outside themselves*. I have in truth another kind of ridicule, but its origin is not contempt but hatred. Hatred is as acceptable as love, and I direct my hate in fullest measure against those *who scorn others*. There is a great number of them, endowed with an absurd superficiality called education or with that dead stuff, learning, who sacrifice the great masses of their fellow men to their scornful egotism. Aristocratic elitism is the most despicable contempt for the holy spirit in human nature. Against this contempt I turn its own weapons: arrogance against arrogance, ridicule against ridicule.—You had better consult my shoeshine-boy about me: my arrogance and contempt of those lacking intelligence or education would find their best subject there. I beg you, ask him sometime . . . I assume you don't consider me capable of the absurdity of condescension. I still hope that I have looked more often with pity at suffering, oppressed beings than I have said bitter words to cold, aristocratic hearts. [. . .]

To Wilhelmine Jaeglé[8]

[Giessen, around March 10, 1834]

[. . .] The first bright moment in a week. Incessant headaches and fever, barely a few hours of inadequate rest. I don't get to bed before two A.M., and then constant sudden awakenings, a sea of thoughts that consume my senses. My silence torments you as it does me, but I couldn't control myself. Dear, dear heart, do you forgive me? I've just come in from outside. A single, sustained tone from a thousand larks' throats resounds through the sultry summer air, heavy clouds wander over the earth, the deep roar of the forest sounds like their melodious footsteps. The spring air dissolved my paralysis. I was afraid of myself. The feeling of having died was always around me. Everyone had a Hippocratic face,[9] with glazed eyes and waxen cheeks, and when the whole machine began to drone, the limbs twitched, the voice grated, and I heard the organ's song warbling endlessly and saw the little cylinders and gears jumping and turning in the organ-box—I cursed the concert, the instrument, the melody and—oh, we poor wailing musicians, is our groaning on the rack only meant to pierce through the clouds, resounding higher and higher, and finally to die away as a melodic breath in heavenly ears?[1] Are we caged in the blazing belly of Peril-

---

8. Büchner's fiancée, nicknamed "Minna" [*Editor*].
9. *Fascies hippocratica* in Latin; the face of one about to die [*Editor*].
1. Cf. Valerio's comments about humans and automatons in *Leonce and Lena* 3.3: "it's highly probable that I'm merely being *made* to speak, and it's actually nothing but cylinders and air hoses that are saying all this" [*Editor*].

lus's bull[2] as sacrificial victims, whose death-cries sound like the ecstatic shouts of the divine animal being consumed by the flames? I'm not blaspheming. But human beings blaspheme. Yet I'm being punished, I'm afraid of my own voice—and of my mirror. I could have sat for a portrait by Herr Callot-Hoffmann,[3] right, my dear? For modelling I could have gotten travel money. I do believe I'm starting to become interesting.

The vacation begins two weeks from tomorrow; if I'm refused permission, I'll go secretly, I owe it to myself to put an end to an intolerable situation. My mental faculties are completely worn out. To work is impossible; I'm overcome by gloomy brooding, which hardly allows me a single bright thought. Everything eats away within me; if only I had an outlet for my inner self, but I have no scream for my pain, no shout for my joy, no harmony for my bliss. This inability to speak is my perdition. I've told you a thousand times: don't read my letters— cold, dull words! If only I could pour one full tone over you—I'm dragging you instead into my desolate aberrations. Now you're sitting in a dark room in tears, soon I'll join you. For two weeks your portrait has been constantly before me, I see you in every dream. Your shadow floats always before me, like a flash of light when one has looked into the sun. I'm thirsting for a blissful feeling—I'll have that soon, soon with you.

To Wilhelmine Jaeglé

[Giessen, after March 10, 1834]

There's no mountain here with an open view. Hill after hill and broad valleys, everywhere a hollow mediocrity; I can't get used to this landscape, and the city is abominable. Spring is here, I can always replace your sprig of violets, it's immortal like the Lama. Dear child, what's the good city of Strassburg doing? All sorts of things are happening there, and you don't say a word. Je baise les petites mains, en goûtant les souvenirs doux de Strasbourg.[4]

"Prouve-moi que tu m'aimes encore beaucoup en me donnant bientôt des nouvelles."[5] And I kept you waiting! Every moment for the last few days I pick up my pen, but I couldn't possibly write a single word. I studied the history of the Revolution. I felt as if I were crushed under the terrible fatalism of history. I find in human nature a horrifying sameness, in the human condition an inescapable force, granted to all and to no one. The individual merely foam

---

2. A bronze bull sculpted by Perillus in which a person would be locked and roasted alive; the victim's screams would issue forth as the roaring of the bull [Editor].
3. E. T. A. Hoffmann wrote a collection of fantastical tales inspired by the engravings of Jacques Callot [Editor].
4. I kiss your little hands and taste sweet memories of Strassburg (French) [Editor].
5. Prove to me that you still love me very much by sending me news soon (French). Possibly a line from an earlier letter from Jaeglé to Büchner [Editor].

on the waves, greatness sheer chance, the mastery of genius a puppet play, a ludicrous struggle against an iron law: to recognize it is
our utmost achievement, to control it is impossible. I no longer
intend to bow down before the parade horses and pillars of history.
I accustomed myself to the sight of blood. But I am no guillotine
blade. The word *must* is one of the curses with which man has been
baptized. The dictum, "It must needs be that offenses come; but
woe to that man by whom the offense cometh"[6]—is terrifying.
What is it within us that lies, murders, steals? I no longer care to
pursue the thought.[7] If only I could lay this cold and martyred
heart on your breast! B.[8] will have reassured you about my condition, I wrote him. I curse my health. I was ablaze, fever covered me
with kisses and embraced me like a lover's arm. Darkness billowed
over me, my heart swelled in infinite longing, stars pierced through
the gloom, and hands and lips bent down. And now? And what else?
I don't even have the ecstasy of pain and longing. Since I crossed the
Rhine, I seem to be dead inside, not a single feeling comes to the
surface. I'm an automaton; my soul has been removed. Easter is still
my only solace; I have relatives near Landau, their invitation and
permission to visit them. I've made the journey a thousand times
already and won't get tired.—You ask me: do you long for me? Do
you call it longing if a person can live only for one thing and is torn
from it and then has nothing but the feeling of one's misery? Please
send me an answer. Are my lips so cold? [. . .] This letter is a
hodgepodge: I'll console you with another.

To Gutzkow[9]

[Darmstadt, February 21, 1835]

Dear Sir:

You may have possibly observed, or in more unfortunate circumstances experienced, that a degree of misery exists that silences all
deference and feeling. There are people who say that in this case
one ought rather starve oneself to death, but I could find a refuta-
tion of this on the street: a captain, recently gone blind, explains
that he would shoot himself if only he were not compelled to
remain alive so that his salary could support his family. That is horrifying. You will realize that similar circumstances may exist which
restrain one from throwing one's body from the wreck of this world
into the water like an anchor, and you will therefore not be surprised that I open your door, step into your room, place a manu-

---

6. Matthew 18:7 [*Editor*].
7. This passage is echoed in Danton's words toward the end of *Danton's Death* 2.5 [*Editor*].
8. Probably Eugen Boeckel [*Editor*].
9. Karl Gutzkow, a leader of the Young Germany group of writers [*Editor*].

script[1] on your chest, and ask for alms. I beg you to read the manuscript as quickly as possible, to recommend it to Mr. Sauerländer[2] if your conscience as a critic should allow you to do so, and to answer immediately.

Concerning the work itself, I can only say that unfortunate circumstances compelled me to write it in about five weeks. I say this to influence your judgment about the author, not about the drama itself. I don't know myself what I should do with it; I only know that I have every reason to blush before history, but I console myself with the thought that all poets, excepting Shakespeare, stand before history and nature like schoolboys.

I repeat my plea for a speedy response. In the event of a favorable reaction, a few lines from your hand—if they reach me before next Wednesday—would save an unfortunate man from a very sorry situation.

If the tone of this letter should disturb you, please consider that it is easier for me to beg in rags than to present a plea in a frock coat, and almost easier to say, with a pistol in my hand: la bourse ou la vie![3] than to whisper with trembling lips: may God reward me!

G. Büchner

To Wilhelm Büchner

[Strassburg, 1835]

[. . .] I wouldn't tell you this if I could believe in the slightest possibility of a political upheaval at this time. For the last six months I've been utterly convinced that nothing is to be done and that anyone who sacrifices himself *right now* is foolishly risking his neck. I can't tell you anything more specific, but I know the situation; I know how weak, how insignificant, how fragmented the liberal party is; I know that purposeful, unified action is impossible and that any attempt won't have the slightest result. [. . .]

To Gutzkow

[Strassburg]

[. . .] The whole revolution has already divided itself into liberals and absolutists, and it will have to be devoured by the uneducated and poor classes; the relationship between poor and rich is the only revolutionary element in the world, hunger alone can become the goddess of freedom, and only a Moses, who brought the seven Egyptian plagues down on our heads, could become a messiah.

---

1. *Danton's Death* [*Editor*].
2. Johann David Sauerländer, a publisher [*Editor*].
3. Your money or your life! (French) [*Editor*].

Fatten the peasants and the revolution will have a stroke. A *chicken* in the pot of every peasant will kill the Gallic *rooster*. [. . .]

To His Parents

Strassburg, July 28, 1835

[. . .] I must say a few words about my drama:[4] first I must point out that my permission to make several changes was used to excess. Omissions and additions occur on almost every page, and almost always to the detriment of the whole. Sometimes the sense is completely distorted or missing entirely, replaced by almost sheer nonsense. Besides, the book is teeming with the most dreadful typographical errors. I received no *proofs*. The title is tasteless[5] and my name is under it, which I had explicitly forbidden; it was not on the title page of my manuscript. The editor has moreover credited me with several obscenities I never would have said in my life. I've read Gutzkow's splendid reviews and noticed, much to my pleasure, that I'm not inclined toward vanity. Regarding the so-called immorality of my book, I have the following to say: the dramatic poet is in my eyes nothing but a writer of history; he is *superior* to the latter, however, in that he creates history a second time for us, and instead of telling us a dry story, he places us into the life of an era, giving us characters instead of characteristics and figures instead of descriptions. His greatest task is to come as close as possible to history as it actually happened. His book must be neither *more nor less moral* than *history itself*; but God didn't create history to be suitable reading matter for young ladies, and for that reason I can't be blamed if my drama is equally unsuitable. I can't make a Danton and the bandits of the Revolution into virtuous heroes! To show their dissoluteness I had to let them be dissolute, to show their godlessness I had to let them speak like atheists. Should you discover any improprieties, then think of the notoriously obscene language of that time; whatever my characters say is only a weak approximation of it. One might reproach me for choosing such material. But such a reproach has long been refuted. If one were to let it stand, then the greatest masterpieces of literature would have to be thrown out. The poet is not a teacher of morality, he invents and creates figures, he brings past times to life, and people can learn from that, just as well as from the study of history and from observation of what is going on around them. If you wished it *otherwise*, you shouldn't be permitted to study history at all, for it tells of many immoral acts; you'd have to walk blindfolded down the street, for you might see indecencies, and you'd have to cry out against a God

---

4. *Danton's Death* [Editor].
5. *Danton's Death* had been published with the added subtitle "Dramatic Scenes of the French Reign of Terror" [Editor].

who created a world in which so much dissoluteness occurs. If someone were to tell me that the poet shouldn't depict the world as it is but as it should be, then I answer that I don't want to make it better than God, who certainly made the world as it should be. As far as the so-called idealistic poets are concerned, I find that they have produced hardly anything besides marionettes with sky-blue noses and affected pathos, but not human beings of flesh and blood, whose sorrow and joy I share and whose actions fill me with loathing or admiration. In a word, I think much of Goethe or Shakespeare, but very little of Schiller. Moreover, it's obvious that highly unfavorable reviews will appear, for the governments must have their paid writers prove that their opponents are either idiots or immoral people. I do not in any way judge my work to be perfect and will accept any truly aesthetic criticism with thanks.

* * *

To His Parents

Strassburg, beginning of August 1835

* * *

We hear everything from the refugees, who know more than anyone, because in most cases they were recently involved in investigations. I know for certain that Minnigerode's[6] hands were chained in Friedberg; I know it from someone who was imprisoned with him. He's said to be mortally ill; would to heaven that his sufferings would cease! It's established that the prisoners are given prison rations and have neither light nor books. I thank heaven that I foresaw what would happen, I would have gone crazy in a hole like that. [. . .]* * *

When one sees how the absolutist powers try to reinstate the old chaos: Poland, Italy, Germany under their thumb again! Only France is missing, it's always hanging over their heads like a sword. * *

To His Parents

Strassburg, January 1, 1836

[. . .] The banning of the *Deutschen Revue* does me no harm. Several articles I prepared for it can be sent to the *Phönix*. It makes me laugh how pious and moral our governments are suddenly becoming; the King of Bavaria bans immoral books! Then he mustn't allow his biography to be published, because that would be the

---

6. Karl von Minnigerode (1814–1894), a school friend of Büchner's from Darmstadt and Giessen and one of those arrested for delivering copies of *The Hessian Messenger*. Imprisoned in Friedberg for three years, he emigrated to the United States after his release. He would ultimately settle in Virginia as a professor of classical literature at the College of William and Mary and a minister of the Episcopal Church [*Editor*].

dirtiest thing ever written! The Grand Duke of Baden, First Knight of the Double Order of Blockheads, makes himself a Knight of the Holy Ghost and has Gutzkow arrested, and every good German believes it's being done for the sake of religion and Christianity and claps his hands. I'm not familiar with the books everyone is talking about; they're not in the lending libraries and they're too expensive for me to spend money on them. If it's all like they say, I can see in it only the misconceptions of a mind led astray by philosophic sophistries. The most common trick to get the masses on one's side is to scream "Immoral!" with a mouth full of food. Besides, it really takes courage to attack a writer who must answer from a German jail. Gutzkow has revealed a distinguished, stalwart nature, he has given proof of great talent; why then suddenly this outcry? It seems to me as if one were fighting for the worldly realm while one pretends to be saving the life of the Trinity. Gutzkow has courageously fought for freedom in his sphere; the few who still stand upright and dare to speak have to be silenced! *I* by no means belong to the so-called "Young Germany,"[7] the literary party of Gutzkow and Heine. Only a complete misunderstanding of our social conditions could lead these people to believe that a complete transformation of our religious and social ideas would be possible through our current literature. I also do not share *in any way their opinions about marriage and Christianity,* but it still annoys me when people who have sinned a thousand times more in practice than these men have in *theory* make moral faces and cast stones at a youthful, vigorous talent. I'm going my own way and staying in the field of drama, which has nothing to do with all of these disputes; I draw my figures as I see fit in accordance with nature and history, and I laugh about people who want to make me responsible for the morality or immorality of these characters. I have my own ideas about that. [. . .].

I just came from the Christmas displays; everywhere crowds of ragged, freezing children who were standing wide-eyed and with sad faces before those wonders of water and flour, dirt and gold foil. The thought that for most people even the most paltry delights and joys are unattainable riches made me very bitter. [. . .]

To Gutzkow

Strassburg, [1836]

* * *

By the way, in all honesty it seems to me that you and your friends didn't exactly take the most sensible path. Reform society

---

7. *Junges Deutschland* in German; a literary and social-reform movement active from roughly 1830 to 1850. Its members included Karl Gutzkow and the poet Heinrich Heine [*Editor*].

through *ideas*, through the *educated* classes? Impossible! Our times are purely *materialistic*; if you had ever worked along more directly political lines, you soon would have come to the point where reform would have stopped on its own. You will never bridge the chasm between the educated and uneducated classes.

I'm convinced that the educated and prosperous minority, as many concessions as it might desire for itself from the authorities, will never want to give up its antagonistic attitude toward the masses. And the masses themselves? For them there are only two levers: material poverty and *religious fanaticism*. Any party that knows how to operate these levers will conquer. Our times demand iron and bread—and then a *cross* or something like that. I believe that in social affairs one must proceed from an absolute *legal* principle, striving for a new mentality among the *people* and letting effete modern society go to the devil. Why should a thing like this walk around between heaven and earth? Its whole life consists only of attempts to dissipate its most dreadful boredom. Let it die out, that is the only new thing it can still experience. [. . .].

To Wilhelm Büchner

Strassburg, September 2, 1836

[. . .] I'm quite cheerful, except when we have a steady downpour or a northwest wind, which turns me into one of those who, when they've taken off one sock before going to bed at night, are capable of hanging themselves on their chamber door because it's too much effort to take off the other one. [. . .] I'm now concentrating totally on the study of natural sciences and philosophy, and I'll soon go to Zurich to lecture to my fellow-beings in my capacity as a superfluous member of society on an equally superfluous topic, namely schools of German philosophy since Descartes and Spinoza.[8]—Right now I'm occupied with letting several people kill each other or get married on paper, and I beg the dear Lord for a simpleminded publisher and a large audience with as little good taste as possible. Many things under the sun require courage—even being a Lecturer in Philosophy. [. . .]

To His Parents

Zurich, November 20, 1836

[. . .] Regarding political activities, you needn't worry at all. Just don't be troubled by the fairy tales in our newspapers. Switzerland is a republic, and since journalists usually don't know what else to say besides: "every republic is barbarous," they tell the good Germans

---

8. René Descartes (1596–1650) and Benedict Spinoza (1632–1677) were two of the most important influences on Kant and German Romantic philosophy [*Editor*].

daily about anarchy, murder, and manslaughter. You'll be surprised when you visit me; already on the way friendly villages everywhere, and then, the closer you come to Zurich and along the lake, widespread prosperity; back home we have no concept of the appearance of these villages and small towns. The streets aren't full of soldiers, job applicants, and lazy bureaucrats, you don't risk being run over by a nobleman's coach; in contrast, a healthy, sturdy people, and for little money a simple, good, purely *republican* government, which sustains itself through a *property tax*, a kind of tax that would be denounced back home as the height of anarchy. [. . .]

Minnigerode is dead,[9] as I've heard in a letter; that is, for three years he was tortured to death. Three years! The men of blood of the French Revolution killed people in a couple of hours—the sentence and then the guillotine! But three years! We have indeed a humane government, it can't stand the sight of blood. And nearly forty people are similarly imprisoned, and that's no anarchy, that's law and order, and the masters feel outraged when they think of anarchistic Switzerland! By God, these people are raising great capital, which may once have to be repaid with heavy interest, very heavy interest. [. . .]

To Wilhelm Büchner

Zurich, end of November 1836
[. . .] I'm sitting with my scalpel by day and my books by night. [. . .]

To Wilhelmine Jaeglé

[Zurich,] January 20 [1837]
[. . .] I caught a cold and was lying in bed. But now it's better. When one is a bit out of sorts like that, one has a great yearning for idleness; but the mill wheel turns without a stop. [. . .] Today and yesterday I've been granting myself a bit of rest and am not reading; tomorrow it'll be back to the old grind, you can't believe how regular and orderly. I'm running almost as well as a Black Forest clock. But it's all right: some rest after all that turbulent mental life, and in addition the joy of creating my poetic products. Poor Shakespeare was a scribe during the day and had to write his own works at night, and I, who am unworthy of untying his shoelaces, am far better off. [. . .] Will you learn to sing the *folk songs* by Easter, if it doesn't fatigue you? One doesn't hear any voices here; the *folk* don't sing, and you know how much I love those women who in a soiree or in concert sing or wail a couple of notes to death. I'm coming ever closer to the

9. Although Karl Minnigerode was arrested on August 1, 1834, and subsequently tortured, he was not in fact dead [*Editor*].

folk and to the Middle Ages, every day I feel more clearheaded—and you'll sing the songs, right? I become half homesick, when I hum a melody to myself. [. . .] Every evening I sit in the casino for one or two hours; you know my liking for beautiful halls, lights, and people around me. [. . .]

To Wilhelmine Jaeglé

[Zurich, 1837]
[. . . I'll] release *Leonce and Lena* along with two other dramas[1] for publication in a week at most. [. . .]

KARL VOGT

[Impression of the Giessen Student Georg Büchner][†]

Frankly, we didn't like this Georg Büchner. He wore a big top hat that always sat back on his neck, constantly made a face like a cat in a thunderstorm, kept completely to himself, only associated with a somewhat seedy and ragged genius, August Becker, who was usually just called "Red August." His reclusiveness was seen as arrogance. Because he was clearly involved with political activities and once or twice also let slip revolutionary pronouncements, when returning from the pub in the evening we not infrequently stood outside his apartment and offered up an ironic cheer: "Long live the upholder of balance in Europe, the abolitionist of the slave trade, Georg Büchner!"—He acted as though he didn't hear the jeering, even though his lamp was burning and showed he was home. He was very eager in Wernekinck's private seminar, and his discussions with the professor soon showed us that he possessed thorough knowledge, which made us respect him. But we never got at all close to him; his gruff, reserved temper always repelled us.

1. Presumably *Woyzeck* and the lost play *Pietro Aretino* [*Editor*].
† Karl (or Carl) Vogt (1817–1895) was a classmate of Büchner's in the medical school at Giessen and in later years was a prominent scientist and politician. This excerpt is taken from his memoir, *Aus meinem Leben* (Stuttgart: Erwin Nägele, 1896), p. 121. Translated by Matthew Wilson Smith.

2493.   Steckbrief.

Der hierunter signalisirte Georg Büchner, Student der Medizin aus Darmstadt, hat sich der gerichtlichen Untersuchun˙ seiner indicirten Theilnahme an staatsverrätherischen Handlungen durch die Entfernung aus dem Vaterlande entzogen. Man ersucht deßhalb die öffentlichen Behörden des In- und Auslandes, denselben im Betretungsfalle festnehmen und wohlverwahrt an die unterzeichnete Stelle abliefern zu lassen.

Darmstadt, den 13. Juni 1835.

Der von Großh. Hess. Hofgericht der Provinz Oberhessen bestellte Untersuchungs-Richter, Hofgerichtsrath

Georgi.

Personal-Beschreibung.

Alter: 21 Jahre,
Größe: 6 Schuh, 9 Zoll neuen Hessischen Maases,
Haare: blond,
Stirne: sehr gewölbt,
Augenbraunen: blond,
Augen: grau,
Nase: stark,
Mund: klein,
Bart: blond,
Kinn: rund,
Angesicht: oval,
Gesichtsfarbe: frisch,
Statur: kräftig, schlank,
Besondere Kennzeichen: Kurzsichtigkeit.

Wanted poster for Büchner issued by the Hessian police, 1835.

WANTED POSTER[†]

WANTED

The hereafter described Georg Büchner, a medical student from Darmstadt, has absented himself from the Judicial Inquiry into his alleged participation in treasonable activities by leaving the Fatherland. Both local and foreign public authorities are therefore requested to arrest this man on sight, and to deliver him safely to the office below.

Darmstadt, 13 June 1835.

Supreme Court Justice, appointed Judge to the Court of Inquiry for the Province of Upper Hesse by order of the Supreme Court of the Archduchy of Hesse

Georgi.

Description
Age: 21 years,
Height: 6 shoes 9 thumbs (new Hessian measure),
Hair: blond,
Forehead: very arched,
Eyebrows: blond,
Eyes: grey,
Nose: prominent,
Mouth: small,
Beard: blond,
Chin: round,
Face: oval,
Coloring: fresh,
Figure: robust, slender,
Particular Characteristics: nearsighted.

JOHANN FRIEDRICH OBERLIN

From Pastor Oberlin's Diary[†]

[The events described here fill the gap in Büchner's text immediately prior to Lenz's departure from Waldbach.]

. . . The nursemaid, deathly pale and trembling all over, came to my wife: Mr. Lenz had thrown himself out of the window. My wife called to me in confusion—I ran out, but Mr. Lenz was already back in his room. I just had a moment to tell a maid: "Go quickly to

† Translated by Matthew Wilson Smith.
† Translated by Henry J. Schmidt. From *Georg Büchner: The Complete Collected Works*, translated and with commentary by Henry J. Schmidt; New York: Avon, 1977. Reprinted by permission.

the bailiff and have him send two men," and I ran up to Mr. Lenz's room.

I led him to my room with friendly words; his whole body shivered. Above the waist he wore only an undershirt, torn and completely soiled like the rest of his clothes. We warmed a shirt and a robe for him, and we dried his clothes. We discovered that during the short time he was outside he must have attempted to drown himself again, but God had provided once more. His clothes were soaked.

Now, I thought, you have deceived me enough, now *you* must be deceived, now it's at an end, now you must be watched. I waited for the men with great impatience. Meanwhile I continued to write my sermon as Mr. Lenz sat at the stove, a step away from me. I didn't dare leave him for a moment, I had to wait. My wife stayed also, worried about me. I really would have liked to send for the men again, but I could not speak of it to my wife or anyone else. If I had spoken openly he would have understood; we didn't want to speak in secret, because the slightest opportunity for suspicion excites such people far too much. At eight-thirty we went to eat. My wife trembled in fear and Mr. Lenz in cold and confusion.

After less than fifteen minutes he asked me whether he could go up to my room.—What do you want to do, my dear friend?—To read something.—Go in God's name.—He went, and pretending I had eaten enough, I followed him.

We sat: I wrote, he leafed through my French Bible with terrifying speed and finally grew quiet. I went for a moment into the study without delaying in the slightest, only to get something from my desk. My wife stood at the door and watched Mr. Lenz. I was stepping out of the study when my wife screamed in a gruesome, hollow, broken voice: "Lord Jesus, he's going to stab himself!" Never in my life have I seen such an expression of deathlike, despairing terror as in that moment, in the wild, horribly distorted features of my wife.

I was outside.—What are you up to, my dear friend?—He put down the scissors. He had been looking about with dreadful, rigid glances, and since he saw no one in his bewilderment, he had quietly picked up the scissors, placed them with a tight fist against his heart—all this so quickly that only God was able to prevent the blow until my wife's scream frightened him and returned him somewhat to his senses. After a few moments I took away the scissors, as if lost in thought and paying him no mind. Since he solemnly assured me that he hadn't intended to kill himself with them, I didn't want to act as if I didn't believe him at all.

Because all previous arguments against his suicidal mania had been fruitless, I tried another tack. I said to him: "You were a total stranger to us, we didn't know you at all, we had only heard your name once before we knew you, we took you in with love, my wife cared for your injured foot with such patience, and you do us so much harm, you cast us from one fright into another." He was moved by this, jumped up, wanted to beg my wife's pardon, but she was still so afraid of him and ran out the door. He wanted to follow, but she held the door shut. Now he wailed that he had murdered my wife, the child she was carrying—everything, he killed everything wherever he went.—No, my friend, my wife is still alive and God can temper the harmful consequences of her fright, nor would her child die nor be harmed by that.—He calmed down again. Soon it was ten o'clock. Meanwhile my wife had sent for urgent help among the neighbors. Everyone was in bed, but the schoolmaster came, pretending as if he had something to ask me, gave me some news, and Mr. Lenz, becoming active again, took part in the conversation as if nothing had happened.

Finally I received a sign that the two men had arrived—oh, how happy I was! It was time. Mr. Lenz had just asked to go to bed. I said to him: "Dear friend, we love you, you know that, and you love us, we are certain of that, too. Your suicide would worsen, not improve your condition; we must therefore be concerned about your survival. But when depression overcomes you, you lose control of yourself. That's why I've asked two men to sleep in your room (to watch, I thought to myself), so that you have company and help if necessary." He agreed to this.

One should not be surprised that I spoke to him and treated him in this manner. He was always quite reasonable and had an exceptionally sympathetic heart. When the attacks of depression had passed, everything seemed so secure, and he was so amiable that one almost had a bad conscience while suspecting or troubling him. Add to that our fondest pity for his immeasurable torment, that we had so often witnessed. What he endured was terrible and hellish, and it pierced and broke my heart when I was compelled to suffer with him the consequences of his disobedience toward his father, his erratic way of life, his aimless occupations, his frequent association with women. I was horrified and felt tortures never experienced before when he was on his knees, his hand in mine, his head resting on my knee, his pale face covered with cold sweat, hidden in my robe, trembling and shivering all over—not confessing, but not able to contain the outpouring of his tormented conscience and unfulfilled longing. The more difficult it became to calm him, the more pitiable he was to me, since our respective attitudes were in strong opposition—or at least appeared to differ.

Now back to the facts: I said he permitted two men to be in his room. I accompanied him into it. One of his guards stared at him with rigid, frightened eyes. To calm the guard somewhat, I said to Mr. Lenz in French in the presence of the two guards what I had already told him in my room. . . . I concluded with several kisses which I pressed on the unhappy youth's mouth with all my heart, and I went to bed with exhausted, quivering limbs.

While in bed he said among other things to his guards: "Listen, we don't want to make any noise, but if you have a knife, give it to me quietly and without fear." After he had requested this time and again without a response, he began to beat his head against the wall. In our sleep we heard much thumping, appearing to increase and decrease, which finally woke us up. We thought it was in the attic but could not guess the cause. The clock struck three and the thumping continued. We rang for a light; our servants were all deep in horrible dreams and had difficulty waking up. We discovered at last that the thumping was coming from Mr. Lenz and in part from the guards, who were summoning help by stamping on the floor, since they could not leave him alone. I rushed to his room. As soon as he saw me, he stopped trying to struggle out of his guards' arms. They then also stopped restraining him. I gave them a sign to let him go, sat on his bed, talked with him, and prayed with him as he requested. He stirred a bit, and once he smashed his head against the wall with great force. The guards jumped up and held him again.

I went to summon a third guard. When Mr. Lenz saw him, he mocked them all, saying that all three would not be strong enough for him. Secretly I ordered my coach to be made ready, to be covered over, to have two extra horses brought besides mine. I sent for Sebastian Scheidecker, the schoolmaster of Bellefosse, and Johann David Bohy, the schoolmaster of Solb, two sensible, determined men whom Mr. Lenz was fond of. Johann Georg Claude, Waldbach's churchwarden, came as well; the house was astir although it was not yet day. Mr. Lenz noticed this, and whereas earlier he had shown such cunning, such violence to free himself, to smash his head, to obtain a knife, he was now suddenly so quiet.

After I had arranged everything, I went to Mr. Lenz, saying to him that I had asked several men to accompany him to Strasbourg in my coach so that he might receive better care in accordance with his condition.

He lay quietly with only one guard sitting by him. At my words he sobbed, asking for only one more week's patience with him (one had to cry at his demeanor). But he said he would think about it. Fifteen minutes later he sent word: yes, he would go; he stood up, got dressed, was quite reasonable, packed his things, thanked everyone individually most tenderly, including the guards, looked for my wife and the maids who had concealed themselves from him, because just previously his rage had increased whenever he heard or believed to have heard a woman's voice. Now he asked to see everyone, thanked them, begged their forgiveness; in short, he took leave from everyone so movingly that all eyes were bathed in tears.

And so the pitiable youth departed from us, with three companions and two coachmen. During the journey he never became violent, seeing himself outnumbered, but he attempted various ruses, especially at Ensisheim where they spent the night. But the schoolmasters matched his cunning politeness with their own, and everything ended admirably.

JOHANN CHRISTIAN AUGUST CLARUS

From The Legal Accountability of the Murderer Johann Christian Woyzeck, Demonstrated with Documentary Evidence According to the Principles of the Science of Public Health[†][1]

By Dr. Johann Christian August Clarus, Royal Saxon Privy Councillor, Knight of the Royal Saxon Civil Order of Merit and of the Russian Order of St. Vladimir 4th Class, Professor of Clinical Medicine, Minister of Public Health of the District Office, the University and the City of Leipzig and Doctor at St. Jacob's Hospital, etc.

Preface

An act of penal justice is impending such as most people in the present generation have not yet experienced. At this moment, after three years of investigation, the murderer *Woyzeck* is awaiting recompense at the hands of the executioner for his deed. Only the dullest egoist can face this day of judgment coldly and unreflectingly, only the degenerate half-human look to it with crude voyeuristic curiosity. The educated and feeling man is overcome by deep, anxious sympathy, for in the criminal he still sees the man, the former fellow citizen and fellow beneficiary of the blessings of a common religion, of a beneficent and mild government, and of the many local advantages and conveniences of this community—a man who,

---

[†] Translated by Peter J. Schwartz.

1. "Die Zurechnungsfähigkeit des Mörders Johann Christian Woyzeck, nach Grundsätzen der Staatsarzneikunde aktenmässig erwiesen." In: *Zeitschrift für die Staatsarzneikunde, 4. Ergänzungsheft* (1825): 1–97. Also in Georg Büchner, *Woyzeck, Marburger Ausgabe, Band 7.2: Text, Editionsbericht, Quellen, Erläuterungsteile,* ed. Burghard Dedner, Arnd Beise, Ingrid Rehme, Eva-Maria Vering and Manfred Wenzel (Darmstadt: Wissenschaftliche Buchgesellschaft, 2005), 259–97 [translator's note].

having sunk through an unstable, debauched, thoughtless and idle life from one level of moral ferality to another, then finally, in a dark tumult of brutal passions, destroyed a human life; and who now, cast out from society, is to lose his own life on the scaffold through human hands.

But besides the sympathy and besides the feeling for everything there is about the death penalty that is terrible and repugnant, still, if things are not to end simply in sickly sentimentalism or even in farce, the thought must arise of the *inviolable sanctity of the law;* which, to be sure, is capable, like mankind itself, of a progressive mitigation and improvement, but which, so long as it exists, must, in defense of the throne and of the cottages, weigh on a strict scale where it shall spare and where it shall punish, and which demands from those who serve it, and from whom, as witnesses or as experts, it seeks enlightenment, *truth*—and not feelings.

Such enlightenment was requested of me, as a physician of this city, when in Woyzeck's criminal trial it had become questionable *whether he was in his right mind*, and thus *accountable for his actions*, or not; and there is no doubt that the investigation of his state of mind thus occasioned and the expert opinion that resulted have had a decisive influence on his fate.

*   *   *

Therefore, may those who accompany that unhappy man to his death, or who will be its witnesses, combine the sympathy that the criminal deserves as a man with the conviction that the law must still be applied for the sake of the general order, and that Justice, who carries her sword for a reason, is *God's* servant.—May teachers and preachers, and all those who watch over institutions of public education, keep in mind their high calling, and never forget that it is from them that a better civilization must flow and a new age must come, in which it will be possible for the wisdom of governments and of legislators to make legal penalties even more mild than they have already become.—May the generation of youth now coming of age, gazing upon the bleeding criminal or thinking of him, take good note of the truth that the reluctance to work, gambling, drunkenness, unlawful satisfaction of sexual lust, and bad company can lead, gradually and unexpectedly, to crimes and to the gallows.—Finally, may all return from this dreadful event with the firm resolution: To *be* better, so that things may *become* better.

Leipzig, August 16, 1824.
Clarus

On June 21 of the year 1821, at half-past nine in the evening, the barber *Johann Christian Woyzeck*, forty-one years old, dealt the forty-six-year-old widow of the late surgeon *Woost, Johanna Christiane* née *Otto*, in the front hall of her house on the Sandgasse, seven wounds with the broken blade of a rapier to which he had that very afternoon had a handle affixed, from which she died after some few minutes, and one of which, a penetrating breast wound that cut through the first intercostal artery and both sacs of the pleura and punctured the descending part of the aorta in a location completely inaccessible to medical help, was declared *unconditionally* and *absolutely lethal* at the legal autopsy that took place the next day and in the report on that autopsy dated July 2, 1821.

٭   ٭   ٭

1. On inspection of the documentary evidence

The examinee Woyzeck is the child of thoroughly upstanding parents, who retained their common sense until the end, and never showed any sign of melancholy or derangement of their rational faculties. After losing his mother when he was eight, and his father when he was thirteen—who may have paid little attention to his education, but who also did not treat him harshly, and who saw to it that he had an education at the Free School of a sort commensurate with his means and his social position—he trained for the profession of wigmaker; in which, although he left his first master of his own accord, he behaved, according to witnesses who knew him at the time, always very well, calmly and rationally, up to the age of eighteen, when he embarked on his journeyman year, and never showed any sign of mental illness or melancholy.

٭   ٭   ٭

There are no testimonies present in the records regarding his conduct and his state of mind during [the intervening] 12-year period; he himself, however, assured me in the conversations that I had with him in the month of August 1821, and during which I asked very specific questions regarding his life circumstances, that he had had it good everywhere, behaved to the satisfaction of his superiors, never took part in duels or fistfights, harbored secret grudges even less, did not care particularly for pleasures or distractions, preferring to occupy himself in his spare time with attempts at all sorts of mechanical work, e.g. with handwork in paper or acquiring tailoring skills, and, while not actively seeking out relations with the female sex, also did not scorn the opportunity of them, tending however increasingly to restrict himself to the company of a single person, in which case it was a matter of indifference to him whether she kept society with several men, or not. In later interrogations he provided more detail, some of it contradicting his earlier account, regarding relations in the year 1810 with a single female named *Wienberg*, with whom he fathered a child, noting that at this time, during which he was serving with the Mecklenburg troops, when he heard that this person was going with other men, he had noticed for the first time a change in his mood, and had on her account transferred to Swedish service, and had continued his former relations with her. This change had revealed itself in a tendency to become very quiet and often to feel vexed by his comrades, without being able to help himself, so that even if he tried as hard as possible to direct his attention to a task he had set himself, he still performed the task incorrectly, because for periods of as long as half an hour, sometimes shorter, *his mind would go blank*. Later, in Stettin, a resentment of certain persons combined itself with this absentmindedness, so that, feeling bitter at people in general, he withdrew from them, often walking about alone out of doors. Besides this he reported having disturbing dreams about Freemasons, and bringing these into relation with things that happened to him. One afternoon, when together with his comrades in a pub, he heard footsteps outside, without in this case discovering anything there, and he thought it a ghost, because he had dreamed of one several days before. His restlessness continued after he moved from Stettin to the garrisons of Schweidnitz and Graudenz, and he believed, when a dream revealed to him the Freemasons' secret signs of recognition, that this knowledge could become dangerous to him, and that he was being pursued by the Freemasons. Also, in Graudenz one evening he saw a vision at the Schlossberg and heard the sound of bells; another time, someone he could not see in a churchyard at night had wished him good morning in a gruff voice.

* * *

After living [in the Steinbrücks' house in Leipzig] for six weeks [* * *] he went to live in the home of the Jew *Samson Schwabe* in Dessau, whom he took care of in sickness and with whom he stayed for 6–7 weeks. The latter attests that when [Woyzeck] was not drunk he behaved well and very reasonably and never gave any reason to doubt his powers of common sense, that however he loved drink to a high degree, and that the exclamation that [Schwabe] made to him once, when, in such a period of great drunkenness, he did everything wrong—"Man, you're crazy and you don't know it"—had been directed solely to his drunken state, and had nothing to do with true insanity.

* * *

From February 1819 to midsummer 1820 [he lived] with the widow *Woost's* stepmother, the widow *Knobloch*, in the house of the brass-founder *Warnecke*, in which the latter's tenant *Jordan* runs a tavern; where he sometimes found work in Herr Knobloch's business, sometimes did handwork with paper for the bookbinder *Wehner* in Volkmarsdorf on the recommendation of Knobloch, sometimes did illumination for the bookseller *Klein*, and also helped out the accountant Mr. *Lang* and Mr. M. *Gebhard*, as well as the foreigner *Benedix* during the fair. According to the testimony of the latter, and also those of *Warnecke, Jordan, Wehner*, Mr. *Lang* and Mr. M. *Gebhard*, during this time as well he behaved in a very rational way, calmly and modestly, took care of the tasks they set him to their satisfaction, and showed no signs of melancholy or insanity, indeed nothing at all remarkable, in his conduct. Several of these witnesses, namely Warnecke and Wehner, remarked that he had loved brandy and sometimes had drunk too much; the widow Knobloch had also complained of this to Jordan.

[Knobloch] says also that *Woyzeck* had had relations with her daughter, but had become jealous on account of her frequent association with soldiers, had abused the widow *Woost* on several occasions, and had made so much noise and disturbance that she had been compelled, at Warnecke's request, to evict him from lodgings. Warnecke relates as follows the incident that led to this: he, Warnecke, had once said to Woyzeck in Jordan's tavern: "Here, *Woyzeck*, killer, want to drink a glass of schnaps?" Woyzeck, however, had given him a vulgar answer, and he himself had turned with surprise to Jordan, exclaiming: "The bloke's whistling dark blue,"[2] and had left. When Warnecke had then said to the widow Knobloch that she would have to leave the premises if she did not evict Woyzeck, the latter, before he was finally evicted, had written him several letters, in one of which he had written the (rhymed) words: "The Saxon offers the Turkish sultan peace, but he's unhappy if he can't slug him, at least."—When now Warnecke, reading this letter, said: "Now the bloke's gonna get slugged if he shows up again," Woyzeck, who had delivered the letter himself and, standing in the kitchen, had heard these words, replied that that was what he'd been waiting

---

2. "Der Kerl pfeift dunkelblau" (literally, "The bloke's whistling dark blue"). In *Woyzeck* 4,14, Büchner modifies this to "Der Kerl soll dunkelblau pfeifen" ("The bloke's going to whistle dark blue"). The sense of the idiom is unclear. Although Clarus's phrase would seem to mean "He's showing off," Büchner's modification suggests something closer to "I'll throttle the fellow." Cf. Christiane Wanzeck, *Zur Etymologie lexikalisierter Farbwortverbindungen: Untersuchungen anhand der Farben Rot, Gelb, Grün und Blau* (Amsterdam: Rodopi, 2003), 146–147 [Translator's note]. (Also see p. 148 in this volume.]

for, Warnecke gave him several blows, and [Woyzeck], having received them, said: "Fair's fair, now we're even, tit for tat!" On the subject of this encounter, during which, so Warnecke suspects, Woyzeck may have been somewhat drunk (which Jordan finds unlikely), Woyzeck says he believed Warnecke was making fun of him.

* * *

In this room, he declared, he was disturbed frequently, by day and by night. He heard voices speaking, although no one was sleeping in the vicinity. Sometimes he heard tapping noises on his bedcovers, and when he had grasped at the noise, thinking it was mice or rats, he had found nothing. Once when he had wanted to return to his room after 10 one evening, he had heard near him a loud rustling noise and, very clearly, a voice saying: *Oh, do come!* He had been very startled and had run down to fetch the innkeeper, who had however entered the room with a lantern and found nothing. Because he had very much feared to sleep there alone, he had spent three nights on a mattress in the innkeeper's tavern room, and when afterwards he had returned to sleep in his own room, he had continued to hear voices speaking, not loudly, but softly and often. Around the same time he felt as if a needle were boring through his heart and he ascribed the disquiet this caused him to the Devil, believing of him that while he prayed the latter had called out to him: "There you have the good Lord."

* * *

Finally, until about May 20, 1821, he had a bed at the Black Board Inn, run by one Mrs. *Wittig*, who passed away at about that time. He himself maintained that he had heard voices here as well. This included the story he told that when he had purchased a broken rapier a voice had called to him: "Stab the Woost woman dead!" In response to which he had thought: "You won't do that," but the voice had answered: "Yes, you *will* do it."

At around the same time, he had punched the widow Woost in the face in the allee of Bose's garden because she had refused to go with him, which had caused bruising and swelling to her face, and shortly thereafter, on encountering her with a rival on the dance floor, he had thrown her down the stairs, and picked up a stone to throw at her, but had then let it fall again from his hand.

* * *

Further, the documents reveal * * * that Woyzeck's thoughts were circling constantly about Woost and her infidelity; that after he had tried to speak with her on an invented pretext the morning of the same day, he had run about idly the rest of the day, and had also been on the Funkenburg; that, however, because he believed that in fact she would fail to come meet him, he had gone back and forth only a couple of times; * * * that, further, towards evening he had had the rapier blade inserted into a handle *with the intention of stabbing Woost with it*, and then, on meeting Woost by chance and hearing from her that she had not been on the Funkenburg, he had accompanied her home, on the way there not thinking again of his intention; in the front hall of the house where she lived, however, she had said something to make him angry, and he had accomplished the deed, afterwards leaving quickly, attempting on his arrest to throw the dagger away, and directly thereafter, when nobody answered his query as to whether Woost was dead, he had said: "God grant that she is dead, she deserved it for what she did to me."

* * *

II. On inspection of the examinee

* * *

1) REGARDING HIS EXTERNAL APPEARANCE AND HIS PHYSICAL HEALTH:

Gaze, facial expression, posture, gait and language are completely unchanged, the color in the face somewhat paler on account of lack of open air and exercise, breathing, skin temperature and tongue fully natural. Otherwise the examinee asserted that his sleep was calm and without disturbing dreams, his appetite was good, and his natural excretions completely in order. * * *

I remarked, however, that the shaking throughout the entire body which I had noticed during the first minutes of the interview, especially when my visit to him came very unexpectedly, lasted somewhat longer, and that his pulse and heart rates, albeit regular and even, were not only fuller and faster, but also that the pulse, each time I measured it in the course of the interview, was always somewhat agitated, and that the heartbeat remained stronger and more distinct, with a greater volume than in the natural state. When however he had been advised of my coming a half hour before my arrival, I noticed all this in a much lesser degree.

2) REGARDING THE PRESENT MENTAL CONDITION OF THE EXAMINEE AND PARTICULARLY

a) his faculty of reason, I observed in him neither unsteadiness and distractibility, nor exaggeration, straining, obsession with or confusion of thoughts and ideas, but rather undivided attentiveness to the subject of our discussion lasting several hours at a time, such that he seemed uninterruptedly absorbed therein, even when I took notes now and then, after which he often took up the thread of discussion where I had let it fall, correcting himself when he strayed from chronological order in his narrative, or went off on a tangent, also always returning unprompted to the point at issue by a natural and coherent train of thought. He understood without hesitation the sense of questions directed to him, so that I was never required to repeat a question, and not only did he answer my questions quickly and accurately, he was also prepared to reformulate their sense in his own words as often as I requested him to do so, which seemed to me especially necessary with questions concerning his state of mind directly before, during and after the deed. His memory had remained entirely accurate, so that he could repeat accounts of events that he had made to me a year and a half before, including identical accessory circumstances. His ideas, as far as they concern objects and conditions in the external world, are correct and in keeping with the level of his intellectual education, and although he is not free from certain errors and prejudices in matters of religion and the supernatural such as are common to people of his class and degree of education and which lead him to false views and opinions, as I will further explain below, still he shows no sign of *pathological* exaltation, dullness, or confusion of ideas, and through continued discussions of the object of these errors I was able to convince myself that his reason is capable of instruction in this regard and accessible to better convictions.

* * *

He will not admit to hearing voices during the period of his incarceration. He has however been very preoccupied with presentiments and dreams. Thus in one of his interviews with me he asserted that he had had the feeling, a moment before, that I would now come. Upon his dreams, which he is very happy to relate, and which he interprets after his manner, he also builds his hopes. Thus he related to me once, with great pleasure, that he had dreamed he was lying in a ditch, around which several people were busy trying to pull him out. Even when such dream-visions have nothing directly to do with him, he still tries to read his fate in them and takes e.g. dreams of fire or clear water for good omens.

* * *

*Medical-physiological conclusions from the facts drawn partly
from the documentary evidence, partly from personal
observation*

* * *

The examinee maintains all sorts of erroneous, fantastic and
superstitious delusions regarding hidden and supernatural things,
at the root of which is partly a lack of knowledge and education,
partly gullibility, delusions nourished and sustained by a natural
inclination to brood over such things and by a reluctance, grounded
in his hypochondriacal disposition, to communicate. These include,
above all, his idée fixe regarding the secret arts of the Freemasons,
which preoccupies him very urgently and which has led him to
make all sorts of fantastic deductions and hypotheses.

* * *

To the second type [of fantastic delusion] belong the tones and
articulated voices which he asserts he heard frequently; when judg-
ing these phenomena, one must take into account, above all, that
on several earlier occasions, during his attacks of anxiety and heart
palpitations, he had noticed a throbbing in the arteries and heat in
the head, a feeling as if something were moving from his heart into
his head, and *at the same time* a hissing, crackling, purring and
humming in the nape of his neck or in front of his ears.

Daily experience teaches that these and similar auditory illusions
frequently result from congestion of the blood, and given his constitution and in view of preceding and concurrent events it cannot
be doubted that this will have been their cause in Woyzeck's case as
well. Just how involved in such coincidences his imagination was,
and to what degree he was inclined to disregard natural causes in
favor of imagined exceptional and supernatural ones, is proven by
the incident, noted above, in which he took heart palpitations occasioned by drills and running in high heat for the effect of secret
arts.—A higher degree of this kind of auditory illusion consists in
similarly affected persons perceiving the sounds heard in the ear as
externally caused, believing the while that they are hearing tones now
at a distance and now up close, e.g. knocking, the sound of bells,
music, etc. We may therefore conclude, within the bounds of the
certainty possible when it comes to establishing pathological facts
and according to the principles of rational medicine, that the rustling and rumbling that Woyzeck attests to having heard in the night
and afterwards also by day at the wooden partitioning wall in his
room (assuming that it did not have some external cause that he left
unexplored) was nothing other than an auditory illusion of precisely
this kind, arising in connection with the *simultaneous* roaring

before the ears and with the sensation of heat rushing to the head, and that it was promoted through his prior fear of ghosts to an *objective* cause.

* * *

From the facts related and for the reasons argued in the foregoing, I conclude: that *Woyzeck's* alleged visions and other unusual encounters must be regarded as *hallucinations* provoked by disorders of blood circulation and then promoted by his superstitions and prejudices to objective and supernatural causes, and that there are *no grounds whatsoever* for the assumption that he was of unsound mind at any time in his life, and in particular directly before, during and after the homicidal act perpetrated by him, or that at that moment he acted under the compulsion of a necessary, blind or instinctual urge, or at all otherwise than according to ordinary passionate impulses.

* * *

Leipzig, February 28, 1823

CAROLINE SCHULZ

From Diary Account of Büchner's Last Days[†]

16th.[1] It was a restless night; the sick man repeatedly wanted to leave because he imagined he was going to be imprisoned or believed himself already to be so and wanted to escape. In the afternoon his pulse merely fluttered and his heart beat 160 times a minute; the doctors abandoned hope. My otherwise pious disposition bitterly asked of providence: "Why?" Then Wilhelm entered the room, and when I shared with him my despairing thoughts he said, "Our friend has answered you himself: just now, after a violent storm of fantasies had passed, he spoke these words in a calm, elevated, solemn voice: 'We do not have too much pain, we have too little, because through pain we make our way to God!'—'We are death, dust, ashes, how can we complain?'" My misery resolved itself into melancholy, but I was very sad and will be so for a long time.

[†] Née Sartorius (1801–1847), Caroline was the wife of the Hessian officer and liberal journalist Wilhelm Schulz (1797–1860). The Schulzes were friends of Büchner in Zurich and cared for him in his last days. Caroline Schulz's full account of Büchner's last days may be found in Georg Büchner, *Werke und Briefe*, ed. Fritz Bergemann (Wiesbaden: Insel-Verlag, 1958), pp. 575–583. Translated by Matthew Wilson Smith.

1. Of February 1837.

CRITICISM

General

HERBERT LINDENBERGER

Forebears, Descendants, and Contemporary Kin[†]

Büchner and Literary Tradition

Büchner's revolt against a classicism gone stale was by no means the first such revolt in German drama. The Storm-and-Stress writers of the 1770's, in the name of spontaneity and truthfulness to nature, and with Lessing's criticism and Shakespeare's example to back them, had succeeded in clearing the German stage of its dreary, "correct" neoclassical drama—a development of the mid-eighteenth century which, as we now see it, never produced anything of lasting value anyway and whose best-known work, Gottsched's *Dying Cato* (1730), is nothing more than a pale, academic imitation of French and English plays on the same theme. One can, indeed, look at the history of German drama as a kind of alternation between relatively tight "classical" forms of one sort or another, and looser forms which derive much of their energy from their conscious revolt against an out-going theatrical tradition. Bertolt Brecht's demand for an "epic theater" can be interpreted as the latest of a number of war cries which have resounded in German dramatic criticism at various times in the last two hundred years.

Büchner's work bears only superficial resemblances to the major single achievement of the Storm-and-Stress drama, Goethe's *Götz von Berlichingen* (1773). Like *Danton's Death*, *Götz* presents a vast historical panorama composed of short, loosely connected scenes. Through their common attempt to render what they saw as Shakespeare's truthfulness to nature, both writers achieved a fullness and earthiness of detail and created a multitude of characters who seem to breathe with a life of their own. Yet two works could scarcely be more different in spirit than *Götz* and *Danton's Death*, for Goethe's play above all demonstrates the possibility of heroic action and

† From *Georg Büchner*. Carbondale: Southern Illinois University Press, 1964, pp. 115–44. Reprinted by permission.

211

meaningful human relationships—the very values toward which Büchner's work expresses the most uncompromising skepticism.

But there was one dramatist of the '70's for whom Büchner felt a fundamental affinity, and that was Lenz. Büchner was drawn to Lenz not only through the personal sympathy he obviously felt toward him, but also through his interest in his plays, especially *The Private Tutor* (1774) and *The Soldiers* (1776), which he mentions in his story on Lenz. These two plays are essentially like miniature paintings, if I may borrow a term which Brecht applied to *The Private Tutor*, a play he adapted for his Berlin Ensemble.[1] In their fusion of comic and tragic moods, in their uncondescending representation of ordinary people, above all, in the concreteness and fullness with which they depict a contemporary environment, they look forward to *Woyzeck* more than any other works in earlier German drama. In his slightly ridiculous, pathetic heroes—the young cloth merchant Stolzius in *The Soldiers*, the private tutor Läuffer—Lenz presents a type of passive hero which Büchner could later develop in the character of Woyzeck. Like Büchner, Lenz allows his characters to reveal themselves through their peculiarities of language; within a single play, in fact, he presents a generous selection of human beings, each asserting his individuality by his manner of speech. Lenz' characters often seem sharply individualized in the way Büchner suggested through the words he put into Lenz' mouth: "If only artists would try to submerge themselves in the life of the very humblest person and to reproduce it with all its faint agitations, hints of experience, the subtle, hardly perceptible play of his features."[2]

The discussion of aesthetics in Büchner's story, partly drawn as it is from Lenz' own critical pronouncements, provides some clues to the aims the two writers hold in common. Among other things, the discussion stresses the dignity and the poetry inherent in the lives of ordinary people. Speaking of the characters he had tried to create in *The Private Tutor* and *The Soldiers*, Büchner's Lenz calls them "the most prosaic people in the world, but the emotional vein is identical in almost every individual; all that varies is the thickness of the shell which this vein must penetrate." For the artist to capture the individuality of every being, he cannot create his characters according to conventional "types" or preconceived molds of any sort, but must observe concretely, indeed, "submerge himself" as he puts it, in his individual characters. The doctrine of realism which Büchner propounds is something far removed from the much more

1. "Über das Poetische und Artistische," *Stücke* (Frankfort, 1959), XI, 216.
2. Walter Höllerer's analysis of *The Soldiers* includes some penetrating remarks on those aspects of Lenz' work which anticipate Büchner's. In Benno von Wiese, ed., *Das deutsche Drama vom Barock bis zur Gegenwart* (Düsseldorf, 1962), 1, 127–146.

"scientific" doctrines of many writers in the later nineteenth century. For instance, Büchner's Lenz finds an attitude of love prerequisite to all successful artistic creation: "One must love human nature in order to penetrate into the peculiar character of any individual; nobody, however insignificant, however ugly, should be despised; only then can one understand human kind as a whole." By what seems a kind of paradox, a writer can create a world of autonomous human beings only through the love he feels for them; as soon as he begins to despise them, his characters lose their individuality and become mere puppets. The artist, in fact, plays a role analogous to God's, both in the plenitude and the variety with which he creates his world: "I take it that God has made the world as it should be and that we can hardly hope to scrawl or daub anything better; our only aspiration should be to recreate modestly in His manner." And, like God, the artist has the ability to breathe life into inert matter; indeed, the artist's central function lies in his life-giving powers: "In all things I demand—life, the possibility of existence, and that's all; nor is it our business to ask whether it's beautiful, whether it's ugly. The feeling that there's life in the thing created is much more important than considerations of beauty and ugliness; it's the sole criterion in matters of art." To illustrate his theories, Büchner's Lenz contrasts the two types of art—the one represented by the Apollo Belvedere and a Raphael Madonna, the other by two Dutch or Flemish genre paintings he had recently seen. He finds the former works too "idealized," and as a result "they make me feel quite dead." The genre paintings, which he goes on to describe in detail, "reproduce nature for me with the greatest degree of truthfulness, so that I can feel [the artist's] creation."

Except for a few remarks here and there in his letters, the discussion of aesthetics in *Lenz* is Büchner's only commentary on his own artistic ideals. But this discussion by no means provides a full rationale for his work; what it tells us—and quite appropriately so—is the points of contact he must have felt with the real Lenz. The analogy which it sets up between their literary art and genre paintings itself suggests the limits within which one may profitably compare their work. Lenz' best plays have something of the charm and the unpretentiousness which we associate with genre art, but they do not attempt to reach beyond the social frame of reference in which they are so securely rooted. (At the end of *The Private Tutor* and *The Soldiers* Lenz, in fact, shamelessly draws a pedantic social moral from his tale—a moral which, in each play, is quite inadequate to account for the richness of life which the play had seemed above all to depict.) Still, Lenz knew better than to attempt to ask the existential questions which echo so naturally out of Büchner's world. The range of reference encompassed by Büchner's plays is immeasurably wider than that of Lenz'. The discussion of aesthetics in Büchner's story, though it provides a rationale for his dramatic objectivity and his richness of detail, takes no account of many elements funda-mental to his work—for example, the grotesque characterizations in *Woyzeck*, the verbal complexity and virtuosity of all three plays, the images of an inverted world which emerge out of *Danton's Death* and *Woyzeck*. Though Büchner's critics often depend on the discussion of aesthetics in *Lenz* to provide a theoretical framework for his art, one wonders if the statement, "I take it that God has made the world as it should be" (a statement, incidentally, which Büchner drew from Lenz' *Notes on the Theater*—1774), is really applicable to a body of work which continually voices its despair at the results of God's creation.

"The idealistic movement was just beginning at that time"—with these words, so fateful for Lenz, Büchner begins the discussion of aesthetics in his story. In 1778, the time in which the story takes place, Goethe was already firmly entrenched in the courtly world of Weimar and was working on *Iphigenia in Tauris*, the first of his major plays in his so-called "classical" manner. The Storm-and-Stress revolt had by this time spent its force (except for Schiller's explosive early plays, which date from the early '80's). For Lenz the advent of the "idealistic" period meant the end of a world in which he could feel himself significantly creative; the very basis of his talent was an earthy realism which the new art-ideals which were to emanate from Weimar for the next generation could scarcely accommodate.

By the time Büchner began to write, the "idealistic movement" (which German literary historians have conventionally divided into two phases—Classicism and Romanticism, the latter itself sub-divided into two phases) had also spent its force. It was only natural for Büchner to seek a model in a writer from an earlier era. But Büchner's obvious antipathy to the plays which the idealistic move-ment produced must not blind us to the real and enduring achieve-ment which marks this drama at its best. The major dramatic works of German Classicism, Goethe's *Iphigenia* (completed in 1786) and *Torquato Tasso* (1789) and Schiller's *Wallenstein* trilogy (1799), though they are little known today outside Germany, can easily hold their own among the world's great dramas. But a contemporary audience can scarcely approach them without some conception of the artistic and cultural premises on which they are based. For one thing, these plays are part of Goethe and Schiller's attempt to found a national culture, of which they saw a national drama as an indispensable cornerstone. Unlike England, France and Spain dur-ing their major periods of dramatic writing, Germany lacked a vital popular theatrical tradition; as a result, the plays of Goethe and

Schiller often seem a kind of hothouse growth, nurtured with a deliberateness and high-mindedness which can all too easily create a barrier to modern taste.

The dramaturgy on which these plays is based is far more closely related to that of French seventeenth-century drama than it is to Shakespeare, though it is by no means a slavish imitation of earlier models, as was the earlier type of German drama represented by *The Dying Cato*. Compared to the Storm-and-Stress plays and Büchner's work, the German Classical plays remain essentially within the Aristotelian dramatic tradition. Their characters are invariably of high station. Their chief dramatic effects emerge out of a carefully contrived, though often relatively simple plot. In striking contrast to the Storm-and-Stress drama, they cultivate an economy of means, with the result that they sacrifice richness of detail for a more austere, lofty effect. Whereas the Storm-and-Stress plays, like Büchner's, were generally in prose, most of the Classical dramas are in blank verse—a verse, indeed, of a rather formal sort, with a diction and syntax deliberately removed from those of ordinary conversation. A work such as *Wallenstein* (which, though publicized and translated into English verse by so powerful a voice as Coleridge's, is scarcely known today to English-speaking readers) succeeds in creating a type of effect quite foreign to that of the various German anti-Aristotelian dramas before and after it. For in *Wallenstein* Schiller, like the ancient Greek tragedians, is centrally concerned with the mysteries inherent in a man's relation to his destiny; his dramatic method, with its cunning contrivance of plot, its disdain for "extraneous" detail, and its careful balance of concrete situation and abstract idea, allows the larger metaphysical questions to emerge naturally out of his fable with an intensity and singularity of effect which dramatists such as Büchner and Brecht have chosen to do without.

A sympathetic reading of the major German plays in the "classical" manner suggests that the distinction which Büchner's Lenz draws between "idealized" and "real" characters is not altogether fair to the actual practice of Goethe and Schiller. The characters of *Wallenstein*, for instance, are "idealized" only to the extent that they speak a somewhat heightened language and are not depicted in the informal situations in which Büchner customarily presents his characters. But Schiller's characters at their best are also concretely differentiated from one another and, once one accepts the premises of his dramatic method, the reader or audience quite naturally comes to believe in them as living beings. Büchner, like any artist confronting a mode of art antithetical to his own, probably did not bother to distinguish between Schiller at his best and at his worst: his two recorded comments on Schiller, both of them negative, attack him for being too "rhetorical" and for creating characters who are essentially "puppets with sky-blue noses and affected pathos, but not flesh-and-blood human beings."[3] And with the notable exception of *Wallenstein* (and perhaps also his uncompleted play *Demetrius*—1805), one must admit that Büchner's view of Schiller's "classical" plays is more or less a just one. In a play such as *The Bride of Messina* (1802), a much more conscious attempt than *Wallenstein* to re-create the effect of Greek tragedy, Schiller's high-mindedness comes to seem virtually unbearable. And, quite in contrast to *Wallenstein*, such later historical plays as *The Maid of Orleans* (1801), *Mary Stuart* (1800) and *William Tell* (1804) fail to embody their lofty central "idea" in any concrete dramatic situation in which a modern audience can honestly believe.

By the time Büchner wrote his first play Schiller had been dead for thirty years and was firmly entrenched as the chief classic of the German theater. Indeed, the rhetoric and the "affected pathos" of which Büchner complains had become standard conventions of German drama—conventions so deeply rooted that the major German dramatists of our century have felt a continuing need to challenge them. It seems only natural that writers like Gerhart Hauptmann and Brecht would look back to Büchner—as the latter looked back to Lenz—as a forerunner in their revolt against the Classical tradition in German drama.

But Büchner was not the first writer in his own century to challenge this tradition. At least two writers, Heinrich von Kleist and Christian Dietrich Grabbe, experimented with significantly new ways of dramatic expression. On the surface, at least, Kleist's plays seem to continue the Classical framework, for they utilize the basic conventions which Goethe and Schiller had established in their Classical plays. Kleist's major plays, *The Broken Jug* (1806), *Penthesilea* (1808), and *The Prince of Homburg* (1810), all maintain the formality of blank verse, and all are marked by the most rigorous economy of structure. Like the Classical plays before them, they are built out of a closely connected chain of events which lead up to the climax (the first two of these plays, though they are full length, each consist of a single, sustained act); and quite unlike Büchner's dramas they allow their central conflicts to develop through the direct confrontation of characters with one another.

Yet, despite his apparently traditional form, Kleist was far less an imitator than an innovator. His language, though elevated in diction, has a taut and breathless quality which, more than any other dramatic blank verse in German, creates the illusion of being spo-

3. Georg Büchner, *Sämtliche Werke und Briefe*, ed. Fritz Bergemann (Wiesbaden, 1958), pp. 553, 400.

ken by living beings. Moreover, despite his Classical dramaturgy, which is predicated on the assumption that characters can express their conflicts with one another in verbal terms, his plays, like Büchner's, ultimately suggest the inability of human beings to communicate meaningfully at all. In *Penthesilea*, for example, the two chief characters appear to communicate with one another in an idyllic love scene, but the heroine, discovering that their relationship is based on a fundamental misunderstanding, ends up tricking her lover into a brutal death-trap. Kleist, one might say, exploits a dramatic method based on character relationships only to lay bare the deceptiveness inherent in these relationships. Like Büchner, Kleist was little known or appreciated in his own time; there is, in fact, no reason to think that Büchner discerned his real significance, if he read him at all. Yet despite their basic differences in dramatic technique, Kleist and Büchner share a certain kinship through the skepticism and the despair which their works voice with a notable lack of pretentiousness; and it hardly seems accidental that Kleist's plays, like Büchner's, achieved no general acclaim until our own century.

Grabbe, too, was little understood in his age. Although the quality of his achievement is considerably below that of Kleist and Büchner, his experiments in dramatic form anticipate much that Büchner was to develop in his own way. Grabbe's early plays are still largely in the grand style, and their blank verse betrays the staleness into which the language of Classical drama had fallen in the generation after Schiller. His heroes, quite in contrast to Büchner's, are also conceived in the grand manner; all, in fact, are men of titanic proportions—Napoleon, Hannibal, the Hohenstaufen emperors—who go to their doom through no fault of their own, but through the pettiness of a world which cannot support such titans. But Grabbe's later plays, above all *Napoleon or the Hundred Days* (1831) and *Hannibal* (1835), seem just as boldly "experimental" as *Danton's Death*.

Napoleon, which Büchner doubtless knew when he wrote his first play, presents a vast panoramic view of the events immediately leading up to Waterloo. Grabbe makes no attempt, as would a dramatist in the Classical tradition, to present these events in any causal chain. The play, in fact, is essentially a vivid and bounteous chronicle which focuses on such diverse phenomena as the crowds on the streets of Paris, soldiers in barracks on the eve of battle, the newly restored Bourbon court, and Napoleon vainly attempting to re-establish his past glory without realizing he lacked the means to do so. *Napoleon* is written in a terse and racy prose, a style which, unlike the verse of his earlier tragedies, is able to accommodate a wide variety of tones and to portray the historical milieu with a lively intimacy. In its mixture of comic and tragic elements, its technique of short, contrasting scenes, and its treatment of the common people caught up by vast historical forces, it may well have served as a model for *Danton's Death*. Though *Napoleon* still reads with a certain vitality, Grabbe did not, like Büchner, succeed in fusing the quite diverse components of his play to create a single, closely organized whole; and as a result, the play remains far more interesting in its individual details than in its totality. Above all, Grabbe lacks that quality of dramatic objectivity which I have tried to describe in Büchner's work. Karl Gutzkow tried to define this difference between the two writers in a letter he wrote to Büchner to encourage him in his work: "If one observes [Grabbe's] stiff, forced, bony manner, one must make the most favorable predictions for your fresh, effervescent natural powers."[4] If Gutzkow's statement is perhaps a bit unfair to Grabbe, it is also notable as the most powerful critical praise Büchner was to receive either in his lifetime or until half a century after his death.

ii

It is a tribute to the richness and variety of Büchner's achievement that each of the writers who have felt his impact have absorbed a different aspect of his work. Gerhart Hauptmann, the first major figure whom Büchner influenced, shares Büchner's sympathy for the sufferings of lowly people. Hauptmann's career, which spans almost six decades, includes a vast variety of forms and themes, from contemporary social realism to symbolic fantasy to grand-style tragedy based on Greek myth. But Hauptmann seems closest to Büchner in his early, largely realistic period. His short story, *The Apostle* (1890), a study of a modern religious fanatic, attempts to imitate the narrative method of Büchner's *Lenz*; yet Hauptmann's interior monologue today reads like a somewhat dated technical experiment, while Büchner's retains a freshness and naturalness which belie its great distance from us in time. Hauptmann perhaps came closest to the spirit of Büchner's work in his drama *The Weavers* (1892) which depicts an actual peasant uprising of the 1840's such as Büchner might have stirred up in his Giessen days. But Hauptmann's play is no socialist tract, as its early audiences often thought. Like Büchner in *Danton's Death*, Hauptmann questions the value of revolution while at the same time showing a high degree of sympathy for the grievances of the common people he is portraying.

4. *Ibid.*, p. 523.

In two later plays, *Henschel the Carter* (1898) and *Rose Bernd* (1903), Hauptmann, like Büchner in *Woyzeck*, succeeds in giving a traditional tragic dignity to inarticulate and passive characters of humble background. Hauptmann goes much further than Büchner in attempting to paint a detailed and authentic social milieu; indeed, the Silesian dialect of the original version of *The Weavers* would have proved so difficult for German readers that he had to "translate" the play into a more easily comprehensible form. Hauptmann's figures often have the brooding, explosive quality that he doubtless discerned in many of Büchner's figures, perhaps even in Büchner himself, whose genius Hauptmann once characterized as "glowing lava hurled out of Chthonic depths."[5] The characters and backgrounds of Hauptmann's best "realist" plays still seem impressive today, though his dramaturgy, with its well-wrought plots and his carefully planned motivations and foreshadowings, seems somewhat old-fashioned next to Büchner's, which shares the disdain for traditional theatrical effect of much contemporary drama.

If Hauptmann drew largely from the realistic side of Büchner's work, Frank Wedekind drew from the "unreal" side of Büchner, above all, the grotesque element which he discerned in the doctor, captain and carnival figures in *Woyzeck*. In his early play, *The Awakening of Spring* (1891), a violent and impassioned protest against the suppression of sexual knowledge in the education of the young, Wedekind depicts his middle-class characters as the kind of grotesque, perverted beings Büchner had presented before him. But Wedekind's entire poetic world is made up of grotesque types: the naturalness and dramatic objectivity with which characters such as Büchner's Marie, Marion and Danton are presented were totally foreign to Wedekind's talent. Ideologically, however, Wedekind's plays attempt to propagate a doctrine of naturalness; thus, in his character Lulu, the heroine of *The Earth Spirit* and its sequel, *Pandora's Box* (1895), Wedekind created a symbol of amoral and instinctual nature. As a literary type, Lulu is perhaps less akin to Büchner's Marie than to his drum major, whom she resembles in the exaggerated manner in which her "naturalness" is depicted.

Wedekind's success as a dramatic artist, one realizes today, falls short of his success as a liberating force in German culture at the turn of the century; though he was often capable of crudely powerful effects, he rarely succeeded in finding an adequate dramatic embodiment for the new ideas he was so intent on disseminating. Even if one admires his integrity, his Lulu, one must admit, is a rather dated creature who lives less surely in Wedekind's plays than

---

5. Quoted in Ernst Johann, *Georg Büchner in Selbstzeugnissen und Bilddokumenten* (Hamburg, 1958), p. 166.

in the opera which Alban Berg built around her. Through Wedekind, however, one side of Büchner—the rebel against bourgeois convention and the creator of the grotesquely extravagant language which Wedekind found in parts of *Woyzeck*—was transmitted to the Expressionist dramatists who followed him and, above all, to Bertolt Brecht.[6]

The fact that Berg's only two operas are based on *Woyzeck* and the Lulu plays is, I think, a testimony to the continuity which Berg's generation felt between Büchner's and Wedekind's work. Berg's setting (1921) of Büchner's play is itself an important instance of the impact of Büchner on our own century. Berg prepared his own libretto, and at first sight one feels amazed at how closely he followed Büchner's text. To be sure, he used only about two thirds of Büchner's scenes, and even these were sometimes pared down for economy's sake. But Berg stuck to the original dialogue to a relatively high degree and managed to retain much of the flavor of the play. His musical method, indeed, often succeeds in heightening Büchner's most original dramatic effects. For example, in Marie's repentance scene the music shifts back and forth in mood as Marie alternately reads from the Bible and expresses her own thoughts, and at the end of the scene it reaches a climax as piercing as any one might imagine from the text.

In its total effect, however, the opera seems a work of a very different kind from the play. Through the heavy orchestral commentary, which presents the composer's point of view on the events, the characters seem far less autonomous beings than they do in the original. The orchestra, in addition, serves to underline that sense of a malign fate which, because of the difference between the two media, hovers over the play in a far less distinct way. Indeed, the atonality of much of the music seems ideally suited to producing the eerie effects which Berg so obviously sought, especially in the final scenes. The character Wozzeck (whose name Berg spelled as it appeared in the Franzos edition of Büchner) seems even more passive and inarticulate than he does in the play. Among the passages which Berg cut out are those in which he asserts his dignity, for example the scene in which he gives Andres his belongings and reads his identification papers. Berg quite deliberately emphasized the abnormality and the suffering of his hero, who thus emerges as a helpless, crazed animal. Berg's version also stressed the economic degradation of the characters; in fact, the musical phrase which accompanies Wozzeck's words, "Wir arme Leut'"—"We poor folk"—is the chief leitmotif of the opera, achieving its fullest force

---

6. Wolfgang Kayser defines several parallels between Büchner and Wedekind in their use of the grotesque in *Das Groteske* (Oldenburg, 1957), pp. 141–43.

in the long and powerful orchestral interlude which directly follows Wozzeck's suicide.

Berg's emphasis on the play's psychological and social aspects is accompanied by a lack of emphasis on the existential questions which Büchner poses so persistently throughout his work, for example in the complex man-animal imagery and in the grandmother's tale (of which Berg uses only a fragment). Büchner's existential questions depend, above all, on strictly literary means of expression for which Berg wisely did not seek a direct musical equivalent. Indeed, Büchner's basic dramatic method, with its loosely connected scenes which could seemingly be placed in several different combinations, in the opera becomes transformed into an entirely different mode of dramaturgy. Through the constant orchestral commentary, and, above all, through the interludes between scenes, each event seems to follow the last with the most frightening inevitability. Berg concentrates almost exclusively on the "main line" of plot and excludes everything that he must have thought subsidiary to it—for example, the carnival scenes, the conversation with the Jewish pawnbroker, in fact that whole crowded larger world which hovers around the edges of Büchner's play. Even the comic touches, grim as they are in the play, are almost missing from the opera; one is scarcely tempted to laugh during the scene between Wozzeck and the doctor, and largely, I think, because of the quite uncomic effect of the musical accompaniment (partly also because Berg, who was perhaps worried about getting his work performed, shifted the doctor's experiment from the excretory to the respiratory functions). The opera, as a result, has a kind of classical starkness and solemnity quite foreign to the spirit of the play. It seems to me symptomatic of Berg's classicism that every scene consists of a different musical form, each systematically different from the others. The following summary,[7] based on Berg's stated intentions, suggests the form-consciousness which governs the opera (scene numbers in parentheses, music in italics):

Act I. Exposition, Wozzeck and his relation to his environment / *five character sketches*: (1) the captain / *suite*; (2) Andres / *rhapsody*; (3) Marie / *military march and cradle song*; (4) the physician / *passacaglia*; (5) the drum major / *andante affettuoso* (*quasi rondo*).

Act II. Dénouement, Wozzeck is gradually convinced of Marie's infidelity / *symphony in five movements*: (1) Wozzeck's first suspicion / *sonata form*; (2) Wozzeck is mocked / *fantasie and fugue*;

7. Adapted from Willi Reich's analysis of the opera, "A Guide to *Wozzeck*," *Musical Quarterly*, XXXVIII (1952), 1–20. For a very different critical approach to the opera, see the chapter on *Wozzeck* and *The Rake's Progress* in Joseph Kerman's *Opera as Drama* (New York, 1959), pp. 219–49.

(3) Wozzeck accuses Marie / *largo;* (4) Marie and drum major dance / *scherzo;* (5) the drum major trounces Wozzeck / *rondo martiale.*

Act III. Catastrophe, Wozzeck murders Marie and atones through suicide / *six inventions:* (1) Marie's remorse / *invention on a theme;* (2) death of Marie / *invention on a tone;* (3) Wozzeck tries to forget / *invention on a rhythm;* (4) Wozzeck drowns in the pond / *invention on a six-tone chord; instrumental interlude* with closed curtain; (5) Marie's son plays unconcerned / *invention on a persistent rhythm* (*perpetuum mobile*).

Berg himself tells us that he chose such diverse forms to embody each scene in order to avoid the effect of musical monotony.[8] One must admit, surely, that even after repeated hearings the listener remains unaware of the nature of the various forms which Berg employs. Yet the form-consciousness which is manifest in the above chart is indicative, I think, of a kind of classicism peculiar to much of the art of the 1920's. It seems to me analogous, for instance, to the mythological framework and charts of correspondences around which James Joyce constructed *Ulysses;* T. S. Eliot's well-known description of the function of Joyce's mythological framework—"It is simply a way of controlling, of ordering, of giving a shape and a significance to the immense panorama of futility and anarchy which is contemporary history"[9]—is perhaps applicable to the function of the tight musical forms which Berg employs to contain the chaotic and characteristically modern materials that he found in Büchner's play. The resulting opera achieves a greatness that remains independent of that of the play; one recognizes it as a work of equal, though by no means kindred genius. Since Berg's work has made its way in recent years into the repertory of all the major opera houses, one hopes that the strong competition it offers will not exclude the play from theatrical performance, which, up to now, it has rarely achieved in the English-speaking countries.

Our sense of Büchner's modernity has been shaped to a large degree through his impact upon, and his affinities with the two most significant developments in European theater during the last few decades—the work of Bertolt Brecht, on the one hand, and the *avant garde* theater in Paris after World War II. It was only natural that Brecht should look back to Büchner as an example: not only did Brecht view Büchner as a fellow political revolutionary, but Büchner's work stood for many of the same values that Brecht throughout his life sought to articulate. Both writers, for instance, succeeded in creating a vital and glowing dramatic language by

---

8. See Berg's note on the opera reprinted with Reich's analysis, pp. 20–21.
9. "'Ulysses,' Order, and Myth," in *Criticism: The Foundations of Modern Literary Judgment,* ed. Mark Schorer, Josephine Miles, and Gordon McKenzie (New York, 1948), p. 270.

first refusing to be poetic in any traditional way. Like Büchner, Brecht created an idiom of his own, colloquial, earthy, ironical—an idiom, moreover, which appears to imitate the language of real men, yet which in its total effect has a richly poetic resonance. Brecht's, like Büchner's, is a realism which refuses to be pedantically realistic: the red moon which hovers menacingly over the murder scene in *Woyzeck* was conceived in something of the same spirit as the red moon which, at the end of Brecht's early play *Drums in the Night* (1919), turns out to be a Chinese lantern which the embittered hero angrily destroys.

Brecht's language is perhaps most directly imitative of Büchner's in his first play, *Baal* (1918), whose bohemian hero speaks a wildly extravagant language which Brecht, like Wedekind before him, developed from such examples as Woyzeck's descriptions of his visions and such caricatures as Büchner's doctor, captain and carnival figures. But Brecht's affinities with Büchner cannot be defined simply through such instances of imitation; one could argue, in fact, that the personal idiom he achieved in his more mature work, through its poise and control, has more in common with Büchner's language than anything in *Baal*. Both writers, moreover, attain much of their creative impulse through their conscious opposition to the conventions of the German Classical drama. For Brecht, as for Wedekind, Büchner served as a kind of liberating force, not only against the Classical drama, but against the middle-class values with which this drama was associated in their minds. The Schiller-like rhetoric which Büchner parodies in the speeches of the drunken stage-prompter Simon in *Danton's Death* is sustained through two full-length plays by Brecht, *St. Joan of the Stockyards* (1930) and *The Resistible Rise of Arturo Ui* (1941), whose intentionally pompous blank verse succeeds in parodying not so much the Chicago capitalists who are made to speak it as the middle-class Germans whose slavish awe of their theatrical classics was for Brecht a sure symptom of their false cultural values.

Not only must Brecht have discerned in Büchner a fellow enemy of theatrical rhetoric, but the forms of organization which Büchner developed in his three plays provided the most successful German example before Brecht of a non-Aristotelian serious drama. In certain crucial respects—for instance, in their disdain for linear plots and their stress on the relative independence of individual scenes—Büchner's plays can surely be seen as ancestors of Brecht's "epic" theater. But Brecht's much-publicized theoretical pronouncements on the nature of epic theater cannot be applied literally to Büchner's plays, nor, it could be argued, to Brecht's own best works; the so-called "alienation effect," whereby the audience is discouraged from believing in the literal reality of the events enacted onstage, is scarcely applicable to plays such as *Danton's Death* and *Woyzeck*, whose dramatic reality we are made to accept wholeheartedly and with whose heroes we sympathize to a high degree. Although Brecht attempted to create most of his heroes as didactic negative examples and to hold back the audience's sympathy with them, some of his greatest figures—for instance, the cowardly Galileo, the greedy vendor Mother Courage, the alternately hearty and sour Finnish businessman Mr. Puntila—despite their author's intentions, achieve something of the autonomous life and the sympathetic quality which we find in Büchner's Danton and Woyzeck.

Like Büchner, Brecht has a penchant for passive heroes who allow the world to shape them as it will; Brecht, indeed, has perhaps gone further than any major dramatist in exploring the psychology of passivity—for instance, in the well-meaning porter Galy Gay in *Man Equals Man* (1926), who is cajoled into assuming the identity of another man and becoming a brutal soldier; in the hero of *The Life of Galileo* (1939), who compromises his principles for the sake of bodily comfort and privacy to pursue his writings; in the good soldier Schweik, who, transferred by Brecht from Jaroslav Hašek's novel (itself an extension of the comic possibilities in the character of Woyzeck) to a more modern setting in *Schweik in the Second World War* (1944), manages to survive and sometimes even to confound the Nazis by pretending to comply with them.

The essential humanitarianism which underlies both Büchner's and Brecht's work finds expression partly through their common skepticism toward older forms of humanitarianism which they see as false or stale. The skepticism with which Büchner treats the doctor's traditionally idealistic definitions of the human being finds its modern equivalent in such Brechtian formulations as the title and theme of *Man Equals Man*, which attempts to demonstrate that one human being *can* be changed into another, or Macheath's cynical refrain in *The Threepenny Opera* (1928):

> *What does a man live by? By grinding, sweating,*
> *Defeating, beating, cheating, eating some other man*
> *For he can only live by sheer forgetting*
> *Forgetting that he ever was a man.*[1]

The title of the parable play *The Good Person* [*Der gute Mensch*] *of Setzuan* (1940) seems almost an echo of the phrase which Büchner ironically puts into the captain's mouth time and again—"Woyzeck, du bist ein guter Mensch, ein guter Mensch"; the captain's phrase is

---

1. Translated by Eric Bentley and Desmond Vesey, *The Modern Theatre* (New York, 1955), I, 168.

as empty of real meaning as is the title of Brecht's play, whose parable attempts to demonstrate the impossibility of being "good" in
the world as it is. Just as the work of both writers achieved a poetic
quality only after their deliberate rejection of older, staler forms of
poetic language, so it succeeds in expounding a humanitarianism
through their tough-minded distrust of smug, traditional ethical
statements.

It seems no accident that Büchner achieved his first major
acclaim outside Germany in the French theater of the last two
decades, for his plays anticipate many of the themes and techniques of the so-called "theater of the absurd." One might note, for
instance, the following passage from the promenade scene in *Danton's Death* (Act II, Scene 2), in which Büchner records the conversation of two gentlemen walking along the street:

FIRST GENTLEMAN   You know, it is the most extraordinary discovery! I mean, it makes all the branches of science look entirely
different. Mankind really is striding towards its high destiny.

SECOND GENTLEMAN   Have you seen that new play? There's a great
Babylonian tower, a mass of arches and steps and passages, and
then, do you know, they blow the whole thing up, right into the
air, just like that! It makes you dizzy. Quite extraordinary. [*He
stops, perplexed.*]

FIRST GENTLEMAN   Why, whatever's the matter?

SECOND GENTLEMAN   Oh, nothing, really! But—would you just
give me a hand—over this puddle—there! Thank you very much.
I only just got over it. That could be extremely dangerous!

FIRST GENTLEMAN   You weren't afraid of it, were you?

SECOND GENTLEMAN   Well, yes—the earth's only a very thin crust,
you know. I always think I might fall through where there's a hole
like that. You have to walk very gently or you may easily go through.
But do go and see that play—I thoroughly recommend it!

This passage could easily be mistaken for one of the random street
conversations which one finds, say, in *The Killer* (1957) by Eugène
Ionesco, who himself once listed Büchner, in company with Aeschylus, Sophocles, Shakespeare, and Kleist, as the only dramatist of
the past whom he still found readable.[2]

Büchner, like Ionesco in similar passages, provides no context for
this conversation: we are never told, for instance, what sort of scientific discovery the first gentleman is even talking about; much of
the comic effect, indeed, comes from Büchner's deliberate failure

to provide any context at all for the gentleman's pretentious remarks. Like the recent French dramatists, Büchner is concerned with exposing the emptiness inherent in the clichés with which people customarily express themselves ("Mankind . . . striding towards its high destiny"). By attempting to record conversation as it is really spoken—not, as in earlier drama, as it *ought* to be spoken—he exposes, as well, the absurdity of the transitions within ordinary human speech: the second gentleman, for example, moves unself-consciously from his enthusiasm for a new play to his fear of the hole in the street and then, at the end of the passage (which is also the end of the scene) directly back to the play in question. If one examines the transition (or lack of it) from the first to the second speech, one notes that the characters are shown talking *past* one another instead of *with* one another. Indeed, there is no real contact between them: the first is fully concerned with his statement about some scientific discovery, the second with his enthusiasm for a play he has seen. In thus demonstrating that human beings often fail to make contact even while they appear to be conversing, Büchner anticipates a technique that was not to be exploited to any great degree in drama until Chekhov and the recent French dramatists. The difficulty of human communication is not merely the theme of this small passage, but is, after all, one of the central themes of *Danton's Death* as a whole: one need only remember Danton's statement to his wife, on the first page of the play, of the impossibility of people really knowing one another. And it is a central theme, moreover, in such otherwise diverse contemporary plays as Arthur Adamov's *The Parody* (1947), Ionesco's *The Bald Soprano* (1948), and Beckett's *Waiting for Godot* (1952).

In fact, to catalogue the themes of the "theater of the absurd" is at once to catalogue many of Büchner's essential themes. The terror, absurd and frightening at once, which lurks behind Adamov's *The Large and the Small Maneuver* (1950) and *Each against Each* (1952) is similar in kind to the terror in the background of *Danton's Death*, which Adamov had himself translated into French a few years before completing these plays; moreover, the totalitarian political rhetoric which resounds in both plays is essentially a modern version of the brutally lifeless language of Robespierre's and St. Just's public pronouncements. The skepticism towards their self-identity which plagues the central characters of *Waiting for Godot* and Adamov's *Professor Taranne* (1951) has much in common with Leonce's skepticism in Büchner's comedy. The vaudeville routines which Beckett's clowns use to while away the time that hangs so oppressively on them corresponds quite precisely to the *commedia dell'arte* techniques employed by Leonce and Valerio to fulfill the same purpose.[3] Indeed, the very words with which Didi in *Waiting for Godot* voices his boredom and despair might easily have come from one of Danton's, or Leonce's, or Lenz' speeches: "We wait. We are bored. No, don't protest, we are bored to death, there's no denying it. Good. A diversion comes along and what do we do? We let it go to waste. Come, let's get to work! In an instant all will vanish and we'll be alone once more, in the midst of nothingness!"[4]

In the face of such an insight, voiced with equal emphasis by Büchner and Beckett, all human endeavor comes to seem futile, meaningless, and absurd. As Lee Baxandall has suggested in his essay on *Danton's Death*, the agonized lyricism of Büchner's first play "finds its closest modern counterpart" in *Waiting for Godot*.[5] And it is through this lyricism, one might add, that Beckett, more than any of his contemporaries, has captured that sense of mystery which ultimately stands behind the despair in Büchner's plays. Moreover, through its plotlessness, its vagueness of setting, and its lack of any real social framework, *Waiting for Godot* seems a kind of Büchner play with its narrative and its background removed. Or, rather, one could view it as a more radical step than the ones Büchner had taken in *Danton's Death* and *Woyzeck* to break down the canons of classical drama.

Yet a comparison of Büchner with the recent French dramatists also suggests some vital differences in purpose and form between his work and theirs. However strikingly Büchner's work may anticipate the significant experiments of our time, it also, for instance, employs certain traditional methods of characterization which the French dramatists have largely abandoned. Thus, Büchner attempted, as the French have chosen not to, to create the illusion of a full and varied world of real beings rooted in a real and recognizable environment. Marie in *Woyzeck* has a completeness and a reality that go well beyond her dramatic function in the play; when she sits before the mirror admiring her new earrings she gains our sympathy in a way that no character—except, perhaps, some of Beckett's—in any of the recent French plays can. Directly after the execution of the Dantonists, a woman passerby makes the sort of statement one often finds in Ionesco's plays: "I always say you ought to see a man in different surroundings; I'm all for these public executions, aren't you, love?" But the effect of these lines is shattering in a way that they could not be in Ionesco. Because of

3. Martin Esslin, in his study of the contemporary "absurd" drama, cites especially *Leonce and Lena* as an ancestor of this movement (*The Theatre of the Absurd* [New York, 1961] pp. 238–39).
4. *Waiting for Godot* (New York, 1954), p. 52.
5. "Georg Büchner's *Danton's Death*," p. 148.

the interest and sympathy which Danton and his friends have aroused in us throughout the play, the passerby's statement causes us to feel at once the tragedy and the absurdity of their death. In contrast, the ironic statements made by the maid in Ionesco's *The Lesson* (1950) after the professor, in a fit of ire, has stabbed his pupil, suggest only the absurdity of the pupil's death. Ionesco, one might say, has dehumanized his characters in order to portray the precariousness and isolation in which they exist, while Büchner has demonstrated a similar precariousness and isolation by more traditional means—by first making us believe in the reality of his characters and their background. In the world of Büchner's plays we still feel the plenitude of creation, even if God's traditional beneficence is missing and his existence is, at most, a questionable thing.

iii

The vitality and the fullness of vision which characterize Büchner's dramatic world have rarely been achieved by those whom he has influenced, perhaps only by Brecht, but these qualities are present in far greater abundance in the dramatist whose impact Büchner felt more strongly than that of any other, namely, Shakespeare. Shakespeare, indeed, is the one writer for whom Büchner expressed the highest and most unqualified admiration. "Poor Shakespeare was a clerk by day and had to write his poetry at night, and I, who am not worthy to untie his shoelaces, have a much easier time," Büchner wrote to his fiancée a few weeks before his death.[6] In his first letter to Gutzkow, when excusing himself for not being entirely true to history in *Danton's Death*, he consoled himself with the notion that "all poets, with the exception of Shakespeare, confront history and nature as though they were school-boys."[7] The "fullness of life" which Büchner's character Lenz upholds so passionately as the central goal of art can be found only—thus we are told in the story—in Shakespeare and in folk poetry, and sometimes in Goethe—"everything else should be thrown in the fire." Like nearly all German writers for at least a generation before him, Büchner had been smitten by Shakespeare's plays since childhood; one of his Darmstadt schoolmates, in fact, testifies how Büchner and his friends would go to a nearby beech forest to read Shakespeare to one another on Sunday afternoons.[8]

6. "Some Letters," trans. Maurer, p. 54.
7. Bergemann, p. 390.
8. *Ibid.*, p. 556.

The many verbal echoes from Shakespeare in Büchner's work have been scrupulously recorded by various scholars,[9] and I shall not attempt to add to their findings here. It seems no surprise to find that Büchner echoed *Hamlet* more than any other Shakespearean play, indeed more than any other literary work. The influence of *Hamlet* went considerably beyond the verbal level. In their passivity, their introspectiveness and their verbal ingenuity, characters like Danton and Leonce obviously have something of Hamlet in them, though they derive as much from the various Hamlet-like heroes of German Romanticism as from the character actually created by Shakespeare. In her pathos and madness Lucille, in *Danton's Death*, has certain affinities with Ophelia. The deathly atmosphere, moreover, which permeates Büchner's first play has much in common with the atmosphere of Shakespeare's play.

It is worth noting, furthermore, that Büchner sometimes resorted to Shakespeare during the tensest dramatic moments of his plays. When Lucille laments the death of her husband, she speaks like Lear on the death of Cordelia: "Dying—dying—! But everything lives, everything's got to live, I mean, the little fly there, the bird. Why can't he?" Woyzeck's last words, in turn, echo Lady Macbeth's feelings of guilt: "Am I still bloody? I better wash up. There's a spot and there's another." Only a dramatist in another language would dare echo such familiar lines at such crucial moments in his own work; for an English dramatist to do so would be to risk writing a parody.

More significant than such echoes is the fact that Büchner succeeded—better, perhaps, than any other German dramatist—in imitating Shakespeare's manner while at the same time integrating it fully into the contexts he himself was creating. His Shakespearean imitation is most fully evident in *Danton's Death*, and it becomes progressively less evident in each of his two other plays. The following passage, in which the carters standing outside the Conciergerie are waiting to take Danton and his friends to the guillotine, has a genuinely Shakespearean quality about it (more so, I might add, in the German than in translation):

SECOND CARTER   Well, who would you say was the best carters?
FIRST CARTER   Whoever goes farthest and quickest.
SECOND CARTER   Well, you old fool, you can't cart a man much
    further than out of this world, can you, and I'd like to see anyone

9. See, for instance, the echoes and parallels cited by Heinrich Vogeley, *Georg Büchner und Shakespeare* (Marburg, 1934), pp. 30–51; Rudolf Majut, "Some Literary Affiliations of Georg Büchner with England," *Modern Language Review*, L (1955), 30–32; and Bergemann, p. 672. There is no evidence that Büchner read Shakespeare in English. His echoes are based on the standard German translation by Ludwig Tieck and August Wilhelm Schlegel.

do it in less than a quarter of an hour. It's exactly a quarter of an hour from here to Guillotine Square.

JAILER   Hurry up, you lazy slugs! Get in nearer the gate. Get back a bit, you girls.

FIRST CARTER   No, don't you budge! Never go round a girl, always go through.

SECOND CARTER   I'm with you there. You can take your horse and cart in with you, the roads are nice, but you'll be in quarantine when you come out again. [*They move forward.*] What are you gawping at?

A WOMAN   Waiting to see our old customers, dearie.

SECOND CARTER   My cart's not a brothel, you know. This is a decent cart, this is; the King went in this, and all the big nobs in Paris.

The bawdy and far-fetched jokes are obviously typical of the banter of Shakespeare's clowns and fools. But Büchner has not only captured the tone of this banter, he has also understood the dramatic function which this sort of banter has in a Shakespearean tragedy. Like the gravedigger scene in *Hamlet*, this passage creates a needed slackening of tension between the two anguished scenes in the Conciergerie immediately before and after it. Yet, also like the gravedigger scene, it functions as something more than "comic relief." Although we laugh at the jokes, the dramatic context in which they are placed powerfully qualifies the effect they have on us. There is something rather grotesque, after all, in the carter's concern for his social status ("this is a decent cart, this is; the King went in this") in the inverted world of the Reign of Terror: indeed, there is something even frightening about it, since he is about to cart the play's hero to his death. The fusion of comic and tragic which we see here and elsewhere in Büchner is a peculiarly Shakespearean one—a fusion, moreover, which is effected not only through the alternation of comic and tragic scenes, but through the multiplicity of levels (ironic, grotesque, pathetic, or whatever) with which a single speech, a single image even, may be interpreted. One could argue, in fact, that Büchner seems modern to us in many of the same respects in which he seems most Shakespearean. Through his use of comic techniques to express the most desperate human situations, his plays as surely look backward to Shakespeare—for instance, to Lear's scenes with his fool—as they look forward to the clowning in *Waiting for Godot*.

Büchner's Shakespearean quality is discernible not only through his echoes and his conscious attempts at imitation, but in certain fundamental affinities he shares with Shakespeare. Büchner is

Shakespearean, for instance, in the dramatic objectivity with which most of his characters are conceived and in the consequent impersonality he achieves in relation to his work. His talent is akin to that which Keats, in a famous passage from one of his letters, was trying to define when he distinguished his own and Shakespeare's mode from that of Wordsworth: "A Poet [by which Keats here means one like Shakespeare or himself] is the most unpoetical of any thing in existence; because he has no Identity—he is continually . . . filling some other Body—The Sun, the Moon, the Sea and Men and Women who are creatures of impulse are poetical and have about them an unchangeable attribute—the poet has none."[1] Like Shakespeare, Büchner expunges his own identity in favor of that of his characters, who seem to live with an autonomous and spontaneous life of their own. Of the major German dramatists before Büchner, only Goethe, I think, possessed this quality, though the severely classicist directions which Goethe's work, including his methods of characterization, took after his Storm-and-Stress years gave it an increasingly less Shakespearean character.

Büchner's most fundamental Shakespearean quality lies, perhaps, in his conception of a drama as a fully embodied poetic world of its own, relying as much on its richness of verbal texture as on its narrative to achieve its effects. The image of a crazy upside-down world which Büchner achieved in *Woyzeck* is comparable in kind, if not in degree, to the image out of which a play such as *King Lear* is built. The power that emanates from both these works is due as much to the atmosphere created by such indirect means as images and ironic thematic parallels as it is to the simple facts of "plot"; both plays, in fact, create their image of a distorted world partly, at least, through their constant insistence on the animallike nature of men—*Lear*, for instance, through its persistent imagery of wild animals, *Woyzeck* through such passages as the animal demonstrations in the carnival scenes. The non-Aristotelian conception of drama in which Büchner seems so conspicuously a pioneer is in certain respects, at least, a Shakespearean conception, as it was, indeed, for the German Storm-and-Stress writers, with whom Büchner felt such obvious affinities. Modern Shakespeare critics such as G. Wilson Knight and William Empson no longer read Shakespeare in terms of the expositions and dénouements with which their classicist-minded predecessors were all too often concerned, but attempt instead to describe and explore the larger poetic whole which they

1. *Letters*, ed. H. E. Rollins (Cambridge, Mass., 1958), I, 387.

see in each play.[2] Büchner, I think, discerned Shakespeare's dramatic method in something of the way we see it today, and to the extent that his plays achieve a Shakespearean thickness of texture and concentration of meaning, he seems to me the most Shakespearean of German dramatists.

iv

Even though Büchner's most striking affinities are with dramatists who lived long before or after him, in certain limited respects he is peculiarly of his own time. His work seems little related, however, to the German drama of the period; except for Grabbe, whose possible influence I noted earlier, the significant dramatic writing of the 1830's took directions quite different from Büchner's. The work of the Viennese comic writers Ferdinand Raimund and Johann Nestroy derives directly from the popular theater of Vienna, the only German-speaking city which had maintained a living *commedia dell'arte* tradition. Franz Grillparzer, also a Viennese, succeeded in giving new life to the forms of the German Classical drama, which he was able to fuse with elements derived from Spanish drama and the Viennese folk tradition. If there was any contemporary dramatist for whom Büchner could feel any real affinities, it was one who did not write in German at all, namely Musset, from whom, as I indicated in my chapter on *Leonce and Lena*, he borrowed what he found useful, and no more.

Nor can one discern many significant relationships between Büchner and the German nondramatic writers of his time. When Büchner was mentioned by nineteenth- and early twentieth-century literary historians his name was usually lumped together with those of the Young Germany group, men such as Gutzkow, Heinrich Laube, and Ludwig Wienbarg—and for no better reason than that he was politically on the left and had been sponsored by Gutzkow. Even without Büchner's firm denial of sympathy with the aims and ideas of the Young Germans,[3] one need only set their works next to his to note a fundamental difference both in their essential thematic concerns and their artistic stature. Gutzkow's best-known work, his short novel *Wally the Doubter*, written in the same year (1835) in which Büchner began his correspondence with him, attempts, far more than any of Büchner's works, to deal with a characteristic contemporary problem, the "problem of the modern woman"; when

---

2. See, for example, G. Wilson Knight's study of the imagery of *Lear*, "The Lear Universe," in *Wheel of Fire* (London, 1930), pp. 194–226, or Empson's study of the functions of a single word in the play, "Fool in *Lear*," in *The Structure of Complex Words* (London, 1951), pp. 125–57.
3. Bergemann, p. 408.

we read it today, however, *Wally* seems less about any real woman than about a problem which Gutzkow lacked the means to embody in any artistically convincing way.

Of the most notable German poets writing in the 1830's—namely, Heinrich Heine, Annette von Droste-Hülshoff, and Eduard Mörike— only Heine shares something of Büchner's world. Büchner himself probably never appreciated Heine's real distinction, for he listed his name with those of the Young Germans (to whom Heine can be linked only superficially) whom he rejected.[4] The common spirit of the age which shapes the work of both manifests itself in their ironi- cal perspectives and their ability to endow seemingly trivial and pro- saic situations with poetic meaning; yet the sensibility that emerges from the writings of each—Heine's work is built around his per- sonality, whereas Büchner's is notable for the deliberate absence of the author's personality—is as different as that of any two writers can be.[5]

The spirit of Büchner's age cannot be defined merely by the orga- nized movements of the time—Young Germany, for instance, or Romanticism in France and Italy—but by the work of certain lonely figures who, in one way or another, were at war with their time. Büchner's closest contemporaries were perhaps less his fellow writ- ers in German than such figures as Stendhal and Lermontov. Each of these, though rooted in the Romantic Movement within his par- ticular country, is distinguished by the concretely real world he created in his fiction and by the steadfast ironic control he main- tained over his material.

The major novels of Stendhal, who was thirty years older than Büchner, were written during the same decade which wit- nessed Büchner's brief career; Lermontov, who was a year younger than Büchner and died only four years after him, reached his artistic maturity in the last years of the decade. Both writers, like Büchner, have succeeded in making contact with our own cen- tury with an immediacy which few other nineteenth-century writers were able to achieve. Büchner was further removed from Romanti- cism (which had waned in Germany far earlier than in France or Russia) than were the authors of *Racine and Shakespeare* or the

---

4. *Ibid.*
5. Walter Höllerer, in *Zwischen Klassik und Moderne*, has made the best attempt thus far to define a common ground between Büchner and his contemporary writers in Ger- man, above all, Grabbe, Heine, Raimund, Nestroy, and Büchner's fellow Hessian writer, Ernst Elias Niebergall. (See the chapter on Büchner, pp. 100–42, and also pp. 36, 37, 63, 65, 67, 68, 80, 85, 151, 168, 169, 176, 178–79, 184, 189, 198–99.) Among the features which Höllerer distinguishes as common to most of these figures are a persistent skepticism, a fusion of wit and pathos, and the development of peculiarly terse ways of expression. Höllerer's fine argument does not deny the fact that Büchner has spoken to our age with a greater degree of contemporaneity than any of these other writers.

Byronic narratives that marked Lermontov's early period.[6] Yet it could be argued that each of these writers seems most modern to us in precisely those areas in which he found the means to distance himself from the various Romantic themes and conventions which he inherited. Pechorin, the protagonist of Lermontov's *A Hero of Our Time* (1840), speaks more directly to us than any of Byron's heroes (including even Don Juan) because Lermontov has created a recognizable social environment for him and, above all, has been willing to view him ironically from a number of points of view. We are willing to accept Julien Sorel, in *The Red and the Black* (1830), as a hero only because Stendhal has placed his heroic gestures in an environment in which they come to seem useless and absurd. At one point in this novel (Book II, Chapter XII) Mathilde looks back longingly to the heroic days of the Revolution and imagines her lover Julien in the role of Danton. Büchner, one might say, went one step further than Stendhal: the banality which Stendhal attributed to the world of the Restoration is much the same as the banality which Büchner discerned in the Revolution as well. The imaginary commonwealth which Stendhal depicted in *The Charterhouse of Parma* (1838) is much akin—above all, in its attempt to hold on to long-outmoded institutions—to the grand duchy of Hesse in which Büchner grew up. If Büchner had lived on to write a drama or novel on Hesse, the image that might have emerged would, I think, have had more in common with Stendhal's ironic portrait of Parma than with the more simple-minded revolutionist's image of Hesse which Büchner presented in *The Hessian Messenger*.

---

6. Despite his antipathies to German Romanticism, in a few respects his work represents a continuation of the aims and methods of this movement. *Leonce and Lena*, in its wordplay, its concern with boredom, and its attempt to re-evoke the world of Shakespearean comedy, has something in common with Clemens Brentano's charming but impossibly diffuse comedy *Ponce de Leon* (1803), which, exactly thirty-five years before, had been submitted to the same competition for which Büchner prepared his play. Gutzkow, in fact, pointed out the parallel between the two plays in his memorial tribute to Büchner (in Bergemann, p. 595). Büchner's attempts, in *Danton's Death* and *Woyzeck*, to fuse comic and tragic elements and to break down the conventions of German Classical drama were among the central aims of the German Romantic school, which, however, was unable to produce a dramatist who could realize these aims. The apocalyptic grandeur with which the prisoners voice their despair in *Danton's Death* has something in common with the tone of *Night Watches* (1804) by Bonaventura (*pseud.*), one of a number of German Romantic works which anticipate the nihilistic attitudes of Büchner's characters. The grotesqueness of figures such as the captain and doctor in *Woyzeck* perhaps owes something to the grotesque characterizations of E. T. A. Hoffmann, with whose poetic world Büchner momentarily identified himself in one of his letters to his fiancée (in Bergemann, pp. 379–80). The sense of fullness with which Büchner characterizes the landscape in parts of *Lenz* ("he stretched himself out and lay on the earth, dug his way into the All") is perhaps the only aspect of his story which would keep it from being mistaken for a work of our own century. For studies of the relationship of *Leonce and Lena* with German Romanticism, see Armin Renker, *Georg Büchner und das Lustspiel der Romantik* (Berlin, 1924) and Gustav Beckers' *Georg Büchners "Leonce und Lena,"* pp. 73–102.

In Stendhal, Lermontov, and Büchner the modern reader recognizes a complexity of intelligence and a dramatic objectivity relatively rare in the work of their Romantic contemporaries and predecessors, whose virtues are of a different, less characteristically modern kind. The realism of these three writers is less amply detailed than that of Balzac or such later writers as Flaubert and Zola; yet it is a realism as surely rooted in their contemporary worlds as that of any writer who came after them. The ironical perspectives which govern the work of all three are centrally directed to laying bare pretensions and uncovering the shades of meaning that lie beneath pat assertions and dramatic postures. Büchner's skepticism, more than that of Stendhal or Lermontov, is a skepticism without poses; the dramatic form he employed (as well as the type of fiction with which he experimented in *Lenz*) gave him little opportunity to put on masks of his own. His manner is perhaps less urbane than that of Stendhal or Lermontov; yet his irony is reinforced more powerfully than theirs by memorable images of terror and suffering. Whatever labels we ultimately attach to such writers—post-Romantic, say, or proto-Modern—their work leads us to question the conventional time divisions with which we have learned to look at literary history.

LAURA GINTERS

Georg Büchner—A Selective Stage History[†]

We cannot say for certain that Büchner ever actually attended the theatre during his own short life, and it was nearly sixty years after his death that *Leonce and Lena* received its first (amateur) production in 1895. Since then, however, his plays have become an established part of the classical repertoire, although with two quite distinct performance histories. On the German-speaking stages—Germany (in all its political incarnations), Austria, and Switzerland—all have been in constant production since the early twentieth century when Büchner's work was "rediscovered." The plays are an integral part of the German stage repertoire, and actors and directors often return to them repeatedly throughout their careers; Bernhard Minetti, for example, played the role of Robespierre five times over four decades. Almost all the great German directors of the twentieth century have directed one or more of Büchner's works, some

---

[†] Written especially for this Norton Critical Edition. All translations are the author's own, unless otherwise noted. Some reviews consulted did not give full references: those in English are from the Büchner files of the New York Public Library's Performing Arts Library; those in German are from the Büchner production files of the Georg Büchner Forschungsstelle, Marburg.

more than once: Max Reinhardt, Gustaf Gründgens,[1] Fritz Kortner, and more recently Claus Peymann, Christoph Marthaler, and
Thomas Ostermeier, to give just a few examples. Elsewhere in the
world productions have been markedly fewer, but often done by
significant directors—Orson Welles, Ingmar Bergman, Jonathan
Miller, JoAnne Akalaitis, Robert Wilson—and for significant occasions: Jean Vilar directed (and starred in) *Danton's Death* for his
first Avignon Festival in 1948; New York's Vivian Beaumont Theater at the Lincoln Center for the Performing Arts opened in 1965
with a production by Herbert Blau of the same play; most recently
the 2010 National Theatre *Danton* has been seen as Michael
Grandage's "try out" as possible successor to Nicholas Hytner.
There have, literally, been thousands of professional productions of
Büchner's works; this essay can only provide the barest sketch of
some notable ones.[2]

Büchner's plays have proved fertile ground for other artists, too:
there have been numerous theatrical adaptations of *Woyzeck* in
particular, operas of all three, ballets and other dance works based
on *Woyzeck* and *Leonce and Lena*, as well as a multitude of films,
notably Werner Herzog's *Woyzeck* (1979), starring Klaus Kinski.
Büchner's novella, *Lenz*, has also been adapted theatrically, incorporated into productions of his plays, as well as filmed and turned
into an opera. And to this we might add a clutch of plays *about*
Büchner, and even inspired by his lost play, *Pietro Aretino*.

1. Gründgens acted in *Danton's Death* and directed it multiple times (and *Leonce and Lena* once) between 1920 and 1958. His influence was profound and enduring: as late as 1974 his directorial interpretation of *Danton's Death* was serving as an explicit (and credited) model in a production in Freiburg.
2. For more detailed production histories, see: Axel Bornkessel, 1970, *Georg Büchners Leonce und Lena auf der deutschsprachigen Bühne*, PhD Dissertation, Universität zu Köln (production history 1895–1945 and an outline 1945–62); Wolfram Viehweg, 1964, *Georg Büchners Dantons Tod auf dem deutschen Theater*, Munich: Laokoon-Verlag GmbH (production history 1902–61); Laura Ginters, 2000, *History and Her Story: Georg Büchner's Dantons Tod on Page and Stage*, PhD Dissertation, University of Sydney (includes production history 1962–1998). Particular aspects of the production history in this period are also covered in Laura Ginters, 1996, "Georg Büchner's *Dantons Tod*: History and Her Story on the Stage," *Modern Drama* XXXIX:4 (Winter), pp. 650–67; Laura Ginters, 2008, "'Wir sind das Volk!' How a Failed Revolutionary Wrote about the French Revolution—and Thereby Helped Cause One 154 Years Later: Georg Büchner's *Dantons Tod* on the German Stage," pp. 165–98 in *Where Culture and Politics Intersect: German Theatre and Reunification*, ed. Denise Varney, Bern: Peter Lang; Wolfram Viehweg, 2001–8, *Georg Büchners Woyzeck auf dem deutschsprachigen Theater*, 2 Teile, Krefeld: Selbstverlag/Books on Demand. For *Woyzeck*'s Canadian production history, see: William C. Reeve, 1987, "Büchner's *Woyzeck* on the English-Canadian Stage," *Theatre Research in Canada/Recherches Théâtrales du Canada* 8:2 (Fall), available at www.lib.unb.ca/Texts/TRIC/bin/get.cgi?directory=vo18_2/&filename=Reeve.htm. Ingeborg Strudthoff has written a production history of Büchner's plays (1957, *Die Rezeption Georg Büchners durch das deutsche Theater*, Berlin-Dahlem: Colloquium Verlag), but it contains numerous errors, and both Bornkessel and Viehweg dispute her analysis of some productions. Dietmar Goltschnigg's three-volume collection, *Georg Büchner und die Moderne. Texte. Analysen. Kommentar* (2001–4, 3 Bände, Berlin: Erich Schmidt Verlag) also contains valuable materials and analyses.

Leonce and Lena

The performance history of Büchner's plays begins on a beautiful May evening in 1895, in a park outside Munich, when a group of literary aficionados and artists gathered to put on an amateur production of *Leonce and Lena* under the guidance of Ernst von Wolzogen. But the play had to wait another sixteen years for its first professional public production, in Vienna. Even then it was an afternoon performance, part of a Saturday series to expose works which were better known as literature. Bornkessel notes that it was indeed something of a "literary exhumation,"[3] but the play's initially rather lukewarm reception was steadily overtaken as all three of Büchner's works began to be produced regularly from 1913. *Leonce and Lena* was popular throughout the 1920s with over forty German-language productions (including productions by Gustaf Gründgens and Max Ophuls) and an opera based on the work[4] but, as was the case with Büchner's other plays, there was a significant drop in the number of productions of the play during the Nazi era and immediately after World War II. This slowly rebuilt to another high point: the anniversary of Büchner's 150th birthday in 1963, when nine productions of *Leonce and Lena* premiered in West Germany.

By 1963, when he directed *Leonce and Lena* at Munich's Kammerspiele, Fritz Kortner had been making theatre for over fifty years.[5] Several reviews indicated viewers knew what to expect from a Kortner production, and some expressed hesitations about his tendency to use the Büchner text as mere impetus for his directorial vision, but generally the response was warm to this (very long) "wonderful"[6] production which used a "hall of mirrors" set and an echoey soundscape to produce an unsettling waking dream atmosphere. One critic noted that Erwin Piscator (who had himself directed a production of the play a decade earlier) had recently commented, "It requires courage to stage [Hochhuth's] *The Representative*, but not *Leonce und Lena*."[7] The critic begged to differ, praising Kortner's treatment of the play as a social satire, commenting further that "Nobody would have guessed [. . .] that this was the genius of a septuagenarian at work, and not the outrageous non-conformism of a young experimenter."

3. Bornkessel, p. 56.
4. Composed by Julius Weisman, 1924.
5. This included some earlier encounters with Büchner: he played Danton in Berlin in 1924 and the same role in a radio play version in 1948.
6. Albert Schulze Vellinghausen, 1963, "Entdeckung Büchners durch Kortner," *Theater heute* 12:22.
7. Quoted by "Special Correspondent," "The Uncompromising Fritz Kortner," *The Times*, 14 January 1964. Piscator was presumably flush with the *succès de scandale* of his recent premiere of Hochhuth's play.

Four years later, and a few blocks away, a young experimenter did take on the play: Rainer Werner Fassbinder muscled his way into Munich's underground collective action-theatre. At just twenty-two, he parlayed attending their production of *Antigone* into playing a small role in it when an actor was injured—and from there to directing their next (and his first) play; *Leonce and Lena*.[8] The play's subject matter—young idealists rebelling against the establishment—appealed to this nascent group of Gen 68ers, and while it was initially proposed that it be co-directed by two men and two women (playing the roles of Leonce, Valerio [Fassbinder], Lena, and the governess) Fassbinder's was "the defining [directorial] voice."[9] What resulted was a pop culture bricolage resonant with contemporary cultural references (including the Beatles' "When I'm Sixty-Four" and images of the Shah of Persia) which was quite well received—even if one reviewer in fact felt "the weaker sections showed too much reverence towards Büchner"![1] Within two years Fassbinder was to become a leading light of the contemporary cultural scene in Germany, though his film work would then increasingly preoccupy him.

Leonce and Lena was the first of Büchner's works to be produced in the United Kingdom too, and it was by far the most popular of Büchner's plays in the UK, right up to the end of the 1960s; even so it was performed just once each decade from 1927 until the late 1950s, and never by a major company.[2] In the United States it was not performed at all until 1960, and thereafter mostly by university groups.

It took a Romanian director/designer to really bring the play to the attention of the English-speaking world. Liviu Ciulei, Artistic Director of the Bulandra Theatre, had already had a great success with *Danton's Death* when he toured his production of *Leonce and Lena* to the Edinburgh Festival in 1971. It garnered great praise, particularly the "startling and audacious," "towering central performance"[3] of a young Ion Caramitru[4] as Leonce. Performed on an

---

8. See David Barnett, 2005, *Rainer Werner Fassbinder and the German Theatre*, Cambridge: Cambridge University Press; and Hanna Bauer, 2010, *"Ich glaube, wenn man Filme macht, muss man etwas vom Theater verstehen": Die Theaterarbeit Rainer Werner Fassbinders am action-theater und antitheater*, Diplomarbeit, Universität Wien, for further background to this era and production.

9. Barnett, p. 33.

1. See Barnett, p. 35 for his analysis of the critical reception of the production.

2. London audiences had also had the chance to see Oscar Fritz Schuh's production (designed by Caspar Neher) from the Freie Volksbühne (West Berlin) in 1957 with Maximilian Schell as Leonce. It toured to London in a double bill with his production of *Woyzeck*.

3. Michael Billington, "Leonce and Lena," *The Times*, 1 September 1971.

4. Caramitru would later become Romania's Minister of Culture (1996–2000) and since 2005 has led the National Theatre Bucharest.

open scaffold set in "timeless costumes,"[5] the eclectic production (it opened with a prologue where the cast members limbered up on stage before performing[6]) embraced an exhilarating mixture of styles and was hailed as a modern fairy tale (with more than a touch of Absurdist theatre), where Büchner's romantic melancholy was "converted into the bored scepticism of today's youth."[7] Ciulei went on to give his American debut and the play its first major professional production in the USA in 1973[8] when he recreated this production with American actors, and it became "one of the year's most extraordinary theatrical experiences."[9]

Ciulei later became Artistic Director at the Guthrie Theater in Minneapolis, with Garland Wright as his associate director. When Wright himself took over the Guthrie he proposed to JoAnne Akalaitis that *she* might like to direct *Leonce and Lena* for the theatre in 1987.[1] Well known for her sometimes polarizing interpretations of the classics, Akalaitis relocated the play to a contemporary American Southwest of "lonely highways [and] big blue skies,"[2] included country and western songs and a multi-ethnic cast, and renamed it *Leon and Lena (and lenz)*. Lenz—Leonce's alter ego— was incorporated into the play through a silent black-and-white film spliced through the production, as well by the onstage characters reading from *Lenz*.[3] King Peter, a cartoon-like corporate cowboy, became the CEO of "Money well."[4] Akalaitis's choices indicate an astute political awareness as a director, but in Germany the connection between theatre and politics has always been stronger and more explicit—with sometimes more direct consequences for directors.

5. Irving Wardle, "Rumanian Theatre: The Classics Scraped Clean," *The Times*, 8 June 1971. Also published (in slightly different form) as "Rumanian Theatre Plays Vital Part in Daily Life," *The New York Times*, 12 June 1971.
6. In the American version the prologue contained lines from all of Büchner's plays. It is not clear if this was part of the original Romanian production.
7. Wardle, "Rumanian Theatre."
8. Washington, Arena Stage. He also directed it in Vancouver (Playhouse Theatre Company) in 1976.
9. Jack Kroll, "Tushi and Wiwi," *Newsweek*, 22 April 1974.
1. She had initially wanted to do *Danton's Death*. See Sarah Bryant-Bertail, 2000, "JoAnne Akalaitis's Postmodern Epic Staging of *Leon and Lena (& lenz)*," pp. 152–70 in *Space and Time in Epic Theater: The Brechtian Legacy*, Rochester (NY) and Woodbridge (Suffolk): Camden House; and Mark Bly, 1989, "Joanne Akalaitis's *Leon and Lena (and Lenz)*: A Log from the Dramaturg," *Yale Theater* 3:81–95 for further discussion of this production.
2. Mike Steele, "*Leon and Lena (and Lenz)* Should Be Vintage Akalaitis," *Star-Tribune*, 18 October 1987.
3. Büchner's other works were also quoted in the production. In 2002 Matthias Langhoff directed *Lenz, Léonce et Lena* for the Comédie Française. He too interwove the two texts and used film as a backdrop for Lenz's flight.
4. Multinational corporation Honeywell had its corporate headquarters in Minneapolis— and was a sponsor of the production.

In 1978 Jürgen Gosch, in his directorial debut at the East Berlin Volksbühne, delivered a highly provocative *Leonce and Lena*.[5] He portrayed the play's Staatsrat (also the name for the GDR's highest state authority) as a bunch of senile, blind, lame geriatrics and alluded clearly to the censorship, travel restrictions, and Stasi surveillance of Honecker's regime. While the East German critics were cautious about drawing explicit contemporary parallels, audiences were not (neither were West German critics), and the production enjoyed sold out houses . . . when it was shown.[6] Finding it difficult thereafter to get employment, however, Gosch defected to the West. His sponsor was Jürgen Flimm, who soon brought Gosch to his theatre in Cologne.

Flimm himself is clearly a Büchner fan. He has directed two productions of *Leonce und Lena*,[7] two of *Woyzeck* (including one in Beijing)[8] and *Danton's Death*.[9] Making a virtue of necessity (his theatre was undergoing renovations), his acrobatic 1981 production of *Leonce and Lena* was staged in a circus tent.[1] Leonce and Lena's first encounter on a giant swing, flying through the air under a blue light, was much remarked on, but the charming production had its darker topical undercurrents; critics read Leonce and Lena as "the last of the flower children"[2] and "two 68-ers in 1981,"[3] with the production commenting on the way in which youthful idealism is inevitably crushed by the prevailing powers that be.[4] The production was invited to the 1982 Theatertreffen, where it elicited a comparison with Peter Brook's *Midsummer Night's Dream*.[5]

The two production histories converge in Robert Wilson, an American who has worked regularly in the German theatre over many years. His *Leonce and Lena* for the Berliner Ensemble in 2003 was the last of his Büchner trilogy. His eagerly anticipated collabo-

---

5. For a discussion of the context and reception of the production, see Laura Bradley, 2006, "Stealing Büchner's Characters? *Leonce und Lena* in East Berlin," *Oxford German Studies* 35, no. 1: 66–78.
6. The production is often mistakenly described as having been "banned" and Gosch as having been sacked from the theatre. In fact, as Bradley points out, the SED sought to avoid controversy by *not* ordering an immediate ban, with the Culture Department merely recommending that "the number of performances should be kept low and that the production should be dropped quietly in the near future" (p. 77).
7. 1973 Mannheim, Nationaltheater; 1981 Cologne, Schauspiel.
8. 1987 Beijing, with Lin Zhaohua; 1990 Hamburg, Thalia Theater.
9. 1976 Hamburg, Deutsches Theater.
1. One wonders at the Flimm dinner table conversations around this time: Flimm's wife Inga also directed the play in Wuppertal in 1980.
2. Brigitte Desalm, "Sehnen nach Liebe," *Kölner Stadt-Anzeiger*, 12 October 1981.
3. See Günther Rühle, 1981, "Leonce und Lena," *Theater heute* 12:24.
4. See Rühle 1981, pp. 24–26. An American critic came to the directly opposite conclusion: "If the cheerful animal spirits of this circus entertainment enforced any special meaning, it was surely the idea that youthful energy can burst the fetters that the older generation imposes." (Henry Popkin, "Berlin Festival Theatertreffen," *Christian Science Monitor*, 9 August 1982, p. 18.)
5. See, for example: Ned Chaillet, "Theatertreffen," *The Times*, 23 June 1982.

ration with German "Rockbard" Herbert Grönemeyer was (almost inevitably) a great popular success,[6] but critics were a little ambivalent, a number commenting on the effective disappearance of Büchner or any exploration of the underlying themes of the play under the imposition of the Wilson treatment. A sense, too, of "more of the same" from Wilson was balanced against a production which well displayed Wilson's facility to craft beautiful theatrical imagery through his striking stylized light and stage design.[7]

Woyzeck

Büchner is most well known outside the German-speaking world for *Woyzeck*, and it is the most produced of his plays the world over. Both its form and subject matter encourage this. As an unfinished collection of scenes the play invites adaptation and reworking.[8] Its subject matter too, centering on the disenfranchised, powerless, and socially excluded Woyzeck, has an enduring strong appeal, both in interpretation (there have been a number of productions, for example, which portray Woyzeck as a contemporary African American soldier) and indeed for those who produce it: *Woyzeck* has been produced by several companies of homeless people.[9] It has also long been the stalwart of student theatre groups, and of emerging directors—so much so that there is a standing joke about the Edinburgh Festival Fringe always having at least one production of the play. Deborah Warner even recalls that her debut at the Festival in 1981 (which also marked the beginning of her long collaboration with actor Fiona Shaw) was "only one of the 10 productions of *Woyzeck* which appear annually on the Fringe"![1]

Woyzeck premiered in 1913 at the Residenztheater in Munich within weeks of the centenary of Büchner's birth.[2] This was quickly followed by a production in Berlin, and just six months later in a

---

6. It reached its 150th performance in 2010 (Irene Bazinger, "Musicalmuster für die Satire," *Berliner Zeitung*, 4 February 2010).
7. See for example John Rouse, 2004, "Two by Büchner in Berlin," *Western European Stages* 16, no. 1 (winter): 35–38.
8. Many well-known playwrights have adapted the play, including Neil LaBute and David Harrower. In Germany, playwrights Franz Xaver Kroetz (1996, Hamburg, Deutsches Schauspielhaus) and Igor Bauersima (2003, Hanover, Schauspielhaus) have directed their own adaptations of *Woyzeck*. There are also a number of plays loosely based on *Woyzeck*, such as Simon Stephen's *Motortown*, Naomi Lizuka's *Skin*, Lynn Manning's *Private Battle*, and Brett Leonard's *Guinea Pig Solo*.
9. Cardboard Citizens (2003 and 2008), London, Southwark Playhouse; Ratten 07 (1995), Berlin, Volksbühne.
1. Al Senter, "Edinburgh Festival; Not Like It Was In My Day," *The Independent on Sunday*, 16 August 1992.
2. Price notes that it was originally scheduled to take place on his birthday, but was postponed so that it didn't clash with the anniversary of the Battle of Leipzig. Victor Price, trans., "Introduction," in *Georg Büchner: Danton's Death, Leonce and Lena, Woyzeck*, Oxford: Oxford University Press, p. xxi.

new production the same Woyzeck (Albert Steinrück[3]), who had won unanimous praise for his interpretation of the role, stunned audiences in Vienna. In the audience that night was composer Alban Berg, who emerged "deathly pale and perspiring profusely," gasping as he left the theatre: "Isn't it fantastic, incredible? [. . .] Someone must set it to music."[4] He did, and *Wozzeck*, which premiered in 1925, became one of the most significant operatic works of the twentieth century.[5]

Woyzeck had been popular throughout the 1920s, with sixty-three productions in Germany alone between 1918 and 1930, but Büchner's works in general—and *Woyzeck* in particular—were unpopular with the National Socialists, and consequently much less frequently performed: *Woyzeck* only twice in Germany in the period 1933–1945.[6] It made a very speedy comeback after the war, however, with three German productions (two in the Russian zone and one in the Western zone) in the first month of the new theatre season in 1945, and there were ten new productions of the play in the years 1945–1947.[7]

One of these was Wolfgang Langhoff's production at the Deutsches Theater in East Berlin—one chapter in a long family history with Büchner's work.[8] Langhoff was *Intendant* of the Deutsches Theater from 1946 to 1963, and his reputation as a director is founded on his production of classic plays there: this production was praised as "one of the most powerful theatre experiences since the end of the war."[9] In a change that divided critical opinion, Langhoff's Woyzeck did not commit suicide by drowning; instead, the play concluded with the scene between the fool and Woyzeck's son. Langhoff believed that this ending was truer to Büchner's rejection of a

3. Steinrück played the role in four productions between 1913 and 1919. The last production in Frankfurt featured a young Helene Weigel in her professional debut.
4. Paul Elbogen, quoted in Douglas Jarman, 1989, *Alban Berg: Wozzeck*, Cambridge Opera Handbook, Cambridge: Cambridge University Press, p. 1.
5. As such it has been produced by many major opera directors, including Götz Friedrich, Harry Kupfer, Ruth Berghaus, Adolf Dresen, Oscar Fritz Schuh, Hans Neugebauer, Hansgünther Heyme, Dieter Dorn, Willy Decker, Luc Bondy, Wolf Sesemann, Otto Schenk, Patrice Chéreau, Barrie Kosky, Deborah Warner (who made her opera debut with it), and Christoph Marthaler.
6. See Viehweg, *Georg Büchners* Woyzeck, 2. Teil, Band 2: 1933–1945, p. 105.
7. See Viehweg, *Georg Büchners* Woyzeck, 2. Teil, Band 2: 1933–1945, p. 110.
8. The Langhoff family's engagement with Büchner spans three generations and more than eighty years. Wolfgang Langhoff performed in *Leonce and Lena* in 1926 (Wiesbaden), directed and performed in *Danton's Death* (1940, Zurich), and directed *Woyzeck* (1947, Berlin; 1958, Berlin). His son Matthias has directed *Woyzeck* (1980, Bochum), *Leonce and Lena* (2002, Paris, Comédie Française), and *Lenz* (2010, Institut für Angewandte Theaterwissenschaft, Justus-Liebig-Universität Gießen). One grandson, Lukas, has directed *Leonce and Lena* (2002, Magdeburg, Freie Kammerspiele); another, Tobias, co-directed a graduating production of *Lenz* (1987, Berlin, Hochschule für Schauspielkunst Ernst Busch) and starred in Jürgen Flimm's *Woyzeck* (1990, Hamburg, Thalia Theater).
9. Paul Rilla, "Georg Büchner und die soziale Wirklichkeit." *Berliner Zeitung*, 16 November 1947.

society whose "soulless and cruel behaviour"[1] resulted in Woyzeck's execution. His lead actor, Ernst Wilhelm Borchert, is still referred to as the first postwar Woyzeck: while not strictly true, the impression he made on critics—"wonderful and unforgettable"[2]—was such that his is the most remembered.

A "first" genuinely did take place in 1964 in Vienna. This was its famous Burgtheater's rather belated premiere of *Woyzeck*—also a belated 150th anniversary celebration of Büchner's birth.[3] Erich Neuberg had previously directed a live broadcast of the play for Austrian television and worked with the same Woyzeck (Bruno Dallansky, making a welcome return to the Burgtheater in his first major role there) and Marie (Martha Wallner) in this production. Stefan Hlawa created a set with no curtain and a black stage space, filled with three platforms on steel posts as playing spaces. A striking use of light—spotlights, fade in/out, and blackouts—to pick out the scenes from the dim background characterised the production. One critic judged this "one of the best acts of direction in this year's Vienna theatre season,"[4] and it was invited to the Berlin Theatertreffen[5] that year.

Like Fassbinder, Ingmar Bergman is now better known for his films, but also made an important contribution to the theatre of his time. His 1969 *Woyzeck* for the Dramaten, Stockholm's Royal Dramatic Theatre, like Fassbinder's *Leonce and Lena*, was responding to the spirit of the times: Bergman envisaged a radical rethinking of the role of theatre and the relationship between actor and audience. His rehearsals were open to the public; he abolished the "opening night" and curtain calls; all seats were general admission and cost 5 krona (the equivalent of one U.S. dollar); and it was staged arena-style on the mainstage.

Another theatre experimenter made a much-anticipated return to the stage as Woyzeck in 1976. Joseph Chaikin had spent most of the previous decade and a half directing for the Open Theater, but had long wanted to either stage or perform in *Woyzeck*. In the event he performed it for the Shaliko Company at the Public Theater in New York, directed by Leonard Shapiro. Chaikin's early investigations

1. Wolfgang Langhoff, 1948, "Die verschiedenen Fassungen des *Woyzeck*," reproduced in Goltschnigg, *Georg Büchner und die Moderne*, Band 2: 1945–1980, p. 166.
2. Paul Rilla, "Georg Büchner und die soziale Wirklichkeit," *Berliner Zeitung*, 16 November 1947.
3. The date of the premiere made it slightly belated, but it was part of the 1963–64 theatre season.
4. H.Z., "Modernes Stuck aus dem Jahr 1836," [publication not given], 14 March 1964.
5. The ten "most remarkable" German-speaking productions (selected from around 400) of the previous season are invited to the Theatertreffen festival, held each May in Berlin. North Rhine-Westphalia runs its own Theatertreffen, honouring the best of that state's productions: in 2008 and 2009 productions of *Woyzeck* by David Bösch (Theater Essen) and Joan Anton Rechi (Theater Oberhausen) were featured.

into acting (which resulted in the formation of the Open Theater) had resulted from his discovery that his own Method training
was not well suited to the Brecht plays he worked on at the Living
Theater. Brecht's insistence that the actor maintain a critical distance from his/her character, as well as an active engagement on the
part of, and with, the audience, became part of Chaikin's approach,
and this was at odds with a Method-dominated theatre scene (and
critical reception). Chaikin strove to bring this Brechtian sensibility
to the role ("I must depict Woyzeck, tell about him, not *be* him"[6]);
for example, after being beaten violently, Woyzeck props himself up
and addresses his line "It happens all the time," confidentially,
directly to the audience, rather than as a lament to an unheeding
God. While some critics praised Chaikin's "masterly," "complex and
arresting," "harrowing"[7] performance, those who resisted this interpretation were rejecting the Brechtian impulses supporting it: Chaikin's interpretation was one that "can only lecture an audience, not
move it," said one reviewer.[8] Another found the production "lacking
in feeling" because the cast *played* the characters, rather than
becoming them,[9] again revealing the implicit Method "norm" which
informed much of the criticism.

Shaliko's production had been part of Joseph Papp's Shakespeare
Festival, and *Woyzeck* was programmed again for the festival in
1992: JoAnne Akalaitis, now the Public Theater's Artistic Director,
directed, working again with Jesse Borrego (who had played Leon/
Lenz) in the title role. The production opened with one of the Lenz
film sequences, from her *Leon and Lena (and lenz)*, visually completing the connection she had drawn between Büchner's existen-
tially strung out, doomed "heroes" (though it nonplussed critics
unaware of the previous production). This interpretation across
productions, and Büchner's oeuvre, was further underlined by the
audience's last sight of a naked, concentration camp intern–like
Woyzeck cowering in a shower—a far cry from the strappingly beautiful, nonchalant Leon who rose elegantly from his bath at the
beginning of her production of *Leon and Lena (and lenz)*. Such a
visual juxtaposition served to underscore the intensely tragic fate of
Woyzeck in this "ravishingly grim"[1] production.

6. Elenore Lester, "I Am the Audience in Action," *New York Times*, 7 March 1976.
7. Arthur Sainer, Eileen Blumenthal, and Erika Munk, respectively, all in "A Dream Production Falls Flat," *The Village Voice*, 5 April 1976.
8. Sylviane Gold, "A Shell of a Play," *New York Post*, 25 March 1976.
9. Linda Lawrence, "Neatly Staged Work Lacks Feeling," *Chelsea Clinton News*, 1 April
   1976.
1. David Richards, "*Woyzeck* Ricochets Through a Mad World," *New York Times*, 13
   December 1992.

Commenting on Akalaitis's production, Robert Brustein mused that "*Woyzeck* is a mountain that every auteur director, at some career point or other, feels compelled to climb."[2] In Germany, where a tradition of *Regietheater* (directors' theatre) remains strong, *Woyzeck* has proved enduringly attractive. We might take as an example the years 1980–1992, when no fewer than five directors were invited to the annual Theatertreffen in Berlin with their production of *Woyzeck*.

Following in his father's footsteps, Matthias Langhoff (and his long-term collaborator Manfred Karge, who also played Woyzeck) directed *Woyzeck*—or rather *Marie. Woyzeck*—for the Schauspielhaus Bochum in 1980. The theatre was transformed into a circus tent for this production, which was set in the "folksy atmosphere of a fair,"[3] complete with a real horse on stage. Possibly setting a record for the longest *Woyzeck* ever (at three and a half hours), it opened the 1981 Theatertreffen and was also invited to the Avignon Festival.

Peter Fitz's Woyzeck in Benjamin Korn's production for the Munich Kammerspiele in 1984 was celebrated as having overturned the clichéd portrayal of the role which had developed over the previous seventy years.[4] His was no "passive, mute sufferer,"[5] no victim; instead he delivered a "perceptive tragic hero."[6] His Marie, Eva Mattes, had already played Marie in Herzog's film, but this is the role "for which she was born";[7] "through her presence alone [she] fills the stage."[8] An effectively simple set was created two weeks out from the premiere when Korn and designer Klaus Hellenstein dumped the previous design. The new set was comprised of two grey-green walls (behind which was an endless red-streaked yellow sky), which formed a corner for interior scenes, and separated to become exterior scenes: these walls finally collapsed before the murder scene.

Achim Freyer followed Korn's lead in the interpretation of the character Woyzeck for his production in 1989. After a late start with *Woyzeck*, Vienna's Burgtheater has done well with its productions; its second (and only other, to date), directed and designed by Freyer

2. Robert Brustein, "Büchner in an Unfurnished Room," *The New Republic*, 4 and 11 January 1993. As he noted, Richard Foreman had also directed a production of the play in 1990 for the Hartford Stage Company.
3. Günther Engelhard, "Korsett für den Abgrund," *Die Weltwoche*, 19 November 1980.
4. See Peter von Becker, "Der wahre Woyzeck," *Theater heute*, June 1984: 8–15, at 10. Fitz was in fact a ring in from the Berlin Schaubühne: playwright/actor Franz Xaver Kroetz was to play the role but withdrew four weeks into rehearsal. Kroetz would later go on to adapt and direct the play in 1996.
5. See von Becker, "Der wahre Woyzeck," 10.
6. See von Becker, "Der wahre Woyzeck," 15.
7. Georg Hensel, "Was man mit Woyzeck alles machen kann," *Frankfurter Allgemeine Zeitung*, 25 April 1984.
8. Marie-Helene Lammers, "Woyzeck intellektuell," *Bayern Kurier*, 5 May 1984.

was, like Neuberg's, invited to the Theatertreffen. Freyer, initially a designer by profession,[9] "thinks visually, not analytically."[1] A comment from his *Regiebuch*—"don't want to direct, rather create constellations of scenes"[2]—indicates an approach founded on a series of three images (clock; razor; blood) which became leitmotifs for the production.[3]

Like Freyer, Andreas Kriegenburg works as both director and designer: he moved into designing when, preparing for his production of *Danton's Death* at the Burgtheater in 2001, he had such a clear vision for what he wanted that he decided to design it himself.[4] Well before this, though, Kriegenburg had had an immediate success with his first production as resident director at the Berlin Volksbühne in 1991. His deconstructed *Woyzeck* ("with a mania for quotation, playfully associative, and saturated with musical choreography [. . .] No ongoing plot, just splinters of scenes with pantomime, *tableaux vivants*, song"[5]) drew comparisons with the work of Frank Castorf (who in fact only joined the Volksbühne the following year). It caused a stir—not least because it was the only production from the former GDR deemed to be of sufficient merit to be invited to the Theatertreffen in 1992.

The last of this series of outstanding productions was that by Valentin Jeker for Bonn's Schauspielhaus in 1992. Rudolf Kowalski[6] was a "gruff and moving, unsentimental and buffeted"[7] Woyzeck. Atmospherically charged, "a cold fever lies over the performance, grief without tears."[8] Thomas Dreissigacker's stage design realised elements of Büchner's text quite literally: the play opened with children playing on a wooden platform; it then swung up in the sky and there it hung, this giant moon of "rotten wood," until the end of the play, when—after Woyzeck, shot, slumps to the ground—it closed over the stage, becoming its/his coffin lid.

That year another *Woyzeck* premiered on the other side of the world: William Kentridge directed *Woyzeck on the Highveld* for Johannesburg's Handspring Puppet Company. Set in a 1950s Johan-

---

9. He had earlier designed Hans Neugebauer's production of *Wozzeck* in 1975 in Cologne. One reviewer of this *Woyzeck* was reminded of the work of that other designer/director, Robert Wilson (Benjamin Henrichs, "Der zerbrochene Gott," *Die Zeit*, 18–28 April 1989).
1. Sigrid Löffler, "Uhr-Rasiermesser-Blut," *Theater heute*, August 1989: 25–27, at 26.
2. His *Regiebuch* was quoted extensively in the production's programme.
3. See Löffler, "Uhr-Rasiermesser-Blut," 26.
4. Kriegenburg has also directed *Leonce and Lena* (1998 Munich, Residenztheater) and *Wozzeck* (2008 Munich, Bayerische Staatsoper).
5. Harmut Krug, trans. Marjorie Gelus, 1993, "Form as Goal—Art as Message: The 29th Berlin Theatertreffen," *Theatre Journal* 45, no. 1 (March): 91–97, at 94.
6. Kowalski would go on to play Danton for Jeker in his 1994 production for the theatre, which also staged *Leonce and Lena* in 1993.
7. Heinz Klunker, "Büchner in Bonn," *Die Deutsche Bühne*, June 1993: 30–32, at 32.
8. Gerhard Jörde, "Bonn: Armer Teufel, trotziger Täter," *Theater heute*, March 1993: 51.

nesburg, Woyzeck, a poor migrant worker (not a soldier: under Apartheid, South Africa's soldiers were seen as part of the state's oppressive forces), and Marie are black; the other characters white. The production, with nearly life-size, rough-hewn wooden puppets manipulated by five puppeteers (whose real hands became the puppets' hands and who voiced the puppets live), was played out against Kentridge's black and white charcoal animation backdrop. The animation was also used to visually portray the disintegration of Woyzeck's mind. It toured the world then and was remounted for another extensive tour from 2008.

Just occasionally it is the productions at the smaller end of the scale which have a disproportionately large effect on their audiences. Controversial playwright Sarah Kane directed *Woyzeck* for the Gate Theatre in London's Notting Hill, as part of the company's ambitious 1997 programme to stage all of Büchner's works.[9] Kane had wanted to direct *Woyzeck* since she was seventeen,[1] and as Michael Shannon (Woyzeck) later reflected: "Sarah was Woyzeck in her [own] life," "she'd never write anything or direct anything that she hadn't already been through in some way, or experienced."[2] This tiny theatre, located above a pub, offered her an opportunity to create a *Woyzeck* that was confronting and deeply moving. Its simple set of planks, closely surrounded by the audience, concealed props under small hatches: the play concluded with Woyzeck disappearing, "drowning," beneath the stage. The *Guardian*'s Michael Billington described it as a "hypnotic, hermetically powerful production" and for this veteran critic, even years later, this production remained "the best *Woyzeck*."[3] It is a benchmark for other London critics too, even in the light of other recent outstanding, and much more lavish, productions, such as that by Gisli Örn Gardarsson.

In 2005 the Icelandic Vesturport theatre premiered a dazzling production, adapted and directed by Gardarsson, with songs and music by pop icon Nick Cave and Warren Ellis. The set was dominated by a scaffolding of industrial pipes and platforms in front of which was a gigantic aquarium trough which curved around the

9. *Leonce and Lena* and *Danton's Death* were directed by the company's Artistic Director, David Farr. In 2004 the Gate produced *Woyzeck* again, adapted and directed by Daniel Kramer. Another great success for the company, it made several "10 best of 2004" lists, was nominated for a number of awards, and toured successfully to New York.

1. See James Christopher, "Backstage," *The Observer*, 2 November 1997. Kane's play *Cleansed* was also structurally based on *Woyzeck* (see Sarah Kane, interviewed by Dan Rebellato, Royal Holloway, University of London, 3 November 1998, available at www .rhul.ac.uk/drama/staff/rebellato_dan/sarahkane/S_KANE_1998.pdf).

2. Marti Lyons, 2008, "'How Skinny I Got, and How Fucking Weird I Was': Michael Shannon, Sarah Kane, Woyzeck, and Experiential Theatre," Honors thesis, Illinois Wesleyan University, p. 32, quoting from Lyons's interview with Shannon.

3. Michael Billington, *The Guardian*, 13 October 2005, reviewing the Vesturport production.

front of the stage and in which characters played, were tortured, had sex, swam, escaped one another—and eventually died. The production, which also featured aerial trapeze and rope work, was visually flamboyant and athletically performed. It toured very successfully to London (twice), New York, and Germany and has since been produced by other companies.[4]

In this it followed in the footsteps of Robert Wilson, who had continued his collaboration with Tom Waits[5] in Wilson's music-heavy production for the Betty Nansen Theatre in Copenhagen (2000): the catchy, gritty songs (evoking Brecht/Weill) brought an added dimension to the tragedy. It was a production filled with Wilson's inimitable visual richness and inventiveness (the Doctor was played by two actors as Siamese twins); a macabrely humorous, strictly choreographed work. As with most of Wilson's works, the production toured widely internationally, and this version has been produced by other theatres repeatedly since.[6]

One of the most striking German productions of the play in the past decade has been Thomas Ostermeier's for the Berlin Schaubühne (2003). Set in East Berlin's poverty-stricken slums, Jan Pappelbaum's set featured a huge drainage pipe, emptying its sewage water into a scummy pool. On the top of the ditch's walls was another playing space (complete with functioning fast food kiosk), surrounded by backdrops of depressing high rises. The first half hour of the production was entirely silent: an early morning pantomime as the kiosk vendor (Andres) sets up his stall, serves his first customers and so on. In this underclass world peopled by the unemployed, neo-fascist thugs, rappers (the Drum Major), prostitutes, and drug dealers, Woyzeck is everyone's victim. In an Ostermeier twist, his vicious murder (and postmortem rape) of Marie gives him entrée into this hierarchy. Ostermeier was invited to become the Avignon Festival's first Associate Artist in 2004, and this production opened the Festival.

To finish where we began: in 2007 the Edinburgh Festival Fringe presented Sadari Movement Laboratory's inventive *Woyzeck*. Performed partly in English, partly in Korean—and set to tango music by Piazzolla—its main performance language was dance. This was a stripped-back version which relied on the highly skilled physical

---

4. This version has since received a production at the Malthouse Theatre in Melbourne, Australia (2009). Directed by Michael Kantor, this production took a less ironic stance towards the material and by playing it "straight" ramped up the tragedy. The rock musical element contributed by the Cave/Ellis songs was enhanced by You Am I frontman Tim Rogers, exuberantly playing the "Entertainer" role.
5. They had previously created *The Black Rider* together in 1990. Waits and collaborator Kathleen Brennan wrote the music and songs for *Woyzeck*.
6. For example, of the ten *Woyzeck* productions premiering in Germany and Switzerland in 2009, three productions used the Wilson/Waits/Brennan text, songs, and music.

performers and their clever manipulation of eleven chairs which variously represented locations (a forest, a medical cage), objects (a weapon, a bed), and even emotional states. It won several awards at the Festival and has toured internationally since.

Danton's Death

Little information remains about the first performances in Berlin of *Danton's Death* in 1902 (directed by Friedrich Moest and Alfred Halen) under the auspices of the Neue Freie Volksbühne;[7] it received its first full professional production in 1910 in Hamburg under the direction of Leopold Jessner at the Thalia Theater.

It was in 1916, though, that the production history of the play reached its first real high point with Max Reinhardt's production in Berlin at the Deutsches Theater. As Viehweg notes, it was not only a great personal success for him, but provided a model for numerous productions that followed.[8] A simple, open two-level stage, connected by a few steps, was the only set, and the production was characterised by its overlapping scenes and intensely contrasting use of light and dark. It was especially memorable for its mass scenes with "six hundred extras," according to poet Kurt Tucholsky, who immortalised this production in verse.[9] Reinhardt's production would be staged again in Berlin in 1921, he would go on to produce it twice more in 1929,[1] and it was he who introduced Büchner to the North American stage when he toured *Danton's Death* (and five other plays) to New York in 1927.

Büchner's plays had only just that year appeared in translation in the UK, and as one reviewer noted "we know nothing of Georg Buechner on the [American] stage."[2] Reviewers were underwhelmed by the play's episodic structure, but raved about the "sweep and imagination"[3] of Reinhardt's stagecraft, and the performances which "blew the audience right out of their upholstered seats."[4] The production was classic Reinhardt with its massed crowd scenes (there were forty-seven named characters and a total cast of 250), and critics especially singled out the extraordinary scene in the Tribunal. Paul Hartmann as Danton won great praise for his performance, one critic declaring "he should share with [Reinhardt star

---

7. See Viehweg, *Georg Büchners Dantons Tod*, p. 27.
8. Viehweg, *Georg Büchners Dantons Tod*, p. 56.
9. *"Dantons Tod"* by Kurt Tucholsky, published originally under the pseudonym Kaspar Hauser in *Die Weltbühne* (4 March 1920, 10: 311).
1. An open air production in Vienna and one at the Residenztheater in Munich, with Gustaf Gründgens playing St Just in both.
2. Gilbert Gabriel, "Last Night's First Night," *The Ne[w York Sun? New York American?]*, [21 December 1927?], p. 22.
3. "The Death of Danton," *World*, 21 December 1927.
4. Robert Littell, *"Danton's* [sic] *Tod* [. . . ?]," *[New York?] Post*, 21 December 1927.

actor] Mr Moissi the honor of being celebrated as Germany's John Barrymore."[5]

Hartmann's opposite number was Vladimir Sokoloff, who went on to reprise the role of Robespierre, in English this time, just over a decade later. The occasion was Orson Welles's production of the play at the Mercury Theatre in New York.[6] Welles was just twenty-three, the same age as Büchner when he died. Like Büchner he too was fascinated by the continued relevance of historical events,[7] though at least one reviewer was to note that contemporary events were more "compelling, dramatic and interesting"[8] than the production. The critic was referring to political developments in Europe—but could easily have been pointing to Welles's infamous *War of the Worlds* radio broadcast (it panicked thousands who believed a real Martian invasion was taking place) which occurred during the rehearsals for *Danton*, and incidentally generated valuable publicity for the theatre company. With a tiny stage and much smaller cast at his disposal than Reinhardt, Welles conjured up the mass scenes by the clever lighting of thousands of masks attached to a curved cyclorama. While this was much praised, and the production moved along at the cracking pace of under ninety minutes, the critics, who had been supportive of the Mercury's rapid rise, were generally less than fully enthusiastic about both play and production, and it suffered from comparisons to the larger-scale Reinhardt production.

As director, Welles had himself resisted taking on the role of Danton, settling for the smaller role of St Just, but Jean Vilar had no such qualms. He directed *La Mort de Danton* (in an adaptation by Arthur Adamov) for his first Festival at Avignon in 1948 (the first time the play had been seen in France) and played the role of Robespierre. A stripped back production "without décor, without curtains, without proscenium"[9] was produced for the bare, open-air stage at Avignon. Vilar's success with the festival led to him being appointed to direct the Théâtre National Populaire, and he staged

5. Percy Hammond, "*Danton's* [sic] *Tod* in Which Mr. Reinhardt Exercises His Great Gifts as a Picture-Maker," *Herald Tribune*, 21 December 1927. Alexander Moissi, who had twice previously played the role for Reinhardt, was part of the ensemble touring to New York. He was Germany's best-known actor in the 1920s and 1930s, and several critics were, in fact, pleased he was not appearing in this production as it gave other actors a chance to shine!

6. For a detailed account of this production, see John Houseman, 1972, "Orson Welles and *Danton's Death*," *Yale/Theatre* 3:3 (winter): 56–67. Apparently Welles let Sokoloff play Robespierre's great scenes "exactly as he had played them in German for Reinhardt" (p. 62).

7. The previous year he had directed an acclaimed production of *Julius Caesar* set in Fascist Italy.

8. Walter Winchell, "*Danton's Death* Slow Drama of the Fre[nch Revolution?]," *Daily Mirror*, 3 November 1938.

9. See Anthony Curtis, quoting Vilar: "Arts: Jean Vilar—Avignon Festival," *Financial Times*, 22 July 1991.

the play again there in 1953, although not without controversy. Vilar was strongly criticised by the extreme left-wing press for portraying Danton in too favourable a light (the Communist party accused him of insulting the Revolution), and the production came close to being banned by the Minister for Culture.

In recent years it has been more frequently produced in Paris, with, among others, an acclaimed production by Karl Michael Grüber for the bicentenary of the French Revolution in 1989[1] (the first since Vilar's 1953 production), and one by Georges Lavaudant which was "one of the biggest successes of [2002's] Parisian theatre season."[2]

A cast of nearly fifty came together for Herbert Blau's inaugural production for a (novel for the New York theatre scene) repertory company in the new Vivian Beaumont Theater at Lincoln Center in 1965. As an event this was much anticipated, and the new theatre and its modern technical setup got rave reviews—not so the play (adapted by Blau) and players. There was a notable level of discontent that Blau and co-Artistic Director Jules Irving had brought with them so many actors from San Francisco when they took up their post in New York, and the uneven acting was heavily criticised. In another controversial move, Blau had written—and been forced to remove—a program note in which he had aligned President Johnson (in his actions in Vietnam) with Mao Tse-Tung and Fidel Castro as all supporting a policy of terror as "the moral whip of virtue"; commentators were unsympathetic to his attempt to draw such forthright comparisons. It was an inauspicious beginning for the new company, which had programmed an adventurous first season, and such was the devastating effect of the critical response that Blau even held a press conference to acknowledge this "failure," promising to do better in future.[3]

Henry Popkin, reporting from Romania the following year, in fact noted: "I briefly watched Ciulei direct *Danton's Death*, in which he was to play Danton, and, in five minutes of rehearsal, Ciulei conveyed more of Danton's sensuality than the Lincoln Center Repertory did in an entire evening."[4] This marked the beginning of Liviu Ciulei's longstanding engagement with Büchner's works, and in 1967 he was invited to the Berlin Festwochen to restage his production of *Danton's Death*. Ciulei described the production as

1. Théâtre des Amandiers, Paris Nanterre.
2. Bruce Kirle, 2003, "Paris, Summer 2002," *Western European Stages* 15:1 (winter): 4–10, at 6.
3. See Whitney Bolton, *"Danton's Death* a Lesson for Repertory Producer," *Morning Telegraph*, 23 November 1965.
4. Henry Popkin, 1967, "Theatre in Eastern Europe," *Tulane Drama Review* 11:3 (spring): 23–51, at 44.

"the biggest success of my life,"[5] and it was invited back to the The-atertreffen the following year. That year, however, it encountered intense opposition from some of the younger theatre-makers and student protesters attending the festival who wanted to see what they regarded as more radical and politically relevant works staged. Ironic, perhaps, that a director from behind the Iron Curtain should encounter the ire of the protesting left-wing youth, but it had long been the case in West Germany that "revolution" had been regarded with suspicion and fear and depicted as such in produc-tions of the day—in contrast, of course, to East Germany.

Gosch's production of *Leonce and Lena* has been described as hav-ing broken "the locks on Büchner's legacy"[6] in the GDR. *Danton's Death*, with its ambivalent attitude towards revolution, had been an even more difficult play for the East German regime to incorporate into a canon of suitably socialist-leaning dramas. Decades of internal debate and vigorous attempts to make Robespierre (or even St Just) the hero of the piece in the very few productions of the play[7] ended finally in Alexander Lang's brilliant production at the Deutsches Theater in East Berlin in 1981. In a series of ten "working theses" for his produc-tion Lang made clear that the play was "a theatrical model and not a naturalistic replica of reality."[8] By casting Christian Grashof as *both* Danton and Robespierre,[9] suggesting two sides of a conflicting/con-flicted personality, he put to bed the hitherto prevailing ideological insistence on Danton as the "baddie" of the piece, Robespierre the "goodie." The production, incidentally, continued in the reper-toire until the summer of 1989—and that autumn, following the the-atre holidays, members of the Deutsches Theater were among those organising the mass demonstrations and protests which resulted in the fall of the Wall—Germany's own successful revolution. Quotes from the play adorned protest banners and, indeed, this peaceful revo-lution's motto—"Wir sind das Volk"—is taken from the play.[1]

5. "The biggest success of my life was (the play) *Danton's Death* in Berlin, where there were 63 curtain calls, while in Romania just eight" (see: www.evenimentul.ro/articol/press-review-65.html). It was described by reviewers as the high point of the festival and by one as "one of the most complete and unified productions of a classic that has ever been seen in post-war Berlin" (H.U.K., "*Dantons Tod* in Berlin," *Basler Nachrich-ten*, 14 October 1967).
6. See Bradley, "Stealing Büchner's Characters?" 78.
7. Especially notable is a production in 1962 in Rostock, in a radical adaptation by Kurt Bartels (KuBa).
8. Alexander Lang, 1983, "Arbeitsthesen zu Georg Büchners *Dantons Tod*," pp. 12–16 in Michael Funke, ed., *Dantons Tod von Georg Büchner: Eine Dokumentation der Auffüh-rung des Deutschen Theaters; Berlin 1981*, Theaterarbeit in der DDR, Nr. 8, Berlin: Verband der Theaterschaffenden der DDR.
9. Roman Kaminski played Camille/St Just.
1. This was pointed out by Wolf Biermann, the dissident artist who had been stripped of his GDR citizenship while on tour in the West in the 1970s, when he accepted the Büchner Literature Prize in 1991 ("Der gräßliche Fatalismus der Geschichte," in Deutsche Akademie für Sprache und Dichtung, *Büchner-Preis-Reden 1984–1994*,

Berlin had, of course, been the scene of many famous productions of the play—its premieres (amateur and professional), the productions by Reinhardt and Gründgens—and after the Wall fell, this tradition continued. Robert Wilson had, already in 1992, directed *Danton's Death* for the Alley Theatre in Texas. His 1998 production[2] premiered at the Salzburg Festival and then went on to a season at the Berliner Ensemble: the first for that theatre, which had been wanting to produce it since the early 1970s under Ruth Berghaus. It took design elements from Wilson's original production and developed them into an exquisite production, using light and moving set panels to great effect to carve the space into a series of "portrait" and "landscape" "paintings," as well as evoking actual art works (Robespierre in his bath as David's "The Death of Marat," for example).

In such a vibrant theatre culture, later productions, then, can have much to live up to. When rising star Thomas Ostermeier produced *Danton's Death* in 2001—the first classic play he did at the Schaubühne, and one he had long wanted to direct—several of the critics noted that it suffered by comparison to other Berlin productions (Lang and Wilson were specifically cited). This was, especially for Ostermeier, a perhaps surprisingly conventional production which reproduced the play's metaphors quite literally (actors as puppets, the world as a theatre; the set evoked a fairground stage). A number of critics also felt that the Schaubühne actors, who had until that point been entirely engaged with contemporary texts, were challenged by the demands of the classic play—and were perplexed that the women's roles were played by men (except for Lucile), though this last may well have just been a practical staging solution, as a cast of just twelve required much doubling.[3]

In 2003 Ostermeier would introduce his (much more acclaimed) production of *Woyzeck* into the Schaubühne's repertoire, contributing to a rich Berlin theatre season for Büchner lovers: Christoph Marthaler's 2003 *Danton* production for the Zurich Schauspielhaus would score him his tenth invitation to the Theatertreffen in

Stuttgart: Philipp Reclam jnr, 1994, pp. 165–89, at 185). On this era, see also Ulrich Kaufmann, 1992, *Dichter in 'stehender Zeit': Studien zur Georg Büchner Rezeption in der DDR*, Erlangen: Verlag Palm und Enke/Jena: Universitätsverlag Jena GmbH.

2. See also Laura Ginters, 1998, "Robert Wilson's *Dantons Tod* at the Berliner Ensemble," *About Performance* 4, "Performance Analysis": 65–75.

3. Ostermeier himself was feeling the pressure of being successful at his new theatre, and acknowledged the failure: "Just before [*Nora*], I had done Georg Büchner's *Dantons Tod* [. . .], which I had wanted to do completely right, but I did everything wrong, because I wanted to be 100 per cent right and on the mark, at the very central point of the play, *and* I was completely in love with the play" (James Woodall, 2010, "Thomas Ostermeier on Europe, Theatre, Communication and Exchange," pp. 363–76 in *Contemporary European Theatre Directors*, ed. Maria M. Delgado and Dan Rebellato, London and New York: Routledge, p. 363).

Berlin, and that year's Theaterpreis (with designer Anna Viebrock) for an outstanding contribution to German theatre. Marthaler was in good company in his choice of play; one could see nine other productions of the play in Germany alone in 2004,[4] but Marthaler's was especially pointed and poignant. It took place on one of Viebrock's classic "waiting room" sets, which began as a pub on the "morning after" and was stripped back to a bare prison cell by the end of the three-and-a-half-hour production. Dressed in polo necks and jeans, Danton and his cronies were resigned, post-68 revolutionaries. Invisibly layered over this, but well known to the Theatertreffen jury,[5] and indeed audiences, was Marthaler's real life situation: he had recently resigned his artistic directorship, and this was his last production, his own farewell to the theatrical revolution he had attempted to carry out in Zurich.

In contrast to its rich history in Germany, and especially in Berlin, the play had been seen relatively infrequently in England. Following its premiere in 1959 at London's Lyric Hammersmith it languished. An RSC production was planned and cast but never staged in 1969. The National Theatre had also long been wanting to programme *Danton's Death* as part of its mission to stage European classics[6] and, finally, in 1971 Jonathan Miller agreed to direct it before his (ultimately temporary) retirement from the stage to concentrate on medical research. Critics remarked favourably on the way "Dr Miller" brought his forensic talents of analysis to his interpretation. Activating the puppetry metaphor so central to Büchner's works, the set was peopled with gauze-covered boxes containing headless mannequins, and the actors too took on the qualities of automatons—a little uncomfortably in the case of Christopher Plummer, who was a towering, weary Danton.[7]

In 2010, the National produced the play again, with Michael Grandage in his directorial debut for the company. Starring well-known screen actor Toby Stephens as a swaggering, heroic Dan-

---

4. See Bernhard Doppler, 2007, "*Dantons Tod* 2004 auf deutschsprachigen Bühnen: Ein Jahresbericht," pp. 310–16 in *Georg Büchner: Neue Perspektiven zur internationalen Rezeption*, ed. Dieter Sevin, Berlin: Erich Schmidt Verlag.

5. Klaus van den Berg noted that one of the jury's express selection criteria was that "productions chosen for the festival should be ones that pursued innovative strategies to reclaim the authenticity of political acts" as "politicians of every stripe have drained political discourse of its substance by theatricalising political events" (2005. "Theatertreffen Festival Berlin, Germany. 1–17 May 2004," *Theatre Journal* 57, no. 2 (May): 289–94, at 289).

6. See Fiona Fearon, 2007, *The Selection, Production and Reception of European Plays at the National Theatre of Great Britain, 1963–1997*, PhD thesis, University of Sheffield, p. 75.

7. See Jonathan Marks, 1972, "Jonathan Miller's *Danton's Death*," *Theater* 3, no. 3 (winter): 99–105 for further description of the production.

ton, the production was popular and critically well received, though several writers felt that the production would have been better suited to the Donmar Warehouse, Grandage's own much smaller theatre, in terms of both choice of play[8] and staging. This adaptation[9] had a running time of under two hours; cutting the street theatrical scenes (and some of the women's scenes) focused attention on the Danton/Robespierre relationship, but risked polarising the audience into pro-Danton, anti-Robespierre camps: Elliot Levey, playing Robespierre, looked taken aback to be hissed when he took his bow at the first preview. Its intimate focus on the two protagonists thus delivered an engaging chamber play—though the text, and the Olivier stage, both offered the possibility of something altogether more epic. The production was distinguished by guillotine executions "so convincing that you are surprised that several prominent members of the cast don't take the curtain call with their heads neatly tucked beneath their arms."[1]

Büchner's work continues to engage each new generation of theatre-makers. This is most clearly so on the German-speaking stages, and especially in Germany itself. Accepted as a classic, whose influence on later figures such as Brecht further reinforces his contemporary currency, he features regularly in a thriving, vital theatre scene: there have been, for example, over eighty productions of Büchner's plays in Berlin alone since *Danton's Death* premiered there in 1902.[2] The familiarity of the plays, and indeed their performance history, to both theatre-makers and audiences also allows for a more nuanced interpretative engagement with his works: productions go beyond merely staging the story to engage with the particular political and cultural concerns of the moment. Outside of the German-speaking world, *Woyzeck* is the only one of Büchner's plays that even the avid theatre-goer is likely to have encountered more than once, and the alienated social outcast will probably always

8. One reviewer noted that *Danton's Death* "returns [Grandage] to his core repertoire concerns at the Donmar [. . .] to mount re-investigations from the relatively obscure European repertoire, presented in new versions by leading contemporary playwrights" (Mark Shenton, "Danton's Death," *The Stage*, 23 July 2010, available at www.thestage .co.uk/reviews/review.php/28994/dantons-death).

9. This was a second, much shorter adaptation by playwright Howard Brenton, who had previously done a "version" of it for Peter Gill's National Theatre production in 1982.

1. Charles Spencer, "Danton's Death, National Theatre, Review," *The Telegraph*, 23 July 2010, available at www.telegraph.co.uk/culture/theatre/theatre-reviews/7906168 /Dantons-Death-National-Theatre-review.html.

2. We might contrast this with the writer who described *Danton's Death* as a "perennial favourite" of the National Theatre as it was staging its *third* production of the play in 2010 (Glen's Theatre Blog, http://gpearce.blogspot.com/2010/07/dantons-death -national-theatre-olivier.html, 24 July 2010)!

remain a familiar and compelling figure, resonating with theatre-makers and audiences alike. While Büchner's other plays may not feature as prominently on the world's stages, they are welcome occasional visitors which allow us to enjoy the precocious theatrical sensibility of a young playwright decades ahead of his time.

The Hessian Messenger

HANS MAGNUS ENZENSBERGER

[*The Hessian Messenger* in the Political Context of 1964][†]

Old books, magically transformed into classics, bequeath riddles to posterity. Not the least of these are the admirers who find them. *The Hessian Messenger* has many readers in our country, and we can be glad of that. Admittedly, it hasn't entered the schoolbooks—it hasn't reached that point yet—but it has been printed and praised. Not even Joseph Goebbels banned it. From time immemorial there hasn't been anyone in Germany who would speak against the text. At most a voice of regret might be raised here and there, saying that some country parson diluted it with the pious milk of human kindness and so detracted from its unconditional message, defusing its explosive revolutionary force.

So that's how we appear: a united nation of radical readers, enraptured by a classic that compensates us for one and a half centuries of bypassed revolutions. We insist on the overthrow of all social conditions—in the counterfactual of the past—and do so all the more the less that actual change is actually thinkable. After all there is only one weak, demoralized, lost party in our country that intends something of that kind, and that party is banned. You don't hear the scholars who disdain the compromises of Weidig advocate for the removal of that ban and the acceptance of the Communist Party.

This clearly isn't how it was meant to be. The textual criticism that took Büchner's radical side with such commendable enthusiasm

† Originally published as "Zum Hessischen Landboten. Zwei Kontexte" in *Georg Büchner und Ludwig Weidig, Der Hessische Landbote. Texte, Briefe, Prozeßakten*, 162–168. Frankfurt: Insel Verlag, 1965. © Insel Verlag Leipzig und Frankfurt am Main 1965. All rights reserved by Insel Verlag Berlin. Translated by Matthew Wilson Smith. One of Germany's most important postwar poets and essayists, Hans Magnus Enzensberger (1929) is also a distinguished playwright, novelist, and translator. He won the Georg Büchner Prize in 1963, the first of many major literary awards. The following is excerpted from an edition of *The Hessian Messenger*, including source materials and commentary, that he edited in 1965.

doesn't want to take him at his word, not at all. That's understandable. Because conditions aren't like that.[1]

Conditions, leaving aside two world wars we senselessly unleashed and their consequences, are really quite rosy. Admittedly the guardians of our constitution haven't forgotten how to move a little outside legality, and admittedly the emergency legislation they prepare brings back certain memories of the past century, and admittedly we remember whose whore the German justice system made itself just a few years ago. But there is no hunger, and the government can run ads in the paper saying: The class struggle is over. Who has won and who has lost isn't mentioned.

"If it should occur to the princes to improve the material conditions of the people," Büchner said over a hundred years ago to his friend "Red" Becker, "then the matter of the revolution in Germany is lost forever, if heaven has no mercy. Look at the Austrians, they're well fed and satisfied! Prince Metternich, the cleverest of them all, took all the revolutionary spirit that could rise up among them and suffocated it forever in their own fat." And to Karl Gutzkow he wrote: "Fatten the peasants and the revolution will have a stroke." You only need to replace the word "peasant" with some favorite catchphrase of pluralistic sociology—say, "employee" or "labor association"—to measure how deeply Büchner's gaze reached into the future—in this case, further than Friedrich Engels and Karl Marx.

The status quo in West Germany as throughout all advanced-industrial Europe is: full employment, continual increase of production and consumption, concealment rather than abolition of class differences. The bourgeoisie has become unrecognizable through the assimilation of all other classes, the workers' movement has become its appendix, and the political parties capable of governing have become a single cartel. The great mass of the people—this wasn't yet true in Büchner's time—is no longer willing to form an opposition. That's why any comparison with the conditions of the German Vormärz is simply misleading.

The status quo in the Federal Republic of Germany can't be christened with the name of restoration either. We don't have a Metternich, we have Herr Höcherl,[2] and even Herr Höcherl seems inflated and expendable: the status quo can afford such reminiscences—they give it a certain Germanic local color—and it isn't reliant on them since the regime isn't based on repression but on compliance.

---

1. "Denn die Verhältnisse, sie sind nicht so"—an allusion to a refrain from "Die Unsicherheit Menschlicher Verhältnisse," a song by Brecht from *The Threepenny Opera*.
2. Klemens von Metternich (1773–1859), Austrian statesman and one of the central architects of European power in the first half of the nineteenth century. Hermann Höcherl (1912–1989), West German Minister of the Interior, 1961–1965.

Whatever else a classic may be, it cannot serve as an alibi for posterity, as a laurel wreath for toastmasters. The most brutal thing you can do to a dead writer is to celebrate him without taking him seriously. The respect we owe to authors such as Büchner and Weidig demands that we say that, in our situation, in regard to our country, *The Hessian Messenger* is an anachronism. Büchner wrote from Strassburg on April 5, 1833: "If anything can help in these times, it is violence." In the same letter he wrote: "The indifference of the Germans really thwarts every plan." The political context in Germany in the year 1964 can be characterized by the judgment that the second sentence is valid while the first is false.

Violence cannot help us, much less our neighbors. The high-flying spokesmen of capital have long since understood this; they're dealing in all the trade shows of Eastern Europe and drumming up business in the great détente. Even among the military the word has spread that the state of emergency imposed on us is called peace. Only resentful old communists and hard-right desperados dream of civil war. So long and so far as international capital is able to keep large protest movements under its control, the status quo is secured.

And yet the lesson of *The Hessian Messenger* has not been refuted and its message for the future is not lost. Today the old text has readers in our country but no addressees. Because it wasn't aimed at passive observers and rich beneficiaries. Thus it doesn't speak to us but against us. Today every thought of Büchner's was for those who "lie on the ground like manure" before us. What was regional politics in 1834 has become world politics. What the student from Giessen and the country parson from Butzbach wrote concerns billions of people today. What is valid about *The Hessian Messenger* in 1964 is no longer valid for Hesse; it is valid for the Middle East, the Indian subcontinent and Southeast Asia, for large parts of Africa and for many countries in Latin America.

*   *   *

The relation between poor and rich peoples is the only revolutionary element in the world. Only with violence can this relation be perpetuated, only with violence can it be remedied. As this comes closer to a crisis every day, the poor peoples know what they can expect from us. Everything we grant them is forced from us by necessity, and we toss them even this favor like a panhandled blessing and a wretched toy, to make ever-gawking Asia forget our good business deals. Apart from that we've turned our palaces into protected historical monuments and devoted ourselves to a new motto: Peace to the condos on the Rhine and the Hudson! War on the huts on the Congo and Mekong!

Whoever can invoke Büchner, it is not us.

VICTOR BROMBERT

[Büchner and Rhetoric]†

Büchner's antiheroic stance is * * * related to an antihistorical bias and a growing distrust of rhetoric. His grim view of history, and specifically of ideological bloodbaths, is quite logically bound up with the noxiousness of inflated language. Such a language becomes the accomplice of brutality and injustice. Büchner's Danton seems to be allergic to speechmaking and poses. Early in the play, he makes it known that he could never look at the pompous Catos of this world without an irresistible desire to kick them in the behind (I.1).[1] Büchner's theatre of antirhetoric is thus to be understood as a reaction against the excesses of rhetorical flourish and the lofty tones of "idealistic" dramaturgy. Schiller was his *bête noire*. Danton, the well-known revolutionary orator, paradoxically questions with utmost skepticism what Herbert Lindenberger aptly calls "the validity of rhetoric in voicing any human ideals."[2]

The problem of rhetoric seems indeed to be at the heart of Büchner's perceptions and themes. As a pupil at the classical *Gymnasium* in Darmstadt, he had been an outstanding practitioner of the *ars rhetorica* and the *ars oratoria*. His talent for oratory was repeatedly recognized by the headmaster of the school, Carl Dilthey, who on three occasions chose him for the honor of giving a public speech, twice in German and once in Latin. The Latin speech has been lost, but we do have the two German school exercises: a speech on Cato's suicide ("Rede zur Verteidigung des Kato von Utica") which glorifies the Stoic virtues of antiquity, and an earlier speech belonging to the genre known as the *genus demonstrativum*, in commemoration of the sacrificial death of the burghers of Pforzheim ("Helden-Tod der Vierhundert Pforzheimer")—a heroic episode of the Thirty Years' War. The word "hero" (*Held*) recurs in various combinations: "Helden-Tod," "Heldenzeit," "Heldenstamm," "Heldenschläfe," together with the related lexicon of virtue ("Tugend"), courage ("Kühnheit") and magnanimity ("Seelengrösse"). In both texts, these terms are contemptuously opposed to the slavish spirit of the masses that grovel in the dust.

The speech about Cato of Utica is particularly interesting. Young Büchner was obviously conversant with all the structures and fig-

---

† From *In Praise of Antiheroes*, 14–16. Chicago: University of Chicago Press, 1999. Reprinted by permission.
1. The numbers in parentheses refer to the numbers of the acts and scenes of the play.
2. Herbert Lindenberger, *Georg Büchner*, Carbondale: Southern Illinois University Press, 1964, p. 27.

ures of rhetoric; he knew all about the order of discourse: proemium, propositio, narratio, argumentio, refutatio, peroratio. But the speech is not just a rhetorical and stylistic exercise. The political implications of a suicide conceived as an act of protest against tyranny are inescapable, especially if one takes into account that the school ceremony took place barely two months after the July 1830 revolution in Paris; that uprisings were occurring in Hessen; and that the Darmstadt bourgeoisie had good reason to be alarmed. Moreover, Büchner had already referred glowingly to the French Revolution of 1789, and to its struggle for liberty, in his oration on the heroic burghers of Pforzheim.[3]

Rhetoric, the heroic tradition, and political action were thus from the start closely linked in Büchner's mind. The opening of his Cato speech stresses the exhilaration of witnessing the noble struggle with fate any time man dares intervene in the march of world history (". . . wenn er es wagt einzugreifen in den Gang der Weltgeschichte"). *Der Hessische Landbote*, a violent diatribe and call to arms against the ruling classes and officialdom in the State of Hessen, was surely Büchner's attempt to translate such a notion of heroic political intervention into militant practice. *The Hessian Messenger* is a most interesting document, not only for the obvious historical and political reasons, but because of what it reveals of the contradictions of Büchner's thought—contradictions nonetheless held together by an inner logic that was to give an enigmatic resonance to his literary work.

The opening statement of *Der Hessische Landbote* is a declaration of war ("War on the Palaces!") and a call to violence. In a letter to his family written a year earlier, the young Büchner had indeed asserted that the only way to fight the "eternal, brute force" inflicted on the have-nots is revolutionary *violence*. "My opinion is this: if anything can help in these times of ours, it is violence."[4] The language in which *The Hessian Messenger* is couched reflects metaphorical violence more than a precise program for violent struggle. The metaphors are earthy, rooted in vivid images of sweat and manure. On the other hand, the metaphorical language is strongly Biblical, and repeatedly inspired by the style of prophecy, especially toward the end. This Biblical vehemence is attributable in large part to the coauthor and editor of the pamphlet, Pastor Friedrich Ludwig Weidig, though there can be no doubt that Büchner

3. Georg Büchner, *Werke und Briefe*, Munich: Carl Hanser Verlag, 1988, pp. 17–34. See the excellent notes provided in this edition, pp. 420–25, 426–34. See also Gerhard Schaub, "Der Rhetorikschüler Georg Büchner. Eine Analyse der Kato-Rede," in *Diskussion Deutsch 17*, 1986, H. 92, pp. 663–84.
4. *Werke und Briefe*, op. cit., p. 278.

himself was well versed in religion and intimately acquainted with the Bible. In any case, the experience of writing the political tract in collaboration with Weidig encouraged the overlapping of the socio-political and religious themes, and further complicated the link between rhetoric and heroism.

But what is distinctly new in *The Hessian Messenger* is that heroic political action is given a consistently anti-elitist character, and thus conceived in exact opposition to the rhetorical school exercises grounded in the classical humanistic tradition which extolled the "hero" as totally different in nature, and superior to, ordinary humanity. Both the "Helden-Tod der Vierhunderdt Pforzheimer" and the "Rede zur Verteidigung des Kato von Utica" refer disdainfully to the millions of slavish creatures who crawl like worms in the dust and deserve to be forgotten.[5]

The tone is altogether different in *The Hessian Messenger*, and in a letter written to his family at about the same time Büchner underlines the following words: "*I have contempt for no one.*" Least of all, he adds, does he scorn those who did not have the benefit of an education. And he concludes that elitism ("Aristokratismus") represents "the most despicable contempt for the holy spirit in a human being." Such a denunciation of arrogant scorn for the humble and the underprivileged is in itself consonant with Biblical language. Walter Hinderer quite aptly recalls the passage from St. Matthew (18:10) that may have been on Büchner's mind when he denounced the elitism of the "gebildete Klasse": "Take heed that ye despise not one of these little ones."[6]

That Büchner's concern for unidealized, ordinary humanity became a permanent motif is made explicit in the programmatic statement of the poet Lenz: "One must love human nature in order to penetrate into the unique character of any individual; one must not consider anybody too insignificant, too ugly. Only then can one understand humankind." *Menschheit* is a notion that can have meaning only if it is rooted in understanding and love of the most ordinary human being. A similar idea appears in a different context in the romantic comedy *Leonce und Lena*: ". . . even the most insignificant of human beings is so important that a whole lifetime is far too short to love him."[7]

As Büchner reached literary maturity—in his case this occurred at a surprisingly early age—he tended systematically to undermine the classical rhetoric of his school exercises and polemical writings. Through parody he thematized the uses and misuses of idealistic

5. Ibid., pp. 17, 27.
6. Walter Hinderer, Introduction to *Complete Works and Letters*, tr. Henry J. Schmidt, ed. Walter Hinderer and Henry J. Schmidt, New York: Continuum, 1986, p. 14.
7. *Werke und Briefe*, op. cit., pp. 145, 181.

rhetoric, while fully aware of its resources for multivalence. For it could camouflage political meanings, as in the Cato speech, or be ironic in praising an absence of ambiguity (Cato, for instance, was expressly lauded for his onesidedness, his "Einseitigkeit").[8] But rhetoric, Büchner knew, could also be a despotic and murderous weapon, as in the case of Robespierre. And it could be a framework for vacuity, a tool for illusions and untruths about human nature, an accomplice in the most fundamental betrayal of human values.[9]

It is hardly surprising that Büchner consistently scorned literary "Idealismus," accusing it, much in the same terms as elitism, of representing the most shameful contempt ("schmählichste Verachtung") of human nature. A writer must not attempt to be a lofty teacher of morality. Büchner repeatedly takes to task those he calls "Idealdichter," who construct puppets with "sky blue noses" and "affected pathos," mere marionettes or wooden dolls, instead of creatures of flesh and blood whose failings and human passions might fill us with awe and compassion. Schiller, it would seem, was his chief target. "I think highly of Goethe and Shakespeare, but very little of Schiller," he writes to his family. Instead of seeking effects of bombast and amplification, Büchner would like to find a human idiom suited to human matters (". . . für menschliche Dinge müsse man auch menschliche Ausdrücke finden").[1]

8. Ibid., p. 33.
9. Ibid., pp. 144, 306, 284. See also Lindenberger, *Georg Büchner*, op. cit., pp. 23–24, with reference to parodistic effects; and Maurice R. Benn, *The Drama of Revolt. A Critical Study of Georg Büchner*, Cambridge: Cambridge University Press, 1976, pp. 81–82, 97, concerning Büchner's aesthetic revolt against idealization, ennoblement, and his fundamental suspicion of "high" art.
1. *Werke und Briefe*, pp. 110–11, 88.

Danton's Death

BERTOLT BRECHT

[On *Danton's Death*]†

[*October 4, 1921*]

* * *

Büchner's *Danton* at the municipal theatre.[1] A superb melodrama. Without Shakespeare's roundedness, edgier, more intellectualised, more fragmentary, an ecstatic sequence of scenes, philosophically a panorama. This kind of thing is no longer a model, more a powerful aid.

* * *

March 3, 1949

* * *

Would Engel be interested in Büchner's *Danton's Death* (in case we have trouble with *The Defeat*)?[2] It would have to be supplemented: Danton actually betrays the Revolution, because he associates with aristocrats, protects them, admires them, lets them admire him, and in general behaves like a prima donna etc. So he's to blame for the necessary terror (necessary against him), which then devours

---

† The German dramatist, poet, and theorist Bertolt Brecht (1898–1956) is one of the central figures of modern theater history. Many of his plays (including *The Threepenny Opera*, *Mother Courage and Her Children*, and *The Caucasian Chalk Circle*) are standards of the international repertoire, and his performance methods have profoundly transformed the modern stage. The first excerpt following is from Brecht's diary; the second, from a letter to his second wife, the distinguished German actress Helene Weigel. *Diaries: 1970–1922*, ed. Herta Ramthun, trans. John Willett; London: Methuen, 1979, p. 132. *Letters*, ed. John Willett, trans. Ralph Manheim; London: Methuen, 1990. Reprinted by permission.

1. Max Reinhardt's 1921 production at the Grosses Schauspielhaus in Berlin, a revival of his highly successful 1916 production at the Deutsches Theater in Berlin.
2. Erich Engel (1891–1966), German stage and film director. *The Defeat*: reference to Brecht's adaptation of *Die Niederlage* (*The Defeat*, 1937), by Norwegian playwright Nordahl Grieg; Brecht would ultimately title his version *Die Tage der Commune* (*The Days of the Commune*).

Robespierre. Seyferth would be good for Robespierre if we could get Dahlke[2] for Danton (and if he filled the bill).

* * *

EDWARD McINNES

Scepticism, Ideology, and History in Büchner's *Dantons Tod*[†]

When *Dantons Tod* first appeared in 1835 it was widely rejected as a work devoid of all creative originality. Many commentators saw it simply as a dramatization of some chapters out of Thiers' history of the French Revolution and as such necessarily defective as a literary work.[1] In this century one of the main concerns of critics has been to show precisely how radical and prophetic is this attempt by Büchner to accommodate the dramatic form to the actuality of history. At the same time they have also been keen to emphasize the power with which this work evokes an awareness of an existential dilemma which goes far beyond any specific historical preoccupation. This two-fold concern is apparent in almost all recent discussions of the play.[2] On the one hand critics have spent much time examining the historical materials Büchner studied and the ways in which he assimilates and utilizes them. But they have also tried to

---

2. Wilfried Seyferth (1908–1954) and Paul Dahlke (1904–1984), German stage and film actors.

† From *For Lionel Thomas: A Collection of Essays in His Memory*, ed. Derek Attwood, Alan Best, and Rex Last, pp. 53–69. Hull: Department of German, University of Hull, 1980.

1. See Ulrike Paul, *Vom Geschichtsdrama zur politischen Diskussion*, Munich, 1974, p. 43ff.

2. See, for example:
Karl Viëtor, *Georg Büchner*, Bern, 1949, pp. 95–158.
Benno von Wiese, *Die deutsche Tragödie von Lessing bis Hebbel*, 2nd ed., Hamburg, 1952, pp. 513–34.
Gerhart Baumann, *Georg Büchner. Die dramatische Ausdruckswelt*, Göttingen, 1961, p. 9ff.
Walter Höllerer, '*Dantons Tod*' in: Benno v. Wiese (ed.), *Das deutsche Drama vom Barock bis zur Gegenwart, Interpretationen II*, Düsseldorf, 1962, pp. 65–68.
Wolfgang Martens, 'Ideologie und Verzweiflung. Religiöse Motive in Büchners Revolutionsdrama' in: *Euphorion* 54 (1960), 83–108.
J. P. Stern, 'A World of Suffering: Georg Büchner' in: *Reinterpretations*, London, 1964, pp. 78–155.
Margaret Jacobs (ed.), '*Dantons Tod*' and '*Woyzeck*', with introduction and notes, 3rd ed., Manchester, 1971, pp. ix–xxxviii.
Jürgen H. Petersen, 'Die Aufhebung der Moral im Werk Georg Büchners' in: *DVjs* 47 (1973), 245–66.
Paul, op.cit., p. 40ff.
M. B. Benn, *The Drama of Revolt. A Critical Study of Georg Büchner*, Cambridge, 1976, p. 107ff.
David G. Richards, *Georg Büchner and the Birth of the Modern Drama*, Albany, 1977, p. 37ff.

show—albeit from very different points of view—how the dramatist constantly strives beyond this historical impetus and uses it as a means of embodying a personal vision of great imaginative force. The problem which is at the centre of these discussions is that of relating the distinctive drive to historical documentation (about one sixth of the text of the play is taken more or less directly from historical sources[3]) to other kinds of insight and concern which do not seem necessarily grounded in Büchner's particular historical enquiry. And, as Ulrike Paul has pointed out, interpreters tend ultimately to give clear priority either to the 'public' documentary parts of the play or to those which express an inward or speculative preoccupation, that is to see one at the expense of the other.[4]

One of the great enigmas of Büchner criticism is that commentators who seem to start from a strong impression of the inner coherence of the work should have found such difficulty in elucidating this in critical terms.[5] The sheer variety of the interpretations which have been put forward in an attempt to meet this central problem is itself evidence that a genuine dilemma exists. There seems to be some deep ambiguity in the conception of the work which lends itself readily to quite contradictory interpretations but which is strangely difficult to analyse. In this essay I would like to re-examine Büchner's play from a rather different point of view in an attempt to probe the sources of its peculiar elusiveness—an elusiveness which, paradoxically, must somehow be bound up with the dramatist's relentless quest for historical objectivity.

It seems to me that any attempt to re-examine *Dantons Tod* has to begin by accepting the peculiar force with which Büchner seeks to penetrate a concrete historical situation. His contemporaries were surely right in seeing this as a work in which the dramatist's imagination is focused with a quite new intensity upon the recorded facts. This play is born, as critics like Mayer have stressed, of a real attempt to explore specific historical developments which Büchner clearly felt were of immediate relevance to the world of the 1830s.[6] To get to grips with the conception of this work we have to begin by looking more clearly at the way Büchner actually sees history and attempts to embody it in dramatic form. This is not as easy as it might seem because his dependence on historical sources is much more complex and ambivalent than critics have generally assumed. His concern as a dramatist to make such full use of the available

3. See L. F. Helbig, *Das Geschichtsdrama Georg Büchners*, Bern and Frankfurt, 1973, p. 16ff.
4. Paul, op.cit., p. 44f.
5. Peacock is one of the very few critics who have seen a fundamental formal incoherence in *Dantons Tod*. See Ronald Peacock, *The Poet in the Theatre*, New York, 1960, p. 181ff.
6. Hans Mayer, *Georg Büchner und seine Zeit*, Berlin (East), 1960, p. 198.

records of historical events does not arise out of a straightforward,
positivist desire to transcribe and substantiate; it also involves a
disconcerting sense of the ambiguity of historical documentation
and of its frequently problematic relation to the circumstances it so
confidently claims to describe. As a playwright Büchner seems intent
on utilizing all the exploratory possibilities of the dramatic form to
question and undermine where at first sight he appears simply
to demonstrate and clarify.

Büchner was fully aware that as a dramatist he had at his disposal
means of enquiry and expression which were different from those
available to the historian, and in the letter of 28 July 1835 which is
so often quoted to show his wholehearted commitment to historical
actuality he makes important distinctions which critics have largely
ignored:

> Der dramatische Dichter ist in meinen Augen nichts als ein
> Geschichtsschreiber, steht aber über letzterem dadurch, daß
> er uns die Geschichte zum zweiten Mal erschafft und uns
> gleich unmittelbar statt eine trockene Erzählung zu geben, in
> das Leben einer Zeit hinein versetzt, uns statt Charakteris-
> tiken Charaktere und statt Beschreibungen Gestalten gibt.
> Seine höchste Aufgabe ist, der Geschichte so nahe als möglich
> zu kommen.[7]

While he sees both the historian and the dramatist as obliged to pursue the truth of history, Büchner emphasizes the distinction between
these two ways of approaching history by pointing to the different
kinds of imaginative effect they produce. While the historian presents the past indirectly, from the outside as it were, the playwright
brings it to life as an immediate present which envelops the spectator or reader with the force of its reality. Unlike the historian, who
renders a phase of history as a limited, completed and thus 'over-
seeable' entity, the playwright, who strives to realize it as a living,
dramatic present, has to address it as a flux or impetus which is
forward-moving and open-ended. In other words, he brings a period
of the past to life by immersing himself imaginatively in its shaping
energies and tensions as they are working themselves out at a specific moment of their development. If this is so, then it would seem
that for Büchner the dramatist confronts a particular historical
situation in something like the same way as the spectator who is
fully caught up in the illusion of a dramatic present. He must, like
the spectator, seek to suspend the conclusive certainty which comes

7. [See p. 188: "the dramatic poet is in my eyes . . ."—Editor]. Georg Büchner, *Sämtliche
Werke und Briefe*, Hist.-krit. Ausgabe mit Kommentar, hrsg. von Werner R. Lehmann,
Bd.2, Hamburg, 1971, p. 443. All references to Büchner's works are to this edition.
Dantons Tod is in vol. I (1967); the correspondence is in Vol. II.

from the foreknowledge of developments which lie beyond the immediate dramatic action. To come 'as close as possible' to actual historical events, he must open himself to the pulsating surge of complex, disordered events whose final consequences are still not clear.

Reflections of this kind, although to some extent speculative, are useful because they can help us grasp and respond to the peculiarities of the dramatic structure which Büchner has developed in *Dantons Tod*. He presents the action in a way which is calculated to enforce an attitude of tense, questioning uncertainty about the prevailing historical crisis and what may lie ahead. This is apparent in the setting of the play. The action covers the twelve days leading up to the death of Danton in early April 1794,[8] but Büchner presents the events of these days as a fragment in the drawn-out, disjointed history of the Revolution. They do not mark a climax or a completion, but appear as part of a vast, amorphous movement whose beginnings are not clear and whose end is not foreseeable.

This distinctive tendency in Büchner's conception becomes clearer if we compare his play with more conventional attempts in the nineteenth century to dramatize the same historical material. Works like Griepenkerl's *Maximilian Robespierre*, Hammerling's *Danton und Robespierre*, Gensichen's *Danton* all embrace a much wider sweep of historical events and portray the dramatic action as the outcome of a clear, unified process of historical development in which the playwright demonstrates the character of the Revolution.[9] The dramatic action in all these plays represents, in other words, a clear and explicit attempt to interpret history.

Büchner's play is most sharply distinguished from these works by his use of a complex, intensely searching form which is in a strange way both outward and inward directed, both 'open' and analytical. Critics have often noted the great flexibility of this form and stressed its capacity to present action in terms of single, discontinuous incidents, but they have not, I think, sufficiently emphasized its counteracting tendency to qualify the scope of this unfolding action by pointing to the shaping force of preceding developments. These belong to a past which is not represented directly and can only be glimpsed intermittently through the fragmentary accounts of characters whose attitudes and aims are in conflict with one another.

---

8. See Helbig, op.cit., p. 33. The assumption that Büchner is giving a coherent and conclusive *interpretation* of the Revolution has led some critics like Mayer, op.cit., p. 200f., to speak as if the fall of Robespierre were part of the dramatic action. In the play itself, however, this does not appear as an inescapable event: it is fleetingly envisaged by one dramatic figure as a possibility in the future.

9. Robert Griepenkerl, *Maximilian Robespierre*, 2nd ed., Bremen, 1851, p. xviiif; p. 154. Robert Hamerling, *Danton und Robespierre*, 2nd ed., Hamburg, 1871, p. 173f. O. F. Genischen, *Danton*, Berlin, 1870, p. 88ff.

The dramatic present in *Dantons Tod* involves a past which, for all its power, is diffuse, ambiguous and, to the spectator, largely inaccessible.

Büchner sets the action of *Dantons Tod* at a point of severe crisis in the development of the Revolution. The first triumphant acts of destruction with all their promise of liberation are over, and the leaders now face the urgent problem of determining the course of future developments. A bitter conflict of outlook has arisen between them.[1] While Robespierre, St Just and their supporters are convinced of the necessity of continuing and even intensifying the terror, Danton and his associates insist that they must bring it to an end and introduce a period of stabilization (10ff; 17ff). This opposition of view, as the dramatist presents it, is complex and confusing. He shows that each group tries to establish the authority of its view by claiming to be able to survey the whole process of the Revolution, its origins and ultimate destiny, and this, Büchner makes clear, involves on both sides profound metaphysical assumptions which cannot be directly related to any specific historical events. The dramatist seems to be inviting the spectator to question this conflict of outlook and to probe its position in the world of the drama as a whole.

The belief of Robespierre and St Just in the ultimate triumph of the Revolution is, as Büchner portrays it, essentially teleological and has much of the deep, unsearchable force of a religious assurance. They have a vision of the Revolution which accords a necessary place to violence and destruction, and both men claim to see in the immense disruption they have lived through the first decisive development towards a new society in which the ideals of the Revolution will be realized.

Robespierre's confidence in the power of the Revolution grows out of an *a priori* moral conviction. The revolutionary process, as he sees it, is the expression of a moral energy which lies in the collective consciousness of the people (15f; 18f). This energy is still necessarily in conflict with forces of depravity and injustice, but he has no doubt that it will lead, under the conscientious direction of the people's leaders, to the establishment of a new regenerate community (44f).

---

1. Critics like Viëtor, op.cit., p. 100f., von Wiese, op.cit., p. 523ff., Richards, op.cit., p. 37, Paul, op.cit., p. 55ff., have tended to see Büchner as exposing unambiguously the breakdown of the Revolution. This is determined largely, I think, by a concern, conscious or unconscious, to see it through Danton's eyes—to regard his cynical indictments as the expression of the dramatist's point of view. Petersen, op.cit., p. 251, and M. McCoglan, 'The True Dialectic of *Dantons Tod*,' *New German Studies* 6 (1978): 151–74, have rightly warned against this tendency.

It is noticeable that St Just also sees the Revolution as a force released, but not created, by human agents. Those who channel its creative power are, he claims, the instruments of the World Spirit; they merely help to guide or direct developments which are fore-ordained and must sooner or later be realized in the course of history (45f). Their role as leaders of the Revolution is just to put into effect what is inescapably decreed. Both men, as Büchner presents them, share the belief that the Revolution is not an arbitrary human initiative, not dependent on contingent historical-social circumstances, but in the last analysis a response to dynamic controlling forces which are inherent in the nature of reality itself.

It is not possible to dismiss these views of the revolutionary leaders as essentially public statements through which they merely seek to strengthen their power over the people. Certainly these views are at times restated in ways calculated to confirm their claim to leadership, but it seems certain that the teleological assurance they imply has informed the idealism of the Revolution from the beginning. It is this assurance which enables them to see the apparently chaotic situation of 1794 as a stage in an ultimately constructive process. For both men the Revolution is a movement of such immense scope and such utterly transforming potentiality that its struggle with opposing forces must necessarily be violent and prolonged. Even the serious divisions in their own ranks do not appear to diminish their confidence that all obstacles will one day be overcome by its irresistible progress towards ultimate fulfilment.

These claims of the committed revolutionaries must necessarily perplex the spectator. They embrace such wide vistas of historical development and go so far beyond the narrow scale of the concrete action that they cannot, as far as I can see, be disproved by any evidence established in the course of the dramatic development. This is something to which we must return.

Even if they could accept that the historical situation is essentially opaque, many critics would, however, claim that Büchner is intent on demonstrating the falseness of the revolutionary idealism in another way. They have seen in Danton's indictment of Robespierre evidence of the dramatist's concern to discredit the revolutionary leader and so expose by implication the ideology of the Revolution as a whole.[2] It seems to me that this reading almost always involves too ready an assumption that Danton speaks here with the authority of the dramatist, that he expresses a view demonstrably given in the conception of the play. It is worth looking again at this encounter and its aftermath (26ff).

---

2. Baumann, op.cit., p. 29ff.; Paul, op.cit., p. 40ff.

There can be no doubt that Robespierre is badly shaken by Danton's attack. The charge that he is driven not by selfless idealism but by an unacknowledged will to power strikes at the very heart of his understanding of himself and of his involvement in the Revolution. He is disturbed, naturally enough, by the sheer comprehensiveness of Danton's attack and he is forced to examine his relationship with his former colleague, not just because it represents the most pressing, practical problem facing him but because it is, as it were, the one concrete point by which he can test the truth of the whole accusation (28). This relationship becomes for Robespierre the acid test of his own moral nature, for he is obviously troubled by the possibility—implicit in Danton's charge—that his opposition to Danton is determined not by political necessity but by personal resentment. It is noticeable that Robespierre does not in the end admit this possibility (28). He is forced, it is true, to concede some degree of personal antagonism in his attitude to Danton, but in the end he reasserts that he wills his death for the sake of the Republic.

Now most critics have assumed that in this monologue of Robespierre's which follows Danton's visit, the dramatist is laying bare by indirect and subtle means a process of massive self-deception, and there is no doubt that it can be read in this way. But it would seem equally possible, if one approaches the scene with different preconceptions, to come to quite opposite conclusions.[3] One could argue that this scene, which critics have read as a demonstration of hypocrisy, in fact vindicates Robespierre's basic good faith. One could claim, for instance, that the fact that he is so shaken by Danton's attack and does not in the end try to exonerate himself completely is a sign of the essential sincerity of his most private intentions. It would also be possible to regard his tortured admission that he cannot understand the deepest motives as evidence of a perplexity which is inconsistent with that blind will to self-justification which critics have generally seen as determining his behaviour. I would not want to claim that such a reading is true but merely to suggest that, given certain prior assumptions about the figure, it would be possible to see things in this way. In the end, however, we have to suspend judgement. We cannot come to a conclusive understanding of Robespierre's behaviour here because we cannot know to what extent his conscious mind is operating under the constraint of

---

3. Viëtor, op.cit., p. 138, claims for example that Robespierre's abrupt exclamation: 'Ja, ja! die Republik! Er muß weg.' shows that this will to power overcomes the accusations of his conscience. But it could equally well be that in the notion of the Republic he comes as an agent face to face with a *value* which he cannot question. It is noticeable that Danton invokes the Republic in this way when attempting to vindicate his involvement in the September murders (p. 41).
    Petersen, op.cit., p. 251ff., is one of the very few critics who have given a more differentiated and subtle analysis of Büchner's presentation of the figure of Robespierre.

subconscious pressures. For all Danton's cynical assurance this must remain a matter of speculation.

I have been suggesting that Büchner does not (as most critics have assumed) unequivocally expose the Revolution. He does not show its objectives as clearly refuted by the prevailing situation nor its ideals as obviously incompatible with the real determining motives of its protagonists. At the same time, however, it is just as important to stress that those aspects of the Revolution—social, institutional or psychological—which clearly come to light in the course of the dramatic action, do not seem for the most part to endorse the claims of the revolutionaries. These seem indeed often strangely divorced from the actual social-historical crisis revealed in the action. The revolutionary leaders, as Büchner presents them, have little concern with immediate problems of corporate development. Their gaze seems firmly fixed on absolute goals. They never try to show in concrete terms how the situation here and now will lead to the formation of a new order, and in most respects seem strangely indifferent towards short-term, intermediate solutions. This is especially evident in their attitude to the grave economic situation of the new Republic. There is no sign that the revolutionary leaders regard the persisting poverty and famine of the people as an urgent problem which can only be solved by means of extensive and carefully co-ordinated planning, and in this as in other respects they seem to make no effort to relate their ultimate claims to actual circumstances or test their ideals against their ability to cope with specific problems. Now one might claim that in emphasizing this apparent indifference to the pressures of the immediate situation Büchner is in fact ironically undermining the general aspirations of the revolutionaries. But this would be to over-simplify. The scope of the Revolution as a historical movement is so vast, the character of its future leadership and policies so uncertain, that from the vantage-point of the dramatic situation we can pass no judgement. Such a judgement would presuppose a clear conception of the nature of history and this, I have argued, we cannot derive from the action of the play itself. Büchner's presentation of the Revolution, it seems to me, forces us to question both the relation between the individual's behaviour and the aims he claims to pursue, as well as that between the idealist's perception of historical possibility and actual historical-social circumstances.

It is important to emphasize these pervading uncertainties because they necessarily affect the way we confront the experience of the central figure, Danton. There can be no doubt that this complex figure is at the centre of the dramatist's concern. This should not, however, mislead us into identifying him with Büchner and attributing a near-choric authority to the views he expresses. Certainly,

Danton does articulate insights which, as critics have noted, are very close to those which Büchner himself expresses in his correspondence and elsewhere.[4] It is also true that, as Koopmann points out, Danton functions to a large extent not just as a character caught up in the action but as a commentator who stands outside and reflects upon it.[5] Nonetheless in the end it seems to me that if we see this character within the structure of tensions which the play generates, then, for all our sympathy, we have to respond to Danton with the same sceptical reserve with which we view all the other dramatic figures. For Büchner also presents Danton as the proponent of a metaphysical outlook which can neither be confirmed nor refuted by any of the specific developments in the play. Although Danton regards himself as someone who has outgrown the illusory hope and self-deceit of those who claim to lead the Revolution, he too, as the dramatist makes clear, is trapped in his own obsessive vision of life and moved by the insights it imposes on him.

Danton's rejection of the Revolution does not flow from mere political scepticism but from a fundamental moral disillusion. It is rooted in the conviction that man is incapable of free ethical action and must always remain the victim of dark, implacable forces in his own nature. He expresses this nihilistic assurance in his encounter with Robespierre. He leaves no doubt that he rejects revolutionary idealism because, like every other form of supposedly moral action, it is a pretence: the devious means by which the individual pursues power and satisfaction (26f). At the heart of Danton's disillusion is the certainty that no human being can escape the imprisoning egotism of his own nature:

> Es giebt nur Epicuräer und zwar grobe und feine, Christus war der feinste; das ist der einzige Unterschied, den ich zwischen den Menschen herausbringen kann. Jeder handelt seiner Natur gemäß d.h. er thut, was ihm wohl thut (27).[1]

This view denies the possibility of any personal relationship which transcends mutual need and precludes any real cooperative endeavour. It also implies that there can be no progress in history. History, as Danton sees it, can be no more than the sum of an infinite number of colliding processes, each of which is determined by the drive of an isolated self towards its own gratification. In this view life must always remain, in every society and at every time, an anarchy of competing wills.

4. See Viëtor, op.cit., p. 95ff.; McCoglan, op.cit., p. 157f.
5. Helmut Koopmann, 'Dantons Tod und die antike Welt. Zur Geschichtsphilosophie Georg Büchners' in: ZfdPh 84 (1965) Sonderheft, Moderne deutsche Dichtung, 22–41.
1. See p. 40: "There are only epicureans . . ." [Editor].

Büchner does not show directly how Danton, the revolutionary idealist, falls prey to such overwhelming disillusion. In fact, it is clear that Danton himself recoils from the memory of this agonizing process of breakdown and seeks to banish it from his conscious awareness. Only once does he lay bare for a few moments the source of this disabling torment and this is, significantly, at a time when his mind is struggling to emerge from the stark compulsions of a nightmare (40f). Here Danton gives an involuntary glimpse of the experience of guilt and horror which seems to have shattered all his hopes. The nightmare, it becomes clear, has forced him to re-live his involvement in the massacre of the imprisoned aristocrats in September 1792. It is not as if Danton were racked by a sense of his responsibility for this atrocity; looking back he can only re-affirm what he has felt from the first—that it was inescapable. With the royalist armies advancing on Paris (he tells himself again) the presence of the aristocrats in the city represented a threat to the very survival of the Republic and the massacre was thus an act of self-defence for which no one is to blame. But this seems to be the crucial point for Danton, for it is precisely the realization that he did not will this atrocity, nor was responsible for it, which seems to have undermined his faith in the effectiveness of the Revolution. This realization seems to have released in him the awareness of a terrible compulsion in all things. In this experience of utter dependence upon circumstances which he could not have foreseen and over which he had no control he apparently senses the ultimate power of contingent and impersonal forces which nullify all moral aspiration. Here, it seems, is born that racking, nightmare vision of the Revolution as a blind, self-perpetuating momentum of destruction beyond human will and leading nowhere (25; 32f).

Danton's conviction of the final futility of everything possesses him with the force of a consuming certainty. It is not something which he can question or which he feels he has to prove to someone else. This awareness seems to have overcome him with the immediacy and force of a revelation and has all the power inherent in such a convulsive experience to crystallize latent feelings and intuitions and to draw them together into a coherent pattern which compels his acceptance. Danton's vision of absurdity has an irresistible force which seems able to transform every experience into further confirmation of its truth.

This emphasis on the inward character of Danton's vision, on its rootedness in the sensitivity and experience of this one man, has the effect of relativizing its position in the structure of the play. It seems to me—and here I know I am at odds with most Büchner critics—that though the dramatist draws us deeply into Danton's experience, making us see things to a considerable extent through his eyes, he also forces us to recognize that his outlook is determined by his involvement in the overwhelming complexities of an immense historical upheaval. Büchner sets this vision of Danton's in opposition to other views which, although equally subjective and vulnerable, are yet also coherent on their own terms.

But Büchner goes even further. He does not just qualify Danton's outlook dramatically but presents it at times in a questioning, ironical light. He seems intent on driving the spectator to look beneath the surface by suggesting a tension between the emotional-spiritual crisis Danton has lived through and his attempt to come to terms with it—between what he has actually experienced and the significance he has subsequently attached to it. Clearly Büchner presents Danton's disillusion with intense, sympathetic seriousness, but by emphasizing its passionate and essentially religious character he seems concerned to vindicate the power of his former revolutionary idealism, and in so doing to undermine Danton's conviction of the narrowly egoistic character of all human behaviour. For here as always Danton's present experience is seen in its relation to a determining past and his visionary nihilism appears in this perspective as the obverse side of a longing to which he has been wholly and selflessly committed. Such has been the force of this longing that its destruction has left him empty and helpless before a disintegrating conviction of meaninglessness. The nature of Danton's despair, as Büchner presents it, seems to deny his nihilism. The fury with which he embraces the vision of absurdity reflects the force of an idealism which transcended self in its commitment to a regenerate world.

In thus suggesting a contradiction at the heart of Danton's outlook, Büchner seems to be emphasizing again the essentially individual and determinate character of his experience. Danton's belief that he has achieved a dispassionate, rational insight into the laws which govern human existence is (as the dramatist makes clear) ambiguously bound up with tensions in his own consciousness which he himself clearly cannot fully understand. But even if Danton's philosophy does appear as conditioned and contradictory this does not, as far as I can see, necessarily invalidate the original insights from which it springs. The recognition that the Revolution is futile, that there is no progress in history, is essentially intuitive and is by no means disproved. At the same time, however, it is important to stress that this view, like that of the revolutionaries, is not clearly substantiated by the actual developments in the play. Here too the dramatist seems intent on denying the spectator any final certainty.

This brings me to the crucial point. In *Dantons Tod* the Revolution is not presented as part of a clearly definable process of development.

It is seen to a large extent obliquely through the colliding perspectives of the different factions, each of which pursues its own ends and has its own standards of value. What is more, these perspectives are deeply bound up with metaphysical assumptions which, as I have argued, cannot in principle be confirmed or disproved by specific empirical events. But the uncertainty does not end here. To respond to the radical impetus of Büchner's vision we have to go on and admit that this clash of views, whatever its apparent philosophical significance, may not after all be at the heart of the play's conception. By emphasizing the precariousness of each view in turn, by showing its involvement with the needs and purposes of particular individuals, Büchner seems to be drawing us to question the relationship of both to actual historical circumstance. It may well be that he is forcing us not so much to choose between them as to query the adequacy of any coherent world-view, to confront the harsh, impenetrable complexities of history. The dramatist's method implies that, ironically, he may be intent on exposing both the nihilism of Danton and the revolutionary aspirations of his opponents.

This seems to me central to Büchner's apprehension of history in *Dantons Tod*. His distinctive concern to take over records of actual speeches and events does not show a passive adherence to historical sources but is (I have suggested) part of a far-reaching and concerted attempt to come to terms with them imaginatively. If we re-read, for instance, Thiers' account of the events leading up to Danton's death after having studied the play, we can feel at once the full force of this probing scepticism of Büchner's. Where the historian seems to postulate continuity and coherence, the dramatist senses possible disjunction and disorder.[6] Büchner appears to be intent on undermining Thiers' confidently positivist view of the Revolution as a coherent process of development and in particular on questioning the two-fold connection which the historian presupposes between the individual's aims and actions on the one hand, and between these actions and their historical consequences on the other.

Büchner, as we have seen, shows that the aims which the agent professes are bound up with pressures in himself which he cannot recognize and that as a result the actions by which he attempts to influence the corporate situation may in fact be quite dissociated from the values he attributes to them. At the same time he also suggests that any individual or group who tries to shape the course of

6. M. A. Thiers, *Histoire de la Révolution Française*, Paris, 1823–27. See especially vol. VI (1825). For a detailed discussion of Büchner's sources see Karl Viëtor, 'Die Quellen von Büchners *Dantons Tod*' in: *Euphorion* 34 (1933): 357–79; and Richard Thieberger, *La mort de Danton et ses sources*, Paris, 1953.

historical events is committing himself to a flux of circumstances so overwhelmingly complex and ambiguous that he cannot surely predict the scope and effect of any action he initiates. This means that Büchner is in the end questioning the crucial assumption of all traditional forms of historiography: that of a determining continuity between the personal realm of responsible, purposive agency and the empirical sphere of historical-social circumstance. He is questioning the nature of man's claim to apprehend value and pursue moral ends and its assumed relevance to the actual movement of historical force, which determines his existence.

In *Dantons Tod* Büchner is not just re-stating in dramatic terms a preconceived, rationally formulated view of man's helplessness before the impersonal power of history. To say even this is to claim a degree of certainty which the play does not provide. The dramatist, as I have tried to show, does not demonstrate the falseness of either the revolutionary ethos or the fatalistic vision, but he presents both in a way which queries the fundamental capacity of human beings to achieve an objective, systematic understanding of their existence in history. The real power of the play lies in the intensity with which it seeks to penetrate beyond the assurance of inherited assumptions—an intensity which refuses any even partial or tentative solutions. This is a work which *explores* all dogmatic certainties and demands from the reader or spectator a corresponding attitude of robust, enquiring openness.

HENRY J. SCHMIDT

Women, Death, and Revolution[†]

Büchner's Danton's Death

At the end of the third act of *Danton's Death*, the dramatic action has played itself out. Danton and his faction have been arrested, his self-defense before the National Convention has failed, and the masses have shifted their allegiance from him to Robespierre. Robespierre himself has disappeared from view; after displaying a trace of humanity in act 1, he has reverted to being nothing more than a speech-making functionary derided behind his back by his own supporters. The epoch-making events of the Revolution—the fall of the Bastille, the arrest and execution of King Louis XVI, the September massacres, the purge of the Girondists—exist only as memories.

† From *How Dramas End: Essays on the German* Sturm und Drang, *Büchner, Hauptmann and Fleisser,* by Henry J. Schmidt, 91–106, 166–170. Ann Arbor: University of Michigan Press, 1992. Reprinted by permission.

The leaders have failed to serve the needs of the masses, who continue to call for bread although the aristocrats have been deposed. The downfall of Danton presages the downfall of Robespierre, signaling the Thermidorian reaction and the end of the Revolution. Both figures have no further historical function than to wait for death. History appears to have come to a stop; act 4 of *Danton's Death* justifiably begins with the words, "It's all over,"[1] and what follows is stasis.

The analogy to Büchner's situation is apparent. The revolutions of 1830 in France, Belgium, and Poland had failed; attempts to foment revolt in Hesse through agitational pamphlets such as the *Hessian Messenger* were unsuccessful; and the disparity between the trivial political reforms granted by the aristocracy and the necessity for fundamental social change was enormous. In his letters, Büchner often deplored how unsuitable the times were for revolution.

> . . . I have recently learned that only the essential needs of the masses can bring about change, that all activity and shouting by *individuals* is vain folly. (*CWL*, 252 [June, 1833])

> I wouldn't tell you this if I could believe in the slightest possibility of a political upheaval at this time. For the last six months I've been utterly convinced that nothing is to be done and that anyone who sacrifices himself *right now* is foolishly risking his neck. . . . Let's hope for times to come! (*CWL*, 273 [1835])

Danton's Death is a product of the post-1830 malaise of a clearsighted social activist who considered impromptu rebellion to be "vain folly." His drama is a critique of the shortcomings of the Jacobin hegemony; his choice of the year 1794 rather than 1789 was motivated by his conviction that the ideals of the French Revolution had remained unrealized and that the excesses of the Reign of Terror were an attempt to conceal the failures of the ruling factions. Büchner's dilemma as a student of history and as an artist was: how does one go on when historical progress appears to stagnate? How does one fill the void? The play's final act takes place during such a historical hiatus; understanding how Büchner resolves this formal and ideological problem can help us map the intersections between his personal, political, and literary concerns.

In classical drama, the cessation of action is followed by ritual, such as an execution, which in turn evokes a concluding lament bewailing the tragic fall of the protagonist. Although *Danton's Death*

---

1. Quotations from Büchner's works are from Georg Büchner, *Complete Works and Letters*, trans. Henry J. Schmidt, ed. Walter Hinderer and Henry J. Schmidt (New York: Continuum, 1986). References in the text to plays are by act and scene, otherwise page numbers, using the abbreviation *CWL*.

can be considered, on one level, to be a requiem for the Dantonists and their ideals, the play does not sustain the traditional hierarchical focus on one or more primary figures. As the drama concludes, a significant gender shift takes place: the last act is framed by women, who dominate the dramatic action even though the bulk of the dialogue occurs in the prison scenes, during which the Dantonists sit passively, waiting to be executed. The mood of the play changes as well, as the historical models for his female characters are displaced by literary ones. Büchner allows Julie Danton and Lucile Desmoulins, who begin and end act 4, to deviate considerably from reality: Julie Danton (actually named Louise) did not precede her husband in death but married a baron in 1797 and eventually outlived even Büchner; Lucile Desmoulins did not become deranged and sacrifice herself to the authorities but was arrested at the same time as her husband and went to her death fully in control of her mental faculties. In the course of the last act, Büchner's primary sources for these figures, Thiers's *History of the French Revolution* and Strahlheim's *Our Times*, give way to Shakespeare;[2] the women's French-Revolutionary identities seem to blend into an amalgam of Shakespearean heroines. Why Büchner focuses on women and allows literary figures to overshadow historical ones in the final scenes of a drama about the French Revolution deserves exploration.

In act 1, scene 2, Portia and Hamlet are mentioned nearly in the same breath by the prompter Simon. Unwittingly, Simon has found a highly appropriate analogy for Danton and Julie; in his introspection and doubt, Danton is surely a Hamlet in extremis, and Julie imitates Portia's actions down to the detail of sending a servant to inquire after her husband's well-being.[3] Beyond the surface image of the loyal wife performing the ultimate sacrifice, however, the similarities end. Portia has, as she herself says, "a man's mind" (2,4). She attempts to transcend the proverbial weaknesses of her sex in a drastic manner: she makes "strong proof of [her] constancy" by inflicting a "voluntary wound" on her thigh (2,1)—the equivalent of a dueling scar as a proof of manliness. Her eventual suicide, prompted by her husband Brutus's misfortunes, is gruesome: Brutus reports that she "swallow'd fire" (4,3). (That is, she "tooke hote burning coles and cast them into her mouth, and kept her mouth so

2. Louis Adolphe Thiers, *Histoire de la Révolution Française* (Paris, 1823–27) and *Unsere Zeit, oder geschichtliche Übersicht der merkwürdigsten Ereignisse von 1789–1830*, ed. Carl Strahlheim (Stuttgart, 1826–30). See also Ilona Broch, "Die Julia und die Ophelia der Revolution: Zu zwei Frauenfiguren in *Dantons Tod*," in *Georg Büchner: 1813–1837: Revolutionär, Dichter, Wissenschaftler*, ed. Susanne Lehmann, Stephen Oetterman, Reinhard Pabst, and Sibylle Spiegel (Basel and Frankfurt am Main: Stroemfeld/Roter Stern, 1987), 241–46.
3. *Danton's Death* 4,1; *Julius Caesar* 2,4.

close that she choked herselfe.")[4] Julie, on the other hand, drinks a
vial of poison and pronounces her death "pleasant." Obviously, she
is meant to project an image of femininity closer to that of her near
namesake, Juliet, for whom poison is "a restorative."[5] Julie's description of the dying earth: "She's becoming ever paler; she's sinking
like a corpse into the flood of the ether. Will no arm catch her by
her golden locks and pull her from the stream and bury her?" (4,6)
recalls yet another Shakespearean woman, namely Ophelia, who
also materializes in Lucile's apparent insanity and self-sacrifice.
The lyrical tranquillity of Julie's and Lucile's final monologues
expresses a peaceful acceptance of mortal endings. However, within
the larger context of male-female relationships in *Danton's Death*,
Büchner's portrayal of such uncompromising wifely devotion is
quite problematic.

Dorothy James has recently pointed out that male Büchner commentators have tended to idealize Julie and Lucile uncritically.[6]
These characterizations, she maintains, are "obviously to many an
appealing fantasy."[7] Büchner's women are, indeed, often lauded
for what is perceived to be their incorporeal purity, their naive
innocence, and their emotional nature untainted by rational contemplation. Until the final act, Julie is nothing more than Danton's
nurturing wife, and Lucile, worse yet, adores Camille so mindlessly
that she cheerfully admits to not understanding a bit of the intellectual conversation that goes on around her (2,3).[8] Julie's and
Lucile's self-chosen deaths, James maintains, "are depicted totally
without cynicism, as acts of beauty, of poignancy, something to
shed unsophisticated tears over." "Büchner is very good at this,"[9]
she writes, which is true. There is no distancing at work here, at
least not *within* the scenes devoted to the women. In a woman's

---

4. From Shakespeare's source, Plutarch's *Lives of the Noble Grecians and Romans*, trans.
Sir Thomas North (1579). Quoted in William Shakespeare, *The Tragedy of Julius Caesar*, in *The Modern Reader's Shakespeare*, ed. Henry Norman Hudson (New York: Big-
elow, Smith, 1909), 8:98. Another literary model is *Egmont's* Klärchen, who poisons
herself while Egmont awaits his end in prison.

5. Juliet dies, to be sure, of a self-inflicted stab wound. Concerning Julie's "Come, dearest
priest" when she produces her vial, Broch indicates a similarity to Juliet's "Come, vial"
and to Faust's "Come down, you glass of crystal purity." See Broch, "Die Julia," 242.

6. Dorothy James, *Georg Büchner's* Dantons Tod: *A Reappraisal* (London: Modern
Humanities Research Assn., 1982), 21. She justly takes my *Satire, Caricature, and Perspectivism in the Works of Georg Büchner* (The Hague: Mouton, 1970) to task on this
account.

7. James, *Büchner's* Dantons Tod, 27.

8. Karl Viëtor interprets this approvingly as an example of "unconscious correspondence
to nature" (Karl Viëtor, *Georg Büchner: Politik, Dichtung, Wissenschaft* [Bern: Francke,
1949], 147), which testifies to the endurance of gender stereotyping based on the
nature/intellect dichotomy of preromantic philosophy. Not until recent decades was
there much objection in German secondary literature to the belief that women's self-
abasing subservience to men was "natural" and hence an enhancement of their aesthetic appeal.

9. James, *Büchner's* Dantons Tod, 25, 24.

death, some critics sense classical grandeur: Danton and Camille, after all, *have* to die, but Julie and Lucile may choose to live if they wish; their demise thus glorifies free will.[1] Yet to a certain extent, Julie's death in particular is simply a fulfillment of Danton's unambiguous wish: "Oh, Julie! If I had to go *alone*! If she were to abandon me! (3,7). And after he receives her assurance that she will accompany him in death, he even thanks her in absentia: "I won't go alone—thank you, Julie" (4,3). She dies, in fact, not only *with* him but *for* him; that is, she dies the aesthetic death unavailable to him: "DANTON: . . . And yet I'd have liked to die in another way, as effortlessly as a falling star, as an expiring tone kissing itself dead with its own lips, as a ray of light burying itself in clear waters" (4,3)—a close anticipation of the imagery Julie employs before ending her life three scenes later. Her surrogate death-as-a-work-of-art restores substance to his life and his death, both of which have lost their meaning within the political sphere. Her death offers him satisfying closure, in keeping with his epicurean philosophy, which extends to the pleasurable anticipation of one's own death as drama.[2]

What prevents audiences from viewing this as an act of supreme selfishness on Danton's part and supreme stupidity on Julie's is the ageless perception of woman as victim, whose fulfillment lies in renouncing herself and serving the needs of others. Analogous to this is the literary convention that decrees: a good man dies for his ideals, which is tragic, whereas a good woman dies for her man, which is beautiful. A male's ending is traditionally endowed with sociopolitical resonances, whereas the female's is restricted to its aesthetic effect. When a man's political effectiveness has been neutralized, as has Danton's, he is merely displaying established patriarchal reflexes when he attempts to create for himself a vicariously experienced "feminine" ending.

Although Büchner was indisputably far ahead of his contemporaries in his depiction of women, he was nonetheless capable of creating such male fantasies as Danton's. One need only take cues from *Leonce and Lena* (1,4; 2,3; 3,1) to justify, for example, the reduction of women to flowers and other forms of vegetation.[3] Some

1. "Here . . . arises in this gloomy tragedy of fatalistic necessity the idea of freedom, in which the extinct world of idealistic belief would have perceived humankind's divinity" (Viëtor, *Büchner*, 148). For William H. Rey, a woman's suicide offers "the purest possibility of human fulfillment—when it is accomplished in the spirit of love." William H. Rey, *Georg Büchners* Dantons Tod: *Revolutionstragödie und Mysterienspiel* (Bern: Lang, 1982), 111.
2. Cf. Burghard Dedner, "Legitimationen des Schreckens in Georg Büchners Revolutionsdrama," *Jahrbuch der deutschen Schillergesellschaft* 29 (1985): 374.
3. Critical commentary on Büchner has readily fallen in line with, for example, a chapter heading such as: "Woman's Naive Security in Her Vegetative Substance" (Gustav Beck-

of his female figures retain traces of the Madonna stereotype inherited from romanticism and its forebears; in his eclectic readings, Büchner surely encountered a host of female "beautiful souls" who influenced his perceptions of women. In the characterizations of Julie and Lucile, biographical as well as literary models become discernible. An obvious source is Büchner's relationship with Minna Jaeglé, to whom he became engaged in 1834. Most of what we know about their romantic attachment is based on letters he wrote to her from Giessen in February and March 1834, and from Zurich in January, 1837, in which he confides to his fiancée the agonies of his loneliness and political disillusionment. His expressions of love for this pastor's daughter, however, never transcend much beyond nineteenth-century middle-class propriety, leaving us at a loss to know whether or not his extraordinary insights into the psyche of a Marion or of *Woyzeck*'s Marie derive from personal experience.

The letter to Minna Jaeglé containing the famous passage about the "terrible fatalism of history" is rarely overlooked in analyses of *Danton's Death*. However, citations of it usually end with the lines: "What is it within us that lies, murders, steals? I no longer care to pursue the thought," thereby suppressing Büchner's emotional yearning for a resolution of the crisis: "If only I could lay this cold and martyred heart on your breast!" (*CWL*, 260 [after March 10, 1834]). He desires from Minna what Julie offers Danton during his self-recriminations about the September massacres (2,5): the emotional closure of loving consolation. Büchner's letter is, after all, not exclusively a disquisition on fatalism, because only one-third of it deals with the consequences of studying "the history of the Revolution." It is therefore misleading to metonymize this letter as a "fatalism *letter*,"[4] for it also contains complaints about the mediocre environment in Giessen, his difficulty writing, his recent illness, his decline into an automatonlike existence, inquiries about Strassburg, declarations of his plans for travel, his longing for Minna, and a final ironic disclaimer: "This letter is a hodgepodge: I'll console you with another." As a whole, his letters to her are soul barings to an idealized recipient, who is alternately mother, child, and nurse.[5] His image making, born out of loneliness, is hardly surprising: during the less than five-and-a-half years they knew each other, they were apart approximately as much as they were together. The

---

ers, *Georg Büchners* Leonce und Lena: *Ein Lustspiel der Langeweile* [Heidelberg: Winter, 1961], 111).

4. That is, a *Fatalismusbrief*, as it is so often called by literary critics.

5. *CWL*, 261 et passim, 295. His psychological reaction to "imprisonment" in Giessen resembles, down to numerous linguistic parallels, that of Danton in jail. Compare, for example, his second extant letter to Minna Jaeglé (*CWL*, 258–59) to *Danton's Death* 4,5.

most telling evidence for Büchner's predilection for romantic fantasies is to be found in the diary of his friend Alexis Muston, who
reports that, in Darmstadt in the summer of 1833, Büchner was
seized by "a kind of mystical adoration for a fallen girl, whom he
dreamed of restoring to the ranks of the angels. . . ."[6] Were it not for
the reference to "a fallen girl," one would assume that Büchner was
speaking of Minna Jaeglé. Lacking substantial testimony from Minna
herself or from third parties, we cannot fairly assess the reality
behind the ideal.[7] In the stereotypical aspects of Julie and Lucile in
Danton's Death, the conventionality of such qualities that men
habitually attribute to women emerges: women are products of male
self-absorption, which generates "mystical adoration" that "saves"
women by making them into angels. Such objectification occurs
even during Marion's extraordinary monologue: Danton remains
outside as the voyeur, unable to internalize her identity in any way
but sexually. Büchner emulates his protagonist's wife/prostitute
categorizations to the extent of not allowing, for instance, *Julie* to
utter such emancipated thoughts as Marion does.[8]

My purpose here is not to *blame* Büchner, a nineteenth-century
male author, for occasional lapses into what we now declare to be
female stereotyping. Without doubt his works display an eroticism
of revolutionary potential; not until the "middle" Heinrich Heine
does one find a comparable provocation of bourgeois prudery.[9] But
the "regressive" aspects of Büchner's female characters cannot be
overlooked as long as his interpreters persist in dematerializing
them into a kind of Rilkean "tranquil heart of the stars." In order to
determine to what extent Büchner internalized conventional images
without reflecting upon them and to what extent he challenged
them, a comprehensive assessment of his concept of women, including as well a sociological analysis of women's status within the
nineteenth-century German family and society, would be neces-

6. Heinz Fischer, *Georg Büchner: Untersuchungen und Marginalien* (München: Bouvier,
   1972), 81. See also Heinz Fischer, *Georg Büchner und Alexis Muston: Untersuchungen
   zu einem Büchner-Fund* (Munich: W. Fink, 1987), 272, 274.
7. The only letters from her hand that have survived were written after Büchner's death.
   Several of Büchner's acquaintances, in particular Caroline and Wilhelm Schulz,
   praised her character and devotion to her fiancé.
8. Cf. Dolf Oehler, "Liberté, Liberté Chérie: Männerphantasien über die Freiheit; Zur
   Problematik der erotischen Freiheits-Allegorie," in *Georg Büchner:* Dantons Tod: *Die
   Trauerarbeit im Schönen, Ein Theater-Lesebuch*, ed. Peter von Becker (Frankfurt am
   Main: Syndikat, 1980), 102.
9. See Reinhold Grimm, "Coeur und Carreau: Über die Liebe bei Georg Büchner," *Georg
   Büchner I/II*, ed. Heinz Ludwig Arnold (Munich: Text+Kritik, 1982), 299–326. Klaus
   Theweleit singles out Büchner as one of the few German authors who did not present
   to his readers an idealized image of femaleness. See Klaus Theweleit, *Männerphantasien* (Reinbek and Hamburg: Rowohlt, 1980), 1:295–97. For the political significance
   of Heine's erotic poetry see Jost Hermand, "Erotik im Juste Milieu: Heines 'Verschie-
   dene,'" in *Heinrich Heine. Artistik und Engagement*, ed. Wolfgang Kuttenkeuler (Stuttgart: Metzler, 1977), 86–104.

sary.[1] One would need to investigate whether Büchner's social environment indeed contained "only married women and prostitutes, only sentimental feeling and unadulterated eroticism," without "intermediate levels" that could serve as models for a more independent, more differentiated womanhood.[2] Yet even a thorough investigation of this sort might still not be able to resolve the ambiguity between "regressive" stereotyping and "progressive" insight in such passages as the following.

DANTON: No, Julie, I love you like the grave.
JULIE (*Turning away.*): Oh!

(1, 1)

LEONCE: *Addio, addio* my love, I shall love your dead body.
(*Rosetta approaches him again.*) Tears, Rosetta?

(*Leonce and Lena*, 1, 3)

LEONCE: Dear corpse, you rest so beautifully on the black pall of night that nature begins to hate life and falls in love with death.
LENA: No, let me be. (*She jumps up and rushes off.*)

(*Leonce and Lena*, 2, 4)

One might fault Julie, Rosetta, and Lena for becoming inarticulate when their men's love-death fantasies grow too explicit; or one might commend them, with latent condescension, for being "creatures of nature" with spontaneous nonverbal responses; or one might argue, as does Christa Wolf, that such reactions are the *only* appropriate means to counter what she calls "man's strenuous intellectual activity" that compensates for his "fear of contact . . . [when] he withdraws from reality's abundance. . . ."[3] Gestures of rejection or grief as quoted here would thereby signify the undesirability of further entanglements in male discourse—an insight that would serve to confirm anew Büchner's modernity.

Such ambiguous passages can sometimes be clarified by placing them in context. For example, Büchner juxtaposes Marion's utopian sexuality against the unromantic life of starving prostitutes,[4] and in such contrasts lies a complex realism that breaks down stereotypes.

1. For an example of such a study with respect to Lessing's dramas, see Karin Wurst's *Familiale Liebe ist die "wahre Gewalt": Die Repräsentation der Familie in G. E. Lessings dramatischem Werk* (Amsterdam: Rodopi, 1988).
2. Hermand, "Erotik," 101.
3. Christa Wolf, "'Shall I Garnish a Metaphor with an Almond Blossom?': Büchner-Prize Acceptance Speech," trans. Henry J. Schmidt, *New German Critique* 23 (Spring/Summer, 1981), 6. However, Wolf consigns Danton and his colleagues without differentiation to the "citadel of reason," overlooking the occasional similarity of their sensibilities to those of the women.
4. Cf. Dedner, "Legitimationen," 352.

Büchner's dramatic language has a similar effect: Julie's final lyrical, "atmospheric" monologue (4,6) cannot be called specifically
feminine, for her evocation of the dying earth is stylistically very
similar to Danton's musings on death a few scenes earlier. Moreover, Hérault speaks almost exactly in her idiom in the lines immediately preceding her death scene: "The clouds hang in the quiet
evening sky like a dying Olympus with fading, sinking, godlike
forms" (4,5). If Julie's language is to be thought of as feminine,
romantic, even sentimental, then that of Danton's faction must be
adjudged so as well. Linguistic categorizations according to gender
or political conviction do not exist in Büchner's plays; the Danton
and Robespierre factions often share the same cynical idiom, and in
his monologues at the end of act 1, Robespierre himself uses language that would be wholly appropriate in the mouths of Danton,
Leonce, or even Lena. Büchner destroys stereotypes through a kind
of stylistic democracy that obliterates conventional distinctions
between "higher" and "lower" characters.[5]

Deviating both from the ennobling verse of classical historical
drama and the class-specific prose of the Sturm und Drang tradition, Büchner's dramatic dialogue mixes poetic and political rhetoric, cynicism, obscenities, and artless simplicity without regard for
conventional distinctions between public and private spheres. A
drama that presents "common folk" who speak like politicians who
speak like prostitutes who speak like philosophers who speak like
"common folk" without subjecting them all to a uniform verse or
prose form is subversively egalitarian even today, since such a perspective anticipates a reordering of social structures. Henri Poschmann correctly notes that, in *Danton's Death*, the democratic
idealism of the constitution of 1793 "becomes formative as an aesthetic principle for the creation of a new type of drama."[6] The classical concept of character as a "bearer of ideas," which implies a
trickle-down process of enlightenment, is supplanted by a dramaturgy that highlights the limitless diversity of the subject. Since any
representational medium can only hint at such diversity, this aesthetic strategy must remain extremely open-ended by definition.

However, despite Büchner's numerous quotations from historical sources, little of the dramatic dialogue in *Danton's Death* can
be called realistic. Artistic intensification—rather than naturalistic
reproduction—of human experience dominates, especially toward
the end of the play. Significantly, Büchner's emphasis on lyrical
expression arises not arbitrarily but organically out of the dramatic

5. See Henri Poschmann, *Georg Büchner: Dichtung der Revolution und Revolution der
Dichtung* (Berlin and Weimar: Aufbau, 1985), 116.
6. Poschmann, *Büchner*, 116.

situation. His figures resort to poetic flights and musical prose as a form of self-aestheticization intended to counter their inability to affect their environment. As in numerous dramas of the Sturm und Drang, lyricism in *Danton's Death* represents a means of sublimating alienation and political impotence. Words rush in to fill the void or, to paraphrase Goethe's Werther, to decorate the walls that imprison one.[7] Both the poetic imagery in *Danton's Death* and the drama as a whole can be viewed as cultural responses to the Zeitgeist of disillusionment in 1794 and 1835. Both Danton contemplating the guillotine and Büchner the playwright produce lasting meaning for themselves by converting language into art. As death approaches them in act 4, the Dantonists, Julie, and Lucile indulge in a lyricism that sustains the spirit of revolt in an increasingly mechanized society.[8] Lyricism's relativizing, anarchistic impact—like that of sexuality and other pleasures throughout the play—provides at least the illusion of defying one's mortality. By poeticizing death, one compensates for its horror—unlike *rationalizing* death, which increases its horror, as St. Just unintentionally demonstrates. Behind the postromantic epigrams, the ceaseless questions without answers, there is no longer any definable belief system. The characters construct rhetorical circles around metaphysical concepts, undermining simplistic concepts of linear historical progress. Their idiom restores dialectical openness to what they perceive as an oppressively controlled existence.[9]

Death is the theme of the play's lyrical prose; in fact, the title, *Danton's Death*, is itself an ending. Death is not merely the final stage of a natural cycle ("The Life and Death of . . ."); in Büchner's genitive formulation, death is a personal possession, a nearly material entity that can be yearned for or rejected. Death is already present at the outset of the play; Danton's comment to Julie: "You sweet grave—your lips are funeral bells, your voice my death knell, your breasts my burial mound, and your heart my coffin" anticipates the structural premise of the last act, namely a theme and variations on death. To alter a phrase from *Leonce and Lena*: "how many scenes does one need to sing up and down the scale of death?"—Büchner achieves extraordinary variety in nine scenes filling less than twelve pages.

7. Johann Wolfgang von Goethe, *Die Leiden des jungen Werthers*, letter of May 22.
8. "The creativity of [their] sentence making realizes itself as a shaping of the world to which those sentences relate" (Martin Swales, "Ontology, Politics, Sexuality: A Note on Georg Büchner's Drama *Dantons Tod*," *New German Studies* 3 [1975]: 122).
9. William H. Rey is among the numerous critics who have maintained that Büchner creates "a tender lyrical language . . . that floats above all of life's contradictions" (Rey, *Büchner's* Dantons Tod, 111). But the *elimination* of contradictions would signify a relapse into epigonal romanticism. For a contrary view, see Poschmann: "[Büchner's] play rotates phenomena in a way . . . that contradiction becomes apparent and they lose their false simplicity" (*Büchner*, 102). The statement could also apply to Lenz's dramaturgy.

1. Julie prepares to die with Danton.
2. Dumas announces to a shocked citizen that he is anticipating without any remorse whatsoever the guillotining of his wife.
3. Lacroix and Hérault contemplate their physical deterioration in jail; Danton meditates over his imminent demise; Camille fears that Lucile might be harmed and, after a brief nightmare, fears losing his reason.
4. A jailor and two cart-drivers who transport prisoners to the guillotine joke about their trade;[1] Lucile searches for Camille and tries to grasp the concept of "to die."
5. Prisoners are dying; Danton predicts Robespierre's downfall; Camille ponders his separation from the "deranged" Lucile; the Dantonists philosophize about mortality.
6. Watching the sun set, Julie takes poison and dies.
7. A woman distracts her children from their hunger by letting them see the executions; jeered by the crowd, the Dantonists ascend the scaffold one after another.
8. Lucile tries to cope with death by attempting to bring time to a halt; three women comment approvingly about public executions.
9. Two executioners finish their work at the guillotine; Lucile sings of Death the Reaper, shouts "Long live the king!" and is led off by the watch.[2]

These final scenes constitute both a lament and its negation—tragedy accompanied by irony, as in a Heine poem. They are suffused by death imagery: night, sleep, decay, the grave, Charon, and so forth. Death is individual and collective; we hear of the death of the self, the death of ideals, the death of love, the death of the revolution. Death and birth come together in Lucile's contemplation of the guillotine as a "dear cradle."[3] Death is both extraordinary and ordinary; the agony of the condemned individual contrasts with the all-in-a-day's-work attitudes of the carters and executioners, who are as human as their victims. Laughter in the face of death is a recognition of mortality, the destruction of heroic illusion. Death becomes theater, savored both by spectators and participants. Those sentenced to die sustain themselves, like the incarcerated protagonists of Sturm und Drang dramas, with dreams and visions. Yet Danton believes that death is no solution because it is distressingly conventional and predictable: "There's no hope in death; it's only a

---

1. This scene and the beginning of scene 9 recall the gravedigger scene in *Hamlet*.
2. For an elaborate scene-by-scene analysis, see Alfred Behrmann and Joachim Wohlleben, *Büchner: Dantons Tod, Eine Dramenanalyse* (Stuttgart: Klett, 1980), 126–36.
3. See Grimm, "Coeur und Carreau," 304.

simpler—and life a more complicated, organized—form of decay; that's the only difference!" (3,7). Danton wishes to die a noninstrumentalized death, dissolving Ophelialike rather than becoming a monument, but he knows he cannot evade the public appropriation of his demise.[4]

The emphasis on love and death in the final scenes of *Danton's Death* has prompted critics such as Peter Michelsen to maintain that the theme of ongoing revolution has become secondary—or has vanished entirely: "*Danton's Death* is a drama about the end of history, a play not so much about the Revolution as about how humans prepare for death."[5] I would counter that Büchner had no intention of writing about the *end* of history, which would indeed be fatalistic if not nihilistic, but about its seeming *pauses*, when the present appears to be a rupture between the past and the future. *Danton's Death* is an open-ended analysis of the ideals and failures of the French Revolution;[6] Danton's question in the drama's first scene: "Who's going to accomplish all these beautiful things?"—as well as "how?"—remains unanswered, because the 1830s offered Büchner no models for the possible synthesis of revolutionary idealism and human needs. Then, as during the 1790s, political reform was centered in the middle classes, who feared that a broadly based social revolution would turn against them. But Büchner's drama does not lose sight of the French Revolution's "categorical imperative," as articulated by Hérault: "The Revolution must stop and the Republic must begin" (1,1). *Danton's Death* depicts both the actual and the ideal transition from Revolution to Republic, real versus fundamental change. By piling such contrasts upon each other, he penetrates ever more deeply into the details of French-Revolutionary reality. Instead of deviating into revolutionary agitation that, according to Lenin, allows "no orgiastic occurrences,"[7] Büchner highlights these "occurrences" in order to explore their origins and contradictions. Such complexity creates a pessimism that is, as Herbert Marcuse writes, not leveled against the idea of revolution itself but against "the trivialization of change."[8] Pessimism and Utopian

---

4. A prime example of a "profiteer" from death is the artist David, who sketches victims in order to capture "the last spasms of life in these villains" (2, 3).
5. Peter Michelsen, "Die Präsenz des Endes: Georg Büchners *Dantons Tod*," *Deutsche Vierteljahrsschrift* 52, no. 3 (1978): 487.
6. See Thomas Michael Mayer, "Büchner und Weidig—Frühkommunismus und revolutionäre Demokratie: Zur Textverteilung des 'Hessischen Landboten,'" in *Georg Büchner I/II*, ed. Arnold, esp. 108–36.
7. Quoted in Peter von Becker, "Die Trauerarbeit im Schönen: 'Dantons Tod'—Notizen zu einem neu gelesenen Stück," in *Büchner: Dantons Tod*, ed. von Becker, 89.
8. The quotation continues: "as if that to which great art had given shape was now thought to be conquered and resolved by the class struggle. Such pessimism prevails even in literature that thematizes revolution: Büchner's *Danton's Death* is a classical example." Quoted in von Becker, *Büchner: Dantons Tod*, 75.

visions coexist within the realistic framework of conflicting perspectives. Rather than cancelling each other out, they mutually
illuminate each other. Formally, the drama's comedy contextual-
izes and heightens its tragedy, and vice versa; thematically, the
people's hunger and the pleasure of the more affluent in "beautiful
things" do not negate each other.[9] Rather than a "neither/nor,"
Büchner's aesthetics produces a "both/and." Instead of allowing history to appear first as tragedy, then as farce,[1] Büchner reveals their
simultaneity.

As *Danton's Death* progresses toward the inevitable reductionism
of an ending, which of the thematic "balls in the air" will drop?
Which note, which gestus will dominate, silencing the others?
What will be the ideological and aesthetic consequences of formal
closure? That the question can have political ramifications is demonstrated by the efforts of East German critics and directors during
the 1950s and 1960s to subvert what they perceived to be the drama's
excessively ambivalent, pessimistic, "bourgeois" conclusion. Renate
Zuchardt, for example, suggested (in 1959) that the ending be altered
in performance so that the spectator would accept Danton's fall as
political necessity and welcome the victory of the "uncompromising
revolutionaries" over the moderates, instead of becoming overly
involved in "pity with those to be executed." Her solution: placing
speeches by Robespierre or St. Just at the end, in order to elevate the
conclusion from "the private sphere once again to the level of political drama," insuring that the final voice be one of "all-controlling
rationality."[2]

Significantly, the drama ends after four rather than five acts,
recalling the Baroque tradition where, according to Walter Benjamin, the plot (if not the drama) ended after the fourth act, evoking
the idea of repeatable actions.[3] To what extent is *Danton's Death's*
ending cyclical? Had Büchner ended his play with the words Danton
speaks to the executioner: "Do you want to be crueler than death?
Can you prevent our heads from kissing at the bottom of the basket?" (4,7), the moment of closure would be powerfully symmetrical:
the lines strongly echo the love-death dialogue that opens the

9. See Dedner, "Legitimationen," 352.
1. See Karl Marx, *The Eighteenth Brumaire of Louis Bonaparte* (New York: International, 1963).
2. Renate Zuchardt, "'Wagt!' lehrt uns Danton: Vorschläge zur szenischen Realisierung des Büchner-Dramas," *Theater der Zeit* 14, no. 9 (1959): 14, 18–19. In his Mercury Theatre (New York, 1938) production of the play, Orson Welles—who played St. Just—placed his speech at the conclusion for dramatic effect. See John Houseman, *Run-Through: A Memoir* (New York: Simon and Schuster, 1972), 379–90. See also Henry J. Schmidt, "Büchner in Amerika: Ein Überblick," in *Georg Büchner,* ed. Henri Poschmann (Bern: Peter Lang, forthcoming).
3. Walter Benjamin, *Ursprung des deutschen Trauerspiels* (Frankfurt am Main: Suhrkamp, 1972), 148–49.

play, and the title's message would be reinforced (that is, after Danton's death, all else is insignificant). The play's self-referentiality as historical drama would be emphasized, because Danton's lines derive nearly verbatim from Büchner's sources. The final spotlight would frame the fallen hero, a self-serving aphoristic lament on his lips—a potent generator of emotional identification. Left to the spectator's imagination would be the historical aftermath as a largely undefined "terrible confusion" (4,5)—Danton's "après moi le déluge" testament. If Büchner ever considered this alternative, he presumably would have rejected it because of its counterrevolutionary implications.[4]

Instead, Lucile, a woman not even related to Danton, is granted a second and third appearance in the drama before it ends. Alone on the street after the executions, she is the "last rebel," challenging the insensitivity of nature and the very passage of time with her scream. Christa Wolf calls this dramaturgy of the scream "an absurdity for the theater of more or less resolvable contradictions";[5] it counterposes an individual's pain against man-made systems of social control. Lucile's insight after the failure of her scream experiment: "I suppose we must bear it," turns out in retrospect to be not just passive resignation but acceptance of present and future suffering. After her separation from Camille, her blunt, disjointed discourse invokes the image of "poor Ophelia / Divided from herself and her fair judgment."[6] But we cannot, therefore, simply pronounce her "insane," even though Camille says so ("Insanity lurked behind her eyes" [4,5]). To stigmatize her as such would create yet another condescending stereotype and would reduce *Danton's Death's* conclusion to a modernist cliché: the insane have the last word, ergo the world is absurd, quod erat demonstrandum. Büchner's nonjudgmental portrayal of her can be best understood by comparing it to his fictionalization of Jakob Michael Reinhold Lenz: for Büchner, Lenz's mental imbalance is a "possibility of existence" (*CWL*, 146) worthy of investigation because it breaks through conventional perceptions of reality, heightening the creative potential of the human

---

4. "Had Büchner ended the drama directly after the execution, the effect of the ending would have been similar to the effect of K's death at the end of Kafka's *The Trial*: a passive, meaningless death as a final, none-too-surprising confirmation of the worldview that has been suggested throughout the work" (Herbert Lindenberger, *Georg Büchner* [Carbondale: Southern Illinois University Press, 1964], 53).

5. Wolf, "Shall I Garnish," 7.

6. *Hamlet* 4, 5. Male literary predecessors also seem to have left their mark: Lucile's "Everything may live, everything, the little fly there, the bird. Why not he?" recalls King Lear's despair over Cordelia's corpse: "Why should a dog, a horse, a rat, have life, / And thou no breath at all?" (*King Lear* 5, 3). Likewise her "I suppose we must bear it" evokes Goethe's "wild youth" who was stung by "the rose in the meadow," and he "just had to bear it." (My thanks for these references to Jerry Wasserman and Ingrid Oesterle.) Like Goethe himself (see chap. 2), Büchner does not classify emotional response according to gender.

imagination. Like Lenz, Lucile opens herself up to her environment totally and voices her uncensored reactions. An instinct
within her transforms the unspeakable into familiar memories,
prompted by what Raymond Williams calls "the nostalgia for ballad
experience"[7]—the guillotine becomes an angel of death, and her
song of Death the Reaper is interrupted by: "You dear cradle, who
lulled my Camille to sleep, who smothered him under your roses.
You death knell, who sang him to the grave with your sweet tongue."
Like Danton and Julie, she succeeds in aestheticizing death by
placing her unique linguistic stamp upon the experience. She
externalizes and confronts death with poetry and song in an act of
self-assertion that cannot save the body from the "logic" of death
but that manages to rescue a bit of immortality through art.

   Lucile's language, if not its context, derives from romanticism.
Although her utterances are relativized by the cynical comments of
"several women" about the executions and by the earthy songs of
the executioners, a curtain falling immediately after her verse, "A
hundred thousand, big and small, / His sickle always makes them
fall" would nonetheless generate such an emotional impact that the
play's tensions between the individual and the Revolution would be
obliterated by sentimentality.[8] *Danton's Death* actually ends with
lines wholly free of romantic overtones:

A CITIZEN: Hey—who's there?
LUCILE: Long live the king!
CITIZEN: In the name of the Republic! (*She is surrounded by the
   watch and is led off.*)

The conclusion is so laconic that it prompted Büchner's first editor,
Karl Gutzkow, to preface Lucile's "Long live the king!" with the
stage direction, *"pensively and as if making a decision, suddenly."*
The stage direction is not in Büchner's manuscript, yet for unknown
reasons he did not delete it from the "Darmstadt" and "Hamburg"
copies of the play's first edition, in which he made many other corrections. Consequently, Franzos, Bergemann, and several recent
editors have retained Gutzkow's stage direction, apparently
believing it to be, as Bergemann insisted, indispensible for the

---

7. Williams maintains that this nostalgia is "a nostalgia for prerevolutionary society,"
   implying not a reactionary but an idealized, stable world. See Raymond Williams,
   "Georg Büchner: A Retrospect," in *Drama from Ibsen to Brecht* (New York: Oxford
   University Press, 1971), 234.
8. This mood is emphasized by critics who seize upon the "atmospheric" qualities of the
   final scenes involving Julie, Danton, and Lucile in order to cloud the drama's political
   issues with vague emotionalism. See, for example, Michelsen, who calls the atmospheric mood the "medium . . . that envelops the soul like a veil of music" ("Die
   Präsenz," 493). Similarly, the play's conclusion does not allow one to absolutize love as
   the *only* "positive message"; see Helmut Krapp, *Der Dialog bei Georg Büchner* (Darmstadt: Gentner, 1958), 121.

motivation.[9] To retain it seems wholly inappropriate, however, because it introduces a note of calculated rationality into Lucile's spontaneity, resulting in a didactic tableau similar to the conclusion of Schiller's *Wallensteins Tod*: after receiving a letter of promotion for his betrayal of Wallenstein, Octavio Piccolomini *"is startled and looks mournfully heavenward."* Schiller achieves closure here by anticipating divine retribution. Gutzkow's editorializing stage direction enjoins Lucile to carry out a deliberate, logical, even heroic action that brings the play to a close. The drama's aesthetic, however, would seem to preclude such Schillerian explicitness and measured ethical balance.

Lucile's "Long live the king!" is an age-old cliché, but it becomes deadly because it is a "misquotation" of the obligatory slogan, "Long live the Republic!"[1] Her phrase is the language of the counter-revolution, recalling the monarchy and anticipating the Thermidorian Reaction, the Napoleonic Restoration, and Büchner's Germany, when "Long live the king!" once again became obligatory. She utters a sentence she does not believe because she knows it will destroy her. Heretofore one of the drama's most powerless figures, she manipulates political language in order to fulfill private desires. She achieves a *Liebestod* without the pathos of suicide, without the sentimentality of bourgeois resignation. Instead of compromising with the forces of reaction, she involuntarily compels her oppressors to reveal their inhumanity, which Büchner evokes but does not sensationalize. With muted, spontaneous irony, she exits in a burst of "meaning."[2] Yet her unadorned exclamation lacks the rhetorical flourish, the self-stylized theatrical posing that often characterizes the speech of the male figures. The spareness of her statement prevents art from silencing history, which reemerges in this final moment in the form of a quotation from one of Büchner's sources. Lucile's action is documented more than once in *Our Times*.

---

9. *Georg Büchners Sämtliche Werke und Briefe*, ed. Fritz Bergemann (Leipzig: Insel, 1922), 677; *Georges Büchner: La Mort de Danton*, ed. Richard Thieberger (Paris: Presses Universitaires de France, 1953), 148.
1. Cf. Lacroix: "The asses will bray 'Long live the Republic!' as we go by" (4, 5). As Hans-Georg Werner points out, these phrases have degenerated into slogans that have lost their ethical correlatives. See Hans-Georg Werner, *"Dantons Tod* im Zwang der Geschichte," *Studien zu Georg Büchner,* ed. Hans-Georg Werner (Berlin and Weimar: Aufbau, 1988), 47–48.
2. At the conclusion of Alexander Lang's production of the play at the Deutsches Theater (East Berlin), two clownish representatives of the "folk" stroke her cheek tenderly before they lift her slightly off the floor and dance toward the back of the stage, to piano improvisations on the "Marseillaise." The back curtain lifts for the first time, revealing blackness, and the three dance off into the void as the curtain falls. The unexpected intimacy, even lightness of this finale serves to make the contrast to the Revolution's brutal reality yet more poignant. See *Dantons Tod von Georg Büchner: Eine Dokumentation der Aufführung des Deutschen Theaters Berlin 1981,* ed. Michael Funke (East Berlin: Verband der Theaterschaffenden der DDR, [1983]), 179–81.

I saw more than ten women who, not having the heart to take poison, shouted "Long live the king!" and through this dreadful device they left the task of ending their lives to the Tribunal—some wished not to survive a husband, others a lover, . . . none because of passionate love of royalty.[3]

The wife [of the Commandant of Longwy] had tried every means to save her husband, but in vain; when his sentence was announced, she cried out, in order to die with him, in a strong voice: "Long live the king!"[4]

In fact, Lucile's "Long live the king!" is both historical *and* fictional. Whereas other women went to their deaths in precisely this fashion, her historical namesake did not—although it would have been in character for her to do so, as Thiers reported.[5] However, Büchner's highlighting of Lucile's self-sacrifice at the drama's close, reinforcing Julie's prior death, results in a kind of gender imbalance: men love women and men die, but they do not die *because* they love women, whereas the reverse is true. Although Büchner did not distort history simply to suit a fantasy, the drama's ending conforms, at least in part, to the conventions of male wish-fulfillment.

The drama's last spoken word is not "love" nor "death" but "Republic." The juxtaposition of the two final lines creates an absurd yet illuminating effect: "Long live the king / in the name of the Republic!" The authoritarian regimentation of the monarchy has, in fact, been resurrected in the police state atmosphere of the Jacobin reign. Lucile's imminent death is grotesque—her compatriots consider the words "Long live the king!" to be a capital crime.[6] Here Büchner emphasizes the discrepancy between the policies of the Jacobin state and the Dantonists' vision of what a republic ought to be (1, 1), analogous to his diatribes against sham constitutional reforms in Germany.[7] Yet at the final curtain he does not explicitly denounce the Revolution of 1789, nor does he allow Jacobin barbarity to reign absolute. Lucile is indeed led off to prison, which recalls how the "motors of history" were throttled in Dan-

---

3. Thiers, *Unsere Zeit*, supplement vol. 5, 84, quoted in Broch, "Die Julia," 244.

4. Thiers, *Unsere Zeit*, 12, 156–57, quoted in Walter Hinderer, *Büchner-Kommentar zum dichterischen Werk* (München: Winkler, 1977), 128.

5. "The unfortunate [Lucile] Desmoulins died with a courage worthy of her husband and his character. Since Charlotte Cordai and Madame Roland, no victim had inspired a more tender interest and more sorrowful regrets" (Thiers, *Unsere Zeit*, 6, 235, quoted in Büchner, *La Mort de Danton*, ed. Richard Thieberger [Paris: L'Arche, 1953], 52).

6. Ironically, the historical Camille Desmoulins demanded the death penalty for this offense in his *Le Vieux Cordelier*. See Broch, "Die Julia," 244.

7. "Our legislatures are a satire against good sense" (*CWL*, 250 [letter of April 5, 1833])— the result of "republican" idealism and aristocratic concessions in Büchner's Hesse-Darmstadt. See also Büchner's letter to Edouard Reuss (*CWL*, 253–54 [August 31, 1833]), recently discovered by Jan-Christoph Hauschild.

ton's and Büchner's time, and she, like Danton and Julie, articulates the desire to "dissolve" passively out of an intolerable environment. Through her instinctive self-assertion, however, she single-handedly prevents the play from lapsing into fatalistic resignation. As Büchner indicated to the last in his letters, one must persist, even in stagnant times, to combat the absurdities of history. The potential of what will yet happen "in the name of the Republic" is counterposed against Lucile's spontaneity, lyricism, and the multilayered irony of her situation—a contrast that anticipates impending defeats as well as inextinguishable resistance.

ACCOUNTS OF THREE PRODUCTIONS

Ernst Stern

[*On Max Reinhardt's* Danton's Death][†]

* * *

Whilst the final rehearsals of "The Green Flute" were still taking place Reinhardt decided to stage Georg Büchner's play "The Death of Danton", whose theme is the conflict between Danton, Camille Desmoulins and their friends and Robespierre. The action takes place in the Convention, before the Revolutionary Tribunal, at the Conciergerie and in the streets and squares of Paris in 1793. When I read the play my impression was of dramatic, tragic and fantastic scenes which flamed up for a short space and then disappeared. The chaos of the revolution struck me as a terrible storm to the accompaniment of the constant rolling of thunder, sometimes near, sometimes in the distance, the scene lit up with flashes of lightning, the passionate actors in the drama appearing for a while as though in the spotlight and then fading into the background. In one respect my work on "The Green Flute" helped me here because it struck me forcibly that "lighting" was the solution for the problem of staging "Danton" just as it had been for the fantastic Chinese fairy tale. The revolving stage was quite out of the question, and fortunately Reinhardt agreed with me that "Danton" required a special system of décor and I was allowed to carry out my own ideas on the subject.

"Reinhardt undertook the daring experiment of producing a famous realistic piece whilst abandoning realism in the scenery

---

† From *My Life, My Stage,* translated by Edward Fitzgerald, 161–163. London: Gollancz, 1951. Reprinted by permission of the Orion Publishing Group, London. This account of the 1916 Max Reinhardt production at the Deutsches Theater in Berlin was written by Reinhardt's longest-serving designer.

and presenting the visual aspect of the great revolutionary drama
chiefly as human bodies and lighting effects. The stage was a neu-
tral construction which was neither obviously interior nor exterior
and therefore served as both. To the right and left of it great pillars
reared up into the flies. The changing background of the play was
represented very simply by various coloured hangings, and steps, on
which the members of the Convention or of the Revolutionary Tribunal sat. At the same time these steps served to represent the front
of the Palais de Justice up which the turbulent masses raced to
storm the building. Here and there railings were used, a wall with
bookshelves, a barred prison window. Perhaps two or three times
throughout the play, not more, a sombre silhouette of old Paris
appeared in the distance. All this would change, merge and disappear in a moment or two. The thing that constantly remained
was the two columns at either side of the stage, and they were constantly treated as an integral part of the play and drawn into the
action. It was in this framework that the tragedy of Danton was
allowed to unroll—from the beginning of the play, which showed
him in lighter mood at the gaming table, or with his head resting in
a woman's lap, right until the last when a ray of moonlight austerely
picked out the guillotine in the background. The two columns
appeared as rocky banks between which the stream rolled, sometimes calm, sometimes tumultuous, carrying the action to its inevitable end. . . . The impression of a tremendous plenitude and variety
of life, the impression of passionate movement, was obtained by
lighting up only one small part of the stage at a time whilst the rest
remained in gloom. Only individuals or small groups were picked
out in the spotlight whilst the masses always remained in semi-
darkness, or even in complete darkness. But they were always there
and they could be heard murmuring, speaking, shouting. Out of
the darkness an upraised arm would catch the light, and in this way
thousands seemed to be where hundreds were in fact. This principle of the rapid play of light and darkness was maintained throughout. Scenes would flash up for a second or two. Lights would go
out, darkness would persist for a fraction, and then lights would go
up elsewhere, and this rapid and often abrupt change reinforced the
rhythm of the piece. The last words of one scene were still being
spoken when the first words of the next would sound and the light
change to it. The sound of singing, the whistling of "The Marseillaise", the tramping of many feet, booing, the echo of a speech being
delivered somewhere, applause from out of the darkness. A lamppost lights up and the mob is seen hanging an aristocrat. Half-
naked furies in colourful rags dance "La Carmagnole". And already
the light turns to a peaceful room in which Danton is resting in the
arms of a *grisette*. And because whatever is the important thing for

the moment is suddenly illuminated out of the darkness in a fiery or ghostly white light, the producer is able to stress the main figures of the play and their action to the utmost: Danton, the People's Tribune; the young Desmoulins; the sea-green Robespierre; St. Just with the fair-haired, girlish head and the heart of ice—they appear for a moment or two and disappear again. And at the end the slim Lucille who has lost her Desmoulins leans exhausted against the guillotine. A short and deeply moving moment in the cold light of the moon".[1]

My name is nowhere mentioned in all this, but, in fact, it was I who had tried something completely new, namely, to paint with light, to stress only the essentials. Fortunately, in Germany the scenic artist does the lighting and not the producer as in England, and that is because, after all, it is part and parcel of the scene and can make or mar it.

*   *   *

John Houseman

[*On Orson Welles's* Danton's Death][†]

*   *   *

Danton's Death had been written, just over a century before, by a boy who died at the age of twenty-four, leaving behind him this and two other more or less finished plays (*Leonce und Lina* and *Wozzeck*). Scribbled in a student's notebook in the attic of his father's house, where Georg Buechner was hiding from the police repression that swept Europe after the Congress of Vienna, it is a play of keen political and human insights—one that seemed to offer us scope for creative and experimental production and, at the same time, reflected significant aspects of the modern scene. Laid in that violent period of the French Revolution when it was making the transition from new-won liberty to dictatorship, it is a very young man's play with a fragmentary and defective structure. It had been seen in New York in 1927 when Max Reinhardt presented it (in an augmented version with vast crowd effects) as one of the great successes of his American season. This success, far from helping us, made our undertaking more hazardous: it conditioned Orson's approach to the play and influenced the nature of his production. Since Reinhardt had made a mass spectacle of it and Orson himself

---

1. Heinz Herald, "Reinhardt und seine Bühne".
† From *Run-through*, by John Houseman, 378–390. New York: Simon and Schuster, 1972. Reprinted by permission. This account of the 1938 Orson Welles production at the Mercury Theatre in New York was written by Welles's long-time producer and collaborator.

had already demonstrated his ability to handle crowd scenes, *Danton's Death* would be performed as a "drama of lonely souls and the mob," with the mob ever-present but rarely visible.

Except for such general notions, Welles came to the play unprepared and uncertain. He was a great improviser but he needed a strong structure (as in *Caesar*) or a brilliant texture (as in *Faustus*) around which to develop his inventions and variations. Both were missing in *Danton*. He brought to it, as he could not fail to do, intermittent genius, spasmodic energy and an occasional flash of vision, but none of that impregnable personal conviction that had carried him irresistibly through his first seven productions.

Casting, for all our disagreements, had always been an exhilarating and spontaneous process. That this was not true of *Danton* had to do with a basic flaw that weakened the entire structure of the new season's Mercury company.

The hero of Buechner's tragedy is a giant of a man: as a role, Danton calls for heroism, magnanimity, lethargy and great personal magnetism. I was confident that Orson had them all—until I discovered that he had no intention of playing the part, which he had already offered to Martin Gabel. We argued bitterly for two days, in the darkness of his air-conditioned hotel room and under the bright lights of Studio One. Orson maintained, not unreasonably, that he could not play Falstaff and Danton and direct both plays in addition to the radio show. Since when, I objected, had we conducted our affairs reasonably? The show needed him and he must do it. Finally, in an unsatisfactory compromise, he agreed to appear in the brief but flashy role of Saint-Just, in which he could be replaced without damage when the *Five Kings* rehearsals began—or whenever the ballerina summoned him, I might have added.

Meantime we had begun to reassemble what was left of the Mercury Company. Chubby and Whitford were gone; so were Vincent Price and Edith Barrett (married and off to California); Mady Christians was playing the Queen in Maurice Evans' *Hamlet*; Norman Lloyd was getting ready to play Johnny Apple-seed in a Broadway musical. George Duthie was sick and Orson, predictably, had decided he did not want Joseph Holland around.

One of my first calls had been to the company's leading malcontent, George Coulouris. When I informed him that he was about to cap his series of Mercury triumphs with the great role of Robespierre, he took it coolly and asked who would be playing Danton. I told him—

"Gabel."

"Martin Gabel?"

"Martin Gabel."

The silence that followed should have alerted me, but I said cheerfully that I was sending over the script. Two days later Coulouris informed me that he found the part monolithic and the play turgid. I told him to go to hell.

After I hung up I remembered that Sokoloff, who had created the role for Reinhardt, was in Hollywood, where he had just played with Paul Muni in *Zola*. We called him and he was interested. After hearing him talk I began to worry about his English; Orson reminded me that I had worried about Mady Christians.

Finally we had only seven carry-overs from previous Mercury shows—not counting the slaves and the extras. Gabel was with us again; so were Joe Cotten, Eustace Wyatt, Ruth Ford, Ross (formerly Ted) Elliot, Erskine Sanford and Arlene Francis, whom we cast as Danton's mistress.[1] Most of the extras were still around: they had kept alive during the summer as Keystone Cops and Cuban peons; now, as they prepared to go back underground as Parisian sans-culottes, I added a few new faces, principally female, of which the most vividly remembered is that of a lovely child named Betty Garrett, from the Neighborhood Playhouse, whose arms and legs were perpetually covered with bruises incurred while repelling sexual attacks in the basement. (She was also frequently covered, rather more mysteriously, with bright patches of violet ink.) Most of our female apprentices had gone back to college: in their place we had two new male slaves—Howard Teichmann from Wisconsin and Richard Baer from Princeton, both of whom soon achieved positions of importance in the Mercury hierarchy.[2]

Teichmann may be exaggerating when he claims that during the final rehearsals of *Danton's Death* he was required to stay in the theatre for thirteen days and thirteen nights without a break. It is true that the show was prepared in an anxious mood that fluctuated between uneasy inertia and almost unbearable tension. It was rehearsed, almost from the first day, in a set of which the dominant element was a huge, curved wall, formed entirely of human faces that filled the rear of the stage from the basement to the grid. Called on to execute this in a hurry and at reasonable cost, Jean Rosenthal went out and bought five thousand unpainted Halloween masks, each of which was colored by hand and glued onto a curved,

1. Once again the Mercury acted as marriage broker. Arlene and Gabel found each other on stage on a "Directoire" sofa that resembled a bathtub and, in due course, came together in what has proved to be one of the most durable marriages in show business.
2. Howard Teichmann became a successful writer for radio and theatre (*The Solid Gold Cadillac*) before becoming administrator of what remains of the great Shubert theatrical empire. Richard Baer (later Barr) is president of the League of New Theatres, producer for Edward Albee of *The Zoo Story*, *Who's Afraid of Virginia Woolf*, *A Delicate Balance* and other successful plays including *The Boys in the Band*.

stiffened canvas cyclorama by rotating crews of assistants; volun-
teers, slaves, wardrobe women, secretaries, visitors—anyone who
could be persuaded or pressured into joining in the loathsome task.
When finished and lit, it was an effective and active device that
suggested different things to different people: in one light it was
"the hydra-headed mob, impersonal but real, omnipresent as a reality," in another "it looked like a huge canopy of staring faces which
gave the strange ominous effect of a rigid dance of death." At the
climax of Danton's self-destruction, blood-red lights were thrown
upon it; during Robespierre's midnight meditation it turned to vicious,
steely gray, which made it seem, for a moment, "as though the whole
pile of skulls was about to fall upon him and stone him to death." In
the last scene, as Danton and his followers went to their execution,
this whole rear wall opened up and revealed a narrow slit against a
bright blue sky topped by glittering steel. At the final curtain drums
rolled and the blade of the guillotine flashed down through the slit as
the lights blacked out.

In front of this wall, starting immediately behind the forestage,
was a yawning pit thirty feet long and twenty wide, hacked out of
the center of the stage floor we had so lovingly and proudly rebuilt
the year before. Out of this hole, rising in steep steps from the
basement, like a miniature Aztec pyramid, was a four-sided structure the center of which was occupied by an elevator shaft through
which a small platform traveled up and down, descending to the
basement to unload and rising to a maximum height of twelve feet
above the stage. This was successively used, at various levels, as a
rostrum, a garret, an elegantly furnished salon, a prison cell and a
tumbril until, in the final scene, it rose slowly to its full height to
become the raised platform of the guillotine.

It was a brilliant conception but mechanically it was a horror. The
only kind of elevator we could afford was a swaying, rickety, man-
driven contraption. When I complained to Jean of its instability she
explained that it was precisely this flexibility that made it safe. We
spent days trying to make it stop at the right places; dozens of hours
lighting it at its various levels. When it was all set and lit, it looked
wonderful; it was also constricting and exceedingly dangerous.

The actors might have been less conscious of their physical problems if they had been more assured in their action. *Danton* was a
play of many scenes and for most of the company it was difficult to
create characters out of such brief, fragmented episodes. In the
rehearsals I attended (between working on the weekly radio shows
and trying to track down investors) it seemed to me that Orson was
working with less patience and intimacy than usual. This was particularly evident in his work with Martin Gabel. In *Caesar* there
had been mutual understanding and faith between them: none of

that was evident now. Gabel was aggressive in his insecurity: he knew he was not ideally cast and that Orson should have been playing Danton. This suspicion hung, between them, unspoken and corrosive, all through rehearsal. It something only Welles could have dispelled: unconsciously competitive and vaguely annoyed at himself for having refused to play the part, he did little to help Gabel overcome his natural handicaps.

For Vladimir Sokoloff (with whom we all fell in love and who entertained the company with anecdotes of Reinhardt and Stanislavski) Welles had that awed and childlike respect which he showed for theatrical figures whom he admired. Most of Robespierre's great scenes were solos—orations and soliloquies. Orson let him play them exactly as he had played them in German for Reinhardt. It was very impressive and the company used to applaud at each rehearsal, but it made it more difficult for Sokoloff to assimilate the part in English than if the scenes had been restaged and redirected. He worried about his speech and requested and received hours of special coaching—to no perceptible effect.

With the extras herded in the basement and emerging only for occasional street scenes during which they sang Blitzstein's updated version of *"La Carmagnole,"* Orson was less painstaking and demanding than he had been in *Caesar*. He turned them over to the stage management and to Marc Blitzstein for musical and sound effects. Indeed, for a time, Marc seemed to be the only completely content and confident person in the organization. Besides the crowd sounds, he had composed some Mozartian harpsichord music and two vocal numbers: an "Ode to Reason" and a duet entitled "Christine" to be sung by Joseph Cotten and Mary Wickes. Then, suddenly, midway through rehearsal, he was seized with a deep anxiety which he lost no time passing on to Orson and myself and, in due course, to the entire company.

In forming the Mercury we had always counted on the solid support of an assured and loyal public—the organized, left-wing, semi-intellectual audiences that consisted predominantly of the Communist Party, its adherents and sympathizers. It was they who had been our main support during the various runs of *The Cradle Will Rock*, who had encouraged us during the early, shaky previews of *Julius Caesar* and who had already bought up the numerous previews on which we hoped to hone the ragged edges of *Danton's Death*.

Ever since the great night of *The Cradle*, Marc Blitzstein had constituted himself our political counsellor. He came to me now, ten days before our first scheduled preview, in a state of extreme agitation. In producing *Danton's Death* at this time, he explained, we were all guilty of a serious and dangerous error: perhaps we should cancel the production immediately. I said this was a hell of a time to tell me and pressed him for an explanation—which Marc now gave me straight from the cultural bureau of the Party: with the Moscow trials still fresh in people's minds and the Trotskyite schism growing wider by the day—couldn't I see the inescapable and dangerous parallel? To the politically uneducated and even to some of the younger emotional members of the Party, Danton, the hero of the Revolution, who had raised and commanded the armies of the young republic, would inevitably suggest Trotsky, while his prosecutor, the incorruptible, ruthless Robespierre, would, equally inevitably, be equated with Joseph Stalin.

When I smilingly minimized his fears he informed me, rather white around the gills, that unless we did something drastic to bring our production into line, our theatre parties (on which it was customary to receive a small deposit on signing and the rest a few days before the performance) would all be canceled. We might even be picketed. Having wiped the smile off my face, he suggested that a meeting be held as soon as possible with V. J. Jerome to discuss the matter.

In the days that followed we held a number of meetings, two of them in Stewart's Cafeteria on Union Square. I remembered Mr. Jerome from the MacLeish symposium, but I hardly knew him. As the result of these meetings we became better acquainted: I visited him at his apartment, where tea was served by an English spinster, his sister; he came to my new, half-furnished apartment on Ninth Street, where we ate some of my mother's *oeufs en gelée*. But over *Danton's Death* we were deadlocked. To placate him, we removed a few of the more obvious Trotsky-Stalin parallels. In exchange, the Party agreed not to boycott us: they merely withheld their support. When we needed them desperately after our mixed notices in the capitalist press they did nothing to help us survive.

These negotiations took place amid rising anxiety and tension. Night after night, and sometimes all night, Welles went through the motions of rehearsal—endlessly shifting the order of scenes and the sequence of speeches. Each time such a change was made it called for a complete rerouting and relighting of that entire section of the play. The wall of faces, effective as it was, was horribly difficult to light; each of its five thousand rounded masks seemed determined to get itself into the light. If one single lamp was moved, even slightly, to accommodate an actor's changed position on the stage, it was likely, a moment later, to illuminate a hundred masks behind him.

Days and nights went by and nobody left the theatre. Mattresses were dragged into the aisles to take care of our twenty-four-hour shifts. Jeannie grew smaller and grayer. Still Orson would not stop. He drove himself and the company with no sense of time, to no apparent purpose and with no perceptible feeling. It was as though he expected, by continuously increasing the pressure, to strike some new well of inspiration that would save us all.

Our mood matched that of the world around us. If anyone, in a moment of restlessness, turned on the small radio that George Zorn kept in the rear of the box office, it was to hear increasingly alarming news: Hitler's armies poised for invasion, Prague vowing resistance, France mobilizing, the British fleet massing in the North Atlantic. In mid-September, while Neville Chamberlain, with his umbrella, was flying between London and Munich to insure "peace in our time," a strange cloud of tragi-comic madness seemed to hang over the Mercury and its inmates.

There was an evening, a week before our first preview, when Orson suddenly announced that the script still wasn't right and he was going to do something about it. Calling the cast together on the stage, he explained that he was sending them home early (it was then after 11:00 P.M.) while he spent the night doing a final and definitive rewrite. He called a rehearsal for ten the next morning, and a moment later the theatre was empty except for Orson, Blitzstein, the slaves and myself. Vakhtangov was sent out to the Astor for cigars and Wilson to 21 for a bottle of brandy. By 1:30 A.M. no work had been done, and I went upstairs to the projection room for a nap while Orson, Marc and Teichmann discussed the Spanish-American War as a subject for a musical. At three I descended and suggested we get back to *Danton's Death*. Orson said no. He was going to do the rewrite by himself. It was better that way. He knew exactly what must be done. I offered to stay with him. He said he could work better alone in his room at the St. Regis. Vakhtangov went off to find him a taxi and they left.

I told Teichmann to cancel the next morning's rehearsal and to call the St. Regis at noon for instructions. Vakhtangov answered in a whisper. He said Orson had worked all night but still wasn't done. We called again at five and again Vakhtangov answered. He said Welles would be working all through the night and wanted the cast called for noon of the next day—at which time he would read them the new script. Rosenthal was to be there, also Augusta with two expert typists.

At twelve the cast assembled, refreshed from its first real sleep in two weeks. At one-thirty Welles arrived, smiled wanly as he crossed the stage and vanished into his dressing room, the slaves following to help him remove his coat and make final preparations for the reading. Seconds later an agonized howl was heard. Then Dick Baer, followed by Wilson and Vakhtangov, came flying out, rushed across the stage and out the stage door onto the street. Finally, Orson himself appeared, his eyes rolling, wringing his huge hands, patting himself all over and announcing in a sepulchral voice that the script on which he had worked for two nights and a day had been left in the cab which brought him from the St. Regis. There was no copy. After an hour had been spent calling police stations and trying to trace the missing cab, rehearsal resumed exactly where it had left off thirty-nine hours before.

Five nights later we had our first real disaster. The night had started badly. The Longchamps Restaurant next door, to which Orson owed several hundred dollars, had refused to release his double steak and triple pistachio ice cream (which he was in the habit of eating, seated in the aisle, while conducting rehearsal) unless they were paid for in cash, and no one in the theatre was able or willing to advance the necessary sum. Augusta Weissberger, hastily summoned from home, took care of that. Then Zolotow of the *Times* called on the box-office phone to ask if we were still going to open when we said we were. I said yes. When I got back into the theatre the run-through had begun. There was a crowd of citizens on the forestage—assorted couples, spies, drunks, market women, hawkers, agitators and lynchers—all calling for "death for those with no holes in their coats." Off stage, in the basement, they were singing *"La Carmagnole."* Then as the street scene faded—behind it, slowly rising out of darkness into light—the elevator platform came into view, revealing a delicate, civilized, eighteenth-century drawing-room scene, all silk and elegance and laughter—three men and two women drinking tea to the soft playing of a harpsichord. It had just cleared the level of the stage, swaying gently as was its wont, when it was shaken by a slight tremor, barely perceptible from the front but enough to make the actors glance at each other. For a few seconds it continued to rise—a charming sight. It had almost reached its mark when it stopped, shuddered (so that a tea cup fell off the table and smashed) and began to sink—slowly at first, but gathering speed as it vanished from sight.

There was a silence that seemed eternal, then a girl's scream followed by a crash that shook the theatre. More screams and a man's groan. It came from Erskine Sanford, whose leg was broken; the rest were shaken but unhurt.

Jean Rosenthal, after examining the debris and determining the cause of the crash, which she said would never occur again, asked for three days to repair and reconstruct the elevator. So once again I called Zolotow of *The New York Times* and the rest of the press, canceled two previews and postponed our opening for the third time—"due to technical problems." Sanford was replaced, and Orson continued to rehearse while morale deteriorated.

Our preview situation was becoming a disgrace. Torn between my reluctance to lose the income we so desperately needed and my aversion to giving performances that could only result in bad word of mouth, I postponed one preview after another—five in all. Finally we could delay no longer. Sylvia Regan had begged me not to lose this one—a full house sold to a friendly middle-class group that had seen all our shows and would forgive our imperfections. The elevator had been tested and pronounced safe. There were still a few minor adjustments to be made, but Jeannie, standing over her reeking, oil-smeared mechanics as they tinkered with the cables and gears of what looked like some primitive, medieval siege engine, assured me that all would be well by curtain time. They were still tinkering when the cast came in at half-hour and Jeannie looked troubled. At nine they were still struggling and Welles insisted we cancel. Thinking of the $750 we would have to refund and didn't possess, I refused.

The audience was friendly when I appeared before the curtain at 9:15, spoke smilingly of "technical difficulties" and begged their indulgence. When I went back through the curtain Jeannie said she needed another twenty minutes. At 9:40, to keep them in patience, Welles and Gabel, wearing the tight silk breeches and high neck-pieces of their late-eighteenth-century costumes, went out on the forestage and performed the tent scene from *Julius Caesar*. There was applause and all was well for another twenty minutes; then they began to get restless again and started to clap and to stamp their feet. Orson came out of his dressing room and yelled that we should give them their money back and send them home. I said we didn't have it and he went back inside and slammed the door. Again I asked Jeannie how long. She was looking gray and she said fifteen minutes. Beyond the curtain the clapping and stamping was getting louder. Once again, I went out. I told them how grateful we were for their patience—so grateful that we were now giving them two alternatives. They could leave now, if their patience was at an end (and I couldn't blame them), and keep their present preview tickets, which would be honored at the box office at any time during the run of *Danton's Death*. Or, having waited this long, they could, if they preferred, remain in their seats and witness the performance, which we had every intention of beginning any minute now. I had not quite finished formulating my offer when I felt myself poked in the back. Turning, I saw a small hand protruding through the crack in the curtain, holding out a card on which I could make out the scrawled message:

SORRY NO SHOW TONIGHT—JEAN

With perfect sang-froid I turned back to the audience, concluded my offer, leaped the short distance from the forestage to the orchestra floor, walked quickly up the aisle, and ordered the doorman to open all doors including the safety exits. Returning to the edge of the stage, I vaulted up, faced the audience and raised my hand for silence. "A vote has been taken," I declared quietly, "and the sentiment of this house is overwhelmingly in favor of returning on another night." I wished them goodnight, then slipped back through the curtain onto the stage, from where I listened anxiously to the receding sound of voices as the house rapidly and peacefully emptied. Hardly were the lights out and the door bolted when the phone rang in the box office. It was Sam Zolotow of the *Times* calling to inquire if this meant still another postponement. I told him yes.

We did give two perfectly smooth previews on the following nights, which were Friday and Saturday. Our press opening was now set for Wednesday, November 3. It could not take place any sooner because over the weekend we had to do our regular weekly radio show which, on this particular Sunday, was *The War of the Worlds,* better known as *"The Men from Mars."*

* * *

Richard Thomas

Wilson, Danton, and Me†

Before coming to Houston, I began trying to find ways into the role. I thought of Danton as a kind of "Natural Man" among the Revolution's politicians, idealists and dogmatists. He has been called a passive character, but I did not—could not—think of him that way. He is, rather, trapped between a nihilistic world-view and a passionate love of life—one moment letting go, surrendering to the tidal wave of history, and the next engaged and fighting. Never still, he is continually changing, at times even in a matter of lines, of words.

Danton faces a great contemporary dilemma between private identity and social identity, between what he wants as a human being and what he does as an icon of the Revolution. We have this dilemma in our own lives. Of course this tension between the private individual and the individual in society, has existed throughout history. It produces an isolation, an aloneness. In the opening scene Danton's wife says, "You know me, don't you Danton?" And he replies, "I know I've touched you many times. I've tried to reach into you, to rub through your skin, but our skins are so thick and in the end we're as lonely as ever."

†   American Theatre (July / August 1993): 24–28. Published by American Theatre Magazine. Used by permission of Theatre Communications Group. This account of the 1992 Robert Wilson production at the Alley Theatre in Houston, Texas, was written by the actor playing Danton.

So in June we came together to work on this fragmented, disjointed (and very wordy) play. Most of us had never worked with Bob before. We had certain notions of what the production would be like, but not the process. After reading through the play, we immediately got "on our feet." For each scene, Bob worked with the actors to create the movements, usually with an idea of how many moves it should contain or how long it should be. We worked without the text, adhering to all the requirements of the scene—who enters, who leaves, how many are in the room, what is happening—but the creation of this movement was not generated by specific lines. We created more or less an abstract movement sequence that had its own life, its own rhythms.

After these movements were created they were numbered and learned, as one would learn a dance. Then we spoke the text while doing the movements. Sometimes the words and gestures reinforced each other, sometimes they had nothing to do with one another, and sometimes the pairings revealed something new and extraordinary— some third idea between gesture and text.

What Bob wants to avoid is illustration, the movements being secondary to the text. He often said that what is seen should stand on its own in the same way that the text does. We didn't rely on psychology and emotional response to provide the "appropriate" or "required" gestures. Working within the framework of this new pairing of text and movement, we made adjustments, alterations, and eventually began to make sense of how these words and gestures went together. The pairing could not seem arbitrary. We very much had to "suit the action to the word and the word to the action," but not in a behaviorally realistic relationship, since the actions were not generated by the words.

The wonderful and surprising thing about this method is that I felt a great freedom as well as a great sense of purpose. I had the movements and the text—separately created and equally important—and I was in the middle, required to perform a kind of alchemy to bond them together and eventually transform them into something else completely.

It was, also surprisingly, a very relaxed process. Many of the things an actor usually has to work out—How do I come in? How do I leave? What am I thinking as I do all these things?—were approached in purely theatrical, often utilitarian, terms. We spent time working on the technical aspects of walking, or entering— finding the correct placement of body weight, or the exact number of steps required to arrive in the same place every time.

This method of working was new to most of us, but because we worked pretty much the same way on each scene, we always knew how to begin. There was no question of mental or artistic blocks.

We could look at the sketches to see what the space looked like. Within that framework we would continually adjust our moves, our line-readings, our gestures. We tried something, and if it seemed right it stayed and if not we changed it. And if it was too soon to tell, it was too soon to tell; we didn't worry about it. Bob had very clear ideas about some things, but he also relied on input from the entire company. The actors always had a voice, always had a vote, sometimes literally: "How many of you like the box in this position? How many in the other?" The most challenging aspect of the work was trying to figure out what Bob was looking for while at the same time having my own experience of the play and the role. I never knew how I stood in relation to "Wilsonian theatre." "Is this too real?" I would ask myself. Then: "Is this too Robert Wilson?" Eventually I just had to figure out where this character is in this production, how to play the performance and, ultimately, truly make it my own.

When Bob directs or choreographs a scene for the first time, or when he imagines a sequence, I believe he sees himself as the performer. This may be especially true since he had worked with so few of us before. He's a performer. It's beautiful to watch him demonstrate a move or explain—verbally and physically—the way a line should be read. Part of what occurs in rehearsal is a shift of the characters moving from him to the performers.

When we finally moved out of the rehearsal hall and onto the stage, the focus shifted to the technical aspects of the piece. The composer and sound designer were with us in almost every rehearsal, and Bob was thinking about light from the beginning, but there was still much work to do. The technical rehearsals were a slow meticulous process. Nothing is an "extra" or secondary element. Everything is important.

During the previews Bob told us: "Make the piece yours. This is not my play anymore now. You know the form is boring. It's how you embody the form that counts." An actor who had worked with him before turned to me and said, "I've never heard him talk like this."

Once in performance, the production continued on that course that all plays take; rhythms change, people relax in certain scenes where they haven't been able to relax, people take little chances that they were not able to take before. The evolutionary process continued, as with any other production. It might not have been as noticeable because the form was so strict, but it was happening. It may have been most evident in the tribunal scenes. But for me, the last prison scene, right before Danton's execution, was the most changed. It became clearer and clearer. All of the elements were the same—the

lines, the lights, the sound, certainly the gestures—but somehow it
had evolved. Something was different. The form was becoming filled,
the alchemy was working.

An actor never really knows what the experience of the audience is. In *Danton's Death*, however, each element of the production has a structure of its own. Amidst these many different—and
autonomous—structures it was almost impossible to know how
much of the experience of the play was being conveyed by the
performers.

Of course, the experience of a production is always created by all
the elements. But in playing Hamlet, for instance, I had a sense that
all the other elements were supporting me—especially the text. In
this production I never had that sense. Sometimes the sound and
lights supported the scenes, and sometimes they didn't. Like the
pairing of movement and text, all the elements were brought together
to make one thing, but without sacrificing their autonomy. I always
had the feeling that the production was communicating on many
levels simultaneously, and my performance was one of those equally
important levels.

Bob's idea is to keep from imposing an interpretation—his or the
actors'—on an audience and to allow them space to enter into the
production. For an audience that goes in with a more conventional
idea of theatre, expecting to be told what to think and how to follow
the play, the production can seem impenetrable. They just can't
find a way into the piece. But because people have that response,
doesn't mean Bob doesn't think about the audience. Not only is he
attempting to let interpretation rest with the audience, to let them
make up their own minds, but he is also thinking about them in the
rehearsal process, as he shapes the piece.

Wilson is a theatre craftsman and a pragmatist—he likes a good
show. In rehearsals, he makes himself a part of the audience. In
many ways he becomes the audience member that should never go
to a Robert Wilson production. He'll become impatient. "This is
too boring. This is too slow. This isn't working. Things have to be
linked more, we need more bridges. I can't understand what the
main points of this speech are." And he is so meticulous because he
doesn't want things to be muddled. He wants each part, each level,
to be clear. That is thinking about the audience.

I heard a lot of praise for the production and I, of course, heard
a lot of criticism. On the one hand there were those people who
found it too avant-garde: "There is no point in producing a great
play," they say, "if you're not going to do the play."

On the other hand there were some Wilson aficionados who felt
that it was too conventional! They thought the elements were not

autonomous enough, that the lights and sound, *did*, in fact, serve too much to support the text.

But with this production, Wilson was directing a *play*—a play written by someone else and with a long production history. He's only recently started doing that. There was no mistaking this was a Robert Wilson production, and the "visual book" of the piece was a Robert Wilson creation; but the production also did a service to the play, to Büchner's text in Bob Auletta's adaptation.

If audiences feel free to have a non-judgmental approach, to "experience" the play, they will see things they love, things they hate, things that confuse them and things that make perfect sense. Pretty much like life.

Lenz

ERIKA SWALES

Büchner, *Lenz*[†]

'Was nennt Ihr denn *gesetzlichen Zustand?* [. . .] dies Gesetz ist
eine *ewige rohe Gewalt*, angetan dem Recht und der gesunden
Vernunft.'[1]
'Ich bin ein Automat; die Seele ist mir genommen' (p. 257).[2]

These two extracts from Büchner's letters articulate the intense
patterns of explosive and implosive energy which mark the author's
short life (1813–37) and works. On the one hand there is the radical, who studies French utopian socialism, co-founds, in despair at
the conditions in Hessen, a 'Gesellschaft der Menschenrechte', and
collaborates with Ludwig Weidig on the revolutionary pamphlet
Der hessische Landbote (1834). In his letters of this period, Büchner
denounces the prevailing power relations—'Der Aristokratismus ist
die schändlichste Verachtung des Heiligen Geistes im Menschen'—
and he is unambiguous in his insistence that only violence can
change the 'ewigen Gewaltzustand' (p. 248).[3] His reflections on the
necessity of violence within a violent system echo eighteenth-century
French materialist philosophy and anticipate Darwinian or Marxian
thought—but one notes an inherent friction: on the one hand,
there is a humanist stance which abhors contempt for any human
being—'*Ich verachte Niemanden*' (p. 253)[4]—yet, on the other hand,
his language is as ruthless as his advocacy of fiercest struggle.

It is this tension which Karl Gutzkow pinpointed when he told
Büchner: 'Sie haben selbst viel Ähnlichkeit mit Ihrem Danton:

[†] From *Landmarks in German Short Prose*, edited by Peter Hutchinson, 79–94. New
York: Peter Lang, 2003. Reprinted by permission.

1. Georg Büchner, *Werke und Briefe*, (Munich, 1980), p. 248. All subsequent page references are to this edition. ["What do you call a lawful state? . . . this law is *eternal, brute
force,* insulting justice and good sense" (p. 182)—*Editor*.]

2. "I'm an automaton; my soul has been removed" (p. 186) [*Editor*].

3. "Aristocratic elitism is the most despicable contempt for the holy spirit in human
nature"; "eternal state of violence" (pp. 184, 182) [*Editor*].

4. "*I scorn no one*" (p. 183) [*Editor*].

genial und träge' (p. 301).[5] The letters of the depressive Büchner
are shot through with references to feelings of collapse, of
'Starrkrampf', and 'das Gefühl des Gestorbenseins' (p. 255).[6] The
motif of being buried alive haunts all his works and is particularly
pronounced in *Dantons Tod* and in *Lenz*. It reflects not only Büchner's individual disposition, but the temper of his times: the philosophical 'Weltschmerz', as epitomized in Arthur Schopenhauer's
philosophy, and the sense of political frustration which dominates
the 1830s. As a cultural mood and mode, melancholia also haunted
the would-be rebels of the *Sturm und Drang* in the 1770s, in particular the writer Jakob Michael Lenz, whom Büchner's narrative remembers as a kindred spirit in kindred times, a mixture of provocation
and resignation.

In order to situate my argument, let me briefly recall the outlines
of the text: it traces the mental breakdown which Lenz suffered in
the winter of 1778. Following in the footsteps of his father, he had
studied theology, but then turned to creative writing and incurred
unforgiving paternal anger. As is apparent from his own writings
and comments by his contemporaries, Lenz was of highly unstable
disposition, notorious for his unsettling whimsicality.

Büchner's text starts with Lenz crossing the Alsatian mountains,
hoping to find a measure of peace in the isolated village of Waldbach, in the vicarage of Pastor Oberlin, who was known for his
Pietist humaneness. To a degree, Oberlin's fatherly calm has a soothing effect: Lenz experiences moments of serenity, and his parish
sermon gives him a sense of meaning. Roughly at the centre of the
story, an oasis of clarity opens up: Lenz is visited by Kaufmann, a
close friend, and in the ensuing debate on aesthetics, Lenz utterly
dominates. But when Kaufmann pleads with him to heed his father's
will and return home, he violently refuses. The consequences are bitterly ironic—Kaufmann and Oberlin leave for a trip to Switzerland,
and the loss of his adoptive father proves catastrophic for Lenz: his
mental health rapidly declines. Compelled by a 'fixe Idee' (p. 81),[7] he
attempts to resurrect a dead girl, and the failure drives him into the
grip of atheism, yet also sheer horror at the enormity of his sin. After
a few days, Oberlin returns, but cannot stop Lenz's slide into the
'wüste Chaos seines Geistes' (p. 80).[8] Finally, he is transported back
to Strasbourg—Büchner's last sentence reads: 'So lebte er hin' (p. 89).

The historical Lenz lived for another fourteen years, trapped in
his illness. Büchner owned his collected works, and he started to

---

5. "You have a strong resemblance to your Danton: brilliant and lethargic" [*Editor's translation*].
6. "paralysis"; "the feeling of having died" (p. 184) [*Editor*].
7. "obsession" (p. 96) [*Editor*].
8. "wild chaos of his spirit" (p. 95) [*Editor*].

focus on the figure of Lenz in the spring of 1835 when he was working on *Dantons Tod*. He also had access to some letters by Lenz and
a written account by Pastor Oberlin which records those distress-
ing three weeks. Intriguingly, Büchner's references to the project
vary strikingly: he speaks of an 'Aufsatz' (p. 276) and of a 'Novelle'
(p. 303).[9] The text was to be published in the *Deutsche Revue*, but,
under the pressures of censorship, the journal closed down. It was
only in 1839 that Gutzkow published *Lenz* in *Telegraph für Deutschland*. Editorial problems have kept academics busy over decades:
the original manuscript is lost, as is the copy which Büchner's
fiancé, Minna Jaeglé, had made.

In the history of German literature, *Lenz* figures as a scandalous
text, on a par with Goethe's *Die Leiden des jungen Werthers* (1774).
Such notions as consolation and redemption, which are central to
many nineteenth-century German *Novellen* do not come into play
in Büchner's text. Or rather, they *do*, but, as in all his works, only in
negated form, in possibilities glimpsed and lost. In this sense, the
opening chords foreshadow the essence of the subsequent text: they
sound such motifs as 'suchen', 'nicht finden', and 'verlorene Träume'
(p. 69).[1] In other words: the quest is there, overwhelmingly so, but,
as the dominant mode of the subjunctive suggests, it is doomed. As
Lenz slips into the night, there is no comfort—and we are not even
granted the solace of aesthetic beauty, for *Lenz* is uncompromising:
it is writing of utter provocation.

Perhaps this is the reason why, over the years, critics have striven
to tame it, to hold it on the leash of the familiar German 'Novelle'
genre by focusing on such traditional norms as the 'sich ereignete,
unerhörte Begebenheit' or a central 'Wendepunkt'.[2] Nowadays, critical reception is largely free from constraining classification. Some
of us have even come to cope with the gaps and view the fragmentary
aspect of the text as an integral part of the whole: the text is, after all,
'about' processes of fragmentation.

The landmark status of *Lenz* is beyond dispute. Ever since Gerhart
Hauptmann's lectures on Büchner in 1887, the text has figured as a
seminal work in German prose writing. Even in the history of medicine, it stands as an unsurpassed, literary study of schizophrenia.[3]
Also, it is a measure of its force that the narrative reverberates in
such twentieth century variations as Peter Schneider's *Lenz* (1973) or

9. "essay"; "novella" [*Editor*].
1. "searching"; "not finding"; "lost dreams" [*Editor*].
2. Goethe defined the subject matter of the *Novelle* (novella) as "an unheard-of event that
   has already occurred," while Ludwig Tieck (among others) emphasized the novella's
   need for a decisive "turning point." [*Editor*].
3. See, for example, Burghard Dedner, *Georg Büchner: 'Lenz'. Text und Kommentar*,
   Suhrkamp Basis Bibliothek (Frankfurt am Main, 1998), p. 110.

Ulrich Plenzdorf's *Die neuen Leiden des jungen W.* (1973), which is
driven not only by Goethe's *Werther*, but also by its intertextual connections with *Lenz*.

   Given this extraordinary degree of fame, it is difficult to add anything new to the vast secondary literature. In the following, therefore, I shall touch on familiar aspects, but combine them with a
structural argument and its interpretative ramifications. In the concluding section, I shall focus on those features which make the work
so distinctively part of its surrounding culture.

   Let me begin by addressing the basic presupposition on which
Lenz rests and which, I think, may affect our interpretative
approach. The story-line is perfectly clear, even in the above summary form. But, in fact, my account includes extra-textual information, some details in respect of the historical Lenz, Pastor Oberlin,
and Christoph Kaufmann. I now add that such names as Stilling
(p. 75) and Lavater (p. 78) refer to figures central to German culture in the late eighteenth century. This extra-textual aspect is, in
my view, highly significant: Büchner's text presupposes a degree of
knowledge which is most unusual for a nineteenth-century *Novelle*.
But: what if we do not have this knowledge? Is an ignorant reading
bound to be inadequate—or could it actually enrich our response,
generating interpretative issues beyond the historical specificity of
the text? The double-edged function of knowledge acquires particular urgency in respect of *Lenz*: to put it in a nutshell, I would
argue that the more knowledge we have of Lenz as a historical figure, the more likely are we to view the text in terms of a psychological documentary.

   This was clearly the case in the 1830s. At that time, the image of
Lenz was very much fixed, both positively and negatively. For the
radical intelligentsia, he was an icon of revolt, as though their frus-
trations were mirrored in his doomed 'Sturm und Drang' voice of
protest. In this context, the title under which Gutzkow published
the text is most revealing—it reads: *Lenz. Eine Reliquie von Georg
Büchner.* 'Reliquie', like our term 'relic' can mean a mere remnant
or a fragment held in reverence, be that in a religious or secular
sense. Gutzkow's edition clearly banks on both meanings: the text
is a fragment, yet it is proffered in a spirit of reverence. Placed at
the very centre, the term 'Reliquie' lends both Lenz and Büchner a
saintly aura. At the other end of the scale, the counter-image of
Lenz was equally fixed. For example, G. G. Gervinus sees Lenz as
both victim and perpetrator of the excesses associated with 'Sturm
und Drang' and 'Empfindsamkeit', and he condemns his lack of
'Sittlichkeit', his disorderly mind-set.[4] Julian Schmidt, advocate of

4. Quoted by Dedner, op. cit., pp. 94–6.

Poetic Realism, recognises Büchner's genius, but accuses him of wasting and degrading artistic energy by focusing on an unworthy protagonist, trapped in notions of 'absolutes Nichts'.[5] In short, in the nineteenth century, knowledge of the historical Lenz is such that Büchner's text tends to be read through ideologically tinged lenses: *Lenz* figures either as an elegiac tribute to the doomed hero of freedom, or as a documentary which warns against extravagant subjectivity. This polarisation again reminds one of *Werther*, its fluctuating reception history.

Whilst twentieth-century interpretations are much subtler, the interpretative model of *Lenz* as a documentary remains in place—in the modern guise of pathography, the writing of suffering. By far the best account is by Burghard Dedner, but he, too, imposes a purpose on the work: he holds that the text will refine our perception of mental illness, change our 'moralischen Reaktionen und Urteile',[6] and further our humane, compassionate capacity. This conception probably captures most readers' experience—the story is indeed compelling as an account of mental agony.

However, on a critical-theoretical perspective, the model of pathography poses a problem which, in the case of *Lenz*, is particularly acute. Generally speaking, pathography, unless it is autobiographical, figures its protagonist as an object, which is, in quasi-voyeuristic manner, spectated by the author as writing subject and by the reader. In this sense, non-autobiographical pathography runs at the very least the risk of exerting a measure of coercion over its object. As Christa Wolf reflects on the re-figuring of protagonist Christa T.: 'Ich verfüge über sie. [. . .] Etwas von Zwang ist unleugbar dabei.'[7] Given this element of coercion, a reading of *Lenz* along the lines of pathography may go against the very grain of Büchner's aesthetics, their ethical and political foundations which denounce any form of domination. To put it somewhat crassly: if we adopt pathography as an interpretative model, we are potentially in danger of replicating the Doktor in *Woyzeck* who presides as lofty subject over his abject medical object. Arguably, Dedner's conception of *Lenz* as pathography in the service of compassionate comprehension is a way out— but the function of pity has been a controversial issue since antiquity: at the very least potentially, pity is a form of domination.

Is *Lenz*, then, irrevocably caught up in power relations which run counter to Büchner's ethically grounded aesthetics? I do not think so. Rather, as I shall argue in the following, the poetic construction is such that the work moves beyond the traps of pathography. In

5. *Georg Büchner: 'Lenz'. Erläuterungen und Dokumente* (Stuttgart, 1987), pp. 96–7.
6. Dedner, op. cit., p. 55.
7. *Nachdenken über Christa T.*, (Berlin und Weimar, 1968), pp. 7, 9. ["I control her. . . . There is undeniably some coercion there."—*Editor's translation*].

this context, let us look at Büchner's main source, Pastor Oberlin's account, *Der Dichter Lenz, im Steinthale*.[8] His report is a documentary, and it shows all the marks of domination. He narrates as subject in the first person, and Lenz figures as object, monitored and, at times, judged. Oberlin follows the conventions of his time and argues, for example, that Lenz's mental agonies are due to a loose life-style and his rebellion against paternal authority.[9] However, at the very end of his account, Oberlin adopts a strikingly different stance: he now concedes that moral judgment is subjective—and, far more crucially, he admits that his account is fundamentally deficient because it remains trapped in descriptive representation, in the sayable:

> Jeder urteilt nach seinem besonderen Temperament [. . .] und nach der Vorstellung, die er sich von der ganzen Sache macht; die aber unmöglich getreu und richtig sein kann [. . .] weil es unmöglich wäre sie getreu zu beschreiben, und doch oft in einem Ton, in einem Blick, der nicht beschrieben werden kann, etwas steckt, das mehr bedeutet, als vorhergegangene erzählbare Handlungen.[1]

By stressing three times that the truth about Lenz lies beyond 'beschreiben', 'beschrieben werden' and 'erzählbare Handlungen', Oberlin abrogates the power of the narrating subject over narrated object.

As though heeding Oberlin's insights, Büchner situates his narrative at the margin of description, and adopts a compositional mode which turns narrative convention on its head. This much is anticipated at the very start of the text. As Lenz crosses the mountains, we are told 'Müdigkeit spürte er keine, nur war es ihm manchmal unangenehm, daß er nicht auf dem Kopf gehn konnte' (p. 69).[2] Similarly, at a later point, we read 'er amüsierte sich, die Häuser auf die Dächer zu stellen' (p. 86).[3] These two passages link back to my reflections on the hermeneutic function of knowledge and ignorance: if we are familiar with the historical figure of Lenz, we are likely to view these lines as documentary references to his noto-

---

8. Reprinted in Dedner, op. cit., pp. 63–76. See also John J. Parker: 'Some Reflections on Georg Büchner's *Lenz* and its principal source, the Oberlin record', *German Life & Letters*, 21 (1967–8), 103–11.

9. Dedner, op. cit., p. 73.

1. Dedner, op. cit., p. 76. ["Everyone judges according to his particular temperament . . . and according to the opinion he has of the whole matter; but it cannot be accurate and true, . . . because it would be impossible to describe it accurately, and indeed often in a tone, in a look that cannot be described there is something more meaningful than all those bygone events we can speak about"—*Editor's translation*].

2. "He felt no fatigue, but at times he was irritated that he could not walk on his head" (p. 84) [*Editor*].

3. "He amused himself by standing houses on their roofs" (p. 100) [*Editor*].

rious whimsicality. Conversely, if we do not have that knowledge—or choose not to bring it into play—we might see them as self-reflective pointers to precisely those narrative strategies in *Lenz* which turn conventional narrative and conceptual 'Häuser' on their 'Dächer'.

Let me elaborate on the key features. As we know, Büchner reduces the traditional narratorial voice to a minimum. True, he records 'erzählbare Handlungen', and such temporal markers as 'den andern Tag' (p. 71) or 'gegen Abend' (p. 72) establish a chronological sequence.[4] But overall, the narrator does not figure as a guiding, interpreting voice. Instead, he largely disappears in free indirect speech, the perspective of the protagonist. In other words: although there is narratorial distance in such recurrent phrases as 'er meinte' (p. 69) or 'es war ihm' (p. 74),[5] the overall momentum of the narrative is so strong that it overrides such fine points of distinction.

Consider here the extraordinary extent to which Büchner turns his back on narrative gradualness: he replaces it by suddenness, non-mediation, and sheer speed. We may know such traits from the works of Kleist, but in *Lenz* they are radicalised. They are systemic properties, informing every aspect—the narrative and stylistic structure, and the very lexis of the text. Take the opening paragraph which plunges us into the midst of things. Without the slightest exposition, we join Lenz suddenly, mid-walk, as he gropes his way across the mountain.

> er stand, keuchend, den Leib vorwärts gebogen, Augen und Mund weit offen, er meinte, er müsse den Sturm in sich ziehen, Alles in sich fassen, er dehnte sich aus und lag über der Erde, er wühlte sich in das All hinein, es war eine Lust, die ihm wehe tat; oder er stand still und legte das Haupt in's Moos und schloß die Augen halb [. . .]. Aber es waren nur Augenblicke, und dann erhob er sich nüchtern, fest, ruhig. (pp. 69–70)[6]

Both referentially and stylistically, these lines anticipate pervasive patterns in the subsequent text: unmediated twists and turns of Lenz's mood, behaviour, and dress, and the unpredictable flux of expansive sentences abruptly alternating with sharp, short, often syntactically incomplete phrases. On the level of lexis, there are similar discontinuities: for example, Lenz's urge to walk on his head may

---

4. "events we can speak about"; "the other day"; "towards evening" [*Editor*].
5. "he thought"; "it seemed to him" [*Editor*].
6. "He stood, panting, his body bent forward, eyes and mouth wide open, he though he must draw the storm into himself, contain all within him, he stretched out and lay over the earth, he burrowed into the cosmos, it was a pleasure that hurt him; or he stood still and rested his head on the moss and half-closed his eyes [. . .]. But these were only moments, and then he rose, calm, steady, quiet" (p. 85) [*Editor*].

take us aback, but the real sting lies in the fact that his inability to do so strikes him as 'unangenehm'. The word belongs to the social code of inconvenience, irritation, and hence is sharply discordant within the context. This one word anticipates the increasing collapse of common lexical and conceptual distinctions as epitomised in Lenz's reference to a screaming, 'entsetzliche Stimme [. . .] die man gewöhnlich die Stille heißt' (p. 88), or the passage: 'Er jagte mit rasender Schnelligkeit sein Leben durch und dann sagte er: "konsequent, konsequent"; wenn Jemand was sprach: "inkonsequent, inkonsequent" ' (p. 87).[7]

For the reader, all this generates a sense of increasing dizziness. As Friedrich Gundolf observes of *Lenz*: 'Die Grammatik selbst hat Eile'.[8] But, crucially, all this speed amounts to stasis. This text runs on the spot, for the protagonist's medical fate is sealed. This conjunction of speed and stasis is such that we are sucked into the maelstrom of both the narrative and its protagonist: the objectively distinct blends into a dense continuum—the continuum of circularity, the vicious circle of Lenz's mind-set. Here, Goethe's *Werther* may again come to mind: *Lenz* is in many ways a highly accelerated version of that novel. However, within the mono-perspectival narrative, Goethe does grant some space for critical reflection—Büchner does not.

Given that both the author and the reader double the vortex of Lenz's perception, the question arises if this is a textual black hole—textual matter so dense that it threatens to suck everything into its own abyss, on a par with some of Kafka's works, or, say, Samuel Beckett's *Krapp's Last Tape* and Thomas Bernhard's *Beton*. Not quite. Büchner's elliptic text and its protagonist are poised on the brink of the void, but on that very brink something remarkable happens: here, the force of the poetic turns Lenz on his head—turns him from object to subject.

True, on the referential level, Lenz is and will remain a powerless object, trapped in the grip of his medical condition, the all-pervasive 'Es' of drives beyond his control. But, in contrast to Oberlin's account, the very fabric of Büchner's text absorbs and reworks the pathology of schizophrenia such that key symptoms turn into poetic properties: Lenz's speech, with its fractured syntax and abrupt changes, turns into the very art of parataxis and ellipsis, the mastery of construction without connective particles; the violent changes of his behaviour and the frenzied 'Schnelligkeit' (p. 87) of

7. "The terrible voice, usually called silence"; "He rushed with blinding speed through his past life and then he said: consistent, consistent; when someone said something: inconsistent, inconsistent" (pp. 102, 101) [*Editor*].
8. In *Georg Büchner*, ed. by Wolfgang Martens, (Darmstadt, 1965), p. 92. ["The grammar itself is in a hurry"—*Editor's translation*].

his movements re-appear as musical tempo and rhythm; and his illogical associations are transmuted into passages of lyrical intensity. In short, Lenz as a patient is doomed, but by his very condition he becomes the poetic voice, the subject of the narrative. As such, he attains, to quote a key phrase from the 'Kunstgespräch', 'Leben, Möglichkeit des Daseins' (p. 76).[9]

As this suggests, I view the compositional principle of inversion as the most far-reaching aspect of *Lenz*. It re-interprets two features which were later to become central criteria of the German *Novelle*: the 'unerhörte Begebenheit' and the 'Wendepunkt'. Of course, on the referential level, the extraordinary event is retained in the shape of Lenz's mental condition. But far more radically, the narrative act itself, with its uncompromising provocative disposition, constitutes the 'unerhörte Begebenheit'. Hence, the notion of 'Wendepunkt'— *peripeteia*—also takes on a new meaning: it does not figure as a specific *point*, but becomes a *process*, a ceaseless flux of in-, re- and diversion as epitomised in this passage:

> Er lag in den heißesten Tränen, und dann bekam er plötzlich eine Stärke, und erhob sich kalt und gleichgültig, seine Tränen waren ihm dann wie Eis, er mußte lachen. Je höher er sich aufriß, desto tiefer stürzte er hinunter. (p. 80)[1]

Admittedly, Büchner's subject matter, the condition of schizophrenia and the historical data, have in themselves a disorientating energy; but it takes a poetic genius to condense and re-configure those facts such that they acquire highest destabilising intensity.

Take the very title: cut down to a minimum, it gains an interpretative potency which is utterly lacking in Oberlin's *Der Dichter Lenz, im Steinthale*: in the nineteenth century, the word 'Lenz' would signal poeticised, romantic spring-time. The opening setting—the figure of the 'Wanderer', the motifs of 'Wald', 'Wasser', 'grün' (p. 69), and of the village Waldbach (p. 70), crucially abridged from the real name Waldersbach, reinforce this expectation. One thinks of the 1820s, of Schubert's songs, of Heine's *Harzreise*. Yet: *Lenz* as a bitterly ironic *peripeteia* traces the descent into the permafrost of mental winter. Similarly, the name Friederike spells peace, but generates horror instead. I also suspect that Büchner, so attuned to word play, was aware of the semantic tensions in the name Oberlin: the conjunction of the comparative 'upper' with the diminutive 'lin' may be read as a pointer to the Pastor's superior position modified

9. "life, the possibility of existence" (p. 90) [*Editor*].
1. "He lay bathed in the hottest tears, and then suddenly strength returned, and he arose cold and indifferent, his tears were like ice then, he had to laugh. The higher he raised himself up, the deeper he fell" (p. 95) [*Editor*].

by his profound kindness, or as a quasi ironic pointer to the discrepancy between his spiritual authority and powerlessness over Lenz.

Whilst this is debatable, it is a matter of textual fact that Büchner builds frequently a 'Wendepunkt' into the very lexis and the motifs of his narrative. As we know, the text is dominated by such binary oppositions as cold/hot, close/far, high/low, 'weinen'/'lachen', and several others. These oppositions turn things quite literally on their head, and are thus central to the text's strategies of inversion. But above all, there are leitmotifs whose meaning is split. Take for example the most dominating—'Ruhe'. At times, it signifies total union, the Romantic dream of German 'Naturphilosophie': 'die mächtige Ruhe, die uns über der ruhenden Natur, im tiefen Wald, in mondhellen schmelzenden Mondnächten überfällt, schien ihm noch näher, in diesem ruhigen Auge' (p. 72).[2]

But 'Ruhe' also figures as the opposite, the calm of the void. The grip of atheism seizes Lenz 'ganz sicher und ruhig und fest' (p. 82), and at the end, 'Ruhe' spells the catatonic sense of resignation: on the journey back to Strasbourg, 'blieb er ganz ruhig sitzen; er war vollkommen gleichgültig' (p. 88).[3] Or take the leitmotif of 'Traum' and 'träumen'. On one level, it echoes *Werther*, the dream for harmonious fusion, Lenz's urge to 'traumartig jedes Wesen in der Natur in sich aufzunehmen' (p. 75).[4] It also figures as the dream of domestic paradise. The vicarage, with its 'heimliche Zimmer und die stillen Gesichter' (p. 70), brings back memories of yore: 'Er wurde ruhig, es war ihm als träten alte Gestalten, vergessene Gesichter wieder aus dem Dunkeln, alte Lieder wachten auf, er war weg, weit weg' (p. 71).[5]

But on another level, the motif denotes Lenz's loss of grip on reality—'als sei alles nur sein Traum' (p. 71)—his waning sense of selfhood—'er war sich selbst ein Traum' (p. 71)—and finally the nightmare of 'fieberhafte Träume' (p. 80).[6]

If such dominating terms are riddled with split meaning, it is hardly surprising that entire thematic strands may tip over and stand on their head. Take the clusters to do with religious faith, church, prayer. In one sense, they underwrite established Christian values: Oberlin's vicarage and the Sunday service suggest humane spiritual communion—'die Menschenstimmen begegneten sich im reinen

---

2. "the immense peace that comes upon us in nature at rest, in the deep forest, in moonlit, melting summer nights seemed even nearer to him in these calm eyes" (p. 87) [*Editor*].
3. "quite securely and calmly and firmly"; "he remained sitting quite calmly; he was totally indifferent" (pp. 97, 102) [*Editor*].
4. "to assimilate each being in nature as in a dream" (p. 90) [*Editor*].
5. "cozy room and the quiet faces"; "he grew calm, it seemed to him as if old shapes, forgotten faces were stepping out of the dark once again, old songs awoke, he was far, far away" (p. 86) [*Editor*].
6. "that all was but a dream"; "he felt himself to be a dream"; "feverish dreams" (pp. 87, 86, 95), [Editor].

hellen Klang' (p. 74).[7] Yet, turned upside down, the same clusters
take on a critical edge and pinpoint religiosity as a sinister, oppressive force. We remember the peaceful image of Oberlin's family
(p. 70), the Dutch painting of a woman who 'sitzt in ihrer Kammer,
das Gebetbuch in der Hand' (p. 77), the calm figure of Madame
Oberlin with her 'schwarze Gesangbuch' (p. 80), and the women of
the parish in their 'ernsten schwarzen Tracht, das weiße gefaltete
Schnupftuch auf dem Gesangbuche' (p. 72).[8] Yet this comforting
strand turns into its opposite when Lenz visits an isolated dwelling:
here, 'das heimliche Zimmer' (p. 70) of the vicarage is terrifyingly
transformed into a nightmarish scenario. A critically ill girl writhes
on her bed, an old woman sings in the shadows 'mit schnarrender
Stimme aus einem Gesangbuch', and they are joined by an old man,
'lang und hager', 'mit unruhigem, verwirrten Gesicht' (p: 79).[9] All
three figures are trapped in manic religiosity: throughout the night,
the singing continues, the girl, in her religious hallucinations, joins
in; and as morning dawns, the narrator conjures up a horrendously
inverted vision of resurrection:

> Der Mann erwachte, seine Augen trafen auf ein erleuchtetes
> Bild an der Wand, sie richteten sich fest und starr darauf, nun
> fing er an die Lippen zu bewegen und betete leise, dann laut
> und immer lauter. Indem kamen Leute zur Hütte herein, sie
> warfen sich schweigend nieder. Das Mädchen lag in Zuck-
> ungen, die Alte schnarrte ihr Lied und plauderte mit den
> Nachbarn. (p. 80)[1]

At such points, religiosity figures as a terrifying, dehumanising
force—and it is but a small step from these critical illuminations to
Lenz's rebellion against God and his contemptuous response to
Oberlin's faith: 'Ja, wenn ich so glücklich wäre, wie Sie, einen so
behaglichen Zeitvertreib aufzufinden [. . .] Alles aus Müßiggang.
Denn die Meisten beten aus Langeweile' (p. 84).[2]

A similar inversion affects the motif of domesticity, which is so
prevalent in nineteenth-century German writing, particularly in the
era of Biedermeier. Oberlin, his vicarage and his wife's calm presence
spell blissful security. Here, Lenz, the restless 'Wanderer', finds

7. "voices joined in clear, bright sound" (p. 89) [*Editor*].
8. "sits in her room holding a prayer book"; "black hymnal"; "somber black dresses, a
   folded white handkerchief on the hymnal" (pp. 92, 95, 88) [*Editor*].
9. "from a hymnal in a droning voice"; "tall and thin"; "with a restless, perplexed face"
   (pp. 93–94) [*Editor*].
1. "The man awoke, his eyes met an illuminated picture on the wall, he stared at it fixedly,
   then he began to move his lips and pray softly, then ever louder. Meanwhile people
   entered the hut, they sat down in silence. The girl was in convulsions, the old woman
   droned her song and chatted with the neighbors" (p. 94) [*Editor*].
2. "yes, if I were as happy as you to have found such a comforting pastime [. . .] Everything out of boredom. For most people pray out of boredom" (p. 98) [*Editor*].

peace—just as, back in the 1770s, Goethe's Faust and Werther find peace in the domestic order of Gretchen and Lotte. The motif of idyllic domesticity is further underpinned by Lenz's invocation of Dutch painting in the seventeenth century: 'Es ist sonntäglich aufgeputzt, der Sand gestreut, so heimlich rein und warm' (p. 77).[3] And yet: at the most critical point of the narrative, the very notion of domesticity is violently rejected: Lenz the prodigal son refuses to return home. Büchner only hints at the conflict between the historical Lenz and his father, but he stresses the sheer stifling force of domesticity, the family as a breeding ground of neurosis. As Lenz exclaims: 'und dann wieder herunter in's Haus, durch den Garten gehn, und zum Fenster hineinsehen,—ich würde toll! toll!' (p. 78)[4] The tensions which inform Büchner's representation of domestic space culminate in his handling of traditional spatial markers of security, of law and order: overall, he both invokes and erases them. The 'Pfarrhaus' and the 'Schulhaus', where Lenz sleeps, epitomise spaces of *nomos*, representing stabilising systems and institutions, be that in the religious or secular sense. However their force disintegrates as Lenz invades and, like a menacing Poltergeist, plays havoc.[5] As the disturbance reaches crisis point, Oberlin finds a guard, the schoolmaster Sebastian, who in turn calls for further help from his brother: 'und nun hatte Lenz zwei Aufseher start einen' (p. 85).[6] Yet even now he escapes, 'wie ein Blitz' (p. 85),[7] the clutches of control, until, exhausted, he finally surrenders.

The above patterns of split meaning and inversion reflect deep-seated patterns of irresolution, and they link with some of the most crucial intellectual currents of his time. So let us now, in conclusion, look at the literary-cultural location of *Lenz*. Of course, in the most immediate sense, the discontinuities which I have traced reflect Lenz's medical condition. But beyond this, they mirror the cultural schizophrenia of both the late eighteenth century and above all the 1830s. Here, mutually incompatible strands merge: late Romanticism alongside Biedermeier, Christian legacy alongside the growing critique of religion, humanist thought next to the materialist discourse of science, and conservatism next to revolutionary politics. Like a cultural kaleidoscope, *Lenz* mirrors the shifting patterns of these often contrary aspects and in this sense it is, to use Gérard Genette's term, truly transtextual.

3. "Everything is cleaned up for Sunday, the sand strewn on the floor, so comfortably clean and warm" (p. 92) [*Editor*].
4. "and then back into the house, walk though the garden and look in through the window. I'd go mad! Mad!" (p. 92) [*Editor*].
5. This culminates in the struggle between Lenz and Oberlin's cat. Quite overtly, Büchner's description relies here on the code of the horror tale (p. 100). The motif of the 'Katze' reappears in *Woyzeck*.
6. "now Lenz had two guardians instead of one" (p. 99) [*Editor*].
7. "like a flash" (p. 99) [*Editor*].

As there is no space here to touch on the many links with nineteenth-century thought, I shall largely focus on the issue of religion which is a thematic centre in the text. Let us turn first to the anthropological thinker Ludwig Feuerbach (1804–72). He would, I suspect, keenly appreciate that both *Woyzeck* and *Lenz* focus on mental illness and that even *Dantons Tod* is as much about the mind as it is about politics: in his search for a better humanity in the here and now, Feuerbach invokes the method of medical diagnosis and is driven by the aim to explore the internal and external factors which contribute to the diseases of the head and of the heart of mankind. Like Büchner, he vehemently rejects German idealism and replaces the abstract 'Idee' by a fundamental stress on sensuous love and interpersonal community. However, as regards the representation of religion in *Lenz*, he would have some reservations. As we know, Feuerbach dismantles the notion of a transcendental deity and instead advocates faith in the divine force of love inherent in humanity. Hence he would approve of Lenz's rebellion against god: its revolutionary energy anticipates his own equation of orthodox theology and oppressive monarchy:

> Er rannte auf und ab. In seiner Brust war ein Triumph-Gesang der Hölle. Der Wind klang wie ein Titanenlied, es war ihm, als könnte er eine ungeheure Faust hinauf in den Himmel ballen und Gott herbei reißen und zwischen seinen Wolken schleifen. (p. 82)[8]

However, Feuerbach would abhor the nihilism of the concluding moment—'als könnte er die Welt mit den Zähnen zermalmen und sie dem Schöpfer in's Gesicht speien' (p. 82).[9] To this degree, he would share Lenz's subsequent horror, but would re-interpret 'die Sünde wider den heiligen Geist' (p. 82)[1] as sin against the divine spirit of love for humanity. Overall, Feuerbach would argue that Lenz's schizophrenia is an acute case of self-alienation, of man split from himself, brought about by his preoccupation with Christian theology. In particular, he would trace neurotic feelings of guilt back to Lenz's reading the Bible, above all the apocalyptic visions of Revelations (p. 75). At this juncture we might recall Karl Marx (1818–83)—not the young Marx, who still invokes the traditional deity, but the later thinker who defined the task of philosophy as the critique of religion which would ultimately lead to the exposure of all conditions

8. "He ran up and down. Hell's song of triumph was in his breast. The wind sounded like a song of titans, he felt as if he could thrust a gigantic fist up into Heaven and tear God down and drag Him through His clouds" (pp. 96–97) [*Editor*].

9. "as if he could grind up the world in his teeth and spit it into the Creator's face" (p. 97) [*Editor*].

1. "the sin against the Holy Ghost" (p. 97) [*Editor*].

debasing the human being. As we know from his *Thesen über Feuerbach* (1845), Marx would remind us that although Feuerbach remains trapped in abstraction, his efforts to reveal religion as a form of self-alienation are praiseworthy. As regards *Lenz*, I suspect the greatest stumbling block for Marx would be the recurrent passages of idyllic domesticity, and above all those sections which seem to endorse the Christian theology of suffering. Take the verse which Büchner adds to a standard Pietist hymn and which speaks of 'heil'gen Schmerzen', of suffering as worship:

> Leiden sei all mein Gewinst,
> Leiden sei mein Gottesdienst. (p. 74)[2]

At this point, discussion would get rather heated: Marx would either condemn the passage, or he would propose to read it as a bitterly ironic reflection of Christian false consciousness, which veils the stifling socio-economic and cultural conditions in Waldbach— and all the communities which it represents in both the eighteenth and nineteenth century. In his defence, Marx would invoke those sections in the text where, as in *Dantons Tod*, suffering functions as the bedrock of atheism. As Lenz puts it: 'wär' ich allmächtig, sehen Sie, wenn ich so wäre, ich könnte das Leiden nicht ertragen, ich würde retten, retten' (p. 87).[3] Marx has a point: the function of religious faith in Büchner's life and work remains an open question.[4]

To lend this debate a twentieth-century angle, let us turn briefly to Freud. He would of course agree that religion is an illusory comfort, but would then, presumably, launch into a lengthy psychoanalytical reading of the text. One can imagine him homing in on Lenz's feelings of guilt towards his father on earth and in heaven, his mother and his beloved Friederike—and, surely, he would theorise Lenz's compulsive urge to 'baden' in the fountain of the vicarage. In his account, Oberlin notes at one point: 'Er stürzte sich, wie gewöhnlich, in den Brunnentrog, patschte drin, wieder heraus und hinauf in sein Zimmer, wieder hinunter in den Trog, und so einige Mai—endlich wurde es still' (p. 364).[5] Büchner quotes this passage almost verbatim, and the motif of 'baden' recurs with such intensity that Freud would, rightly, insist on reading it as Lenz's neurotic need to cleanse himself of his feelings of guilt and to re-enact the ritual of Christian baptism. I would suggest, however, that we might

---

2. "May pain be my reward / Through pain I love my lord" [*Editor*].
3. "but I, if I were almighty, you see, if I were, and I couldn't bear this suffering, I would save, save" (p. 101) [*Editor*].
4. See, for example, the letter to his family of 1 January 1836 (*Werke*, p. 279).
5. "He threw himself, as usual, into the basin of the fountain, splashed about in it, out again and up to his room, down again into the basin, and so on several times—at last it was quiet" [*Editor's translation*].

adopt a further interpretative perspective: given that patterns of inversion are so central to *Lenz*, we might give the motif a Feuerbachian twist as it were: on this perspective, Lenz's urge to 'baden' shifts from a pathological trait to a rebellious contrafacture, which turns the submissive immersion of Christian baptism on its head.

This brings us back to the centre of my argument—*Lenz* as a text of and about inversion. It is this aspect which, I think, links the work most profoundly to nineteenth-century German thought. Inversion is, in one form or the other, central to the thought of Feuerbach, Marx and Engels with their trope of the Camera obscura or retina which perceive things 'auf den Kopf gestellt', as 'Umdrehung',[6] and it culminates in Friedrich Nietzsche. The connections between Büchner and Nietzsche are considerable, but let me sketch in some key points in respect of *Lenz*.

Take the issue of 'beschreiben' and 'erzählbare Handlungen'. Like most critics, I pointed out that the sequence of facts, which are often closely observed, remains unexplained in the absence of an interpretatively guiding narrator. As Arnold Zweig put it so succinctly: 'Ein Mensch wird wahnsinnig, punktum, und das wird erzählt.'[7] As we know, the reader, let alone the critic, finds it hard to live with the non-mediated given, with the 'Punktum' that is also the very basis of Kafka's *Die Verwandlung* or *Der Proceß* where the chaplain, at the end of the penultimate chapter, drives home the tantalising point of interpretation: 'Die Schrift ist unveränderlich, und die Meinungen sind oft nur ein Ausdruck der Verzweiflung darüber.'[8] It is Nietzsche who captures that sense of despair when he notes: 'Wir beschreiben besser—wir erklären ebensowenig, wie alle Früheren.'[9] As regards Lenz, he would, with Büchner, turn him from object to subject. Even without philosophical knowledge, most readers surely sense that the protagonist's dislocated perception has at times that revelatory authority which we associate with so-called mad figures, be that in ancient Greek mythology, in Shakespeare, or in Büchner's *Woyzeck*. At their most unsettling, such voices show up both the sanity of insanity and the insanity of sanity.[1] As Gräfin Orsina, the abandoned, 'mad' woman, in Lessing's *Emilia Galotti* (1772), points out: 'Wer über gewisse Dinge den

6. See *Die deutsche Ideologie*, in Karl Marx, Friedrich Engels, *Werke*, [East] Berlin, 1969, Vol. 3, p. 26.
7. Quoted by Dedner, op.cit., p. 105. ["A person goes crazy, period, and that's the story"—*Editor's translation*.]
8. "The text is unalterable, and opinions are often just an expression of despair about it." [*Editor's translation.*]
9. *Die fröhliche Wissenschaft*, *Werke*, Vol. 2, ed. by K. Schlechta (Munich, 1955), p. 119. ["We describe better—we explain just as little as our predecessors"—*Editor's translation*].
1. See, for example, Janet K. King, 'Lenz viewed sane', *The Germanic Review*, 4 (1974), 146–53.

Verstand nicht verlieret, der hat keinen zu verlieren' (IV, 7); and if
Büchner's Danton could have read *Lenz*, he would surely have commented: 'Das lautet verrückt, es ist aber doch was Wahres daran'
(p. 55).[2] In *Lenz*, the pathological condition of schizophrenia repeatedly takes on an epistemological force. Within nineteenth-century
philosophy, Lenz's (and Woyzeck's) difficulty with articulation, the
common meaning of things, and the elliptical nature of the text as
such acquire a powerful anticipatory force: they point forward to
Nietzsche's conclusion that the authority of language and logic is
but illusory, that 'die Worte liegen uns im Wege'[3]—and, ultimately,
they anticipate the very basis of 'Sprachkritik' in twentieth-century
philosophy.

The deadly calm of Lenz's life back in Strasbourg may remind us
of the recognition at the heart of Nietzsche's *Morgenröte*—the
insight into 'die Unmöglichkeit der Erkenntnis'?[4]—and of his insistence on that highest form of wisdom which simply endures personal
and the world's suffering: a 'Weisheit [. . .] die sich ungetäuscht
[. . .] mit unbewegtem Blicke dem Gesamtbild der Welt zuwendet'.[5]
But the difference is telling: Nietzsche insists on the cathartic force
of the tragic—*Lenz* grants us no such solace:

> Er schien ganz vernünftig, sprach mit den Leuten; er tat Alles
> wie es die Andern taten, es war aber eine entsetzliche Leere in
> ihm, er fühlte keine Angst mehr, kein Verlangen; sein Dasein
> war ihm eine notwendige Last.—So lebte er hin.[6]

2. "Anyone who doesn't lose their mind over certain things, doesn't have one to lose" [*Editor's translation*]. "That sounds crazy, but there's some truth to it" (p. 69) [*Editor*].
3. *Morgenröte*, ed. cit., Vol. 1, p. 1045. ["Words lie in our way"—*Editor's translation*.]
4. Loc. cit., p. 1242. ["the impossibility of knowledge"—*Editor's translation*].
5. *Die Geburt der Tragödie*, ed. cit., Vol. 1, p. 101. "wisdom . . . undeceived . . . turns with
a fixed gaze toward the total picture of the world"—[*Editor's translation*].
6. The last two sentences of *Lenz* [*Editor*].

Leonce and Lena

THOMAS BERNHARD

Leonce and Lena: Tragic Comedy by Georg Büchner[†]

Leonce is the hereditary prince of Georg Büchner's poetic "fairy tale" of the middle of the last century, which is to say he is the young Büchner himself, that spirit who wants "to be someone else for once! Just for one minute." What he seeks is unfathomable, his life exhausts itself on the surface and in the baseness of the environment. He is "so young and yet so old," a king's son and an idler, a person without a name and without knowledge of Creation, a "fool" in a world of shamelessness that consists largely of calculation and greed.

The play is a tragedy from beginning to end. In it uncanny things happen. People appear like shadows around Leonce, the "useless one," and he has to use them as one might use a toy and then throw it away: Valerio, the valet, "his happiness," the man without cares, the friend of all things, for whom the sun is a pub sign and the earth a table on which one eats oneself to death. What really matters to him is not meaning but being!—Rosetta, the dancer, lightfooted, profound and heart-wrenching in her simplicity; she just wants to love and nothing more. And, as the high point of Büchner's "that which is and cannot be otherwise," there appears the court of the "marionettes of the flesh," the world of officials that he felt at first hand, that he hated to the core: King Peter, who wants to marry Leonce with Lena, the Master of Ceremonies, the President of the State Council, the General, the Court Chaplain (perhaps the best of the supporting characters), the District Magistrate, and a doctor; caricatures such as the day draws for us. "It is not the brotherhood of man I love—and lament," Leonce might say. And he calls them but creatures, cripples of the will, have-nots of the

† From *Georg Büchner und die Moderne, Band 2,* edited by Dietmar Goldschnigg, 252–253. Berlin: Erich, Schmidt Verlag, 2002. Translated by Matthew Wilson Smith. One of the most prominent Austrian writers of the twentieth century, Thomas Bernhard (1931–1989) is known for his novels (including *Das Kalkwerk* [*The Lime Works,* 1970], *Korrektur* [*Correction,* 1975], and *Holzfällen* [*Woodcutters,* 1984]), as well as plays and short stories.

spirit, the sweet topping atop the wobbly cake of life that one must spit out to so as not to upset one's gut. Even Lena, the beautiful princess to whom he finally turns with a sort of ludicrous reasonableness just before going mad, is not of flesh and blood. If the play ends with the "wedding" of the couple, Büchner does not mean to say that this is the final and only happiness, because for him happiness, which humanity craves so bitterly, is no earthly thing. *Leonce and Lena* scarcely has a storyline, only a frame, it is like a monologue that works in a fatally direct way and cuts into the flesh; for any of us, whoever we may be. It smells of roses, of putrefaction, and of the stars of the firmament. The humor here is so serious that there is no point in the play where one can laugh! Büchner's label "comedy" is comprehensible only as a bitter pill: that life is just that, a comedy.

ANDREW WEBBER

Büchner, *Leonce und Lena*†

Like *Woyzeck, Leonce und Lena*—the courtly, or pseudo-courtly comedy of 1836 that was written in parallel with Büchner's tragedy of the common man—is only available to us as a reconstruction, based on manuscript material that is largely lost. While the generally accepted form of the text is certainly more finished than *Woyzeck*, questions of incompletion and uncertain transmission prevail, undermining any claim to authenticity of origin. This equivocal status is, in fact, peculiarly suitable for a drama like *Leonce und Lena*, one that, as we shall see, teasingly resists ideas of literary originality and authenticity.

Also like *Woyzeck*, or indeed *Dantons Tod, Leonce und Lena* is a hybrid form of drama. Just as Büchner's versions of social and historical tragedy involve a dialogue with other generic forms which have more affinity with comedy—deploying the techniques of burlesque, pantomime, and puppet theatre—so his exercise in comedy maintains a relationship to the darkness and nihilism of his tragedies, and so to the last questions of life and death. While early commentators tended to bracket *Leonce und Lena* off from the serious dramas, as what Hans Mayer called a 'romantisch-ironisches Zwischenspiel',[1] the interlude in fact has more in common with the canonical tragedies with which it ostensibly breaks than they supposed. This 'Zwischenspiel' actively *plays between* the other dramas,

---

† From *Landmarks in German Comedy*, edited by Peter Hutchinson, 79–94. New York: Peter Lang, 2006. Reprinted by permission.
1. *Georg Büchner und seine Zeit* (Wiesbaden, 1946), p. 307. ["romantic-ironic interlude"— *Editor's translation*.]

pointing up the elements of romantic irony and burlesque that they share with it,[2] while reflecting in less obvious forms their earnest existential and political concerns.

Much criticism of the play has to do with its more or less blatantly derivative character. Scholars have identified in it a tissue of borrowings and echoes, explicit or implicit, from a whole series of earlier comic works by authors ranging from Shakespeare to Musset, Tieck, and Brentano.[3] While *Dantons Tod* and *Woyzeck* both derive much of their shape (in the case of *Dantons Tod* a large part of the dialogue) from documentary sources, this form of textual appropriation has tended to be seen as legitimate, while the co-option of ideas and linguistic turns from other texts in the a-historical and self-consciously literary *Leonce und Lena* has provoked antagonism.[4] Mayer's criticism of Büchner's characters as voracious readers who have come to speak like the books they have read, leading second-hand literary lives, is characteristic of this tendency.[5] And while Maurice Benn resists that sort of judgement in his account of the play's 'kaleidoscope of tones',[6] he too finds the 'fertility of Büchner's comic imagination' wanting, its comedic repertoire mechanical and repetitious (p. 180).

More recent critics have been willing to give *Leonce und Lena* its due as a masterpiece of comic invention and reinvention, as well as a play with a more serious aesthetic and ethical basis. John Reddick, for instance, sees in the play not empty derivation but a 'brilliant montage' of source materials.[7] The following reading will follow Reddick's lead in seeing the play's lack of originality, its recycling of received material, as an aesthetic strategy. And so, it will stake a claim to the play's status as a landmark of the German comedy tradition. In a scholarly climate more attuned to dialogical relations than the singular voice of the author, more to questions of construction than of originality, the extensive, playful intertextuality of *Leonce und Lena* demands to be seen anew. It is a drama

---

2. Thus both *Dantons Tod* and *Woyzeck* have versions of the fool figure. In *Woyzeck* there is the 'Narr' who idiotically mocks the protagonist and his powers of speech at the height of his tragedy. And in *Dantons Tod* there is Simon the burlesque prompter, as much a fabrication of theatrical quotations as the characters of *Leonce und Lena*. He has, as it were, wandered onstage out of the prompter's pit to suggest that the life-and-death action of this drama is always also a theatrical construction.

3. For an account of many of the sources, see Walter Hinderer, *Büchner-Kommentar zum dichterischen Werk* (Munich, 1977), pp. 129–58.

4. Perhaps most extremely, Peter Hacks accuses Büchner of brazen artistic theft from Tieck's *Zerbino* in 'Die freudlose Wissenschaft', *Sinn und Form* 43,1 (1991), 76–90.

5. 'Leonce, aber, Lena, Valerio und alle die anderen Gestalten des Märchenspuks haben vor allem sehr viele Bücher gelesen. Prinz und Vielfraß, Prinzessin und empfindsame alte Jungfer führen ein Leben aus zweiter Hand.' Hans Mayer, *Georg Büchner und seine Zeit*, p. 310.

6. *The Drama of Revolt: A Critical Study of Georg Büchner* (Cambridge, 1976), p. 162.

7. *Georg Büchner: The Shattered Whole* (Oxford, 1994), p. 217.

which, in its citational excesses, can be seen to preview—and to have a melancholic laugh at—what has come to be called the post-modern condition, a condition given to simulacra, without meta-physical bearings and grand narratives to guide it. It could be seen, in this light, as a precursor to Beckett's *Waiting for Godot*, a play in which very little happens, repeatedly, but which gives a compelling and darkly comic form to the drama of being.

That Büchner understood the writing of his 'Lustspiel' as a fabri-cation can be seen from references to it in his letters. Here, the composition of the play is ironically distanced from the idea of the original creation of literary life by being aligned with processes of compilation, imitation, and masquerade. If one of the play's early readers, Friedrich Gundolf, criticised it and its origins as 'papiern',[8] then Büchner pre-empts this criticism of the paper construction in his own account of the drama's genesis in a letter to his brother of September 1836: 'Dabei bin ich gerade daran, sich einige Men-schen auf dem Papier totschlagen oder verheiraten zu lassen, und bitte den lieben Gott um einen einfältigen Buchhändler und ein groß Publikum mit so wenig Geschmack, als möglich' (p. 321).[9] Creative writing is a material necessity for the impoverished Büch-ner, who produces the play as an entry for a comedy competition run by the Cotta Verlag. Writing is thus reduced to the tasteless work of putting text to page, with life and death as scripted effects of paper and ink. As Ferdinand Knapp has pointed out in his dandy-istic reading of *Leonce und Lena*, the text is also figured as costume and shaped around the body.[1] Thus, the manuscript is a tailored covering for life rather than embodying the thing itself. Out of the text he spreads, Büchner cuts the means to clothe himself, as described in a letter of June 1836: 'Ich muß eine Zeitlang vom lieben Kredit leben und sehen, wie ich mir in den nächsten 6–8 Wochen Rock und Hosen aus meinen großen Papierbogen, die ich vollschmieren soll, schneiden werde' (p. 317).[2] And yet he also resists the idea of such an instrumental tailoring of the text, sug-gesting in a letter to his family of September 1836 that works such as *Leonce und Lena* cannot be cut to order 'wie der Schneider mit

8. *Romantiker* (Berlin, 1930), pp. 390–91.

9. All references to Büchner's writings are to Georg Büchner, *Werke und Briefe*, ed. by Karl Pörnbacher et al. (Munich, 1988). ["Right now I'm occupied with letting several people kill each other or get married on paper, and I beg the dear Lord for a simple-minded publisher and a large audience with as little good taste as possible" (p. 191).— Editor.]

1. *Dandyism as a Principle of Aesthetic Composition: A Study of Georg Büchner, Franz Kafka and Oswald Wiener* (Unpublished dissertation, University of Cambridge, 2002), pp. 55–87. Various ideas in the current essay derive from discussions with the author of that dissertation.

2. "I need to live for a while on credit and see how I'll cut myself a jacket and pants from my big sheets of paper, which I should be scribbling all over" [*Editor's translation*].

seinem Kleid' (p. 321).[3] Both of the figures deployed here, papering
and tailoring, recur in the drama itself and suggest an awareness of
the constructed character of the literary text, where life—to evoke
the play's dénouement—is only ever present *in effigie*, in the mode
of the simulacrum. And yet Büchner's wish to distance himself
from, even as he embraces, the role of literary tailor suggests that
the costumed effigy following the fashion of Romantic comedy,
might make certain claims on the realities of life in spite of itself.

The motto to the play's first act, derived from Shakespeare's *As
You Like It*, indicates something of the ambivalent character of the
style that it adopts:

O wär' ich doch ein Narr!
Mein Ehrgeiz geht auf eine bunte Jacke.

The lines, derived from a play so given to doubling, travesty, and
usurpation, announce above all the adoption of role-play. Shakespeare's Jacques is one of that play's double figures, a melancholy
courtier whose courtly ambition is strangely skewed, ambitious as
he is 'for a motley coat'. He yearns to be a proper fool like Touchstone, but is only able to conceive of wearing the clothes of folly.
Folly here then is seen as a costume, a function of performance,
but one to which the melancholy Jacques can only aspire second-
hand. Melancholy and folly are thus tailored into a reversible coat,
one fashioned—as we shall see—around their peculiar, and peculiarly correlative, anatomies.[4] The motto, ventriloquised from Shakespeare, is less an act of hubris, as some critics have suggested, than
an imitation of the ambivalent configuration of melancholy and
comedy. While the comic fool and the melancholic share an affinity, folly remains a fantasy costume that the melancholic is ill able
to adopt, whatever his ambitions. By this citational gesture, Büchner's 'Lustspiel' at once tries on the clothes of Shakespearean comedy as an element in its motley garb of literary stylings and suggests
that that costume cannot simply be taken as the authentic identity
of the drama. Beneath the costume of folly is a deep-seated historical and existential melancholy.

Leonce und Lena has three such 'jackets' around it, with a further
motto at the head of the play and another at the start of the second
act. They have an ambiguous status as at once part of the text and
yet, presumably, unspoken—operating on a literary rather than
a performance level. The double character of the Shakespeare

---

3. "like a tailor with his dress" [*Editor's translation*].
4. The misshaping of bodily behaviour in comedy shares certain features of exaggeration
   with that of melancholy, as, famously anatomised by Burton in 1632. The special relationship between comedy and melancholy is recognised by both Kierkegaard and
   Freud.

quotation is also in evidence in the other two. The opening motto
introduces the idea of citation as imposture, with the lines 'e la
fama?' ('and what of fame?') and 'e la fame?' ('and what of famine?'),
misattributed to two eighteenth-century Italian writers: the trage-
dian Alfieri and the comic dramatist Gozzi (p. 160). If these lines
are emblematically juxtaposed at the head of the drama as equiva-
lents of the comic and tragic masks, then they are masks in a more
dissimulating sense. The snatch from a fantasy drama, played out
by dramatists, works as a kind of false mirroring; it is a structure of
repetition that reverses the ideal (fame) into the material (hunger),
plenitude into lack, the tragic into the comic, the offstage world of
dramatists into the onstage world of the play. It prepares us for a
drama of imposture, repetition, and switching. And the motto at
the start of the second act is no less teasing a piece of motley. Here,
the voice is quoted from the poem 'Die Blinde' by the Romantic
poet Chamisso—or, rather, misquoted. While it appeals to the idea
of a Romantic voice, bringing about an elision of memory and the
inner self ('Erinnern' and 'Innern'), the voice is operating here in
masquerade (p. 174). The difference between the poise of the original verse and Büchner's more laboured rendition indicates once
more that the versions of the Romantic voice that we hear within the
drama proper are at an ironic remove from the 'real' thing, symptomatic perhaps of the lapsed memory described in the lines. At the same
time it introduces a melancholic tension, a gesture of existential loss,
of oblivion, into the version of Romantic comedy that Büchner con-
structs here.

The motley costume of Shakespearian comedy comes to Büchner
second-hand, via the fashionable German Romantic dramas of the
early nineteenth century. Like Heine or Hoffmann, Büchner shows
himself here to be, or to be performing as, a Romantic ironist of the
second order.[4] He takes the fantasy flights of first-order Romantics
like Brentano and Tieck, with their fairy-tale frameworks and capri-
cious humour, and subjects these to ironic reworking, to a form of
performance that is always looking awry at itself, aware of its own
character as pastiche. Not for nothing does the fool Valerio masquerade in the clothes of Goethe's Werther, enacting a mock version of
the proto-Romantic hero *par excellence* and turning Werther's blue
and yellow costume into a kind of motley.

While *Leonce und Lena* is confected out of an extensive intertextual network, Brentano's comedy, *Ponce de Leon* (1801), is its
prime source. Büchner's title in itself, eliding Ponce and Leon into

---

4. The discussion here of Büchner's second order Romanticism expands on a section on
   Leonce und Lena in my essay 'The Afterlife of Romanticism', in *German Literature of
   the Nineteenth Century, 1832–1899*, ed. by Clayton Koelb and Eric Downing, Vol. 9 of
   Camden House History of German Literature (Rochester, 2005), pp. 23–43.

the figure of Leonce, indicates that the play will be an echoing fabrication after Brentano's model, an exercise in the ludic performance of citation. Büchner develops a fantasia on the principal themes of Brentano's drama, with Leonce following the eponymous Ponce in cultivating aristocratic melancholy born of existential langour, or *far niente*, and a plot which leads through playful, masquerading diversions towards a resolution of the romance intrigue. While Brentano borrows the clothes for his play from a range of sources—Shakespeare, Spanish Golden Age drama, and *commedia dell'arte*—Büchner's text is a borrowing at second hand, one which takes the figures of ambiguous or artificial identity in *Ponce de Leon* and subjects these to hyperbolic reworking. In particular, the mask and the automaton, which Brentano employs as theatrical devices in order first to complicate and then to resolve riddles of identity and relationship in his drama, are redeployed by Büchner to leave the distinction between artifice and authenticity profoundly unclear to the end. While the couples at the end of *Ponce de Leon* are revealed and made ready for true wedding in the conventional romance style, the marriage of Leonce and Lena is conducted under false pretences, a performance by automata that is set to be replayed at will. And the figure of the masked performing automaton also stands for a fabricated, repetitive performance of human discourse. Büchner adopts the wordplay of Brentano's characters, their playful linguistic masquerading, and produces out of it an intense self-reflexivity. Like the masks within masks that Valerio peels off, or his puns within and upon puns, the play is constructed in the style of an elaborate *mise-en-abyme* or Chinese box. And at the core of the self-reflexive playing is a sense of absence: the possibility that Valerio might peel himself away to nothing, revealing nonentity at the heart of identity, or that Leonce might smash the walls of the theatrical 'Spiegelzimmer' of a world in which he finds himself (p. 174). The broken mirrors, which are one of the figures that Büchner cites from *Ponce de Leon*, serve as an emblem of the fragmentary reflection of his source text and its Romantic conventions that Büchner undertakes. Behind the 'Lustspiel' of mirrorings, both external and internal, lies the prospect of naked emptiness.

The play's reiterative Romantic theatricality has a profoundly ambivalent character. While the engineering of comedy under the sign of romance is mocked here, and thus used as a vehicle for the satirical exposure of feudal structures, the comic drama seems ready to take on a less instrumental life of its own. Romantic fantasy is certainly parodied in the play, but it also exerts a seductiveness that threatens to become autonomous, freeing itself from the playwright's declared political agenda. The rhetorical postures of the Romantic prince and princess or the exuberant playfulness of Valerio's punning create an aesthetic surplus which seems to be produced for its own sake, perhaps not without a degree of nostalgic indulgence in the creative licence and political irresponsibility which the Romantic model allows.

At the same time, the figure of the masked automaton embodies a darker side to the appropriation of the Romantic model. While in *Ponce de Leon*, the automaton is unmasked at the end as a figure in the role of *deus ex machina*, resolving the play of false identities and introducing order into the play's relationships, *Leonce und Lena* effects a different sort of resolution *ex machina*, transforming its protagonists into repeating machines. Büchner appears to expose here the sort of cultural apparatus of fantasy which sustains prevailing systems of oppression (not for nothing does Leonce propose to build a theatre and fashion his puppet-subjects after his own fantasies). But he also perhaps recognises, in a more uncanny sense, the limitations of his own attempts at theatrical intervention in the course of history, exposing himself as another Leonce, indulging in play and replay. The marriage of the automata Leonce and Lena incorporates into the mock-Romantic drama the writer's real sense of Romantic hauntedness, the idea that he is surrounded by human automata and might himself be nothing more than an undead character in a *Fantasiestück* by Hoffmann.[5] In other words, Büchner's text seems to be inwardly transformed by the darker implications of its Romantic intertext, unable to keep it at an ironic distance.

In order to consider in more detail how Büchner's version of Romantic comedy works, it is worth thinking about the workings of comedy on a more theoretical level. If comedy is relatively under-theorised, compared with other generic categories, there is a theoretical literature that can be useful to us here. While the second part of Aristotle's *Poetics*, devoted to Comedy, has been lost, the extant text does give some indication of the direction it might have taken. Comedy, for Aristotle, follows the same fundamental principle of mimesis—imitation of the real—as Tragedy and Epic, but with a particular twist: 'Comedy, as we said, is mimesis of baser but not wholly vicious characters: rather, the laughable is one category of the shameful. For the laughable comprises any fault or mark of shame which involves no pain or destruction: most obviously, the laughable mask is something ugly and twisted, but not painfully.'[6]

---

5. In a letter of March 1834 to his fiancée, Büchner describes a feeling of living death and a morbid fear of himself such that he could pose for "Herrn Callot-Hoffmann" (p. 287). The doubling of Hoffmann with the artist Jacques Callot, whose etchings inspired his *Prinzessin Brambilla*, indicate the sort of chain of identification which Büchner's own citational practices establish, not least in relation to Romantic sources.

6. *Poetics*, ed. and transl. by Stephen Halliwell (Cambridge, Mass., & London, 1995), p. 45.

The mimetic mask of Comedy is thus cast in a distorted form as a figuration of shame at the laughable vices and debasements of the human condition. Whether that twisting remains without pain is, however, cast into question by a play like *Leonce und Lena*, where the comedy is certainly sometimes painful.

In *Leonce und Lena*, this sense of shame is focused on the idea of exposure that attends the play's concern with costume and masquerade. The comedy is saturated with the discourse of shame, with inadvertent nakedness, both spiritual and physical. Comedy's alternative to *anagnorisis*, the moment of recognition that Aristotle posits as a key topos of Tragedy and Epic, is such exposure: the pathos of recognition is turned into the bathos of a more shameful revelation. Comedy thus has an attachment to the anatomical, and especially to the genital, as a focus for sexual and toilet humour. The play is set between the two mock duodecimo states of Pipi (Weewee) and Popo (Botty), mirroring the mirror-image alliteration of the opening motto. It thus takes place in a diminutive, nursery version of that anatomical territory, a place of arrested development, where obsessive sexual and scatological curiosity holds sway. Büchner follows Shakespeare in putting the conventionally private and shameful on public view, from the phallus in the mock form of the elongated nose or the cuckold's horns to the excremental functions of the toilet.[7] In the context of König Peter's mock-Kantian disquisition on the meaning of things, the exposure of the shameful is effected as a kind of involuntary exhibitionism—his trouser buttons are open and his 'free will' on view (p. 164). The masquerade of exalted monarchic philosophy is punctured by a spectacle of physical shame, and free will subjected to involuntary lapses, taking unacceptable liberties. The scene follows the model of Jean Paul's comic theory, whereby the sublime is doubled in a laughable and diminutive form (the Kantian discourse of sublimity projected into the laughable form of the King's free 'will').[8]

Copying or repetition and physical exposure serve as the guiding principles of other key theories of the comic. Thus Henri Bergson, in his influential study on laughter, *Le Rire*, aligns the comic with the structures of children's games following principles of '*repetition, inversion*, and *reciprocal interference of series*'.[9] While comedy works mimetically, it also introduces into its mirroring of the real

---

7. Shakespeare's Jacques takes his name from a colloquial term for a toilet. Cuckoldry is a leitmotif of the suggestive humour in *As You Like It*, as in other Shakespeare plays, and it is duly transmitted to *Leonce und Lena* in the form of Valerio's ribald play with the 'Cape of Good Hope' and 'Cape Horn' (p. 169).

8. Jean Paul, *Vorschule der Ästhetik, Werke in zwölf Bänden*, ed. by Walter Höllerer (Munich and Vienna, 1975), vol. 9, p. 105.

9. *Laughter: An Essay on the Meaning of the Comic*, transl. by C. Brereton and F. Rothwell (London, 1911), p. 89 (italics as original).

reversals and interferences. This describes nicely the sort of linguistic play that is at work in the protracted punning of *Leonce und Lena*. This structuring of speech finds its corollary for Bergson in the performance of the body, which, in its comic mode, is understood by him as a dysfunctional machine, whose mechanical repetitions are interfered with and exposed to ridicule. When Leonce trips up (p. 169), this is part of the physical comedy of the drama, and at the same time provides an opportunity for Valerio to play with ideas in language. It also appeals, in this play that aligns the human body and its behaviour with machinery, to Bergson's idea of tripping or other physical lapses as comic evidence of the 'mechanical inelasticity' that afflicts the human condition (pp. 9–10).

For Bergson, comedy is at once an effect and a cause of repression: the unruly element in speech or physical behaviour emerges, 'goes off like a spring', and is then repressed once more by its comic management (p. 73). This in turn makes his theory of comedy amenable to Freud when he writes his classic study *Der Witz*. Freud sets out a theory of comedy, more especially of verbal wit, which is consonant with his theory of dreams: comedy works technically, through 'Witzarbeit', in much the way that the dream-work works, giving expression to the repressed through condensed and displaced forms. It exposes hidden connections, but does so in disguise. Freud follows illustrious progenitors here in focusing on two types of exposure. He follows Jean Paul in foregrounding the idea of weddings or couplings of ideas, however inappropriate the match may seem: 'Der Witz ist der verkleidete Priester, der jedes Paar traut.'[1] This sort of marriage, or what he calls elsewhere a short circuit (p. 114), has particular effect where that pair are the sublime and the ridiculous (p. 186). And he follows Lichtenberg and Heine in focusing the comic on the idea of exposures below-the-belt, as the 'Hose des guten Anstandes' (Lichtenberg) or the 'Hose der Geduld' (Heine) burst open to reveal what Lichtenberg calls the 'moralische Backside' or other conventionally hidden parts, sexual or excremental (p. 81).[2] *Leonce und Lena* nicely works according to both of these models, as do its principal sources, *As You Like It* and *Ponce de Leon*: the comedy of doublings and couplings is combined in each case with the classic exhibitionist devices of farce, as buttons are undone, trousers dropped, and skirts lifted, whether literally or metaphorically.

---

1. *Der Witz und seine Beziehung zum Unbewußten*, in *Studienausgabe*, ed. by Alexander Mitscherlich and others (Frankfurt a. M., 1969–75), Vol. 4, p. 15. Freud's citation here is marked by a repression of its own; the original aphorism had 'kopuliert' rather than 'traut' (Jean Paul, *Werke*, Vol. 9, p. 173). "A joke is a priest in vestments, whom every couple trusts" [*Editor's translation*].

2. "pants of good grace"; "pants of patience"; "moral backside" [*Editor's translation*].

While comic effect turns for both Bergson and Freud on varieties of mistake or mistaken identity, which are governed by techniques of repetition, reversal, interference, and distortion, in both theories there is a darker aspect in play, albeit not fully acknowledged in its significance. Their focus on automatism, repetition, and the effects of chance leads both writers into an encounter with the uncanny. At the end of their respective texts a classic practitioner of comic writing, Mark Twain, is introduced, in each case focusing on his account of the confused, at once absurd and traumatic relations between himself and his brothers. Bergson relays an interview in which Twain describes his twin brother, who was switched with the writer in his infancy and subsequently died, as having a distinguishing mark that in fact belonged to the writer himself. Thus the exemplary structure of *anagnorisis* is turned into a more radical uncertainty of identity. While Bergson cites this as an example of absurd humour, it seems equally appropriate to understand it as an uncanny case of the living dead for an author who had an abiding interest in doubling and twinning.

This points, in its turn, to a blind spot in Freud's account. Although he makes a connection between joking and aggression, the general tenor of his study is rather idealised and pleasure-seeking, enjoying the familiarity of comedy and its situations. Following Aristotle, Freud describes the recognition of the familiar as pleasurable, giving the example of Faust's return to his study after his encounter with the uncanny.[3] However, in his later work on the uncanny and repetition compulsion, this return to the familiar was to become confounded with darker aspects of the psyche. Both Bergson and Freud make light of the encounter with the uncanny through Twain's brothers at the end of their respective studies, but the inclination for the repetitive mechanisms of comedy to turn uncanny should be borne in mind when we consider their operation in *Leonce und Lena*. The scenario of automata taking over from humans is a key aspect of the repertoire of the uncanny, and the condition of being lost, which appears so innocent in the mock nursery-tale kingdom of Popo, in fact leads Leonce into an experience of uncanny darkness: 'welch unheimlicher Abend' (p. 177). It remains unclear whether this uncanny evening is merely another part of the Romantic scenery or truly experienced as such. Humour, at any rate, is always ambivalently cast here between creative vitality and melancholic morbidity; the 'Lustspiel' modulates between pleasure, the free play of 'Lust', and the more uncanny demands of what Freud would call 'Unlust', its dialectical counterpart. As Freud argues, while repetition of play or jokes can stimulate pleasure in

3. *Der Witz*, p. 115.

children, hearing the same joke or seeing the same play twice will
tend to produce indifference or degrees of unpleasure in adults.[4] At
its limit, this unpleasure is experienced in the 'demonic' experience
of the repetition compulsion, and those suffering from psycho-
pathologies repeat compulsively like children but beyond the control of the pleasure principle. Caught between the infantile and the
adult, the repetitive character of the wit of *Leonce und Lena*—both
in local instances and on a more general, structural level—is always
ready to tip into the performance of madness (the 'Narr' as fool
becoming the 'Narr' as psychopath) or back into the desperate *tae-
dium vitae* from which it is designed to provide release.

The doubled and mixed performances of language and physical
behaviour that characterise comedy in Bergson's and Freud's
accounts and apply to its operation in *Leonce und Lena* are also
consonant with the ideas of a further key theorist of the comic,
Bakhtin. A principal aspect of the play's genealogy is the *commedia dell'arte*, and its version of the harlequinade aligns it with
Bakhtin's discussion of carnival humour. For Bakhtin, comedy
under the sign of carnival functions at once in mock forms of
language that double or dialogise orthodox discourse and in grotesque performances of the human body. Carnival, as a site of
role-reversal and excess, is defined spatially and temporally—given
licence to happen at certain places (classically Venice) and at a
specific time, as long as order prevails at other places and times—
but its subversive energy resists that sort of containment. *Leonce
und Lena* is not least a play about the obsessive regulation of time
and space, which in the diminutive duodecimo state ruled by a
dynasty with nothing to do takes on a grotesquely excessive,
because empty form. Here, the carnivalesque is a continuous condition, everyday life a masquerade; but by being turned into the
norm, carnival also loses its holiday energy and threatens to
become a form of empty labour. Carnival in this mock feudal form
is grotesquely at odds with the working life of the under-classes,
who are made to play supernumerary roles in its ceremonies. The
'Vivat' that the peasants are required mechanically to repeat is
empty of living meaning for them. Indeed, it gives the potential for
the peasants to perform their incomprehension by converting the
Latin acclamation into 'Wie? Wat?' ('Wat?' as a low German version of 'Was?'). 'Ennui' and perplexity are suspended here between
an existential condition shared by all and a socially selective one, a
privilege of the under-active upper classes.

Throughout the play, a tension is maintained between the ability
of its carnival performance to create pleasure and the exposure of

4. *Jenseits des Lustprinzips*, in *Studienausgabe*, Vol. 3, pp. 217–72 (p. 245).

that performance as an empty and ideologically abhorrent charade. The body is used here as a marker of time and space, a clock and a measure, with the heart beating time for Lena as a mortal body-clock (p. 178),[5] Rosetta dancing a rhythm for time (p. 166), and Leonce spitting on a stone, once for each day of the year (p. 161), and seeking to take the measure of his grace with his legs (p. 171). In their carnival, Rabelaisian form, these measurements become grotesquely distorted, as the governess's protuberant nose threatens to bump against the horizon and Valerio's overactive mouth opens a hole in the governess's view (p. 178). The boundaries of time and space, the clocking of appointments and the crossing of frontiers, become confused and distended along with the bounds of the body. Not for nothing are the courtiers afraid, according to Leonce, of the word 'Platz' (p. 170): secure placement is confused with ideas of bursting here. Space is at once too big, in Valerio's experience, and too tight, in Leonce's (p. 174). The agoraphobic fool and the claustrophobic prince suffer from versions of the 'Platzangst' that runs through the play, as indeed through Büchner's other works.[6] The classical body that Leonce wishes for at the end of the drama, a perfectly formed vessel providing a golden mean for the placing and spacing of things, is squeezed out by more grotesque and incontinent body-shapes. The human body and its clothing become, to cite a neologism from the play, 'philobestialisch' (p. 181), taking after the forms of animals, with the cuckold horns and extravagant snouts already mentioned, and collars turning into 'melancholische Schweinsohren' (p. 183). And just as the lack of control over bodily functions reduces Woyzeck to a 'Hund' in the diagnosis of the Doktor, here the animal transformation of the various characters is associated with excremental flows. By leaving the water ('das Wasser lassen') at Valerio's behest after his attempted suicide (p. 180), Leonce is also passing water on the level of word-play; and when König Peter is first described by the epithet 'ein höchster Wille' (p. 170), and so metonymically identified with the 'Wille' that was hanging free from his trousers in the dressing scene, and then as wanting to pass his 'Willensäußerungen' into his son's hands (p. 170),[7] so the play becomes saturated with uncontained body fluids (with references also to spitting, crying, and nose-wiping). The idealised pretensions of the characters are constantly subverted by these grotesque extensions and

---

5. The converse is the clock dictating the workings of the body, specifically in Leonce's reference to Sterne's Tristram Shandy (p. 171), whose father was reminded of his conjugal duties once a month when his clock needed winding up.
6. For a discussion of the claustrophobic condition of Woyzeck, see my essay on *Woyzeck* in *Landmarks in German Drama*, ed. by Peter Hutchinson (Oxford, Berne, etc, 2002), pp. 95–110 (pp. 98–9). Lenz and the protagonists of *Dantons Tod* are also plagued by alternations between spatial dilation and constriction.
7. "the Highest Will"; "disposition of Will" (p. 114) [*Editor*].

overflows of the body and its functions. As the 'Zeremonienmeister' says of the 'Hofprediger': 'Ich glaube er hat Ideale und verwandelt alle Kammerherrn in Kammerstühle' (p. 183).[8] As Idealism is twisted into the grotesque, so chamberlains are convertible into chamber pots, receptacles for the play's scatological excesses.

A common feature of these comic figures is a linguistic structure that imitates the physical distortions that are conjured up. As the play's comic effects depict the body as grotesque in its extensions, repetitions, and incontinences, so it represents that condition through a collateral distortion of the linguistic corpus. This is especially the case in the discourse of Valerio, a 'Wortspiel' (p. 171)[9] incarnate, purveying pleasurably and painfully twisting puns with incontinent abandon. Language games here play out the principles of carnival performance, as words are repeated, coupled, reversed, extended, and let loose without conventional inhibition. Comedy is of course always a performative phenomenon, played out by the body and in language, but in *Leonce und Lena* that performativity is raised to a more self-conscious level. The workings of comedy, its staging and enactment, become the object of performance here, and what emerges is at once comic and tedious, vital and mechanical.

In its conclusion, the play enacts a stock performative act: the marriage ceremony. We recall that marriage is used by both Jean Paul and Freud as a figure for the wedding of ideas in jokes, pronouncing apparently inappropriate couples to be made for each other. Not for nothing is marriage routinely used as a ceremonial *ex machina* device for closing comedy, as in *As You Like It* or *Ponce de Leon*. While in *Ponce de Leon*, marriage is a multiple ceremony that resolves all tensions and errors, in *Leonce und Lena* the resolution is a more ambiguous contrivance. When the automata played by Leonce and Lena and performing the marriage *in effigie* turn out indeed to have been playing Leonce and Lena, the wedding seems less a device for achieving a happy ending than a mechanism that is out of the control of its performers, cast between chance and providence, and subjecting the masked performers in their turn to deceits.[1] The line 'Ich bin betrogen',[2] repeated by them, becomes a subversive supplement to the marriage ceremony: this is a marriage broken by deception before it has started. While Leonce takes up

---

8. "Master of Ceremonies"; "Court Chaplain"; "I think he has ideals and is changing all the chamberlains into chamber stools" (p. 124) [*Editor*].
9. "wordplay" [*Editor's translation*].
1. The final 'joke' that is the wedding is therefore suspended between legitimate comic management (Jean Paul's priest who couples every pair) and a more illegitimate, chance mechanism, registered by Leonce's exclamation 'O Zufall!'. Significantly, for Jean Paul, 'Zufall' is 'eine wilde Paarung ohne Priester' (*Werke*, Vol. 9, p. 193).
2. "I've been deceived" (p. 128) [*Editor*].

the role of master of ceremonies for a repeat performance of the wedding, Lena is bewildered and silenced, reduced it seems by her unmasking to the condition of shame that has run through the drama, not least in her performance.[3]

If the wedding is described by Valerio as an enactment of biblical paradise, it also involves a fall from grace, hence the elaborate playing on the painful coincidence of the 'Fall' contained within 'Zufall'. When Leonce suggests building a theatre, Lena can only shake her head and become a punning physical enactment of her name in the act of leaning: '(*Lena lehnt sich an ihn und schüttelt den Kopf.*)' (p. 189).[4] One of the marriage partners over-performs and the other is reduced to a marionette-like dumb-show. We are reminded that König Peter sanctions the marriage in effigy after the example of execution;[5] there is perhaps more affinity between the performative ending of the comedy and that of *Dantons Tod*, with its theatrical execution ceremony, than meets the eye. The bodies of the bride and groom in this melancholic comedy are also versions of the body of the condemned, set up for public exhibition.[6] As Danton and his colleagues go to the execution machine in order to perform their final appearances in the drama of the Revolution, so the Romantic lovers who do not know each other are 'zusammengeschmiedet' (p. 181)[7] in the mechanical execution of theatrical resolution. The comic ending is it seems as much a function of compulsion as the tragic one, and Valerio's 'Ich muß lachen' (p. 188),[8] which is repeated in one version of the play, should perhaps be read less as an expression of involuntary comedy than as one of compulsive behaviour in the comic style.[9] To follow the ambivalent intonation adopted by Stefan Kurt, the actor playing Valerio in the recent Berliner Ensemble production of the play, a character whose role as fool is defined by a compulsion to laugh and to make laugh, repeatedly: 'Ich muß lachen. Ich *muß* lachen'.

Büchner's dark-edged comedy, combining human vitality with mechanical morbidity, new clothes with second-hand ones, complicates idealised notions of the originality of the work of art and its ability to recreate meaningful life. Bergson writes that: 'We are strangely mistaken as to the part played by the poetic imagination,

---

3. Being married to a man she does not love is, for Lena, a cause for shame: 'Pfui! Siehst du, ich schäme mich.' (p. 173).
4. *"Lena leans against him and shakes her head"* (p. 129) [*Editor*].
5. This juristic move is reminiscent of the reference in *As You Like It* to dying 'in attorney' rather than in one's 'own person' (IV, 1).
6. The term is taken from Foucault and describes the attachment of systems of correction to the spectacle of physical punishment.
7. "joined" (p. 123) [*Editor*].
8. "I can't help laughing" (p. 128) [*Editor*].
9. It is a version, in other words, of the accursed 'Muß' that is lamented by Büchner in one of his letters (p. 288) and is compulsively repeated by Danton (p. 100).

if we think it pieces together its heroes out of fragments filched from right and left, as though it were patching together a harlequin's motley. Nothing living would result from that.'[1] What Büchner shows, however, is that motley of that kind, tailored in the right way, can be a viable ambition for a playwright and yield alternative, sometimes also uncannily death-like, forms of dramatic life. He tries out the clothes of comedy and plays it out in an effigy at once beguiling and troubling in its physical and linguistic workings. We have here, in other words, a 'Lustspiel'[2] as paranomastic 'Wortspiel', a comedy of the body and of words, and of the body in words, at which we have to laugh. But it is also a comedy that is twisted towards its generic opposite, incorporating both the melancholy of the 'Trauerspiel'[3]—this is a comedy, after all, that almost ends prematurely in the suicide of the leading man—and the compulsive rhythms of what might be termed an 'Unlustspiel'.

---

1. *Laughter*, p. 167.
2. "comedy" [*Editor's translation*].
3. "tragedy" [*Editor's translation*].

Woyzeck

RAINER MARIA RILKE

[On *Woyzeck*][†]

218. *Rilke to Marie Taxis*
Munich, Widenmayerstr. 32[III] c/o Koenig,
9th July 1915

* * *

. . . Are you reading anything, and what? I have been busy with
Hermann Keyserling, furthermore Strindberg (the Strindberg of the
truly unbelievable *Ghost-Sonata*, which has been played here most
movingly) the most positive event in the theatre next to *Wozzeck*
by Georg Büchner, which the Court Theatres very generously produced just before the holidays.[1] A tremendous play, written more
than eighty years ago (G. Büchner died young and was a brother of
the better known Ludwig Büchner)—nothing but the fate of a common soldier (round about 1848) who stabs his unfaithful mistress.
But it expounds magnificently how all the greatness of existence is
a frame even to the most insignificant life, one for which even the
uniform of an infantryman seems too large and too individual,
even round this recruit Wozzeck; how here, there, and everywhere,
on all sides of his dumb soul he is unable to prevent the horizons
from bursting open into the mighty, the tremendous, the infinite;
an incomparable spectacle, this ill-used man in his drill coat standing in the universe, *malgré lui*, in the boundless dimension of the
stars. That is real theatre, that is what the theatre could be. . . .

---

† From *The Letters of Rainer Maria Rilke and Princess Marie von Thorn und Taxis*, translated by Nora Wydenbruck, 141. London: Hogarth Press, 1958. Used by permission of
The Random House Group, Ltd. One of the best-known German-language poets, Rilke
(1875–1926) was an Austrian-Bohemian whose work includes the poetic cycles *Duine-
ser Elegien* (*Duino Elegies*, 1922) and *Sonette an Orpheus* (*Sonnets to Orpheus*, 1922)
and the novel *Die Aufzeichnungen des Malte Laurids Brigge* (*The Notebook of Malte
Laurids Brigge*, 1910). The following is an excerpt from a letter to the Countess Marie
of Thurn und Taxis.
1. Rilke saw the production of *Woyzeck* at the Residenztheater in Munich on June 24,
1915. The production was a revival of Eugen Kilian's 1913 staging of the play.

GEORGE STEINER

[*Woyzeck* and *Lear*]†

* * *

* * * Once Goethe had written [*Faust*], there was no further need in German literature for a dissociation between prose and tragedy. Nearly at one stroke, German prose had ripened to the highest dramatic purpose.

That purpose was, in part, fulfilled by Georg Büchner. In part only, because Büchner died at twenty-three. Throughout this book, I have to consider dramatists who failed because they lacked talent, because their natural bent lay in poetry or fiction rather than in drama, or because they could not reconcile their ideal vision of the theatre with the requirements of the actual stage. To Büchner these causes of defeat are not applicable. Had he lived, the history of European drama would probably have been different. His absurdly premature death is a symbol of waste more absolute than that of either of the two instances so often quoted in indictment of mortality, the deaths of Mozart and Keats. Not that one can usefully set Büchner's work beside theirs; but because the promise of genius in his writings is so large and explicit that what we have is like a mockery of that which was to come. There is some flagging in Keats's late poetry. Büchner was cut down in full and mounting career. One can scarcely foresee the directions in which might have matured a young boy who had already written *Dantons Tod, Leonce und Lena, Woyzeck*, and that massive torso of prose narrative, *Lenz*. At a comparable age, Shakespeare may have been the author of a few amorous lyrics.

Büchner's instantaneous ripeness staggers belief. The mastery is there from the outset. There is hardly an early letter or piece of political pamphleteering which does not bear the mark of originality and stylistic control. If we make exception of Rimbaud, there is no other writer who was so completely himself at so early an age. Usually passion or eloquence come long before style; in Büchner they were at once united. One marvels also at Büchner's range. In Marlowe, for example, there is a voice prematurely silenced, but already having defined its particular timbre. Büchner commits his powers to many different directions; all in his work is both accomplishment and experiment. *Dantons Tod* renews the possibilities of

† From *The Death of Tragedy*, by George Steiner, 271–281. New Haven: Yale University Press, 1996. © 1961, 1980 by George Steiner. Reprinted by permission of Georges Borchardt, Inc., for the author.

political drama. *Leonce und Lena* is a dream-play, a fusion of irony and heart's abandon that is still in advance of the modern theatre. *Woyzeck* is not only the historical source of "expressionism"; it poses in a new way the entire problem of modern tragedy. *Lenz* carries the devices of narrative to the verge of surrealism. I am mainly concerned with Büchner's dramatic prose and with his radical extension of the compass of tragedy. But every aspect of his genius reminds one that the progress of moral and aesthetic awareness often turns on the precarious pivot of a single life.

It turns also on trivial accidents. The manuscript of *Woyzeck* vanished from sight immediately after the death of Büchner in 1837. The faded, nearly illegible text was rediscovered and published in 1879, and it was not until the first World War and the 1920's that Büchner's dramas became widely known. They then exercised a tremendous influence on expressionist art and literature. Without Büchner there might have been no Brecht. But the long, fortuitous gap between the work and its recognition poses one of the most tantalizing questions in the history of drama. What would have happened in the theatre if *Woyzeck* had been recognized earlier for the revolutionary masterpiece it is? Would Ibsen and Strindberg have laboured over their unwieldy historical dramas if they had known *Dantons Tod?* In the late nineteenth century only Wedekind, that erratic, wildly gifted figure from the underworld of the legitimate theatre, knew and profited from Büchner's example. And had it not been for a minor Austrian novelist, Karl Emil Franzos, who rescued the manuscript, the very existence of *Woyzeck* might now be a disputed footnote to literary history.

Büchner knew the prose scene in *Faust* and cites one of Mephisto's derisive retorts in *Leonce und Lena*. He was familiar, also, with the energetic, though rather crude, uses of prose in Schiller's *Die Räuber*. But the style of *Woyzeck* is nearly autonomous; it is one of those rare feats whereby a writer adds a new voice to the means of language. Van Gogh has taught the eye to see the flame within the tree, and Schoenberg has brought to the ear new areas of possible delight. Büchner's work is of this order of enrichment. He revolutionized the language of the theatre and challenged definitions of tragedy which had been in force since Aeschylus. By one of those fortunate hazards which sometimes occur in the history of art, Büchner came at the right moment. There was crucial need of a new conception of tragic form, as neither the antique nor the Shakespearean seemed to accord with the great changes in modern outlook and social circumstance. *Woyzeck* filled that need. But it surpassed the historical occasion, and much of what it revealed is as yet unexplored. The most exact parallel is that of a contemporary of Büchner, the mathematician Galois. On the eve of his death in a ridiculous duel at the age of twenty, Galois laid down the foundations of topology. His fragmentary statements and proofs, great leaps beyond the bounds of classic theory, are still to be reckoned with in the vanguard of modern mathematics. Galois's notations, moreover, were preserved nearly by accident. So it is with *Woyzeck*; the play is incomplete and was nearly lost. Yet we know now that it is one of the hinges on which drama turned toward the future.

Woyzeck is the first real tragedy of low life. It repudiates an assumption implicit in Greek, Elizabethan, and neo-classic drama: the assumption that tragic suffering is the sombre privilege of those who are in high places. Ancient tragedy had touched the lower orders, but only in passing, as if a spark had been thrown off from the great conflagrations inside the royal palace. Into the dependent griefs of the menial classes, moreover, the tragic poets introduced a grotesque or comic note. The watchman in *Agamemnon* and the messenger in *Antigone* are lit by the fire of the tragic action, but they are meant to be laughed at. Indeed, the touch of comedy derives from the fact that they are inadequate, by virtue of social rank or understanding, to the great occasions on which they briefly perform. Shakespeare surrounds his principals with a rich following of lesser men. But their own griefs are merely a loyal echo to those of kings, as with the gardeners in *Richard II*, or a pause for humour, as in the Porter's scene in *Macbeth*. Only in *Lear* is the sense of tragic desolation so universal as to encompass all social conditions (and it is to *Lear* that *Woyzeck* is, in certain respects, indebted). Lillo, Lessing, and Diderot widened the notion of dramatic seriousness to include the fortunes of the middle class. But their plays are sentimental homilies in which there lurks the ancient aristocratic presumption that the miseries of servants are, at bottom, comical. Diderot, in particular, was that characteristic figure, the radical snob.

Büchner was the first who brought to bear on the lowest order of men the solemnity and compassion of tragedy. He has had successors: Tolstoy, Gorky, Synge, and Brecht. But none has equalled the nightmarish force of *Woyzeck*. Drama is language under such high pressure of feeling that the words carry a necessary and immediate connotation of gesture. It is in mounting this pressure that Büchner excels. He shaped a style more graphic than any since *Lear* and saw, as had Shakespeare, that in the extremity of suffering, the mind seeks to loosen the bonds of rational syntax. Woyzeck's powers of speech fall drastically short of the depth of his anguish. That is the crux of the play. Whereas so many personages in classic and Shakespearean tragedy seem to speak far better than they know, borne aloft by verse and rhetoric, Woyzeck's agonized spirit hammers in vain on the doors of language. The fluency of his tormentors, the Doctor and the Captain, is the more horrible because what they have to say should not be dignified with literate speech. Alban Berg's operatic version of *Woyzeck* is superb, both as music and drama. But it distorts Büchner's principal device. The music makes Woyzeck eloquent; a cunning orchestration gives speech to his soul. In the play, that soul is nearly mute and it is the lameness of Woyzeck's words which conveys his suffering. Yet the style has a fierce clarity. How is this achieved? By uses of prose which are undeniably related to *King Lear*. Set side by side, the two tragedies illuminate each other:

GLOUCESTER: These late eclipses in the sun and moon portend no good to us. Though the wisdom of nature can reason it thus and thus, yet nature finds itself scourg'd by the sequent effects. Love cools, friendship falls off, brothers divide. In cities, mutinies; in countries, discord; in palaces, treason; and the bond crack'd twixt son and father. This villain of mine comes under the prediction; there's son against father; the King falls from bias of nature; there's father against child. We have seen the best of our time. (*I, ii*)

WOYZECK: Aber mit der Natur ist's was anders, sehn Sie; mit der Natur das is so was, wie soll ich doch sagen, zum Beispiel. . . .

. . . .

Herr Doktor, haben Sie schon was von der doppelten Natur gesehn? Wenn die Sonn in Mittag steht und es ist, als ging' die Welt in Feuer auf, hat schon eine fürchterliche Stimme zu mir geredt!

. . . .

Die Schwämme, Herr Doktor, da, da steckt's. Haben Sie schon gesehn, in was für Figuren die Schwämme auf dem Boden wachsen? Wer das lesen könnt! (*"Beim Doktor"*)

LEAR: Down from the waist they are Centaurs, though women all above; but to the girdle do the gods inherit, beneath in all the fiend's. There's hell, there's darkness, there's the sulphurous pit; burning, scalding, stench, consumption. Fie, fie, fie! pah, pah! (*IV, v*)

WOYZECK: Immer zu—immer zu! Immer zu, immer zu! Dreht euch, wälzt euch! Warum bläst Gott nicht die Sonn aus, dass alles in Unzucht sich übereinander wälzt, Mann und Weib, Mensch und Vieh?! Tut's am hellen Tag, tut's einem auf den Händen wie die Mücken!—Weib! Das Weib is heiss, heiss! Immer zu, immer zu! (*"Wirtshaus"*)

LEAR: And when I have stolne upon these son in lawes,

Then kill, kill, kill, kill, kill, kill! (*IV, v*)
WOYZECK: Hör ich's da auch?—Sagt's der Wind auch?—Hör
ich's immer, immer zu: stich tot, tot! (*"Freies Feld"*)[1]

There are direct echoes. Lear calls upon the elements to "crack
nature's mould" at the sight of man's ingratitude; Woyzeck wonders
why God does not snuff out the sun. Both Lear and Woyzeck are
maddened with sexual loathing. Before their very eyes, men assume
the shapes of lecherous beasts: the polecat and the rutting horse in
Lear; the gnats coupling in broad daylight in *Woyzeck*. The mere
thought of woman touches their nerves like a hot iron: "there's the
sulphurous pit; burning, scalding"; "Das Weib is heiss, heiss!" A sense
of all-pervading sexual corruption goads the old mad king and the
illiterate soldier to the same murderous frenzy: "kill, kill"; "stich
tot, tot!"

But it is in their use of prose that the two plays stand nearest to
each other. Büchner is plainly in Shakespeare's debt. Prose style is
notoriously difficult to analyse, and there is a great and obvious
distance between post-romantic German and Elizabethan English.
Yet when we place the passages side by side, the ear seizes on
undeniable similarities. Words are organized in the same abrupt
manner, and the underlying beat works toward a comparable stress
and release of feeling. Read aloud, the prose in *Lear* and in *Woyzeck*
carries with it the same shortness of breath and unflagging drive.
The "shape" of the sentences is remarkably similar. In the rhymed
couplets of Racine there is a quality of poise and roundedness
nearly visible to the eye. But in the prose of *Lear* as in *Woyzeck*, the
impression is one of broken lines and rough-edged groupings. Or,
to paraphrase a conceit in *Timon of Athens*, the words "ache at us."

Yet the psychological facts with which Shakespeare and Büchner
deal are diametrically opposed. The style of Lear's agony marks a

---

1. WOYZECK: But with Nature, you see, it's something else again; with Nature it's like
this, how shall I say, like. . . .

....

Herr Doktor, have you ever seen anything of compound Nature? When the sun is at
midday and it feels as though the world might go up in flame, then a terrible voice has
spoken to me!

....

In toadstools, Herr Doktor, there, there's where it lurks. Have you already observed in
what configurations toadstools grow along the ground? He that could riddle that!

* * * * * * * *

Ever and ever and ever and ever! Whirl around, wind around! Why does God not blow
out the sun so that all may pile on top of one another in lechery, man upon woman,
human upon beast?! They do it in broad daylight, they do it on your hands like gnats!
Woman! Woman's hot, hot! Ever and ever!

* * * * * * * *

Do I hear it here also?—Does the wind say it also?—Shall I hear it ever and ever: stick
her dead, dead!

ruinous fall; that of Woyzeck, a desperate upward surge. Lear crumbles into prose, and fearing a total eclipse of reason, he seeks to preserve within reach of his anguish the fragments of his former understanding. His prose is made up of such fragments arrayed in some rough semblance of order. In place of rational connection, there is now a binding hatred of the world. Woyzeck, on the contrary, is driven by his torment toward an articulateness which is not native to him. He tries to break out of silence and is continually drawn back because the words at his command are inadequate to the pressure and savagery of his feeling. The result is a kind of terrible simplicity. Each word is used as if it had just been given to human speech. It is new and full of uncontrollable meaning. That is the way children use words, holding them at arm's length because they have a natural apprehension of their power to build or destroy. And it is precisely this childishness in Woyzeck which is relevant to Lear, for in his decline of reason Lear returns to a child's innocence and ferocity. In both texts, moreover, one important rhetorical device is that of a child—repetition: "kill, kill, kill"; "never, never, never"; "immer zu, immer zu!"; "stich tot, tot!" as if saying a thing over and over could make it come true.

Compulsive repetition and discontinuity belong not only to the language of children, but also to that of nightmares. It is the effect of nightmare which Büchner strives for. Woyzeck's anguish crowds to the surface of speech, and there it is somehow arrested; only nervous, strident flashes break through. So in black dreams the shout is turned back in our throats. The words that would save us remain just beyond our grasp. That is Woyzeck's tragedy, and it was an audacious thought to make a spoken drama of it. It is as if a man had composed a great opera on the theme of deafness.

One of the earliest and most enduring laments over the tragic condition of man is Cassandra's outcry in the courtyard of the house of Atreus. In the final, fragmentary scene of *Woyzeck* there are implications of grief no less universal. Woyzeck has committed murder and staggers about in a trance. He meets an idiot and a child:

> WOYZECK: Christianchen, du bekommst ein Reuter, sa, sa: da, kauf dem Bub ein Reuter! Hop, hop! Ross!
> KARL: Hop, hop! Ross! Ross![2]

In both instances, language seems to revert to a communication of terror older than literate speech. Cassandra's cry is like that of a sea

2. WOYZECK: Christianchen, you'll get a gee-gee, ho, ho: there, buy the lad a gee-gee! Giddy-up, giddy-up, horsey!
   KARL: Giddy-up, giddy-up! Horsey! Horsey!

bird, wild and without meaning. Woyzeck throws words away like
broken toys; they have betrayed him.

* * *

JOHN A. McCARTHY

Some Aspects of Imagery in Büchner's *Woyzeck*†

Although the views of *Woyzeck* are varied, surprisingly little attention
has been focused on the play's imagery. In fact several of the most
salient analogies which contribute decisively to a pervasive sense of
vertigo in the drama have been hitherto neglected.[1] A detailed analysis of some prominent images is, one should think, prerequisite to a
judicious appraisal of the basic tension between free will and deter-
minism long noted in the play. In this study I cite the Bergemann text
because his arrangement of the scenes does greater justice to the
centrality of certain images and their relationship to the underlying
idea of the work: "what is man?"

The opening lines in Bergemann's version are spoken by the captain who is admonishing his subordinate to slow down: "Langsam,
Woyzeck, langsam; eins nach dem andern! Er macht mir ganz
schwindlig."[2] They set the tone and tempo for the rest of the play
which is marked by dizzying activity. The very first scene introduces the image of a harried and restless man with no hope for a
better future or release from his relentless existence, who says of
himself: "Unsereins ist doch einmal unselig in der und der andern
Welt. Ich glaub, wenn wir in Himmel kämen, so müßten wir donnern helfen" (i, 114).[3]

The image of frenzied activity sounded here assumes the proportions of a leitmotif in the ensuing scenes. Woyzeck is so pressed in
the third scene that he barely greets Marie and takes no notice of the
child. He rushes off to work, darts home, bolts out of the inn to

---

† From *MLN* 91:3 (German Issue, April 1976), pp. 543–51. © 1976 The Johns Hopkins
University Press. Reprinted with permission of The Johns Hopkins University Press.

1. Only a few studies have been expressly devoted to images in the play. See, for example,
G. Bell, "Windows: A Study of a Symbol in Georg Büchner's Work," *GR*, 47 (1972),
95–108; A. P. Messenger, "'Barefoot into Hell': Clothing Imagery in *Woyzeck*," *Modern
Drama*, 13 (1971), 393–397; F. Mautner, "Wortgewebe, Sinngefüge und 'Idee' in Büchners *Woyzeck*," *Wege der Forschung*, 53 (Darmstadt: Wissenschaftliche Buchgesellschaft, 1965), 507–554.
2. G. Büchner, *Werke und Briefe*, ed. Fritz Bergemann, 6th ed. (München: DTV, 1965),
p. 113. Hereafter scene and page number will be cited in the text. All quotations from
the play refer to the Bergemann arrangement. [The Bergmann version begins with 4,5
(p. 141)—*Editor*.]
3. "The likes of us are wretched in this world and the next; I guess if we ever got to
Heaven, we'd have to help with the thunder" (p. 142) [*Editor*].

return to the scene of the crime; he races feverishly and irrevocably into the arms of his fate. This precipitation is mirrored in the fairy tale of the child who dashes off first to the moon, then the sun, then the stars, and finally back to an upside down world in a fruitless search for the meaning of life. The abrupt change of scenes and their terseness contribute further to the mood of unrest. Yet Woyzeck's life is not to be considered goal-oriented. The ineluctable urgency of his actions results in no economic or social improvement; the purpose of his life consists only in the procurement of hand-to-mouth sustenance for his small family. The hopelessness of his incessant activity is underscored by the progressive deterioration of his mental and physical health. In vain does the reader look for a spiral development to a higher state. Woyzeck's life runs its course in a desolate circular motion which knows no higher purpose than its own bleak continuance. Life appears as the existential plight of a senseless, swirling *perpetuum mobile*.

At first sight the cause of the protagonist's agitation would seem to lie solely in his extreme social and economic exploitation. However, the imagery offers us a second view and points toward a deeper, more disturbing source, a sort of *primum mobile*. The somewhat tepid Hauptmann is not quite so empty headed as is generally assumed,[4] for the initial "philosophic" interpretation in the play of the "horrifying sameness of human nature" comes from him. It comes in the form of a symbol: the mill wheel. But it bears no resemblance to the Romantic symbol of *Taugenichts*.

The mill wheel is a most significant symbol in the drama. Incorporated in it are both the busyness of men ("Beschäftigung") designed to kill time and the daily revolution of man's world on its own axis, headed nowhere but in a circle ("Was 'n Zeitverschwendung!"). Gone the Romantic aura of reassuring tranquility and optimism, gone the sense of security under the watchful eye of Providence. The ceaseless, aimless turning of the mill wheel now poignantly symbolizes the eternal sameness and the inconsequence of human existence which gives rise to a feeling of melancholy.[5] We

---

4. The affinity which Büchner felt for the captain has not gone completely unnoticed. Wolfgang Martens, "Zur Karikatur in der Dichtung Büchners (Woyzecks Hauptmann)," *GRM*, 39 (1958), 70–71, has delineated the several parallels between Woyzeck and the officer. For example, both are gripped by giddiness at the sight of man, both are experimental objects for the doctor, and neither can tolerate utter quiet. Martens concludes that these traits lift the captain out of a purely satirical role, reveal a "trans- and suprasocial ('übergesellschaftliche') wretchedness of the world order," and bring the captain to the brink of the tragic and comic. These considerations of imagery should strengthen the view of the captain as a reflection of Büchner's *Weltschmerz* and Woyzeck's disorientation.

5. B. von Wiese, *Die deutsche Tragödie von Lessing bis Hebbel* (Hamburg: Hoffman & Campe, 1964), p. 520, points out that the monotonous return of the same thing day in and day out leads to "Ermüdung am Leben" and to "Ernüchterung durch die Wirklichkeit." In a word, boredom. M. Hamburger, "Georg Büchner," *Contraries* (New York,

are reminded of Büchner's letter to Wilhelmine Jaeglé which is filled with despair over man's impotence in the face of human nature, social relationships, and the flow of history ("Schaum auf der Welle").[6] "Wo soll das hinaus?",[7] the captain asks, since even the revolutions of the earth are a waste of time. As soon as the endless stream of time enters the present it becomes something momentary and thus transitory. In either case, whether seen from the standpoint of the persistent stream of time or from its momentary actualization, life has no substance; it has lost its metaphysical framework. The passing of time (or the killing of time from the human point of view) has become a purely mechanical process, much like the turning of the mill wheel.

In a letter written a month before his death Büchner again alluded to the mill wheel. Its recurrence tends to stress the profundity of its import for the poet. He writes: "Wenn man so ein wenig unwohl ist, hat man ein so groß Gelüsten nach Faulheit; aber *das Mühlrad dreht sich als fort ohne Rast und Ruh.* . . . Heute und gestern gönne ich mir jedoch ein wenig Ruhe und lese nicht; morgen geht's wieder im alten Trab, du glaubst nicht, wie regelmäßig und ordentlich. Ich gehe fast so richtig, wie eine Schwarzwälder Uhr" (II, 463; italics mine).[8] In this context the mill wheel undergoes an expansion of meaning wrought by the clock simile in the concluding sentence. The world, or life, is represented by the wheel; the individual caught on the tread mill of life is depicted as a mechanical device. The imagery seems to say that the movements of man (like the figurine on the *Schwarzwälder Uhr*) and the cycle of life are both controlled by an unseen, lifeless mechanism.[9] The clock image, so popular in the seventeenth and eighteenth centuries as an expression of admiration for the powers of the Supreme Engineer, returns now stripped of its transcendental glorification. The teleological, divine world-machine appears as an instrument of

---

Dutton, 1970), p. 182, indicates that boredom is the "apathy that springs from despair." The resultant melancholiness from which the captain suffers was part of a wide-spread phenomenon in the early nineteenth century which was expressed as "dämonische Zerrissenheit und sentimentaler Weltschmerz." See Fr. Sengle, *Biedermeierzeit* (Stuttgart: Metzler, 1971), I, 2.

6. G. Büchner, *Sämtliche Werke und Briefe*, ed. Werner P. Lehmann (Hamburg: Chr. Wegner, 1971), II, 425–426. Hereafter cited in text by volume and page number.
7. "What will come of that?" (p. 142) [*Editor*].
8. See the letter to Wilhelmine Jaeglé from Zurich on Jan. 20, 1837 [*Editor*].
9. The clock motif in Büchner's writings is expanded even further in *Leonce und Lena* to include the death aspect when Leonce is made to say: "Das Picken der Totenuhr in unserer Brust is langsam, und jeder Tropfen Blut mißt seine Zeit, und unser Leben ist ein schleichend Fieber" (II, ii, 101). The remark can be seen as a summation of Woyzeck's situation. The once vital function of the three sisters Clotho, Lachesis, and Atropos, who spun the thread of life, assigned each man's destiny, and severed the thread at death, has been replaced by a machine.

torture, a dim foreshadowing of Kafka's hideous device in the "Strafkolonie."

The imagery of the mill wheel and the clock intensify the "entsetzliche Gleichheit der Menschennatur"[1] lamented by Büchner. Combined they convey the picture of man and his world as part and parcel of an automated system which allows for no alteration of the predestined cycle of vertiginous repetition. Man is a programmed robot. The mechanicalness of human nature itself, connoted in the first scene, is subsequently developed into a major image in *Woyzeck*. The mechanical repetition of human actions parallels the involuntary revolutions of the wheel of life. The question of morality raised in this same scene serves as a springboard for reflection on human nature itself. Of interest in this regard is not the captain's definition of morality, but rather Woyzeck's striking reply to the officer's reproof. As a well-disciplined soldier Woyzeck doesn't contradict his superior, but simply states in justification: "Man hat auch sein Fleisch und Blut" and further: ". . . es kommt einem nur so die Natur" (i, 114).[2] The officer reiterates the phrase "Fleisch und Blut" and develops the thought further in a manner which elucidates its sexual overtones. The captain intends only to explain to Woyzeck that he knows what Woyzeck means because he too has experienced the sensation; however, much more is revealed for the mechanicalness of human love is poignantly expressed: "Fleisch und Blut? Wenn ich am Fenster lieg, wenn's geregnet hat, und den weißen Strümpfen so nachseh, wie sie über die Gassen springen— verdammt, Woyzeck, da kommt mir die Liebe! Ich habe auch Fleisch und Blut" (i, 114).[3] The impression conveyed is not one of love, but one of unadulterated lust, which is activated automatically when the appropriate stimulus is present ("weiße Strümpfe"). Woyzeck's reply, therefore, is an implicit admission, that he has a child because he was unable to control his sexual impulses. The captain's explanation thus serves to illustrate the mechanical aspect of love, which ultimately obfuscates the original spiritual quality of Woyzeck's specific love for Marie. Because the scene "Beim Hauptmann" introduces the decisive images of the mill wheel and of man as a sexual automaton there appears to be greater justification for placing it at the beginning of the drama as Bergemann does.

The mechanical characteristics of sexual love become more pronounced in the liaison between the drum major and Marie. In the

---

1. "horrifying sameness of human nature"; see the letter to Wilhelmine Jaeglé, p. 185 [*Editor*].
2. "After all, we're flesh and blood"; "we act like nature tells us" (p. 142) [*Editor*].
3. "Flesh and blood? When I'm lying at the window after it has rained, and I watch the white stockings as they go tripping down the street—damn it, Woyzeck, then love comes all over me. I've got flesh and blood, too" (p. 142) [*Editor*].

terminology used to describe the incipient affair the many references
to animals or animal husbandry are designed to underscore the further dehumanization (i.e., despiritualization) of love. At their first
encounter Marie remarks with admiration that "he walks like a lion"
(iii, 115) and begins immediately to make eyes at him. Later Marie
compares his chest to that of a steer and his beard to a lion's (vii,
121). She calls him simply "Mann" (vii, 121), because for her, to put it
colloquially, he is just a good lay. For his part, the drum major treats
Marie like a sex object, "ein Weibsbild . . . zur Zucht von Tambour-
majors" (iv, 117). He admires her carriage and her coloration as if he
were examining a fine horse. In the "seduction" scene Marie and the
drum major encounter one another like prime specimens of the two
sexes, more animal than human in their attitude.[4] When the drum
major attempts to take his "wild Tier" (vii, 121), Marie half-heartedly
resists but immediately yields remarking: "Meinetwegen! Es ist alles
eins!" (vii, 121).[5] Her comment suggests the spiritual emptiness of
the act. Her animal appetite is too powerful to be denied; she is just
as compelled to act according to nature as Woyzeck is. It should be
clear that animal attraction forms another vital part of the "horrifying sameness of human nature," of the relentless gyration of the mill
wheel, for a few scenes later Woyzeck despondently laments: "Er, er
hat sie—wie ich zu Anfang" (xii, 125).[6] Büchner intimates here a
kind of *Reigen* which is continued somewhat by Woyzeck and Käthe
after Woyzeck has returned to the inn from the pond.

The unthinking bestiality of man becomes even more apparent
in scenes four ("Buden. Lichter. Volk"), five ("Das Innere der heller-
leuchteten Bude"), and seven ("Beim Doktor") where animals are
compared to man and man to an animal. The monkey ("nix, gar
nix"; iv, 117) and the horse ("Staub, Sand, Dreck"; v, 118) represent
an unidealistic[7] view of man for they are presented void of any
ennobling traits, just as God made them. However, the animals
undergo an "humanization" process, the monkey when it is clothed
and taught human mannerisms, the horse in view of its (albeit "viehische") "Vernünftigkeit." This "humanization" process contrasts
with the "dehumanization" of Marie and the drum major. A comment the poet once made elsewhere demonstrates further that for

---

4. von Wiese, p. 531, calls them "instinktsicher." Mautner, p. 513, notes the "körperlich-
   animalische" overtones of Marie's language. Hermann Pongs, *Das Bild in der Dichtung*
   (Marburg: Elvertsche Verlagsbuchhandlung, 1969), III, 632, compares the actions of
   the drum major and the non-commissioned officer in the market scene with the horse's
   "vernünftigen Viehigkeit."
5. "For all I care. What does it matter?" (p. 143) [*Editor*].
6. "He—he's got her now, like I used to have her" (p. 147) [*Editor*].
7. The phrase "unideale Nàtur" in this context (v, 118) is reminiscent of the author's use
   of it in rejecting idealism in literature and science. See the letter to his family dated
   July 28, 1835 (II, 444); also *Lenz*, I, 87 and "Über Schädelnerven," II, 292.

him there was no basic difference between man and beast: "Boire sans soif et faire l'amour en tout temps, il n'y a que ce qui nous distingue des autres bêtes.[8]

Two scenes later we learn that Woyzeck has "pissed" on the street like a dog (vii, 119). Büchner establishes an obvious parallel to the horse's behavior when it relieved itself during the performance in order to contradict the doctor's theory of free will. In answering the question why he did it, Woyzeck uses the same explanation cited earlier to explain his illegitimate child: "Aber, Herr Doktor, wenn einem die Natur kommt" (vii, 119).[9] By association Büchner seems to imply that "love" is as mechanical and automatic as the renal function. Man is thus nothing but a marionette. Aesthetically, it is striking that Büchner has so effectively intertwined the nascent love affair between Marie and the drum major with the development of the animal and puppet motifs, so that they are seen as complementary movements. In the final analysis Marie and the drum major are mere puppets on the wheel of life acting like the figurine of the *Schwarzwälder Uhr* with the passing of time.[1]

Besides the images of the mill wheel and the puppet-man, the *Menschenbild* of the play is accentuated by the dance image. One naturally thinks of the scene in the inn where Marie and the drum major are dancing. That moment is not an isolated instance but rather the culmination of the vertiginous motion which underlies the entire play, and which has been prefigured in the mill wheel's circular path, in Woyzeck's gyrating haste, and in ths characters' relentless animalism. Once again it is the opening scene in Bergemann's arrangement which first prepares us for the dance image, albeit in an indirect manner with respect to a sense of vertigo. There the captain urges Woyzeck: "Langsam, Woyzeck, langsam. . . . Er macht mir ganz schwindlig" (i, 113).[2] The dizziness caused by the protagonist's sense of urgency in the first scene is later associated with the dizzying plunge into the depths of despair upon learning of Marie's infidelity. Horrified, Woyzeck bolts from the captain presumably

---

8. Cited by Wolfgang Martens, "Zum Menschenbild Georg Büchners *Woyzeck* und die Marionszene in *Dantons Tod*," *Wege der Forschung*, 53 (Darmstadt: Wissenschaftliche Buchgesellschaft, 1965), p. 379, n. 11.

9. "But Doctor, the call of nature . . ." (p. 144) [*Editor*].

1. The puppet-like aspects of human nature play a prominent role in *Leonce und Lena* as well. For example, Valerio says of the princely pair: "Sehen Sie hier, meine Herren und Damen, zwei Personen beiderlei Geschlechts, ein Männchen und ein Weibchen, einen Herrn und eine Darnel Nichts als Kunst und Mechanismus, nichts als Pappendeckel und Uhrfedern! Jede hat eine feine, feine Feder von Rubin unter dem Nagel der kleinen Zehe am rechten Fuß, man drückt ein klein wenig, und die Mechanik läuft voile fünfzig Jahre" (III, iii, 108). Furthermore, Valerio refers to "der Mechanismus der Liebe" (ibid.) which has been set in motion. In keeping with the aristocratic backgrounds of Leonce und Lena, however, the mechanical expression of love is befittingly more sophisticated.

2. "Take it easy, Woyzeck, take it easy. [. . .] You're making me quite dizzy" (p. 141) [*Editor*].

to seek out Marie. The officer follows his flight with his eyes and remarks: "Mir wird ganz schwindlig vor den Menschen. Wie schnell!" (ix, 123).[3] At this point it is unclear whether the captain's vertigo is caused merely by a sense of Woyzeck's alacrity or also by a sense of his despair. However, this additional source of giddiness is blatantly expressed in the confrontation between Woyzeck and Marie. Her infidelity rends the last thread of meaning which had still imparted a purpose to Woyzeck's crazed existence; her faithlessness means for him that man is nothing but a mindless animal, indistinguishable from the *bête*. Woyzeck stands on the brink of the human void and peers into the abyss called man. The intuitive recognition of man's powerlessness makes him reel with anguish as he calls out in terms reminiscent of the captain's sense of vertigo: "Jeder Mensch ist ein Abgrund; es schwindelt einem, wenn man hinabsieht" (x, 123).[4] Thereafter giddiness becomes an openly major motif in the drama and is closely linked with the revelation of man as a volitionless machine; from that moment on Woyzeck is unable to rid himself of a feeling of a downward, swirling motion. From his barracks he hears the dance music and can have no peace. Tortured he cries out: "Es dreht sich mir vor den Augen. Tanz, Tanz!" (xi, 124).[5] Giddiness, implying the maelstrom of the abyss, is paired with the whirling motion of dancing. The vertigo motif thus experiences a further expansion of meaning.

The dizzying sensation rises with the foregoing images to culminate in the passionate giddiness of the dance which abruptly leads to Woyzeck's unrestrainable raving. The inflamed passions of the dancers are expressed in the words "immer zu, immer zu." There can be no doubt about the sexual connotations of the dance when Woyzeck cries in his anguish: "Immer zu, immer zu! Dreht euch, wälzt euch! Warum bläst Gott nicht die Sonn aus, daß alles in Unzucht sich übereinander wälzt, Mann und Weib, Mensch und Vieh?! Tut's am hellen Tag, tut's einem auf den Händen wie die Mücken!—Weib! Das Weib ist heiß, heiß—Immer zu, immer zu" (xii, 125).[6] All the images discussed thus far are joined in this passage: the revolutions of the mill wheel return in the "Dreht euch!" and are coupled with the rampant sexuality of the dance motif: "Wälzt euch!". The unthinking animality of human relationships is forcefully expressed by the word groupings, "Mann und Weib, Mensch und Vieh," as well as by the mental image of men copulating like gnats. Finally, the

3. "These people make me dizzy. Look at them go" (p. 168) [*Editor*].
4. "Everyone's an abyss—you get dizzy when you look down into it" (p. 169) [*Editor*].
5. "Everything's spinning before my eyes. Dance, dance!" [*Editor's translation*].
6. See Woyzeck's lines in 4,11.

rhythmic recurrence of the phrase "immer zu" calls to mind the horrible sameness of nature and embraces Woyzeck's vertiginous terror at the mechanicalness of love and the resultant meaninglessness of life. He collapses in a dizzying swoon (xii, 125).

In his extreme mental state Marie's "immer zu, immer zu" seems to Woyzeck to be reiterated by those mysterious, subterranean voices which have haunted him from the beginning. The voices seem to repeat the words as a command to kill Marie. From the original "immer zu" a new phrase gradually evolves: "stich tot, tot" (xiii, 125).[7] It is a helpless lashing out at an incomprehensible fate.

The phases of development leading up to the stabbing are transparent: from the ineluctable turning of the mill wheel and Woyzeck's nervous agitation arises the passionate frenzy of the dance; from the sexual dance rite comes the murderous rage. The originally circular motion evolves into a frantic perpendicular movement: "auf und nieder, immer wieder" (as the obscene ditty goes).[8] After the bloody deed Woyzeck returns to the inn and dances with Käthe, upon whom his sexual attention is now centered. His advances close the circle; he is still caught in the same cycle of life, trotting along the same vertiginous path, the victim of uncontrollable forces. "Tanzt alle, immer zu! schwitzt und stinkt!" (xxiii, 131)[9] he urges his fellow man, because that is all they have. The "tanzt alle" expresses the whirling motion again, the "immer zu" recalls the headlong passion, the "schwitzt und stinkt" implies man's animality.

The images of the mill wheel, the man-animal, and the whirling dance convey a disconsolate *Menschenbild*. Man is powerless in the face of natural laws; he is "mere foam on the crest of the wave." Other less developed images and metaphors tend to support the antimetaphysical world view of the play. For example, the ground upon which man treads is hollow (ii, 115), the romantic mood is only "a piece of rotten wood," the omnific sun merely a "wilted sunflower," the earth an "overturned pot," man a helpless child who "sits abandoned and cries its heart out" (xxi, 130). The play's imagery has little bearing on the social and economic injustices evident in the drama. The purpose in citing them has been to demonstrate that at least as much, if not more, importance is to be attached to the images and symbols, as to the economic and social indictment in an evaluation of the work. Woyzeck's suffering and ineptitude would seem ascribable first to the mechanicalness of the *condition humaine*, then to the restrictiveness of the *condition sociale*. It

---

7. "on and on"; "stab dead, dead." See 4,12.
8. Mautner, p. 520, has pointed out the psychoanalytic connection here between sexuality and brutality.
9. Woyzeck's opening lines in 1,17.

will be remembered that Büchner referred to both conditions in his oft-quoted letter to his fiancee: "Ich finde in der Menschennatur eine entsetzliche Gleichheit, in den menschlichen Verhältnissen eine unabwendbare Gewalt. Allen und Keinen verliehen" (II, 425).[1]

In the same letter the poet wrote: "Der Ausspruch: es muß ja Ärgerniß kommen, aber wehe dem, durch den es kommt—ist schauderhaft. Was ist das, was in uns lügt, mordet, stiehlt?" (II, 426).[2] Büchner did not want to pursue the thought. But as a scientist he felt obligated to think the thought to its apparent conclusion, for in his Zürich *Probevorlesung* almost three years later, the promising researcher claimed: "Alles, was ist, ist um seiner selbst Willen da. Das Gesetz dieses Seins zu suchen, ist das Ziel der, der teleologischen gegenüberstehenden Ansicht, die ich die *philosophische* nennen will" (II, 292).[3] *Woyzeck*, which was written at the same time, might be looked upon as a literary answer to the question. The solution would appear to be: man lies, steals, and murders because he is a mere man, not divine.[4] As "unideale Natur" he is compelled to obey the commands of his inner nature and his outer world.[5] There is no telos behind these laws; nature is aimless. Only physical laws are of any consequence for man. In the end life is senseless, man a clothed monkey bound to a tread mill, society an extension of human nature. Büchner replaces the *Vernünftigkeit* of bygone idealism with the *Viehnünftigkeit* of modern anti-idealism.

The *Welt- und Menschenbild* articulated through the similes emphasize a relentless, unproductive circumrotation and man's powerlessness to alter his course. The death of the individual

1. "I find in human nature a horrifying sameness, in the human condition an inescapable force, granted to all and to no one" (p. 185) [*Editor*].
2. "The dictum, 'it must be that offenses come; but woe to that man by whom the offence cometh'—is terrifying. What is it within us that lies, murders, steals?" (p. 186) [*Editor*].
3. "All that is, is for its own sake. To seek the law of this Being is the aim of the anti-teleological view, a view I will call the *philosophical*" (p. 175) [*Editor*].
4. von Wiese, p. 524, draws the following conclusion about the statement "es muß ja Ärgerniß kommen" and its implied guilt: "Aber diese Schuld hat mit Freiheit und sittlicher Selbstbestimmung eigentlich nichts mehr zu tun, sondern zeigt die Kreatur nur in ihrer Abhängigkeit von einer als Qual erlebten und dennoch notwendigen Existenz. Der Abfall Gottes von sich selbst, als er in die Welt einging, bedeutet für den Menschen eine als Schmerz und Schuld erlebte Endlichkeit, *die bereits im Ursprung unfrei ist* und unter dem Fluch des Muß steht" (italics mine).
5. This view of man is remarkably similar to one expressed by Fyodor Dosteyevsky twenty-eight years later in the story "Notes from Underground": ". . . [man] is something like a piano key or an organ stop; . . . there are natural laws in the universe, and whatever happens to him happens outside his will, as it were, by itself, in accordance with the laws of nature." *Notes from Underground, White Nights, The Dream of a Ridiculous Man*, trans. A. R. MacAndrew (New York: Signet, 1961), p. 109. The deterministic conception of man is but one of many parallels between the two writers. Another major similarity is the stress on *ennui*. The reason for the parallels lies no doubt in the "Philosophiemüdigkeit" of the age (Sengle, I, 1).

does not bring the mill wheel of life to a halt; the wheel continues undisruptedly along its age-worn path. This disturbing picture of man and his world is poignantly portrayed in the play's
dominant imagery. The powerful effect of the compressed,
intense language of *Woyzeck* is thus augmented by a series of
interrelated likenesses which tend to enhance the sense of vertigo. In Michael Hamburger's words, imagery is used "not only to
'heighten' the prose . . . but to impregnate the whole play with a
hidden, unifying significance not easily conveyed in '. . . the language of men.'"[5]

JOHN REDDICK

Natur and *Kunst*[†]

What are we to make of this extraordinary work, unfinished as it
is? What are the driving concerns, issues, obsessions that underlie
the texts, and condition their particular shape and thrust? After
Dantons Tod and *Leonce und Lena* (not to mention *Lenz*), we
should not expect *Woyzeck* to offer answers, and indeed it does
not: *Woyzeck* is a problem-play *par excellence*. This may well be
one reason why Büchner had not completed it by the time he died.
After all, he wrote *Dantons Tod*—a far longer play—at phenome-
nal speed, and the (lost) competition version of *Leonce und Lena*
was likewise begun and finished within a matter of weeks.
Woyzeck, on the other hand, clearly preoccupied him for many
months, and the fact that he still never managed to finish it is
surely because he had taken on the biggest challenge of his creative life, and found himself struggling to give shape to the most
profound and complex questions.

One particular nettle needs to be grasped at once: although the
opposite is commonly held to be true, *Woyzeck* was clearly not
intended to be a 'social drama'—that is to say, a play principally
aimed at exposing or documenting the iniquities of the given socio-
economic system, as epitomized in the suffering of exemplary victims. One pointer to this is the fact that Büchner makes his
Woyzeck relatively much better off in terms of both money and
social status than the historical Woyzeck. In the period immediately prior to the murder, the real Woyzeck was jobless, homeless,
and in such absolute penury that he could not afford even the

5. Hamburger, p. 197, is referring specifically to *Dantons Tod*, but the same statement
holds true for *Woyzeck* as well.
† Nature and Art. From *Georg Büchner: The Shattered Whole*, by John Reddick, 303–313.
Oxford: Oxford University Press, 1994. Reprinted by permission.

meanest doss-house, and was living rough.[1] By comparison, Büchner's Woyzeck is relatively secure: he has a regular job, and another job on the side; a family of sorts; a place to sleep; and a little spare cash, however paltry. He is an exemplar of the underclass—but not of social deprivation in its extreme form; his circumstances would be enviable even to the down-and-outs of today in the cities of Europe or America. This is not to say that there is no element of social criticism in the texts: there undeniably is—but it is never more than a secondary issue. In H1, indeed, it is not an issue at all: Büchner never once shines a spotlight on socio-economic factors, and they are scarcely even mentioned in passing. The cash-nexus is fleetingly referred to in the 'Barbier's' cryptic remark that 'he is science', and that his 'scientific-ness' earns him half a gulden per week ('Ich bin die Wissenschaft. Ich bekomm für mei Wissenschaftlichkeit alle Woche ein halbe Gulden', 387; this presumably prefigures the Doctor/Woyzeck contract in H2/H4). The only other reference to money is even more fleeting, namely the reference to venal sex in one of the songs in the inn in H1, 17 ('. . . Behalt dei Thaler u. schlaf allein', 403; . . . *Keep your money and sleep alone*). The Grandmother's tale is all about 'a poor child' ('ein arm Kind', 397); but although the child is doubtless to be imagined as economically poor (on the model of countless characters in fairytale lore), the epithet is clearly meant here in the sense of 'pitiable', for the story is patently about the nature of existence, not the nature of society.[2] In H2, economic details are woven slightly more often into the fabric of the text, but they are still not frequent, nor are they given any particular prominence. Poverty is implicitly conveyed when Büchner has Woyzeck tell Louise that they can go to the fair that evening as he has saved a bit of money ('Heut Abend auf die Mess. Ich hab wieder was gespart', 343); and of course poverty and economic exploitation are strongly implied by the monstrous arrangement whereby Woyzeck lets himself be systematically abused and degraded by the Doctor for the sake of a miserable pittance (367). Only twice in H2 does Büchner have his characters refer specifically to their poverty: Louise laments the lot of 'us poor folk' ('Ach wir armen

1. Cf. Alfons Glück, 'Der historische Woyzeck', in Anon. (ed.), *Georg Büchner 1813–1837*, 314–24. But cf. also Alfons Glück, 'Der "ökonomische Tod": Armut und Arbeit in Georg Büchners *Woyzeck*', in T. M. Mayer (ed.), *Georg Büchner Jahrbuch*, 4/1984, 167–226: in this article, Glück maintains that the central focus of *Woyzeck* is indeed the prevailing system of social 'exploitation, suppression and alienation' (167).
2. It is striking that although Büchner almost certainly drew on the fairytale 'Die Sterntaler' (*The Star Talers*), he retained none of its specific insistence on poverty: 'Once upon a time there was a little girl, her mother and father had died, and she was so poor that she had no little house to live in and no little bed to sleep in, and all she had left was the clothes on her body and a crust in her hand that some kind soul had given her.' Cf. Walter Hinderer, *Büchner-Kommentar zum dichterischen Werk* (Munich, 1977), 234.

Leut', 343); and Woyzeck utters his poignant cry when the Hauptmann taunts him about Louise: 'ich bin ein arm Teufel,—und hab
sonst nichts auf der Welt' (375; *I'm a poor devil—and I've nothing
else in the world*).

Things are markedly different in H4. Here, Büchner not only
specifically thematizes poverty, but also projects it in class terms: at
relevant moments, Woyzeck and Marie are no longer presented as
individuals who happen to be poor, but as exemplars of a whole
stratum of society—a grossly disadvantaged and quite literally
'working' class. Büchner does not refashion old H1/H2 scenes in
such as a way as to include this new social-critical dimension
(indeed in his reworking of H2, 2 he cuts out both Louise's 'Ach wir
armen Leut', and Woyzeck's reference to his saved-up money).
Instead, he incorporates the new dimension in brand-new episodes:
the earrings scene, and the shaving scene (H4, 4; H4, 5). The class
element is unmistakable in the remark that Büchner has Woyzeck
make in response to his child's sweating brow—with the phrase
'wir arme Leut' now acquiring a far sharper edge than it had when
Louise spoke it in H2, 2: 'Die hellen Tropfen steh'n ihm auf der
Stirn; Alles Arbeit unter d. Sonn, sogar Schweiß im Schlaf. Wir
arme Leut!' (358/360; *His forehead's all shiny with sweat; nothing in
the world but work, even in your sleep you sweats. That's us poor for
you!*) The class basis of poverty is equally strongly highlighted earlier in this new scene in the speech that Büchner gives to Marie,
particularly through the use of the collective term 'Unsereins' (*our
sort*); and what we also see here (and nowhere else in the text) is a
defiant assertion that, however large the gulf between the poor and
the rich, in their essential humanness they remain the same
(though ironically it is precisely this 'humanness' that is already in
the process of ensuring Marie's own doom):

> Unseins hat nur ein Eckchen in der Welt und ein Stückchen
> Spiegel und doch hab' ich einen so rothen Mund als die großen
> Madamen mit ihren Spiegeln von oben bis unten und ihren
> schönen Herrn, die ihnen die Hand küssen, ich bin nur ein
> arm Weibsbild. (358)
>
> Our sort don't have much, a bare little corner and a broken
> bit of mirror—but my mouth's just as red as them grand
> madames' with their full-length mirrors and their fancy gents
> what kiss their hands; I'm just a poor woman, that's all.

The same kind of argument is propounded minutes later in the
shaving scene, only much more vehemently and programmatically.

The cue, of course, is the Hauptmann's mealy-mouthed accusation that Woyzeck, as the father of a bastard child, is devoid of
'morals':

Wir arme Leut. Sehn sie, Herr Hauptmann, Geld, Geld. Wer
kein Geld hat. Da setz eimal einer seinsgleichen auf die Moral
in die Welt. Man hat auch sein Fleisch und Blut. Unseins ist
doch einmal unseelig in der und der andern Welt, ich glaub'
wenn wir in Himmel kämen so müßten wir donnern helfen.
(362)

>   We're poor folk, we are. Money, you see, sir, money. If you
>   don't have no money. Morality don't get much of a look in when
>   our sort gets made. We're flesh and blood too. Our sort just
>   don't have no chance in this world or the next; I reckon if we
>   ever got to heaven we'd have to help with the thunder.

The class argument is put even more sharply and specifically in
response to the Hauptmann's lament at Woyzeck's lack of 'Tugend'
(*virtue*):

Ja Herr Hauptmann, die Tugend! ich hab's noch nicht so aus.
Sehn Sie, wir gemeine Leut, das hat keine Tugend, es kommt
einem nur so die Natur, aber wenn ich ein Herr wär und hätt ein
Hut u. eine Uhr und eine anglaise und könnt vornehm reden, ich
wollt schon tugendhaft seyn. Es muß was Schöns seyn um die
Tugend, Herr Hauptmann. Aber ich bin ein armer Kerl. (362)

>   Yes, sir, virtue! I'm not that far meself. Us common folk,
>   y'see, we don't have no virtue, it's nature what drives us; but if
>   I was a gent with a hat and a watch and a nice smart coat and
>   could talk all posh, I'd be virtuous alright. Must be a fine
>   thing, sir, virtue. But poor, that's what I am.

This is social criticism writ large, and it is all the more trenchant
for being voiced by an underdog, who not only stands up to his pompous windbag of a master but also leaves him thoroughly deflated and
confused, to the delight of the reader/spectator. It is easy to see why
so many commentators have regarded it as the central issue and purpose of the work, especially given the fact that for many years this
scene was routinely placed at the beginning of edition after edition,
following the practice initiated by Franzos in his garbled edition of
1879, and seemingly validated by the distinguished scholar Fritz
Bergemann in the numerous popular editions first launched by the
publishers Insel in 1958. Franzos and Bergemann no doubt believed
that that was where the scene best 'fitted', but what they did was
nonetheless an act of editorial barbarism, perpetrated in the face of
the incontrovertible evidence of the manuscript: the ordering of
scenes in H4 may in some cases be arguable, but there is no possibility whatever that the shaving scene came first—not least because it
starts part-way down the page, following the last few lines of H4, 4.
Indeed the true position of H4, 5 within the scene-order of the manuscript is highly significant, for it locates Woyzeck's expostulations on

poverty and morality within a far larger context than that of mere social criticism.

By using the word 'mere' I do not mean to disparage the element of social criticism within the work, but to put it in its due perspective. By placing the shaving scene first, Franzos and Bergemann wantonly and enduringly distorted the overall perspective by not only wrenching the scene from its proper context, but arbitrarily re-functionalizing it as the dramatic exposition, which in consequence sets the play going in the wrong direction and with the wrong atmosphere. There can be little doubt that at one level Woyzeck is indeed serving as Büchner's mouthpiece with his sudden and highly effective blasts of rhetoric against the iniquities of the class-system and the speciousness of the Hauptmann's supposed 'morality' (cf. above, pp. 50 ff.). But we can interpret them as straightforward, unambiguous statements of Büchner's own social-political stance only by taking them in isolation. Within their particular dramatic context they are far less clear-cut; in fact they turn out to be part of the most profound and problematic concerns of the play. This is just as well, for if Woyzeck's words represented the ultimate truth of the play, or the premiss upon which it was founded, then we would be dealing not with a sustained and poignant tragedy, but with a *pièce à thèse* embodying an all too simple syllogism: morality is a luxury beyond the means of the poor, who in consequence are driven solely by their nature; Marie and Woyzeck belong to the poor; therefore morality is beyond them, and they are driven solely by their nature. Woyzeck uses this argument vis-à-vis the Hauptmann to explain or excuse the fact that he has a bastard child: 'wir gemeine Leut, das hat keine Tugend, es kommt einem nur so die Natur'. Three scenes later, he uses exactly the same argument—again in relation to the doings of his penis— when the Doctor berates him for pissing in the street: 'Aber H. Doctor, wenn einem die Natur kommt.' (366; Büchner clearly sets up the 'Natur'–'Natur' echo in H4 quite deliberately: at the relevant point in the H2 predecessor-scene, Büchner had Woyzeck use different and much vaguer terms: 'Aber H. Doctor wenn man nit anders kann?', 367; *But Doctor, if you just can't help it?*) But what do we find in the intervening two scenes? In the first of them we see Marie and the Drum-Major in a louche tête-à-tête prickling with sexuality. In the second we see Woyzeck face to face with Marie— not in this case adducing the imperatives of nature as a counter to accusations of immorality and the like, but making such accusations himself, and making them in the most drastic terms of 'mortal sin': 'Eine Sünde so dick und so breit. (Es stinkt daß man die Engelchen zum Himmel hinaus rauche könnt.) . . . Adieu, Marie, du bist schön wie die Sünde—. Kann die Todsünde so schön seyn?'

(364; *A sin so big and so fat. (It stinks enough to smoke the angels out of heaven.)* . . . *Goodbye, Marie, you're beautiful as sin. Can mortal sin be so beautiful?*) In Woyzeck's contradictory responses to the Doctor and the Hauptmann on the one hand, and to Marie on the other, we glimpse the essential skein of fundamental issues that Büchner tries ever more keenly to unravel and illumine throughout the successive drafts: questions of civilization as against nature; moral choice as against animal compulsion; responsibility and accountability; crime and punishment; sin and retribution.

It is in just such terms that Büchner launches the entire project in the opening scenes of H1: before homing in on the doings of individual human beings within their particular society, he conjures up a context that challenges the very idea of humanity, society, civilization. The tone is struck in the first words from the 'Marktschreier' (*Barker*): 'Meine Herren! Meine Herren! Sehn sie die Creatur, wie sie Gott gemacht, nix, gar nix. Sehen Sie jezt die Kunst, geht aufrecht hat Rock und Hosen, hat ein Säbel!' (343; *Gentlemen! Gentlemen! See here the creature as God made it: nothing, just nothing. Now here's civilization for you: walks upright, wears jacket and trousers, has a sword!*) It is not clear what exactly Büchner had in mind here, but it obviously entails animals, perhaps a couple of monkeys, one in its natural state, the other tamed, and togged up like a soldier. But in any case the thrust of the words is clear: 'Kunst', that entire man-made contrivance that is culture, society, civilization, is perhaps merely an overlay that might disguise our essential creatureliness and nothingness, but can never change or overcome it. The challenging of our normal assumptions is then greatly intensified in the second scene through the device of the performing horse, which serves as a visible parody of human pretensions. Twice the horse is said by the Barker to 'put human society to shame' ('Beschäm die menschlich Societät! . . . So beschäm die société', 355)—but for very different reasons on the two occasions. In the first case it is the horse's alleged intellectual brilliance that does the trick: it may stand on four legs and have a dangling 'Schwanz' (a *double entendre* implying both 'tail' and 'penis'), but with its 'Talent' and its 'viehische Vernünftigkeit' (*brutish braininess*) it is a member of every learned society, and a professor to boot. In short, it is no mere specimen of dumb animality, but rates as an individual, a personality, a true human being: 'Ja das ist kei viehdummes Individuum, das ist eine Person. Ei Mensch . . .'. For all its apparent humanness, however, it remains an 'animal human', indeed 'a beast': 'Ei Mensch, ei thierisch Mensch und doch ei Vieh, ei bête.' The point is driven home by the most graphic means: a stage direction requires the horse-cum-human to 'behave improperly', in other words to defecate or urinate in public ('das Pferd führt sich ungebührlich auf'). This is where the horse is said for the second time to 'put society to shame'—by demonstrating not its super-developed intelligence, but its abiding naturalness: 'So beschäm die société. Sehn sie das Vieh ist noch Natur, unideale [Schmid: unverdorbe] Natur!' (*There, put society to shame. See, the animal is still all nature, unideal [Schmid: unspoilt] nature!*) The whole episode turns out to have a moral, which is duly delivered—and carries us with shocking suddenness from piss and shit to ultimate questions of ontology: 'Lern Sie bey ihm. Fragen sie den Arzt, es ist höchst schädlich. Das hat geheiße: Mensch sey natürlich. Du bist geschaffe Staub, Sand, Dreck. Willst du mehr seyn, als Staub, Sand, Dreck?' (*Learn from him. Ask the doctor, it's extremely bad for you. There's the moral: man, be natural. You're made of dust, sand, dirt. Do you claim to be more than dust, sand, dirt?*) The central importance of this proposition is reflected in the fact that Büchner tries it out again later in H1, through the medium of the 'Barbier': 'Was ist der Mensch? Knochen! Staub, Sand, Dreck. Was ist die Natur? Staub, Sand, Dreck. Aber die dummen Menschen, die dummen Menschen. . . . Was ist das? Bein, Arm, Fleisch, Knochen, Adern? Was ist das? Dreck? Was steckt's im Dreck?' (387; *What is man? Bones! Dust, sand, dirt. What is nature? Dust, sand, dirt. But stupid humans, stupid humans. . . . What is this? Leg, arm, flesh, bones, veins? What is it? Dirt? Why's it stuck in dirt?* Büchner's handwriting is particularly problematic here; see also Schmid's readings, and his list of variants.)

Such, then, was the original departure point of *Woyzeck*: the proposition that there is perhaps nothing real beyond the grim materiality of nature and its functional processes; that all else is perhaps mere delusion and absurd pretension. Büchner raised a similar perspective in the climactic final gaol scene of *Dantons Tod*: eating, sleeping, and procreating as the only essential reality; the infinitely replicated and immutable 'Schaafskopf' as the vapid truth behind our speciously individualized masks; our ugly genitals as the true mark of our animality—'das häßliche Ding' that we might just as well not bother to disguise, but instead leave exposed for dogs to lick.

In this context it is notable that Büchner makes mention of the animal world with astonishing frequency in *Woyzeck*. The majority of cases are only passing references, but they nonetheless serve to locate the central story within a kind of menagerie of animal activity: horse, canary, monkey, dog, ass, hare, hedgehog, mole, cat, toad, lice, sundry pondlife and other small organisms, spider, wasp, cow, hornet, mouse, worm, gnat, crab, butcher-bird, beetle. In many cases, however, the animal reference is much more specific and pointed. The fairground scenes present the most elaborate example of this, not least in the H2 version, where Büchner includes a sardonic comment

on the 'advance' of civilization: 'Sehn Sie die Fortschritte d. Civilisa-
tion. Alles schreitet fort, ein Pferd, ein Aff, ein Canaillevogel! Der
Aff ist schon ein Soldat, s'ist noch nit viel, unterst Stuf von menschliche Geschlecht!' (348; *Observe the progress of civilization. Everything's progressing, a horse, a monkey, a canary! The monkey's already
a soldier, though that's not much—bottom-most species of human
kind!*) This has a particular edge to it because—like the fairground
scenes generally—it merges the realms of the animal and the human;
and in the process it also serves to spotlight the way Woyzeck is automatically perceived by those around him: as a soldier he rates as the
lowest form of human life, more or less on a par with the performing
monkey. Elsewhere, too, the lowly perception of him by other characters is expressed through animal associations. Thus the Jew from
whom he buys the knife dismisses him contemptuously as a 'dog'
('Der Hund', 388). When he urinates in the street—thus repeating
the 'natural' but 'improper' behaviour of the horse—the Doctor likewise compares him to a dog ('er hat auf die Straß gepißt, an die
Wand gepißt wie ein Hund', 366; cf. also 367). In the cat-throwing
scene the Doctor not only calls him an 'animal' ('Bestie'), but also
describes him to the students as displaying regressive features that
link him to the ass ('So meine Herrn, das sind so Uebergänge zum
Esel', 396).

    Animal imagery is also used in relation to Marie and the Drum-
Major—but imagery of a very different kind. Interestingly, it occurs
scarcely at all in the earlier drafts: only in H2 do we find a hint of
animality, when Büchner has the Drum-Major instantly see 'Louisel'
as a virtual brood-mare perfectly suited to the mass propagation of
him and his kind: 'Teufel zum Fortpflanzen von Kürassier-regimenter
u. zur Zucht von Tambourmajors!' (356). In H4, however, we find a
whole train of such images. Perhaps the most forceful instance is
H4, 6, the only scene in which we see Marie and the Drum-Major
alone together. If Büchner had been intent on writing a 'social
drama' reflecting the irresistible impact of socio-economic circumstances, then this scene would surely have taken a very different
shape. As it is we see an encounter not between exemplars of a particular society, but between an emblematic male and an emblematic
female who see each other in purely creatural terms. For Marie, the
Drum-Major is not a potential meal-ticket: he is an 'ox' and a 'lion'
in human form: 'MARIE [*ihn ansehend, mit Ausdruck.*] Geh' einmal
vor Dich hin.—Ueber die Brust wie ein Rind [Schmid: Stier] u. ein
Bart wie ein Löw . . So ist keiner . . Ich bin stolz vor allen Weibern.'
(364; *MARIE [with intensity as she gazes at him]. Just walk up and
down, go on.—Chest like an ox, and a beard like a lion . . There's not
another man like you . . I'm the proudest woman in the world.*) As for
the Drum-Major's response to Marie: Büchner recycles the H2, 5

'brood-mare' image ('Sapperment, wir wollen eine Zucht von Tambour-Majors anlegen. He?'); but he also has him see Marie as a 'wild animal' ('Wild Thier').

The Marie/Drum-Major encounter in H4 constitutes a new scene, so that there are no comparators in the earlier drafts; but there are some revealing changes and additions in scenes that do have predecessors. H4, 2 is a notable case in point. In the equivalent H2 scene, Büchner had Louise and her neighbour respond to the Drum-Major as follows: 'MAGRETH. Ein schöner Mann! LOUISE. Wie e Baum.' (341; MAGRETH. *Handsome man, that!* LOUISE. *Like a tree.*); in H4, though, the dialogue is altered to yield a quite new perspective: 'MAGRETH. Was ein Mann, wie ein Baum. MARIE. Er steht auf seinen Füßen wie ein Löw.' (340; MAGRETH. *What a man, like a tree.* MARIE. *Stands there like a lion.*) Even more striking, perhaps, are the changes introduced into Woyzeck's responses. In H1, 6 'Louis' hears the subterranean voices telling him to stab 'the Woyzeck woman': 'Stich, Stich, Stich die Woyzecke todt, Stich, stich die Woyzecke todt!' (383); in H4, 12, however, 'die Woyzecke' is replaced by 'die Zickwolfin': '—stich, stich die Zickwolfin todt? stich, stich die Zickwolfin todt' (382). Büchner even invents a new word here (or borrows it from some unknown source), and no one knows for certain exactly what 'Zickwolfin' is supposed to mean. But the '-wolfin' part is plain enough: Marie is being projected as a 'she-wolf'; and it is more than likely that 'Zick-' is meant as a shortened form of 'Zicke', a variant of 'Ziege' (*goat*), and a word still used today as a pejorative term for a woman (analogous to English 'bitch!')—so that Magreth is implied to be so to speak doubly animal-like. The immediately preceding inn scene (H4, 11) offers the most revealing changes of all. When Woyzeck looks through the window and sees the couple dancing past, his reaction in the original H1, 5 version is simply this: 'LOUIS [*lauscht am Fenster*] Er—Sie! Teufel! [*er setzt sich zitternd nieder*] [*Er späht, tritt an's Fenster*] Wie das geht! Ja wälzt Euch übernander! Und Sie: immer, zu—immer zu.' (379; LOUIS [*listens at the window*]. *Him—her! Hellfire!* [*he sits down, trembling*] [*He looks, steps to the window*] *Such a frenzy! Yes, keep at it, writhe around on top of each other! And her: 'go on, go on'.*) In H4, Woyzeck's reaction is not only far more intense and sustained—it is also critically different in its orientation:

WOYZECK [*erstickt*]   Immer zu!—immer zu! [*fährt heftig auf u. sinkt zurück auf die Bank*] immer zu immer zu, [*schlägt die Hände in einander*] dreht Euch, wälzt Euch. Warum bläßt Gott nicht die Sonn aus, daß Alles in Unzucht sich übernanderwälzt, Mann und Weib, Mensch u. Vieh. Thut's am hellen Tag, thut's einem auf den Händen, wie die Mücken. [etc.] (380)

woyzeck [*choking*]   Go on!—go on! [*starts up violently then sinks back onto the bench*] Go on! go on! [*Claps his hands together.*] Whirl and writhe! Why don't God blow out the sun when he sees the whole world writhing together in lechery, men and women, man and beast. They're doing it in broad daylight, on the backs of your hands, like gnats. [etc.]

What gives this passage particular resonance is the fact that it contains strong echoes of *Dantons Tod*: Danton's 'es ist als brüte die Sonne Unzucht aus' in the 'Promenade' scene; Lacroix's 'die Mücken treiben's ihnen sonst auf den Händen' in the Marion scene (see above, pp. 182 f.); there is also a clear echo of *Der Hessische Landbote*, in which the lords and ladies of court and aristocracy are said to 'sich . . . in ihrer Geilheit übereinander wälzen' (ii. 44; *writhe together . . . in their lasciviousness*). As these resonances tend to confirm, we are not confronted here simply by the spectacle of a man in the grip of insane delusions. What we witness is a critical conjuncture: the point at which the central questions of nature and morality most powerfully intersect.

PETER J. SCHWARTZ

Clarus, Woyzeck, and the Politics of Accountability[†]

"Friede den Hütten! Krieg den Palästen!"—Peace to the cottages! War on the palaces!—If the epigraph to Büchner's political pamphlet "The Hessian Messenger" (1834) weren't so clearly a German translation of the French revolutionary slogan "Guerre aux châteaux! Paix aux chaumières," one might suspect it of being directly a slap in the face to one Dr. Johann Christian August Clarus, the author of an 1824 report on the state of mental health of the murderer Johann Christian Woyzeck.[1] Clarus perversely enlists the phrase in the service, precisely, of the palaces—here understood as the rightful protectors of those in the cottages:

> The educated and feeling man is overcome by deep, anxious sympathy, for in the criminal he still sees the man. . . . But

---

† Written especially for this Norton Critical Edition.
1. See "The Hessian Messenger," in this volume, p. 3. On the French revolutionary phrase, see the commentary in Georg Büchner, *Werke und Briefe*, ed. Karl Pörnbacher, Gerhard Schaub, Hans-Joachim Simm and Edda Ziegler (Munich: Deutscher Taschenbuch Verlag, 1988), 460. On the uncertain dating of Büchner's encounter with Clarus's text, see Georg Büchner, *Woyzeck, Marburger Ausgabe, Band 7.2: Text, Editionsbericht, Quellen, Erläuterungsteile*, ed. Burghard Dedner, Arnd Beise, Ingrid Rehme, Eva-Maria Vering and Manfred Wenzel (Darmstadt: Wissenschaftliche Buchgesellschaft, 2005), 252–54.

besides the sympathy and besides the feeling for everything there is about the death penalty that is terrible and repugnant, still, if things are not to end simply in sickly sentimentalism or even in farce, the thought must arise of the *inviolable sanctity of the law*; which, to be sure, is capable, like mankind itself, of a progressive mitigation and improvement, but which, so long as it exists, must, *in defense of the throne and of the cottages*,[2] weigh on a strict scale where it shall spare and where it shall punish, and which demands from those who serve it, and from whom, as witnesses or as experts, it seeks enlightenment, *truth*—and not feelings.[3]

One can read Büchner's *Woyzeck* as an angry evisceration of the logic informing this passage and this text; a logic that, in rejecting humane sympathy and in distinguishing empathy strictly from truth, knowingly reverses the progressive legacy of the Enlightenment in matters of crime and punishment to suit the conservative politics of the moment.

In September of 1821, Clarus, a prominent Leipzig physician and the city's minister of public health, was engaged as an expert witness to examine Woyzeck, a soldier and sometime barber and drifter who had brutally stabbed his mistress to death on June 2 of the same year. Questions had been raised regarding the murderer's sanity, and members of the public had objected that the crime, if committed *non compos mentis*, might not require capital punishment.[4] In a short testimony dated September 16, 1821, Clarus adjudged Woyzeck's deed a consequence, not of any "involuntary, blind and rabid impulse which nullifies self-determination," but rather of "moral degeneracy, insensibility to natural feelings, and indifference with regard to the present and future."[5] In October, in a judgment based largely on this report, the Leipzig criminal court sentenced Woyzeck to death. Appealed by the defense, the decision was reconfirmed by the court, and a plea for clemency rejected by the Saxon king. In November 1822, however, seven days before the scheduled execution, Woyzeck's defense counsel filed to introduce new witnesses ready to testify to his insanity. The case was reopened;

---

2. Emphasis added.
3. See this volume, pp. 199–200.
4. For a description of the extant archival documents regarding the Woyzeck case, see Ursula Walter, "Der Fall Woyzeck: Eine Quellen-Dokumentation (Repertorium und vorläufiger Bericht)," *Büchner-Jahrbuch* 7 (1988–1989): 351–380. Further archival finds have since been made by Holger Steinberg, Adrian Schmidt-Recla and Sebastian Schmideler (see p. 370, n. 6; also Sebastian Schmideler and Holger Steinberg, "Der 'Fall Woyzeck': Historische Quellen, zeitgenossische Diskurse," in Claude D. Conter, ed., *Literatur und Recht im Vormärz. Forum Vormärz Forschung, Jahrbuch 2009, 15. Jahrgang* (Bielefeld: Aisthesis, 2010), 41–58).
5. In Büchner, *Woyzeck, Marburger Ausgabe, Band 7.2*, 368; also in Büchner, *Werke und Briefe*, 652.

the demand was made for a second medical certificate; and because Woyzeck "was still an inmate of the Leipzig prison, the person providing the certificate was, according to the existing administrative and judicial procedures, the same public health officer, Clarus, as in the first court case. In his lengthier second report of February 28, 1823, Clarus confirmed the findings of his first expert opinion of September 1821."[6] In direct consequence of this second report, Woyzeck was judged responsible for his actions and sentenced a second time to death by beheading; on August 27, 1824, he was publicly executed on Leipzig's Market Square. By this time, however, the Woyzeck case had become a matter of impassioned public discussion, and when in response to criticism Clarus made public his second report in Adolph Henke's *Zeitschrift für die Staatsarzneikunde* (*Journal of Public Health*) in 1825, he unleashed a pamphlet war among German physicians and lawyers regarding the legal accountability of persons adjudged insane.[7]

Büchner's *Woyzeck* bears unmistakeable traces of the playwright's direct engagement with Clarus's text, which he probably first encountered in his father's medical library. Beyond the basic plot of the crime itself and such clearly matching details as Woyzeck's obsession with Freemasons, imagined voices, the miscellany of semiskilled odd jobs that keep him busy, and dreams of fire, there are Büchner's transfigurations of the drunken quarrel in Jordan's tavern (4,14) and of Woyzeck's exchange with a voice that commands him to stab his lover (4,12). Clarus was likely one of the inspirations for the Doctor in 4,8; if so, his coldly clinical observations of Woyzeck's heart rate and pulse are revealed there in their awful absurdity as inhumane condescension. Yet the playwright does more with Clarus than simply mine him for information and pillory him for his callousness, for his work engages this text at far deeper levels of argument. Along with the two other comparable cases on which Büchner is known to have drawn to a lesser degree while writing *Woyzeck*—one the murder trial of Daniel Schmolling, a tobacco-rolling apprentice who had stabbed his lover to death in Berlin in September 1817, the other the trial of the weaver Johann Diess for a similar murder committed in Darmstadt in 1830—the Woyzeck affair became a *cause célèbre* because it raised certain questions of special importance to its time. Like the crimes of suicide and infanticide in Germany in the 1770s, which allowed the

6. The best short account in English of the trial, its historical context, and the documents relating to it is Holger Steinberg, Adrian Schmidt-Recla and Sebastian Schmideler, "Forensic Psychiatry in Nineteenth-Century Saxony: The Case of Woyzeck," *The Harvard Review of Psychiatry* 2007; 15(4):169–180; this quotation, 171.
7. The debate is exhaustively documented in Büchner, *Woyzeck, Marburger Ausgabe, Band* 7.2, 249–440.

writers of the Sturm und Drang to explore rising tensions between the stiffening institutional and ideological constraints of the new bourgeois civil society and that same society's stake in the notion of human individuality, these three cases enjoyed the press they did because they permitted the working-through of recently pressing discursive tensions: tensions partly politically shaped, and partly developments of longer discursive arcs.

Although the major German debates on legal accountability date to the years around 1820, the philosophical framework for recognizing psychological factors in crime originates in the Enlightenment—above all in the 1780s and 1790s—as the nascent sciences of anthropology and psychology interact with new trends in penal reform.[8] An example may be found in a 1784 literary account of a man led by misguided religious enthusiasm to murder his sons so as to rival the biblical Abraham's sacrifice to God. The account ends with the author's approval of the enlightened clemency of the man's judges, who instead of a death sentence recommend lifelong incarceration. The sovereign—Frederick the Great—shows even better insight by striking this sentence and simply writing: "madhouse."[9] This vision of the Prussian king corresponds to that of Immanuel Kant, who in the very same year defined the age of enlightenment as "the century of *Frederick*," and praised that tolerant monarch for opening up for his subjects a horizon not only of intellectual but also of gradual political self-liberation.[1] In contrast, the 1820s, 1830s, and 1840s were an age of political reaction, of state censorship and repression. This period in central Europe—often called in German the *Vormärz*, because it preceded the failed democratic revolution of March 1848—began with the antiliberal measures introduced at Carlsbad in 1819 by the Austrian minister Klemens von Metternich and was characterized above all by tensions between the efforts of ruling elites to banish the spectre of revolution and those of political reformers (such as Büchner, Heine, or Marx) to democratize German political and cultural life. We can measure the distance from 1784 in the way Frederick's enlightened beneficence recurs as a seeming anomaly in the dissenting vote in favor of life imprisonment filed in the

8. On the problem of accountability generally, see Ylva Greve, "Die Unzurechnungsfähig-keit in der 'Criminalpsychologie' des 19. Jahrhunderts," in Michael Niehaus and Hans-Walter Schmidt-Hannisa, eds., *Unzurechnungsfähigkeiten: Diskursivierungen unfreier Bewusstseinszustände seit dem 18. Jahrhundert* (Frankfurt am Main: Peter Lang, 1998), 107–132.
9. August Gottlieb Meißner, "Mord aus Schwärmerey," *Ausgewählte Kriminalgeschichten*, ed. Alexander Košenina (St. Ingbert: Röhrig Universitätsverlag, 2003), 33–35.
1. Immanuel Kant, "An Answer to the Question: 'What Is Enlightenment?'" *Political Writings*, ed. Hans Reiss, trans. H. B. Nisbet (Cambridge: Cambridge University Press, 1970), 58.

Woyzeck case by Duke Friedrich August, the young and fairly liberal heir apparent to the throne of Saxony—an opinion ignored by
the sovereign (his uncle), who would refuse Woyzeck clemency.[2]
This is also precisely where Clarus, paying lip service to the
Enlightenment ideal of "a progressive mitigation and improvement"
(represented for Kant by Friedrich), draws his line "in defense of the
throne and of the cottages."

    If the legal debates of the 1820s and 1830s surrounding the
insanity defense mark a particular discursive threshhold, "a moment
when the sciences of the individual—psychology and psychiatry—
came into contact with the juridical domain,"[3] they also reflect the
self-positioning of professional representatives of these sciences—
such as Clarus—within a newly conservative political climate.
Clarus's introduction to his second opinion on Woyzeck concludes
ninety pages that seem clearly to point to insanity with a dubious
physiological explanation that returns to Woyzeck full agency as a
homicide, leaving little doubt as to the doctor's choice of which
wind to trim his sails to: the truth that the law demands from him is
a truth "in defense of the throne and of the cottages."[4] This is the
venal teleology skewered in *Woyzeck* with the speech of the First
Apprentice ("How could the soldier exist, if men didn't feel the
necessity of killing one another?" [4,11]) and with the Captain's
absurd definitions ("Morality—that's when you're moral, you understand" [4,5]). The manner of reasoning that "understands the individual only as something that achieves a purpose beyond itself" is
also a target in Büchner's inaugural lecture at Zurich in 1836 on
cranial nerves, where he insists that "everything that exists is there
for its own sake."[5] We find similar thoughts in one of his earliest
writings, an essay on suicide of 1831, where he rejects Christian
eschatology as a betrayal of human life, "for it considers life only as
a *means*; I believe, however, that life is *itself* an end."[6] The life of a
man is an end in itself, not a means to salvation—or to political
order. What Büchner resists in satirizing the Doctor's reduction of
Woyzeck to a "case" ("You're an interesting case. Subject Woyzeck,
you're getting a raise!" [4,8])—indeed, with the entire play
Woyzeck—is the making useful of man through forensic discourse
that Michel Foucault would call "biopolitics"; that is, through a mode
of discipline, characteristic of the modern age, that tries to rule and

2. Steinberg et al., "Forensic Psychiatry," 170–71.
3. Dorothea E. von Mücke, *The Seduction of the Occult and the Rise of the Fantastic Tale*
   (Stanford: Stanford University Press, 2003), 109.
4. See Michael Niehaus, "Gutachterlichkeit," in Claude D. Conter, ed., *Literatur und
   Recht im Vormärz. Forum Vormärz Forschung, Jahrbuch 2009*, 15. Jahrgang (Bielefeld:
   Aisthesis, 2010), 23–40, esp. 37; also von Mücke, *The Seduction of the Occult*, 109–117.
5. See this volume, p. 175.
6. Büchner, *Werke und Briefe*, 36.

exploit "a multiplicity of men to the extent that their multiplicity can and must be dissolved into individual bodies that can be kept under surveillance, trained, used, and, if need be, punished."[7] It is thus no coincidence that in the politically restless years around 1830, German positions in the debate on accountability were split fairly evenly between Christian conservative defenders of Clarus and of the law, and liberal or revolutionary proponents of the insanity defense.[8]

7. Michel Foucault, "Society Must Be Defended": Lectures at the Collège de France, 1975–1976, ed. Mauro Bertani and Alessandro Fontana, trans. David Macey (New York: Picador, 2003), 242; see also Nicolas Pethes, "Individuum als >Fall< in Recht- und Naturwissenschaft," in Roland Borgards and Harald Neumeyer, eds., Büchner-Handbuch: Leben-Werk-Wirkung (Stuttgart: Metzler, 2009), 198–204.
8. Büchner, Woyzeck, Marburger Ausgabe, Band 7.2, 334–8; see also 259.

Four Georg Büchner Prize Talks

The Georg Büchner Prize is Germany's most prestigious literary honor. Established in 1923, the prize was originally awarded to artists of all kinds who came from or were closely associated with Büchner's home state of Hesse. In 1951, the Deutsche Akademie für Sprache und Dichtung restricted the prize to authors, but broadened its geographic scope to include all who write in German. At the annual award ceremony, held in Darmstadt, the awardee is asked to deliver an acceptance speech in which he or she reflects on Büchner's work. Four of these talks are reprinted here.

PAUL CELAN

The Meridian[†]

Ladies and gentlemen!

Art, you will remember, has the qualities of the marionette and the iambic pentameter. Furthermore—and this characteristic is attested in mythology, in the story of Pygmalion and his creature—it is incapable of producing offspring.

In this form art constitutes the subject of a conversation which takes place in a room, and not in the Conciergerie, a conversation which, as we see, could be indefinitely prolonged if nothing were to intervene.

But something does intervene.

Art reappears. It is found in another work by Georg Büchner, in "Wozzeck," where it appears as one of many nameless characters,

---

[†] Translated by Jerry Glenn. From *Chicago Review* 29:3 (winter 1978), pp. 29–40. Though he never lived in Germany, Paul Celan (1920–1970) is one of the most influential German-language poets of the twentieth century. Born Paul Antschel into a Jewish family in Romania, Celan was deported to forced-labor camps under the Nazi occupation; his parents were murdered under similar conditions. After settling in Paris in 1948, Celan wrote several volumes of poetry, including *Mohn und Gedächtnis* (*Poppy and Memory*, 1952) and *Lichtzwang* (*Light-force*, 1970). This speech, given on the occasion of his winning the Georg Büchner Prize in 1960, is a touchstone of his work and of postwar aesthetics.

and "in the more livid light of a thunder storm,"—if I might be permitted to convey a phrase coined by Moritz Heiman in reference
to "Danton's Death." Art makes another appearance, unchanged,
although the times are totally different, introduced by a barker. Here
it has no connection with a "glowing," "surging," and "shining" creation as it did in the conversation mentioned above. This time art
appears with a member of the animal kingdom and the "nothin'" that
this creature "has on." This time art appears in the form of a monkey. It is, however, one and the same—we are immediately able to
recognize it by the "coat and trousers." And art is also introduced to
us in a third work by Büchner, "Leonce and Lena." Time and light
are here no longer recognized. We find ourselves "in flight to Paradise"; "all clocks and calendars" are soon to be "destroyed" or "pro-
scribed." But first "two persons, one of each sex" are presented, "two
world-famous robots have arrived," and a person who announces that
he is "perhaps the third and most remarkable of the two" challenges
us in a raspy tone to gaze with astonishment at what is before our
eyes: "Nothing but art and mechanism, nothing but cardboard and
watch springs."

Art appears here with a larger retinue than before, but we immediately see that it is in the company of its own kind; it is the same
art, the same art we have seen before. Valerio is but another name
for the hawker.

Art, ladies and gentlemen, with all that pertains to it and remains
to be applied to it, is indeed a problem, as one sees, a problem which
is hardy, long-lived, and transformable—that is to say, eternal.

A problem which allows a mortal, Camille, and a person who can
be understood only in the context of his death, Danton, to string
words together at great length. It it easy enough to talk about art.

But when art is being talked about there is always someone present who doesn't listen very carefully.

More precisely: someone who hears and listens and looks . . .
and then doesn't know what the conversation was all about. But
who hears the speaker, who "sees him speak," who has perceived
language and form, and at the same time—what doubt could there
be in the world of this drama?—at the same time has perceived
breath, that is, direction and fate.

This person is—as you have guessed, since she, who is so often
quoted, and rightly so, makes her appearance before you every
year—this person is Lucile.

That which intervened during the conversation relentlessly presses
on. It arrives with us at the Place de la Révolution, "the carts are
driven up and stop."

Those who made the ride are there, Danton, Camille, the others. Even here they are not at a loss for words, words rich in artistry, which are effectively disposed, and here Büchner is often able to rely on direct quotations. There is talk of going-to-our-deaths-together, Fabre even wants to be able to die "twice over." Everyone is in top form. Only a couple of voices, "a few"—nameless—"voices" observe that they've seen it all before and find it rather boring.

And here, as the end approaches, in the long drawn-out moments, Camille—no, not he, not he himself, but merely one who rode along—this Camille is dying a theatrical—one is almost tempted to say iambic—death, which only two scenes later, on the basis of a dictum so foreign, yet so appropriate, to him, we recognize as his own death. As pathos and bathos surround Camille and confirm the triumph of "puppet" and "wire," Lucile appears, the one who is blind to art, this same Lucile, for whom language is something personal, something perceptible. She appears once again, with her sudden "Long live the king!"

After all the words spoken on the platform (the scaffold)—what a statement!

It is a counterstatement, a statement that severs the "wire," that refuses to bow before the "loiterers and parade horses of history." It is an act of freedom. It is a step.

To be sure, it sounds like an expression of allegiance to the ancien régime—and that might not be a coincidence, in view of what I am venturing to say about the subject now, today. But these words—please allow one who also grew up with the writings of Peter Kropotkin and Gustav Landauer expressly to emphasize the point—these words are not a celebration of the monarchy and a past which should be preserved.

They are a tribute to the majesty of the absurd, which bears witness to mankind's here and now.

That, ladies and gentlemen, has no universally recognized name, but it is, I believe . . . literature.

"Alas, art." As you see, I remain entangled in these words of Camille.

I am well aware that it is possible to read these words in various ways, one can insert different accents: the acute of the present, the gravis of the historical (including the literary historical), the circumflex—a mark indicating length—of the eternal.

I insert—I have no choice—I insert the acute.

Art—"alas, art": it possesses, aside from its ability to transform, the gift of ubiquity; it is also found in "Lenz," and here—I must emphasize this point—as in "Danton's Death," it is an episode in nature.

"At table Lenz recaptured his good mood; literature was the topic of conversation and he was in his element . . ."

". . . The feeling that there is life in the thing that has been created is more important than these two factors. Indeed, it is the sole criterion in matters of art. . . ."

My guilty conscience with regard to the gravis forces me to make you aware of the passages I have just quoted. Above all, these lines have significance for literary history. They must be read in conjunction with the conversation from "Danton's Death" which I have already cited. In them one finds a concise formulation of Büchner's conception of aesthetics. When one leaves them and Büchner's "Lenz" fragment behind, it is but a short distance to Reinhold Lenz, the author of the "Notes on the Theatre," and by way of him, the historical Lenz, still further back to Mercier's "Elargissez l'Art," which is of great significance in the history of literature. This maxim opens vistas. It is naturalism, it anticipates Gerhart Hauptmann. And in it are contained the social and political roots of Büchner's thought.

Ladies and gentlemen, I have appeased my conscience, if only temporarily, by making this point. But at the same time it disquiets my conscience anew—it also shows you that something continues to concern me, something that seems to be related to art.

I am also seeking it here, in "Lenz"—I am taking the liberty of calling this to your attention.

Lenz, that is, Büchner, has—"alas, art"—disdainful words for "Idealism" and its "wooden puppets." He contrasts them—and they are followed by the unforgettable lines about the "life of the most humble," the "movements," the "suggestions," the "subtle, scarcely perceptible play of their facial expressions"—he contrasts them with that which is natural, with all living creatures. And he illustrates this conception of art by relating a recent experience:

"Yesterday, as I was walking along the edge of the valley, I saw two girls sitting on a rock; one was putting up her hair and the other was helping; and the golden hair was hanging down, and the face, pale and serious, and yet so young, and the black dress, and the other one so absorbed in helping her. The most beautiful, the most intimate pictures of the Old German School can convey but the vaguest impression of such a scene. At times one might wish to be a Medusa's head so as to be able to transform such a group into stone, and call out to the people."

Ladies and gentlemen, please take note: "One would like to be the Medusa's head," in order to . . . comprehend that which is natural as that which is natural, by means of art!

One would like to, not: *I* would like to.

Here we have stepped beyond human nature, gone outwards, and entered a mysterious realm, yet one turned towards that which is human, the same realm in which the monkey, the robots, and, accordingly . . . alas, art, too, seem to be at home.

This is not the historical Lenz speaking, it is Büchner's Lenz. We hear Büchner's voice: even here art preserves something mysterious for him.

Ladies and gentlemen, I have inserted the acute. But we must not deceive ourselves. I have approached Büchner, consciously, if not voluntarily, with my question about art and literature—one question among many—in order to identify his question.

But as you see, whenever art makes an appearance Valerio's raspy tone cannot be ignored.

Büchner's voice leads me to the suspicion that these are the most ancient mysteries. The reason for my persistent lingering over this subject today is probably to be found in the air—in the air which we have to breathe.

And I must now ask if the works of Georg Büchner, the poet of all living beings, do not contain a perhaps muted, perhaps only half conscious, but on that account no less radical—or for precisely that reason in the most basic sense a radical calling-into-question of art, a calling-into-question from this direction? A calling-into-question, to which all contemporary literature must return if it is to continue posing questions? To rephrase and anticipate myself somewhat: may we proceed from art as something given, something to be taken for granted, as is now often done; should we, in concrete terms, above all—let's say—follow Mallarmé to his logical conclusion?

I have gotten ahead of myself (not far enough, I know), and now I will return to Büchner's "Lenz," specifically to that—episodic—conversation held "at table," during which Lenz recaptured his "good mood."

Lenz spoke for a long time, "smiling one minute, serious the next." And now, when the conversation is over, a statement is made about him, about the person who is concerned with problems of art, but also about the artist Lenz: "He had completely forgotten himself."

As I read that, I find myself thinking of Lucile; I read: *He*, he himself. Whoever has art before his eyes and on his mind—I am now referring to the story about Lenz—has forgotten himself. Art produces a distance from the I. Art demands here a certain distance, a certain path, in a certain direction.

And literature? Literature, which, after all, must travel the path of art? In that case we would in fact be shown here the path to the Medusa's head and the robot!

At this point I am not searching for a way out, I am just asking, along the same line, and also, I believe, in the line suggested in the Lenz fragment.

Perhaps—I'm just asking—perhaps literature, in the company of the I which has forgotten itself, travels the same path as art, toward that which is mysterious and alien. And once again—but where? but in what place? but how? but as what?—it sets itself free.

In that case art would be the path travelled by literature—nothing more and nothing less.

I know, there are other, shorter paths. But after all literature, too, often shoots ahead of us. *La poésie, elle aussi, brûle nos étapes.*

I will take leave of the one who has forgotten himself, the one concerned with art, the artist. I think that I have encountered poetry in Lucile, and Lucile perceives language as form and direction and breath. Here, too, in this work of Büchner, I am searching for the very same thing. I am searching for Lenz himself, I am searching for him, as a person, I am searching for his form: for the sake of the location of literature, the setting free, the step.

Büchner's "Lenz," ladies and gentlemen, remained a fragment. Would it be proper for us to search out the historical Lenz, in order to learn which direction his existence took?

"His existence was an inescapable burden.—So his life went on." Here the story breaks off.

But literature, like Lucile, attempts to see form in its direction; literature shoots ahead. We know *where* his life went, and how it *went on.*

"Death"—one reads in a work about Jakob Michael Reinhold Lenz by the Moscow academician M. N. Rosanow which appeared in Leipzig in 1909—"Death the redeemer was not slow in coming. Lenz was found dead on one of the streets of Moscow during the night of May 23–24, 1792. A nobleman paid for his burial expenses. His final resting place is unknown."

So *his* life had *gone on.*

This person Lenz: the true Lenz, Büchner's Lenz, the one we were able to recognize on the first page of the story, the Lenz who "walked through the mountains on the 20th of January"—this person, and not the artist and the one concerned with questions about art—this person as an I.

Can we now, perhaps, find the place where strangeness was present, the place where a person succeeded in setting himself free, as an—estranged—I? Can we find such a place, such a step?

"... but now and then he experienced a sense of uneasiness because he was not able to walk on his head."—That is Lenz. That is, I am convinced, Lenz and his step, Lenz and his "Long live the king!"

"... but now and then he experienced a sense of uneasiness because he was not able to walk on his head."

Whoever walks on his head, ladies and gentlemen, whoever walks on his head has heaven beneath him as an abyss.

Ladies and gentlemen, nowadays it is fashionable to reproach literature with its "obscurity." Permit me now, abruptly—but hasn't something suddenly appeared on the horizon?—permit me now to quote a maxim by Pascal, a maxim that I read some time ago in Leo Schestow: *Ne nous reprochez pas le manque de clarté puisque nous en faisons profession!* That is, I believe, if not the inherent obscurity of poetry, the obscurity attributed to it for the sake of an encounter—from a great distance or sense of strangeness possibly of its own making.

But there are perhaps two kinds of strangeness, in one and the same direction—side by side.

Lenz—that is, Büchner—has here gone one step further than Lucile. His "Long live the king" no longer consists of words. It has become a terrible silence. It robs him—and us—of breath and speech.

Literature: that can signify a turn-of-breath. Who knows, perhaps literature travels its path—which is also the path of art—for the sake of such a breath turning? Perhaps it succeeds, since strangeness, that is, the abyss *and* the Medusa's head, the abyss *and* the robots, seem to lie in the same direction—perhaps it succeeds here in distinguishing between strangeness and strangeness, perhaps at precisely this point the Medusa's head shrivels, perhaps the robots cease to function—for this unique, fleeting moment? Is perhaps at this point, along with the I—with the estranged I, set free *at this point* and *in a similar manner*—is perhaps at this point an Other set free?

Perhaps the poem assumes its own identity as a result ... and is accordingly able to travel other paths, that is, the paths of art, again and again—in this art-less, art-free manner?

Perhaps.

Perhaps one can say that every poem has its "20th of January"? Perhaps the novelty of poems that are written today is to be found in precisely this point: that here the attempt is most clearly made to remain mindful of such dates?

But are we all not descended from such dates? And to which dates do we attribute ourselves?

But the poem does speak! It remains mindful of its dates, but—it speaks, to be sure, it speaks only in its own, its own, individual cause.

But I think—and this thought can scarcely come as a surprise to you—I think that it has always belonged to the expectations of the poem, in precisely this manner to speak in the cause of the strange—no, I can no longer use this word—in precisely this manner to speak *in the cause of an Other*—who knows, perhaps in the cause of a *wholely Other*.

This "who knows," at which I see I have arrived, is the only thing I can add—on my own, here, today—to the old expectations.

Perhaps, I must now say to myself—and at this point I am making use of a well-known term—perhaps it is now possible to conceive a meeting of this "wholly Other" and an "other" which is not far removed, which is very near.

The poem tarries, stops to catch a scent—like a creature when confronted with such thoughts.

No one can say how long the pause in breath—the thought and the stopping to catch the scent—will last. The "Something quick," which has always been "outside," has gained speed; the poem knows this; but it continues to make for that "Other," which it considers to be attainable, capable of being set free, and, perhaps, unoccupied—and, accordingly, attuned—like Lucile, one might say—attuned to it, to the poem.

To be sure, there can be no doubt that the poem—the poem today—shows a strong inclination towards falling silent. And this, I believe, has only an indirect relationship to the difficulties of word selection (which should not be underestimated), the more pronounced vagrancies of syntax, or the more finely tuned sense of ellipsis.

It takes its position—after so many radical formulations, permit me to use one more—the poem takes its position at the edge of itself; in order to be able to exist, it without interruption calls and fetches itself from its now-no-longer back into its as-always.

But this as-always can be nothing more than verbal communication—not, then, the abstract concept of speech—and presumably a "correspondence to," and not only because this is suggested by another form of communication, a "correspondence with."

But language become reality, language set free under the sign of an individuation which is radical, yet at the same time remains mindful of the boundaries established for it by language, of the possibilities laid open for it by language.

This as-always of the poem can, to be sure, only be found in the poem of that person who does not forget that he speaks from under the angle of inclination of his existence, the angle of inclination of his position among all living creatures.

Then the poem would be—even more clearly than before—the language of an individual which has taken on form; and, in keeping with its innermost nature, it would also be the present, the here and now.

The poem is alone. It is alone and underway. Whoever writes it must remain in its company.

But doesn't the poem, for precisely that reason, at this point participate in an encounter—*in the mystery of an encounter?*

The poem wants to reach the Other, it needs this Other, it needs a vis à vis. It searches it out and addresses it.

Each thing, each person is a form of the Other for the poem, as it makes for this Other.

The poem attempts to pay careful attention to everything it encounters; it has a finer sense of detail, of outline, of structure, of color, and also of the "movements" and the "suggestions." These are, I believe, not qualities gained by an eye competing (or cooperating) with mechanical devices which are continually being brought to a higher degree of perfection. No, it is a concentration which remains aware of all of our dates.

"Attention"—permit me at this point to quote a maxim of Malebranche which occurs in Walter Benjamin's essay on Kafka: "Attention is the natural prayer of the soul."

The poem becomes—and under what conditions!—a poem of one who—as before—perceives, who faces that which appears. Who questions this appearing and addresses it. It becomes dialogue—it is often despairing dialogue.

Only in the realm of this dialogue does that which is addressed take form and gather around the I who is addressing and naming it. But the one who has been addressed and who, by virtue of having been named, has, as it were, become a thou, also brings its otherness along into the present, into this present.—In the here and now of the poem it is still possible—the poem itself, after all, has only this one, unique, limited present—only in this immediacy and proximity does it allow the most idiosyncratic quality of the Other, its time, to participate in the dialogue.

When we speak with things in this manner we always find ourselves faced with the question of their whence and whither: a question which "remains open" and "does not come to an end," which points into openness, emptiness, freedom—we are outside, at a considerable distance.

The poem, I believe, also seeks this place.

The poem?
The poem with its images and tropes?

Ladies and gentlemen, what am I really speaking of, when, from *this* direction, in *this* direction, with *these* words, I speak of the poem—no, of *the* poem?

I am speaking of the poem which doesn't exist!

The absolute poem—no, it doesn't exist, it cannot exist.

But each real poem, even the least pretentious, contains this inescapable question, this incredible demand.

And what, then, would the images be?

That which is perceived and to be perceived one time, one time over and over again, and only now and only here. And the poem would then be the place where all tropes and metaphors are developed ad absurdum.

Topos study?

Certainly! But in light of that which is to be studied: in light of u-topia.

And human beings? And all living creatures?

In this light.

Such questions! Such demands!

It is time to turn back.

Ladies and gentlemen, I have reached the conclusion—I have returned to the beginning.

Élargissez l'Art! This question comes to us with its mysteries, new and old. I approached Büchner in its company—I believed I would once again find it there.

I also had an answer ready, a "Lucilean" counterstatement; I wanted to establish something in opposition, I wanted to be there with my contradiction.

Expand art?

No. But accompany art into your own unique place of no escape. And set yourself free.

Here, too, in your presence, I have travelled this path.

It was a circle.

Art—and one must also include the Medusa's head, mechaniza-
tion, robots; the mysterious, indistinguishable, and in the end perhaps the only strangeness—art lives on.

Twice, in Lucile's "Long live the king" and as heaven opened up
under Lenz as an abyss, the breath turning seemed to be there.
Perhaps also, when I attempted to make for that distant but occupi-
able realm which became visible only in the form of Lucile. And
once, proceeding from the attention devoted to things and all living
creatures, we even reached the vicinity of something open and free.
And finally the vicinity of utopia.

Poetry, ladies and gentlemen—: this pronouncement of the
infinitude of mere mortality and futility.

Ladies and gentlemen, now that I am again at the beginning,
permit me once more—briefly, and from a different direction—to
pose my old question.

Ladies and gentlemen, a few years ago I wrote a little quatrain
which reads: "Voices from the path of the nettles:/*come on your
hands to us.*/Whoever is alone with the lamp/has only his palm to
read from."

And last year, in commemoration of a proposed encounter in
Engadine which came to naught, I composed a little story in which
I had a person walk, "like Lenz," through the mountains.

In each instance I started to write from a "20th of January," from
my "20th of January."

I encountered . . . myself.

Does one, when one thinks of poems—does one travel such
paths with poems? Are these paths but circuitous paths, circuitous
paths from thou to thou? There are, however, among possible paths,
paths on which language acquires a voice; these are encounters, a
voice's paths to a perceiving thou, creaturely paths, sketches of
existence perhaps, a sending oneself ahead to oneself, in the process of searching for oneself. . . . A kind of homecoming.

Ladies and gentlemen, I am approaching the conclusion. With
the acute, which I inserted, I am approaching the conclusion of . . .
"Leonce and Lena."

And here, with the final two words of the drama, I must pay care-
ful attention, lest, like Karl Emil Franzos, the editor of that "First
Complete Critical Edition of Georg Büchner's Collected Works and
Posthumous Papers," which the Sauerländer Press published in

Frankfurt am Main eighty-one years ago—I must pay careful attention, lest, like *my countryman Karl Emil Franzos, whom I have here found again*, I read "coming" for "accommodating," which is now the accepted variant.

But on second thought: aren't there quotation marks present in "Leonce and Lena," quotation marks with an invisible smile in the direction of the words? And perhaps these are to be understood not as mere punctuation scratches, but rather as rabbit ears, listening in, somewhat timidly, on themselves and the words?

From this point, that is, from "accommodating," but also in light of utopia, I will now embark upon the study of topoi:

I will search for the region from which Reinhold Lenz and Karl Emil Franzos came, they who encountered me on the path I have taken today, as well as in Georg Büchner's works. I am also seeking the place of my own origin, since I have once again arrived at my point of departure.

I am seeking all of that on the map with a finger which is uncertain, because it is restless—on a child's map, as I readily confess.

None of these places is to be found, they do not exist, but I know where they would have to exist—above all at the present time—and . . . I find something!

Ladies and gentlemen, I find something which offers me some consolation for having travelled the impossible path, this path of the impossible, in your presence.

I find something which binds and which, like the poem, leads to an encounter.

I find something, like language, abstract, yet earthly, terrestrial, something circular, which traverses both poles and returns to itself, thereby—I am happy to report—even crossing the tropics and tropes. I find . . . a *meridian*.

With you and Georg Büchner and the state of Hesse I believe that I have just now touched it again.

Ladies and gentlemen, a great honor has been bestowed upon me today, an honor I will remember. Together with people whose personal contact and works constitute an encounter for me, I am the recipient of a prize which commemorates Georg Büchner.

I extend my sincerest thanks to you for this honor, for this moment, and for this encounter.

I extend my thanks to the state of Hesse, the city of Darmstadt, and the German Academy of Language and Literature.

I extend my thanks to the president of the Germany Academy of Language and Literature, to you, my dear Hermann Kasack.

Thank you, my dear Marie Luise Kaschnitz.

Ladies and gentlemen, I thank you for your presence.

CHRISTA WOLF

Speaking of Büchner[†]

I thank the German Academy of Language and Poetry of the city of Darmstadt for awarding me this year's Georg Büchner Prize. On an occasion like this, the dissatisfaction a writer feels about her own work rises to fever pitch and her doubts about her chosen way of life intensify. I will skip over my ongoing struggles with this subject, my account of them being vain and maybe futile, too. I will also omit the pages I wrote about how hard it is for me to talk here today. With Büchner's example confronting me, I feel more troubled than ever by the hidden links between writing and life, between responsibility and guilt, which produce the person who lives by writing and writes while living, and which threaten to tear that person apart by the same process. Today, I believe that these links must be not only endured but accepted. In moments of weakness, it may seem desirable to be innocent and without responsibility; but it is escapist. In the concrete conditions in which we live, write, grow up, learn to see, get involved, fail, rebel again, and crave new experiences, no space is provided for a state of irresponsible innocence. We cannot get away from the here and now, and our masks are torn off as we go along. When the masks come off, "Do the faces come off with them?"

To read Büchner again is to see your own situation more clearly. "I accustomed my eye to the sight of blood, but I'm no guillotine!" The laborious, often dislocated, plodding, violent, depraved march of the Germans through history might suitably be paved with the words of their poets. I'd like to give a speech that was made up of lines from Büchner, which would sound as if it had been written

† From *The Author's Dimension: Selected Essays*, by Christa Wolf, translated by Jan Van Heurck, 176–186. New York: Farrar, Straus and Giroux, 1993. Translation copyright © 1993 by Jan Van Heurck. Reprinted by permission of Farrar, Straus and Giroux, LLC. A central figure of postwar German letters, Christa Wolf (1929–) rose to prominence in the former East Germany. She established her reputation with the novels *Der geteilte Himmel* (*Divided Heaven*, 1963) and *Nachdenken über Christa T.* (*The Quest for Christa T.*, 1968), though the latter was banned in her home country. Her essays have been collected in several volumes, including *Auf dem Weg nach Tabou* (1997, translated as *Parting from Phantoms*). She was awarded the Georg Büchner Prize in 1980.

today. But we cannot make up now for what we failed to achieve in his lifetime.

Büchner could never have gotten himself into the embarrassing scrape of having to issue a public thank you. How justified we are to look to him and to his work, the work of this very young man— revolutionary, poet, and scientist—who accepted every risk in order to pluck a livable alternative from the dark conditions of his time. A young man whose feverishly sober dialogues, whose clairvoyant, terse lines of prose must have been wrung out from the press of hellish pain. "The pain began to restore him to consciousness. He told his tale rapidly, but like a prisoner on the rack."

The consciousness that comes out of the pain of madness is no longer the same consciousness he had before. And the tortured language to which it is confined to express itself is alien to the man. Lenz goes mad when he loses his agreement with common sense. We who have sobered up right through to the bones stand deject- edly, face to face with the dream products of a type of thinking which still refers to itself as "reason" but which treats things as means to an end and which long ago abandoned the Enlightenment's quest for emancipation and independent maturity, in exchange for the delusion of naked expediency with which we entered the indus- trial age. The metaphor of the sorcerer's apprentice, which today is a harmless fairy tale, was initially a stern warning. Once the drive for profit had fused with technological progress, the slogan "Everything is permitted" could be used to cover up every act of violence. Then bourgeois literature, galled enough to fight back, drew the portrait of the aged, blind Faust, who, in a grotesque act of self-deception, inter- prets the sound of the shovels which are digging his grave as a part of his happy vision of the future. That is a metaphor which sends a shudder through us, more than it could through any previous genera- tion. We are contemporaries of that civilization which treasures money and flawless technology above all else, and which is insane and benighted enough to devote these treasures to products which will bring about its own destruction. We are contemporaries, too, of the new Faust, the "father of the atomic bomb," a man with a human- ist education who, when he is blinded by the light of a bomb that is brighter than a thousand suns, remembers lines from a sacred East Indian epic: "I am death, the thief of everything, the shaker of worlds."

What abuse will we see befall literature the next time? What more can happen before words fail us altogether? Into what snarls and what deaths will literature follow us, as the faithful attendant at mankind's funeral? No longer assisting our lives but only our deaths? Confined as we are by a past which for the most part we do not understand, banished into a present which is virtually stripped of alternatives, and full of evil premonitions of the future—how are we to speak? A new cycle of historical conflicts is preparing itself. Will it have time to evolve, in this age when there are means enough to kill each of us many times over? If we imagine a literature whose language and forms express the intellectual and behavioral models of the West, and whose structures have been developed to portray contradictions and to build upon a productive bond among people at a time when we can no longer count on the existence of such a bond—must that literature not be the accomplice of the whole process of alienation? No matter how much it may struggle, twist, and turn? Isn't it true that the only choice literature has left is between crude and refined techniques of deception? In an age when the word is technologically reproducible, isn't it, too, turning against us, who produced it? And isn't all that can be said about our time being said in plastic, concrete, and steel? Isn't what is said monstrous, grim, self-betraying, and mighty, with a might which language cannot attain? So, is the language of literature going to fail us?

"Noble is man!" Goethe said. And Büchner said, "We were created wrong." A fifty-year gap separates Goethe's statement from Büchner's. Büchner saw that the hallmark of the new age was paradox. His century, which resolutely refused to regard itself as paradoxical, quite logically punished him—by ignoring him. Early in life, he experienced that loss of meaning and certitude with which we are so familiar now, and which brings with it a disgust with language. A whole host of words has been taken from us—words which we believed we could rely on, like "liberty," "equality," "fraternity," "humanism," "justice"—and turned over to news journalists, now that these words no longer correspond to any reality and no longer command belief. By the logic of language, their opposite numbers have also lost their meaning, because words such as "terrible," "disastrous," "hideous," "threatening," and "barbarous" do not adequately describe our realities either. In their place—in place of all the well-informed and know-it-all words, all the judgmental, air-of-triumph, or giving-up words—comes the plain quiet word: *wrong*.

"The state of the world is wrong," we say, testing the phrase. And we hear that it rings true. We have found a sentence that we can stand by. It isn't beautiful, it's only accurate. And so it soothes our ears, which have been ravaged by shouts of the grand words. It also soothes our consciences, which are troubled by too many words which proved false, or were falsely used. Could this phrase become the first in a new, accurate language which we would hear with our ears but not yet speak with our tongues? Perhaps a train of other accurate phrases might emerge out of this one, phrases which are not just the negative of the old phrases but express a different sense of values tailored to our times. (Although we must not forget for a moment that naming things is not the same as putting them right, or repairing or changing them.) But with such new phrases we could say something to each other again, and tell each other stories without having to feel ashamed.

Those who would search for this language, however, must be able to tolerate the almost complete loss of their self-esteem, of their self-confidence, because all the patterns in which we are used to speaking, narrating, thinking, and writing poetry would no longer be available. Such people would no doubt learn what it really means to lose your grip.

We are not the first to go through this. What gets fractured, at the fracture points between different eras, is: courage, backbone, hope, direct contact—all things that you need to be able to speak. Fear jumps in to fill the gaps. In poetry, the precursors are almost always premonitors, too: they sense the fear which later will overtake many.

"Dance, Rosetta, dance, so that time keeps step with the beat of your dainty feet."

"My feet would rather go out of time."

There is a rhythm which pounds into your sleep, into your dreams. It can nail you down, it can drive you crazy.

My feet would rather go out of time.

Dance, Rosetta.

Rosetta dances. Sings: "Ah, dear pain." Goes away, because Leonce cannot love her but only the corpse of her love. "Tears, Rosetta?" "Diamonds, I expect, they are cutting into my eyes." Leonce, alone: "It's a funny thing about love." Meanwhile, his "brother" Danton, on the next stage over, announces: "I will retreat into the citadel of reason. I will burst out with the cannon of truth and mow down my enemies."

But where are the women, while the man holes up in the citadel of reason? Where are Rosetta, Marie, Marion, Lena, Julie, Lucile? Outside the citadel, of course. Unprotected in the foreground. No edifice of thought will shelter them. They have been made to believe that rational thinking is something you can do only if you are dug into the trenches! And they have neither the education nor any real inclination to do so. From a vantage point below and outside the citadel, they observe the strained mental activity of the male, which he directs increasingly toward safeguarding his fortress with exact measurements, calculations, and ingenious number and design systems. This activity thrives in the iciest abstraction, and its ultimate truth is a formula. How could Rosetta suspect that it is the fear of contact which causes the man to retreat from reality's abundance? That his fragility, and his fear of recognizing it, is what drives him to take refuge in his insane systems? That wounded and torn, and robbed of his wholeness by the ruthless division of labor, he is hounding himself, driving at reckless speeds, just to avoid having to make the "descent into hell" that is self-knowledge—even though, Kant says, reason cannot exist without self-knowledge? And how could Rosetta guess that a man who does not know himself cannot know a woman either?

And so their ways divide. Rosetta keeps silent. Loves. Suffers. In the person of Marie in *Woyzeck*, she is murdered. As Julie in *Danton's Death*, she follows her husband into death. As Lucile in the same play, she goes mad. Sacrifices herself. In the role of Lena from *Leonce and Lena*, she laments: "So, am I like the poor helpless well which must reflect in its silent depth any image which leans down over it?" One of Büchner's women, the prostitute Marion from *Danton's Death*, listens to her own nature. That is how far Büchner pushes his realism.

People did not know how to read him. They refused to recognize that the progress which was just beginning to unfold on a grand scale had in it the stuff of a new mythology. That progress could produce craving, but not love. And that its most powerful engine was the fear people felt of their own inner emptiness.

Büchner recognized very quickly, and with horror, I think, that the pleasure people took in the new age was rooted partly in a desire for destruction. But he did not see its full-blown grimace, the paradox that yokes creation to destruction. He did not know words like "megadeath," the multiple deaths that the new weapons hold in store for each living person. He gave his fictional characters a love of death. But it would not have entered his head that people would refer to a flawless but murderous technological solution as "sweet," or would write the names of women on missile hulls. His character Leonce feels confined in a room lined with distorting mirrors; but Büchner could not guess what later Leonces would resort to, just in order not to go without any mirror. For Leonce and his more powerful and industrious successors fall prey to a deadly fear as soon as they have no mirror—no eyes or body of a woman, no theater, no corporate mergers, no powerful organization, no nation, no earth, no cosmos to reflect their own image back to them, magnified to larger than life-size.

"Oh, if we could just once see the top of our own heads!" If any man ever wanted to do the impossible, to make visible the blind spot in our civilization, it must have been Büchner. He surrounded that blind spot with a ring of his characters and drove them to the limits of what could be said in words. Once, he tried using a scream: when Lucile loses her reason over Camille's death in *Danton's Death*. But "that doesn't help, everything is still the way it was before," she says. A dramaturgy of screams is an absurdity to a the-ater based on more or less soluble contradictions. You cannot bring an adequate representation of reality onto the stage. That was another fact that Büchner collided with. So, in his drama of the As-if—which he attached loosely to traditional dramatic structure so that the audience could still just barely imagine that they under-stood what they were seeing—he created a space in which to put sentences which have to be spoken tonelessly, one breath before a scream: "My feet would rather go out of time."

It is Rosetta's fate to live invisible to herself and to Leonce, speech-less, stripped of reality, in a space that is denied, soundproofed, manipulated away, and which the rest of her world cannot see no matter how hard they try. Her character is definable by what she is *not*.

She lets her own history be taken away from her. Lets her soul be taken away. Her reason. Her humanity. Her responsibility for her-self. Lets herself be married. Serves her husband. Gives him heirs. Is forced to believe that the pleasure he enjoys is denied to her for-ever. She hides her unhappiness. Dances. Hears him reproach her: "I want to sleep, but you have to dance."

Rosetta lets her rights be taken away. Lets herself be forbidden to speak. Forbidden to grieve. To feel joy. To feel love. To work. To know art. She lets herself be raped. Be prostituted. Locked up. Driven crazy. In the role of Rose, she lets herself be worked to death, exploited; "twice over," as the play says. Lets herself be forced to bear children. To abort children. Lets her sex be analyzed away. Gets caught in the net of impotence. Becomes a nag. A whore. A vamp. A cricket. In the role of Nora, she leaves the Doll's House.

At last—her name is Rosa now—she begins to fight. Then she is murdered, thrown into the canal. In persecution, her rights equal those of the man, who is oppressed and persecuted, too. Dance, Rosetta. She dances. Now her name is Marlene: "I'm supposed to laugh? Fine, then I'll laugh./I'm supposed to dance? Okay, I'll dance./I'm supposed to captivate you? Absolutely. At your service."

It's a funny thing about love. Rosetta, under her many names, would rather be destroyed than admit what is happening to her: that when Leonce the thinker says "I, the autonomous self," he is never referring to her, to a real woman. That he classes her among the objects. That is, that he . . .

There she stops. She does not struggle through to the final insight. Prefers to deny herself. Suppresses her talent. Under her many names, some of which are no doubt familiar to you, she sup-ports the genius of the man who thinks, writes, paints. "You love me, Leonce?" "Sure, why not?" Sometimes she can become peculiar, even harsh, jealous, bitter. She cries out, she screams at him. Gets hysterical. Starts drinking. Commits suicide.

During the wars, she replaces the man, proves her worth on his machinery of production and destruction. Her ultimate admission is that now she has become like him. She sets out to prove it to him. Progress, for her, is that she works like a man. And it *is* progress. She stands beside him, tending the machine, day and night. Sits next to him in the lecture hall and in the board room (although she is in the minority there, of course). She writes, paints, composes poetry like him—*almost* like him. Here one sees the first fine cracks in her performance. People attribute them to her oversensitivity and make allowances; or they don't make allowances. To some extent, she sticks to the mental and visual framework which the man evolved, and to the forms in which he couched his attitudes, and his melancholy, too. So she walks out of the "blind spot" and gets discovered. She is found worthy of being put into print. Worthy of being critiqued. Becomes a "talent," a name. Is found worthy of praise—in the right circumstances.

Will people believe her when she talks about her ambivalent feelings? It took her a long time to understand herself. To understand why she still goes on feeling so strange. Why she goes on feeling that the praise and blame she reaps don't apply to her but still apply to that other woman, somewhere off to the side of her, to that false image she pretends to be. Why she feels that she herself has barely been mentioned yet.

Once she enters the citadel of reason, she, too, succumbs to its paradoxical laws, so she finds herself—paradoxically—forced to abet the misunderstanding of who she really is. For the sake of being free, she has put on new chains. To achieve self-realization, she is driven into new kinds of self-denial. Her intentions were good. She staked her hopes on the scientific age. She trusted in its rationality, only to fall prey to the irrationalism where it fled for refuge and which it made impregnable with expert scientific testimony. Time has never kept step with the beat of her feet, she has to confess now. But in an oddly persistent and sometimes uncanny way, she is ready to take herself seriously. And now she meets resistance. In the past, whenever things got serious, she was looked after, spared this seriousness. People did not trouble her about the construction of weapons and super-weapons systems which could make old-fashioned individual death obsolete and which have already reduced each one of us to radiation, ashes, and dust seven, eight, twenty times over, in the fantasies of nuclear planning staffs. She—the woman Rosetta under her many names—is allowed no further initiation into the secret meaning of the military, economic, and political strategies which encircle the globe. She sees the man, the upholder of the balance of terror, sitting exhausted in front of the TV set—the planner of economic monstrosities heading for a heart attack—the worldwide distributor of hunger reaching for the bottle. They are working themselves to death—and not only themselves.

Dance, Rosetta, dance.

She does raise her voice at last: admittedly it may be too late. She asks: "Gentlemen. Friends. Colleagues. Comrades. Don't you think that the ground has gotten rather thin, even for light feet?"

She is not allowed to talk that way. Now she has really become ungrateful. She is really dancing to her own tune. She drops out of the net of her helplessness—as if this is a joy ride that she is free to skip if she wants to—even though the meshes of that net were as finely knit as the stuff dreams are made of: the nightmares of thought alienated from self.

Now the fear sets in.

Her fear *and* his. For now they share the terrible secret, the taboo of taboos. Leonce, under his many names, cannot love; he can love only what is dead. ("Beautiful corpse, you rest so sweetly on the black pall of night that you make nature hate life and fall in love with death.") So, does Rosetta, under her many names, have no other option but to be driven back into her dead space, or to become like Leonce? Doesn't every step she takes toward freedom increase his fear, his defensiveness? So, is *she* supposed to hole up now in the citadel of reason, and from it fire "the cannon of truth"? Is she supposed to regard the man as her enemy whom she must "mow down"? And: Is there no way for them to work together, to bring each other to their senses? Are the two of them, both wedded to the same paradox, incapable of taking a single step toward each other that isn't wrong? And is this unprecedented moment in history already a failure?

Once again, the old beat is heard—loud, very loud, especially at night. My feet would rather go out of time. Then fantasies stir beneath the threshold of consciousness, where perpetual threat sets off perpetual alarm, and a ceaseless hunt goes on for alternatives that can be lived with. The troubled consciences of the men or women who feel compelled to write help to feed the fantasies. But can one write on this paper-thin ground? No longer "for hope's sake" but only "for the emergency case"?

"Nothing pleases me anymore" begins the last poem of Ingeborg Bachmann.

> *Should I*
> *deck out a metaphor*
> *with an almond blossom?*
> . . .

> *Should I*
> *take a thought captive, lead it*
> *into the lit-up cell of a sentence?*
> *Feed eye and ear*
> *with word-tidbits,*
> *Grade A?*

The poem ends:

> *(Yup, I should. Let the others do it.)*
> *My portion is meant for loss.*

That is language beyond faith, but it's still language, all the same. A metaphor is used to break with metaphors. The lines which renounce the grade-A tidbits are grade-A themselves. The poem to give up art with paradoxically is forced to be a work of art. All the products of our age (or almost all) carry the seed of self-destruction inside them. Or at least the seed is inside the anti-product which they give rise to. Art cannot cancel itself as art, nor can literature cancel itself as literature. A woman does not eliminate herself by a complete act of self-expression. Her desire to eliminate herself remains, bearing witness. Her portion will not be lost.

We all know only too well that books can be burned. But a literature which despairs of itself, and is sick of itself, must endure—canceling out both despair and self-disgust. It must endure, unless it fails to come into being in the first place because its authors have gone away: into another country, another profession, another name, into an illness, into madness, into death—all of those being metaphors for silence, insofar as the affected person is a writer. To be silenced. To choose silence. To be forced into silence. At last, to be allowed to be silent.

But—before this "But," you have to picture a long pause whose color (if it had a color) would be black—the three languages which Büchner held together in his own person, at the cost of excessive strain to his body and mind, the languages of politics, science, and literature, have been separated beyond repair since his day. It is, strangely, the language of literature which seems to come closest to the reality of man today, and which knows him best, regardless of what statistics, numerical descriptions, standardized tables, and performance charts may say to the contrary. The reason for this, perhaps, is that the moral courage of the author—the courage for self-knowledge—always enters into literature. Contracts are written into literature which over the centuries have woven the fabric we call "civilization," however laborious the process, and however fragile and frequently broken the contracts may be. Our surprise at this old-fashioned word "civilization" may make us realize the threat that exists to what the word stands for. And yet this word—unlike the terms used in politics and science—has a halo, an aura, similar to that of other words which just happen to occur to me: "peace," "moon," "town," "meadow," "life," "death." Do we really want to discard them? Replace them with words like "nuclear stalemate," "earth satellite," "settlement area," "grassland cultivation," "matter in its motion modality," "exitus"?

Scientists have devised a specialized language to safeguard their inventions from their own emotions. Pseudo-logical linguistic constructions support the fixed idea of politicians that the way to save mankind lies in the ability to annihilate it many times over.

Literature has to be peace research.

Writing has not become easier since we learned that our two countries—both of which once bore the name "Germany" and forfeited it through the name of "Auschwitz"—that the land on both sides of the Elbe River would be among the first to suffer extinction in the event of a "nuclear confrontation." I expect that maps already exist which record the phases of our extinction. Cassandra, I think, must have loved Troy more than herself when she dared to prophesy to her countrymen the ruinous end of their city. I wonder, have our two countries not been loved enough by their people? And do they consequently desire to destroy themselves and others, like a person who has not been loved and thus is incapable of love himself? I ask this only to vehemently deny it. As evidence to the contrary—absurd as it may seem—I take literature. I know that literature does not give a people enough of a homeland on its own. Yet—because any proposal, however farfetched, deserves a hearing—I propose that literature should be allowed to draw its own map, to counteract those maps of death. The villages, landscapes, and human affairs which literature describes with precision, accuracy, and bias—describes painfully, critically, devotedly, fearfully, and joyfully, ironically, rebelliously, and lovingly—should be removed from the death map and counted as saved. And finally, just for once, the literature of the Germans should not remain ineffectual. Whatever grief work and joy work literature in the two Germanys has achieved over the last three decades, whatever "worldly truth" it has confronted, should be entered in the books now, should be credited to both nations. Finally, just once, literature should be taken at its word, and should be applied to help ensure that the things of this earth endure.

"That's lucid madness," you say. Fine. So in psychiatric terms I lack insight into my illness, and I give way to this lucid madness, in order not to succumb to the dark side of reason. Maybe a member of the General Staff will really find it harder to wipe out a city which has been tenderly and exactly described in a book than a city

which no one has read about, which no one cared about enough to
feel the need to portray it as the city of her childhood, the place of
her humiliation or of her first love.

Now you are smiling at my naïveté, at my irrationality. Büchner
describes the mad Lenz this way: "He seemed completely rational.
He conversed with people. He did everything just as other people
did. But there was a ghastly emptiness inside him. He no longer felt
any fear, any desire. He experienced his life as a burden which could
not be avoided."

People speak, albeit softly, even in that country beyond faith. A
conversation about trees, about Water, Earth, Sky, Man, strikes me
as more realistic than the sheer insanity of speculations about the
end of the world. Once we had thoroughly investigated the truth
contained in the word "wrong," no doubt we would happen on some
other words which we could say, too, not boastfully but warily. We
would know that none of them, not even the most sincere, is the
last word. We would hope that none is the *last* word.

This skin, too, will be stripped away and turn to rags.

HEINER MÜLLER

The Wounded Woyzeck[†]

for Nelson Mandela

1

Woyzeck still is shaving his captain, eating his prescribed peas, tor-
turing Marie with the torpor of his love, the play's population has
become a state, surrounded by ghosts: The Fusilier Runge is his
bloody brother, proletarian tool of Rosa Luxemburg's murderers; his
prison is called Stalingrad where the murdered woman faces him in
the mask of Kriemhild; her monument is erected on Mamaia Hill,
her German monument the Wall in Berlin, the armored train of the
Revolution curdled to politics.[1]

† Performing Arts Journal 10:3 (1987): 73–75. © 1985 by Performing Arts Journal.
Reprinted by permission of Suhrkamp Verlag and MIT Press Journals. Translated by
Carl Weber. The dramatist, director, and poet Heiner Müller (1929–1995) was one of
the most prominent theatrical artists of East Germany. Sometimes viewed as Bertolt
Brecht's artistic successor, Müller pioneered a post-Brechtian form of theater that
combined sharp critique with openness of form. His plays include *Mauser* (*Mauser*,
1970), *Die Hamletmachine* (*Hamletmachine*, 1977), and *Quartett* (*Quartet*, 1981). He
was awarded the Georg Büchner Prize in 1985.
1. Müller's texts are typically dense with allusion. Fusilier: a soldier armed with a musket.
Runge: Otto Runge (1875–1945), a member of the rightist *Freikorps* militia and one of
the murderers of the socialist activist Rosa Luxemburg in 1919. Stalingrad: site of one

HIS MOUTH PRESSED AGAINST THE SHOULDER OF THE
POLICEMAN WHO NIMBLY LEADS HIM AWAY, that is how
Kafka has seen him disappear from the stage, after the fratricide
WITH DIFFICULTY STIFLING THE LAST NAUSEA.[2] Or as the
patient, in whose bed the doctor is placed, with his wound open like
a mine pit from which the worms are swarming. Goya's giant was his
first appearance, he who sitting on the mountains counts the hours
of the rulers, father of the guerilla. On a mural in a cloister cell in
Parma I have seen his broken off feet, gigantic in an Arcadian landscape.[3] Somewhere, his body perhaps swings itself onward on his
hands, shaking with laughter perhaps, toward an unknown future
that perhaps will be his crossbreeding with a machine, propelled
against the force of gravity in the frenzy of rockets. In Africa he is
still on his Way of the Cross into history, time doesn't work for him
any more, perhaps even his hunger isn't an element of Revolution any
longer since it can be quenched with bombs, while the Drum Majors
of the world devastate our planet, a battlefield of Tourism, runway for
the final emergency; they won't see the Fire that the Rifleman Franz
Johann Christoph Woyzeck saw race around the sky near Darmstadt
as he was cutting switches for the gauntlet. Ulrike Meinhof, a daughter of Prussia and late born bride of another erratic block of German
letters who buried himself on Wannsee shore, female protagonist in
the last drama of a bourgeois world, the armed RESURRECTION
OF THE YOUNG COMRADE FROM THE LIME PIT, she is his
sister with Marie's bloody necklace.[4]

2

A text many times raped by the theatre, a text that happened to a
twenty-three-year-old whose eyelids were cut off at his birth by The
Weird Sisters,[5] a text blasted by fever to orthographic splinters, a
structure as it might be created when lead is smelted at New Year's
Eve since the hand is trembling with anticipation of the future; it

---

of the bloodiest battles of World War II, between German and Soviet forces. Kriemhild: a figure in the *Nibelungenlied* who is ultimately cut to ribbons; Müller compares
her here to Luxemburg. Mamaia Hill (also Mamayev Hill): site of a Stalingrad war
memorial in the form of a woman brandishing a sword.

2. Reference to the Kafka tale *"Ein Brudermord"* ("A Fratricide," 1920).
3. Likely a reference to *The Colossus* (1808–1812), a painting often attributed to Francisco Goya (1746–1828).
4. Ulrike Meinhof (1934–1976) was a German leftist militant and cofounder of the Red
Army Faction. Erratic block of German letters: reference to the writer Heinrich von
Kleist (1777–1811), who shot another and himself in a double-suicide pact on the
shores of the Kleiner Wannsee, a lake near Berlin; the Wannsee was also the site of a
high-level Nazi conference that planned the mass extermination of Jews. LIME PIT:
reference to Brecht's *Die Maßnahme* (*The Measures Taken*, 1930), a *Lehrstück* (teaching play) that Müller subsequently reworked in plays such as *Mauser* (1970). Marie's
bloody necklace: see *Woyzeck* 1,19.
5. *Parzen* in the original German: the three Fates of Greek mythology.

blocks as a sleepless angel the entrance to Paradise where the innocence of playwriting was at home. How harmless the Pill's equivalent in recent drama, Beckett's WAITING FOR GODOT, faced with this fast thunderstorm that moves with the speed of another age, in its baggage Lenz, the extinguished lightning from Livonia, the time of Georg Heym bereft of utopia in his space under the Havel river's ice, of Konrad Bayer in Vitus Bering's eviscerated skull, of Rolf Dieter Brinkmann in the right-hand traffic in front of SHAKESPEARE'S PUB; how shameless the lie of POSTHISTOIRE in the face of the barbaric reality of our prehistory.[6]

3

THE WOUND HEINE begins to scar over, crooked; WOYZECK is the open wound. Woyzeck lives where the dog is buried, the dog's name: Woyzeck. We are waiting for his resurrection with fear and/ or hope that the dog will return as a wolf. The wolf will come from the South. When the Sun is in its Zenith, he will be one with our shadow and in the hour of white heat History will begin. Not until History will have happened will our shared destruction in the frost of entropy or, abridged by politics, in the nuclear lightning, be worthwhile; the destruction which will be the end of all utopias and the beginning of a reality beyond mankind.

DURS GRÜNBEIN

Breaking the Body[†]

What do the cranial nerves of vertebrates have to do with poetry? What is comparative anatomy doing in the monologue of the dramatic hero? What path leads from the gill chambers of fish to the

6. Georg Heym (1887–1912): German Expressionist writer who drowned in the icy Havel river. Konrad Bayer (1932–1964): Austrian avant-garde writer and suicide; author of the novel *der kopf des vitus bering (the head of vitrus bering)*. Dieter Brinkmann (1940–1975): experimental writer of German *Pop-Literatur* who died because he looked the wrong way while crossing a street in front of a London pub called "The Shakespeare." POSTHISTOIRE: theory of "post-history," principally propounded by the sociologist Henri de Man (1885–1953) and the anthropologist Arnold Gehlen (1904–1976), in which the history of ideas is said to have exhausted itself.

† From *The Bars of Atlantis: Selected Essays*, by Durs Grünbein, 12–21. New York: Farrar, Straus and Giroux, 2010. Copyright © 2010 by Durs Grünbein. Translation copyright © by Farrar, Straus and Giroux, LLC. Reprinted by permission of Farrar, Straus and Giroux. One of the most prominent German-language poets of his generation, Durs Grünbein (1962–) was born in the former East Germany and has lived in Berlin since 1985. His poetry collections include *Grauzone morgens* (1988) and *Den teuren Toten* (1994) and the translated volume *Ashes for Breakfast* (2006). Many of his essays are collected in *Gedicht und Geheimnis* (2007) and the translated volume *The Bars of Atlantis* (2010). He was awarded the Georg Büchner Prize in 1995.

human comedy, from rhythmicized prose to the brain's outpouching into the facial nerve? Peculiar questions—they alone suggest what was bound to happen if literature engaged with the real, if the study of nature shaped style, if zoological fact and the medical report found their way into the novella and the drama . . . until the genre lay in pieces, with fragments as the result, delirious notations, somatic poetry. One of the few who could have answered these questions is dead. He died young of typhus, which he contracted, it is believed, while dissecting fish specimens—a poet, unique, his name: Georg Büchner. I admit I was shaking at the knees at the idea of having to talk about him on this occasion. Now the time has come, and I am trying to keep my cool.

For there is more at stake here, at least as I see it, than the annual visit of an unclassical classic. Thinking Büchner's project through to its logical conclusion, we are dealing here with a turning point in literature, a shifting of perspective at the very moment when a German philosopher conjured the specter of the death of art.

If the verdict is correct, then Büchner was one of the first at the grave, and his oeuvre is the earliest commentary on the reading of the will. Büchner—and although this could be demonstrated, I merely want to state it here—braved a sortie, an act of liberation under the most severe duress. With a *salto mortale*, he freed literature from the imposition of having to remain playfully oblivious both to the misery of the real and to real misery. What he managed to achieve was nothing less than a complete transformation: physiology absorbed into literature. And this was no *Sonderweg*, as it turned out; it was the beginning of a series of experiments that have continued to this day. If poetry is understood as one language among others, then this meant the modification of the majority of its forms of inflection. What emerged was a harder grammar, a colder tone: the appropriate tool for an intelligence amputated from the heart.

The road there was long, and he went down that road with giant steps, growing stronger under the force of circumstance, parrying each blow ever more rapidly with every piece, pushing the limits with every new draft. *Danton's Death*—that great song of farewell—spread out across several voices, speech punctured by groans, the hunger for life and the longing for death embodied in a handful of immortal characters. Or *Lenz*—that breathless report on self-dissolution, a self that evaporates in the mountains like steam. *Woyzeck*—the criminal case as medical record, with a symptom as large as all of small-state Germany of Büchner's day. How humiliating for later ages is the speed with which he rushed through the forms, as if he wanted to leave all literary genres behind as quickly as possible so as to be able to devote himself wholly to the study of

nature . . . as if only here he would be able to find the key to understanding the real driving forces, the energies inside the body: the
affects, the stuff history is made of. Everyone knows the famous
lines, as well as their echo. "We'd have to smash our skulls open
and tear the thoughts from the very fibers of each other's brains,"
says Danton in the first act, only to cut himself short in the second
act: "A mistake crept in when we were made, there's something
missing, I don't have a name for it, we'll never discover it by groping
around in each other's guts, so why smash open each other's bodies
to try to find it?" Between the first and the second statements an
abyss opens. It is the abyss bodies vanish into. In the new, gruesome light shining up from down there, history appears as that
intermediate age in which the Last Animal meets the First Man: he
himself *is* that Last Animal. In the darkness of enlightenment,
deep in the sleep of reason, in the night of conscience that keeps
falling again and again, Büchner saw that creature appear. And
sometimes his shock tipped over into laughter, into monological ire.

Caravaggio captured the scene. One of his fleeting sketches depicts
a nighttime dissection: two half-cloaked persons settling down to
work on a lifeless body by the light of a candle sticking out of the
cut-open belly. It is a drawing in the manner of the horror stories
man tells himself about his end. In its feverishness, it resembles the
terse events in Büchner's fragments.

Here I would like to pause briefly . . . in order to highlight one of
the central moments at the heart of an oeuvre replete with pivotal
passages (German Studies can tell you a thing or two about it). The
scene is a study in Strasbourg, and in it sits a young man with a
very high forehead, bent over books, magnifying glasses, and dead
fish. For three long months, he doesn't leave his study. Dissecting
and drawing, he spends the next-to-last winter, the next-to-last
spring of his life writing his dissertation, half-dead from exhaustion, driven by the promise of a professorship, which meant the
safety of Swiss exile for the political refugee. The short text he
writes during these weeks—a study of the nervous system in the
heads of barbels—will later become his job talk at the University of
Zurich, bearing the simple title "On Cranial Nerves." I have always
read this text as the fragment of a confession, as a kind of literary
manifesto. Putting aside all period-related and soon-to-be-dated
hypotheses, what is immediately striking about this text is Büchner's
meticulousness in isolating and studying each individual nerve. Isn't
this—given Büchner's caliber as a poet—more than merely a coincidence? An important lead, perhaps? Without wanting to gloss over
the rift between literature and natural history in Büchner, or to

reduce his view of humanity to a handful of zoological assumptions—doesn't Büchner's very subject suggest that he was looking for answers here, of all places, about something that gave direction to all creaturely existence? His insistence on the importance of the sensory apparatus can hardly be understood any other way. Büchner pursues by way of biology what had long been subterraneously growing "sensitive roots" in him by way of literature.

What is a nerve? he wonders. Where does it lead, and where does it come together? What is its evolutionary purpose? Are there basic forms of nerves that always reappear from one animal species to another, in different arrangements but with the same origin? What does this structure mean for physical sensation, pain, and the fear of death . . . which he once writes about as follows: "They say it lasts only a moment, but pain has the subtlest sense of time: a fraction of a second can last an eternity." And, finally: What is the body, considered in terms of the nervous system? What is history considered in terms of the body thus scrutinized? These are questions to which that autopsy may have led him. And these are also the questions that, even today, provide the basis for raising objections to every kind of social contract, social reform, revolution, or Utopia. In their light, Büchner's perhaps most desperate question reveals its radical thrust: "But are we not in a perpetual state of violence?"

Make no mistake about it: what is significant here is not that his research engages the natural philosophy of his age so much as that he puts the nerve in first place, declaring the body the highest authority. Here we have a poet who derives his principles from physiology as others before him did from religion or ethics. From pure zootomy, he extracts the insight that life is sufficient unto itself and not subject to the strictures of external or higher purposes.

"Everything that exists, exists for its own sake."

In the dissected body, the skull (violently) pried open, he discovers the principles of a viable and free coexistence . . . as well as its ever-threatening negation: radical failure, from within the guts. For autopsy is the surest path to the loss of faith, or, for those for whom this is not enough, to the fortification of faithlessness. Dissecting the body is the royal road to the absurd as much as to utmost pragmatic humility. Where else if not inside the moribund body may we hold equality—the blueprint we all share in common—in our very hands? And doesn't such gut-gazing ultimately entail something as unheard-of and cogent as the invention and proclamation of universal human rights? Büchner, a doctor's son, tried to right society from this physiological vantage point. Could it be that his passion for politics was nothing but resuscitated fatalism and self-motivation, comparable to the experiments of Galvani, who applied electric shocks to torn-off frog legs? His signal question—Are our senses too crude, or are they sufficiently fine-tuned?—remains open. Whether only the flaws in the fabric of creation stand out or its organic beauties as well, whether freedom of spirit among individuals prevails over inscrutable desire, violence, and thick-skinned loneliness will depend on how we answer it. A century later, coming from a different direction, the painter Francis Bacon reached the same insight. In words not unlike Büchner's, he summed it up as follows in the course of an interview: "One's basic nature is totally without hope, and yet one's nervous system is made out of optimistic stuff."

Georg Büchner examined this stuff; again and again, he turned this lining of nerves inside out and made it flash forth in the spoken word, in the frozen moment of shock. The new, dramatic driving forces appear in the light of medical microscopy, they are exploratory forays into the vegetative realm, case studies performed on the living object, *en détail*. Beneath the writing, the nerve is at work; behind the play of facial expressions, the affects reign supreme; and only there, in the bodies of the pushed-around and pushing-around protagonists can be localized the driving forces that make histories and stories seem plausible. Büchner registered early on, and not at all coldly, the cracks that run through each of us. He was the first to observe this lying, stealing, murdering individual with diagnostic curiosity, one hundred years before the great bourgeois catastrophes and long before Kafka's futile attempt to retire it, operetta-style: "Who can fathom human nature!"

As a high school student, Büchner had already watched his father dissect at the hospital. At eighteen, he is a student of comparative anatomy and psychopathology in Giessen, used to working with cadavers on a daily basis. He quickly begins letting off steam in sarcastic witticisms. Among friends and in letters, he sends greetings from cadaver to cadaver. *Danton's Death*, written fifty years after the French Revolution, scraped together from historical documents, emerges amid zoology books and anatomical atlases. It is the final report on a sickness unto death. Original quotations from standard works on the revolution are incorporated like transplants into Büchner's own dramatic text. The blood does not want to clot at the tissue's edges. Like chopped-off limbs, the dead heroes' words continue to twitch on the dust-covered stage. This is how he creates his own style—modeled on Shakespeare, branded by medicine, treacling with juvenile vanitas. According to the Young German Karl Gutzkow, he suffered from a ubiquitous "autopsy compulsion."

The active, collecting spirit of order had run aground, the acceleration had begun. What Goethe referred to as the "appropriate euphemism" is completely absent in Büchner. His language does not gloss over anything; it's just as torn and full of nervous tension as the situation it stumbles up from. Psychomotor activity now determines the plot: the show booth as moral institution is closed; opened in its place is the theater of anatomy.

Although Goethe, the humanist, still collected bones while walking across a battlefield as material for his osteological studies, his travel report *The French Campaign* is conspicuously silent about it. Decades later, he held Schiller's skull in his hands; thus end the humanist's dreams—as a cannibalistic swan song in terza rima on viewing the remains of a friend. Büchner listened to all these dreams, including the involuntary ambient noise, the scratching and scraping of regular versification. Jacques-Louis David, the history painter, is said to have studied the twitching of the dying in the interest of graphic realism. In his diary, the executioner Sanson describes how the cart going to the guillotine went past a café where Citizen David, sitting on a windowsill, was drawing the condemned. Büchner holds on to the individual nerve, and not just for research purposes. One senses how a jolt has gone through the metaphors. Once and for all, they have been released from their artificial supports: the end of shadow boxing, of the clanging of automatons. Büchner opposes his anthropological realism to the "tremendous work of idealization" that Schiller still thought he had to perform. From now on, all that counts is what takes place in the "world of the body"—a world that, according to St. Just, must be ruled by brute force, by terror and mass murder. In this world, Büchner sees the new sufferings piling up and, hidden behind its forces, the future laws of nature. From the beginning, his landscapes are those "graveyards of the spirit" that Hegel talked about from the bird's-eye view of the philosopher. Even where, in good Hegelian fashion, Büchner takes up the idea of a world spirit wending its way through society, he first stops to look at the mounds of dead bodies left by the wayside. There is no democracy without its barbaric episodes; a constitution without dismembered bodies can no longer be imagined. "Just follow your slogans through," says Mercier, "to the point where they turn into flesh and blood." And Danton agrees with him: "These days, everything is fashioned out of human flesh. It's the curse of our age. And now my body's to be used as well." History and revolution cut deeply into the flesh, they leave crushed bodies in their wake—this is what creates such a distance between them and redemption. And this is why every social model is worthless that doesn't take into account the fragility of these pitiful bodies. It may be that Utopias are sought with the soul, but they are carried out on the bones of mangled bodies, paid for with the biographies of those who are dragged along into each successive ugly paradise.

In *Demise of the Egoist Fatzer*, Bertolt Brecht has captured the temporary conclusion to this historical sequence, just in time for standardized killing to make it to the factory floor: the reduction of the body to mere waste material. In the First World War, while the Woyzecks were croaking by the millions in the trenches, a deserter in Mülheim scribbles his new equation on the wall. What is a dead body? ". . . 170 lbs. of cold meat, 4 buckets of water, 1 packet of salt."

Back in the present, I will close quickly and simply, with one final scene. In Berlin, on the evening of October 7, 1989, when I woke up from the initial euphoria of the first day of a wave of demonstrations that washed away the other Germany, I found myself astonished by the sight of a monstrous machine. On the median of one of the typical colossal thoroughfares in the city center (which, like the Parisian boulevards or the Muscovite prospects, followed the model of postrevolutionary city planning and were laid out as pure marching zones for the military or the police) stood a Russian tank that had emerged from nowhere or from one of the bunkers that served as underground garages. Its turret, painted with the emblems of the GDR's National People's Army, was screwed down, the cannon pointed across the roadway toward Alexanderplatz. I no longer know if it was the tremendous tonnage of its appearance or the (Asiatic) distance it seemed to rule so easily: a loiterer heading home from the battles, straggling far behind the others, I was suddenly overcome by a desire to lie down, right there, in the shadow of the tank and lean against its steel chains and wheels for minutes on end with my eyes closed. The threatening vehicle, the machine of the civil wars, had awoken a primeval need for sleep in me. The body had come this far, now it sought rest, a break from history. It had had enough of all that, enough of the streets as wide as runways, of Peace Squares and death strips, of morning roll call and skewed prefab high-rises, of urban monotony and delusions of security, of conditioned stirrings and simple-minded languages, and, finally, of the long socialist twilight, the lethargy of an entire landscape which that body had blundered into by accident as if into a giant trap. I wanted to rest, to cut myself off from East *and* West, from the disastrous clamping together of the divided sides of all relationships and brains, to lie down and sleep in the middle of the minefield, to forget the powerlessness, the physiological dictatorship, and all the years of collective humiliation . . . to fall asleep, to forget the insults to the intellect, to find a moment's peace, leaning against this heavy, tracked vehicle that stood there as if unmanned.

Here it was the body that, on a sudden and childlike whim and *prior* to all words, desired to yield to its own exhaustion: after all, it had had to endure longer, having been more oppressively stifled than my ever-ready-to-defect thoughts. It was as if with the tank behind me I wanted to oversleep history, just this once, for minutes on end, before everything gathered momentum again, to forget the body in a dreamless sleep.

I thank the Darmstadt Academy for a prize that I could hardly refuse and that (so much still lies ahead of me) I would have nevertheless preferred to see in other hands, awarded for an entire oeuvre, a life's work. Büchner's age at his death can hardly be a source of comfort to me, much less an alibi. Thinking of him, I don't see any of my other ancestors, I see this unique, meteorlike image: the young poet as sphinx.

Georg Büchner: A Chronology

Broader historical events from 1813 to 1837 are listed in italics.

1813   October 16–19. *The Battle of Leipzig, a catastrophic loss for Napoleon that ultimately leads to his abdication and exile to Elba.*

October 17. Karl Georg Büchner born in the town of Goddelau, west of Darmstadt, in the Grand Duchy of Hesse-Darmstadt. He is the first child of Dr. Ernst Karl Büchner (1786–1861), a prominent surgeon, and Caroline, née Reuss (1791–1858).

1814   September 1814–June 1815. *The Congress of Vienna reorganizes Europe in the wake of the Napoleonic Wars. Results in the formation of the German Confederation, a loose alliance of thirty-eight states.*

June 18. *Napoleon, having escaped from Elba and reorganized his army, is decisively defeated at Waterloo.*

1815   Birth of sister Mathilde.

1816   The family moves to Darmstadt, where Ernst Büchner eventually becomes director of the medical college.

1816   Birth of brother Wilhelm, who will become a pharmacist, factory owner, and politician.

1819   *The Carlsbad Decrees are issued across the German states, enforcing censorship of periodicals, tighter political control of universities, and the establishment of a central investigating commission to uncover potential insurrection.*

1821   Birth of sister Louise, who will become a poet, novelist, and campaigner for women's rights.

1824   Birth of brother Ludwig, who will become a philosopher, physician, and physiologist. In 1850 he will publish the first collected edition of his brother's work (omitting *Woyzeck*) and subsequently make a name of his own as the author of *Force and Matter* (*Kraft und Stoff*, 1855), among other influential works.

1825–31   Studies at Ludwig-Georg-Gymnasium, a humanistic secondary school in Darmstadt.

1827   Birth of brother Alexander, who will fight in the 1848
            revolutions and subsequently resettle in France, becom-
            ing a professor of literature in Caen.
1830   *Series of revolutionary uprisings, first in France (where
            the July Revolution overthrows Charles X and establishes
            the more liberal Louis-Philippe), and thereafter, unsuc-
            cessfully, in Poland and parts of Italy and Germany. Bel-
            gium declares independence from the Netherlands.*
            September. *Peasant uprising in upper Hesse is crushed by
            Hessian dragoons in an event dubbed the "bloodbath at
            Södel."*
            September 29. Delivers a speech in defense of the sui-
            cide of Cato, a Roman republican who preferred death
            to life under Caesar's dictatorship.
1831   November 9. Enrolls in the medical school of the Uni-
            versity of Strassburg.
            December 4. The Polish freedom fighter and former
            Napoleonic officer Girolamo Ramorino passes through
            Strassburg. Students, including Büchner, march in sup-
            port, singing the *Marseillaise* and the *Carmagnole*.
1832   May 24. Delivers an address to a Strassburg student
            organization ("Eugenia"), in which he criticizes the
            backward social and political situation in Germany.
1833   Becomes secretly engaged to Wilhelmina ("Minna")
            Jaeglé (1810–1880).
            April 3. *Armed students, largely from the local fraternities,
            attack the main guardhouse in Frankfurt in an attempt to
            spark a pan-German revolution. The uprising is betrayed
            to the police before it begins and quickly suppressed.*
            October. Study-abroad regulations force him to leave
            Strassburg, and with disappointment he returns to
            Hesse to continue his medical studies at the University
            of Giessen.
1834   Winter. Meets and befriends Friedrich Ludwig Weidig
            (1791–1837), a pastor, schoolteacher, and revolutionary
            activist.
            March. Founds the Society of Human Rights (*Gesell-
            schaft der Menschenrechte*) in Giessen.
            April. Engagement to Minna Jaeglé made public.
            May. Founds a second branch of the Society in Darm-
            stadt. Completes a draft of *The Hessian Messenger*, which
            Weidig then rewrites.
            July. Smuggles the manuscript of *The Hessian Messenger*
            to a secret printing press in Offenbach. The conspiracy is

betrayed by a professional informant and Büchner attempts to warn his comrades. Several conspirators are arrested and Büchner's rooms searched.

November. Weidig prints a second edition of the *Messenger*.

September. Returns to Darmstadt.

Creation of the Zollverein, or Customs Union, establishing limited free trade across Germany and marking a significant step toward reunification.

1835   January–February. Writes *Danton's Death*, which he sends to Karl Gutzkow.

March. Flees to Strassburg.

April. Weidig arrested and imprisoned.

May. Begins work on *Lenz*.

May–July. Translates Victor Hugo's plays *Lucrèce Borgia* and *Marie Tudor* for Gutzkow.

June 13. Hessian authorities issue a warrant for Büchner's arrest.

July. Publication of a bowdlerized version of *Danton's Death*.

October. Publication of Hugo translations.

Winter. Works on his dissertation on the nervous system of the barbel fish. Composes lectures on Greek philosophy, Descartes, and Spinoza.

1836   April–May. Reads his dissertation to the Natural History Society of Strassburg, which inducts him as a corresponding member.

Summer–mid-October. Works on *Leonce and Lena* and *Woyzeck*.

September 3. Granted a doctorate for his dissertation by the University of Zurich.

October 18. Moves to Zurich.

November 5. Delivers his trial lecture, *On Cranial Nerves*, in Zurich.

November. Begins to teach a course on comparative anatomy of fish and amphibians. Returns to work on *Leonce and Lena*, *Woyzeck*, and possibly the lost play *Pietro Aretino*.

1837   Late January. Falls ill with typhus.

February 17. Minna Jaeglé meets him in Zurich.

February 19. Dies.

February 23. Weidig dies in prison, possibly by suicide.

1838   Publication of *Leonce and Lena*, edited by Gutzkow.

1839   Publication of *Lenz*, edited by Gutzkow.

1850   Publication of the first edition of Büchner's collected works, edited by his brother Ludwig. This edition omits *Woyzeck*.

1875   September–October. Publication of *Wozzeck*, reconstructed by Karl Emil Franzos, in the Viennese journal *Neue Freie Presse*.

1877   January. Publication of Franzos's reconstruction of *Wozzeck* in the Berlin journal *Mehr Licht*.

1879   First publication of Büchner's collected works, edited by Franzos.

1895   May 31. Premiere of *Leonce and Lena* at the Intimes Theater in Munich.

1902   January 5. Premiere of *Danton's Death* by the Volksbühne at the Belle-Alliance Theater in Berlin.

1911   December 31. First public performance of *Leonce and Lena*, at the Residenztheater in Vienna.

1913   November 8. Premiere of *Woyzeck* at the Munich Kammerspiele, directed by Eugen Kilian.

1916   Max Reinhardt's highly popular production of *Danton's Death* at the Deutsches Theater in Berlin. A second Reinhardt production of the play is staged in 1921.

1923   Publication of Alban Berg's opera *Wozzeck*.

1925   December 14. Premiere of Berg's *Wozzeck* at the Berlin Staatsoper.

1927   First English-language edition of the plays of Georg Büchner, translated by Geoffrey Dunlop. Reissued in the United States in 1928.

         Reinhardt includes *Danton's Death* in the repertory for his United States tour.

1967   Publication of Werner Lehmann's Hamburg edition of Büchner's complete works.

Selected Bibliography

•Indicates works included or excerpted in this Norton Critical Edition

I. Collected Primary Works in German

Büchner, Georg. *Sämtliche Werke und Briefe*. Historisch-kritische Ausgabe mit Kommentar. Ed. Werner R. Lehmann. Hamburg: C. Wegner, 1967.

———. *Sämtliche Werke, Briefe und Dokumente in Zwei Bänden*. Ed. Henri Poschmann & Rosemarie Poschmann. Frankfurt am Main: Deutscher Klassiker Verlag, 1992.

———. *Werke und Briefe*. Münchner Ausgabe. Ed. Karl Pörnbacher, et al. Munich: Carl Hanser Verlag, 1988.

II. Secondary Works in English

1. GENERAL

Benn, Maurice B. *The Drama of Revolt: A Critical Study of Georg Büchner*. Cambridge: Cambridge University Press, 1976.

Gilman, Richard. "Büchner." *The Making of Modern Drama: A Study of Büchner, Ibsen, Strindberg, Chekhov, Pirandello, Brecht, Handke*. New Haven, CT: Yale University Press, 1999. 3–44.

Grimm, Reinhold. *Love, Lust, and Rebellion: New Approaches to Georg Büchner*. Madison: University of Wisconsin Press, 1985.

Hilton, Julian. *Georg Büchner*. New York: Grove Press, 1982.

•Lindenberger, Herbert. *Georg Büchner*. Carbondale: Southern Illinois University Press, 1964.

Lukács, Georg. "The Real Georg Büchner and His Fascist Misrepresentation." *German Realists in the Nineteenth Century*. Ed. Rodney Livingstone. Trans. Jeremy Gaines & Paul Keast. Cambridge, MA: MIT Press, 1993. 69–94.

Perraudin, Michael. "Towards a New Cultural Life: Büchner and the 'Volk.'" *The Modern Language Review* 86.3 (1991): 627–44.

•Reddick, John. *Georg Büchner: The Shattered Whole*. 1994.

Richards, David. *Georg Büchner and the Birth of the Modern Drama*. Albany: State University of New York Press, 1977.

Schmidt, Henry J. *Satire, Caricature and Perspectivism in the Works of Georg Büchner*. The Hague: Mouton, 1970.

•Steiner, George. *The Death of Tragedy*. 1961. New Haven, CT: Yale University Press, 1996. 270–81.

Stern, J. P. "A World of Suffering: Georg Büchner." *Re-interpretations: Seven Studies in Nineteenth-Century German Literature*. London: Thames & Hudson, 1964. 78–155.

2. THE HESSIAN MESSENGER

Schmidt, Henry J. "The Hessian Messenger." *Georg Büchner: The Complete Collected Works*. Ed. Henry J. Schmidt. New York: Avon, 1977. 241–57.

3. Danton's Death

Buckley, Matthew S. "Reviving the Revolution: *Dantons Tod*." Baltimore: Johns Hopkins University Press, 2006. 120–48.

Ginters, Laura. "Georg Büchner's *Dantons Tod*: History and Her Story on the Stage." *Modern Drama* 39.4 (1996): 650–67.

James, Dorothy. *Georg Büchner's "Dantons Tod": A Reappraisal.* London: Modern Humanities Research Association, 1982.

•McInnes, Edward. "Scepticism, Ideology, and History in Büchner's *Dantons Tod.*" *For Lionel Thomas: A Collection of Essays Presented in His Memory.* Ed. Derek Attwood, Alan Best, & Rex Last. Hull, England: Department of German, University of Hull, 1980.

•Schmidt, Henry J. "Women, Death, and Revolution: Büchner's *Danton's Death.*" *How Dramas End.* Ann Arbor: University of Michigan Press, 1992. 91–106.

Taylor, Rodney. "The Convergence of Individual Will and Historical Necessity in Büchner's Danton." *Neue Germanistik* 4.2 (1986): 25–43.

4. Lenz

King, Janet K. "Lenz Viewed Sane." *Germanic Review* 49 (1974): 146–53.

Madland, Helga Stipa. "Madness and Lenz: Two Hundred Years Later." *German Quarterly* 66.1 (1993): 34–42.

Pascal, Roy. "Büchner's *Lenz*: Style and Message." *Oxford German Studies* 9 (1978): 68–83.

•Swales, Erika. "Büchner, *Lenz.*" *Landmarks in German Short Prose.* Oxford & New York: Peter Lang, 2003.

5. Leonce and Lena

Lukens, Nancy. *Büchner's Valerio and the Theatrical Fool Tradition.* Stuttgart: Akademischer Verlag H.-D. Heinz, 1977.

Musolf, Peter M. "Parallelism in Büchner's *Leonce und Lena*: A Tragicomedy of Tautology." *The German Quarterly* 59.2 (1986): 216–27.

•Webber, Andrew. "Büchner, *Leonce und Lena.*" *Landmarks in German Comedy.* Oxford & New York: Peter Lang, 2006.

6. Woyzeck

Dunne, Kerry. "Woyzeck's Marie: 'Ein schlecht Mensch'? The Construction of Female Sexuality in Büchner's *Woyzeck.*" *Seminar: A Journal of Germanic Studies* 26.4 (1990): 294–308.

Gray, Richard T. "The Dialectic of Enlightenment in Büchner's *Woyzeck.*" *German Quarterly* 61.1 (1988): 78–96.

Harding, James M. "The Preclusions of Progress: *Woyzeck's* Challenge to Materialism and Social Change." *Seminar: A Journal of Germanic Studies* 29.1 (1993): 28–42.

James, Dorothy. "The 'Interesting Case' of Büchner's *Woyzeck.*" *Patterns of Change: German Drama and the European Tradition* (1990): 103–19.

Martin, Laura. "'Schlechtes Mensch/Gutes Opfer': The Role of Marie in Georg Büchner's *Woyzeck.*" *German Life and Letters* 50.4 (1997): 429–44.

•McCarthy, John A. "Some Aspects of Imagery in Büchner's *Woyzeck.*" *MLN* 91.3 (1976): 543–51.

Mills, Ken. "Moon, Madness and Murder: The Motivation of Woyzeck's Killing of Marie." *German Life and Letters* 41.4 (1988): 430–36.

Patterson, Michael. "Contradictions Concerning Time in Büchner's *Woyzeck.*" *German Life and Letters* 32 (1979): 115–21.

Richards, David G. *Georg Büchner's* Woyzeck: *A History of Its Criticism.* 2001.

7. Trial Lecture

Müller-Sievers, Helmut. "Of Fish and Men: The Importance of Georg Büchner's Anatomical Writings." *MLN* 118.3 (2003): 704–18.